Frommer's®

W9-AXY-764

Maryland & Delaware

7th Edition

by Mary K. Tilghman

Here's what the critics say about Frommer's:

"Amazingly easy to use. Very portable, very complete."
—*Booklist*

"Detailed, accurate, and easy-to-read information for all price ranges."
—*Glamour Magazine*

"Hotel information is close to encyclopedic."
—*Des Moines Sunday Register*

"Frommer's Guides have a way of giving you a real feel for a place."
—*Knight Ridder Newspapers*

WILEY

Wiley Publishing, Inc.

About the Author

Maryland native **Mary K. Tilghman** is a journalist and editor and has lived and worked all over the state, from small towns to a farm on the Eastern Shore. She and her family have seen just about every corner of their home state and Delaware, by land and on their sailboat on the Magothy River. She lives in Baltimore.

Published by:

Wiley Publishing, Inc.

111 River St.
Hoboken, NJ 07030-5774

ISBN-13: 978-0-471-77884-4
ISBN-10: 0-471-77884-2

Editor: Leslie Shen
Production Editor: Jana M. Stefanciosa
Cartographer: Anton Crane
Photo Editor: Richard Fox
Production by Wiley Indianapolis Composition Services

Front cover photo: The historic tug *Delaware* in St. Michaels, Maryland
Back cover photo: Winfields Farm, Chesapeake City

For information on our other products and services or to obtain technical support, please contact our Customer Care Department within the U.S. at 800/762-2974, outside the U.S. at 317/572-3993 or fax 317/572-4002.

Wiley also publishes its books in a variety of electronic formats. Some content that appears in print may not be available in electronic formats.

Manufactured in the United States of America

5   4   3   2   1

Contents

13 Dover & Central Delaware 320

List of Maps

Acknowledgments

Special thanks to Kerry Osborne of the Greater Wilmington Convention and Visitors Bureau, Connie Yingling and Joanne Calhoun of the Maryland Office of Tourism Development, Susan Steckman of the Annapolis and Anne Arundel County Conference and Visitors Bureau, John Fieseler of the Tourism Council of Frederick County, Stacey Fox of Gettysburg Convention and Visitors Bureau, Christine Serio of the Delaware Economic Tourism Office, Deborah Dodson of Talbot County Office of Tourism, and Mary Callaway of Dorchester County Tourism. I would especially like to thank the hotel/inn owners and the staff at all the museums and other tourist destinations for their help and their hospitality. They made my visits a pleasure. And, finally, I want to thank my family, several Maryvale Preparatory School families, and Good Samaritan Joe Fleischman, who helped make it easier for me to research this book.

—Mary K. Tilghman

An Invitation to the Reader

In researching this book, we discovered many wonderful places—hotels, restaurants, shops, and more. We're sure you'll find others. Please tell us about them, so we can share the information with your fellow travelers in upcoming editions. If you were disappointed with a recommendation, we'd love to know that, too. Please write to:

Frommer's Maryland & Delaware, 7th Edition
Wiley Publishing, Inc. • 111 River St. • Hoboken, NJ 07030-5774

An Additional Note

Please be advised that travel information is subject to change at any time—and this is especially true of prices. We therefore suggest that you write or call ahead for confirmation when making your travel plans. The authors, editors, and publisher cannot be held responsible for the experiences of readers while traveling. Your safety is important to us, however, so we encourage you to stay alert and be aware of your surroundings. Keep a close eye on cameras, purses, and wallets, all favorite targets of thieves and pickpockets.

Other Great Guides for Your Trip:

Frommer's Virginia
Frommer's Washington D.C.
Frommer's Philadelphia & the Amish Country
The Unofficial Guide to the Mid-Atlantic with Kids

Frommer's Star Ratings, Icons & Abbreviations

Every hotel, restaurant, and attraction listing in this guide has been ranked for quality, value, service, amenities, and special features using a **star-rating system.** In country, state, and regional guides, we also rate towns and regions to help you narrow down your choices and budget your time accordingly. Hotels and restaurants are rated on a scale of zero (recommended) to three stars (exceptional). Attractions, shopping, nightlife, towns, and regions are rated according to the following scale: zero stars (recommended), one star (highly recommended), two stars (very highly recommended), and three stars (must-see).

In addition to the star-rating system, we also use **seven feature icons** that point you to the great deals, in-the-know advice, and unique experiences that separate travelers from tourists. Throughout the book, look for:

Finds	Special finds—those places only insiders know about
Fun Fact	Fun facts—details that make travelers more informed and their trips more fun
Kids	Best bets for kids and advice for the whole family
Moments	Special moments—those experiences that memories are made of
Overrated	Places or experiences not worth your time or money
Tips	Insider tips—great ways to save time and money
Value	Great values—where to get the best deals

The following **abbreviations** are used for credit cards:

AE	American Express	DISC	Discover	V	Visa
DC	Diners Club	MC	MasterCard		

Frommers.com

Now that you have the guidebook to a great trip, visit our website at **www.frommers.com** for travel information on more than 3,000 destinations. With features updated regularly, we give you instant access to the most current trip-planning information available. At Frommers.com, you'll also find the best prices on airfares, accommodations, and car rentals—and you can even book travel online through our travel booking partners. At Frommers.com, you'll also find the following:

- Online updates to our most popular guidebooks
- Vacation sweepstakes and contest giveaways
- Newsletter highlighting the hottest travel trends
- Online travel message boards with featured travel discussions

What's New in Maryland & Delaware

Arriving by plane? You'll now be landing at **Baltimore/Washington International Thurgood Marshall Airport** (© **800/I-FLY-BWI;** www.bwiairport. com). State legislators approved the name change in 2005 to honor the Maryland native and the first African American to sit on the U.S. Supreme Court.

Accommodations in Maryland and Delaware never seem to stop updating their rooms. The newest thing is high-speed Internet access—most hotels now offer it in guest rooms as well as public areas. Often it's wireless; often it's free. Check when making reservations, as policies keep changing.

Both Maryland and Delaware have a number of new museums—or newly refurbished museums.

MARYLAND

BALTIMORE Baltimore's **Heritage Walk** (© **877/BALTIMORE;** www. heritagewalk.org) gives visitors another way to stroll around the city. Using new maps and brochures, guides, and signage all around the downtown area, visitors can learn a little about the history and culture of Charm City. See p. 103.

Don't want to walk? The **Big Bus Company** (© **410/396-6611**) operates new double-decker buses that tool about town, enabling visitors to get on and off as they please—and going far beyond the Inner Harbor to must-see attractions in western and northern Baltimore. See p. 71.

The city welcomed several new hotels this year, including a **Residence Inn,** 17 Light St. (© **410/962-1220**), right in the heart of the business district (p. 76). Over in Fells Point, the **Henderson's Wharf Inn,** 1000 Fell St. (© **800/522-2088**), suffered mightily when Hurricane Isabel blew through in 2003. We're happy to report that after months of reconstruction, the inn on the harbor is welcoming guests back with style (p. 79).

Baltimore diners have become an adventurous lot in recent years—but the city and its visitors still like a thick steak and a good pub. One of the new Irish eateries isn't your usual Guinness-and-corned-beef place. With a gleaming oak bar—no, make that two bars—plus white tablecloths and sweeping city views, **Tir Na Nog,** newly opened at Harborplace (© **410/483-8968**), is worth the hassle of finding a parking space (p. 83). If beef is what's for dinner, stop at either downtown branch of **Ruth's Chris Steak House,** at 600 Water St. (© **410/783-0033**), or at the Pier 5 Hotel, 711 Eastern Ave. (© **410/230-0033**) (p. 81). Or you can try the terrific new **Capital Grille,** 500 E. Pratt St. (© **443/703-4064**), right downtown (p. 82). Sadly, the **Joy America Cafe,** at the American Visionary Art Museum, shut its doors in 2006 after 6 years in business.

With a brand new exhibit, "Australia: Wild Extremes," Down Under has come to the **National Aquarium in Baltimore,**

501 E. Pratt St. (© 410/576-3800). Anyone walking past the giant glass cube in the past year or so couldn't help but marvel at the contents visible from outside. Timed, advance-purchase tickets are now available online at www.aqua.org. See p. 94.

Baltimoreans are justly proud of their newest museum, the **Reginald F. Lewis Museum of Maryland African American History & Culture,** 830 E. Pratt St. (© 443/263-1800). It's the East Coast's largest museum chronicling African-American history. Architecturally, the soaring black, red, and yellow edifice is breathtaking; inside, the exhibits are designed to inspire young people. See p. 97.

The **B&O Railroad Museum,** 901 W. Pratt St. (© 410/752-2490), is back. Heavy snows a few years ago made a mess of the building and its priceless contents, but the staff has revived this jewel in West Baltimore. Some damaged pieces are still on display, but the place looks as good as new—maybe even better. See p. 97.

Sports fans will revel in the new **Sports Legends at Camden Yards,** 301 W. Camden St. (© 410/727-1539), right beside Camden Yards. It's a delight for anyone who loves Bawlamer's local teams. See p. 98.

New to this edition of the guide are two bright spots in Maryland. Just 14 miles from Baltimore, **Ellicott City,** the country's first railroad town, is a great place to spend a day antiquing, sightseeing, and eating out (p. 115). **Havre de Grace,** a Colonial crossroads at the top of the Chesapeake Bay, has plenty of shopping, attractions, and water activities, as well as a handful of delightful bed-and-breakfasts (p. 117).

ANNAPOLIS In Annapolis, walking is *so* 18th century. The Segway, the newfangled way to get around, has come to Maryland's capital thanks to **Segs in the City** (© 800/SEGS-393). See p. 140.

The **Annapolis Maritime Museum,** Second Street and Back Creek (© 410/295-0104), was pretty much ransacked by Hurricane Isabel in 2003. It has now reopened with exhibits on the Thomas Point Lighthouse and the venerable oyster. See p. 136.

The **Banneker–Douglass Museum,** 84 Franklin St. (© 410/216-6180), has added new space, doubling its capacity and enabling its staff to add changing exhibits to its permanent displays about local African Americans. See p. 136.

The Historic Annapolis Foundation spent 2005 readying its newest museum, **HistoryQuest at the St. Clair Wright History Center,** 99 Main St. (© 410/267-7619). The restored 1790s building will be home to exhibits that highlight the capital's history, architecture, and culture. See p. 138.

THE EASTERN SHORE The **Tidewater Inn,** 101 E. Dover St., Easton (© 800/237-8775), has been the centerpiece of Easton's downtown district for, well, forever. The aging lady wasn't looking her best, though, when she was auctioned off in mid-2005. The good news is that new owners are giving her a major makeover, with elegant results promised by 2007. See p. 158.

Motorists can follow in the path of Harriet Tubman by taking the 105-mile **"Finding a Way to Freedom"** self-guided driving tour, available from the Route 50 Visitor Center in Cambridge (© 410/228-1000; www.tourdorchester. org). The route visits Underground Railroad sites around Dorchester County. See p. 175.

MARYLAND & DELAWARE'S ATLANTIC BEACHES Ocean City has gotten too big for its barrier island—so development has spread across the bay to what's been dubbed "West Ocean City." Housing and shopping outlets have been around for years; now the local restaurant scene is getting tasty. The

Southern-inspired **Plantation House,** 12308 Ocean Gateway (Rte. 50), West Ocean City (© **410/213-7786**), is one of the most welcome new additions. See p. 275.

FREDERICK & THE CIVIL WAR CROSSROADS Antietam National Battlefield, a place with sad history but sweeping mountain vistas, has several new attractions. Its licensed Battlefield Guides, similar to those at Gettysburg, will take families and groups on tours of the battlefield. A new field hospital exhibit has been set up in the house where Gen. George McClellan had his headquarters. And hiking aficionados should look for the trails now marked around the battlefields. It's a new way to look and learn—and to enjoy the scenery. See p. 202.

WESTERN MARYLAND Mush! Anyone who has ever dreamed of running the Iditarod can now try dogsledding in the parks of Western Maryland with two local outfitters, **Husky Power Dogsledding** (© **301/746-7200**) and **Yellow Snow Dog Sled Adventures** (© **301/ 616-4996**). Since snow can be a chancy proposition here, some sleds are even outfitted with wheels. Okay, so maybe it isn't quite the same experience as sledding across the snow . . . but those furry creatures are still hauling you around at top speeds. See p. 230.

Maryland's only ski area, **Wisp Resort,** at Deep Creek Lake (© **301/387-4911**), is expanding again. Open now for 50 years, the resort has added 10 trails and two quad lifts to the north side of the mountain. Skiers will rejoice at the chance for new trails—and a new view. See p. 230.

DELAWARE

Routes 52 and 100, the two main routes from Wilmington through the Brandywine Valley, have been recently named Delaware's first **Scenic Byway,** a national designation. Before you visit, go to www. byways.org for information and a map of the 5½-mile route. That, along with this guide, will make visiting the Brandywine Valley a snap. See p. 307.

WILMINGTON & THE BRANDY-WINE VALLEY Downtown Wilmington has its first wine bar. **Domaine Hudson,** 1314 N. Washington St. (© **302/655-WINE**), which has paired a cellar full of wines from all over with a creative tasting menu—and Wilmingtonians are eating it up. See p. 299.

Wilmington has welcomed the **Delaware Art Museum,** 2301 Kentmere Pkwy. (© **302/571-9590**), back into its original quarters—spiffed up, very elegant, and quite impressive (p. 300).

On the Pennsylvania side of the Brandywine Valley, **Simon Pearce,** 1333 Lenape Rd., West Chester (© **610/793-0948**), has opened its second restaurant (the other is in New England). The company well known for fine crystal is now also known for fine dining near Longwood Gardens. See p. 310.

At **Longwood Gardens,** Route 1, Kennett Square, Pennsylvania (© **610/ 388-1000**), the newly restored East Conservatory has opened to dazzling effect, expanding the *wow* factor at a place that already had plenty of it. See p. 312.

DOVER & CENTRAL DELAWARE Dover is known for its really good little museums, but now it has packaged them all as the **First State Heritage Park at Dover.** See p. 324.

After being closed for several years, the **Historic Houses of Odessa** (© **302/ 378-4119**), which were once the property of Winterthur Museum, are under new ownership and are once again open to the public. See p. 326.

1

The Best of Maryland & Delaware

Maryland and Delaware are often overshadowed by their neighbors, including the nation's capital. But thanks to the always-dazzling Chesapeake Bay, ocean beaches, and gently rolling mountains, these two states offer plenty of outdoor charms. The cities of Baltimore, in Maryland, and Wilmington, in Delaware, are filled with intriguing museums, sophisticated restaurants, and delightful waterfronts that make for a romantic summer evening stroll.

Add charming small towns—including Maryland's capital, Annapolis, and Delaware's capital, Dover—and friendly people and a wealth of historic sites, and you've got two states worth a visit—whether you have a day, a weekend, or a whole week.

These two states have been shaped by history, from the Colonial days to the Revolutionary and Civil wars; by industry, from the commercial fisheries of ocean and bay to high-tech banking and information technology; and even by sports. What would NASCAR do without Dover twice a year? And what Baltimoreans don't keep up-to-date with their beloved Orioles or stop whatever they're doing for the Preakness?

Every corner of Maryland offers something for those who look. Get off I-95 at the Mason-Dixon Line and you'll find scenic Havre de Grace. Wander through the Eastern Shore for a table full of hot steamed crabs. Park the car outside Frederick and you'll find the leafy glens that surround Cunningham Falls.

And don't be fooled by Delaware's small size. Sure, it's got beaches and NASCAR, but it also has mansions tucked in the Brandywine Valley, good food and wine on quiet Wilmington nights, and the town of Lewes—which is so charming, you might forget the ocean is just a short walk across a bridge.

Marylanders and Delawareans look into the future, but they remember where they've been, too. They remember their fallen friends with monuments, battlefields, and aging forts that recall battles in 1776, 1812, 1917, and 1945. You can see places where George Washington stood, where brothers died, and where slaves ran for freedom. You can get a glimpse of how people lived when these states were just small colonies, or when the Golden Age made industrialists millionaires.

Whether you visit Maryland and Delaware because they're on the way to someplace else or because you're drawn to their style, charm, and friendliness, you won't be disappointed.

1 Frommer's Favorite Maryland & Delaware Experiences

- **Sipping Tea at Bertha's** (Baltimore, Md.; © 410/327-5795): Bertha's tea is an afternoon delight. Cup after cup of Earl Grey with scones and clotted cream, Scotch eggs, and an assortment of savories and sweets are perfect in the shabby-chic dining room of this Fells Point eatery. See p. 86.

- **Raising the Star-Spangled Banner at Fort McHenry** (Baltimore, Md.): The park rangers ask visitors to help with the raising and lowering of the huge flag each day. The nooks and crannies and views keep young ones interested. Outside the fort, the sprawling waterfront park is perfect for families and picnics. See p. 92.

- **Going to Any Baseball Game:** Maryland has baseball's most beautiful stadium—Oriole Park at Camden Yards—and the best team in the world (the Orioles, of course!). Players toss balls to kids in the stands, and the Oriole Bird has been known to loft T-shirts and even (wrapped) hot dogs to the fans. The many minor league teams are also fun, and more affordable. See "The Best Baseball in Maryland" (p. 12).

- **Attending the Preakness** (Baltimore, Md.): If you're young and want some serious partying, check out the infield. If you actually want to see the second jewel in the Triple Crown, head for the grandstand. The race is held the third Saturday in May. If you want grandstand tickets to the Preakness, held at **Pimlico Race Course** (© **410/542-9400**), it's best to call up to a year ahead. Infield tickets are available up to the week before and are sold at some area gas stations. See p. 105.

- **Rafting the Yough:** The Youghiogheny (generally just called the "Yock") is Maryland's great whitewater river. Its churning waters race through class III/IV rapids, with names like Gap Falls, Bastard, Triple Drop, Meatcleaver, Lost and Found, and Backbender. The water levels are controlled by dam release, so the river can be ridden almost year-round. See chapter 9.

- **Taking in the View from the O.C. Ferris Wheel** (Ocean City, Md.): Fork over the $5 for a ticket and climb aboard the vintage wheel. Go just before sunset and you won't wait in line. It's the perfect time to watch the charter boats heading in for the night and to see the sun set over Assawoman Bay. As darkness falls, you can watch the boardwalk light up. See p. 279.

- **Going "Downy Ocean":** Head for the crowded beaches of Ocean City, Maryland (with all those restaurants, shops, and golf courses), or to the quiet public beaches of Rehoboth or Bethany, Delaware. Both have their charms. The sand is white and clean; the waves can be gentle or furious (watch for the red warning flags). The sand crabs are used to being dug up, and the seagulls will keep an eye on your snacks. (Don't give in and feed them—it can be pretty scary.) See chapter 10.

- **Off-Roading on Assateague Island** (Md.): Most people who visit Assateague see only the 4- or 5-mile stretch of guarded beach and the federal and state camping facilities. They've missed the best part: the 20 miles of undisturbed beaches. This part of the island is only accessible on foot, by canoe or kayak, or over off-road-vehicle trails, the fastest way to get to those secluded areas. See p. 288.

2 The Best Lodging Bets

- **Annapolis Inn** (Annapolis, Md.; © **410/295-5200**): This sumptuous Georgian-style house was originally the home of Thomas Jefferson's physician in the 1770s. A three-course breakfast is served on fine china in the cranberry-red dining room. Selling points include Jacuzzis,

Maryland & Delaware

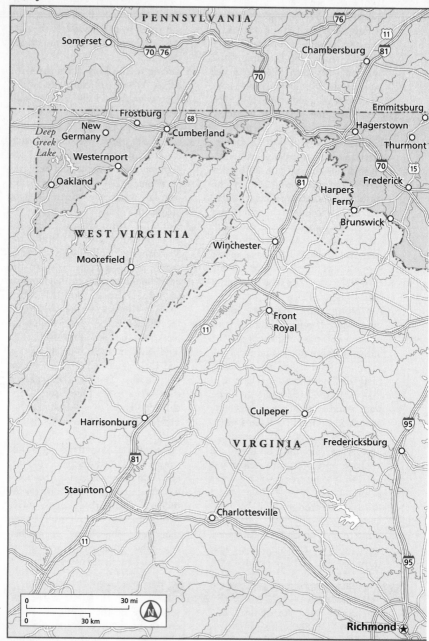

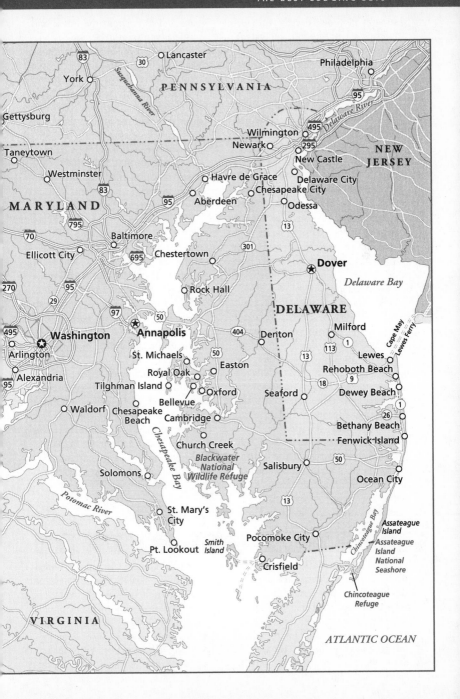

a room with its own deck, a patio surrounding a koi fishpond, and experienced, welcoming hosts. See p. 126.

• **Tilghman Island Inn** (Tilghman, Md.; © **800/866-2141**): Waterfront rooms take full advantage of the inn's setting on Knapps Narrows on the Eastern Shore. The bedrooms are spacious, the amenities are comfy, and the welcome is warm. See p. 167.

• **Waterloo Country Inn** (Princess Anne, outside Crisfield, Md.; © **410/651-0883**): This 1775 Georgian manor on Maryland's Eastern Shore sits right on the banks of Monie Creek. It offers seclusion, peace, and tranquillity, whether you're wandering the grounds, canoeing the lovely tidal creek, or biking the back roads of Somerset County. See p. 180.

• **Inn at Osprey Point** (Rock Hall, Md.; © **410/639-2194**): Who can resist a room with a view? This modern Eastern Shore inn has plenty of charm in its individually designed guest rooms. Amenities include an acclaimed restaurant, a pool, a marina, and those views of the Chesapeake Bay. See p. 187.

• **Stonebow Inn** (Grantsville, near Deep Creek Lake, Md.; © **800/272-4090**): Location makes the Stonebow, a restored 1877 Victorian, a good bet. It's right on the Casselman River beside the Spruce Forest Artisan Village, a few minutes from Deep Creek Lake and as far from the hustle and bustle as you want to be. See p. 234.

• **Addy Sea Bed & Breakfast** (Bethany Beach, Del.; © **800/418-6764**): In a resort filled with condos and rental houses, this B&B offers cozy charm surrounded by beach and surf. It's quiet enough for romance, but close enough to beach fun. See p. 259.

• **Lighthouse Club Hotel** (Ocean City, Md.; © **800/371-5400**): This hotel was designed for romantic beach getaways. Leave the kids at home and come here for secluded luxury with a view of the bay. Some rooms have fireplaces and Jacuzzis, too. See p. 272.

• **Hotel du Pont** (Wilmington, Del.; © **800/441-9019**): Not only is this a showcase of marble, carved paneling, and DuPont's latest fibers, but it also offers its lucky guests palatial surroundings, terrific amenities, and some of the best dining in town. See p. 295.

• **Inn at Montchanin Village** (Montchanin, Del.; © **800/COWBIRD**): This cluster of buildings was once home for workers of the DuPont powder mills. Now they're charming guest rooms and suites, set in beautiful gardens, located just a few miles from the du Pont homes and gardens. See p. 296.

3 The Best Dining Bets

• **Charleston** (Baltimore, Md.; © **410/332-7373**): Southern cuisine takes center stage at this restaurant in the trendy Harbor East neighborhood. Expect to be treated like royalty as the waitstaff serves your micro-greens salad, grilled yellowfin tuna with andouille sausage, and a perfect crème brûlée. See p. 80.

• **Carrol's Creek** (Annapolis, Md.; © **410/263-8102**): The best views of the waterfront and Annapolis's skyline are paired with imaginative food here. Dine indoors or on the porch from a menu that is always changing, but might pair rockfish with polenta or free-range chicken with truffle-scented mashed potatoes. The cream of crab soup is always a winner. See p. 132.

- **Green Room** (Wilmington, Del.; ⓒ **302/594-3154**): Delaware's top restaurant wows diners the minute they see the impressive decor. But the real star here is the food: classic sauces, perfectly cooked entrees, and desserts prepared as art. See p. 298.

- **Krazy Kat's** (Wilmington, Del.; ⓒ **302/888-4200**): The Brandywine Valley's finest inn also has the finest classic dining. Enjoy a leisurely meal of exceptionally prepared food in the cozy candlelit dining rooms. See p. 299.

4 The Best Affordable Dining

- **Sabatino's** (Baltimore, Md.; ⓒ **410/727-9414**): Good food at reasonable prices is the norm at most of Little Italy's restaurants. But Sabatino's also offers cozy dining rooms, an attentive waitstaff, and dinner served late into the night. See p. 85.

- Eat at the museum: **Gertrude's,** at the Baltimore Museum of Art (ⓒ **410/889-3399**), is a delightful spot that goes perfectly with a trip to view the exhibits or as a destination in itself. Gertrude's (as in Gertrude Stein) boasts artfully prepared food and outdoor dining (in season) with beautiful views. See p. 89.

- **Grill Art Cafe** (Baltimore, Md.; ⓒ **410/366-2005**): The stylish bistro setting and inventive sandwiches, salads, and brunch menu make Grill Art a great addition to the quirky Hampden scene. And the prices make this a good value, too. See p. 90.

- **Harpoon Hanna's** (Fenwick Island, Del.; ⓒ **800/227-0525**): The food is good; the fresh breads and muffins are outstanding. For a beach restaurant, this one is worth the trip. Set on a canal, its big windows let the sunset in. The fish is fresh, the staff hardworking, and children are always welcome. Come early or be prepared for a substantial wait. See p. 262.

5 The Best Shopping Bets

- **Antique Row** (Baltimore, Md.): In a single block of Howard Street a few blocks north of downtown, serious antiques fans can find old silver, chandeliers, assorted porcelain, and chairs of all sizes and shapes. See p. 108.

- **Downtown Annapolis** (Md.): Main Street and Maryland Avenue offer all kinds of choices in little shops. Tuscan kitchenware, Christmas ornaments, antique mirrors, and Navy sweatshirts are only a few of the items on these charming streets. There are a few chain stores, but the best shops are locally owned. See p. 142.

- **Tanger Outlet Centers** (Rehoboth Beach, Del.): Wear comfortable shoes for this colossal (tax-free) shopping extravaganza. The three centers have everything from Waterford crystal to OshKosh B'Gosh overalls. There's lots of clothing and home decor, as well as books, food, and other stuff. See p. 255.

6 The Best Views & Vistas

- **From the Severn River Scenic Overlook** (near Annapolis, Md.): On Route 450 outside of Annapolis, a beautiful stone porch offers stunning views of the Severn River and the U.S. Naval Academy. It's also now the site of a World War II Memorial, with summaries of the major battles and obelisks bearing the names of Marylanders who gave their lives in World War II. See p. 140.

- **At Great Falls of the Potomac** (near Potomac, Md.): On a sunny Sunday, the walkways will be crowded, but who cares? Just outside of Potomac, a Maryland suburb north of Washington, D.C., on the C&O Canal, a series of walkways will take you over the Great Falls of the Potomac. Stand above the piles of jagged rocks as the Potomac River rushes over them and down to the sea, the steepest and most spectacular fall line rapids of any Eastern river. See p. 146.

- **On the Bay Bridge** (Md.): When you get to the middle of this bridge, you'll have a wonderful view of the Chesapeake. Maryland's Eastern Shore stretches down one terminus, while the view of the Western Shore includes Annapolis south of the bridge and two lighthouses north of the bridge. The closest is the Sandy Point Light, and the farther one is the Baltimore Light. Believe it or not, state officials considered obstructing this view because motorists keep slowing down!

- **Atop the Mountain at Wisp Resort** (Western Md.): Ride the ski lift to the top, and before you go schussing down, take a good look. You'll see snow-covered slopes, the vast white expanse of Deep Creek Lake lined with the tracks of an occasional snowmobile, and a sky as blue as it can be. See p. 231.

- **From the Brandywine River Museum** (Chadds Ford, Pa., in the Brandywine Valley): While the art at this museum is dazzling, don't forget to look out the windows: The view of the river meandering under the canopy of trees is peaceful, though in fall a riot of color. See p. 314.

7 The Best Hiking

- **Calvert Cliffs State Park** (near Solomons, in Calvert County, Md.): This park offers a wide variety of wilderness scenery and trails for moderate-length day hikes. They wind through forests and then descend into a primordial tidal marsh with grasses, waterfowl, and cypress trees. Most hikes include at least one view of the Chesapeake Bay from atop the cliffs or from a small beach at the base of the marsh. See p. 151.

- **Swallow Falls State Park** (Garrett County, Md.): A great place for families to hike in Western Maryland, this park's short trails wind through dark, peaty forest and offer relatively easy access to some stunning scenery. There are overlooks to three waterfalls—Swallow Falls, Tolliver Falls, and the 63-foot-high cascading Muddy Creek Falls. See p. 216.

- **Big Savage Trail in Savage River State Forest** (Garrett County, Md.): This rugged trail extends 17 miles along the ridge of Big Savage Mountain, passing impressive vistas along the way. A tough hike through almost total wilderness, it's the best choice for serious backpacking in Western Maryland. See p. 216.

8 The Best Fishing & Crabbing

- **Calvert County Charter Fleets** (Solomons and Chesapeake Beach, Md.): For charter fishing on the Chesapeake, Calvert County south of Annapolis is the place to go. The small harbor of Chesapeake Beach is home to the largest charter fleet on the bay. Solomons, south of Chesapeake Beach, has a good fleet, too—with over 30 charter boats and a few headboats of its own. From either one, the captains are glad to take you trolling or chumming along the Western and Eastern Shores of the Chesapeake. See p. 149.
- **Point Lookout State Park** (St. Mary's County, Md.): Location is everything at this peninsular park, with the Chesapeake Bay on one side and the Potomac River on the other. Fish from the pier on the bay, or rent a boat at the camp marina. If they aren't biting in the bay, simply stroll over to the Potomac and try again. See p. 153.
- **Casselman River** (near Grantsville, Md.): Cleanup efforts in this area of Western Maryland have paid off. The beautiful and wild Casselman River, once empty of fish because of acid draining from local mines, is now teeming with trout. Fish tales include catches of up to 40 fish a day—and fly-fishing with the bears. One thing is for certain, though: The Casselman is a great place to fish. See chapter 9.

9 The Best Birding & Wildlife Watching

- **Blackwater National Wildlife Refuge** (Eastern Shore, Md.): The Delmarva Peninsula is dotted with wildlife refuges and protected lands, havens for migrating waterfowl and other wildlife. Blackwater is the largest of these. During peak migration season, you'll see ducks, tundra and mute swan, and snow geese, as well as the ever-present herons, Canada geese, and osprey, plus the occasional bald eagle. If you explore the wooded areas, you may even catch sight of the endangered Delmarva fox squirrel. See p. 176.
- **Butterfly-Watching at Eastern Neck National Wildlife Refuge** (Eastern Shore, Md.): The trees here fill up with the colorful little travelers as they make their way to South America every fall. Fans of the tundra swan also await the waterfowls' arrival to this resting place. The refuge's website keeps nature lovers up-to-date on the migrating creatures' arrival. See p. 186.
- **Whale- & Dolphin-Watching on the Mid-Atlantic:** The Atlantic coast of Maryland and Delaware, particularly near Cape Henlopen State Park (Del.), is a good place to spot whales and dolphins. The Great Dune at Cape Henlopen is a great vantage point (bring binoculars). There are also whale- and dolphin-watching cruises available—even sea kayaking with the dolphins. See p. 244 and chapter 10.
- **Bombay Hook National Wildlife Refuge** (Central Del.): The largest of Delaware's wildlife refuges, Bombay Hook, northeast of Dover, has nearly 16,000 acres of tidal marsh, freshwater pools, and timbered swamps. You'll see a lot of migratory waterfowl in fall and spring; then the migrant shorebirds and songbirds appear in April, May, and June. See p. 328.

The Best Baseball in Maryland

Marylanders love baseball. The Orioles are the big-league team, of course, but the state is also home to six minor-league teams, three baseball museums, and a monument to a storied slugger.

The **Baltimore Orioles** (© 888/848-BIRD; baltimore.orioles.mlb.com) play at Oriole Park at Camden Yards. The stadium is easy to get to, right off I-95 to I-395 at the bottom of the ramp into town. Parking in lots around the stadium usually costs about $10. The Light Rail stops here for every game. The ballpark was designed to bring spectators closer to the action, and it does. Watch out for foul balls! A promenade follows the warehouse building along the outfield wall. Stop at the deck overlooking the bullpen to watch the pitchers warm up. The food here is pretty good, ranging from hot dogs to Italian sausage to crab cakes. Former Oriole Boog Powell's barbecue stand sends a cloud of smoke up over the scoreboard wall—the pit-beef sandwiches are worth the wait in line. The park also offers tours that give visitors a chance to sit in the dugout and in the press box from April to September.

An Orioles game might be a great place to bring a client (the stands are full of them), but a minor-league game is the place for families. In addition to lower ticket prices (less than $10) and more intimate stadiums, many minor-league games offer playgrounds, fireworks, and special family events.

The **Aberdeen IronBirds** (© 410/297-9292; www.ironbirdsbaseball.com), a Class A affiliate of the Orioles, are owned by Aberdeen natives Cal and Billy Ripken. The stadium was an instant hit when it opened in 2002. It also houses the **Ripken Museum,** which moved here in late 2005 from downtown Aberdeen. A temporary exhibit is part of group tours (call © 410/297-9292 for reservations). A permanent home—a testament to the "Ripken Way," which took six Ripkens to professional baseball—will open in 2007. Nearby youth-size fields copy the dimensions of famous parks; Cal Sr.'s Yard, for instance, is a miniature replica of Oriole Park at Camden Yards (a "warehouse" like the one at the real Camden Yards will house a 200-room hotel by late 2006). The Ripken Academy operates a series of baseball clinics, tournaments, and the Cal Ripken World Series here.

10 The Best Camping

- **Janes Island State Park** (Eastern Shore, Md.): For sunset vistas over the Chesapeake Bay, the campsites at this park north of Crisfield can't be beat. Many sites sit on the water's edge, offering unobstructed views and access to the canoe trail. If you prefer less primitive accommodations, there are a few waterside cabins as well. See p. 181.

- **New Germany State Park** (Garrett County, Md.): It's small, with only 37 well-spaced sites, but they are clean, well kept, and offer easy access to hiking trails, fishing spots in the park's lake, and the facilities of several other Western Maryland state parks and forests. The 11 cabins are great options for winter cross-country skiing trips. See p. 216.

The **Bowie Baysox** (© 301/464-4865; www.baysox.com), a Class AA Orioles affiliate, usually have a fireworks display after Saturday home games. The team plays in Prince George's Stadium, in Prince George's County, northeast of Washington, D.C.

The **Delmarva Shorebirds** (© 888/BIRDS96 or 410/219-3112; www.theshorebirds.com), an Orioles affiliate in the Class A South Atlantic League, play near Ocean City, at Arthur W. Perdue Stadium in Salisbury, Maryland. An Eastern Shore Hall of Fame here celebrates Delmarva baseball from amateur to pro.

The **Frederick Keys** (© 877/8GO-KEYS; www.frederickkeys.com), the 2005 Carolina League champions and a Class A Orioles affiliate, play at Harry Grove Stadium in Frederick, off I-70 and Route 355 (Market St.). The Keys draw fans from Baltimore and Washington, D.C.

The **Hagerstown Suns** (© 800/538-9967 or 301/791-6266; www.hagerstownsuns.com), a Class A team of the New York Mets, play at Municipal Stadium, on Route 40, in Hagerstown, Western Maryland.

Baltimore City has two sports museums celebrating baseball. Yes, the Babe *was* a Yankee, but he was born in Baltimore in the narrow rowhouse that is now the **Babe Ruth Birthplace and Museum,** 216 Emory St. (© 410/727-1539; www.baberuthmuseum.com). Next door to Oriole Park at Camden Yards is **Sports Legends at Camden Yards,** 301 W. Camden St. © 410/727-1539; www.sportslegendsatcamdenyards.com), filled with mementos of Orioles history as well as other local sporting memories. For details of these two museums, see p. 97 and p. 98.

If you visit **Chestertown,** on the Eastern Shore, look for the life-size statue of **Bill Nicholson** next to the town hall on Cross Street. In the 1940s, the Chestertown native was a home-run king with the Chicago Cubs. He led the majors in home runs and RBIs in 1943 and 1944. During the 1944 season, the New York Giants intentionally walked him with the bases loaded, rather than risk a grand slam. He died in his hometown, Chestertown, in 1996.

- **Potomac–Garrett State Forest** (Garrett County, Md.): For primitive camping in the mountains, head to this state forest in Western Maryland. Nearly all the campsites are within walking distance of one of the forest's mountain streams, and they're so spread out, you may never know if you have camping neighbors. See p. 217.
- **Cape Henlopen State Park** (near Lewes, Del.): Summer beach camping is always a tenuous venture, with the heat, the bugs, and the sand. But the facilities at Cape Henlopen make for the best beach experience: There are 159 wooded sites, several with full hookups, and all with access to bathhouses and running water. Within the park, you'll find several miles of hiking and biking trails, guarded beaches, and great fishing. See p. 236.

11 The Best Festivals & Events

- **Flower Mart** (Baltimore, Md.; **410/ 323-0022;** www.flowermart.org): This 2-day festival is held the first weekend in May, beside the Washington Monument on Charles Street. You'll see ladies wearing flower-bedecked hats, plenty of flowers, and traditional Baltimore foods such as crab cakes and the yummy lemon stick. (Halve a lemon, stab it with a peppermint stick, and suck the juice through the candy.)

- **United States Sailboat Show** (Annapolis, Md.; *©* **410/268-8828;** www.usboat.com): Boat dealers fill the city dock with an array of sailboats, some spartan racing boats and others luxurious floating living rooms. Wear sneakers or boat shoes, and you can climb aboard them all and dream. It takes place the first weekend in October. The **Powerboat Show** is held the following weekend.

- **Waterfowl Festival** (Easton, Md.; *©* **410/822-4567;** www.waterfowl festival.org): You'll see paintings of canvasbacks, herons, and Canada geese; decoys both practical and fanciful; and sculptures so lifelike you'll want to smooth their feathers. There are sometimes even tiny sculptures worked in gold. For fun, stop by the duck-calling contest, too. The festival is held the second week in November.

- **Christmas at Longwood Gardens** (Kennett Square, Pa., in the Brandywine Valley; *©* **610/388-1000**): Thousands of lights—or maybe it's millions—turn the gardens into pure magic. Everyone forgets that it's cold as they slow down to gaze at all those twinkling lights. Then they go into the conservatories to see all the poinsettias and Christmas decorations. "Winter wonderland" is so cliché, but it's really true in this case.

12 The Best Family Activities

- **B&O Railroad Museum** (Baltimore, Md.): Kids of every age are entranced by the gigantic iron horses that fill the roundhouse where American railroading got its start. See p. 97.

- **Art and Industry** (Baltimore, Md.): Baltimore's museums have a few attractions the kids are sure to like. The **Walters Art Museum** (p. 101) has a great armor collection, while the sculpture garden at the **Baltimore Museum of Art** (p. 101) delights even the youngest children. And the guides at the **Baltimore Museum of Industry** (p. 92) offer insights on the kids' levels and even let them try out some of the machines.

- *Harbor Queen* **Boat Ride** (Annapolis, Md.): The kids love leaning over the rail as waves hit the boat, and it's a great way to see the bay. There's a little history lesson, but mostly this is a wind-in-your-face, sun-in-your-eyes ride. See p. 141.

- **Delaware History Museum** (Wilmington, Del.): Toddlers can run up and down the ramps, school-age children can try out the interactive displays, and everybody will get a kick out of the "Distinctly Delaware" exhibit. Grandma's Attic adds hands-on activities to the fun. See p. 301.

2

Planning Your Trip to Maryland & Delaware

Maryland and Delaware are relatively visitor-friendly states—they're compact and have good roads, fair public transportation, three international airports, and one national airport within a 3-hour drive. But even in such an accessible region, a little advance planning can make your trip run more smoothly. This chapter will answer many questions you may have while planning your trip: When is the best time to visit? Which festivals and events will coincide with my trip? How much time (and money) should I plan to spend? What's the best way to get there?

1 The Regions in Brief

MARYLAND

Maryland and Delaware, two of the smaller states, contain a wide variety of terrain, weather, topography, and urban and rural areas. Here's a brief description of the major regions in the two Mid-Atlantic States, starting from the mountainous west to the coastal east.

WESTERN MARYLAND Lovers of the outdoors adore this part of Maryland. It has biking and hiking trails, lakes, and white water. It has the Catoctin Mountains and Deep Creek Lake, charming towns, and historic sites.

Everything west of Frederick County is considered Western Maryland. Although development is beginning to touch the area, particularly around Hagerstown and Cumberland, the atmosphere is peaceful. You can expect a smile and a welcome from the people you meet.

It used to take hours driving over small winding roads to get to the far reaches of Western Maryland. That's no longer true since the construction of Route 68, which continues westward when Route 70 heads north near Hancock. Route 68

bypasses the small towns and slices right through a mountain at Sideling Hill.

Now skiing at Wisp Resort is just a few hours away from the more populous eastern part of the state. Hiking a trail at Swallow Falls can take longer than driving to it. And many visitors frequent Deep Creek Lake and Rocky Gap State Park and Resort.

Summer and winter are the best times to visit. Spring is a little cold for most activities except shopping, limited sightseeing, and relaxing. Fall is the prettiest time for sightseeing trips. Wisp Resort has added an 18-hole golf course on its gentler slopes and made the ski lifts available for hikers and bikers once the snow melts. In the state parks, visitors can go cross-country skiing, snowshoeing, and tobogganing, or ride in a horse-drawn sleigh. Spring and fall are the seasons for hiking, biking, horseback riding, fishing, and sometimes boating. Summer offers warm breezes, hot sunshine, and cool shade for outdoor activities and relaxing afterward.

Wine, Maryland Style

The state has an array of wineries, from Western Maryland to north of Baltimore City to the Eastern Shore. New wineries open every year.

Visit the wineries either in summer, while the grapes are growing, or in September, when winemaking begins. The tours are most interesting when you see those vats brimming with fermenting grape juice. On weekends, several wineries host festivals with live music, food, and their own wines. All are in picturesque country, characterized by rolling hills and fresh air, and all have tastings and can help you choose a bottle or case to take home.

In Western Maryland, **Deep Creek Cellars**, 177 Frazee Ridge Rd., Friendsville (© **301/746-4349**; www.deepcreekcellars.com), is a tiny family-run operation near Deep Creek that uses mostly organic techniques. Tours are offered Wednesday through Saturday from 11am to 6pm between April 20 and November 20. Take I-68 west to Exit 6. Go north on Route 42 and turn right on Frazee Ridge Road; the winery is on the left.

In Frederick County, **Berrywine Plantations/Linganore Winecellars**, 13601 Glissans Mill Rd., Mount Airy (© **410/795-6432**; www.linganore-wine.com), **Elk Run Vineyards**, 15113 Liberty Rd., Mount Airy (© **410/775-2513**; www.elkrun.com), and **Loew Vineyards**, 14001 Liberty Rd., Mount Airy (© **301/831-5464**; www.loewvineyards.net), are all close enough to each other to visit in a day. Make a day trip by combining the wineries with a stop in New Market for lunch and antiques shopping. Take I-70 to Route 75 and follow signs to New Market and Berrywine; then continue north to Route 26 East to reach nearby Elk Run and Loew. Berrywine is the largest winery in the state, with a yield of 300,000 bottles yearly. Elk Run and Loew are much smaller, but friendly and fun. On weekends, all three have tours Saturday from 10am to 5pm and Sunday from noon to 5pm. Elk Run also has tours Tuesday through Friday from 10am to 5pm, and Berrywine offers weekday tours from 10am to 5pm. Berrywine hosts festivals with lots of music about twice a month.

In Carroll County, **Cygnus Wine Cellars**, 3130 Long Lane, Manchester (© **410/374-6395**; www.cygnuswinecellars.com), has tastings and tours on Saturday and Sunday from noon to 5pm. It specializes in late-harvest vidal and sparkling wines. It's located near Westminster.

In northern Baltimore County, **Basignani Winery**, 15722 Falls Rd., Sparks (© **410/472-0703**; www.basignani.com), produces varietals such as cabernet sauvignon, chardonnay, and Riesling. It's open Wednesday through Saturday from 11:30am to 5:30pm, Sunday from noon to 6pm. Take I-83 north to Exit 24B, Belfast Road. Follow signs to the winery; turn right on Route 25; the winery is on the left.

An easy drive from Basignani Winery is **Woodhall Wine Cellars**, 17912 York Rd., Parkton (© **410/357-8644**; www.woodhallwinecellars.com), farther north on I-83 off Exit 27, next to the Gunpowder River. One of the oldest wineries in the state, Woodhall makes a wide variety of wines, including Gunpowder Falls Estate Chardonnay and Parkton Prestige, a red wine. Woodhall has festivals twice a month. Tours are offered Monday through Saturday from 10am to 6pm, Sunday from noon to 6pm.

Also in northern Baltimore County, **Boordy Vineyards,** 12820 Long Green Pike, Hydes (© 410/592-5015; www.boordy.com), is one of Maryland's most highly regarded wineries. It hosts regular festivals and tastings. Tours are offered daily on the hour from 1 to 4pm, though the winery is open Monday through Saturday from 10am to 5pm, Sunday from 1 to 5pm. From the Baltimore Beltway (I-695), take Exit 31 North and go 4 miles to Long Green Pike.

About a half-hour drive from Woodhall or Boordy is **Fiore Winery,** 3026 Whiteford Rd., Pylesville (© 410/879-4007; www.fiorewinery.com), run by a winemaker whose family made wine in Italy for 400 years. Wines range from chambourcin to merlot and chardonnay. Get here by driving through the countryside or taking I-95, Exit 74. Turn left on Route 152, then right on Route 1 North to Route 24 North to Route 136 to Whiteford Road.

In Montgomery County, southwest of Baltimore, **Catoctin Winery,** 805 Greenbridge Rd., Brookeville (© 301/744-2310), is known for its cabernet sauvignon, Riesling, and especially Eye of the Oriole. Tastings are Saturday and Sunday from noon to 5pm. Take I-95 south to Exit 38B, Route 32 West. Turn left on Route 108, right on Ten Oaks Road, left on Brighton Dam Road, right on New Hampshire Avenue, and right on Greenbridge Road to the winery.

Also in Montgomery County, **Sugarloaf Mountain Vineyard,** 18101 Comus Rd., Dickerson (© 301/605-0130; www.smvwinery.com), is one of Maryland's newest, opened in 2006. It produces cabernet sauvignon, cabernet franc, and chardonnay. Call for visiting hours. Take I-270 south to Exit 22, Route 109 to Comus Road.

In Calvert County, **Cove Point Winery,** 755 Cove Point Rd., Lusby (© 410/326-0949; www.covepointwinery.com), specializes in ice-style wines, along with merlot and gewürztraminer. Located on Route 4 toward Solomons, it's open Saturday and Sunday from noon to 5:30pm.

Over on the Eastern Shore, **St. Michaels Winery,** 605 S. Talbot St., St. Michaels (© 410/253-2552), opens for business in mid-2006 in the old Flour Mill Complex, which also houses a bakery, art studios, and shops. Call for visiting hours.

Also on the Eastern Shore, **Tilmon's Island Winery,** 755 Millington Rd., Sudlersville (© 443/480-5021; www.tilmonswine.com), has tastings of its cabernet franc and chambourcin on Saturdays from 11am to 5pm. It uses primarily Eastern Shore–grown grapes. Call for directions.

In addition to the wineries, Maryland has two festivals celebrating the grape. The largest—drawing more than 20,000 people—is the **Maryland Wine Festival,** held on a mid-September weekend, Saturday from 10am to 6pm and Sunday from noon to 6pm, at the Carroll County Farm Museum in Westminster. There's music and food to accompany the 10 tastings of Maryland wines. **Wine in the Woods** has a lovely setting, under the trees of Symphony Woods in Columbia, about 45 minutes west of Baltimore. The festival is usually held on Preakness Weekend in mid-May, Saturday and Sunday from noon to 6pm. Admission includes 10 tastings. For exact dates of both, call © 800/313-7275 or visit www.marylandwine.com.

THE WASHINGTON, D.C., SUB-URBS   A lot of territory is dumped into this region. All roads—or at least highways—go to Washington, D.C., and so do many of the people who live in these Maryland counties. But the counties of Frederick, Montgomery, Prince George's, Howard, and Carroll are distinctly different. Frederick's history is tied more to that of Western Maryland, though you'd never know it if you're driving the highways around rush hour. It's part of the Civil War crossroads, so you can't go far without finding another reminder of the War Between the States. The area is also home to Camp David, the presidential retreat, and rolling hills covered with orchards and dairy farms. A drive up Route 15 toward Gettysburg offers one of Maryland's best day trips.

The other four counties have mostly given themselves over to urban sprawl. There are still some gems, like the Great Falls of the Potomac and the home of Clara Barton, the founder of the American Red Cross. Theme-park fans can head for Six Flags America in Prince George's County.

BALTIMORE   METROPOLITAN AREA   With Baltimore and Annapolis as its crown jewels, this heavily populated region is home to most Marylanders. Baltimore keeps attracting more businesses and new residents as it continues to transform itself from aging industrial town to up-to-the-minute cosmopolitan city. It's got plenty of restaurants, museums, and attractions to keep both tourists and locals happy. Annapolis, 25 miles away, works hard at staying just the way it has always been. That Colonial style, with the U.S. Naval Academy and Chesapeake Bay as charming backdrops, still attracts plenty of visitors to this day.

SOUTHERN MARYLAND   Tobacco was king in Southern Maryland in the old days, and reminders are still evident. As you drive down rural routes through Charles, Calvert, and St. Mary's counties, you can see tobacco-curing barns with the long narrow slits that open up to the air.

St. Clements's Island, where Maryland's first settlers stepped upon the New World on March 25, 1634, is still a very remote place. St. Mary's City disappeared after Annapolis became the capital, but archaeologists are rediscovering and restoring the 371-year-old buildings in a fascinating work in progress.

Surrounded by the mouth of the Potomac River and the Atlantic Ocean, this is fishing territory. At Point Lookout State Park, anglers can try their luck in both. In Calvert County, both Chesapeake Beach and Solomons offer many a fishing-charter boat.

THE EASTERN SHORE   This is the home of corn, oysters, and geese. On a flat spit of land that stretches up the eastern side of the Chesapeake Bay, from the Atlantic to the Susquehanna River, the Eastern Shore is different from the rest of Maryland. Natives have their own accent. They're sun- and wind-burned from long hours on a tractor or a workboat.

The Eastern Shore's flatness makes biking easy. There are rivers for fishing, boating, and swimming. Towns are small, and though many are more businesslike than pretty, some have deserved reputations for charm and history. The wide-open spaces attract waterfowl from fall to spring, a delight if you're a hunter or a birder.

The Mid-Shore—Talbot County, Kent Island, and Dorchester County along the Choptank—is the most developed part of the Eastern Shore and the most tourist-friendly. Though fishing and crabbing are important, the main industry here has historically been shipbuilding. Talbot County has the most hotels, inns, and restaurants.

Kent and Cecil counties comprise the North Shore, an area of highlands and rolling hills. The countryside is beautiful, but accommodations for travelers are few and far between.

Don't care about any of that? You'll love Route 50 because it will get you "downy ocean" in a hurry, hon.

DOWN THE OCEAN The Atlantic rules here. Sun, beach, and miniature golf as far as the eye can see! Here, too, are the lifesaving stations that once housed those who saved sailors in distress and the concrete watchtowers that once housed those on the lookout for World War II enemy ships.

Ocean City's condos, shops, and highways dominate the state's coastline; in summer, it's Maryland's second-largest city. South of the inlet is Assateague Island, a seashore park renowned for its wild ponies and its pristine landscape.

DELAWARE
DOWN THE OCEAN, CONTINUED
In Delaware, much smaller resorts, such as Bethany Beach and Dewey Beach, are located between long stretches of public beach and national seashore. Rehoboth, Delaware's premier beach, retains its small-town charm in spite of the crowds that can make north–south Route 1 impassable on holidays or summer weekends. An ever-expanding district of outlet stores on Route 1 makes the traffic worse (and the bargains more plentiful). Just north of Rehoboth Beach is Lewes, a quaint Victorian town known as the terminus of the Cape May–Lewes Ferry. It's a nice diversion thanks to its shops, its

Delaware Bay beaches with gentle waves, and its many charter fishing boats.

CENTRAL DELAWARE Kent County, which is primarily farmland, is Delaware's central county and home of Dover, the state capital. Bombay Hook National Wildlife Refuge on the Delaware Bay is a stop along the East Coast for migrating waterfowl and is less developed than Blackwater on Maryland's Eastern Shore. State capital Dover, a striking contrast to Annapolis, is a quiet town, with charming museums and historic sites—but twice a year on race weekends, Dover and most of the state fill up with fans of the big NASCAR auto races.

THE BRANDYWINE VALLEY This is du Pont country. The American branch of the du Pont family has been in this region since E. I. du Pont opened his black powder mill on the banks of the Brandywine River in 1802. Their legacy is everywhere, from Longwood Gardens to Winterthur. You could easily spend a week here and not see all the sights. It's not hard to see why the du Ponts, or anyone, would settle here: The rolling hills, the fertile land, and the river itself have served as inspiration for the region's other famous family, the Wyeths.

Wilmington lies at the mouth of the Brandywine River. It's a convenient spot for visiting the Brandywine Valley, but it's also got interesting restaurants and museums of its own. The city's newly developed Riverfront is worth a visit, too.

2 Visitor Information

MARYLAND For information about the entire state, contact the **Maryland Division of Tourism, Film, and the Arts** (© **800/MD-IS-FUN** or 410/767-3400; www.mdisfun.org). Its website has links to county websites as well. For information on Baltimore and the vicinity, contact the **Baltimore Area Convention and Visitors Bureau** (© **877-BALTIMORE** or 410/659-7300; www.baltimore.org).

For information on state parks, forests, and wildlife refuges, contact the **Maryland Department of Natural Resources** (© **800/830-3974** or 410/260-8DNR; www.dnr.maryland.gov).

In addition, look for **"Visitor Information"** or blue question-mark signs near your destination. They are on all major highways and, especially in Frederick and Western Maryland, will lead you to an office filled with knowledgeable people. **Maryland Welcome Centers** are on I-95, Route 50, Route 68, Route 70, and Route 301, as well as at BWI Airport.

DELAWARE   Delaware's tourism agencies are regional. **The Delaware Tourism Office** (© **800/VISITDE** or 302/739-4271; www.visitdelaware.com) offers general information, but local tourism offices and chambers of commerce will provide more detailed information in a more timely fashion. In southern Delaware (Sussex County), contact **Southern Delaware Tourism** (© **800/357-1818** or 302/856-1818; www.visit southerndelaware.com). For information on Wilmington and the Brandywine Valley, contact the **Greater Wilmington Convention and Visitors Bureau** (© **800/422-1181** or 302/652-4088; www.visit wilmingtonde.com).

3 Money

As you might expect, prices in restaurants and hotels in the larger cities are higher than prices in small towns and roadside diners. Resort towns like Ocean City can be quite expensive in summer, but far more reasonable in the shoulder and off seasons.

Expect expenses to rise the closer you get to Washington, D.C. Wilmington, as a corporate headquarters and destination for business travelers, has many high-end hotels and restaurants. Baltimore is, overall, a less expensive city. Compared to American cities like New York and European destinations like London and Paris, both Wilmington and Baltimore are much less expensive as tourist destinations.

ATMs   The easiest way to get cash away from home is from an ATM (automated teller machine). The **Cirrus** (© **800/424-7787;** www.mastercard.com) and **PLUS** (© **800/843-7587;** www.visa. com) networks span the globe; look at the back of your card to see which network you're on, then call or check online for ATM locations at your destination. Be sure you know your personal identification number (PIN) before you leave home and be sure to find out your daily withdrawal limit before you depart. Also keep in mind that many banks impose a fee every time a card is used at a different bank's ATM (where they're usually around $1.50). On top of this, the bank from which you withdraw cash may charge its own fee. To compare banks' ATM fees within the U.S., use www.bankrate.com. For international withdrawal fees, ask your bank. You can also get cash advances on your credit card at an ATM.

TRAVELER'S CHECKS   Traveler's checks are something of an anachronism from the days before the ATM made cash accessible at any time. Given the fees you'll pay for ATM use at banks other than your own, however, you might be better off with traveler's checks if you're withdrawing money often.

You can buy traveler's checks at most banks. **American Express** offers denominations of $20, $50, $100, $500, and (for cardholders only) $1,000. You'll pay a service charge ranging from 1% to 4%. By phone, you can buy traveler's checks by calling © **800/807-6233.** American Express cardholders should dial © **800/221-7282;** this number accepts collect calls, offers service in several foreign languages, and exempts Amex gold and platinum cardholders from the 1% fee.

Visa offers traveler's checks at Citibank locations nationwide, as well as at several other banks. The service charge ranges between 1.5% and 2%; checks come in denominations of $20, $50, $100, $500, and $1,000. Call © **800/732-1322** for information. AAA members can obtain Visa checks at most AAA offices or by calling ✆ **866/339-3378. MasterCard** also offers traveler's checks. Call ✆ **800/ 223-9920** for a location near you.

If you choose to carry traveler's checks, be sure to keep a record of their serial numbers separate from your checks in the event that they are stolen or lost. You'll get a refund faster if you know the numbers.

CREDIT CARDS Credit cards are a safe way to carry money, they provide a convenient record of all your expenses, and they generally offer good exchange rates. You can also withdraw cash advances from your credit cards at banks or ATMs, provided you know your PIN.

If you've forgotten yours, or didn't even know you had one, call the number on the back of your credit card and ask the bank to send it to you. It usually takes 5 to 7 business days, though some banks will provide the number over the phone if you tell them your mother's maiden name or some other personal information.

MasterCard and Visa are by far the most commonly accepted credit cards in both Maryland and Delaware. American Express is nearly as common, although many small businesses, especially B&Bs, don't accept it. Diners Club isn't very common, although Discover is becoming more accepted.

4 When to Go

The resort towns on the Atlantic are most popular in summer, and usually quite crowded. The fringe season, May and especially September, is a great time to find cheaper rates, comfortable temperatures, and quieter beaches.

Peak season for the Eastern Shore, Annapolis, and Southern Maryland is April through October, when the weather clears up for boating and the fish start biting.

Most everything is open in Baltimore year-round, though because of its boating culture and baseball season, summer is the most popular and crowded time to visit. The best time is usually in May or fall, when the weather is likely to be sunny but not so humid.

Western Maryland attracts visitors year-round, though spring can be too cool and soggy. Fall is magnificent, especially around mid-October; when it snows, winter is beautiful; summers are cooler here than in the rest of the state.

Baltimore's Average Monthly Temperatures & Precipitation

	Jan	Feb	Mar	Apr	May	June	July	Aug	Sept	Oct	Nov	Dec
Temp (°F)	32	35	44	53	63	73	77	76	69	57	47	37
Temp (°C)	0	1	6	11	17	22	25	24	20	13	8	2
Precip (in.)	3.05	3.12	3.38	3.09	3.72	3.67	3.69	3.92	3.41	2.98	3.32	3.41

Cumberland's Average Monthly Temperatures & Precipitation

	Jan	Feb	Mar	Apr	May	June	July	Aug	Sept	Oct	Nov	Dec
Temp (°F)	30	33	43	54	63	71	75	74	67	55	45	35
Temp (°C)	0	0	6	12	17	21	23	23	19	12	7	1
Precip (in.)	2.38	2.29	3.08	3.19	3.66	3.34	3.37	3.30	3.08	2.77	2.76	2.61

Wilmington and the Brandywine Valley are year-round destinations.

Most attractions offer festivals and events year-round. In the temperature chart above, Baltimore information applies generally to Wilmington and the Brandywine Valley as well; expect summer temperatures to be slightly higher on the southern Eastern Shore and on the coast. Remember that monthly averages can be deceiving: Even though the average temperature in Baltimore during July is 77°F (25°C), days in the 90s (32°C and up) are common.

MARYLAND & DELAWARE CALENDAR OF EVENTS

January

Historic Annapolis Antiques Show (© 410/267-8146; www.annapolis. org), Medford National Guard Armory, Annapolis, Md. Fine country and period furniture and decorative arts to benefit London Town Foundation. Second weekend in January.

Chesapeake Bay Boat Show (© 212/984-7000; www.discoverboating.com), Baltimore Convention Center, Baltimore, Md. Dream of summer while climbing aboard all kinds of motor- and sailboats. Nine days in mid-January.

February

Hunt Valley Antiques Show (© 410/961-5121; www.armacostantiques shows.com), Marriott's Hunt Valley Inn, I-83 and Shawan Road, Hunt Valley, Md. As good as Annapolis's show. Call for tickets. Last weekend in February.

March

St. Patrick's Day Parade and Festival (© 800/OC-OCEAN), Coastal Highway, Ocean City, Md. Saturday nearest the actual day.

Maryland Day (© 800/762-1634 for St. Mary's or 410/267-8146 for Annapolis), Historic St. Mary's City and Annapolis, Md. Special tours and ceremonies at historic sites. On or near March 25.

April

My Lady's Manor Steeplechase Races (© 410/557-9466), Ladew Topiary Gardens, Route 146 and Pocock Road, Monkton, Md. Annual running of the steeplechase. Saturday in mid-April.

Baltimore Waterfront Festival, Harborplace, Baltimore, Md. Free celebration of the Chesapeake Bay, with boating, activities, food, and entertainment. Last weekend in April.

Maryland Maritime Heritage Festival (© 410/266-3960; www.mdmhf. org), City Dock, Annapolis, Md. Late April to early May.

May

Maryland Film Festival (© 410/752-8083; www.mdfilmfest.com), venues around Maryland. First week in May.

Decoy and Wildlife Art Festival (© 410/939-3739; www.decoy museum.com), Havre de Grace Decoy Museum, Havre de Grace, Md. First weekend in May.

Bay Bridge Walk (© 877/BAYSPAN), Chesapeake Bay, Md. Arrive early to walk the 4¼-mile span across the Chesapeake Bay Bridge. First Sunday in May at 9am.

Preakness Week (© 410/542-9400; www.preakness.com), Baltimore area, Md. The Preakness Stakes, the second jewel of horse racing's Triple Crown, is held at Pimlico Race Course. Gates open at 8:30am. The celebration begins the previous week with a parade and other events. Third Saturday in May.

Wine in the Woods (© 410/313-7275; www.wineinthewoods.com), Symphony Woods, Columbia, Md. Sample Maryland wines and gourmet foods, enjoy entertainment, and browse arts and crafts. Preakness Weekend (just by coincidence) from noon to 6pm.

Flower Mart (© 410/323-0022; www.flowermart.org), Mount Vernon, Baltimore, Md. A charming tradition by the Washington Monument, known for its flowers, lemon sticks, and crab cakes. First weekend in May.

Chestertown Tea Party (✆ 410/778-0416; www.chestertownteaparty.com), Chestertown, Md. Bostonians weren't the only ones throwing tea overboard in the 1770s. This festival has a reenactment of the 1774 Tea Party, a parade, a crafts and art show, entertainment, and food. Last weekend in May.

U.S. Naval Academy Commissioning Week (✆ 410/263-6937), Annapolis, Md. Activities include an air show by the Blue Angels, several dress parades, and graduation. The air show stops traffic near the Severn River and attracts lots of spectators. Other events are closed to the general public. Mid-May.

June

"Monster Mile" NASCAR Weekend (✆ 800/441-RACE; www.doverspeedway.com), Dover, Del. This 2-day stock-car race draws top drivers from the circuit to Dover International Speedway. Early June.

Arts Alive (✆ 800/0C-OCEAN), Northside Park, Ocean City, Md. Juried art contest and exhibition. First weekend in June.

Columbia Festival of the Arts (✆ 410/715-3044; www.columbia festival.com), Lake Kittamaqundi, Columbia, Md. Celebration of the arts with local and national stars of theater, music, dance, and visual arts. Ten days in mid-June.

July

Salute to Independence (✆ 301/432-5124; www.nps.gov/anti/salute.htm), Antietam National Battlefield, Sharpsburg, Md. The Maryland Symphony Orchestra's annual concert of classical and patriotic music, with cannon fire and fireworks. Saturday after July 4th.

Artscape (✆ 410/837-4636; www.artscape.org), Baltimore, Md. A weekend festival celebrating the visual and performing arts. Nationally known performers join local artists; children's activities are also offered. Mid-July.

Delaware State Fair (✆ 302/398-3269; www.delawarestatefair.com), State Fairgrounds, Harrington, Del. Annual agricultural showcase, as well as stock-car races, a demolition derby, harness racing, rides, games, and live concerts. Third week in July.

J. Millard Tawes Crab and Clam Bake (✆ 410/968-2500), Crisfield, Md. An all-you-can-eat celebration of crabs, clams, and corn on the Eastern Shore. Wednesday in mid-July.

August

Kunta Kinte Celebration (✆ 410/349-0338), Annapolis, Md. African-American cultural heritage festival with music, dance, arts, and crafts. Mid-August.

Maryland State Fair (✆ 410/252-0200; www.marylandstatefair.com), Timonium Fairgrounds, Md. Eleven days of farm animals, crafts, produce, rides, entertainment, and thoroughbred racing. From the week before Labor Day through the holiday weekend, daily from 10am to 10pm.

September

Duck Fair (✆ 410/939-3739; www.decoymuseum.com), Havre de Grace Decoy Museum, Havre de Grace, Md. A celebration of wildlife art, along with food, entertainment, and children's activities. Weekend after Labor Day.

Star-Spangled Banner Weekend (✆ 410/962-4290; www.nps.gov/fomc), Fort McHenry, Baltimore, Md. Reenactments of the War of 1812, with musket firing and children's activities. Fall weekend near Defender's Day, September 12 (a Baltimore City holiday).

Maryland Wine Festival (© 800/ 654-4645), Carroll County Farm Museum, Westminster, Md. Maryland wines, food, entertainment, and tours of the farm museum. Weekend in mid-September.

Baltimore Book Festival (© 888/ BALTIMORE or 410/837-4636), Baltimore, Md. Features local bookstores and publishers, authors and story-tellers, art, entertainment, and food. Weekend in mid-September.

Bethany Beach Boardwalk Arts Festival (© 800/962-7873), Bethany Beach, Del. Juried show attracts crafts-people, artisans, and spectators, and takes up the length of the boardwalk. First Saturday in September.

"Monster Mile" NASCAR Weekend (© 800/441-RACE; www.dover speedway.com), Dover, Del. This 2-day stock-car race, like June's event, draws dozens of top drivers from around the world. Second or third weekend in September.

October

Fells Point Fun Festival (© 410/675-6756), Baltimore, Md. Largest urban festival on the East Coast. First weekend in October.

United States Sailboat Show (© 410/ 268-8828; www.usboat.com), City Dock, Annapolis, Md. Nation's oldest and largest in-water sailboat show. Columbus Day weekend, Thursday through Monday.

United States Powerboat Show (© 410/268-8828; www.usboat.com), City Dock, Annapolis, Md. Nation's oldest and largest in-water powerboat show. Weekend after sailboat show.

Autumn Glory Festival (© 301/387-4386; www.garrettchamber.com), Oakland, Md. State banjo and fiddle championship, crafts, and antiques.

Second week in October, Thursday through Sunday.

Catoctin Colorfest (© 301/271-4432), Thurmont, Md. Arts and crafts and the beauty of the mountains. Second weekend in October.

Tilghman Island Day (© 410/886-2677), Tilghman Island, Md. Local seafood, music, watermen contests, and rides on skipjacks and workboats. Saturday in October.

Maryland Million (© 410/252-2100; www.mdhorsebreeders.com), Laurel Park, Laurel, Md. Maryland's own are celebrated in this race of Maryland-bred, trained thoroughbreds. Saturday in mid-October.

November

Waterfowl Festival (© 410/822-4567; www.waterfowlfestival.org), Easton, Md. An Eastern Shore celebration of decoys, artwork of waterfowl, duck-calling contests, kids' activities, and food. Second weekend in November.

December

New Year's Eve Spectacular (© 888/ BALTIMORE), Inner Harbor, Baltimore, Md. Nonalcoholic parties suitable for families, featuring entertainment, food, and fireworks. December 31.

Yuletide at Winterthur (© 800/448-3883 or 302/888-4600; www.winter thur.org), Winterthur, Del. Celebrate the holidays in 19th-century style, with a festive program at the Brandywine Valley museum, featuring entertainment and guided tours. Mid-November through early January.

First Night Annapolis (© 410/268-8553; www.firstnightannapolis.org), Annapolis, Md. Ring in the new year with performing arts and festivities for families.

5 Travel Insurance

Check your existing insurance policies and credit card coverage before you buy travel insurance. You may already be covered for lost luggage, canceled tickets, or medical expenses. The cost of travel insurance varies widely, depending on the cost and length of your trip, your age, health, and the type of trip you're taking.

TRIP-CANCELLATION INSURANCE Trip-cancellation insurance helps you get your money back if you have to back out of a trip, if you have to go home early, or if your travel supplier goes bankrupt. Allowed reasons for cancellation can range from sickness to natural disasters to the State Department declaring your destination unsafe for travel. (Insurers usually won't cover vague fears, though, as many travelers discovered who tried to cancel their trips in Oct 2001 because they were wary of flying.) In this unstable world, trip-cancellation insurance is a good buy if you're getting tickets well in advance—who knows what the state of the world, or of your airline, will be in 9 months? Insurance policy details vary, so read the fine print—and especially make sure that your airline or cruise line is on the list of carriers covered in case of bankruptcy. For information, contact one of the following insurers: **Access America** (*℃* 866/807-3982; www.accessamerica.com), **Travel Guard International** (*℃* 800/826-4919; www.travelguard.com), **Travel Insured International** (*℃* 800/243-3174; www.travelinsured.com), and **Travelex Insurance Services** (*℃* 888/457-4602; www.travelex-insurance.com).

MEDICAL INSURANCE Most health insurance policies cover you if you get sick away from home—but check before you depart, particularly if you're insured by an HMO. If you require additional medical insurance, try **MEDEX Assistance** (*℃* 410/453-6300; www.medexassist.com) or **Travel Assistance International** (*℃* 800/821-2828; www.travelassistance.com; for general information on services, call the company's Worldwide Assistance Services, Inc., at *℃* 800/777-8710).

LOST-LUGGAGE INSURANCE On domestic flights, checked baggage is covered up to $2,500 per ticketed passenger. On international flights (including U.S. portions of international trips), baggage is limited to approximately $9.05 per pound, up to approximately $635 per checked bag. If you plan to check items more valuable than the standard liability, see if your valuables are covered by your homeowner's policy, get baggage insurance as part of your comprehensive travel-insurance package, or buy Travel Guard's "BagTrak" product. Don't buy insurance at the airport, as it's usually overpriced. Be sure to take any valuables or irreplaceable items with you in your carry-on luggage, as many things (including books, money, and electronics) aren't covered by airline policies.

If your luggage is lost, immediately file a lost-luggage claim at the airport, detailing the luggage contents. For most airlines, you must report delayed, damaged, or lost baggage within 4 hours of arrival. The airlines are required to deliver luggage, once found, directly to your house or destination free of charge.

6 Health & Safety

STAYING HEALTHY
COMMON AILMENTS Maryland and Delaware don't pose any unusual health risks to the average visitor. If you're hiking or camping, be aware that this is deer-tick country, and deer ticks can carry **Lyme disease.** Wear long sleeves and pants tucked into your socks, cover your

head, and inspect yourself for ticks later. Insect repellent containing DEET also helps repel ticks. After your trip, watch for a bull's-eye-shaped rash that can appear 3 days to a month following infection (but be aware that not everyone who is infected will get the rash). There is now a vaccine available for Lyme disease; consult your doctor if you're planning to take an extensive trip to deer tick–infested areas.

For information on West Nile Virus—which has been seen only rarely in Maryland—or Lyme disease, visit www.edcp. org and click on "Fact Sheets."

WHAT TO DO IF YOU GET SICK AWAY FROM HOME   In most cases, your existing health plan will provide the coverage you need. But double-check; you may want to buy **travel medical insurance** as well. (See the section on insurance, above.) Bring your insurance ID card with you when you travel.

If you suffer from a chronic illness, consult your doctor before your departure. For conditions like epilepsy, diabetes, or heart problems, wear a **MedicAlert Identification Tag** (© 800/ 825-3785; www.medicalert.org), which will immediately alert doctors to your condition and give them access to your records through MedicAlert's 24-hour hot line.

Pack **prescription medications** in your carry-on luggage, and carry them in their original containers, with pharmacy labels intact—otherwise they won't make it through airport security. Also bring along copies of your prescriptions in case you lose your pills or run out. Don't forget an extra pair of contact lenses or prescription glasses.

STAYING SAFE

While most of Maryland and Delaware enjoy relatively low crime rates, Baltimore has a nagging problem with property and violent crime, and Wilmington also has neighborhoods where visitors are advised not to go. The major tourist areas of both cities are fairly well policed, but be alert and follow common-sense precautions.

If you're using public transport, it's best to travel during the day and to keep valuables out of sight. It is safer and smarter to drive or take a cab between neighborhoods (unless otherwise noted) rather than to walk, even when the distance is not too great. Keep a good city map at hand to help you out if you're lost. Neighborhoods can go from safe to scary in a matter of a few blocks. It's best to keep on the main routes and turn around if anything looks worrisome.

In parts of Baltimore and Wilmington, panhandlers may approach you. Don't open your wallet or purse to give money. Offer only what's in your pocket. It's okay to say no, too.

7 Specialized Travel Resources

TRAVELERS WITH DISABILITIES

Most disabilities shouldn't stop anyone from traveling. There are more options and resources out there than ever before.

Most hotels in Maryland and Delaware offer accessible accommodations, but be sure to ask when you make reservations. Nearly all of the states' museums are accessible, with the exception of some historic buildings and sites.

Several state parks in Maryland offer accessible facilities. A complete list is available at www.dnr.maryland.gov.

The **Maryland Relay Service** (© 711 or 800/669-0865 TTY) and the **Delaware Relay Service** (© 711 or 800/232-5460 TTY) link standard telephones with text-telephone users.

The **Golden Access Passport** gives visually impaired or permanently disabled persons (regardless of age) free lifetime entrance to all properties administered by the National Park Service, the U.S. Fish and Wildlife Service, the U.S. Forest Service, the U.S. Army Corps of Engineers, the Bureau of Land Management, and the Tennessee Valley Authority. This may include national parks, monuments, historic sites, recreation areas, and national wildlife refuges. You may pick up a Golden Access Passport at any NPS entrance-fee area by showing proof of medically determined disability and eligibility for benefits under federal law. Besides free entry, the Golden Access Passport also offers a 50% discount on federal-use fees charged for such facilities as camping, swimming, parking, boat launching, and tours. For more information, go to www.nps.gov/fees_passes.htm or call © **888/467-2757.**

Organizations that offer assistance to disabled travelers include **MossRehab** (www.mossresourcenet.org), which provides a library of accessible-travel resources online; the **American Foundation for the Blind** (© **800/232-5463;** www.afb.org), a referral resource for the blind or visually impaired that includes information on traveling with Seeing Eye dogs; and **SATH** (Society for Accessible Travel & Hospitality) (© **212/447-7284;** www.sath.org; annual membership fees: $45 adults, $30 seniors and students), which offers a wealth of travel resources for all types of disabilities and informed recommendations on destinations, access guides, travel agents, tour operators, vehicle rentals, and companion services.

For more information specifically targeted to travelers with disabilities, check out the magazines *Emerging Horizons* (www.emerginghorizons.com) and *Open World,* published by SATH (see above).

GAY & LESBIAN TRAVELERS

In Baltimore, the main resource for gay and lesbians is the **Gay and Lesbian Community Center of Baltimore,** 241 W. Chase St. (© **410/837-7748**). The center also produces the *Baltimore Gay Paper* (www.glccb.org), available free at area restaurants, nightclubs, bars, and bookstores.

Rehoboth Beach, Delaware, calls itself the "Nation's Gay Summer Capital." The website **www.gayrehoboth.com** provides a list of gay-friendly hotels and B&Bs as well as information on nightlife and beaches.

The **International Gay & Lesbian Travel Association (IGLTA)** (© **800/448-8550** or 954/776-2626; www.iglta.org) is the trade association for the gay and lesbian travel industry. It offers an online directory of gay- and lesbian-friendly travel businesses; go to the website and click on "Members."

Gay.com Travel (© **800/929-2268** or 415/644-8044; www.gay.com/travel or www.outandabout.com), is an excellent online successor to the popular *Out & About* print magazine. It provides regularly updated information about gay-owned, gay-oriented, and gay-friendly lodging, dining, sightseeing, nightlife, and shopping establishments in every important destination worldwide.

The following travel guides are available at many bookstores and online: *Spartacus International Gay Guide* and *Odysseus,* both good English-language guidebooks focused on gay men; the *Damron* guides, with separate books for gay men and lesbians; and *Gay Travel A to Z: The World of Gay & Lesbian Travel Options at Your Fingertips,* by Marianne Ferrari (Ferrari Publications; Box 35575, Phoenix, AZ 85069), a very good gay and lesbian guidebook series.

SENIOR TRAVEL

Mention the fact that you're a senior when you make your travel reservations. Although all of the major U.S. airlines except America West have canceled their senior discount programs, many hotels still offer discounts for seniors and AARP members. Make sure you ask about these rates, and mention if you are traveling with grandchildren. In most cities, people over the age of 60 qualify for reduced admission to theaters and other attractions, as well as discounted fares on public transportation.

Members of **AARP** (formerly known as the American Association of Retired Persons), 601 E St. NW, Washington, DC 20049 (© **888/687-2277;** www. aarp.org), get discounts on hotels, airfares, and car rentals. Anyone over 50 can join.

The National Park Service offers a **Golden Age Passport** that gives seniors 62 or older lifetime entrance to all properties administered by the National Park Service—national parks, monuments, historic sites, recreation areas, and national wildlife refuges—for a one-time processing fee of $10. It must be purchased in person at any NPS facility that charges an entrance fee. Besides free entry, a Golden Age Passport also offers a 50% discount on federal use fees charged for such facilities as camping, swimming, parking, boat launching, and tours. For more information, go to www.nps.gov/ fees_passes.htm or call © **888/467-2757.**

Many reliable agencies and organizations target the 50-plus market. **Elderhostel** (© **877/426-8056;** www.elder hostel.org) arranges study programs for those 55 and over (and a spouse or companion of any age) in the U.S. and in more than 80 countries around the world. Most courses include airfare, accommodations in university dormitories or modest inns, meals, and tuition.

Recommended publications offering travel resources and discounts for seniors include: the quarterly magazine *Travel 50 & Beyond* (www.travel50andbeyond. com); *Travel Unlimited: Uncommon Adventures for the Mature Traveler* (Avalon); *101 Tips for Mature Travelers,* available from Grand Circle Travel (© **800/221-2610** or 617/350-7500; www.gct.com); and *Unbelievably Good Deals and Great Adventures That You Absolutely Can't Get Unless You're Over 50* (McGraw-Hill).

FAMILY TRAVEL

Maryland and Delaware are very family-friendly destinations (with a few exceptions noted in specific chapters), with many "family-style" restaurants and resorts—and even museums for young people, like Port Discovery in Baltimore, Rose Hill Manor in Frederick, and the Enchanted Woods at Winterthur in Delaware. Don't forget Six Flags America near the Washington, D.C., beltway. And, of course, beach vacations and trips to the mountains were made for families. Attractions tailored for kids are mentioned in just about every chapter.

Recommended family travel websites include **Family Travel Forum** (www. familytravelforum.com), **Family Travel Network** (www.familytravelnetwork. com), and **Family Travel Files** (www.the familytravelfiles.com).

You might also want to pick up *The Unofficial Guide to the Mid-Atlantic with Kids* (Wiley Publishing, Inc.), which includes many ideas for activities, lodging, and restaurants in Maryland and Delaware.

8 Planning Your Trip Online

SURFING FOR AIRFARES

The "big three" online travel agencies, **Expedia.com, Travelocity.com,** and **Orbitz.com,** sell most of the air tickets bought on the Internet. (Canadian travelers should try expedia.ca and Travelocity.ca; U.K. residents can go for expedia.co.uk and opodo.co.uk.). **Kayak.com** is also gaining popularity and uses a sophisticated search engine. Each has different business deals with the airlines and may offer different fares on the same flights, so it's wise to shop around. Expedia, Kayak, and Travelocity will also send you **e-mail notification** when a cheap fare becomes available to your favorite destination. Of the smaller travel-agency websites, **SideStep** (www.sidestep.com) has gotten the best reviews from Frommer's authors. The website (with optional browser add-on) purports to "search 140 sites at once," but in reality only beats competitors' fares as often as other sites do.

Also remember to check **airline websites,** especially those for low-fare carriers such as Southwest, JetBlue, AirTran, or WestJet, whose fares are often misreported or simply missing from travel agency websites. Even with major airlines, you can often shave a few bucks from a fare by booking directly through the airline and avoiding a travel agency's transaction fee. But you'll get these discounts only by **booking online:** Most airlines now offer online-only fares that even their phone agents know nothing about.

Great **last-minute deals** are available through free weekly e-mail services provided directly by the airlines. Most of these are announced on Tuesday or Wednesday and must be purchased online. Most are only valid for travel that weekend, but some (such as Southwest's) can be booked weeks or months in advance. Southwest has a hub at BWI Airport, so it frequently offers excellent fares to Baltimore. Sign up for weekly e-mail alerts at airline websites or check mega-sites that compile comprehensive lists of last-minute specials, such as **Smarter Travel** (smartertravel.com). For last-minute trips, **site59.com** and **lastminutetravel.com** often have better air-and-hotel package deals than the major-label sites.

If you're willing to give up some control over your flight details, use what's called an **"opaque" fare service** like **Priceline** (www.priceline.com) or **Hotwire** (www.hotwire.com). Both offer rock-bottom prices in exchange for travel on a "mystery airline" at a mysterious time of day, often with a mysterious change of planes en route. The mystery airlines are all major, well-known carriers—and the possibility of being sent from Philadelphia to Chicago via Tampa is remote; the airlines' routing computers have gotten a lot better than they used to be. Your chances of getting a 6am or 11pm flight, however, are still pretty high. Hotwire tells you flight prices before you buy; Priceline usually has better deals than Hotwire, but you have to play its "name our price" game. If you're new at this, the helpful folks at **BiddingForTravel** (www.biddingfortravel.com) do a good job of demystifying Priceline's prices and strategies. *Note:* In 2004, Priceline added non-opaque service to its roster. You now have the option to pick exact flights, times, and airlines from a list of offers—or opt to bid on opaque fares as before.

SURFING FOR HOTELS

Shopping online for accommodations is generally done one of two ways: by booking through the hotel's own website or through an independent booking agency (or a fare-service agency like Priceline; see below). Keep in mind that many smaller hotels and B&Bs don't show up on booking-agency websites at all.

Of the big booking sites, **Expedia** offers a long list of special deals and virtual tours of available rooms so you can see what you're paying for. **Travelocity** posts unvarnished customer reviews and ranks its properties according to the AAA rating system. Other reliable options include **Hotels.com** and **Quikbook.com.** An excellent free program, **TravelAxe** (www.travelaxe.net), can help you search multiple hotel sites at once, even ones you may never have heard of.

Frommers.com: The Complete Travel Resource

For an excellent travel-planning resource, we highly recommend **Frommers. com** (www.frommers.com), voted Best Travel Site by *PC Magazine*. We're a little biased, of course, but we guarantee you'll find the travel tips, reviews, monthly vacation giveaways, bookstore, and online-booking capabilities thoroughly indispensable. Among the special features are our popular **Destinations** section, where you'll get expert travel tips, hotel and dining recommendations, and advice on the sights to see for more than 3,500 destinations around the globe; the **Frommers.com Newsletter,** with the latest deals, travel trends, and money-saving secrets; our **Community** area featuring **Message Boards,** where Frommer's readers post queries and share advice (sometimes even our authors show up to answer questions); and our **Photo Center,** where you can post and share vacation tips. When your research is finished, the **Online Reservations System** (www.frommers.com/ book_a_trip) takes you to Frommer's preferred online partners for booking your vacation at affordable prices.

Most of the B&Bs in the Maryland and Delaware area have useful websites. Some of them are listed at www.bbonline. com, but you can find them using a search engine, too. Check with county tourism offices, which can lead you to good websites. Generally speaking, the B&Bs are as good as the websites say they are.

In the opaque website category, **Priceline** and **Hotwire** are even better for hotels than for airfares; with both, you're allowed to pick the neighborhood and quality level of your hotel before paying. For both Priceline and Hotwire, you pay upfront, and the fee is nonrefundable. Some hotels do not provide loyalty program credits or points or other frequent-stay amenities when you book a room through opaque online services. *Note:* Hotwire overrates its hotels by one star—what Hotwire calls a four-star is a three-star anywhere else.

SURFING FOR RENTAL CARS

For booking rental cars online, the best deals are usually found at rental-car company websites, although all the major online travel agencies also offer rental-car reservations services. Priceline and Hotwire work well for rental cars, too; the only "mystery" is which major rental company you get, and for most travelers the difference between Hertz, Avis, and Budget is negligible.

9 The 21st-Century Traveler

INTERNET ACCESS AWAY FROM HOME

Travelers have any number of ways to check their e-mail and access the Internet on the road. Of course, using your own laptop—or even a PDA or electronic organizer with a modem—gives you the most flexibility. But even if you don't have a computer, you can still access your e-mail and even your office computer from cybercafes.

WITHOUT YOUR OWN COMPUTER It's hard nowadays to find a city that *doesn't* have a few cybercafes. Although there's no definitive directory for cybercafes—these are independent businesses, after all—two places to start looking are at **www.cybercaptive.com** and **www.cybercafe.com**.

Aside from formal cybercafes, most **youth hostels** have at least one computer with Internet access. And most **public libraries** offer access for free or a small charge. Avoid **hotel business centers** unless you're willing to pay exorbitant rates.

Most major airports now have **Internet kiosks** scattered throughout their gates. These kiosks, which you'll also see in shopping malls, hotel lobbies, and tourist information offices, give you basic Web access for a per-minute fee that's usually higher than cybercafe prices.

To retrieve your e-mail, ask your **Internet Service Provider (ISP)** if it has a Web-based interface tied to your existing e-mail account. If your ISP doesn't have such an interface, you can use the free **mail2web** service (www.mail2web.com) to view and reply to your home e-mail. For more flexibility, you may want to open a free, Web-based e-mail account with **Yahoo! Mail** (mail.yahoo.com) or **Google Gmail** (gmail.google.com). Your home ISP may be able to forward your e-mail to the Web-based account automatically.

If you need to access files on your office computer, look into a service called **GoToMyPC** (www.gotomypc.com). It provides a Web-based interface for you to access and manipulate a distant PC from anywhere, provided your "target" PC is on and has an always-on connection to the Internet. If you're worried about hackers, use your own laptop rather than a cybercafe computer to access the GoTo-MyPC system.

WITH YOUR OWN COMPUTER

More and more hotels, cafes, and retailers are signing on as Wi-Fi (wireless fidelity) "hotspots," from which you can get high-speed connection without cable wires, networking hardware, or a phone line (see below). You can get Wi-Fi connection in one of several ways. Many laptops sold in the last year or so have built-in Wi-Fi capability (an 802.11b wireless Ethernet connection). Mac owners have their own networking technology, Apple AirPort. For those with older computers, you can plug in an 802.11b/**Wi-Fi card** (around $50). You sign up for wireless access service much as you do for cellphone service, through a plan offered by one of several commercial companies that have made wireless service available in airports, hotel lobbies, and coffee shops, primarily in the U.S. (followed by the U.K. and Japan). **T-Mobile Hotspot** (www.t-mobile.com/hotspot) serves up wireless connections at more than 1,000 Starbucks nationwide. **Boingo** (www.boingo.com) and **Wayport** (www.wayport.com) have set up networks in airports and high-class hotel lobbies. iPass providers (see below) also give you access to a few hundred wireless hotel lobby setups. Best of all, you don't need to be staying at the Four Seasons to use the hotel's network; just set yourself up on a nice couch in the lobby. (Pricing policies can be byzantine, but in general you pay around $30 a month for unlimited access; prices are dropping as Wi-Fi access becomes more common.) To locate other hotspots that provide free wireless networks in cities around the world, go to **www.personaltelco.net/index.cgi/WirelessCommunities**.

Most hotels, especially those catering to business travelers in Baltimore and Wilmington, offer dataports for laptop modems—although wireless service is getting more common. Many hotels now offer free high-speed Internet access using an Ethernet network cable. You can bring your own cables, but most hotels rent them for around $10. Call your hotel in advance to see what your options are.

In addition, major ISPs have **local access numbers** around the world, allowing you to go online by placing a local call. Check your ISP's website or call its toll-free number and ask how you can use your current account away from home, and how much it will cost.

The **iPass** network also has dial-up numbers around the world. You'll have to sign up with an iPass provider, who will then tell you how to set up your computer for your destination(s). For a list of iPass providers, go to www.ipass.com and click on "Individuals Buy Now." One solid provider is **i2roam** (www.i2roam. com; © **866/811-6209** or 920/235-0475).

Wherever you go, bring a **connection kit** of the right power and phone adapters, a spare phone cord, and a spare Ethernet network cable—or find out whether your hotel supplies them to guests.

USING A CELLPHONE

Just because your cellphone works at home doesn't mean it'll work elsewhere in the country (thanks to our nation's fragmented cellphone system). It's a good bet that your phone will work in major cities, but take a look at your wireless company's coverage map on its website before heading out—T-Mobile, Sprint, and Nextel are particularly weak in rural areas. If you need to stay in touch at a destination where you know your phone won't work, rent a phone that does from **InTouch USA** (© **800/872-7626**; www.intouch global.com) or a rental-car location, but beware that you'll pay $1 a minute or more for airtime.

If you're venturing deep into national parks, you may want to consider renting a **satellite phone ("satphone"),** which is different from a cellphone in that it connects to satellites rather than ground-based towers. A satphone is more costly than a cellphone but works in the absence of cellular signal and towers. You'll pay at least $2 per minute to use the phone, and it only works where you can see the horizon (that is, usually not indoors). You can rent Iridium satphones from **RoadPost** (© **888/290-1606** or 905/272-5665; www.roadpost.com). InTouch USA (see above) offers a wider range of satphones but at higher rates.

If you're not from the U.S., you'll be appalled at the poor reach of our **GSM (Global System for Mobiles) wireless network,** which is used by much of the rest of the world (see below). Your phone will probably work in most major U.S. cities; it definitely won't work in many rural areas. (To see where GSM phones work in the U.S., check out www.t-mobile.com/coverage/national_popup. asp). And you may or may not be able to send SMS (text messaging) home. Assume nothing—call your wireless provider and get the full scoop. In a worst-case scenario, you can always rent a phone; InTouch USA delivers to hotels.

10 Getting There

BY PLANE

The gateway to Maryland is **Baltimore/ Washington International Thurgood Marshall Airport (BWI),** 10 miles south of Baltimore and 20 miles north of Annapolis. Hundreds of domestic and international flights arrive daily, and it's a hub for several airlines. Most cities and towns are also convenient to **Washington Dulles International Airport** and **Ronald Reagan Washington National Airport.**

Most major airlines fly into BWI, including **Air Canada Jazz** (© 888/247-2262), **American** (© 800/433-7300), **British Airways** (© 800/247-9297), **Continental** (© 800/525-0280), **Delta** (© 800/221-1212), **Northwest** (© 800/ 225-2525), **Southwest** (© 800/435-9792), **United** (© 800/241-6522), and **US Airways** (© 800/428-4322).

Commuter flights fly into **Salisbury–Ocean City–Wicomico Regional Airport,** near Ocean City, Maryland, and **Cumberland Regional Airport,** in West Virginia, close to Western Maryland destinations.

Delaware does not have its own major airport. Located within easy reach are **Philadelphia International Airport,** 30 minutes from downtown Wilmington and 1½ hours from Dover; **BWI,** approximately 1½ to 2½ hours to most points in Delaware; and **Washington Dulles International Airport** and **Ronald Reagan Washington National Airport,** approximately 2½ to 3 hours to most points in Delaware. In addition, **New Castle County Airport,** about 5 miles south of Wilmington, serves private craft and some limited commercial flights.

GETTING THROUGH THE AIRPORT

Generally, you'll be fine if you arrive at the airport **1 hour** before a domestic flight; if you show up late, tell an airline employee and she'll probably bump you to the front of the line.

Bring a **current, government-issued photo ID** such as a driver's license or passport. Keep your ID at the ready to present at check-in, the security checkpoint, and sometimes even the gate. (Children under 18 do not need government-issued photo IDs for domestic flights.)

The Transportation Security Administration (TSA) has phased out **gate check-in** at all U.S. airports. Passengers with e-tickets, which have made paper tickets nearly obsolete, can beat the ticket-counter lines by using airport **electronic kiosks** or even **online check-in** from their home computers. Online check-in involves logging on to your airline's website, accessing your reservation, and printing out your boarding pass. If you're using a kiosk at the airport, bring the credit card you used to book the ticket or your frequent-flier card. Print out your boarding pass from the kiosk and simply proceed to the security checkpoint with your pass and a photo ID. If you're checking bags or looking to snag an exit-row seat, you will be able to do so using most airline kiosks. **Curbside check-in** is also a good way to avoid lines, although a few airlines still don't allow it.

Security lines remain, particularly during periods of high security alerts. If you have trouble standing for long periods of time, tell an airline employee; the airline will provide a wheelchair. Speed up security by **not wearing metal objects** such as big belt buckles or clanky earrings. If you've got metallic body parts, a note from your doctor can prevent a long chat with the security screeners. Keep in mind that only **ticketed passengers** are allowed past security, except for folks escorting disabled passengers or children.

Federalization has stabilized **what you can carry on** and **what you can't.** The general rule is that sharp things are out, nail clippers are okay, and food and beverages must pass through the X-ray machine—but security screeners can't make you drink from your coffee cup. Travelers in the U.S. are allowed one carry-on bag, plus a "personal item" such as a purse, briefcase, or laptop bag. Carry-on hoarders can stuff all sorts of things into a laptop bag; as long as it has a laptop in it, it's still considered a personal item. The Transportation Security Administration (TSA) has issued a list of restricted items; check www.tsa.gov/public/index.jsp for details.

Airport screeners may decide that your checked luggage warrants a hand search. You can now purchase luggage locks that allow screeners to open and relock a checked bag if hand searching is necessary. Look for Travel Sentry certified locks at luggage or travel shops and Brookstone stores (www.brookstone.com). Luggage inspectors can open these TSA-approved locks with a special code or key—rather than having to cut them off the suitcase, as they normally do to conduct a hand search. For more information on the locks, visit www.travelsentry.org.

FLYING FOR LESS: TIPS FOR GETTING THE BEST AIRFARE

Passengers sharing the same airplane cabin rarely pay the same fare. Travelers who need to purchase tickets at the last minute, change their itinerary at a moment's notice, or fly one-way often get stuck paying the premium rate. Here are some ways to keep your airfare costs down.

- Passengers who can book their ticket **well in advance,** who can **stay over Saturday night,** or who **fly midweek** or **at less-trafficked hours** will pay a fraction of the full fare. If your schedule is flexible, ask if you can secure a cheaper fare by changing your flight plans.
- Search the **Internet** for cheap fares (see "Planning Your Trip Online," earlier in this chapter).
- Keep an eye on local newspapers for **promotional specials** or **fare wars,** when airlines lower prices on their most popular routes. You rarely see fare wars offered for peak travel times, but if you can travel in the off-months, you may snag a bargain.
- **Consolidators,** also known as bucket shops, are great sources for international tickets, although they usually can't beat the Internet on fares within North America. Start by looking in Sunday newspaper travel sections;

U.S. travelers should focus on the *New York Times, Los Angeles Times,* and *Miami Herald.* For less-developed destinations, small travel agents who cater to immigrant communities in large cities often have the best deals. *Beware:* Bucket-shop tickets are usually nonrefundable or rigged with stiff cancellation penalties, often as high as 50% to 75% of the ticket price, and some put you on charter airlines with questionable safety records. **STA Travel** (www.statravel. com) is now the world's leader in student travel, thanks to its purchase of Council Travel. It also offers good fares for travelers of all ages.

- Join **frequent-flier clubs.** Frequent-flier membership doesn't cost a cent, but it does entitle you to better seats, faster response to phone inquiries, and prompter service if your luggage is stolen or your flight is canceled or delayed. And you don't have to fly to earn points; **frequent-flier credit cards** can earn you miles when you do your everyday shopping. With more than 70 mileage awards programs on the market, consumers have never had more options, but the system has never been more complicated—what with major airlines folding, new budget carriers emerging, and alliances forming (allowing you to earn points on partner airlines). Investigate the program details of your favorite airlines before you sink points into any one. Consider which airlines have hubs in the airport nearest you,

---

Tips Don't Just Fly to BWI!

Check all the airports in the Maryland/D.C. area—**Reagan National, Dulles,** and **BWI**—when scouting for low fares. With sales and promotions, one fare could be significantly lower than the others. All three are accessible to the major destinations in the region. Shuttle service will take visitors from **Philadelphia International Airport** to Wilmington and other Delaware sites.

and, of those carriers, which have the most advantageous alliances, given your most common routes. To play the frequent-flier game to your best advantage, consult Randy Petersen's **Inside Flyer** (www.insideflyer.com). Petersen and friends review all the programs in detail and post regular updates on changes in policies and trends. Petersen will also field direct questions (via e-mail) if a partner airline refuses to redeem points, for instance, or if you're still not sure after researching the various programs which one is right for you. It's well worth the $12 online subscription fee, good for 1 year.

BY CAR

The Eastern Seaboard's major north–south link from Maine to Florida, **I-95**, passes through Wilmington and Newark in Delaware as well as Baltimore and central Maryland. Other interstate highways that traverse Maryland are **I-83**, which connects Baltimore with Harrisburg and points north; and **I-70** and **I-68**, which connect Western Maryland to the rest of the state and to Pennsylvania, West Virginia, and Ohio. There are no other interstates in Delaware, but to access the state from Maryland and points south, use U.S. **Route 13** or **Route 113.**

Travel information, including maps and brochures, is available at several locations on I-95, I-70, and I-68. Most are open only from 9am to 5pm. Some locations even offer a hotel reservations service.

BY TRAIN

Amtrak (© **800/USA-RAIL;** www. amtrak.com) offers frequent daily service to Baltimore, at both Pennsylvania Station (downtown) and BWI Airport Rail Station, and to the Wilmington station at 100 S. French St. (at Martin Luther King, Jr. Blvd.). There's also daily service to Newark, Delaware; and Aberdeen and New Carrollton, Maryland. Amtrak has limited service to and from the west at Cumberland and Rockville, Maryland. The high-speed Acela train runs along the Northeast Corridor.

MARC (© **800/325-RAIL**) commuter service runs between Washington, D.C., and Baltimore during the week. MARC also serves Western Maryland in Brunswick and Frederick.

BY BUS

Greyhound (© **800/231-2222;** www. greyhound.com) serves major points in Maryland and Delaware, including Wilmington, Dover, Rehoboth Beach, Baltimore, Ocean City, Easton, Frederick, and Cumberland, with express service from New York City to Newark, Delaware, and Baltimore (both downtown and at East Baltimore's Travel Plaza) via Greyhound and Peter Pan/Trailways (use Greyhound's phone and website for schedule information).

BY FERRY

The **Cape May–Lewes Ferry** travels daily between southern New Jersey and the lower Delaware coast. This 70-minute crossing is operated on a drive-on, drive-off basis and can accommodate up to 800 passengers and 100 cars. Full details on the ferry are given on p. 239.

11 Packages for the Independent Traveler

Before you start your search for the lowest airfare, you may want to consider booking your flight as part of a travel package. Package tours are not the same thing as escorted tours. Package tours are simply a way to buy the airfare, accommodations, and other elements of your trip (such as car rentals, airport transfers, and sometimes even activities) at the same time and often at discounted prices—kind of like one-stop shopping. Packages are sold in bulk to tour operators—who resell them to the public at a cost that usually undercuts standard rates.

One good source of package deals is the airlines themselves. Most major airlines offer air/land packages, including **American Airlines Vacations** (✆ 800/321-2121; www.aavacations.com), **Continental Airlines Vacations** (✆ 800/301-3800; www.covacations.com), **Delta Vacations** (✆ 800/221-6666; www.delta vacations.com), and **United Vacations** (✆ 888/854-3899; www.unitedvacations. com). Several big **online travel agencies**—Expedia, Travelocity, Orbitz, Site59, and Lastminute.com—also do a brisk business in packages. If you're unsure about the pedigree of a smaller packager, check with the Better Business Bureau in the city where the company is based, or go online at www.bbb.org. If a packager won't tell you where they're based, don't fly with them.

Travel packages are also listed in the travel section of your local Sunday newspaper. Or check ads in the national travel magazines such as *Arthur Frommer's Budget Travel, Travel & Leisure, National Geographic Traveler,* and *Condé Nast Traveler.*

Package tours can vary by leaps and bounds. Some offer a better class of hotels than others. Some offer the same hotels for lower prices. Some offer flights on scheduled airlines, while others book charters. Some limit your choice of accommodations and travel days. You are often required to make a large payment upfront. On the plus side, packages can save you money, offering group prices but allowing for independent travel. Some even let you add on a few guided excursions or escorted day trips (also at prices lower than if you booked them yourself) without booking an entirely escorted tour.

Before you invest in a package tour, get some answers. Ask about the **accommodations choices** and prices for each. Then look up the hotels' reviews in a Frommer's guidebook and check rates online for your specific dates of travel.

Finally, look for **hidden expenses.** Ask whether airport departure fees and taxes, for example, are included in the total cost.

12 Escorted General-Interest Tours

Escorted tours are structured group tours, with a group leader. The price usually includes everything from airfare to hotels, meals, tours, admission costs, and local transportation.

Despite the fact that escorted tours require big deposits and predetermine hotels, restaurants, and itineraries, many people derive security and peace of mind from the structure they offer. Escorted tours—whether by bus, motorcoach, train, or boat—let travelers sit back and enjoy the trip without having to drive or worry about details. They take you to the maximum number of sights in the minimum amount of time with the least amount of hassle. They're particularly convenient for people with limited mobility.

On the downside, you'll have little opportunity for serendipitous interactions with locals. The tours can be jam-packed with activities, leaving little room for individual sightseeing, whim, or adventure—plus they also often focus on the heavily touristed sites, so you miss out on many a lesser-known gem.

Before you invest in an escorted tour, request a complete **schedule** of the trip to find out how much sightseeing is planned and whether you'll have enough time to relax or have an adventure of your own. Also ask about the **cancellation policy:** Is a deposit required? Can they cancel the trip if enough people don't sign up? Do you get a refund if they cancel? If *you* cancel? How late can you cancel if you are unable to go and still get a refund? When must you pay in full? If you choose an escorted tour, think strongly about purchasing trip-cancellation insurance, especially if the tour operator asks you to pay in advance. See the section on "Travel Insurance" (p. 25).

The **size** of the group is also important to know upfront. Generally, the smaller the group, the more flexible the itinerary, and the less time you'll spend waiting for people to get on and off the bus. Find out the **demographics** of the group as well. What is the age range? What is the gender

breakdown? Is this mostly a trip for couples or singles?

Discuss what is included in the **price.** You may have to pay for transportation to and from the airport. A box lunch may be included in an excursion, but drinks might cost extra. Tips may not be included. Find out if you will be charged if you decide to opt out of certain activities or meals. If you plan to travel alone, find out if they'll charge a **single supplement** or whether they can pair you with a roommate.

13 Getting Around Maryland & Delaware

BY CAR   The most practical way to see both Maryland and Delaware is by car. Depending on traffic, it takes approximately 2 hours to get from Wilmington to Lewes; from 75 minutes to 2 hours, also depending on traffic, from Wilmington to Baltimore; 1 hour from Baltimore to Annapolis; 90 minutes from Baltimore to Washington, D.C.; 90 minutes from Baltimore to Frederick; 2½ hours from Frederick to Cumberland; and 2½ hours from Annapolis to Ocean City.

If you're planning to drive on the **Baltimore Beltway** (I-695), try to avoid it during rush hour. Congestion, particularly at the junctions north and south with I-95, has gotten terrible. Road widening is underway in some areas, but traffic is at its heaviest from 7 to 9am and 3 to 6pm.

The tourism agencies in Maryland and Delaware both produce good free maps. However, if you plan to do any extensive driving on Maryland's Eastern Shore, you'll need more detail than the state maps provide. Contact the county

tourism agencies (especially Somerset, Dorchester, and Talbot) for free county maps. There are a couple of special-interest maps, too. The best is the **Maryland Scenic Byways** map and guide, which offers some off-the-beaten-path routes with scenic stops. (Get them just so you can see what the black-eyed Susan signs along the road are referring to.) The state also puts out an excellent bicycle map.

BY PLANE   Commuter flights within Maryland are operated from Baltimore and Philadelphia airports to **Salisbury–Ocean City–Wicomico Regional Airport** (✆ **410/548-4827**), 40 minutes west of Ocean City, in the outskirts of Salisbury.

BY BUS & TRAIN   You can travel in Baltimore on the Metro, Light Rail, or bus, all operated by the **MTA** (✆ **410/539-5000;** www.mtamaryland.com). In Wilmington and the Brandywine Valley, **DART First State** (✆ **302/577-3278;** www.dartfirststate.com) runs buses between the downtown business section and outlying suburbs and tourist attractions.

14 Tips on Accommodations

In Baltimore or Wilmington, your best bet is one of the big hotels in the tourist and business sections of town on a weekend or special package. These are pricier

than the motels outside of town, but you'll be closer to major attractions.

Baltimore has three Marriotts, a Hyatt, a Sheraton, and a few independent hotels offering comfortable accommodations near the Inner Harbor.

If you prefer the suburbs, you can find chain hotels and motels near BWI, along Route 40 and I-95, and around the Beltway that circles Baltimore City. Two hotels near the airport are within walking distance of the Light Rail—with stops in downtown Baltimore. That's a good way to avoid the hassles of renting a car, driving in an unfamiliar city, and finding an expensive parking space. The suburbs are home to several Sheratons, a Hilton, and an Embassy Suites. You can usually count on a clean, comfortable room at a Holiday Inn or Best Western, often with a simple continental breakfast included. In most cases, children stay in their parent's room at no extra charge.

Wilmington also has a number of chain hotels in its business district; these usually have plenty of room on the weekends, often with free parking. There are also some comfortable hotels on the outskirts of town, convenient to both Wilmington and the Brandywine Valley. Chains include Holiday Inn, Embassy Suites, Quality Inn, and the Hilton.

For bed-and-breakfasts, head for Annapolis, Frederick, or Western Maryland. These areas are rich in B&Bs. Because they are old and often have delicate furnishings, innkeepers require children to be well behaved, if they are welcome at all. There may be no TV, indoor pool, or hair dryer—but the bread will be fresh from the oven and the furnishings usually reflect the locale. Lots of these places now have their own websites that are accurate, if a bit flowery.

In addition, many B&Bs have made their accommodations as accessible as possible. Call ahead and check to see what can be done for you. Some innkeepers admit they haven't figured out how to accommodate a wheelchair while preserving a fine old house—but they're clearly working on it.

Smokers should be aware that their cigarettes are usually not welcome in the house, not even on the porches.

If you're going to a beach resort in Delaware or Maryland, you've got lots of choices: chains, local hotels, or home and condo rentals. The chains offer predictable accommodations, while the local hotels range from clean and comfy to dazzling.

What makes resort destinations really comfortable and economical for families are house and condo rentals. Real-estate agents in each resort (listed in specific chapters) can help you find a place big enough for a family reunion or cozy enough for newlyweds. At the beach, you'll have to pack linens, towels, and paper products, as these aren't provided. But you can count on a pretty well equipped kitchen, living areas with TVs and often VCRs, and sleeping space and bathrooms.

House rentals have become more popular in Deep Creek Lake as well. There are lots of choices, many with hot tubs, boat piers, or beach access. Here linens are provided, so just bring paper products.

SAVING ON YOUR HOTEL ROOM

The **rack rate** is the maximum rate that a hotel charges for a room. Hardly anybody pays this price, however, except in high season or on holidays. To lower the cost of your room:

- **Ask about special rates or other discounts.** Always ask whether a less expensive room than the first one quoted is available, or whether any special rates apply to you. You may qualify for corporate, student, military, senior, or other discounts. Mention membership in AAA, AARP, frequent-flier programs, or trade unions, which may entitle you to special deals as well. Find out the hotel policy on children—do kids stay free in the room or qualify for a special rate?

- **Dial direct.** When booking a room in a chain hotel, you'll often get a better deal by calling the individual hotel's reservations desk rather than the chain's main number.

- **Book online.** Many hotels offer Internet-only discounts, or supply rooms to Priceline, Hotwire, or Expedia at rates much lower than the ones you can get through the hotel itself. Shop around. And if you have special needs—a quiet room, a room with a view—call the hotel directly and make your needs known after you've booked online.

- **Remember the law of supply and demand.** Resort hotels are most crowded and therefore most expensive on weekends, so discounts are usually available for midweek stays. Business hotels in downtown locations are busiest during the week, so you can expect big discounts over the weekend. Many hotels have high-season and low-season prices, and booking the day after "high season" ends can mean big discounts.

- **Look into group or long-stay discounts.** If you come as part of a large group, you should be able to negotiate a bargain rate, since the hotel can then guarantee occupancy in a number of rooms. Likewise, if you're planning a long stay (at least 5 days), you might qualify for a discount. As a general rule, expect 1 night free after a 7-night stay.

- **Avoid excess charges and hidden costs.** Ask whether your hotel charges for parking. Use your own cellphone, pay phones, or prepaid phone cards instead of dialing direct from hotel phones. And don't be tempted by the room's minibar offerings: Most hotels charge through the nose for drinks and snacks. Finally, ask about local taxes, which can increase the cost of a room by 15% or more.

- **Book an efficiency.** A room with a kitchenette allows you to shop for groceries and cook your own meals. This is a big money saver, especially for families on long stays.

LANDING THE BEST ROOM

Somebody has to get the best room in the house. It might as well be you. You can start by joining the hotel's frequent-guest program, which may make you eligible for upgrades. Always ask about a corner room. They're often larger and quieter, and they often cost the same as standard rooms. Ask for a room that has been most recently renovated; if the hotel is renovating, request a room away from the construction. If you're a light sleeper, request a quiet room away from vending machines, elevators, restaurants, and bars. If you aren't happy with your room when you arrive, ask for another one. Most lodgings will be willing to accommodate you.

In resort areas, ask the following questions before you book a room:

- What's the view like? Cost-conscious travelers may be willing to pay less for a back room facing the parking lot, especially if they don't plan to spend much time in their room.

- Does the room have air-conditioning or ceiling fans? Do the windows open? If they do, and the nighttime entertainment takes place alfresco, you may want to find out when showtime is over.

- What's included in the price? Your room may be moderately priced, but if you're charged for beach chairs, towels, sports equipment, and other amenities, you could end up spending more than you bargained for.

- How far is the room from the beach and other amenities? If it's far, is there transportation to and from the beach?

15 Recommended Books & Films

BOOKS   A number of books about the Chesapeake Bay region will give you historical and cultural perspective for your trip.

James Michener wrote his historical novel *Chesapeake* (Random House, 1978) while living on the Eastern Shore. It offers a good history of the area and the watermen who make their living on the bay.

Anne Tyler's novels are usually set in and around Baltimore—*The Accidental Tourist* (Knopf, 1985) was made into a film with William Hurt and Geena Davis.

Sports writer Frank Deford set his novel *An American Summer* in hometown Baltimore in 1954 (Sourcebooks, 2002).

Alex Haley's *Roots* (Doubleday, 1976) begins in Annapolis—and is remembered with a charming sculpture on City Dock.

William H. Warner's *Beautiful Swimmers* (Little, Brown, 1976) is a Pulitzer Prize–winning study of the blue crab and the culture around the prized crustacean.

Tom Horton's *An Island Out of Time* (Norton, 1996), chronicles his 3 years living on remote Smith Island.

FILMS   Baltimore has been the backdrop of quite a few movies, notably by Baltimoreans Barry Levinson and John Waters, who still maintains a home here. For a look at Baltimore in the 1950s and 1960s, check out Levinson's *Diner, Tin Men,* or *Avalon.* Waters's view of Baltimore is a bit more twisted, but *Hairspray* has some memorable moments; *Serial Mom* stars Kathleen Turner (who graduated from the University of Maryland–Baltimore County).

Local firefighters appeared with John Travolta in *Ladder 49,* also set in Baltimore. The Eastern Shore is featured in *Runaway Bride,* which takes place in the town of Berlin, and in *Wedding Crashers,* which was filmed in Talbot County.

Gettysburg is the backdrop for *Gods and Generals.* In 2005, movie crews were in Baltimore filming Nicole Kidman in *The Visiting* and in Annapolis filming Matthew McConaughey and Sarah Jessica Parker in *Failure to Launch.*

On the small screen, you can still catch repeats of *Homicide: Life on the Street,* a television series based on the nonfiction book by David Simon and shot on location in Baltimore. HBO's *The Wire* is also shot here.

FAST FACTS: Maryland & Delaware

American Express The Baltimore office is at 100 E. Pratt St. (© **410/837-3100**); the Annapolis office is in the Annapolis Mall (© **410/224-4200**). To report lost or stolen traveler's checks, call © **800/221-7282.**

Area Codes The area code for all of Delaware is **302.** Some Brandywine Valley attractions are in Pennsylvania; their area code is **610.** Maryland has four area codes: **301** and **240** in the western half of the state, **410** and **443** in the eastern half, including Baltimore and Annapolis. In Maryland, you must always dial the area code first.

Business Hours Businesses are generally open from 9am to 5pm; government offices are open from 8:30am to 4:30pm. Stores usually open at 10am and close at 5pm or later. In smaller towns, shops may close on Monday or Tuesday but stay open Saturday and Sunday. Shops usually don't open before noon on Sunday.

Car Rentals See "Getting Around Maryland & Delaware," earlier in this chapter.

Climate See "When to Go," earlier in this chapter.

Emergencies Dial ℂ **911** for police, fire, or medical emergency.

Liquor Laws Alcohol is usually available every day at area restaurants and liquor stores. But the regulations do change from county to county—so plan ahead. For instance, Bethany Beach, Delaware, does not allow liquor to be served on Sunday. Neither does Garrett County in Western Maryland. Liquor stores are closed on Sundays in Baltimore County, but not in Baltimore City. You must be 21 to buy alcohol; shopkeepers will ask for ID from anyone who looks to be under the age of 30.

Newspapers & Magazines The **Baltimore Sun** and the **Washington Post** are the major newspapers in Maryland. In Annapolis, look for the **Capital,** and in the Mid-Shore, the **Star Democrat.** You'll find the **Wilmington News-Journal** and the **Philadelphia Inquirer** in Delaware.

Police Dial ℂ **911** or, in Baltimore, ℂ **311** for nonemergency situations that require police attention.

Smoking Smoking in restaurants, bars, and other public places is very rare. Hotels usually offer rooms for smokers—but the majority of bed-and-breakfasts do not.

Taxes State sales tax in Maryland is 5%. Delaware has no sales tax. Hotel tax in both states is between 7% and 8%.

Time Zone Maryland and Delaware are on Eastern Standard Time. Daylight saving time is in effect April through October.

Weather For Baltimore weather, call ℂ **410/936-1212;** for Wilmington, call ℂ **302/429-9000.**

3

For International Visitors

Whether it's your first visit or your tenth, a trip to the United States may require advance planning. This chapter will provide you with essential information, helpful tips, and advice for the more common problems that international visitors may encounter while vacationing in Maryland and Delaware.

1 Preparing for Your Trip

ENTRY REQUIREMENTS

Check at any U.S. embassy or consulate for current information and requirements. You can also obtain a visa application and other information online at the **U.S. State Department**'s website, at **www.travel.state.gov**.

VISAS The U.S. State Department has a **Visa Waiver Program** allowing citizens of certain countries to enter the United States without a visa for stays of up to 90 days. At press time these included Andorra, Australia, Austria, Belgium, Brunei, Denmark, Finland, France, Germany, Iceland, Ireland, Italy, Japan, Liechtenstein, Luxembourg, Monaco, the Netherlands, New Zealand, Norway, Portugal, San Marino, Singapore, Slovenia, Spain, Sweden, Switzerland, and the United Kingdom. Citizens of these countries need only a valid passport and a round-trip air or cruise ticket in their possession upon arrival. If they first enter the United States, they may also visit Mexico, Canada, Bermuda, and/or the Caribbean islands and return to the United States without a visa. Further information is available from any U.S. embassy or consulate. Canadian citizens may enter the United States without visas; they need only proof of residence.

Citizens of all other countries must have (1) a valid passport that expires at least 6 months later than the end of their visit to the U.S., and (2) a tourist visa, which may be obtained without charge from any U.S. consulate.

To obtain a visa, the traveler must submit a completed application form, with a 1½-inch-square photo, and must demonstrate binding ties to a residence abroad. Usually you can obtain a visa at once or within 24 hours, but it may take longer from June through August. If you cannot go in person, contact the nearest U.S. embassy or consulate for directions on applying by mail. Your travel agent or airline may also be able to provide you with visa applications and instructions. The U.S. consulate or embassy that issues your visa will determine whether you will be issued a multiple- or single-entry visa and any restrictions regarding the length of your stay.

British subjects can obtain up-to-date visa information by calling the **U.S. Embassy Visa Information Line** (© **0891/200-290**) or by visiting the "Visas to the U.S." section of the American Embassy London's website at www.usembassy.org.uk.

Irish citizens can obtain up-to-date visa information through the **Embassy of**

Tips **Prepare to Be Fingerprinted**

Many international visitors traveling on visas to the U.S. must now be photographed and fingerprinted at Customs in a new program, called **US-VISIT**, created by the Department of Homeland Security. Non-U.S. citizens arriving at airports and on cruise ships must undergo an instant background check as part of the government's ongoing efforts to deter terrorism by verifying the identity of incoming and outgoing visitors. Exempt from the extra scrutiny are visitors entering by land or those from 28 countries (mostly in Europe) that don't require a visa for short-term visits. For more information, go to the Homeland Security website at **www.dhs.gov/dhspublic**.

the U.S.A. Dublin, 42 Elgin Rd., Dublin 4, Ireland (© **353/1-668-8**777), or by checking the "Consular Services" section of the website at dublin.usembassy. gov.

MEDICAL REQUIREMENTS   Unless you're arriving from an area known to be suffering from an epidemic (particularly cholera or yellow fever), inoculations or vaccinations are not required for entry into the U.S. If you have a medical condition that requires **syringe-administered medications,** carry a valid signed prescription from your doctor—the Federal Aviation Administration (FAA) no longer allows airline passengers to pack syringes in their carry-on baggage without documented proof of medical need. If you have a disease that requires treatment with **narcotics,** you should also carry documented proof with you—smuggling narcotics aboard a plane is a serious offense that carries severe penalties in the U.S.

For **HIV-positive visitors,** requirements for entering the U.S. are somewhat vague and change frequently. According to the latest publication of *HIV and Immigrants: A Manual for AIDS Service Providers,* the Immigration and Naturalization Service (INS) doesn't require a medical exam for entry into the U.S., but INS officials may stop individuals because they look sick or because they are carrying AIDS/HIV medicine. For up-to-the-minute information, contact **AIDSinfo**

(© **800/448-0440,** or 301/519-6616 outside the U.S.; www.aidsinfo.nih.gov) or the **Gay Men's Health Crisis** (© **212/ 367-1000;** www.gmhc.org).

DRIVER'S LICENSES   Foreign driver's licenses are usually recognized in the U.S., although you may want to get an international driver's license if your home license is not in English.

PASSPORT INFORMATION

Safeguard your passport in an inconspicuous, inaccessible place. Make a copy of the critical pages, including the passport number, and store it in a safe place, separate from the passport itself. If you lose your passport, visit the nearest consulate of your native country as soon as possible for a replacement. Passport applications are downloadable from the websites listed below.

Note: The International Civil Aviation Organization has recommended a policy requiring that *every* individual who travels by air have a passport. Many countries are now requiring that even children have their own passports to travel internationally.

FOR RESIDENTS OF CANADA   You can pick up a passport application at any of 28 regional passport offices or most travel agencies. Canadian children who travel must have their own passport. However, if you hold a valid Canadian passport issued before December 11, 2001, that bears the name of your child, the passport remains valid for you and your child until it expires. Passports cost C$87 for those 16 and older (valid 5 years), C$37 for children 3 to 15 (valid 5 years), and C$22 for children under 3 (valid 3 years). Applications, which must be accompanied by two passport-size photographs and proof of Canadian citizenship, are available at travel agencies throughout Canada or from the central **Passport Office,** Department of Foreign Affairs and International Trade, Ottawa, ON K1A 0G3 (© **800/567-6868;** www.dfait-maeci.gc.ca). Processing takes 5 to 10 days if you apply in person, or about 3 weeks by mail.

FOR RESIDENTS OF THE U.K. To pick up an application for a standard 10-year passport (5-year passport for children under 16), visit the nearest passport office, major post office, or travel agency. You can also contact the **United Kingdom Passport Service** at © **0870/571-0410** or visit its website at www.passport.gov.uk. Passports are £42 for adults and £25 for children under 16, with another £30 fee if you apply in person at a passport office. Processing takes about 2 weeks (1 week if you apply at the passport office).

FOR RESIDENTS OF IRELAND You can apply for a 10-year passport (€57), at the **Passport Office,** Setanta Centre, Molesworth Street, Dublin 2 (© **01/671-1633;** www.irlgov.ie/iveagh). Those under age 18 and over 65 must apply for a €12 3-year passport. You can also apply at 1A South Mall, Cork (© **021/272-525**) or over the counter at most post offices.

CUSTOMS
WHAT YOU CAN BRING IN
Every visitor more than 21 years of age may bring in, free of duty, the following: (1) 1 liter of wine or hard liquor; (2) 200 cigarettes, 100 cigars (but not from Cuba), or 3 pounds of smoking tobacco;

and (3) $100 worth of gifts. These exemptions are offered to travelers who spend at least 72 hours in the U.S. and who have not claimed them within the preceding 6 months. It is altogether forbidden to bring into the country foodstuffs (particularly fruit, cooked meats, and canned goods) and plants (vegetables, seeds, tropical plants, and the like). Foreign tourists may carry in or out up to $10,000 in U.S. or foreign currency with no formalities; larger sums must be declared to U.S. Customs on entering or leaving, which includes filing form CM 4790. For details regarding U.S. Customs and Border Protection, consult your nearest U.S. embassy or consulate, or **U.S. Customs** (© **202/927-1770;** www.customs.ustreas.gov).

WHAT YOU CAN TAKE HOME
U.K. citizens returning from a non-E.U. country have a customs allowance of: 200 cigarettes; 50 cigars; 250 grams of smoking tobacco; 2 liters of still table wine; 1 liter of spirits or strong liqueurs (over 22% volume); 2 liters of fortified wine, sparkling wine or other liqueurs; 60cc (ml) perfume; 250cc (ml) of toilet water; and £145 worth of all other goods, including gifts and souvenirs. People under 17 cannot have the tobacco or alcohol allowance. For more information, consult **HM Customs & Excise** at © **0845/010-9000** (or 020/8929-0152 from outside the U.K.), or customs.hmrc.gov.uk.

For a clear summary of **Canadian** rules, request the booklet *I Declare,* from the **Canada Customs and Revenue Agency** (© **800/461-9999** in Canada, or 204/983-3500; www.cra-arc.gc.ca). Canada allows its citizens a C$750 exemption, and you're allowed to bring back duty-free one carton of cigarettes, one can of tobacco, 40 imperial ounces of liquor, and 50 cigars. Canadian citizens under age 18 or 19, depending on their province, cannot have the tobacco or alcohol allowance. In addition, you're allowed to mail gifts to Canada valued at less than C$60 a day, if they're unsolicited and don't contain alcohol or tobacco (write on the package "Unsolicited gift, under $60 value"). All valuables should be declared on the Y-38 form before departure from Canada, including serial numbers of items you already own, such as expensive foreign cameras. *Note:* The C$750 exemption can be used only once a year and only after an absence of 7 days.

HEALTH INSURANCE

Although it's not required of travelers, health insurance is highly recommended. Unlike many European countries, the United States does not usually offer free or low-cost medical care to its citizens or visitors. Doctors and hospitals are expensive, and in most cases will require advance payment or proof of coverage before they render their services. Policies can cover everything from the loss or theft of your baggage and trip cancellation to the guarantee of bail in case you're arrested. Good policies will also cover the costs of an accident, repatriation, or death. Packages such as **Europ Assistance's "Worldwide Healthcare Plan"** are sold by European automobile clubs and travel agencies at attractive rates. **Worldwide Assistance Services, Inc.** (© **800/777-8710;** www.worldwide assistance.com) is the agent for Europ Assistance in the U.S.

Though lack of health insurance may prevent you from being admitted to a hospital in nonemergencies, don't worry about being left on a street corner to die: The American way is to fix you now and bill the living daylights out of you later.

FOR BRITISH TRAVELERS Most big travel agents offer their own insurance and will probably try to sell you their package when you book a holiday. Think before you sign. **Britain's Consumers' Association** recommends that you insist on seeing the policy and reading the fine print before buying travel insurance. The

Association of British Insurers (© 020/ 7600-3333; www.abi.org.uk) gives advice by phone and publishes *Holiday Insurance,* a free guide to policy provisions and prices. You might also shop around for better deals: Try **Columbus Direct** (© 0870/033-9988; www.columbus direct.net).

FOR CANADIAN TRAVELERS Canadians should check with their provincial health plan offices or call **Health Canada** (© 866/225-0709; www.hc-sc.gc.ca) to find the extent of their coverage and what documentation and receipts they must take home if they are treated in the U.S.

MONEY

CURRENCY The U.S. monetary system is very simple: The most common **bills** are the $1 (a "buck"), $5, $10, and $20 denominations. There are also $2 bills (seldom encountered), $50 bills, and $100 bills (the last two are usually not welcome as payment for small purchases). All the paper money was recently redesigned, making the faces on them disproportionately large, but the old-style bills are still legal tender.

Coins come in seven denominations: 1¢ (1 cent, or a penny); 5¢ (5 cents, or a nickel); 10¢ (10 cents, or a dime); 25¢ (25 cents, or a quarter); 50¢ (50 cents, or a half dollar); the gold-colored Sacagawea coin, worth $1; and the rare silver dollar.

Note: The "foreign-exchange bureaus" so common in Europe are rare even at airports in the U.S., and nonexistent outside major cities. It's best not to change foreign money (or traveler's checks denominated in a currency other than U.S. dollars) at a small-town bank, or even a branch in a big city; in fact, leave any currency other than U.S. dollars at home—it may prove a greater nuisance to you than it's worth.

The exceptions in Maryland and Delaware are the exchange desks at

Washington Dulles International Airport, Ronald Reagan Washington National Airport, and Baltimore/Washington International Thurgood Marshall Airport, operated by **Travelex** (© **800/287-7362;** www.travelex.com). Currency exchange is also offered at several banks in Baltimore, as well as American Express in Baltimore and Annapolis.

TRAVELER'S CHECKS Traveler's checks are widely accepted, but make sure they're denominated in U.S. dollars; foreign-currency checks are often difficult to exchange. The three traveler's checks that are most widely recognized—and least likely to be denied—are **Visa, American Express,** and **Thomas Cook.** Be sure to record the numbers of the checks, and keep that information in a separate place in case they get lost or stolen. Most businesses are pretty good about taking traveler's checks, but you're better off cashing them in at a bank (in small amounts) and then paying for purchases in cash. *Note:* You'll need identification, such as a driver's license or passport, to change a traveler's check.

CREDIT CARDS & ATMs Credit cards are the most widely used form of payment in the U.S.: **Visa** (Barclaycard in Britain), **MasterCard** (EuroCard in Europe, Access in Britain, Chargex in Canada), **American Express, Diners Club,** and **Discover.** There are, however, a handful of stores and restaurants that do not take credit cards, so ask in advance. Most businesses display a sticker near their entrance to let you know which cards they accept. (*Note:* Businesses may require a minimum purchase, usually around $10, to use a credit card.)

It's strongly recommended that you bring at least one major credit card. You must have one to rent a car, and hotels and airlines usually require a credit card imprint as a deposit against expenses. In an emergency, a credit card is invaluable.

Some **automated teller machines (ATMs)** will allow you to draw U.S. currency against your bank and credit cards. Check with your bank before leaving home, and remember that you will need your personal identification number (PIN) to do so. Most machines accept Visa, MasterCard, and American Express, as well as ATM cards from other U.S. banks. Expect to be charged up to $3 per transaction, however, if you're not using your own bank's ATM.

One way around these fees is to ask for "cash back" at grocery stores that accept ATM cards and don't charge usage fees. Of course, you'll have to purchase something first. The same is true at most U.S. post offices.

SAFETY

GENERAL SUGGESTIONS Although tourist areas are generally safe, U.S. urban areas tend to be less safe than those in Europe or Japan. You should always stay alert. This is particularly true of large American cities. If you're in doubt about which neighborhoods are safe, don't hesitate to make inquiries with the hotel front-desk staff or the local tourist office.

Avoid deserted areas, especially at night, and don't go into public parks after dark unless there's a concert or similar occasion that will attract a crowd.

Avoid carrying valuables on the street, and keep expensive cameras or electronic equipment bagged up or covered when not in use. If you're using a map, try to consult it inconspicuously—or better yet, study it before you leave your room. Hold on to your pocketbook, and place your billfold in an inside pocket. In theaters, restaurants, and other public places, keep your possessions in sight.

Always lock your room door—don't assume that once you're inside the hotel you are automatically safe and no longer need to be aware of your surroundings.

DRIVING SAFETY Driving safety is important, too, and carjacking is not unprecedented. Question your rental agency about personal safety and ask for a traveler-safety brochure when you pick up your car. Obtain written directions— or a map with the route clearly marked— from the agency showing how to get to your destination. (Many agencies now offer the option of renting a cellphone for the duration of your car rental; check with the rental agent when you pick up the car. Otherwise, contact **InTouch USA** at © **800/872-7626** or www.in touchusa.com for short-term cellphone rental.) And, if possible, arrive and depart during daylight hours.

If you drive off a highway and end up in a dodgy-looking neighborhood, leave the area as quickly as possible. If you have an accident, even on the highway, stay in your car with the doors locked until you assess the situation or until the police arrive. If you're bumped from behind on the street or are involved in a minor accident with no injuries, and the situation appears to be suspicious, motion to the other driver to follow you. Never get out of your car in such situations. Go directly to the nearest police precinct, well-lit service station, or 24-hour store.

Park in well-lit, busy areas when possible. Keep your car doors locked, even if the vehicle is attended. Never leave packages or valuables in sight. If someone attempts to rob you or steal your car, don't try to resist. Report the incident to the police department immediately by calling © **911.**

2 Getting to the U.S.

AIRLINES   In addition to the domestic U.S. airlines listed in chapter 2, many international carriers serve Washington Dulles International Airport and Baltimore/Washington International Thurgood Marshall Airport. These include, among others: **Aer Lingus** (© 01/886-8888 in Dublin; www.aerlingus.ie), **Air Canada** (© 800/776-3000; www.air canada.ca), **British Airways** (© 0845/7733-377 in the U.K.; www.british-airways.com), **Canadian Airlines** (© 800/426-7000), **Japan Airlines** (© 0354/89-1111 in Tokyo; www.jal.co.jp), **Qantas** (© 13-13-13 in Australia; www.qantas.com.au), and **Virgin Atlantic** (© 01293/747-747 in the U.K.; www.fly.virgin.com).

AIRLINE DISCOUNTS   Smart travelers can reduce the price of a plane ticket by shopping around. Overseas visitors, for example, can take advantage of the APEX (Advance Purchase Excursion) reductions offered by all major U.S. and European carriers. For more money-saving airline advice, see "Getting There," in chapter 2. For the best rates, compare fares and be flexible with the dates and times of travel.

IMMIGRATION AND CUSTOMS CLEARANCE   Visitors arriving by air, no matter what the port of entry, should cultivate patience and resignation before setting foot on U.S. soil. Clearing immigration control can take as long as 2 hours, especially on summer weekends, so carry this guidebook or other reading material. This is especially true in the aftermath of the September 11, 2001, terrorist attacks, when U.S. airports have considerably beefed up security clearances. People traveling by air from Canada, Bermuda, and certain Caribbean countries can sometimes clear Customs and Immigration at the point of departure, which is much faster.

3 Getting Around the U.S.

BY PLANE Some large airlines offer transatlantic or transpacific passengers special discount tickets under the name **Visit USA,** which allows mostly one-way travel from one U.S. destination to another at low prices. These discount tickets must be purchased abroad in conjunction with your international fare. This system is the easiest, fastest, cheapest way to see the country. Obtain information well in advance from your travel agent or the airline, since the conditions attached to these discount tickets can be changed without advance notice.

BY TRAIN International visitors (excluding Canadians) can also buy a **USA Rail Pass,** good for 15 or 30 days of unlimited travel on **Amtrak** (© **800/USA-RAIL;** www.amtrak.com). The pass is available through many overseas travel agents. Prices in 2005 for a 15-day pass were $295 off-peak, $440 peak; a 30-day pass was $385 off-peak, $550 peak. With a foreign passport, you can also buy passes direct from some Amtrak locations, including New York, Boston, and Washington, D.C. Reservations are generally required and should be made as early as possible. Regional rail passes are also available.

BY BUS Bus travel is often the most economical form of public transit for short hops between U.S. cities, but it can also be slow and uncomfortable—certainly not an option for everyone (particularly when Amtrak, which is far more luxurious, offers similar rates). **Greyhound/Trailways** (© **800/231-2222;** www.greyhound.com), the sole nationwide bus line, offers an **International Ameripass** that must be purchased before coming to the U.S., or by phone through the Greyhound International Office at the Port Authority Bus Terminal in New York City (© **212/971-0492**). The pass can be obtained from foreign travel agents or through Greyhound's website (order at least 21 days before your departure to the U.S.) and costs less than the domestic version. In 2005, the cost of passes were as follows: 4 days ($179), 7 days ($239), 10 days ($289), 15 days ($349), 21 days ($419), 30 days ($479), 45 days ($529), or 60 days ($639). You can get more info on the pass at the website, or by calling © **402/330-8552.** In addition, special rates are available for seniors, students, and children. Passes can be activated at the downtown Baltimore bus terminal, 2110 Haines St. (© **410/752-7682**), or the Baltimore Travel Plaza, off I-95 (© **410/633-6389**). Both are open 24 hours.

BY CAR Unless you plan to spend the bulk of your vacation in a city where walking is the best way to get around (read: New York City), the most convenient way to travel the U.S. is by car. The interstate highway system connects cities and towns all over the country, with an extensive network of federal, state, and local highways and roads as well. Some of the national car-rental companies include **Alamo** (© 800/462-5266; www.alamo.com), **Avis** (© 800/230-4898; www.avis.com), **Budget** (© 800/527-0700; www.budget.com), **Dollar** (© 800/800-3665; www.dollar.com), **Hertz** (© 800/654-3131; www.hertz.com), and **National** (© 800/227-7368; www.nationalcar.com).

If you plan to rent a car in the U.S., you probably won't need the services of an additional automobile organization. If you're planning to buy or borrow a car, automobile-association membership is recommended. **AAA,** the **American Automobile Association** (© **800/222-4357;** travel.aaa.com), is the country's largest auto club and supplies its members with maps, insurance, and, most important, emergency road service. The cost runs from $63 for singles to $87 for two members, but if you're a member of a foreign auto club with reciprocal arrangements, you can enjoy free AAA service in America. See "Getting There" in chapter 2 for more information.

FAST FACTS: For the International Traveler

Automobile Organizations Auto clubs will supply maps, suggested routes, guidebooks, accident and bail-bond insurance, and emergency road service. The **American Automobile Association (AAA)** is the major auto club in the U.S. If you belong to an auto club in your home country, inquire about AAA reciprocity before you leave. You may be able to join AAA even if you're not a member of a reciprocal club; to inquire, call ✆ **800/222-4357**. AAA offers nationwide emergency road service by calling ✆ **800/AAA-HELP**.

Business Hours Offices are usually open weekdays from 9am to 5pm. Banks are open weekdays from 9am to 3pm or later and sometimes Saturday mornings. Stores typically open between 9 and 10am and close between 5 and 6pm from Monday through Saturday. Stores in shopping complexes or malls tend to stay open late, until about 9pm on weekdays and weekends; many malls and larger department stores are open on Sundays as well.

Drinking Laws The legal age for purchase and consumption of alcoholic beverages is 21; proof of age is required and often requested at bars, nightclubs, and restaurants, so it's always a good idea to bring ID when you go out. Beer and wine cannot be purchased in most Maryland supermarkets, but liquor laws vary from state to state.

Do not carry open containers of alcohol in your car or any public area that isn't zoned for alcohol consumption. The police can fine you on the spot. And nothing will ruin your trip faster than getting a citation for DUI ("driving under the influence"), so don't even think about driving while intoxicated.

Electricity Like Canada, the United States uses 110–120 volts AC (60 cycles), compared to 220–240 volts AC (50 cycles) in most of Europe, Australia, and New Zealand. If your small appliances use 220–240 volts, you'll need a 110-volt transformer and a plug adapter with two flat parallel pins to operate them here. Downward converters that change 220–240 volts to 110–120 volts are difficult to find in the United States, so bring one with you.

Embassies & Consulates If your country isn't listed below, call for directory information in Washington, D.C. (✆ **202/555-1212**) or log on to www.embassy.org/embassies. All embassies are in the national capital, Washington, D.C., which is easily accessible from Baltimore:

Australia: 1601 Massachusetts Ave. NW, Washington, DC 20036 (✆ **202/797-3000**; www.austemb.org).

Canada: 501 Pennsylvania Ave. NW, Washington, DC 20001 (✆ **202/682-1740**; www.canadianembassy.org).

Ireland: 2234 Massachusetts Ave. NW, Washington, DC 20008 (✆ **202/462-3939**; www.irelandemb.org).

Japan: 2520 Massachusetts Ave. NW, Washington, DC 20008 (✆ **202/238-6700**; www.embjapan.org).

New Zealand: 37 Observatory Circle NW, Washington, DC 20008 (© **202/328-4800;** www.nzemb.org).

United Kingdom: 3100 Massachusetts Ave. NW, Washington, DC 20008 (© **202/588-7800;** www.britainusa.com).

Emergencies Call © **911** to report a fire, call the police, or get an ambulance anywhere in the U.S. This is a toll-free call (no coins are required at public telephones). In Baltimore, © **311** is a non-emergency call to police.

If you encounter serious problems, contact **Traveler's Aid International** (© **202/546-1127;** www.travelersaid.org) to help direct you to a local branch. This nationwide nonprofit organization helps travelers in difficult straits. Its services might include reuniting families separated while traveling, providing food and/or shelter to people stranded without cash, and even emotional counseling.

Gasoline (Petrol) Petrol is known as gasoline (or simply "gas") in the U.S., and petrol stations are known as both gas stations and service stations. At press time, the cost of gas in the U.S. was abnormally high ($3 a gallon) and fluctuating drastically. Taxes are already included in the printed price. One U.S. gallon equals 3.8 liters or .85 imperial gallons.

Holidays Banks, government offices, post offices, and many stores, restaurants, and museums are closed on the following legal national holidays: January 1 (New Year's Day), the third Monday in January (Martin Luther King, Jr., Day), the third Monday in February (Presidents' Day), the last Monday in May (Memorial Day), July 4th (Independence Day), the first Monday in September (Labor Day), the second Monday in October (Columbus Day), November 11 (Veterans Day/Armistice Day), the fourth Thursday in November (Thanksgiving Day), and December 25 (Christmas). The Tuesday after the first Monday in November is Election Day, a federal holiday in presidential-election years (held every 4 years, and next in 2008).

Legal Aid If you are "pulled over" for a minor infraction (such as speeding), never attempt to pay the fine directly to a police officer; this could be construed as attempted bribery, a much more serious crime. Pay fines by mail, or directly into the hands of the clerk of the court. If accused of a more serious offense, say and do nothing before consulting a lawyer. Here the burden is on the state to prove a person's guilt beyond a reasonable doubt, and everyone has the right to remain silent, whether he or she is suspected of a crime or actually arrested. Once arrested, a person can make one telephone call to a party of his or her choice. Call your embassy or consulate.

Mail If you aren't sure what your address will be in the U.S., mail can be sent to you, in your name, c/o General Delivery at the main post office of the city or region where you expect to be. (Call © **800/275-8777** for information on the nearest post office.) The addressee must pick up mail in person and must produce proof of identity (driver's license, passport, or the like). Most post offices will hold your mail for up to 1 month and are open Monday through Friday from 8am to 6pm and Saturday from 9am to 3pm.

Generally found at intersections, mailboxes are blue with a red-and-white stripe and carry the inscription U.S. MAIL. If your mail is addressed to a U.S.

destination, don't forget to add the five-digit postal code (or zip code) after the two-letter abbreviation of the state to which the mail is addressed (MD for Maryland, DE for Delaware). This is essential for prompt delivery.

At press time, domestic postage rates were 24¢ for a large postcard and 39¢ for a letter. For international mail, a first-class letter of up to ½ ounce costs 80¢ (60¢ to Canada and Mexico); a first-class postcard costs 70¢ (50¢ to Canada and Mexico); and a preprinted postal aerogramme costs 70¢. For more information, see www.usps.com.

Taxes The U.S. has no value-added tax (VAT) or other indirect tax at the national level. Every state, county, and city may levy its own local tax on all purchases, including hotel and restaurant checks and airline tickets. These taxes will not appear on price tags. Maryland sales tax is 5% on everything except food in a grocery store. Delaware has no sales tax.

Telephone & Fax Private corporations run the telephone system in the U.S., so rates can vary widely, especially for long-distance service and operator-assisted calls. Generally, hotel surcharges on long-distance and local calls are astronomical, so you're better off using a **public pay telephone,** which you'll find clearly marked in most public buildings and private establishments, as well as on the street. Convenience grocery stores and gas stations almost always have them. Many convenience groceries and packaging services sell **prepaid calling cards** in denominations up to $50; these can be the least expensive way to call home. Many public phones at airports now accept American Express, MasterCard, and Visa credit cards. **Local calls** made from public pay phones in Maryland and Delaware cost 50¢. Pay phones do not accept pennies, and few will take anything larger than a quarter.

Most long-distance and international calls can be dialed directly from any phone. **For calls within the United States and to Canada,** dial 1 followed by the area code and the seven-digit number. **For other international calls,** dial 011 followed by the country code, city code, and the number you are calling.

Calls to area codes **800, 888, 877,** and **866** are toll-free. However, calls to area codes **700** and **900** (chat lines, bulletin boards, "dating" services, and so on) can be very expensive—usually a charge of 95¢ to $3 or more per minute, and they sometimes have minimum charges that can run as high as $15 or more.

For **reversed-charge** or **collect calls,** and for **person-to-person calls,** dial the number 0 and then the area code and number; an operator will come on the line, and you should specify whether you are calling collect, person-to-person, or both. If your operator-assisted call is international, ask for the overseas operator.

For **local directory assistance** ("information"), dial 411; for long-distance information, dial 1, then the appropriate area code and 555-1212.

Most hotels have **fax machines** available for guest use (be sure to ask about any charge to use it). Many hotel rooms are even wired for guests' fax machines. A less expensive way to send and receive faxes may be at businesses such as the **UPS Store** (formerly Mail Boxes Etc.), a national chain of packing service shops. (Look in the Yellow Pages directory under "Packing Services.")

Time The continental United States is divided into **four time zones:** Eastern Standard Time (EST), Central Standard Time (CST), Mountain Standard Time

(MST), and Pacific Standard Time (PST). Alaska and Hawaii have their own zones. For example, when it's noon in New York City (EST), it's 11am in Chicago (CST), 10am in Denver (MST), 9am in Los Angeles (PST), 8am in Anchorage (AST), and 7am in Honolulu (HST). Both Maryland and Delaware observe Eastern Standard Time.

Daylight saving time takes effect at 2am the first Sunday in April until 2am the last Sunday in October, except in Arizona, Hawaii, the U.S. Virgin Islands, and Puerto Rico. (Indiana will begin observing daylight saving time in Apr 2006.) Daylight saving moves the clock 1 hour ahead of standard time. *Note:* A new law will extend daylight saving in 2007; clocks will change the second Sunday in March and the first Sunday in November.

Tipping Tips are a very important part of certain workers' income, and gratuities are the standard way of showing appreciation for services provided. (Tipping is certainly not compulsory if the service is poor!) In hotels, tip **bellhops** at least $1 per bag ($2–$3 if you have a lot of luggage) and tip the **chamber staff** $1 to $2 per day (more if you've left a disaster area for him or her to clean up). Tip the **doorman** or **concierge** only if he or she has provided you with some specific service (for example, calling a cab for you or obtaining difficult-to-get theater tickets). Tip the **valet-parking attendant** $1 every time you get your car.

In restaurants, bars, and nightclubs, tip **service staff** 15% to 20% of the check; tip **bartenders** 10% to 15%; and tip **checkroom attendants** $1 per garment.

As for other service personnel, tip **cabdrivers** 15% of the fare; tip **skycaps** at airports at least $1 per bag ($2–$3 if you have a lot of luggage); and tip **hairdressers** and **barbers** 15% to 20%.

Toilets You won't find public toilets or "restrooms" on the streets in most U.S. cities, but they can be found in hotel lobbies, bars, restaurants, museums, larger stores, railway and bus stations, or service stations. Note that restaurants and bars in resorts or heavily visited areas may reserve their restrooms for the use of their patrons.

4

Suggested Itineraries

Two little states. A prospective visitor might think it would be easy to see either one in just a few days. But a leisurely pace is best for this "Land of Pleasant Living." How much time do you have? How much driving do you want to do? You could come by boat, but most visitors do best with a car when exploring both Maryland and Delaware. It's the only way to see the Brandywine Valley or Western Maryland.

So, what are your interests? In a week, you could see the highlights of Maryland or the attractions of the state's Eastern Shore, along with a glimpse of Delaware. But you'll have to make some choices about what to see.

Civil War buffs will want to include a visit to Baltimore with trips to the battlefields around Frederick. Wine lovers might like to plan a long weekend to see local wineries, enjoy fresh seafood, and experience a little culture. History fans should consider taking a walk on the path to freedom trod by slaves on the underground railroad. And outdoorsy types, you're in for a treat: hiking, skiing, fly-fishing, kayaking, and bodysurfing await.

1 The Best of Maryland & Delaware in 2 Weeks

Annapolis is a fairly central place to start this trip—especially for those flying into Baltimore/Washington International Thurgood Marshall Airport. Or if you're coming from the west, start in Western Maryland and just keep heading east. Coming from the south? Take the Chesapeake Bay Bridge Tunnel and visit Delaware and the Eastern Shore before heading across the other Bay Bridge to see the rest of Maryland.

Maryland requires a lot of driving in order to see everything, from the mountains of Western Maryland to the Eastern Shore to the Atlantic Ocean. Delaware's attractions begin at the beach and end in Wilmington. There's a lot to see: Civil War battlefields, museums of all sorts, the Chesapeake Bay, waterfalls and mountain trails, historic homes and veritable castles. The historic districts of Annapolis and Frederick, in Maryland, along with Dover and New Castle, in Delaware, are other options.

I've designed this itinerary for visiting at breakneck speed. Feel free to slow down and savor any place you like.

Day ❶: Annapolis

You could start in Baltimore, but Annapolis offers a slower pace—so you'll feel like you're on vacation right away. **HistoryQuest** at the **St. Clair Wright Center** makes a good first stop for walking tours and an orientation exhibit on

Maryland's capital. Stop for lunch along the **City Dock,** then visit the **State House,** and afterward spend a leisurely afternoon shopping along Maryland Avenue for antiques or gifts. Have dinner on Main Street or West Street and finish with a carriage ride through the historic

The Best of Maryland & Delaware

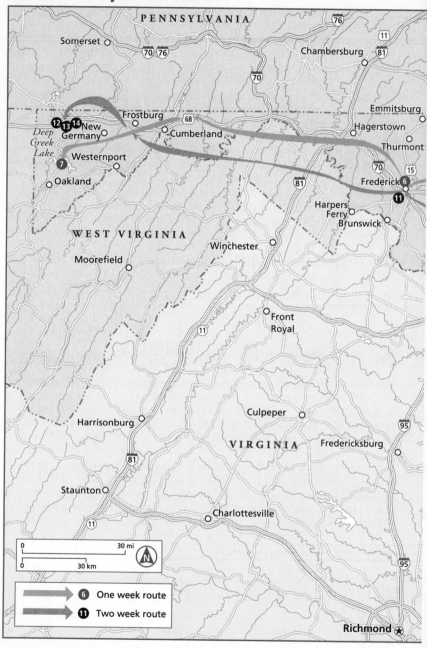

PENNSYLVANIA

Somerset

76
70 76
70

Chambersburg
11
81

Emmitsburg

Frostburg
68
12 13 14 New
Germany
Deep
Creek
Lake
7 Westernport
Cumberland

Hagerstown

Thurmont

70
15
Frederick 6
11

Oakland

Harpers
Ferry
Brunswick

WEST VIRGINIA

81

Moorefield

Winchester

Front
Royal
11

Harrisonburg

Culpeper

95

VIRGINIA
Fredericksburg

81

Staunton

Charlottesville

11

0   30 mi
0   30 km

N

95

6 One week route
11 Two week route

Richmond ★

54

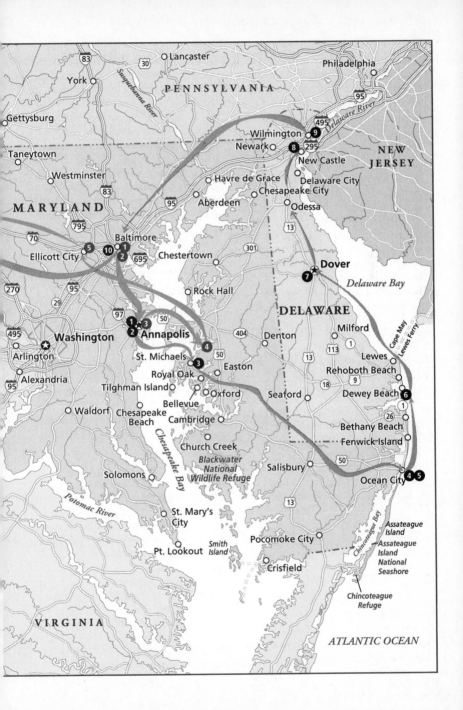

district. You'll need a good night's sleep, so make sure you have a reservation at a local B&B or one of the **Historic Inns.** Since you want an early start tomorrow morning, it's best to stay downtown.

Day ❷: U.S. Naval Academy & Historic Homes

Head to the **Naval Academy** and sign up for a tour at the visitor center—the best one includes a stop at Bancroft Hall about the time the midshipmen line up for noon formation. After they march in for lunch, head into the historic district for a meal of your own. Along and nearby Maryland Avenue are three houses worth a visit: the **Chase–Lloyd House,** the **Paca House and Gardens,** and the **Hammond–Harwood House.** You can probably see all three in an afternoon, or just go to the Hammond–Harwood and then spend a leisurely time in the Paca gardens. (Hours at the Chase–Lloyd are quite limited.) Make reservations at an **Eastport** restaurant and take the water taxi across the harbor for a good seafood meal.

Day ❸: Boat Trip to St. Michaels

You can't be this close to the Chesapeake Bay and not get on it. **Watermark Cruises** offers a boat trip to **St. Michaels,** an Eastern Shore village with a number of interesting shops, restaurants, and the **Chesapeake Bay Maritime Museum.** Not a big boat fan? Try one of the shorter cruises, such as a trip on the *Woodwind,* a sailing schooner with several 2-hour cruises each day, or with **Annapolis by Boat,** which offers a variety of short excursions

Days ❹–❺: Ocean City

Head across the Bay Bridge and down Route 50 to **Ocean City.** The visit to St. Michaels yesterday was your only stop along the Eastern Shore, but if it caught your fancy and you want to see more, stop for lunch in **Easton** or **Cambridge** along the way. Bird lovers may want to make a detour to the **Blackwater National Wildlife Refuge,** which is southwest of Cambridge.

Once you get to Ocean City, take a break: Rent an umbrella and a chair and relax by the surf. Plan an early dinner at one of the local restaurants before heading to the **boardwalk** for a little amusement and shopping. Or spend the evening playing **miniature golf;** this town is full of courses. Repeat this routine for a second day if you want. Marylanders (and plenty of out-of-state visitors) can do this for a whole week or more. Another way to spend your second day is beachcombing and seeing the ponies on **Assateague Island.**

Day ❻: The Delaware Shore

Delaware's beaches are just like Ocean City's, but the area around them is different. **Bethany** is small and quiet. **Rehoboth** has lots of good restaurants, plus spa treatments, live jazz, and a plethora of tax-free outlet stores. **Lewes** forgets it's a beach town while celebrating its history as the First State's First Town with museums and historic sites. Choose one and go exploring.

Day ❼: Dover

Delaware's capital city has a cluster of unusual museums along with the well-regarded **Biggs Museum of American Art.** In fact, the downtown sights, along with the Legislative Hall and state archives, are now known as the **First State Heritage Park at Dover.** You could easily see them all in a day. Or chuck all that culture and head to the slots or horse races at **Dover Downs.** Wildlife fans may prefer to head a little north to **Bombay Hook National Wildlife Refuge** for a little bird-watching. Plan to be there for about 2 hours or more—depending on how much walking you want to do.

Day ❽: Historic New Castle

The original capital of Delaware was the waterfront village of **New Castle.** Its historic sites are still lovingly maintained, including the Federal-style **Read House,** home of the son of a signer of the Declaration of Independence. A number of other Colonial-era homes are open most days (except Mon). Have lunch at a Colonial inn: **Jessop's Tavern,** the **Chef's Table at David Finney Inn,** or the **Arsenal.** Or go modern and stop near the airport outside of town at the **Air Transport Command,** where you can get a bit of World War II history with your meal.

Day ❾: Wilmington
Make this a base for your visit to the **Brandywine Valley.** You're going to want to see one of the du Pont properties: **Winterthur** if you love home furnishings, **Nemours** if you love lavish style (but not until it reopens in 2007), **Longwood Gardens** if flowers are your passion, **Hagley** if you like to learn how things work in a bucolic setting. Or stay in town and visit the 12,000 works of art at the **Delaware Art Museum** or the changing exhibits of the **Delaware Center for the Contemporary Arts.** History buffs should see the **Delaware History Museum** or visit the *Kalmar Nyckel* if it's moored here. Get some rest; it's off to Baltimore tomorrow, a 2-hour drive.

Day ❿: Baltimore
If you have only a day to see Baltimore, your first stop has to be **Fort McHenry,** home of the Star-Spangled Banner. Have lunch at **Harborplace** while you decide where to go next. Should it be the **National Aquarium** to see the new Australia exhibit? Or the new **Reginald F.**

Lewis Museum of Maryland African American History & Culture? Art lovers can choose from the **Baltimore Museum of Art,** the **Walters Art Museum,** or the **American Visionary Art Museum.** History buffs may want to check out the **Maryland Historical Society** or one of its sister museums, the **Civil War Museum–President Street Station** or the **Fells Point Maritime Museum.** Or go to the new visitor center at the Inner Harbor and sign up for a **Heritage Walk** to get a closer look at Charm City. Prefer a view from the top? Then go to the **Top of the World** observation level in the World Trade Center. End the day with dinner in **Little Italy** or **Fells Point.**

Day ⓫: Frederick
The drive to **Frederick** takes about 2 hours along I-70. After checking into your hotel or B&B, spend the afternoon at **Antietam Battlefield.** Head to Frederick's historic district for dinner.

Days ⓬–⓮: Outdoors Maryland
You have a choice: The Deep Creek Lake area off I-70 and I-68 has lots to draw an outdoors enthusiast—snow skiing, dogsledding, white-water rafting, hiking, and fly-fishing. If you have the time, make sure you include this area on your itinerary. But if you're running out of time, head north on Route 15 and spend the day at Cunningham Falls State Park. Here you can hike to a waterfall and swim or canoe in a nearby lake. Stop for local produce or penny candy along the way, and have a meal at one of the roadside restaurants.

2 The Best of Maryland in 1 Week

If you have only a week, put four places on your itinerary: Baltimore, Annapolis, anyplace on the Eastern Shore (or Ocean City, on the Atlantic), and Western Maryland. You can slow down long enough to see a Civil War battlefield, too. But hurry: There's lots to do in 7 little days.

Day ❶: Baltimore Essentials

Baltimore means three things to first-time visitors: Fort McHenry, Harborplace, and the National Aquarium. You can see all three in a day, so put on some comfortable shoes and let's go. Get your all-day ticket on the **water taxi** so you can travel to the fort and Fells Point by water. Start off at the **National Aquarium** (get your tickets online so you don't have to wait in line). You'll want to see the new Australia exhibit as well as the dolphin demonstration. Have lunch and shop a bit at **Harborplace.** Then hop that water taxi and head to **Fort McHenry.** You'll need most of the afternoon for this visit. In fact, if you can be here at sunset, you may be able to help take down the large flag—it takes about 20 people to fold it. Get on another water taxi for an evening in **Fells Point** for dinner and live entertainment at one of the local watering holes.

Day ❷: Baltimore History & Culture

Spend a second day in Baltimore soaking up either the history or the culture. Stop by the new visitor center at the Inner Harbor to sign up for a **Heritage Walk,** which will give you a closer look at Charm City. If you don't want to walk, get on one of the boats or the **Big Bus** for a tour; they all have kiosks at the Inner Harbor. After lunch in **Little Italy,** take in a museum. Baltimore has plenty to choose from: the new **Reginald F. Lewis Museum of Maryland African American History & Culture,** the **Baltimore Museum of Art,** the **Walters Art Museum,** the **American Visionary Art Museum,** or the **Baltimore & Ohio Railroad Museum.** End the day at **Power Plant Live** with dinner and maybe a little dancing.

Day ❸: Annapolis

If you have only a day, you must go to the **Naval Academy** and sign up for a tour at the visitor center. The best tour includes a stop at Bancroft Hall about the time the midshipmen line up for noon formation.

The **State House,** where George Washington resigned as commander in chief, or the **Paca House and Gardens** are also good places to visit. Or skip the history for an afternoon on a boat: **Watermark Cruises,** the *Woodwind,* or **Annapolis by Boat** can get you on the Chesapeake Bay and Severn River. Have dinner on Main Street or West Street and finish with a carriage ride through the historic district. If you haven't clambered aboard a boat yet, make reservations at an **Eastport** restaurant and take the water taxi across the harbor for a good seafood meal.

Day ❹: Boat Trip to St. Michaels or Day Trip to Ocean City

You can't be this close to the Chesapeake Bay and not get on it. **Watermark Cruises** offers a boat trip to **St. Michaels,** an Eastern Shore village with a number of interesting shops, restaurants, and the **Chesapeake Bay Maritime Museum.** If you need to see the ocean, take the day and drive to **Ocean City.** It's only 2½ hours from here. Lots of locals spend just a day on the beach.

Day ❺: Driving to Western Maryland

Take your time so you can see how settlers headed from the rolling valleys around Baltimore to the hills of Appalachia. The drive to Western Maryland will take up to 4 hours. If you want, stop along I-70. **Ellicott City** has a charming historic district with antiques shops, the oldest railroad station in the world, and good restaurants. **New Market** is the state antiques capital. Civil War buffs should plan to stop at **Antietam,** near Frederick. **Frederick** has its own small-town historic district, as does **Cumberland,** a stop along the **C&O Canal.**

Days ❻–❼: Western Maryland's Great Outdoors

Ski at Wisp if it's wintertime, or head to and hike Deep Creek Lake if it's warm. Don't miss a chance to hike to Muddy

Falls at Swallow Falls State Park or enjoy the pristine nature of the Savage River State Forest. Sign up at one of the outfitters for a white-water rafting trip, fly-fishing, or boat or snowshoe rental. Hey, you can even sign up for dogsledding. Take 2 days. Take 3 if you've got 'em.

3 The Best of Maryland for Families

These two 1-week itineraries both focus on the outdoors. Start in Baltimore with either itinerary so the kids can see Fort McHenry, the National Aquarium, and the railroad museum. Then head east to the Eastern Shore and Ocean City (or a Delaware beach, if you prefer) or head west to the mountains. End in Annapolis with a visit to the Naval Academy and a boat ride.

Days ❶–❷: Baltimore for Kids

I've never met a kid who didn't like **Fort McHenry.** The rangers talk on their level, there are lots of cannons to see and nooks and crannies to climb into, and the waterfront lawn outside the fort wall is great for running around or enjoying a picnic. Or have lunch at **Harborplace,** where there's plenty of kid-friendly food. The **National Aquarium** has sharks and dolphins and a sparkling rainforest at the top. You'll probably spend the whole afternoon here. Then head to **Little Italy** for some pasta. Finish with cannoli and gelato at **Vaccaro's.**

On your second day, pick a couple of museums according to your interests—kid-oriented museums are everywhere in Baltimore. **Port Discovery** is a children's museum. The **Baltimore Museum of Industry** has guides who tell great stories and let kids handle some of the artifacts. Everyone likes the massive locomotives and diminutive model trains at the **B&O Railroad Museum.** Give your children some inspiration at the new **Reginald F. Lewis Museum of Maryland African American History & Culture,** where many of the displays tell very personal stories. Sneak a little art education into the day with a visit to the **Walters Art Museum,** home of some pretty impressive armor, or the **Baltimore Museum of Art,** where kids can simultaneously enjoy the outdoors and the arts in the sculpture garden. Baseball fans might want to spend the afternoon in the presence of greatness at **Sports Legends at Camden Yards** or the **Babe Ruth Museum.**

Days ❸–❺, Option A: Ocean City

Enough city life. Throw the bathing suits into the car and head to **Ocean City** for a couple of days of surf and sun. Spend all 3 days building sandcastles and bodysurfing during the day and playing miniature golf in the evening. Or book a fishing trip, rent a kayak, or visit **Assateague Island** or **Frontier Town** amusement park. In the evening, take the kids to **Ocean Downs** to watch the harness races. Admission is free, and the lead horse comes up to the fence so children can pet his nose. Or head to Salisbury for a **Delmarva Shorebirds** minor league baseball game.

Days ❸–❺, Option B: Western Maryland

Get out your hiking boots, your bathing suit, or your skis—whatever the weather, there's something to do in Western Maryland. Base your family at **Deep Creek Lake** so you can ski at **Wisp,** hike to Muddy Falls at **Swallow Falls State Park,** or enjoy the pristine nature of the **Savage River State Forest.** Sign up at one of the outfitters for a white-water rafting trip, fly-fishing, dogsledding or kennel visit, or boat or snowshoe rental.

Days ❻—❼: Annapolis

Two days in Annapolis are plenty for children. Just make sure you visit the **Naval Academy**—try to sign up for a tour that takes visitors by Bancroft Hall in time for noon formation—and then take a ride on the *Harbor Queen.* Children give both of these high marks. You can easily do this all in a day, with lunch at the **City Dock** in between. Take a carriage ride in the historic district in the evening.

Spend your second day hiking or kayaking at nearby **Quiet Waters Park,** or head down Route 2 to **Six Flags America** for some big-time thrills. Children also like the **State House** and the **Annapolis Maritime Museum** in Eastport.

4 The Best of Delaware for Families

Tiny Delaware packs in a lot of fun, history, and culture. This is a 5-day itinerary, but it's easy to pick and choose a couple of days' worth of activity for a long weekend— or stretch out the fun for a whole week's vacation without getting bored even once.

Day ❶: A Day at the Beach

Start slow. Unpack your bathing suit or fishing rod and head to **Bethany Beach** or **Fenwick State Park** for a day at one of the quiet resorts. Doing nothing will make you hungry, so decide whether you want pizza or fine dining at **Sedona** or **Kingston Grille.**

Day ❷: Let's Go Shopping

Sales-tax-free Delaware makes shopping even more fun. Head to the **Tanger Outlet Centers** in Rehoboth. Or visit the little shops in downtown **Rehoboth Beach** or **Lewes.**

Day ❸: Dover

Delaware's capital city has a cluster of unusual museums along with the well-regarded **Biggs Museum of American Art.** In fact, the downtown sights, along with the Legislative Hall and state archives, are now known as the **First State Heritage Park at Dover.** You could easily see them all in a day. Or chuck all that culture and head to the slots or horse races at **Dover Downs.** Wildlife fans may prefer to head a little north to **Bombay Hook National Wildlife Refuge** for a little bird-watching. Plan to be there for about 2 hours or more—depending on how much walking you want to do.

Day ❹: Historic New Castle

The original capital of Delaware was the waterfront village of **New Castle.** Its historic sites are still lovingly maintained, including the Federal-style **Read House,** home of the son of a signer of the Declaration of Independence. A number of other Colonial-era homes are open most days (except Mon). Have lunch at a Colonial inn: **Jessop's Tavern,** the **Chef's Table at David Finney Inn,** or the **Arsenal.** Or go modern and stop near the airport outside of town at the **Air Transport Command,** where you can get a bit of World War II history with your meal.

Day ❺: Wilmington & the Brandywine Valley

The castles of the Brandywine Valley beckon, but the exhibits at the **Delaware Art Museum** and the **Delaware History Museum** are hard to pass by, too. If you've got only a day, you're going to want to see one of the du Pont properties: **Winterthur** if you love home furnishings, **Nemours** if you love lavish style (but not until it reopens in 2007), **Longwood Gardens** if flowers are your passion, **Hagley** if you like to learn how things work in a bucolic setting. But Wilmington's charms are many, too. Try to stay a second day to see the art and history museums, or the

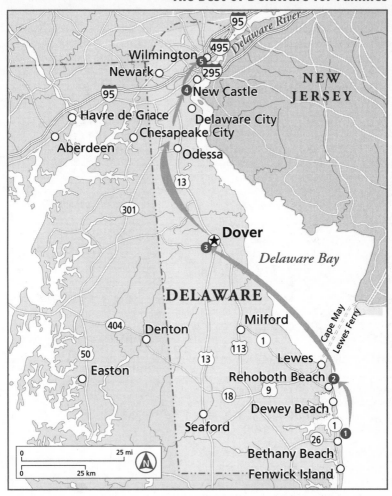

changing exhibits of the **Delaware Center for the Contemporary Arts.** You'll want to have dinner at the **Hotel du Pont** or the trendy **Domaine Hudson,** or perhaps head into the valley for a fabulous meal at **Krazy Kat's** at the Inn at Montchanin Village. Or spend the evening at the Riverfront, where you can pick a restaurant and be entertained at Kahunaville.

5 Walking on the Path to Freedom

African-American history has gotten some well-deserved attention throughout the region. From Baltimore to the Eastern Shore, look for the places where people struggled for freedom and the museums that highlight their courage and faith.

The Path to Freedom

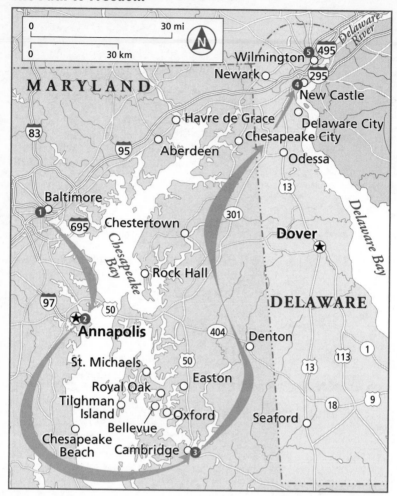

Day ❶: Baltimore Museums

You can learn the stories of individuals who found freedom on the underground railroad or who made the civil-rights movement their own in three museums here. All eyes are on the **Reginald F. Lewis Museum of Maryland African American History & Culture,** the newest jewel in the city's collection of museums, on the east side of the Inner Harbor. Farther east, the **Civil War Museum–President Street Station** tells the story of the underground railroad—complete with a box that recalls how one "passenger" was smuggled to freedom. The **National Great Blacks in Wax Museum** is a bit out of the way for downtown visitors, but the wax figures recall the triumphs and the horrors of slavery in a unique way. The **Eubie Blake Cultural Center** focuses on musical talents, most notably of this Broadway composer, jazzman Cab Calloway, and others.

Day ❷: Annapolis

Alex Haley, author of *Roots,* has a permanent seat at **City Dock,** a place where people were once auctioned off as slaves. The sculpture is only one such tribute. U.S. Supreme Court Justice Thurgood Marshall and North Pole explorer Matthew Henson are honored with statues on the lawn of the **State House.** Stop in the newly expanded **Banneker–Douglass Museum** for a look at the lives of other prominent African-American Marylanders. A tour focusing on African-American history is available at the **Historic Annapolis** museum store.

Day ❸: Following the Underground Railroad

These roads in Dorchester and Caroline counties on the Eastern Shore, which were traveled by underground railroad "conductor" Harriett Tubman, are detailed in the *Finding a Way to Freedom* driving-tour brochure and map, available at visitor centers on I-95 and in Cambridge. The roads remain, though most of the actual buildings, such as Tubman's home, are gone. The **Harriet Tubman Museum,** in Cambridge, offers tours to help interpret the places as you go by. The route is about 100 miles long and takes about 4 hours. Most of it goes through farmland, but there are a few places to stop for food and restrooms.

Day ❹: Delaware

If you have only a day, be sure to stop in Newark, Delaware, to see the nationally recognized **Paul R. Jones Collection of African American Art**—the largest and most comprehensive collection of 20th-century African-American art in the world. Mr. Jones's collection, which includes Jacob Lawrence, Carrie Mae Weems, and Elizabeth Catlett, is on display at the University of Delaware's Mechanical Hall. Stop in nearby New Castle and visit the old Court House to see exhibits on the underground railroad and the legal history of free and enslaved African Americans. If you have time, visit Wilmington and walk along the Riverfront to see the markers recalling Harriet Tubman's efforts here. The riverside Tubman–Garrett Park is named for her and abolitionist Thomas Garrett.

6 Recalling the War Between the States

Frederick is your base for a 3- or 4-day visit to three major battlefields: Gettysburg, Antietam, and Harpers Ferry. Or you could spend a week and add Baltimore's Civil War Museum (site of the first bloodshed in the Civil War) and Federal Hill (where U.S. cannons were trained on the city), plus Delaware's Fort Delaware, which served as a prisoner-of-war camp for 33,000 Confederate soldiers.

Day ❶: Frederick

Begin your day in Frederick at the **National Museum of Civil War Medicine** for a different perspective of the war—that of doctors and nurses. Take a walk through town and look at the signs in the historic district, which feature photos of the troops as they marched through town. Frederick was not only a crossroads for soldiers as they headed off to battle, but also where many came to recuperate after battle. The confrontation between **Barbara Fritchie** and General Stonewall Jackson in 1862 was immortalized in poetry; a reconstruction of her house sits along Carroll Creek.

Day ❷: Antietam

More U.S. soldiers were killed, wounded, or missing after the 1-day battle here than at any other time in American history. Stop in the visitor center at **Antietam**

Recalling the War Between the States

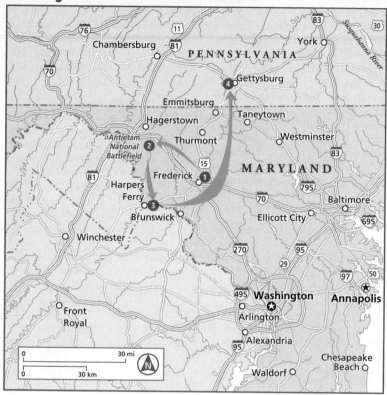

National Battlefield to see a film about the battle and get a tour map. There are maps for biking and hiking along these gently rolling hills, too. Battlefield guides are another option. Take a few minutes to stop by the **Pry House Field Hospital,** which was also Gen. George McClellan's headquarters prior to the battle and a field hospital afterward. A visit here takes only a few hours and could be combined with the Frederick sightseeing if your time is short.

Day ❸: Harpers Ferry
Abolitionist John Brown's plan to start a rebellion was thwarted here by Lt. Col. Robert E. Lee in 1859. The riverfront town was to see Union and Confederate troops several more times before witnessing the war's largest surrender of Federal troops. It's worth a day trip to visit the **Harpers Ferry National Historical Park,** which still appears much as it did during the war. It's a place of natural beauty, too—so bring your hiking shoes or plan a rafting trip on the Shenandoah–Potomac here.

Day ❹: Gettysburg
The 34-mile drive to Gettysburg from Frederick takes you through gently rolling hills and woodlands, orchards, and farms. Take it slowly if you have the time, but if you have just a day you'll need to start early so you can fit in the Gettysburg National Military Park, including the

Gettysburg Cemetery, where President Lincoln delivered his famous address. Driving the battlefield takes a good 2 hours. You'll also want to see the museum at the visitor center. A number of companies, as well as the well-regarded Association of Licensed Battlefield Guides, offer guided tours that give good historical perspective on the sites here. The town itself, with a charming historic district, has lots of privately owned museums. If you have time, don't miss the Schriver House Museum for a view of how citizens fared during the battle here. One day is enough for the highlights here, but 2 days gives you time to savor your visit and take time to shop and have a meal.

5

Baltimore

Baltimore likes to celebrate: Arrive on a sunny May Wednesday and take part in the old-fashioned Flower Mart. Listen to schoolchildren sing. Line up for a crab-cake sandwich or a local treat known as a "lemon stick."

Or come in midsummer and walk around Harborplace, where you'll wonder what the party's for. But it isn't a party: It's just Baltimore having a good time. On a wintry night when it looks like the city has wrapped itself in a blanket and gone to bed, head east to Power Plant Live, historic Fells Point, or the newly redeveloped Canton, and you'll find hot crowds and cool music.

Baltimore celebrates in its historic sites, its endless array of parties and festivals, and its grand museums and neighborhood shops. Picturesque old neighborhoods like Federal Hill, Mount Vernon, Fells Point, and Canton make Baltimore an ever-more-popular tourist destination.

"Charm City" has welcomed visitors since 1729. Founded as a port and ship-building town, manufacturing has always had a big role in this city. General Motors and Bethlehem Steel have been a part of the East Baltimore landscape for decades. Domino Sugar's sign dominates the Inner Harbor. More recently, Baltimore has welcomed a new wave of service industries and nonprofits. Tourism plays an ever-increasing role in the city's economy, and a laid-back population welcomes its visitors with a friendly "Hi, hon!" in the unique Bawlamer accent.

1 Orientation

ARRIVING

BY PLANE   **Baltimore/Washington International Thurgood Marshall Airport** (© **800/I-FLY-BWI** or 410/859-7111; www.bwiairport.com) is 10 miles south of downtown Baltimore, off I-295 (the Baltimore–Washington Pkwy.). It's a major domestic and international hub. Domestic airlines serving Baltimore include **American** (© 800/433-7300), **Continental** (© 800/525-0280), **Delta** (© 800/221-1212), **Northwest** (© 800/225-2525), **Southwest** (© 800/435-9792), **United** (© 800/241-6522), and **US Airways** (© 800/428-4322).

To get to Baltimore from the airport, take I-195 west to Route 295 north, which will take you into downtown. **SuperShuttle** (© **800/258-3826;** www.supershuttle.com) operates vans between the airport and all major downtown hotels. The cost is $11 per person one-way. The **Light Rail** also connects the airport with downtown Baltimore and the Amtrak stations at BWI and at Penn Station.

BY CAR   **I-95** provides the easiest routes to Baltimore from the north and south. From the north, follow I-95 south through the **Fort McHenry Tunnel** ($2 toll) to Exit 53, I-395 north to downtown. Bear left off the exit and follow signs to the Inner

Harbor. From the south, follow I-95 north to Exit 53, I-395 north to downtown. Bear left off the exit and follow signs to the Inner Harbor.

From the west, take **I-70** east to Exit 91, I-695 south (the **Baltimore Beltway**) heading toward Glen Burnie. Take Exit 11A, I-95, to I-395 north to downtown.

From **I-83** (Pennsylvania to the north), follow I-83 south to where it merges with I-695 (the Baltimore Beltway). Continue on I-83 south for 1 mile to Exit 23A (I-83 south, downtown). Continue until the expressway (Jones Falls Expwy.) ends at President Street downtown.

Once you arrive, you'll find lots of parking garages, as well as metered on-street parking throughout the downtown district. Garages charge about $18 a day, or $5 to $8 for special events or evening visits. Parking meters must be fed $1 an hour (in quarters only). New meters in tourist areas enable visitors to use both credit cards and cash to pay parking fees.

BY TRAIN   Baltimore is served by **Amtrak** (© 800/872-7245; www.amtrak.com). Trains on the Northeast Corridor route arrive at and depart from **Pennsylvania Station,** 1500 N. Charles St. (© 410/291-4165), north of the Inner Harbor, and **BWI Airport Rail Station** (© 410/672-6169), off Route 170 about 1½ miles from the airport.

In addition, **MARC** (Maryland Area Rail Commuter) trains provide rail service on two routes from Washington, D.C., stopping at BWI en route. One route ends at Camden Station, closest to the Inner Harbor, and the other ends at Penn Station, about 20 blocks north. From here, you can take a taxi or the Light Rail, which runs Monday through Friday from approximately 6am to 11pm, Saturday from 7am to 11pm, and Sunday and holidays from 11am to 7pm; the fare to the airport is $4 one-way. For more information, call © 800/325-RAIL or go to www.mtamaryland.com.

BY BUS   Regular bus service is provided to and from Baltimore via **Greyhound** (© 800/231-2222; www.greyhound.com) and **Peter Pan/Trailways** (© 800/343-9999; www.peterpanbus.com). Buses serve two stations in the area: in South Baltimore at 2110 Haines St. (© 410/752-7682), and in East Baltimore at the **Baltimore Travel Plaza,** 5625 O'Donnell St. (© 410/633-6389).

VISITOR INFORMATION

Contact the **Baltimore Area Convention and Visitors Association,** 100 Light St., Baltimore, MD 21202 (© 877/BALTIMORE; www.baltimore.org). It has all sorts of information to help you plan your trip, including maps, brochures, and water taxi schedules. In town, the visitor center is located at the Inner Harbor, adjacent to Harborplace. Stop by to pick up a copy of the *Baltimore Quick Guide,* a purse-size guide to events in and around the city. A short film shown several times an hour will introduce you to Baltimore.

You can also stop at the **Downtown Partnership,** 217 N. Charles St., for directions, maps, and other information. Or ask one of the safety guides wearing a purple cap.

BALTIMORE'S NEIGHBORHOODS IN BRIEF

Baltimore has always been a hardworking town, home to fiercely loyal Orioles fans, with close-knit neighborhoods and families. Below are some neighborhoods you may wish to visit, along with a few of the characteristics that make them unique.

Baltimore's **Inner Harbor** is the starting point for most visitors, the focal point of the town's turnaround in the late 1970s. Visitors can get a feel for the city's seafaring days through its attractions on the Inner Harbor, its harbor cruises, and even its water taxis.

The National Aquarium is filled with fish, sharks, and dolphins, and topped with a rainforest. The Maryland Science Center offers an IMAX theater and planetarium. Harborplace and the Gallery are shopping and dining extravaganzas that draw thousands every weekend.

Baltimore has become a destination for pleasure boaters, tall ships, and, more recently, high-tech racing sailboats. The Volvo Ocean Race sailors stopped here in 2002 and 2006.

Just past the Inner Harbor are some of Baltimore's oldest neighborhoods:

Little Italy has been home to Italian immigrants and their descendants since the mid-1800s, when they first opened the restaurants that continue to anchor the neighborhood. Some of the city's oldest buildings line the charming, narrow streets—these survived the 1905 fire that destroyed downtown. Before or after dinner, take a walk to see the rowhouses and their famous marble steps, which dominate the Baltimore streetscape—and notice the shrines with flowers and statues that grace windows here and there.

Harbor East, formerly an industrial area, now boasts the city's newest hotels and condos, some fine restaurants, and a branch of Whole Foods. Young adults moving to Baltimore want to live in this area, which is quite convenient to the other harborside neighborhoods.

Fells Point was Baltimore's original seaport and home to the first shipyards. Baltimore clippers, a swift and elegant topsail schooner, were made here. For many years, immigrants to the U.S. arrived in Fells Point and settled this area as well as the surrounding neighborhoods of Highlandtown and Canton.

Fells Point has long been known as a rowdy part of town. Restaurants and entertainment venues keep this neighborhood hopping all night. But don't miss the history: A maritime museum and walking tours bring the past (and a few ghosts) to life.

The Recreation Pier will be familiar to TV viewers as the site of police headquarters in the series *Homicide.*

Canton is one of Baltimore's newest hot spots. Long a working-class neighborhood, it was once home to families whose breadwinners worked at nearby factories, canneries, and breweries. Today, technology firms rent office space here, while families are moving in to rehab the old brick and Formstone rowhouses. O'Donnell Square is surrounded by bars and eateries, and the Can Company has transformed an abandoned can-making operation into a mixed-use space with offices, a few shops, and restaurants with outdoor patios.

All of the above neighborhoods are connected by a waterfront promenade as well as water taxis.

Mount Vernon, the blocks surrounding the Washington Monument (which, as Baltimoreans will remind you, pre-dates the one in D.C.), offers a collection of beautiful buildings from its heyday as the city's toniest neighborhood. It's home to the Walters Art Museum.

Northern Baltimore City is mostly residential, though **Hampden** and **Mount Washington** offer their own charms, with interesting shopping and some good restaurants. If you happen to be in town during December, visit Hampden's **34th Street** to see how the neighbors dress up their rowhouses for the holidays; people come from all over the city to view the thousands of lights, model trains, and Santas. Mount

Baltimore Neighborhoods

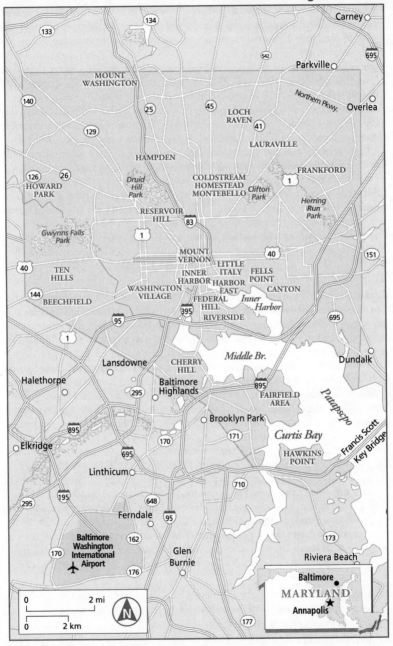

Washington is a short Light Rail trip from downtown, a good side trip if the glitz of the Inner Harbor is too much for you. It's small, but offers a handful of fun eateries, as well as some nice shops and a pottery studio.

2 Getting Around

BY CAR If you plan to stay near the harbor, it is easier to walk or take a water taxi than to drive and park. That said, driving in downtown Baltimore is fairly easy. The streets are on a straight grid; many are one-way. The major northbound streets are Howard, Charles, and Calvert. Cathedral and St. Paul are southbound. Lombard and Pratt are the major east and west streets. On the west side, Martin Luther King Boulevard connects the harbor with the cultural district; it runs both north and south.

Need to find an address? Buildings are numbered east and west from Charles Street; 100 East Lombard is in the first block to the east of Charles. Baltimore Street is the dividing line for north–south addresses; 100 South Charles is a block below Baltimore.

If you need to rent a car, the major agencies at Baltimore/Washington International Thurgood Marshall Airport include **Alamo** (© 800/327-9633), **Avis** (© 800/831-2847), **Budget** (© 800/527-0700), **Dollar** (© 800/800-4000), **Enterprise** (© 800/325-8007), **Hertz** (© 800/654-3131), **National** (© 800/227-7368), and **Thrifty** (© 800/347-4389).

BY LIGHT RAIL, SUBWAY & BUS The Maryland Transit Administration (MTA) operates the **Light Rail,** a 27-mile system of aboveground rail lines reminiscent of the city's old streetcars. It travels on one north–south line, from the northern suburb of Timonium to Glen Burnie in the south, with a spur to Penn Station. The key stop within the city is Camden Station, next to the Orioles' ballpark. The Light Rail is the ideal way to get to a game or to travel within the downtown area between Camden Yards and the Inner Harbor to the train station, the performing-arts district, or Mount Washington. Trains run every 15 to 30 minutes Monday through Friday between 6am and 11pm, Saturday between 7am and 11pm, and Sunday between 11am and 7pm. Tickets, which cost $1.60 one-way, are dispensed from machines at each stop. Better yet, get a day pass for $3.50—it's good on all MTA transportation.

The MTA also operates the **Metro,** a subway system that connects downtown with the northwestern suburbs. Trains run from Johns Hopkins Hospital in East Baltimore through Charles Center and north to the suburb of Owings Mills. Service is available Monday through Friday from 5am to midnight, Saturday and Sunday from 6am to midnight. The fare is $1.60; you can also purchase the aforementioned day pass, which allows unlimited trips on the Light Rail, the Metro, and city buses for $3.50.

A network of **buses,** also operated by the MTA, connects all sections of the city. Service is daily, but hours vary. The base fare is $1.60; exact change is necessary.

To get information and schedules for all MTA services, call © **410/539-5000** or visit www.mtamaryland.com.

BY TAXI All taxis in the city are metered; two reputable companies are **Yellow Checker Cab** (© **410/841-5573**) and **Arrow Cab** (© **410/261-0000**). For airport trips, call **SuperShuttle** (© **410/258-3826**).

BY WATER TAXI The water taxi makes for a pleasant way to visit Baltimore's attractions. **Ed Kane's Water Taxi** (© **800/658-8947** or 410/563-3901; www.the watertaxi.com) runs between about a dozen Inner Harbor locations, including

Harborplace, Fells Point, Little Italy, Canton, and Fort McHenry; the main stop at Harborplace is on the corner between the two pavilions. Just tell the mate where you want to go. The cost is $8 for adults and $4 for children 10 and under for a full day's unlimited use of the water taxi and trolley to Fort McHenry. Tickets include a "Letter of Marque," a set of discount coupons for area restaurants, museums, and shops.

From May through Labor Day weekend, the 13 water taxis generally run about every 15 to 18 minutes, from 10am to 11pm Sunday through Thursday and until midnight Friday and Saturday. From October through April, taxi service runs from 10am to at least 6pm, sometimes later. In April, September, and October, Friday and Saturday service runs until midnight. The trolley service to Fort McHenry is in operation between April 1 and September 1, daily from 10am to 5 or 7pm, depending on when the fort closes. It runs on weekends only in September. The trolley may be discontinued once Fort McHenry water taxi service begins. Service is always weather permitting; you can pick up a schedule at the main stop at Harborplace.

BY DOUBLE-DECKER BUS   New in 2005 is the **Big Bus Company** (© **410/ 396-6611,** or 877/BALTIMORE for reservations), which operates distinctive double-decker buses on a 14-mile guided route around Baltimore, stopping at various downtown attractions as well as more out-of-the-way places, such as the Maryland Zoo, Baltimore Museum of Art, and B&O Railroad Museum. For one price ($25 adults, $22 seniors, $10 children 4–10), you can ride the 90-minute round-trip or get on and off wherever and whenever you like over a 24-hour period. Buses leave from the visitor center five times a day.

ON FOOT   You'll need to know only a few streets to get around. The easiest is the **promenade** around the Inner Harbor, which runs along the water from Federal Hill to Harbor East to Fells Point and Canton. Because of construction, portions of the route are not quite finished—but it's still a pretty walk. You can take it to the American Visionary Art Museum, Maryland Science Center, Harborplace, National Aquarium, USS *Constellation,* and Maritime Museum, as well as to shops and restaurants.

Pratt and **Lombard** streets are the two major east–west arteries just above the Inner Harbor. Pratt heads east to Little Italy, while Lombard extends west to the stadiums. **Charles Street** is Baltimore's main route north and home to some good restaurants, Baltimore's Washington Monument, and the Walters Art Museum, all within walking distance of the Inner Harbor. **St. Paul Street** is the major route south.

FAST FACTS: Baltimore

American Express The office is at 100 E. Pratt St. (© **410/837-3100**).

Area Code The area codes in Baltimore are **410** and **443**.

Car Rentals See "Getting Around" (p. 70) for car-rental agencies at BWI. Two companies have locations at the Inner Harbor: **Budget,** at the Hyatt, 300 Light St. (© **410/783-1448**), and **Enterprise,** at the Sheraton, 300 S. Charles St. (© **410/547-1855**).

Emergencies Dial © **911** for fire, police, or ambulance.

Eyeglass Repair Try **For Eyes,** 330 N. Charles St. (© **410/727-2027**).

Hospitals Downtown options include **Johns Hopkins Hospital,** 600 S. Wolfe St. (© 410/328-8667); **University of Maryland Medical Center,** 22 S. Greene St. (© 410/328-8667); and **Mercy Medical Center,** 301 St. Paul Place (© 410/332-9000).

Liquor Laws Restaurants, bars, hotels, and other places serving alcohol may stay open from 6am to 2am. Some opt to close on Sundays and election days. The legal age to buy or consume alcohol is 21.

Newspapers & Magazines The major daily newspaper is the *Baltimore Sun;* the *Washington Post* is also widely available. *City Paper* is Baltimore's free weekly alternative paper, published every Wednesday; it has excellent listings. The local monthly magazine is *Baltimore.*

Pharmacies Two downtown options are **Rite Aid,** 17 W. Baltimore St. (© 410/539-0838), and **Walgreens,** 19 E. Fayette St. (© 410/625-1179).

Police Dial © **911** for emergencies, or © **311** for nonemergencies requiring police attention.

Post Office The main post office is at 900 E. Fayette St. (© 410/347-4202). It's open Monday through Saturday from 7:30am to 10pm. Other area post offices are at 111 N. Calvert (© 410/539-1947), and 130 N. Greene St. (© 410/659-6853). Both are open Monday through Friday from 8:30am to 5pm.

Safety Baltimore has a nagging problem with both property and violent crime. The Inner Harbor and Mount Vernon areas are fairly safe, thanks to a greater number of police officers, along with the Downtown Partnership's safety guides. Still, be alert and follow some common-sense precautions.

If you're using public transportation, try to travel during peak hours and keep valuables out of sight. It's much safer and smarter to take a cab or drive between neighborhoods (unless otherwise noted in this chapter) rather than walk, even when the distance is not too great. Keep a good city map at hand; neighborhoods can go from safe to scary in a matter of a few blocks. Stick to the main routes and turn around if anything looks worrisome.

Taxes The state sales tax is 5%. The hotel tax is an additional 7.5%.

Transit Information For bus, Light Rail, and Metro info, call the **Maryland Transit Administration (MTA)** at © **866/743-3682** or 410/539-5000, or go to www.mtamaryland.com.

Weather Call © **410/936-1212.**

3 Where to Stay

Baltimore caters to the business traveler—there are more than 6,600 hotel rooms downtown, with all the expected amenities—but has only a few B&Bs and inns.

It can be hard to find a double for under $100 during the week, but some hotels offer weekend rates and packages that represent savings of 35% to 50% off normal Sunday through Thursday tariffs. So don't be scared off by midweek rates—come on a weekend instead.

Every hotel listed is accessible to travelers with disabilities, although specific amenities vary from place to place.

Where to Stay & Dine in Downtown Baltimore

ACCOMMODATIONS ◼
Abacrombie **2**
Baltimore Marriott Inner Harbor **17**
Baltimore Marriott Waterfront **36**
Brookshire Suites **21**
Courtyard by Marriott Downtown/Inner Harbor **38**
Days Inn Inner Harbor **19**
Doubletree Inn at the Colonnade **4**
Harbor Court **30**
Holiday Inn Baltimore Inner Harbor **18**
Hyatt Regency Baltimore **22**
Peabody Court Hotel **8**
Pier 5 Hotel **33**
Radisson Plaza Lord Baltimore **13**
Renaissance Harborplace Hotel **25**
Residence Inn Downtown/Inner Harbor **16**
Sheraton Inner Harbor **31**
Tremont Park **11**

Tremont Plaza **12**
Wyndham Baltimore
  Inner Harbor **14**

DINING ◆
Bay Atlantic Club **15**
Brass Elephant **5**
Cafe Hon **7**
Capital Grille **24**
Charleston **39**
Crepe du Jour **7**
Ethel and Ramone's **7**
Gertrude's **4**
Grill Art Cafe **1**
Hampton's **29**
James Joyce Irish Pub
  and Restaurant **35**
Johnny Rockets **28**

Mount Washington
  Tavern **7**
Owl Bar **3**
Paper Moon Diner **3**
Phillips Harborplace **28**
Pisces **23**
Prime Rib **6**
Ray Lewis' Full Moon Bar-B-Que **34**
Rick's Café Americain **40**
Roy's Baltimore **37**
Ruth's Chris Steak House **32, 34**
Sascha's 527 **9**
Tapas Teatro **5**
Tio Pepe **10**
Tir Na Nog Irish Bar and Grill **27**
Wharf Rat **20**
Windows **26**

INNER HARBOR
VERY EXPENSIVE

Harbor Court ✿✿✿   Baltimore's finest hotel was for sale at press time, but is expected to remain a first-class establishment. It's a treat just to walk in the door; when you spend the night, prepare to be pampered. Accommodations are exquisitely furnished, from the large standard rooms to the suites, which boast hand-painted decor, marble bathrooms, kitchenettes, and canopy beds. The hotel overlooks the harbor, but only a few rooms have a clear harbor view. Dining options include two first-rate restaurants—**Hampton's** (which serves dinner and Sun brunch) and **Brightons Orangerie** (which serves three meals and afternoon tea)—plus the **Explorers Lounge,** which offers music every night and is popular with locals as well as hotel guests.

550 Light St, Baltimore, MD 21202. © 800/824-0076 or 410/234-0550. Fax 410/659-5925. www.harborcourt.com. 195 units. $275–$305 double; $450–$3,800 suite. AE, DC, DISC, MC, V. Self-parking $21, valet parking $29. **Amenities:** 2 restaurants; coffee shop; indoor pool; tennis courts; health club; Jacuzzi; massage; tanning. *In room:* A/C, TV, high-speed Internet access, minibar, hair dryer, iron, trouser press, CD player, additional TV and phone in bathroom.

EXPENSIVE

Baltimore Marriott Inner Harbor ✿   This hotel, with a 10-story crescent-shaped facade, is across from Camden Yards—a couple of blocks from Harborplace and the convention center. (Don't confuse it with the Baltimore Marriott Waterfront in Harbor East.) A waterfall dominates the lobby. Guest rooms are designed in contemporary style and include all the amenities the business traveler might expect.

110 S. Eutaw St., Baltimore, MD 21202. © 800/228-9290 or 410/962-0202. Fax 410/962-0404. www.baltimore marriottinnerharbor.com. 524 units. $189–$324 double. Weekend rates available. AE, DC, DISC, MC, V. Self-parking $18, valet parking $25. **Amenities:** Restaurant; lounge; indoor pool; health club; whirlpool; business center; concierge-level rooms. *In room:* A/C, TV, high-speed Internet access, minibar, coffeemaker, hair dryer, iron.

Baltimore Marriott Waterfront ✿ *Kids*   This Marriott dominates a prime piece of waterfront—even though it's more than a few steps from the city's best-known attractions and the convention center. Luckily, the water taxi stops nearby. The hotel rises 32 floors above the Harbor East neighborhood. Rooms here are pretty standard, with the added pleasures of down duvets and, of course, that skyline vista. The best views are from the 30th through the 32nd floors, which, naturally, come at a premium. For children, the hotel offers cribs and rollaway beds at no charge, plus a kids' menu in the restaurants.

700 Aliceanna St., Baltimore, MD 21202. © 410/385-3000. Fax 410/895-1900. www.baltimoremarriottwaterfront. com. 750 units. $299–$425 double. AE, DC, DISC, MC, V. Self-parking $20, valet parking $30. Water taxi stop nearby. **Amenities:** 2 restaurants; delicatessen; lounge; health club; business center; massage; concierge-level rooms. *In room:* A/C, TV, dataport, Wi-Fi, minibar, hair dryer, iron.

Hyatt Regency Baltimore ✿✿✿   The eye-catching all-glass Hyatt was the Inner Harbor's first hotel 20 years ago, and it's still one of the best. Sure, Baltimore has more luxury hotels now, but the Hyatt still has the best location. It's a short walk across a skywalk to the Inner Harbor, another skywalk to the convention center, and a few blocks to the stadiums. Accommodations are your standard hotel-chain style, but they have breathtaking harbor views. It's often busy, but not too noisy, and the staff here couldn't be nicer.

300 Light St., Baltimore, MD 21202. © 800/233-1234 or 410/528-1234. Fax 410/685-3362. www.baltimore. hyatt.com. 486 units. $199–$359 double. Ask about packages and discounts. Children under 18 stay free in parent's room. AE, DC, DISC, MC, V. Self-parking $19, valet parking $25. **Amenities:** Rooftop restaurant; bar; outdoor pool;

recreation deck w/jogging track, putting green, 2 tennis courts, basketball court; health club; executive-level rooms; Wi-Fi in lobby. *In room:* A/C, TV, high-speed Internet access, minibar, hair dryer, iron, safe.

Pier 5 Hotel ⚓ *Finds*   Be prepared for something wild when you walk into the lobby of the Pier 5. It's bright and airy, with fun, offbeat sofas and a purple, red, and yellow color scheme. The rooms continue the theme, though they're much quieter and more refined. Standard units are comfortable, with lots of conveniences for both business and leisure travelers. Suites are luxurious, with one, two, or even three tiny balconies overlooking the harbor or the National Aquarium. Just about every room has a water view—and a much closer one than at any of the other hotels, as this place is only two stories high and right on the harbor. Ask about their packages; some include attractions that both adults and children will enjoy, while others are geared toward romance. The **Peacock Cafe** is open for breakfast, lunch, and dinner; **McCormick & Schmick's** offers lunch and dinner; and **Ruth's Chris Steak House** serves dinner.

711 Eastern Ave. (at the end of Pier 5), Baltimore, MD 21202. ✆ **866/583-4162** or 410/539-2000. Fax 410/783-1787. www.harbormagic.com. 65 units. $149–$399 double; $329–$1,500 suite. AE, DC, DISC, MC, V. Self-parking $21, valet parking $28. Located at a water taxi stop. Pets welcome. **Amenities:** 3 restaurants; access to exercise room at Brookshire Suites; complimentary shuttle to Brookshire Suites, Admiral Fell Inn, and Johns Hopkins Hospital; free weekend activities; Wi-Fi in lobby. *In room:* A/C, dataport and T1 Internet access, fridge, coffeemaker, iron, robe.

Renaissance Harborplace Hotel ⚓⚓   The Renaissance is in the middle of everything: Business travelers find it convenient to local firms, the convention center, and restaurants, while tourists like its location across the street from Harborplace and the Inner Harbor. It's part of the Gallery at Harborplace, five floors of shops topped by an office tower. Guest rooms are the biggest in Baltimore, with comfortable furniture and wide windows (that really open) overlooking the Inner Harbor. The huge rooms, renovated in 2003, have good views, especially on the upper floors. Need extra luxury? Special suites have bedrooms connected to a parlor with living room, dining room, and kitchenette; some even have Murphy beds for extra guests.

202 E. Pratt St., Baltimore, MD 21202. ✆ **800/HOTELS-1** or 410/547-1200. Fax 410/783-9676. www.renaissance harborplace.com. 622 units. $259–$309 double; $500–$5,000 suite. Children under 17 stay free in parent's room. AE, DC, DISC, MC, V. Self-parking $21, valet parking $28. **Amenities:** Restaurant overlooking harbor; lounge; indoor pool; whirlpool; sauna; health club with harbor view; business center; concierge-level rooms; access to Gallery on 1st and 5th floors. *In room:* A/C, 2-line phone, dataport, high speed Internet access, minibar, coffeemaker, hair dryer, iron, lock box, robe.

MODERATE

Brookshire Suites ⚓ *Kids*   This building was once a parking garage, but only the tallest guests might notice its slightly lower ceilings. Accommodations are comfortable, with room to spread out. The **Cloud Club** has a terrific view, lots of comfortable seating, and TVs. What makes the Brookshire an even better deal for visiting families is the full breakfast buffet served every morning. The hotel is easy to find, located a block from the Inner Harbor on one of the city's main arteries—a convenient base for stepping out to see the sights.

120 E. Lombard St., Baltimore, MD 21202. ✆ **866/583-4162** or 410/625-1300. www.harbormagic.com. 97 units. $119–$269 double. Ask about packages. Rates include full breakfast in Cloud Club. AE, DC, DISC, MC, V. Valet parking $25. Pets welcome. **Amenities:** Cloud Club lounge; health club; complimentary shuttle to Pier 5 Hotel, Admiral Fell Inn, and Johns Hopkins Hospital; free weekend activities; Wi-Fi in lounge. *In room:* A/C, dataport and T1 Internet access, minibar, coffeemaker, iron, robe.

Courtyard by Marriott Baltimore Downtown/Inner Harbor ⚓   Although overshadowed in size by its big sister, the Baltimore Marriott Waterfront, the Courtyard won't be outdone for service or comfortable accommodations. There are eight units with Jacuzzis and 10 corner suites. This hotel is serious enough for business travelers, but casual enough for families on vacation. Though it's not in the midst of the major attractions, it's on the water taxi routes and located near the newly developing promenade, making it an easy walk to the Inner Harbor and Fells Point.

1000 Aliceanna St., Baltimore, MD 21202. © **443/923-4000.** Fax 443/923-9970. www.marriott.com/bwidt. 205 units. $129–$209 double. AE, DC, DISC, MC, V. Self-parking $19. Water taxi stop nearby. **Amenities:** Cafe; lounge; indoor pool; health club; whirlpool; business center; coin-op laundry; complimentary coffee in lobby. *In room:* A/C, TV w/pay movies and PlayStation, Wi-Fi, coffeemaker, hair dryer, iron.

Days Inn Inner Harbor *Value*   If you're willing to give up proximity to the harbor (by 2 or 3 blocks), you can get a great deal at this modern nine-story hotel, located between the 1st Mariner Arena and the convention center, just 3 blocks from Camden Yards. It's got a good setup for business travelers, including "work zone" rooms with large desks, kitchenettes, and plenty of space—but all units have the comfort you expect from this chain. Many rooms received fresh updates in 2005.

100 Hopkins Place (between Lombard and Pratt sts.), Baltimore, MD 21202. © **800/DAYS-INN** or 410/576-1000. Fax 410/576-9437. www.daysinnerharbor.com. 250 units. $99–$189 double. Children under 17 stay free in parent's room. AE, DC, DISC, MC, V. Parking $15. **Amenities:** Restaurant; outdoor pool; health club; business center; courtyard patio. *In room:* A/C, TV w/Nintendo 64, Wi-Fi, coffeemaker, hair dryer, iron.

Holiday Inn Baltimore Inner Harbor *Kids*   For value and location, it's hard to beat this old-timer, the first major chain property in Baltimore. It's between the 1st Mariner Arena and the convention center, a block from Camden Yards, and 3 blocks from Harborplace. Renovations were underway in 2005 and 2006, renewing everything from the hotel's facade to the bedroom upholstery. Guest rooms are a good size, with traditional furniture and wide windows with skyline views. Baseball fans might want to ask for a view of Camden Yards.

301 W. Lombard St., Baltimore, MD 21201. © **800/HOLIDAY** or 410/685-3500. Fax 410/727-6169. www.holiday-inn.com/bal-downtown. 375 units. $129–$189 double; $285 suite. Children under 18 stay free in parent's room. AE, DC, DISC, MC, V. Self-parking $15. **Amenities:** Restaurant; coffee shop; indoor pool; health club; sauna, business center. *In room:* A/C, TV w/PlayStation, Wi-Fi, coffeemaker, hair dryer, iron.

Radisson Plaza Lord Baltimore *Moments*   If you love grand old hotels with modern conveniences, this one's for you. The 23-story French Renaissance–style hotel, which opened in 1928, still retains its old-fashioned charm. The grand lobby boasts soaring columns and a glittering chandelier. Those who need extra space should consider a one-bedroom parlor suite or a corner room, which comes with king-size bed and sleeper sofa. Set in the heart of the financial district, the hotel is convenient to Mount Vernon attractions; the Inner Harbor is only 5 blocks away.

20 W. Baltimore St. (between Charles and Hanover sts.), Baltimore, MD 21202. © **800/333-3333** or 410/539-8400. Fax 410/625-1060. www.radisson.com/lordbaltimore. 439 units. $99–$279 double. AE, DC, DISC, MC, V. Valet parking $25. **Amenities:** Restaurant; bar; coffee shop; health club; Jacuzzi; sauna; business center; gift shop; concierge-level rooms. *In room:* A/C, TV, Wi-Fi, fridge or microwave upon request, coffeemaker, hair dryer, iron, 2-line phone.

Residence Inn Baltimore Downtown/Inner Harbor   Just a block from the Inner Harbor and tucked into the financial district is a branch of this family- and business-traveler-friendly chain. The studio kings, comfortable and reasonably priced, fill up quickly. But families may prefer the other, larger units: One-bedrooms have kitchenettes and pull-out sofas, while two-bedroom suites are reserved for extended-stay guests. A hot breakfast is served every morning, and dinner or filling snacks are offered

Monday through Thursday evenings, all complimentary. Managers stop by to see if their guests need anything—a Residence Inn tradition.

17 Light St., Baltimore, MD 21202. (C) 410/962-1220. Fax 410/962-1221. www.marriott.com/BWIHB. 188 units. $179–$299 double (daily rates decrease for longer stays). Rates include breakfast and evening refreshments. AE, DC, DISC, MC, V. Valet parking $25. **Amenities:** Restaurant; bar; snack shop; access to pool at nearby Marriott hotels; business center w/Wi-Fi; children's playroom; laundry room; complimentary grocery shopping. *In room:* A/C, TV, high-speed Internet, kitchenette, coffeemaker, hair dryer, iron.

Sheraton Inner Harbor   The Sheraton has a perfect location for conventioneers and Orioles fans; the latter will like the location and the packages with tickets to Camden Yards. Guest rooms are fairly dark and not as interesting as those at many other choices in the area. The suites are a good idea, set up with Murphy beds so they can be turned into mini–conference rooms. The **Orioles Grille** has some interesting sports memorabilia, though no view. **Morton's of Chicago** has a restaurant here.

300 S. Charles St., Baltimore, MD 21202. (C) 410/962-8300. Fax 410/962-8211. www.sheraton.com/innerharbor. 337 units. $119–$309 double; $495–$1,500 suite. Children under 18 stay free in parent's room. AE, DC, DISC, MC, V. **Amenities:** Restaurant; casual grill and lounge; indoor pool; health club; car-rental desk; terrace. *In room:* A/C, high-speed Internet access, minibar, fridge and microwave on request in suites, hair dryer, iron, 2-line phone.

Tremont Plaza *Value*   You get the most room for the least amount of money at this all-suite hotel. The "studio" suites are really L-shaped rooms with sleeping and sitting areas, as well as a kitchenette. If that's not big enough for you, there are one- and two-bedroom suites as well. Furnishings are simple but adequate. At first glance, the location may seem out of the way—but Charles Street, Baltimore's main drag, is just a block away. It's 7 blocks to the Inner Harbor and about 4 blocks to the Walters Art Museum. A free shuttle will take guests anywhere within a 2-mile radius. You'll find downtown's only outdoor pool here, but it's too small for laps.

Just around the corner is the hotel's sister property, the **Tremont Park,** 8 E. Pleasant St., which has 58 studio and one-bedroom suites.

222 St. Paul Place, Baltimore, MD 21202. (C) 800/TREMONT. www.1800tremont.com. 303 units. $109–$209 studio; $139–$239 1-bedroom. AE, DC, DISC, MC, V. Valet parking $25. **Amenities:** Restaurant; lounge; deli; pool; health club; sauna; complimentary downtown shuttle. *In room:* A/C, Wi-Fi, coffeemaker, fridge, microwave, hair dryer, iron.

Wyndham Baltimore Inner Harbor *🐾*   You could get lost in here, but the staff is quick to point a confused guest in the right direction. Just remember which tower you're staying in! Maryland's largest hotel, the Wyndham is a popular place for conventions. Rooms in the two towers are set up with the business traveler in mind. Tourists can count on comfortable accommodations about 5 blocks from the Inner Harbor and next door to the 1st Mariner Arena.

101 W. Fayette St., Baltimore, MD 21202. (C) 800/WYNDHAM or 410/752-1100. Fax 410/625-3805. www.wyndham.com. 707 units. $139–$179 double. Weekend packages available. Children under 18 stay free in parent's room. AE, DC, MC, V. Self-parking $20, valet parking $27. Small pets welcome. **Amenities:** Restaurant; lounge w/light fare; outdoor pool; health club, business center. *In room:* A/C, TV w/video games, dataport, Internet access, fridge on request, coffeemaker, hair dryer, iron.

FELLS POINT

Admiral Fell Inn   Updated and expanded over the years, this charming inn sits just across Thames Street from the harbor in the heart of the Fells Point Historic District. It spans eight buildings, built between 1790 and 1996 and blending Victorian and Federal-style architecture. Originally a boardinghouse for sailors, later a YMCA, and then a vinegar bottling plant, the inn now features an antiques-filled lobby and library,

Where to Stay & Dine in Fells Point & Little Italy

ACCOMMODATIONS ■
Admiral Fell Inn **15**
Celie's Waterfront Inn **16**
Henderson's Wharf Inn **18**

DINING ◆
Amicci's **3**
Bertha's **11**
Black Olive **13**
Bonaparte Breads **17**
Chiapparelli's **4**
Della Note **6**
James Joyce Irish Pub
  & Restaurant **7**
Kali's Court **14**
Mezze **14**
Obrycki's **8**
Petticoat Tea Room **12**
Pierpoint Restaurant **10**
Roy's Baltimore **7**
Sabatino's **5**
Vaccaro's **1**
Velleggia's **2**
Ze Mean Bean Café **9**

Inner Harbor

along with individually decorated guest rooms with Federal-period furnishings. Some units have canopy beds and Jacuzzis, two rooms have balconies, and one suite has a fireplace and Jacuzzi. The loft room is quite different from the rest—more rustic, with sloping ceilings that tall guests might not like. But from its three dormer windows, the views are among the best in the inn. The **Petticoat Tea Room** offers lunch, tea, and late-afternoon dining; **True** serves dinner Tuesday through Saturday.

888 S. Broadway, Baltimore, MD 21231. © **866/583-4162** or 410/522-7377. Fax 410/522-0707. www.harbormagic. com. 80 units. $199–$249 double. Rates include breakfast at True. AE, DC, DISC, MC, V. Valet parking $20. Located across the street from a water taxi stop. Pets welcome. **Amenities:** Admiral's lounge; restaurant; tearoom; access to health club at nearby Brookshire Suites; complimentary shuttle to Pier 5 Hotel, Brookshire Suites, and Johns Hopkins Hospital; free weekend activities; complimentary treats in lobby. *In room:* A/C, dataport and T1 Internet access, iron, robe.

Celie's Waterfront Inn ⊛ (Finds)   Walk down the sally port of this 18th-century town house and enter a quiet refuge. It's one of only a few B&Bs in Baltimore, and it's delightful. Two units have fireplaces, whirlpool tubs, and harbor views, while two others—with just as nice city views—have private balconies and whirlpools. Two interior rooms are particularly quiet, as they overlook the flower-filled courtyard. New owners have added two suites (with full kitchens), which can accommodate four and six comfortably. Enjoy breakfast in your room, on the deck, or in the garden.

1714 Thames St., Baltimore, MD 21231. © 800/432-0184 or 410/522-2323. www.celieswaterfront.com. 9 units. $139–$239 double; $299–$349 suites. Rates include hearty continental breakfast. 2- or 3-night minimum stay may be required on weekends or holidays. AE, DISC, MC, V. On-street parking only. Located across the street from a water taxi stop. **Amenities:** Roof deck w/harbor views; access to conveniences such as VCR, coffeemaker, fridge, and iron on request. *In room:* A/C, Wi-Fi, portable phones upon request, robe.

Henderson's Wharf Inn ✧ Hurricane Isabel flooded this tobacco-warehouse-turned-inn in 2003, but repairs have made this place better than ever. From the warm lobby to the courtyard garden, every detail has been chosen for comfort and style. All rooms are on the ground floor (shutters at the windows ensure privacy), with views of the courtyard, the adjacent marina, or the cobblestone streets of Fells Point. Each is outfitted in soothing neutrals, with dark mahogany furniture and luxurious marble bathrooms.

1000 Fell St., Baltimore, MD 21231. © 800/522-2088 or 410/522-7777. Fax 410/522-7087. www.hendersons wharf.com. 37 units. $179–$259 double. Rates include continental breakfast. AE, DC, MC, V. Free parking. **Amenities:** 256-slip marina; business center. *In room:* A/C, flatscreen TV w/DVD player available, coffeemaker, fridge, hair dryer, iron, robes.

NORTH OF DOWNTOWN

Abacrombie *Finds* Guest performers with the Baltimore Symphony Orchestra often choose this inviting B&B across from the Meyerhoff Symphony Hall. Guest rooms, decorated with vintage furnishings, are cheery and bright. The owners, former Ritz-Carlton employees, have added luxe touches such as robes and fine toiletries. Ask for a room at the end of the hall if you'd like more space—these have the most square footage and biggest windows. Single rooms are tiny, with charming beds. Two connect to doubles, making them perfect for families. A good restaurant and bar are located on the ground floor.

58 W. Biddle St., Baltimore, MD 21201. © 410/244-7227. Fax 410/244-8413 www.abacrombie.net. 12 units. $88 single; $115–$155 double. Rates include extended European continental breakfast. AE, DC, DISC, MC, V. Free parking. **Amenities:** Restaurant; bar; book/video library; convenience room w/iron, fridge, and microwave. *In room:* A/C, TV/VCR, hair dryer, robe.

Doubletree Inn at the Colonnade If your visit will take you to the northern reaches of Baltimore, to Johns Hopkins University (which is right across the street), to the Baltimore Museum of Art, or to friends' places in Homeland or Roland Park, this is a good choice. Sleek and elegant, the inn offers comfortable rooms, Biedermeier-style furnishings, and plenty of amenities. Some units have fridges and microwaves. The parking is a bit tricky—you'd do best to pull up and let the valet park your car.

4 W. University Pkwy., Baltimore, MD 21218. © 800/222-8737 or 410/235-5400. Fax 410/235-5572. www.double treehotels.com. 125 units. $139–$225 double. Weekend rates available. AE, DC, DISC, MC, V. Self-parking $18, valet parking $20. **Amenities:** Restaurant; indoor pool; access to nearby tennis courts; health club; whirlpool; access to nearby jogging track; complimentary shuttle to Inner Harbor. *In room:* A/C, dataport, coffeemaker, hair dryer, iron.

Peabody Court Hotel ✧ This Mount Vernon boutique hotel, a Clarion property, continues to offer the first-class service that has kept it in business since 1930. Extensive renovations in 2003 have retained the small lobby's luxurious, European-style ambience. The polished guest rooms are some of the most spacious in the city. The light-bathed corner units have upward of 600 square feet. Ask for a room that overlooks Baltimore's most beautiful and historic square. The hotel is close to the Peabody Institute, Walters Art Museum, and Mount Vernon restaurants and shops. The walk to the Inner Harbor takes 20 minutes or so—and it's all downhill. The casual restaurant, **George's,** has several dinner entrees in the $12 range.

612 Cathedral St., Baltimore, MD 21201. ℭ **800/292-5500** or 410/727-7101. Fax 410/789-3312. www.peabody courthotel.com. 104 units. $150–$300 double. Weekend rates available. AE, DC, DISC, MC, V. Valet parking $25. **Amenities:** Restaurant; health club; business center. *In room:* A/C, TV, high-speed Internet access, fridge, coffeemaker, hair dryer, iron, towel warmers, wet bar in some rooms.

NEAR THE AIRPORT

An alternative to staying downtown and worrying about parking—especially if you plan to see only the Inner Harbor attractions—is a hotel near Baltimore/Washington International Thurgood Marshall Airport that offers free shuttle service to the North Linthicum Light Rail station. About 15 airport hotels have such shuttles. From North Linthicum, it's a 15-minute ride to the Camden Yards station, which is just 6 blocks from the Inner Harbor. For a train schedule, see www.mtamaryland.com.

Closest to the airport are the **BWI Airport Marriott,** 1743 W. Nursery Rd. (ℭ **800/ 228-9290** or 410/859-8300; www.marriott.com), which has an indoor pool; **Country Inn & Suites by Carlson BWI Airport,** 1717 W. Nursery Rd. (ℭ **800/456-4000** or 443/577-1036; www.countryinns.com/bwiairport), which has an indoor pool; and **Four Points by Sheraton BWI Airport,** 7032 Elm Rd. (ℭ **888/625-5144** or 410/859-3300; www.starwoodhotels.com), with an outdoor pool.

4 Where to Dine

Baltimore has always been known for seafood, but the city is also home to a variety of ethnic and regional cuisines. There are plenty of good restaurants in the main tourist areas, with excellent choices in Little Italy, Fells Point, and Mount Vernon.

In recent years, the Inner Harbor has become a bit overrun with chain restaurants serving mediocre fare—but the Hard Rock Cafe and ESPN Zone continue to draw big crowds. Power Plant Live, with its mix of chains, local restaurants, and clubs, is also packed at dinnertime. You'll find it a block north of Pratt Street, a short walk from Charles Street and the Inner Harbor.

A note for your wallet: Restaurant prices are creeping up, and $25 dinner entrees—unheard of in recent years—are becoming more common.

INNER HARBOR & HARBOR EAST
VERY EXPENSIVE

Charleston ✦✦✦ AMERICAN/SOUTHERN   The Charleston is Baltimore's special-night-out place. It's crowded, yes, but the waiters are so attentive you'll think they're serving only you. Chef Cindy Wolf's restaurant celebrates Southern hospitality. With its beautiful setting and imaginative cuisine, the prevailing mood is "gracious." The food is, simply put, the best in Baltimore. The menu changes daily, but might include she-crab soup, shrimp with andouille sausage and grits, pan-fried rockfish, and bacon-wrapped tenderloin with seasonal vegetables. Charleston offers diners a choice of three to six courses: A three-course dinner is $64, while a six-course meal will run $102 (wine is extra). The chef's husband and co-owner, Tony Foreman, has selected 600 bottles for the restaurant's wine list. The lounge has its own menu of small plates ($10–$15), cocktails, and wines by the glass.

1000 Lancaster St. ℭ 410/332-7373. www.charlestonrestaurant.com. Reservations recommended. Prix-fixe dinners $64–$102. AE, DC, DISC, MC, V. Mon–Sat 5:30–10pm. Free valet parking.

Baltimore's Best Crab Cakes

A visit to Baltimore means crab cakes—but what makes a good crab cake is up for heated debate. You can expect jumbo lump mixed with a bit of mayo; fried or broiled is often the diner's choice. But each recipe is different. Is Old Bay seasoning required? How much filler is too much? Should you see a fleck of any plant material besides parsley?

Keep in mind a few things: Crabs run from May to September (more or less), so you have a better chance of getting local crab—not Louisiana or Asia imports—in those months. You don't have to go to a crab house for a decent crab cake. In fact, the number of crab houses has dwindled in recent years, but you can find good seafood at just about every restaurant around. Expect to pay about $12 to $15 for a crab-cake sandwich (served on crackers or a bun). A crab-cake platter will be at least $25 and usually comes with fries, coleslaw, and sliced tomato.

Below is *my* list of where I think you'll find a good crab cake. Are these the best? Have a marvelous time deciding!

Crab Shanty, 3410 Plum Tree Dr. (Rte. 40 W.), Ellicott City (℃ 410/465-9660; www.crabshanty.com). Good-size cake, not too much filler. Open Sunday through Friday for lunch, daily for dinner. Carryout is available.

Faidley Seafood, Lexington Market, 400 W. Lexington St. (℃ 410/727-4898; www.faidleyscrabcakes.com). The Faidley family has been selling seafood from this stall for 120 years. One of the things it does right is a traditional crab cake. Open Monday through Saturday from 8:30am to 6pm. Carryout only; shipping is available, too.

Gertrude's, at the Baltimore Museum of Art, 10 Art Museum Dr. (℃ 410/889-3399; www.johnshields.com). Noted chef John Shields offers traditional Baltimore-style cakes as well as a creative chef's special. Open Tuesday through Sunday for lunch and dinner.

Kali's Court & Mezze, 1606 Thames St., Fells Point (℃ 410/276-4700; www.kaliscourt.net). Crab, crab, and not much else. Open daily for lunch and dinner.

Obrycki's, 1727 E. Pratt St., Upper Fells Point (℃ 410/732-6399; www.obryckis.com). Traditional crab house, traditional crab cake. Open daily for lunch and dinner from mid-March to November.

Pierpoint Restaurant, 1822 Aliceanna St., Fells Point (℃ 410/675-2080; www.pierpointrestaurant.com). Crab cakes here are smoked—different, but well worth a try. Open Tuesday through Friday for lunch, Tuesday through Sunday for dinner.

Ruth's Chris Steak House 🦀🦀 STEAKHOUSE/AMERICAN   Located on the first floor of the Brokerage, the Baltimore branch of this steakhouse chain is a favorite with the suit-and-tie crowd. The dark wood furnishings and globe lanterns contribute to its clubby atmosphere. This is a place to come for beef—there are six choices of steak on the menu, all butter-bathed and prepared to order, plus prime rib and filet mignon. Alternatively, you can opt for lobster, salmon, swordfish, or blackened tuna.

A second downtown Ruth's Chris has opened at the Pier 5 Hotel, 711 Eastern Ave. (© **410/230-0033**).

600 Water St., between S. Frederick and Market sts. © **410/783-0033**. www.ruthschris.com. Reservations highly recommended Fri–Sat. Main courses $27–$73. AE, DC, DISC, MC, V. Mon–Thurs 5–10pm; Fri–Sat 5–11pm; Sun 4–9pm.

EXPENSIVE

Capital Grille STEAKHOUSE Baltimore is a town big enough for two Ruth's Chris steakhouses, plus the ever-popular Prime Rib. And now here comes another steakhouse, creating quite a buzz for its clubby atmosphere and sizzling steaks. The food is expertly prepared and the service professional. Lunchtime choices range from sandwiches to salads to steak. At dinner, steak reigns, but there's plenty of seafood, too. Everything is a la carte.

500 E. Pratt St. © **443/703-4064**. www.thecapitalgrille.com. Reservations recommended. Main courses $11–$23 at lunch, $19–$37 at dinner. AE, DC, DISC, MC, V. Mon–Fri 11:30am–3pm; Sun–Thurs 5–10pm, Fri–Sat 5–11pm.

Pisces 🍴 *Moments* SEAFOOD In a city where lots of restaurants have good views, this one tops them all, literally. Overlooking the Inner Harbor, Camden Yards, and the downtown skyline, this rooftop restaurant spreads the city out before you. The interior is sleek and modern, the menu small but intriguing. Soups can range from cream of crab to grilled seafood miso, while entrees are mostly seafood prepared with creative sauces and seasonings. The well-spaced tables offer a pleasantly intimate dining experience; service is anything but hurried. A pianist plays nightly and at Sunday brunch.

At the Hyatt Regency, 300 Light St., 15th floor. © **410/528-1234**. Reservations recommended. Main courses $18–$38; Sun brunch $40. AE, DC, DISC, MC, V. Mon–Thurs 5:30–10pm; Fri 5:30–10:30pm; Sat 5:30–11pm; Sun 10am–2pm.

Roy's Baltimore HAWAIIAN This well-regarded chain restaurant next door to the Marriott Waterfront features modern furnishings and a menu quite exotic for Baltimore. Known for its incredible blackened ahi tuna and other tropical delights, the restaurant also does local seasonal favorites, including crab cakes, oysters, and softshell crabs. Its prix-fixe menu offers an appetizer sampler, entree, and dessert for about $33. The sleek bar is a great place to try one of Roy's intriguing martinis.

720B Aliceanna St. © **410/659-0099**. www.roysrestaurant.com. Reservations recommended. Main courses $19–$28. AE, DC, DISC, MC, V. Mon–Thurs 5:30–10pm; Fri 5:30–10:30pm; Sat 5–10:30pm; Sun 5–9pm.

Windows 🍴 NEW AMERICAN The sweeping views of the Inner Harbor are only the beginning at this fifth-floor restaurant. Using fresh seasonal ingredients, particularly Maryland produce and seafood, the chef has created a delightful menu. Entrees recently included wonderful rockfish and lump crab grilled with charred tomato vinaigrette, as well as pecan-crusted cod and filet mignon with savory potato hash. Lunchtime is just as adventurous, and breakfast is an occasion here.

At the Renaissance Harborplace Hotel, 202 E. Pratt St. © **410/685-8439**. Reservations recommended. Main courses $8.95–$18 lunch, $16–$39 dinner. AE, DC, DISC, MC, V. Daily 6:30am–11pm.

MODERATE

Bay Atlantic Club 🍴 *Value* CASUAL AMERICAN The students at the Baltimore International College's culinary school work with the chef to produce wonderful meals at their lunchtime restaurant. The dining room is elegant, with chandeliers and high

Family-Friendly Restaurants

With the emphasis on seafood in Baltimore, finding an affordable family restaurant can be difficult. Below are a few places where the younger set is quite welcome. The restaurants and food courts at Harborplace are also a good bet.

Amicci's (p. 85) It's casual; there are usually lots of families here, so you don't have to worry about disturbing other diners; and there's a great selection of pasta dishes. If it's crowded, try Sabatino's or Vellegia's.

Cafe Hon (p. 89) This Hampden eatery is so relaxed and offers so many comfort foods, you know a kid will like it. And the friendly staff caters to children, too. The dining room is filled with knickknacks and other stuff to keep the little ones interested until the food arrives.

Johnny Rockets (p. 84) This branch of the chain of retro '50s diners is located in Harborplace's Light Street Pavilion. It's both fun and affordable. Kids will definitely like the fries, burgers, and shakes. Service is lightning-fast.

Phillips Harborplace (p. 83) Perhaps the city's most affordable good seafood, even if you're visiting with the whole family. The Harborplace location is ideal for lunch or dinner after a day at the aquarium or the science center. The children's menu lists favorites like burgers, fries, and fried chicken.

ceilings painted sky-blue with clouds. And you have to love the young staff, who are obviously proud of their delicious work. The wonderful, creative entrees might include herb-crusted salmon or braised short ribs. There are also sandwiches and meal-size salads. Desserts are a joy. If you're downtown on business or pleasure, this is a pleasant way to break for lunch—and you can either do it in less than an hour or take your time.

206 E. Redwood St. ℂ **410/752-1448.** www.bic.edu. Reservations recommended. Main courses $7–$15. AE, DC, MC, V. Mon–Fri 11:30am–2pm.

Phillips Harborplace *Kids* SEAFOOD   This branch of a successful Ocean City chain consistently draws big crowds. Phillips is known for its seafood, but it isn't worth the wait on a crowded afternoon when the staff is overworked. If you just have to have Phillips's crab imperial, pick a quieter time for an early lunch or dinner. If you want a crab cake, splurge for the higher-priced option—it's much better. The children's menu offers burgers, chicken nuggets, and hot dogs as well as shrimp and fish. A lively singalong piano bar and entertainment draw a crowd at dinner. Phillips also has a seafood buffet and express carryout in the same pavilion.

Harborplace, Light Street Pavilion, Level 1. ℂ **410/685-6600.** www.phillipsseafood.com. Reservations recommended. Main courses $5–$15 lunch, $15–$41 dinner. AE, DC, DISC, MC, V. Sun–Thurs 11am–10pm; Fri–Sat 11am–midnight.

Tir Na Nog Irish Bar and Grill IRISH   This is not your Grandmother O'Malley's Irish pub. Yes, you'll find Guinness stout and fish and chips. But the style here is more cosmopolitan: The sausages come with chanterelle sauce, and those fish and chips are served in a heavenly mustard sauce. At dinner, try the hearty crab soup, followed by the roasted trout and Irish bacon with crab butter. The restaurant is a knockout—you'd think the two beautifully carved bars would dominate, but diners lucky enough to have window seats get to look out on the Inner Harbor.

Harborplace, Pratt Street Pavilion, Level 2. ☏ **410/483-8968.** Reservations recommended. Main courses $9–$15 lunch, $14–$25 dinner; bar menu $9–$14. AE, DC, DISC, MC, V. Daily 11:30am–3pm and 5–10pm; bar menu 3–5pm and until midnight.

Wharf Rat BREWPUB   Located across the street from the convention center, the Wharf Rat is filled with British, Scottish, and Irish beer paraphernalia; a glass wall in the dining room allows diners to peek in on the beer making. The pub's Oliver Brewery offers a wide variety of ales and stouts, plus an especially good porter. Try it with a sandwich, crab cake, or the traditional English pub fare, such as the Ploughman's lunch or Henry VIII's meatloaf.

A second Wharf Rat is in Fells Point, at 801 S. Ann St.; it's closed on Sundays.

206 W. Pratt St. (at Hanover St.). ☏ **410/244-8900.** www.thewharfrat.com. Reservations not accepted. Main courses $7–$10 lunch, $8–$19 dinner. AE, DC, DISC, MC, V. Daily 11:30am–2am.

INEXPENSIVE

James Joyce Irish Pub & Restaurant IRISH   This Irish-style pub in Harbor East attracts conventioneers for hearty fare and beer. It's a handsome, wood-paneled place, with a musician crooning several nights a week. The menu includes lots of Irish favorites as well as seafood. If you don't have room for shepherd's pie, try a crab-cake sandwich or a bowl of potato soup. All go down well with a Guinness or Harp.

616 President St. ☏ **410/727-5107.** www.thejamesjoycepub.com. Reservations recommended. Main courses $8–$21. AE, DISC, MC, V. Daily 11am–2am (late-night menu only 11pm–1am Mon–Sat, 11pm–midnight Sun).

Johnny Rockets *(Kids)* AMERICAN   Sit at the counter or in one of the vinyl booths. Your bow-tied waiter will take your order, offer you a straw for your malt, and pour the ketchup for your fries while you watch the cook put together your hamburger. It almost feels like a movie set, but you'll delight in the hot burgers, the cool shakes, and the inexpensive prices (for Harborplace).

Harborplace, Light Street Pavilion, Level 1. ☏ **410/347-5757.** www.johnnyrockets.com. Main courses $3.35–$6.75. MC, V. Daily 11:30am–9pm.

LITTLE ITALY

In just a few packed blocks, you'll find all the pasta, cannoli, and chianti you could want. Make a reservation if you know where you want to eat beforehand. But if you prefer to wander, then plan to eat early or late and choose a place as you stroll through the basil-scented streets. If you don't have room for dessert, remember, there's always Vaccaro's to go. *Tip:* Parking has gotten easier with the opening of a huge garage at Pratt and President streets. Best of all, many restaurants now offer valet parking.

MODERATE

Chiapparelli's SOUTHERN ITALIAN   Southern Italian dishes in red sauce are the trademark at this longtime favorite, but do try the ravioli stuffed with spinach and ricotta, as well as the Italian wedding soup. Dinner is the main event, when veal is the star of the menu. You'll also find tasty chicken dishes and many classics such as *pescatore* and shrimp parmigiana. The children's menu includes chicken fingers and pizza toast.

237 S. High St. ☏ **410/837-0309.** www.chiapparellis.com. Reservations recommended. Main courses $6–$14 lunch, $12–$25 dinner. AE, DC, DISC, MC, V. Mon–Thurs 11:30am–10:30pm; Fri–Sat 11:30am–midnight; Sun 11:30am–10pm.

Della Notte 🐍🐍 ITALIAN   Della Notte is noted for its circular main dining room, lined with banquettes and a huge tree rising in the center. Lunch can be panini, pizza for one, or pasta. At dinner, choose chicken Marsala, a traditional pasta, or something inventive from the night's specials. The wine list goes on forever, with 1,200 choices that include 16 champagnes. (Prices range from bargain to *wow!*) The lounge is open from 6 to 10pm nightly, and until midnight on Friday and Saturday for piano music and maybe a cigar.

801 Eastern Ave. ℂ 410/837-5500. www.dellanotte.com. Reservations recommended. Main courses $8–$11 lunch, $19–$30 dinner. AE, MC, V. Sun–Thurs 11am–10pm; Fri–Sat 11am–midnight.

Sabatino's 🐍🐍🐍 ITALIAN   For 50 years, Sabatino's has been known for its exceptional Italian cuisine. Everyone will tell you to get the house salad with the house dressing, which is thick and garlicky. Simple pasta dishes come in very large portions. The menu also has seafood and meat dishes—*brasciole,* a roll of beef, prosciutto, cheeses, and marinara, is heavenly. Dining rooms fill three floors of this narrow building. It's worth the wait to be seated upstairs, where it's quieter. This is a good spot for late-night dining and people-watching after the bars have closed.

901 Fawn St. (at High St.). ℂ 410/727-9414. www.sabatinos.com. Reservations recommended. Main courses $8–$15 lunch, $9.25–$28 dinner. AE, DC, DISC, MC, V. Sun–Thurs 11:30am–midnight; Fri–Sat 11:30am–3am.

Velleggia's 🐍 ITALIAN   It's always crowded at Velleggia's. The place is loud and fun, and you'll probably have to wait a few minutes. But then the food will come, and you'll be glad you had patience. The fettuccine al Mare Bianco is wonderful, studded with shrimp, scallops, and crab. Cannelloni is rich and soothing. And there are veal, beef, and chicken dishes cooked the Italian way, too. It's all good.

829 E. Pratt St. ℂ 410/685-2620. www.velleggiasrestaurant.com. Reservations recommended. Main courses $13–$22. AE, DC, MC, V. Tues–Thurs 11am–9pm; Fri 11:30am–10pm; Sat 11:30am–11:30pm; Sun 11am–10pm.

INEXPENSIVE

Amicci's 🇰ids 🇻alue ITALIAN   You'll usually find Amicci's crowded with local families and young couples who don't want to spend a lot on good Italian food, and who also don't want to dress to the hilt. Don't be fooled by the small shopfront—the restaurant is a maze of dining rooms. If you have to wait, it won't be too long. Start with the superb antipasto for two. Seafood lovers might consider the special with mussels, shrimp, and scallops in a Marsala sauce. The sausage Marsala is a lovely take on the traditional chicken or veal versions. Desserts here come from Vaccaro's.

231 S. High St. ℂ 410/528-1096. www.amiccis.com. Reservations recommended. Main courses $6.90-$9.50 lunch, $7.90–$14 dinner. AE, DISC, MC, V. Sun–Thurs 11:30am–10pm; Fri–Sat 11:30am–11pm.

Vaccaro's 🐍 ITALIAN PASTRIES/DESSERTS   To top off a perfect day, stop at the always-busy Vaccaro's for dessert and coffee. The cannoli is famous, the pastries and tiramisu stand up to the competition, and if you love gelato, you'll be thrilled by the huge servings—just one scoop is plenty (really!). Coffee is a standout as well, especially when scented with cinnamon or vanilla. If dessert is your thing, come on Monday for the all-you-can-eat special.

Vaccaro's has a second location in Harborplace's Light Street Pavilion (ℂ 410/547-7169).

222 Albemarle St. ℂ 410/685-4905. www.vaccarospastry.com. Reservations not accepted. Desserts $2.95–$9.50. AE, MC, V. Mon 9am–10pm; Tues–Thurs 9am–11pm; Fri–Sat 9am–1am; Sun 9am–11pm.

FELLS POINT
EXPENSIVE

Black Olive ✿✿ GREEK/SEAFOOD   Slip down a quiet residential street and find this taverna, which specializes in fresh, organic Greek treats and an enormous fish selection. The whole-fish preparations are well known among area foodies. Diners can also choose from a variety of small plates and Greek dishes, including chicken souvlaki and village pie. The wine list is hefty, with a dozen options available by the glass. Service is smooth but friendly, and the four dining rooms are intimate and comfortable. Tea fans should try the iced tea made with Greek flowers—it's fragrant and spicy.

814 S. Bond St. ℂ 410/276-7141. www.theblackolive.com. Reservations required for dinner. Main courses $12–$28 lunch, $25–$36 dinner. AE, MC, V. Daily noon–2:30pm and 5–10pm.

Obrycki's ✿✿ SEAFOOD   Food connoisseurs Craig Claiborne and George Lang have raved about this place in Upper Fells Point. The decor is charming, with stained-glass windows, wainscoting, and brick archways. It's the quintessential crab house, where you can crack open steamed crabs or choose crab soup, crab cocktail, crab balls, crab cakes, crab imperial, or softshell crabs. The rest of the menu is just as tempting, with options such as lobster, haddock, flounder, and steaks. Service is extremely attentive. Note that Obrycki's is open only during the local crab season.

1727 E. Pratt St. ℂ 410/732-6399. www.obryckis.com. Reservations recommended, but accepted only until 7pm Mon–Fri, 6pm Sat–Sun. Main courses $15–$29; lunch and light fare $6.50–$15. AE, DC, DISC, MC, V. Mon–Fri 11:30am–10pm; Sat 11:30am–11pm; Sun 11:30am–9:30pm. Closed late Nov to mid-Mar.

MODERATE

Bertha's ✿ INTERNATIONAL/SEAFOOD   This Fells Point landmark is known for its mussels and music. The decor is shabby chic, with dark walls and plenty of accessories proud of their age. It's a perfect place for a traditional afternoon tea, a dinner featuring Bertha's mussels, or a night of jazz or blues. Mussels are prepared in a dozen different ways—they're delicious swimming in garlic butter. The rest of the menu is heavy on seafood, while at lunch you can get salads, omelets, sandwiches, and burgers. Afternoon tea is a wonderful tradition; it's served Monday through Saturday from 3 to 4:30pm. After 9pm most evenings, the music starts: jazz Tuesday through Thursday, blues on Friday and Saturday.

734 S. Broadway. ℂ 410/327-5795. www.berthas.com. Reservations accepted only for parties of 6 or more for lunch and dinner; reservations required 24 hr. in advance for afternoon tea. Main courses $5.25–$10 lunch, $12–$20 dinner; afternoon tea $10. MC, V. Sun–Thurs 11:30am–11pm; Fri–Sat 11:30am–midnight.

Kali's Court ✿✿ GREEK/SEAFOOD   This two-story cathedral to good food and good times has the most wonderful crab cakes—giant lump crab held together with little more than a prayer and not even a hint of Old Bay. The place is known for its grilled whole fish; its bouillabaisse comes highly recommended, too. Make a reservation and plan to wait. The bar in the front can be raucous, but upstairs, the mood is more intimate. Once seated, you'll be treated well and your palate will be delighted. Sunday brunch was due to be added in March 2006.

   Mezze (ℂ 410/563-7600), right next door, serves Mediterranean-style tapas at affordable prices. It's open daily for lunch and dinner.

1606 Thames St. ℂ 410/276-4700. www.kaliscourt.net. Reservations recommended. Main courses $21–$31. AE, DC, DISC, MC, V. Daily 5–10pm; Sun 11am–3pm and 5–10pm. Free valet parking.

Pierpoint Restaurant ☆☆ AMERICAN   Chef Nancy Longo has won accolades for her creative American cuisine with its Maryland and Italian roots. Smoked crab cakes are a specialty, but you'll also be delighted with the stylish preparations of tenderloin, duck breast, or oysters. Save room for dessert: Everything from the divine crème brûlée trio (ginger, orange, and chocolate) to the sorbet is wonderful. Lunchtime brings special entrees as well as pasta, salads, and soups. The restaurant is a quirky little place with a big bar up front.

1822 Aliceanna St. ✆ **410/675-2080**. www.pierpointrestaurant.com. Reservations required for lunch, recommended for dinner. Main courses $6–$14 lunch, $19–$26 dinner. AE, DC, DISC, MC, V. Tues–Fri 11:30am–2pm; Tues–Thurs 5–9:30pm; Fri–Sat 5:30–10:30pm; Sun 10:30am–1:30pm and 4–9pm.

Ze Mean Bean Cafe ☆ EASTERN EUROPEAN   The name's all wrong, but the restaurant does everything right. At this cozy European-style cafe, you can count on an attentive waitstaff, a menu that maintains its ties to Eastern Europe (this area is rich in Polish and Ukrainian heritage) while trying new things, and food that lives up to its promise. Sample the pierogi or borscht, or try the signature chicken Kiev. Thursday is Slavic night, with $9.95 dinners. The lunch and light-fare menu includes salads and sandwiches. Brunch is served both Saturday and Sunday, with jazz on Sunday.

1739 Fleet St. ✆ **410/675-5999**. www.zemeanbean.com. Reservations recommended. Main courses $5–$10 lunch, $8–$25 dinner. AE, DC, DISC, MC, V. Mon–Thurs 10am–11pm; Fri 10am–1am; Sat 9am–1am; Sun 9am–11pm.

INEXPENSIVE

Bonaparte Breads FRENCH/BAKERY   This wonderful little spot is part bakery, part cafe, all French. You can take out fresh pastries or bread studded with olives and herbs. Or you can stop in for the breakfast or lunch special. At lunchtime, walk up to the counter and choose from the numerous sandwiches and quiches (the seafood version is rich and creamy). Then pull up a leather chair at one of the tables; if you're lucky, you'll sit by the windows looking out at the harbor. After lunch, check out the fresh tarts in the case. Filled with fruit and sugar, they're all good.

903 S. Ann St. ✆ **410/342-4000**. Breakfast special $7; lunch special $11. MC, V. Daily 8am–6pm. Lunch served only until 3pm, but breads and pastries available until 6pm.

Petticoat Tea Room   Everything about this pretty pink-and-lace dining room is sweet. The offerings include scones, tiny sandwiches, fruit and sweets, and hot or cold tea (jasmine and mint are among the many blends). In summer, the tomatoes are local, the cucumber fresh, and the shrimp salad savory. It doesn't look like a lot of food, but you'll be content once you've finished. Lunch options include sandwiches and salads.

814 S. Broadway. ✆ **410/342-7884**. www.petticoattearoom.com. Reservations required for tea, suggested for other times. Lunch $7.95–$13; afternoon tea $20; high tea $26. DISC, MC, V. Daily 10am–5pm.

CANTON

Ray Lewis' Full Moon Bar-B-Que AMERICAN   First-timers come to Ray's because it's Ray's. And the Baltimore Ravens, as well as no. 52 himself, are well represented in the restaurant's purple decor and many photos. Return visitors come for the spicy ribs and pulled pork or chicken sandwiches. The big, two-story space has lots of flatscreen TVs for keeping up with sports. Carryout and delivery are available, too.

Can Company, 2400 Boston St. ✆ **410/327-5200**. www.raylewisfullmoon.com. Reservations recommended, but accepted on weekdays only. Main courses $9–$20. AE, DC, DISC, MC, V. Sun–Thurs 11am–10pm; Fri–Sat 11am–11pm.

Rick's Café Americain AMERICAN   Don't look for Ilsa to come sauntering in—this really is an American cafe. But the decor recalls those romantic days in *Casablanca*. So do the sandwiches. Captain Renault's is quite good, a thick slab of fresh fish between slices of rosemary focaccia. Dinner entrees include pasta, lamb chops, and steaks. The casual cafe is right on O'Donnell Square. Although it can be quiet at lunchtime, it's filled to capacity and quite noisy at night.

2903 O'Donnell St. © **410/675-1880**. www.rickscafecanton.com. Reservations not accepted, but for parties of 8 or more, call ahead for preferred seating. Main courses $11–$18; sandwiches and light fare $6–$10. AE, DC, DISC, MC, V. Daily 11am–2am.

MOUNT VERNON
EXPENSIVE
Prime Rib 🐾🐾 STEAKHOUSE   In the heart of Mount Vernon, this restaurant has been dishing out the beef since 1965. The prime rib is the best in town; the Caesar salad is dressed to perfection; and the lobster bisque is rich and creamy. If you want seafood, there are crab cakes and fish. Everything is a la carte. Tables are squeezed together, making intimate conversation impossible. In fact, the dining room can be noisy—but people come for the food, not the conversation.

1101 N. Calvert St. (between Biddle and Chase sts.). © **410/539-1804**. www.theprimerib.com. Reservations recommended. Main courses $25–$45. AE, DC, DISC, MC, V. Mon–Sat 5–11pm; Sun 4–10pm.

MODERATE
Brass Elephant 🐾🐾 CONTINENTAL   The Brass Elephant prides itself on well-prepared food at reasonable prices. You can count on rockfish or softshell crabs in season, along with hearty American dishes such as stuffed pork chops. And all of this comes in one of Baltimore's most elegant restaurant settings, an 1861 town house with fireplace, chandeliers, and gold-leaf trim.

924 N. Charles St. © **410/547-8480**. www.brasselephant.com. Reservations recommended. Main courses $18–$28. AE, DC, DISC, MC, V. Mon–Thurs 5:30–9:30pm; Fri–Sat 5:30–11pm; Sun 4:30–8:30pm. Free valet parking.

Owl Bar AMERICAN   Housed in the wedding-cake-fancy Belvedere Hotel, the Owl Bar exudes a long-ago charm with its brass-rail bar, paneled walls, and leather furnishings. Yet it's a more casual place than all that suggests, especially as the older diners give way to a younger crowd around 9pm. The menu includes brick-oven pizza, salads, a famous French onion soup, crab and meat dishes, and a raw bar. Sunday brunch is served from noon to 3pm.

1 E. Chase St. © **410/347-0888**. www.theowlbar.com. Reservations recommended for dinner. Main courses $10–$15 lunch, $13–$38 dinner. AE, DC, DISC, MC, V. Mon–Thurs 11:30am–11pm; Fri–Sat 11:30am–midnight; Sun noon–10pm.

Sascha's 527 🐾🐾 AMERICAN   Sascha's has put together an eclectic menu and a colorful but sophisticated dining room, with high ceilings and velvet banquettes. Dinner choices range from burgers to seafood entrees, but the "taste plates" are where Sascha's shines. These adventurous appetizer-size portions include Acapulco High Rise (Sascha's answer to nachos) and Indonesian chicken canes with Asian slaw. At lunch, the restaurant goes buffet style, with salads, panini sandwiches, and soup.

527 N. Charles St. © **410/539-8880**. www.saschas.com. Reservations accepted only for parties of 5 or more. Main courses $4.25–$6.75 lunch, $8.50–$20 dinner; taste plates $4–$9. AE, DC, MC, V. Mon–Fri 11am–3:30pm; Mon–Wed 5:30–10pm; Thurs 5:30–11pm; Fri–Sat 5:30pm–midnight.

Tapas Teatro ★★ TAPAS/INTERNATIONAL   Tapas have gotten big in Baltimore—and as pretty as Sascha's is, the food here is even better. The restaurant, adjacent to the Charles Theatre, is an ode to industrial chic, with its exposed-brick walls and metal accents. The refinement is in the food: colorful salads, tiny bites of rockfish, country bread rubbed with Maryland tomatoes and Asiago cheese. Need something hearty? Try the paella or whole rainbow trout. Sangria makes a nice accompaniment, or try one of the 37 wines or 15 beers. The desserts are a delight to the eye and a pleasure to the palate.

1711 N. Charles St. ✆ 410/332-0110. www.tapasteatro.net. Reservations not accepted. Tapas and main courses $3–$15. AE, MC, V. Tues–Fri 5pm–2am (food served until 11pm); Sat–Sun 4pm–2am (food served until midnight).

Tío Pepe ★★★ MEDITERRANEAN/SPANISH   Walk down the stairs into whitewashed rooms that resemble a wine cellar. Spanish artwork, wrought iron, and pottery decorate the tiny dining rooms that seem to go on and on. Start with the fruity sangria. The menu's highlights include shrimp in garlic sauce, sole with bananas and hollandaise sauce, and a dramatic paella. Dessert is a standout: Try the flan, the chocolate soufflé, or the roll cakes. The servers are so professional, you'll feel like royalty. Tío Pepe is a special-occasion restaurant for Baltimoreans, so reservations are a must.

10 E. Franklin St. (just off Charles St.). ✆ 410/539-4675. Reservations recommended (as far as 3 weeks in advance for Sat night). Jackets suggested. Main courses $11–$25 lunch, $18–$35 dinner. AE, DC, DISC, MC, V. Mon–Fri 11:30am–2:30pm; Mon–Thurs 5–10pm; Fri 5–11pm; Sat 5–11:30pm; Sun 4–10pm.

NORTH OF DOWNTOWN
MODERATE

Gertrude's ★★ (Finds) SEAFOOD   Pause at Gertrude's during a visit to the Baltimore Museum of Art. Chef and cookbook author John Shields has created a restaurant filled with local delights—making this place a destination in itself. The sleek space has tall windows overlooking the sculpture garden, with outdoor seating in warm weather. The menu includes soups (such as rich cream of crab) and sandwiches (with plenty of Old Bay on the shrimp)—or perhaps you're ready for the Trinity (two traditional-recipe crab cakes and one chef's special version). If you're feeling adventurous, you might like the small plates, such as citrus barbecue shrimp or portobello crab imperial. Tuesday dinner specials feature $10 entrees and $18 bottles of wine; Wednesday brings half-price bottles and glasses of wine. Brunch is served Saturday and Sunday.

At the Baltimore Museum of Art, 10 Art Museum Dr. ✆ 410/889-3399. Reservations recommended. www.johnshields.com. Main courses $8–$15 lunch, $11–$40 dinner. AE, DC, MC, V. Tues–Fri 11:30am–9pm; Sat 10:30am–9pm; Sun 10:30am–8pm.

INEXPENSIVE

Cafe Hon (Kids) AMERICAN/DINER   Elvis greets guests, but the real star at this Hampden institution is homey comfort food. The specialty is "Much Better than Mom's" meatloaf with mashed potatoes. At dinner, you'll find spaghetti, pork chops, and roast beef as well. The lunch menu includes chicken salad, grilled cheese, burgers, and blue-plate specials. There are also 20 wines for $20. Come for breakfast and get killer coffee and "Hon Buns," cinnamon rolls as big as your hand. The menu always lists something any kid will eat.

1002 W. 36th St. (at Roland Ave.). ✆ 410/243-1230. www.cafehon.com. Reservations not accepted. Main courses $6–$12 lunch, $6–$18 dinner. AE, DC, DISC, MC, V. Mon–Thurs 7am–9pm; Fri–Sat 9am–10pm; Sun 9am–8pm.

Grill Art Cafe ❀ (Value) ECLECTIC   Among all the kitsch of Hampden is this contemporary little jewel of a restaurant. It's tucked into a narrow rowhouse, complete with stamped-tin ceiling and exposed-brick walls. And the food—what to choose? Come if you like vegetables: Grill Art has wonderful salads, stuffed portobellos, pizzas, and interesting sandwiches, such as a BLT jazzed up with avocado and made with fresh bread. Dinner entrees include enchiladas and tortellini stew. Since there's no liquor license, it's BYOB. Brunch is served on Saturday and Sunday. There's a great coffee bar, too.

1011 W. 36th St. ☎ 410/366-2005. Reservations recommended on weekends. Main courses $6–$13 lunch, $6–$19 dinner. MC, V. Mon–Fri 11:30am–3pm; Tues–Thurs 5–9:30pm, Fri 5:30–10pm; Sat 10am–3pm and 5:30–10pm; Sun 10am–3pm and 5–8pm.

Paper Moon Diner DINER   This funky diner/health-food restaurant is a favorite of the college crowd, but anyone with a sense of fun will like it. It's quite dark, with all sorts of toys and little knickknacks lurking about. The food is good, with burgers, sandwiches, breakfast items, and a few intriguing vegetarian options served all day.

227 W. 29th St. (between Remington Ave. and Howard St.). ☎ 410/889-4444. www.papermoondiner24.com. Reservations not accepted. Main courses $7–$14. MC, V. Daily 24 hr.

MOUNT WASHINGTON

Crepe du Jour FRENCH   The bright yellow-and-blue porch may attract your eye, but the huge savory and sweet crepes will thrill your taste buds. Crepes come with all kinds of fillings: ratatouille; walnuts, blue cheese, and mesclun; sugar and lemon. At dinner, the menu expands to include French-flavored steak, chicken, and seafood entrees. Sidewalk tables and a deck increase the dining space in warm months.

1609 Sulgrave Ave. ☎ 410/542-9000. www.crepedujour.com. Reservations suggested for dinner and weekend brunch. Crepes and sandwiches $3–$11; dinner main courses $17–$23. AE, DISC, MC, V. Tues–Thurs 11am–10pm; Fri–Sat 10am–11pm; Sun 10am–9pm.

Ethel and Ramone's ❀ CAJUN/AMERICAN   On this little street in Mount Washington, you'll be confronted with four intriguing restaurants on the same short block. Ethel and Ramone's is the place for Cajun-style food. The folks who run this offbeat eatery know good food. Get the gumbo—it's spicy, filling, and rich with andouille sausage and chicken. Other Louisiana favorites include red beans and rice, jambalaya, and blackened fish. Lunch is mostly overstuffed sandwiches, including po' boys. Breakfast is offered from 7 to 11am. There's seating outdoors in warm weather.

1615 Sulgrave Ave. ☎ 410/664-2971. Reservations recommended for dinner. Main courses $8–$12 lunch, $15–$26 dinner. AE, DISC, MC, V. Tues–Sat 7am–3pm and 6–11pm.

Mount Washington Tavern ❀❀ AMERICAN   This sprawling restaurant, beloved by locals, has bars where you can watch the ballgame, wood-paneled nooks for intimate dining, and a garden room elegant enough for special occasions. It's big enough that if the Ravens score, those in the dining room would never know it. The eclectic menu offers seafood, steaks, and a raw bar. Light fare, sandwiches, and burgers are available at lunch. Try the nachos grande, perfect with a beer or while you wait for your crab cake. Sunday brunch is served from noon to 3pm.

5700 Newbury St. ☎ 410/367-6903. Reservations recommended on weekends. Main courses $5.75–$11 lunch, $17–$25 dinner. AE, DC, DISC, MC, V. Mon–Sat 11:30am–11pm; Sun 10:30am–10pm. Bar open until 2am daily.

5 Attractions

INNER HARBOR ✸✸✸

Although much of Baltimore's business takes place along Charles Street, the city's focal point for tourism is the Inner Harbor, home of the Baltimore Convention Center, Harborplace shopping pavilions, Oriole Park at Camden Yards, M&T Bank Stadium, National Aquarium, Pier 6 Concert Pavilion, and brand-new Reginald F. Lewis Museum of Maryland African American History & Culture.

Baltimore is still a working deepwater port. Boats from all over dock just beyond the Domino Sugar sign. At the Inner Harbor seawall, it's not unusual to see naval vessels and tall ships and their crews from around the world.

American Visionary Art Museum ✸   Look for the "Whirligig," a 55-foot windpowered sculpture at the front of this curvaceous building. Step inside, and you'll be entranced from the moment you set your eyes on Emery Blagdon's "Healing Machines" mobile hanging down three stories. Visionary art is created by people who lack artistic training but feel compelled to draw, paint, or build a ship with matchsticks. Everything here is fascinating; some of it can be quite troubling. And the artists' stories are as interesting as their art. Some of the work is too strong for children (the museum will alert you about that); other exhibits are a joy that kids will love. The new Jim Rouse Visionary Center, built in a converted whiskey warehouse, expands the space and will feature the social visionary in future exhibitions. On the first Thursday of the month from June through August, the neighbors gather in Federal Hill Park to watch a free movie screened on the side of the museum's building.

800 Key Hwy. ⓒ **410/244-1900.** www.avam.org. Admission $11 adults; $7 seniors, students, and children. Tues–Sun 10am–6pm. Closed Thanksgiving and Dec 25. Take Light St. south, turn left onto Key Hwy. (at the Maryland Science Center); museum is about 3 blocks farther on the right.

Baltimore Maritime Museum   This museum comprises three boats and a lighthouse that tell recent maritime history. The Coast Guard Cutter *Taney* survived the bombing of Pearl Harbor. The submarine USS *Torsk* sank the last two Japanese merchant ships of World War II and still holds the record for the most dives and resurfacings of any sub. The Seven Foot Knoll Lighthouse is worth a climb up the steps to see the Fresnel light and learn about the lighthouse that once welcomed immigrants to Baltimore. The lightship *Chesapeake* spent 40 years anchored near the mouth of the Chesapeake Bay. Each provides an interesting glimpse into the lives of 20th-century sailors.

⟨Value Money-Saving Harbor Pass

Baltimore's top tourism spots have teamed up with **Harbor Pass.** For $46, adults can visit the National Aquarium, Maryland Science Center, Port Discovery, and Top of the World Observation Level—and ride Ed Kane's Water Taxi all day. Kids' passes are $30. The passes are valid for 3 consecutive days, but only one visit per location. They're also good for discounts at a few hotels and restaurants, an Orioles game, and other Inner Harbor attractions. Call ⓒ **877/BALTI-MORE** or visit www.baltimore.org for information. Passes are also available at the Inner Harbor visitor center.

Tip: For a good value, buy the **Seaport Pass,** which includes admission to the Baltimore Maritime Museum and the USS *Constellation,* plus a ticket to ride all day on Ed Kane's Water Taxi. The pass costs $18 for adults, $15 for seniors, and $13 for kids 6 to 14.

Piers 3 and 5. (C) **410/396-3453.** www.baltomaritimemuseum.org. Admission $7 adults, $6 seniors, $4 children 6–14. Buy tickets at the booth near the National Aquarium or on board the *Taney.* Mar–Dec daily 10am–5pm; Jan–Feb Fri–Sun 10am–5pm.

Baltimore Museum of Industry *(Finds) (Kids)*   Housed in a former oyster packing house in a still-industrial part of the city, this museum gives visitors a look at the industries that made Baltimore a manufacturing capital in the 1880s—canning, printing, and garment making. It's geared toward children, with exhibits set up so kids can get their hands on the oyster-shucking stations, antique irons, and moveable type. Tour guides are sensitive to kids' attention spans and will adjust their talks for the younger visitors. You can wander around on your own, but the exhibits aren't as interesting without the guides' stories. Wall-size pictures recall the days before child labor laws, and other displays include a collection of antique delivery trucks and one of only two working steam tugboats in the country. The museum is a few blocks from Fort McHenry; a visit to both—with a picnic on Fort McHenry's lawn—could make a great day. One of the city's least-known museums, this is one of the best for children and anyone who loves industrial history.

1415 Key Hwy. (C) **410/727-4808.** www.thebmi.org. Admission $10 adults, $6 students and seniors. Tues–Sat 10am–4pm; Sun 11am–4pm. Closed Thanksgiving, Dec 24, and Dec 25. Water taxis stop nearby. Bus: 1 to Fort Ave., 1 block south of the museum.

Fort McHenry *★★★ (Moments)*   The flag that flies at Fort McHenry is 30×42 feet, big enough for Francis Scott Key to "see by the dawn's early light." The flag's 15 stars and stripes still fly as boldly as they did that terrible night, when soldiers here stood once again to reclaim American independence. Today, the star-shaped fort looks much as it did in 1814, the year of the British attack. Its buildings, repaired in the days following that attack, still stand.

The Star-Spangled Banner is central to this fort, which is a national monument. Visitors are invited to take part in the daily changing of the flag—in fact, because the flag is so big, around 20 people are needed to keep it off the ground and to fold it. If you'd like to join in, stop by at 9:30am or 4:30pm (7:30pm June–Aug). The large flag flies only during daylight hours, but a smaller flag flies at night. The rangers conclude the flag-raising ceremony with a short historical talk about the fort, the flag, or the national anthem.

Exhibits recall Baltimore under siege during the War of 1812, the fort's Civil War service, and its use as an army hospital during World War I. Allow about 90 minutes for a visit. The fort sits on a point in the harbor, from which visitors can see the Inner Harbor, the Patapsco River, and down to the Chesapeake Bay. Visits to the park outside the fort are free, and picnicking is allowed.

The **Star-Spangled Banner Weekend,** held in mid-September, recalls the British attack on the fort. On select Sundays from 6 to 8pm, military bands perform with a color guard, drill teams, and the Fort McHenry Guard dressed in 19th-century uniforms, a ceremony that began in 1803. Admission to this ceremony is free; call or visit the website for a schedule.

Fort McHenry National Monument, E. Fort Ave. (C) **410/962-4290.** www.nps.gov/fomc. Admission $7 adults, free for children under 16. Sept–May daily 8am–5pm; June to Labor Day daily 8am–8pm. Water taxi stop.

Baltimore Attractions

American Visionary Art Museum **29**
Babe Ruth Birthplace and Museum **12**
Baltimore & Ohio Railroad Museum **11**
Baltimore Civil War Museum/
  President Street Station **21**
Baltimore Maritime Museum **25**
Baltimore Museum of Art **1**
Baltimore Museum of Industry **30**
Basilica of the Assumption **8**
Contemporary Museum **7**
Creative Alliance **21**
Edgar Allan Poe House and Museum **9**
Edgar Allan Poe's Grave **10**
Eubie Blake National Jazz Institute
  and Cultural Center **4**
Evergreen House **2**
Fells Point Maritime Museum **22**

Flag House & Star-Spangled
  Banner Museum **18**
Fort McHenry **30**
George Peabody Library **7**
Holocaust Memorial and Sculpture **16**
Homewood House **2**
Irish Shrine and Railroad Workers
  Museum **11**
Jewish Museum of Maryland **20**
Lacrosse Museum &
  National Hall of Fame **2**
Marine Mammal Pavilion/
  National Aquarium **27**
Maryland Historical Society **6**
Maryland Science Center **28**
National Aquarium in Baltimore **26**

National Great Blacks in Wax Museum **3**
Old St. Paul's Church **14**
PassPort Voyages **17**
Port Discovery Children's Museum **15**
Reginald F. Lewis Museum
  of Maryland African American
  History & Culture **19**
Sports Legends at Camden Yards **13**
Top of the World Observation Level **24**
USS Constellation **23**
Walters Art Museum **7**
Washington Monument & Museum **5**

Holocaust Memorial and Sculpture   In the heart of downtown near the Inner Harbor, this open-air memorial starkly recalls the six million Jews murdered by the Nazis in Europe between 1933 and 1945.

Corner of Gay and Lombard sts. Free admission. Daily 24 hr.

Maryland Science Center 🎭🎭 *Kids*   Three floors of exhibits include the popular Outer Space Place, home of the Hubble Space Telescope National Visitor Center and Space Link, which offers a live connection to NASA. DinoQuest, with its towering dinosaurs, shouldn't be missed. Sometimes the exhibits are too crowded or of limited interest, but the IMAX theater and planetarium are always worth a visit. The IMAX shows, which have been as diverse as *Beauty and the Beast* and *Space Station 3D,* are so popular that extra screenings have been added on Friday and Saturday evenings, for $8 per ticket. The stars are on display at the Davis Planetarium and the Crosby Ramsey Memorial Observatory; the latter is free to the public on Friday nights, weather permitting (call for hours).

601 Light St. (south side of the Inner Harbor). ℂ **410/685-5225.** www.mdsci.org. Admission varies according to special exhibits: core experience with planetarium $14 adults, $9.50 children 4–12; core experience with planetarium and IMAX film $18 adults, $12 children 4–12; core experience with traveling exhibit $17 adults, $12 children 4–12; admission to everything $20 adults, $14 children 4–12. Labor Day to Memorial Day Tues–Fri 10am–5pm, Sat 10am–6pm, Sun 11am–5pm; Memorial Day to Labor Day Thurs–Sat 10am–8pm, Sun–Wed 10am–6pm. Call ahead, as hours change with some exhibits. Water taxi stop.

National Aquarium in Baltimore 🎭🎭🎭   Walk into a room surrounded by patrolling sharks, stroll among coral reefs, and visit a rainforest on the roof at one of best aquariums in the country. The newest exhibit, **Animal Planet Australia: Wild Extremes,** set in a 120-foot-tall glass cube at the front of the aquarium, takes visitors to the floor of an Australian river gorge. In this immersion exhibit, you can wander past tanks filled with death adders, pythons, archer fish, and barramundi, while kookaburras, parrots, and lorikeets fly overhead—there are 1,800 animals in all, as well as plants native to Australia.

On a cold day, it's a joy to skip right to the top of the aquarium and bask in the tropical heat that envelops the brightly colored birds, the shy iguana, and the sloth who reside on this level. (For the best views, come straight here when the aquarium opens, as that's when the animals are most active.) Although you simply walk in front of most of the exhibits, you get to actually walk inside the doughnut-shaped coral reef and the shark tanks, getting up close to these exotic creatures. At feeding time at the coral reef, the divers always draw a crowd.

The **Marine Mammal Pavilion,** connected by covered bridge to the main hall, is where you'll find the dolphins. Don't miss the presentations—reserve a seat (at no additional fee) when you pay your admission. If one has been born recently, the presentations are canceled, but go in anyway and watch the dolphins play. You can stay as long as you want.

Tip: The aquarium draws huge crowds in summer. Beat the crush by purchasing timed tickets in advance, either in person or through the aquarium's website. Nonpeak visiting hours are weekday mornings, Friday evenings, and any day after 3pm.

501 E. Pratt St. (on the harbor). ℂ **410/576-3800.** www.aqua.org. Admission $22 adults, $21 seniors, $15 children 3–11. Mar–June and Sept–Oct daily 9am–5pm; Nov–Feb daily 10am–5pm; July–Aug daily 9am–5pm. Year-round Fri until 8pm. Hours subject to change; call ahead. Exhibits are open 2 hr. after last ticket is sold.

PassPort Voyages   An attraction more suited to a theme park, PassPort offers visitors four "experiences." Each is a 20-minute movie, shown in theaters with seats that bump and twist, accompanied by special effects such as mist and wind. (There are stationary seats, too.) None have any real Baltimore ties, although opening footage was shot on Federal Hill, in city neighborhoods, and at the National Aquarium. The three *Time Elevator* films travel back to Colonial America, ancient Rome, and Jerusalem. But if you love fish, *Oceanarium* is a better choice. PassPort isn't up to Disney quality, but it's a fun, if pricey, diversion in the Inner Harbor.

Pier 4, 624 E. Pratt St. (✆ 410/468-0700. www.passportvoyages.com. Admission for 1st film $14 adults, $9.25 children, $13 seniors and military; 2-film combo ticket $5 additional. Daily from 10am; closing times vary. New show begins every 30 min.

Top of the World Observation Level   For a 360-degree view of the city, head to the 27th floor of the World Trade Center, the world's tallest pentagonal building, next to Harborplace. In addition to the fine view, you can acquire a bit of background about Baltimore from the exhibits, hands-on displays, and multimedia presentations. Renovations have improved viewing conditions and made it more accessible to visitors with disabilities.

401 E. Pratt St. (on the harbor). (✆ 410/837-8439. Admission $5 adults, $4 seniors, $3 children 3–16. Wed–Sun 10am–6pm. Tickets sold in the lobby up to a half-hour before closing.

USS *Constellation*   You can't miss the *Constellation,* docked for years at the Inner Harbor (predating Harborplace). A triple-masted sloop-of-war launched in 1854, the *Constellation* is the last Civil War–era vessel afloat. Tour her gun decks, visit the wardrooms, see a cannon fired, and learn about the life of a sailor. Demonstrations begin with the raising of the colors at 10:30am and continue on the hour. Special events include a Fourth of July picnic and a New Year's Eve reception, both ending with fireworks (tickets are required). A free birthday party is usually held on the Saturday closest to August 26.

Pier 1, 301 E. Pratt St. (✆ 410/539-1797. www.constellation.org. Admission (including audio tour) $8.75 adults, $7.50 seniors, $4.75 children 6–14. Apr–Oct daily 10am–5:30pm (extended hours June–Aug); Nov–Mar daily 10am–4:30pm. Closed Thanksgiving, Dec 25, and Jan 1.

NEAR LITTLE ITALY & FELLS POINT

Baltimore Civil War Museum—President Street Station   Tucked beside the Marriott Inner Harbor in the Harbor East neighborhood is this small brick structure with a curved roof. The first bloodshed of the Civil War occurred here, when Union soldiers arrived in April 1861 on their way south and were attacked by a mob of Southern sympathizers as they marched from this railroad station to Camden Station (now near Camden Yards). The little building, one of the country's oldest railroad stations, has been restored and now has exhibits about that awful day, Maryland's railroad history, and the underground railroad.

601 President St. (✆ 410/385-5188. www.mdhs.org. Admission $4 adults; $3 children 13–17, students, and seniors; free for children 12 and under. Pass for Maryland Historical Society Museum, Baltimore Civil War Museum—President Street Station, and Fells Point Maritime Museum $12 adults, $10 students and seniors, $4 children 3–12. Daily 10am–5pm. Closed Labor Day, Thanksgiving, and Dec 25.

Creative Alliance *Finds*   This Highlandtown venue's gallery and performance space celebrate local arts. Contemporary artwork in all media is on display, and the auditorium is the site of a Wednesday classic-film series as well as special events. The resident

Loyal Opposition comedy troupe, Sound Foundation new-music group, and Charm City Kitty Club play here at least once a quarter. The Baltimore Mandolin Orchestra also holds its annual concert here. Though much of the work is edgy, more mainstream works also have their place. It's worth going out of your way to visit if you'd like a taste of the Baltimore arts scene. Check the website for a schedule of events.

3134 Eastern Ave. (℘ 410/276-1651. www.creativealliance.org. Free admission to gallery. Tickets for films and performances $5–$20. Gallery Wed–Sat 11am–5pm; film and performance times vary. From downtown, take Pratt St. east, head south around Patterson Park to Eastern Ave., and continue on Eastern Ave. to Highlandtown.

Fells Point Maritime Museum   This two-room museum overlooking the harbor recalls the shipbuilding history of Fells Point. With interactive displays, maps, photos, and models of ships of the War of 1812, pilot schooners, and Baltimore clippers, the museum aims to tell about the sailors and shipbuilders who made this part of the city their home. A continuously running video of the *Pride of Baltimore II* offers a glimpse of how sailors handled these ships.

1724 Thames St. (℘ 410/732-0278. www.mdhs.org. Admission $4 adults; $3 students and seniors; free for children under 13. Pass for Maryland Historical Society Museum, Baltimore Civil War Museum—President Street Station, and Fells Point Maritime Museum $12 adults, $10 students and seniors, $4 children 3–12. Thurs–Mon 10am–5pm. Closed Labor Day, Thanksgiving, and Dec 25.

Flag House & Star-Spangled Banner Museum *Kids*   Everyone remembers Betsy Ross and the first American flag. Baltimoreans, however, recall Mary Pickersgill and the 15-star flag she sewed. It flew over Fort McHenry during the bombardment of the War of 1812 that inspired Francis Scott Key to write "The Star-Spangled Banner." Though the flag is now part of the Smithsonian, its seamstress is remembered in the 1793 house where she once lived, located in Little Italy. Guides offer visitors a glimpse of her life and times. You can see period furniture and artifacts of the war, along with the giant glass flag that dominates a 2003 addition—walk up the stairs behind it and get a sense of how big the Star-Spangled Banner really is. The addition, which is handicapped-accessible, has an orientation theater, children's hands-on room, and exhibit space.

844 E. Pratt St., at Albemarle St. (℘ 410/837-1793. www.flaghouse.org. Admission $6 adults, $5 seniors, $4 children. Tues–Sat 10am–4pm; Sun noon–5pm. Closed major holidays.

Jewish Museum of Maryland   A visit here offers insight into local Jewish history, a glimpse of Jewish traditions, and a look at the immigration experience. The two 19th-century synagogues are worth a stop. The 1845 Lloyd Street Synagogue is Maryland's oldest (and one of the oldest in the U.S.). It's plainer than the nearby B'nai Israel Synagogue, but it has a matzo oven, a *mikvah* (ritual bath), and a classroom where the first Hebrew school got its start. There's also a hands-on exhibit for children that focuses on the immigrant experience in this neighborhood over the past 2 centuries. The Greek Revival–style B'nai Israel Synagogue, built in 1876, contains what may be the oldest Jewish star in one of its stained-glass windows. Its Ark is a hand-carved masterpiece. Take a tour of the synagogues at 1 or 2:30pm for the best experience; the guides are full of stories. Between the two synagogues is the exhibit space and library. The exhibits change often, but always focus on Jewish religion and culture.

15 Lloyd St. (℘ 410/732-6400. www.jewishmuseummd.org. Admission $8 adults, $4 students, $3 children under 12. Sun and Tues–Thurs noon–4pm. Travel east on Pratt St.; turn left on Central St., left on Lombard St., and then right onto Lloyd St.

Port Discovery Children's Museum *★★* *Kids*   At this kid-powered museum with three floors of exhibits, children of all ages—though mostly ages 6 to 12—can cross the Nile to explore ancient Egypt, climb through a kitchen drain to solve a mystery in Miss Perception's Mystery House, and play on the three-story-high Kidworks. Walt Disney Company "Imagineers" designed most of the exhibits. There's also a collection of high-tech toys which enable children to compose music, shoot videos, and produce their own cartoons. Story times for toddlers are offered Tuesday through Friday at 11:30am, as well as Saturday at 11am, noon, and 1pm and Sunday at 3:30pm.

Power Plant Live, 35 Market Place. © 410/727-8120. www.portdiscovery.org. Admission $11 adults, $8.50 children 3–12. Oct–May Tues–Fri 9:30am–4:30pm, Sat 10am–5pm. Memorial Day to Labor Day Mon–Sat 10am–5pm (Fri until 8pm July–Aug); Sept Fri 9:30am–4:30pm, Sat 10am–5pm; year-round Sun noon–5pm. Bus: 7, 10, 19, or 20. Metro: Shot Tower.

Reginald F. Lewis Museum of Maryland African American History & Culture ⋆ *Finds*

The building alone makes this a memorable place. It's enormous— out of scale for the neighborhood, really—but striking in its bold use of black, yellow, and red in a distinctly modern design. Inside, the museum is much more personal, detailing individual stories of African-American Marylanders such as Supreme Court justice Thurgood Marshall, gymnast Dominique Dawes, musician Cab Calloway, and religious leader Mother Mary Elizabeth Lange—exhibits designed to give children examples of African Americans who were successful in spite of poverty, discrimination, and poor schooling. On-site are a gift shop and cafe.

830 E. Pratt St. © 443/263-1800. www.africanamericanculture.org. Admission $8 adults; $6 children, students, and seniors. Tues–Sun 10am–5pm. Closed Thanksgiving, Dec 25, Jan 1, and Easter. Bus: 10. Metro: Shot Tower.

WEST OF DOWNTOWN

Babe Ruth Birthplace and Museum ⋆

George Herman "Babe" Ruth was born in this rowhouse, where two rooms have been re-created to look as they would have when the Sultan of Swat was a boy. Other exhibits include a wall enumerating his home runs, plus memorabilia from his major league career and his days at St. Mary's Industrial School in Baltimore, where he learned to play the game.

216 Emory St. © 410/727-1539. www.baberuthmuseum.com. Admission $6 adults, $4 seniors, $3 children 5–16. Apr–Oct daily 10am–5pm (until 7:30pm on days of Orioles home games); Nov–Mar daily 10am–5pm (until 8pm on days of Ravens home games). Closed Thanksgiving, Dec 25, and Jan 1. From Camden Yards, follow the sidewalk baseballs from the Babe Ruth statue at the north end of the warehouse to the house on this tiny street, 3 blocks away.

Baltimore & Ohio (B&O) Railroad Museum ⋆⋆ *Kids*

American railroading got its start here when the B&O was chartered in 1827. The first locomotive, the *Tom Thumb*, was built here. The remarkable roundhouse—whose roof collapsed in a 2003 snowstorm—has been restored and is now even better than before. It's filled with an awe-inspiring collection of engines and rolling stock, including several damaged pieces awaiting repair. A car barn has the largest locomotive ever built, as well as pieces undergoing restoration. Platforms enable visitors to tour trains outside, including a World War II troop sleeper, a caboose, and a refrigerated car where a train movie runs continuously. Recent changes should make it easier for visitors with disabilities and parents with strollers. Admission includes a short ride, with trains departing regularly every day from April through December and weekends only in January; no rides are offered in February and March.

901 W. Pratt St. © 410/752-2490. www.borail.org. Admission $14 adults, $10 seniors, $8 children 2–12. Mon–Fri 10am–4pm; Sat 10am–5pm; Sun noon–5pm. Closed Thanksgiving, Dec 24–25, Dec 31, Jan 1, and Easter. Bus: 31.

Edgar Allan Poe House and Museum

Edgar Allan Poe composed some of his first works in this tiny West Baltimore rowhouse, which contains five rooms (including the

garret where Poe slept and wrote). He lived here from 1833 to 1835 with his grandmother, aunt, and cousin Virginia, whom he later married. You can see portraits, memorabilia, period furniture, changing exhibits, and a video presentation. The house is
located on a small one-way street heading south; there is no number, but you will see
a black antique street lamp out front and two markers on the house itself. Don't try to
walk here from downtown—take a car or cab. Definitely call ahead to verify hours.

203 N. Amity St. $\textcircled{C}$ 410/396-7932. Admission $3 adults, free for children under 13. Wed–Sat noon–3:45pm. Closed
Jan–Feb. Take Charles St. north to Fayette St.; turn left on Fayette and go past Martin Luther King Blvd. to Schroeder
St. Turn right on Schroeder; in 2 blocks, turn right on Saratoga St. and continue about ¼ block to Amity St., the first
street on the right. Turn right on Amity and look for the Poe House on the left side, near the end of the block.

Edgar Allan Poe's Grave (Moments)   Three modest memorials in this old graveyard
recall the poet who wrote "The Tell-Tale Heart" and "The Raven" (the only poem to
inspire an NFL team's name). After his mysterious death in 1849 at age 40, Poe's relatives erected a small gravestone. Before the stone could be installed, however, a train
crashed through the monument yard and destroyed it. In the century since, the site
has been adorned with three newer monuments: the main memorial, which features a
bas-relief bust of Poe; a small gravestone adorned with a raven at Poe's original burial
lot; and a plaque placed by the French, who, thanks to the poet Baudelaire, enjoy
some of the best translations of Poe's works. The poet is remembered on his birthday
every January 19, when a mysterious "Poe Toaster" leaves half a bottle of cognac and
three roses at the grave. On the weekend closest to Poe's birthday, a party is held in his
honor. A Halloween tour is also scheduled each year.

Westminster Cemetery, southeast corner of Fayette and Greene sts. $\textcircled{C}$ 410/706-2072 (answered by a University of
Maryland Law School staffer). Daily 8am–dusk. Closed major holidays.

Irish Shrine and Railroad Workers Museum   Two 100-foot-wide 1848 brick
rowhouses, a block from the B&O Museum, have been restored as a monument to
the thousands of Irish workers who lived here and worked for the railroad. One house,
which still has its plaster walls and floors intact, is sparsely furnished for a family of
eight and a boarder. Next door is a museum devoted to Irish Baltimoreans, with photo
displays and a heartfelt video presentation. Volunteer tour guides are well acquainted
with—and may be related to—past residents; their stories are personal and folksy.
Tours of the neighborhood, including a church and market, can be arranged as well.
Reservations are required. Even if you're not interested in the Irish (gasp!), it's worth
a visit to see a typical pre–Civil War Baltimore home.

918–920 Lemmon St. $\textcircled{C}$ 410/669-8154. www.irishshrine.org. Free admission. Sat 11am–2pm and by appointment.
Call ahead to confirm opening times. Tours are free, but require a group of 10. From the Inner Harbor, go west on
Lombard St., turn left on Poppleton St., and turn right on Lemmon St.

Mount Clare Museum House   Set on a hill with a sweeping view of the Baltimore
skyline, this 1760 building was the summer home of barrister Charles Carroll and his
wife, Margaret Tilghman Carroll. Most of the furnishings belonged to the Carroll
family, including a Charles Wilson Peale portrait and a fine collection of Chinese and
English porcelain. Washington didn't sleep here, but Martha did—and so did the
Marquis de Lafayette.

In Carroll Park, 1500 Washington Blvd. $\textcircled{C}$ 410/837-3262. www.mountclare.org. Admission $6 adults, $5 seniors, $4
students. Tues–Sat 10am–4pm (tours until 3pm). Bus: 11.

Sports Legends at Camden Yards (Kids)   Two floors of the historic 1856 Camden
Station have been lovingly developed as a tribute to local sports. The Orioles have

---

Moments   Only in Baltimore, Hon!

- **Cannoli at Vaccaro's.** All the desserts are divine, but the cannoli is a tradition. Skip dessert wherever you're having dinner and head straight to Little Italy afterward, or stop by the annex at the Light Street Pavilion.
- **Seventh-Inning Stretch at Camden Yards.** There's nothing like a crowd of 45,000 uniting for a rousing rendition of John Denver's "Thank God I'm a Country Boy."
- **Spring in Sherwood Gardens.** This community garden at Highfield Road and Greenway Street, in the Guilford neighborhood of northern Baltimore, is out-of-the-way and hard to find—but it's an oasis in May, when the tulips are in bloom. The trip will take you through lovely neighborhoods that tourists seldom see.
- **View from the Glass Elevators at the Hyatt.** Short of a harbor-view room, this is the best view in the city, especially at night—and it's free!
- **Water Taxi Ride to Fells Point and Little Italy.** It's an inexpensive way to see the harbor—and a great way to avoid the hassle of parking.

---

their own Hall of Fame, of course, as do the Colts, with special attention given to star quarterback Johnny Unitas. The Ravens, the Blast soccer team, and the Negro Leagues, particularly the Baltimore Elite Giants, also have their own exhibits. But where else can you find high-school and college sports teams represented, along with a history of stadiums in Baltimore? Bring your camera if you bring your kids: The locker room has uniforms to try on, and you're going to want a photo in that way-too-big Ravens jersey. The museum is at the baseball stadium, just 3 blocks west of the Babe Ruth Museum.

301 W. Camden St. ✆ 410/727-1539. www.baberuthmuseum.com. Admission $10 adults, $8 seniors, $6.50 children 2–12. Combination tickets with the Babe Ruth Museum available. Apr–Oct daily 10am–6pm (until 7:30pm on days of Orioles home games); Nov–Mar Tues–Sun 10am–5pm (until 8pm on days of Ravens home games).

MOUNT VERNON

Basilica of the Assumption of the Blessed Virgin Mary ☆☆   This church has been a monument to religious freedom since 1806. Designed by Benjamin Latrobe—who was working on the U.S. Capitol at the same time—the neoclassical basilica is considered one of America's most beautiful. A national shrine and historic landmark, it was the first cathedral built in the United States. Notable visitors have included Mother Teresa and Pope John Paul II. A 2-year restoration has closed the church, but reopening is expected in November 2006, the bicentennial of the laying of the cornerstone by America's first Catholic bishop, John Carroll. Changes are expected to be dramatic. Guided tours and historical displays are planned.

400 block of Cathedral St. ✆ 410/727-3564. www.baltimorebasilica.org. Free admission. After reopening, daily 7am–5pm. Masses on Sun at 7:15am, 8:30am, 10am, 11:30am, 4pm, and 5:30pm, plus Mon–Sat 7:15am and 12:10pm. Take Charles St. north; turn left on Franklin St. and left again on Cathedral St.

Contemporary Museum *Finds*   The Contemporary Museum holds shows in its Mount Vernon home, but will sometimes exhibit art on the sides of buildings, on buses, or in other community settings as well. Its small storefront galleries are devoted to distinctly contemporary art, ranging from photography and video to paintings and performance art. It's a nice counterpoint to its neighbors, the elegant Walters Art Museum and the traditional Maryland Historical Society, both a block or so away.

100 W. Centre St. $\textcircled{C}$ 410/783-5720; www.contemporary.org. Free admission; donations accepted. Wed–Sat noon–5pm (Thurs until 7pm). Hours vary depending on exhibit; calling ahead is a must. Closed between exhibits.

Eubie Blake National Jazz Institute and Cultural Center   Baltimorean Eubie Blake, the ragtime pianist and Broadway composer, is remembered in this small museum on Howard Street's Antique Row. Exhibits also feature local musicians Billie Holiday and Cab Calloway. Because the focus here is on music, most of the space is devoted to recitals and programs for children. Open-mic poetry readings are held the last Thursday evening of the month; the Heritage Band has open rehearsals on the first Saturday morning of the month. *Tip:* There usually isn't a lot to see here, but talk to the docents—many of them knew Blake or Calloway personally.

847 N. Howard St. $\textcircled{C}$ 410/225-3130. www.eubieblake.org. Admission $3 adults, $2 school-age children. Tues–Fri 10:30am–5pm; Sat 10:30am–2:30pm.

George Peabody Library ✸✸✸   One of Baltimore's hidden treasures has reopened to the public after a 2-year restoration. The library, part of the Peabody Institute, is an architectural gem set into the historic Mount Vernon neighborhood that is also home to the Walters Art Museum and the Washington Monument. It's an academic gem as well—the resting place of 300,000 volumes, mostly rare books, with some dating back to the days when the printing press was new. Philanthropist George Peabody provided the funds to build this magnificent "cathedral of books" and ordered that it be filled with the best works on every subject. Bibliophiles and lovers of architecture won't want to miss seeing this 1866 beauty. It's open all day to readers, but visitors who just want to see the cast-iron balconies, which soar five levels to a shining glass ceiling, are advised to stop by at 10am or 3pm (though they won't be turned away at other times).

17 E. Mount Vernon Place. $\textcircled{C}$ **410/659-8179.** www.georgepeabodylibrary.jhu.edu. Library Tues–Fri 9am–5pm; Sat 9am–1pm. Exhibits Mon–Sat 9am–5pm; Sun noon–5pm.

Maryland Historical Society Museum ✸✸ *(Kids)*   Francis Scott Key's manuscript of the "Star-Spangled Banner" is the centerpiece of an exhibit called "Looking for Liberty," which includes artifacts that recall Maryland's past. You can find all kinds of stuff here: Cal Ripken's bat, a recording of Eubie Blake playing the piano, Stieff silver, numerous landscape paintings. The collections represent Maryland's 350-plus years of history in a sprawling museum that takes up a city block and includes the town house of Baltimore philanthropist Enoch Pratt, which served as the MHS's first home. Don't miss the museum store: Part consignment store, part gift shop, it has plenty of antiques and other interesting items. It's easy to spend a couple of hours on a visit here, and the society is not far from the Walters Art Museum and the antiques shops of Howard Street.

201 W. Monument St. $\textcircled{C}$ 410/685-3750. www.mdhs.org. Admission $8 adults, $6 seniors and children 13–17; $4 children 3–12. Pass for Maryland Historical Society Museum, Baltimore Civil War Museum—President Street Station, and Fells Point Maritime Museum $12 adults, $10 students and seniors, $4 children 3–12. Wed–Sun 10am–5pm. Open until 8pm first Thurs of every month, when admission is free. Light Rail: Centre St.

Old St. Paul's Church   Originally founded in 1692 as one of Maryland's first Anglican parishes, this building dates to 1856. The church was built in Italian Romanesque style and is filled with Tiffany stained-glass windows and mosaics. The Tiffany rose window, which crowns the entrance, is a jewel many people miss. In addition, two friezes salvaged from the previous church, which burned in 1817, have been incorporated into the portico. A brochure outlining some of the treasures is available in the back of the church. In addition to Sunday services, the church is the site of a Tuesday noontime music series October through May.

Charles and Saratoga sts. © 410/685-3404. www.osp1692.org. Free admission. Sun services at 8am, 10:30am, and 5:30pm; call for services on other days. Church often open during the week for quiet visits.

Walters Art Museum 🏛🏛🏛 The Walters has always been one of Baltimore's great attractions. Begun with the 22,000-object collection of William and Henry Walters, this gem's ancient and medieval galleries got new sparkle in a 2001 renovation. Walk through the galleries of sculpture, jewelry, mummies, sarcophagi, and French 19th-century paintings to see the progress of fine art through 50 centuries. The Knight's Hall displays tapestries, furnishings, and suits of armor from the Middle Ages. The Egyptian collection is one of the best in the U.S. The original Palazzo building has been restored, with 1,500 works from mostly the Renaissance and baroque periods reinstalled. Hackerman House features Asian art. And the Palace of Wonders is the imaginary gallery of a 17th-century Flemish nobleman; it features art, collections from nature, and artifacts from around the world. In 2006, look for a number of exhibits on French painting, as well as architecture, quilts, and glass. The cafe serves light fare.

600 N. Charles St. © 410/547-9000. www.thewalters.org. Admission $10 adults, $8 seniors, $6 students, $2 children 6–17. Free admission to permanent collection first Thurs of every month and every Sat 10am–noon. Wed–Sun 10am–5pm. Closed Thanksgiving, Dec 24–25, and July 4th. Extended hours Dec 26–Jan 1. Bus: 3, 11, 31, 61, or 64. Light Rail: Centre St. Take Charles St. north to the Washington Monument.

Washington Monument and Museum This column, 178 feet tall, stands as the country's first major architectural memorial to George Washington. Begun in 1815, it was designed by Robert Mills, who also designed the Washington Monument (begun in 1848) in Washington, D.C. To learn the whole story, have a look at the exhibit inside the building. The physically fit can also climb the 228 steps to the top of the tower and see why this spot has what's often called the best view in Baltimore.

Mount Vernon Place and Charles St. © 410/396-0929. Suggested donation $1. Wed–Sun 10am–5pm. Take Charles St. north to the monument.

NORTH OF DOWNTOWN

Baltimore Museum of Art 🏛🏛🏛 The BMA is famous for its Matisse collection, assembled by Baltimore sisters Claribel and Etta Cone, who went to Paris in the 1920s and came back with Impressionist and modern art. The $4-million Cone Wing showcases their collection of paintings by Matisse, Cézanne, Gauguin, van Gogh, and Renoir. Visit the special room set up to remember these women, featuring drawers filled with their personal things, pieces of furniture, and a virtual tour of their Baltimore apartments.

The largest museum in Maryland, the BMA offers galleries dedicated to modern and contemporary art; European sculpture and painting; American painting and decorative arts; prints and photographs; the arts of Africa, Asia, the Americas, and Oceania; and a 2¾-acre sculpture garden with 35 major works by Alexander Calder, Henry Moore, and others. Highlights include the 35,000-square-foot West Wing for Contemporary Art, with work by Andy Warhol, Jasper Johns, and Baltimorean Grace Hartigan; Early American decorative arts and a gallery of miniature rooms; European art that includes Impressionist paintings by Monet and Degas; and the Jacobs Wing, a collection of 15th- to 19th-century European art beautifully displayed in rich jewel-toned rooms. Younger visitors can borrow the ART + FUN packs, which will show them museum pieces on their own level as they listen to music or draw. On the first Thursday of the month, admission is free and the museum stays open until 8pm, offering gallery tours, music, and activities for families. A summer jazz series in the sculpture garden is another delight.

10 Art Museum Dr. (at N. Charles St. and 31st St.). ℂ 410/396-7100. www.artbma.org. Admission $10 adults, $8 seniors and $6 students, free for children 18 and under. Free admission and extended hours on first Thurs of every month. Wed–Fri 11am–5pm; Sat–Sun 11am–6pm. Bus: 3 or 11. Take Howard St. north; bear right onto Art Museum Dr., about 3 miles north of the harbor.

Evergreen House *(Finds*   What started as a relatively modest Italianate mansion in the mid-1800s became a 48-room marvel of the Gilded Age, with a 23-karat gold-plated bathroom, a theater painted by noted Ballet Russe designer Leon Bakst, and room after room of art, books, and *objets*. Bought in 1878 by the president of the B&O railroad, John W. Garrett, the home grew over the years and became ever more lavish and more famous. Its last owners, John and Alice Garrett, turned it into a glittering salon, where they entertained statesmen, authors, artists, and musicians.

From the moment visitors arrive at the entrance, a porte-cochere topped by a Tiffany glass awning, they are treated to a multitude of beautiful rooms, fine arts, and decorative items that reflect the Garretts' travels and interests: a red Asian room displaying Japanese and Chinese items; paintings by Picasso, Modigliani, and Degas; glass by Tiffany; a 30,000-book library; and Dutch marquetry furniture. A tour lasts about an hour. The beautiful formal gardens should be visited as well.

4545 N. Charles St. (between Loyola College and the College of Notre Dame). ℂ 410/516-0341. www.jhu.edu/historichouses. Admission $6 adults, $5 seniors, $3 students. Tues–Fri 11am–4pm; Sat–Sun noon–4pm (last tour at 3pm).

Homewood House   If you have time, visit both Evergreen (see above) and Homewood (they're a mile apart) to see how differently the rich lived in different centuries. Homewood was designed and built by the son of Charles Carroll of Carrollton, a signer of the Declaration of Independence. Built in 1801, the five-part classic Palladian home is a dazzling example of Federal architecture. Its interiors boast superb woodcarving, plaster ornamentation, and an array of fanlights. It's painted in a rainbow of soothing colors and decorated in pieces of the time, some from the Carroll family. Highlights are the main hall, the family sitting room with toys and doll furniture, the music room, the long lemon-yellow hall, and the master bedroom with its high cove ceiling and bookcases tucked into the sides of the fireplace. Tours last about 45 minutes. Changing exhibits in the main hall often focus on the decorative arts or architecture.

On the campus of Johns Hopkins University, 3400 N. Charles St. ℂ 410/516-5589. www.jhu.edu/historichouses. Admission $6 adults, $5 seniors, $3 students. Combination ticket with Evergreen House $10. Tues–Fri 11am–4pm; Sat–Sun noon–4pm (last tour at 3:30pm). Drive to the university's north entrance, on University Pkwy., and follow signs to the parking lot. Press the button at the gate to park. The house is on the other side of a building by the lot.

Lacrosse Museum & National Hall of Fame   This museum offers a look at 350 years in the history of lacrosse, America's oldest sport and a passion in Maryland. Displays include photographs and murals of athletes at play, sculptures and paintings, vintage equipment and uniforms, a multimedia show, a documentary, and a Hall of Fame.

113 W. University Pkwy. (C) **410/235-6882**. www.uslacrosse.org. Admission $3 adults, $2 children 5–15. Feb–May Tues–Sat 10am–3pm; June–Jan Mon–Fri 10am–3pm; plus 1st Thurs of every month 11am–3pm. Hours occasionally change, so call ahead.

Maryland Zoo in Baltimore _Kids_   The third-oldest zoo in the U.S. is home to some 2,000 animals, including polar bears, penguins, and chimpanzees. Ongoing renovation includes replacing old cages with more modern habitats. The new Polar Bear Watch allows visitors a better view of the bears. The Chimpanzee Forest, Leopard Lair, and African Watering Hole are also good, but the best part is the children's zoo, with its lily pads, tree slide, farm animals, and Maryland wilderness exhibit. Plan to spend a few hours here. Bring a stroller for the little ones.

Druid Hill Park. (C) **410/366-LION**. www.marylandzoo.org. Admission $15 adults, $12 seniors, $10 children 2–11. Daily 10am–4:30pm. Closed Jan–Feb, 2nd Fri in June, Thanksgiving, and Dec 25. Take Exit 7 (Druid Hill Lake Dr.) off I-83 and follow signs for the zoo.

National Great Blacks in Wax Museum _Finds_   The first thing you hear when you enter is the sound of moaning, coming from the Slave Ship exhibit. This wax museum doesn't shy away from the tough topics—a lynching exhibit is in the basement—but it revels in the African Americans—indeed, all people of color—who made a difference. Some are the expected, like Martin Luther King, Jr., Frederick Douglass, and famous athletes, artists, and entertainers. Some may be people you weren't aware of: rodeo star Bill Pickett, Matthew Henson at the North Pole, and African Americans who made advances in medicine, science, law, and politics.

1601–1603 E. North Ave. (C) **410/563-3404**. www.greatblacksinwax.org. Admission $6.80 adults, $6.30 seniors and students, $4.80 children 12–17, $4.55 children 2–11. Mon–Sat 9am–6pm; Sun noon–6pm. Closed Mon Oct 15–Jan 14.

6 Organized Tours & Cruises

LAND & SEA TOURS

Amphibious sightseeing vehicles take visitors on a cruise of the harbor after touring the city's neighborhoods. **Ride the Ducks** ((C) **410/727-DUCK;** www.baltimore ducks.com) conducts 50-minute tours in converted 1945 DUKWs that accommodate 38 passengers. Tours are offered daily from April to September, and Saturday and Sunday only in October and November. Tickets are $24 for adults, $23 for seniors, $22 for active military, and $14 for children 3 to 12. The ticket kiosk is outside the Light Street Pavilion at Harborplace.

SPECIAL-INTEREST TOURS

Modeled after Boston's Freedom Trail, the **Heritage Walk** _☆_ was unveiled in 2004. Interpretive signs and bronze sidewalk markers highlight 20 historic spots along a 3.2-mile trail. Some are obvious, such as City Hall and the USS _Constellation_. Other sites benefit from explanation, such as the 1771 Friends Meeting House, one of Baltimore's oldest structures. You can take the walk on your own—maps are available for $2 at the _Constellation_ gift shop and at www.baltimore.org—but it's better with a guide. The 90-minute guided tours depart from the Inner Harbor visitor center six times a day. They're $7.50 for adults, $5 for students and seniors, and free for children under 5. Though visitors don't go inside any of the buildings (admission to open sites costs extra), they do get an insider's look at some fascinating streets and learn a few stories about Baltimore in its earliest days. For details, call (C) **877/BALTIMORE** or visit www.heritagewalk.org.

The **Baltimore Mural Tour**—a trip to see the 150 murals painted around town—is one of a number of tours offered by the **Baltimore Office of Promotion & the Arts** (© 410/752-8622; www.bop.org). Tickets range from $10 to $20. Bike tours are also offered.

The **Fell's Point Visitor Center,** 1732 Thames St. (© 410/675-6750; www.preservationsociety.com), offers several historical tours of some of Baltimore's oldest streets. Walking tours, including the Immigration Tour and Secrets of the Seaport, depart from here on Saturday at noon. Ghostwalks are offered Friday and Saturday at 7pm. Tickets are $12 for adults, $8 for children 11 and under; reservations are a must.

The **Mount Vernon Cultural District** (© 410/605-0462; www.mvcd.org) offers 90-minute walking tours of the area around the Washington Monument, on Saturday at 10am from April to November, weather permitting. On Sunday, there's a 12:30pm tour of area churches, known for their architectural and historical impact. Or visit the website for a self-guided tour.

African American Cultural Tours focus on contributions of local African Americans, such as Harriet Tubman and Thurgood Marshall, as well as important landmarks. Call © 410/727-0755; reservations for these bus tours are essential.

Baseball fans should not miss the 75-minute tour of **Oriole Park at Camden Yards** (© 410/547-6234; www.oriolepark.com). Well-informed guides fill you in on where Hall of Famer Eddie Murray hit his 500th home run, why there are no bat racks in the dugout, and how many miles of beer lines run under the seats. The tour visits places the average fan can't see: the dugouts, the umpires' tunnel, and the press box. Buy tickets at least 30 minutes beforehand. They can be purchased at the box office at the north end of the warehouse building at the ballpark; prices are $7 for adults and $5 for seniors and children. Call ahead to confirm the tour schedule.

CRUISES & BOAT TOURS

There's no shortage of options for seeing Baltimore from the water. Several touring boats will inevitably be docked at the Inner Harbor during your visit, but the cheapest way to get on the water is to take **Ed Kane's Water Taxi** (© 800/658-8947 or 410/563-3901; www.thewatertaxi.com). It provides transportation to various destinations, including Harborplace, Little Italy, Fells Point, Canton, and Fort McHenry, but you're welcome to stay on for the entire route. See "Getting Around," earlier in this chapter, for details.

You can't miss the *Bay Lady* and the newly refurbished *Lady Baltimore,* two 450-passenger three-deck ships docked outside the Light Street Pavilion. **Harbor Cruises** (© 800/695-BOAT or 410/727-3113; www.harborcruises.com) offers 2-hour lunch, 3-hour dinner, and 2½-hour moonlight excursions, as well as themed options such as crab feasts and holiday cruises year-round. Prices range from $29 to $60 per person. The food is passable, but the cruise is worthwhile. Also available are 60-minute narrated harbor tours on the *Prince Charming.* Tickets are $11 for adults and $9 for children and seniors.

For a tall-ship adventure, come aboard the *Clipper City* (© 410/539-6277; www.clippercity.com), a 140-passenger topsail schooner. This ship offers 2-hour afternoon excursions, 3-hour evening trips with live calypso and reggae music, and 3-hour Sunday champagne brunch sails, all departing from the dock next to the Maryland Science Center. Afternoon sails cost $20 for adults and $5 for children under 10; calypso and reggae sails cost $30 for adults; and Sunday brunch is $45 for adults. Most Thursdays are pirate nights—come dressed as a pirate and you get a $5 discount. This is a busy boat with lots of cruises; call or check the website for other options.

The *Black-Eyed Susan,* a 150-passenger paddle-wheeler, offers Sunday brunch cruises priced at $38 for adults. This and other excursions depart from the dock in Fells Point. Call © 410/342-6960 or visit www.theblack-eyedsusan.com for details.

Want more than a couple hours on the water? In the fall, the *Mystic Whaler* (© 800/697-8420; www.mysticwhaler.com) offers 3-day Chesapeake Bay cruises from Baltimore. Prices range from $450 to $570.

7 Spectator Sports & Outdoor Activities

BASEBALL   From April to October, you can see the American League's **Baltimore Orioles** play ball. If there's a home game during your visit, try to attend: It's a real Baltimore experience. The team plays at Oriole Park at Camden Yards, 333 W. Camden St. (© 888/848-BIRD or 410/685-9800; www.oriolepark.com). Afternoon games are usually at 1:35pm; evening games start at 7:35pm. Ticket prices range from $9 to $55, with bargain night on Tuesday and college-student discounts on Friday, both for the upper deck.

FOOTBALL   The **Baltimore Ravens** play at M&T Bank Stadium, next to Camden Yards at 1101 Russell St. (© 410/261-RAVE; www.baltimoreravens.com). There are about 5,000 tickets sold per game (the rest are held by season-ticket holders). They are both expensive—$40 to $315—and difficult to get.

HORSE RACING   Maryland's oldest thoroughbred track and the site of the annual Preakness Stakes is **Pimlico Race Course,** 5241 Park Heights (© 410/542-9400; www.marylandracing.com), about 5 miles from the Inner Harbor on the city's northwest side. (This is where Seabiscuit made history beating Triple Crown winner War Admiral.) The **Preakness** ⚐ (www.preakness.com), the middle jewel in racing's Triple Crown, is held the third Saturday in May. Clubhouse and grandstand tickets go on sale in October—and go fast. Infield tickets, at $45, are for sale at the box office or gas stations as the Preakness gets closer. Post time for regular racing days is 1:10pm; admission is $3 for the grandstand. Self-parking is free; valet parking is $3. Call ahead for opening days.

INDOOR SOCCER   The **Baltimore Blast** (© 410/732-5278; www.baltimoreblast. com), 2003 MISL champs, have had a loyal following for more than 20 years. The season lasts October through April; games are played at the 1st Mariner Arena. Tickets cost $14 to $20.

LACROSSE   Baltimore's pro lacrosse team is the 2005 MLL champion **Baltimore Bayhawks** (© 866/99HAWKS; www.baltimorebayhawks.com). Games are played May through August at Johnny Unitas Stadium in Towson. Tickets are $12 to $18.

PADDLEBOATS & ELECTRIC BOATS   Paddleboats and little electric boats are available for rent at the Inner Harbor, adjacent to the World Trade Center. Hours vary according to season. Paddleboats, some built like dragons, cost $8 to $11 per half-hour per boat, depending on the number of people riding. Not that energetic? A half-hour ride on an electric boat will run $12 for two passengers or $18 for three.

PUBLIC PARKS
Baltimore has many green spaces, including a couple that deserve special mention.

Cylburn Arboretum *(Moments* You'll have to look for this one, but when you find it—just off Northern Parkway, a quick run up the Jones Falls Expressway—you'll be thrilled by the fascinating gardens and fancy mansion. The 100-plus acres of grounds include a formal Victorian garden, children's garden, and gardens devoted to butter-flies, shade, roses, and vegetables. Woodland trails wind 2.5 miles through the forests of Cylburn. At the bird sanctuary, 161 species have been spotted, including the Balti-more oriole and bald eagle. The house, an ornate stone building with mansard roof, tower, and cupola, has an equally ornate interior, with inlaid floors, mosaics, and plas-terwork. The Maryland Ornithological Society's bird museum and a nature museum for children are in a carriage house behind the mansion. Tucked in the woods off very busy I-83, Cylburn makes for a peaceful retreat from urban life.

4915 Greenspring Ave., Mount Washington. ② 410/367-2217. www.cylburnassociation.org. Grounds open daily dawn–dusk. Free admission. Mansion museums Mon–Fri 7:30am–3:30pm and selected Sat–Sun (see website for details).

Federal Hill 🕊🕊🕊 Yes, it's that big hill overlooking the Inner Harbor. Take the 100 steps on the Battery Avenue side on the east; or else enter from Warren Avenue on the south side, where you won't have any steps to contend with at all, except maybe a curb-stone. The hill has been valued for its scenic views since the first Baltimoreans came here to watch construction around the harbor. A single cannon recalls the Civil War, when federal guns were trained on this city. Take your dog (on a leash) or your chil-dren. Once the kids get tired of the view, they can play in the fenced-in playground.

Federal Hill Park, Battery and Warren aves. Free admission. Best to visit during daylight hours.

8 Shopping

The Inner Harbor is an obvious choice for shoppers. But those who like an adventure will find Fells Point, Hampden, Mount Washington, Antique Row on Howard Street, and a lot of fun. If your wallet needs emptying, head over to Cross Keys, near Mount Washington, for designer threads.

INNER HARBOR

You can find anything from onion rings to diamond rings at the 160 shops that make up **Harborplace** (② 410/332-0060; www.harborplace.com), which is actually three separate venues: two stand-alone pavilions on Light and Pratt streets; and the Gallery, a vertical mall in the atrium of the Renaissance Harborplace Hotel. The **Light Street Pavilion** has the most food stalls and restaurants, plus some souvenir shops. The **Pratt Street Pavilion** offers specialty stores, clothing and jewelry shops, and more restau-rants. The **Gallery** has three floors of shops, plus a fourth-floor food court. Most of the stores are open Monday through Saturday from 10am to 9pm and Sunday from 11am to 7pm.

Most tenants are franchises of national chains, but a few offer some local color. At the **Fudgery,** in the Light Street Pavilion, employees make amazing music while they make the fudge. **Lee's Ice Cream,** also in the Light Street Pavilion, is made in West Baltimore. **White House/Black Market** has stores all over the country, but the origi-nal's in the Pratt Street Pavilion. The 75 shops in the Gallery (connected via skywalk to the Pratt Street Pavilion) include Banana Republic, Brooks Brothers, Ann Taylor, and the Disney Store. Santa's magical house is located between the Harborplace pavil-ions from Thanksgiving to Christmas Eve.

Sweet Things in Charm City

Sometimes you just need a sweet—and there are a couple sweet spots around town that shouldn't be missed if you're in the neighborhood.

Baltimore Cupcake Company, 1433 E. Fort Ave. (© **410/783-1600;** www. baltimorecupcakecompany.com). This little pink-and-white shop down the street from Fort McHenry sells pretty $2 cupcakes and other sweets along with its Cafe du Monde coffee. Open Monday through Friday from 8am to 6pm, Saturday from 9am to 4pm.

Dangerously Delicious Pies, 2400 Fleet St., at Montford Ave. (© **410/ 522-PIES;** www.dangerouspies.com). These aren't refined, fancily decorated pies. These are honest, homemade, fresh-out-of-the-oven pies. The rock-'n'-roll guys here make all kinds: fruit, Key (Bridge) lime, derby, and a towering lemon meringue. Open Tuesday through Sunday from 7am to 9pm; located between Fells Point and Canton, near Patterson Park.

Patisserie Poupon, 820 E. Baltimore St. (© **410/332-0390**). You'll find this delightful French pastry shop in the shadow of the Shot Tower and near Port Discovery and Little Italy. (It's safer to drive here due to traffic.) Stop for coffee and a croissant or a fabulously decorated pastry. Open Monday through Saturday from 7am to 6pm.

FELLS POINT

AKI   Where else would you put your first American store when you already have locations in Rome and Florence? One of the owners of this shop, which is filled with colorful Italian athletic wear, lives nearby. Open daily. 1500 Thames St. © 410/732-1880. www.aki.it.

Art Gallery of Fells Point   This cooperative gallery features works by regional artists, including paintings, drawings, sculpture, photography, fibers, and jewelry. Open Tuesday through Sunday. 1716 Thames St. © 410/327-1272. www.fellspointgallery.org.

Brassworks   Brass glistens from every shelf here. Fine-quality items include lamps, candlesticks, doorknockers, and a lot more. Open daily. 1641 Thames St. © 410/327-7280. www.baltimorebrassworks.com.

Sheep's Clothing   Irish woolens, ceramics and glass, and Provençal soaps and fragrances. Open Wednesday through Sunday. 1620 Shakespeare St. © 410/327-2222.

Silk Road   Go East, all you shoppers, to this emporium filled with Oriental rugs, copper pots, tiles, and other Eastern gifts. Open Thursday through Monday and by appointment. 905 S. Ann St. © 410/675-1705. www.silkroad-rugs.com.

Strictly Be-More   Art by Baltimoreans, mostly about B-more. Open Thursday through Monday. 1728 Thames St. © 410/675-0075.

Ten Thousand Villages   Using the Body Shop model of commissioning handmade products by indigenous peoples, this large shop (for Fells Point, anyway) is filled with textiles, pottery, baskets, and coffee, all fairly traded and affordably priced. Open daily. 1621 Thames St. © 410/342-5568. www.tenthousandvillages.com.

MOUNT VERNON

A People United   This nonprofit shop features a variety of goods made by women who are part of development cooperatives in India, Nepal, Thailand, Guatemala, Kenya, and other lands. You'll find a colorful selection of clothing, jewelry, and accessories; sweaters here are not your average pullovers. Open daily. 516 N. Charles St. ☎ 410/727-4470. www.apeopleunited.com.

Beadazzled   Be dazzled by the array of beads, which come from everywhere—Europe, South America, Africa—and in every color. There's usually a crowd here looking for just the right combination for a pair of earrings or necklace. Classes are available. Open daily. 501 N. Charles St. ☎ 410/837-2323. www.beadazzled.net.

C. Grimaldis Gallery   Contemporary art is the focus here, with new exhibitions 11 times a year. Open Tuesday through Saturday. 523 N. Charles St. ☎ 410/539-1092. www.cgrimaldisgallery.com.

Woman's Industrial Exchange   Founded in 1880, this shop's mission has always been to help women by selling their handiwork, originally as part of a national movement after the Civil War. Baltimore's effort continues today with this charming crafts shop and newly reopened lunchroom, **Chef's Express.** (Those who remember the quaint old tearoom should note that the dining room has been updated.) The work here is finely done: smocked dresses, handmade afghans, quilts, and other wares, which come from women around the country and change all the time. Open Monday through Friday. 333 N. Charles St. ☎ 410/685-4388. www.womansindustrialexchange.org.

Antique Row

In a single block—the 800 block of Howard Street—lies an amazing string of antiques shops. Not only is it fun, it's also historic. The first antiques shops opened here in the 1840s—they were furniture resellers, really—making this the oldest antiques district in the U.S. Most of the shops are open from around 11am or noon to 5pm. Street parking is metered, so bring lots of quarters. Or take the Light Rail, which runs up this street.

Amos Judd and Sons, Inc. (☎ 410/462-2000) is a dark little store filled with cases of elegant jewelry, as well as some unique lamps and chandeliers. The 20 dealers at **Antique Row Stalls** (☎ 410/728-6363), an 8,000-square-foot co-op, sell, well, just about everything; closed Tuesdays.

The eclectic **Connoisseur's Connection** (☎ 410/383-2624) has a little of everything, from furniture to curiosities. This fun shop often provides set pieces for locally produced movies. **Dubey's Art and Antiques** (☎ 410/383-2881) boasts a wealth of Chinese export porcelain and other American, English, and Asian treasures.

E. A. Mack Antiques (☎ 410/728-1333) specializes in 18th- and 19th-century furniture, all of it in lovely condition. You can also get custom reproductions made here. Check out the old silver at **Imperial Half Bushel** (☎ 410/462-1192)—the shop fairly glitters with flatware and holloware. **20th Century Galleries** (☎ 410/728-3800) stocks American and European art pottery, as well as prints and paintings.

HAMPDEN

Antreasian Gallery   Antreasian Gallery (formerly Paper Rock Scissors) is filled with the work of 50 regional artists. The art varies widely, from painting to jewelry and ceramics—and it's affordable. Call ahead or check the website to see if there's an opening while you're in town. Open Tuesday through Saturday. 1111 W. 36th St. ✆ 410/235-4420. www.antreasiangallery.com.

Fat Elvis   This tiny shop houses a good selection of unusual antiques, but you'll also find some great coats and dresses, old LPs, glassware, and other collectibles. Usually open Friday and Saturday from 10am to 6pm, Sunday from noon to 4pm. 833 W. 36th St. ✆ 410/467-6030.

Hometown Girl *Finds*   If you want a real Baltimore souvenir, Hometown Girl probably has it. You'll find books about Baltimore, books written by Baltimoreans, fun shirts, even screen-painting kits. (If you've walked past the rowhouses of Little Italy or Highlandtown, you've probably seen a window screen sporting a painted landscape.) The shop also has a soda fountain. Open daily. 1001 W. 36th St. ✆ **410/467-1015.** www.celebratebaltimore.com.

Ma Petite Shoe   Splurge on two indulgences—eye-catching footwear and gourmet chocolates—in one shop. It's just two tiny rooms, but what rooms! Open daily. 832 W. 36th St. ✆ **410/235-3442.** www.mapetiteshoe.com.

Mud and Metal   This great little shop specializes in functional art—lamps, tables, business-card holders, jewelry—often created from recycled materials. Most items are made by local artists; the selection is constantly changing. Open daily. 1121 W. 36th St. ✆ 410/467-8698. www.mudandmetal.com.

Oh! Said Rose   The young will love this crowded spot, packed with vintage-style clothes (really all new) and accessories from the wild to the merely fun. Open daily. 840 W. 36th St. ✆ **410/235-5170.** www.ohsaidrose.com.

2 Hot Art Chicks   Fresh, fun art. Open Wednesday through Sunday. 820 W. 39th St. ✆ **410/235-1888.**

Wild Yam Pottery   Hampden has become a center for local artists, and this shop was the first to arrive in the mid-1990s. The handmade pottery is mostly practical—lamps, baking dishes, vases—in soothing earth tones. Special orders and handcrafted jewelry are also available. Open daily. 863 W. 36th St. ✆ **410/662-1123.** www.wildyampottery.com.

MOUNT WASHINGTON

Baltimore Clayworks   This nonprofit center holds classes, rents studio space, and runs a gallery and shop. The main building at 5707, a former convent, has a warren of little gallery rooms where the works change frequently; they're often art pieces rather than mugs and pitchers. The shop has functional pottery, made by local potters. Open daily. 5706–5707 Smith Ave. ✆ **410/578-1919.** www.baltimoreclayworks.org.

Jurus   I go out of my way to shop at this elegant little store filled with jewelry crafted by the owners, tableware, scarves, and crafts. You'll see many one-of-a-kind items. Open Tuesday through Saturday. 5618 Newbury St. ✆ **410/542-5227.** www.jurusjewelry.com.

Something Else   You won't find the clothing here in any department store. Flowing dresses, exotic jewelry, colorful scarves, and South American sweaters are made of flax, wood, and cotton. Open Monday through Saturday. 1611 Sulgrave Ave. ✆ **410/542-0444.**

Sunnyfields With so many funky shops in Baltimore, it's nice to see this one, filled with Williamsburg reproduction furniture and accessories, imported porcelain and crystal, lamps, and party furnishings. Open Monday through Saturday. 6305 Falls Rd. © 410/823-6666.

VILLAGE OF CROSS KEYS

This upscale shopping center, at 5100 Falls Rd. in Baltimore, has some terrific stores that shouldn't be missed, plus a few chains such as Talbots and Williams-Sonoma. Hours are generally from 10am to 6pm or later. From downtown, take the Jones Falls Expressway north to the Northern Parkway East exit. Turn right at the light at Falls Road; the center is on the right. Below is a sampling of the shops here.

Elizabeth Arden Red Door Spa Take care of all of you, from your skin to your toes, at this luxurious spa. Open daily. © 410/323-3636. www.reddoorspas.com.

Gazelle If you like your home decor more organic, more primal, this is the place for you. It specializes in wearable art and American crafts. Open Monday through Saturday. © 410/433-3305. www.gazelleglass.com.

Ruth Shaw You need designer clothes, you come to Ruth Shaw. Where else are you going to get your Jimmy Choo shoes? Open Monday through Saturday. © 410/532-7886.

The Store Ltd. Pared down to their simplest form, these home furnishings and personal accessories are contemporary, bold, and always fresh. Open Monday through Saturday. © 410/323-2350.

MARKETS & MALLS

Baltimore still has several old-fashioned covered markets with vendors selling seafood, baked goods, produce, and sweets. The outdoor farmers' market held under the Jones Falls viaduct is a Sunday tradition for many people.

Arundel Mills It's actually south of Baltimore, but shopaholics might want to make the excursion to this theme-park-like mall. It's *huge,* with some 200 shops. Larger retailers like Off 5th Saks Fifth Avenue Outlet, Neiman Marcus Last Call Clearance Center, and Bass Pro Shops Outdoor World are joined by plenty of smaller shops, a 24-screen movie theater, and lots of restaurants. The combination of games and food at Dave & Buster's is an afternoon's diversion all by itself, and Medieval Times offers dinner and a show. Open daily. © 410/540-5110. www.arundelmillsmall.com. Off Rte. 295, 10 miles south of Baltimore. Take Rte. 295 south; pass BWI exit to the exit for Arundel Mills.

Baltimore Farmers' Market For a look at Old Baltimore, stop at this weekly outdoor gathering—a great source for crafts, herbs, jams, jellies, baked goods, smoked meats, cheeses, local produce, and flowers. Open June to mid-December, Sunday from 8am to noon. Saratoga St., between Holliday and Gay sts. (under JFX). © 410/752-8632 (for office at 200 W. Lombard St.).

Belvedere Square If you're going to be in northern Baltimore, near Hopkins or Loyola College, this is a great place to stop for a bite to eat. A cluster of takeout counters and retail shops offer mouthwatering choices: sushi, fresh fruits and vegetables, baked goods, even organic items. Atwater's soups, breads, and desserts should never be passed up. Open daily; store hours vary. York Rd. and Belvedere Ave. (just south of Northern Pkwy.), Roland Park. © 410/464-9773. www.belvederesquare.com.

Broadway Market   Smell and taste the flavors of Baltimore's original seaport at this 200-year-old market, which has two large covered buildings staffed by local vendors selling produce, flowers, crafts, and an assortment of ethnic and raw-bar foods (ideal for a snack, quick lunch, or picnic). You'll even find an old-fashioned Baltimore tradition: "sweet potatoes," soft white candies powdered with cinnamon. Open Monday through Saturday from 7am to 6pm. S. Broadway, between Fleet and Lancaster sts., Fells Point. No phone. www.bpmarkets.com.

Cross Street Market   First opened in 1846, Cross Street Market is one of Baltimore's public markets. Come for the fresh flowers that seem to be everywhere. Local vendors also have produce, seafood, meats, candy, baked goods, and much more. Open Monday through Saturday from 7am to 7pm. 1065 S. Charles St., at Cross St., Federal Hill. No phone. www.bpmarkets.com.

Lexington Market   Established in 1782, this Baltimore landmark claims to be the oldest continuously operating market in the U.S. Freshly renovated in 2003, it houses more than 140 merchants, selling prepared ethnic foods (for eat-in or takeaway), seafood, produce, meats, baked goods, sweets, even freshly grated coconut. It's worth a visit. Open Monday through Saturday from 8:30am to 6pm. 400 W. Lexington St. ℂ 410/685-6169. www.lexingtonmarket.com.

9 Baltimore After Dark

Baltimore used to be a quiet town after dark, except for the Fells Point bars and the theater district. Now it's jumping when the sun sets: The Inner Harbor, Federal Hill, Canton, and Mount Vernon have all developed lives after dark.

For major events, check the arts and entertainment sections of the *Baltimore Sun* and the *Washington Post.* The free weekly *City Paper* has very complete listings, down to the smallest bars and clubs. On the Web, try www.baltimorefunguide.com.

Tickets for most major venues are available at the individual box offices or through **Ticketmaster** (ℂ 410/547-SEAT; www.ticketmaster.com).

THE PERFORMING ARTS

Baltimore has a solid range of resident performing-arts companies: a nationally recognized symphony (which will welcome an internationally renowned music director in 2006), an opera company, a major regional theater, and several local professional theater companies.

CLASSICAL MUSIC & OPERA

The world-class **Baltimore Symphony Orchestra** (ℂ 410/783-8000; www.baltimoresymphony.org) welcomes renowned conductor Marin Alsop in 2006 as its new musical director. The BSO performs classical and pops concerts at the Meyerhoff Symphony Hall, 1212 Cathedral St., from September through June. In summer, you'll find the BSO outside at Oregon Ridge Park, north of the city off I-83. Its Fourth of July concerts are terrific fun. Tickets are $25 to $75.

The **Peabody Symphony Orchestra** (ℂ 410/659-8100; www.peabody.jhu.edu/583) is a performing unit of the Peabody Institute of Music at the Johns Hopkins University; concerts are held in Friedberg Hall, at 1 E. Mount Vernon Place.

The **Baltimore Opera** (ℂ 410/727-6000; www.baltimoreopera.com), has been a tradition in the city for 50 years. The company presents four operas each year, all with supertitles, at the Lyric Opera House, 110 W. Mount Royal Ave. Acoustics are so good, even spectators in the last row of the balcony will hear every note. Ticket prices range from $45 to $150.

THEATER

For entertainment by local professional actors at affordable prices, check out these area theaters.

In Fells Point, the **Vagabond Players,** 806 S. Broadway (© **410/563-9135;** www.vagabondplayers.com), stages a variety of classics, contemporary comedies, and dramas. The **Fell's Point Corner Theater,** 251 S. Ann St. (© **410/276-7837;** www.fpct.org), presents eight productions a year.

The city's prominent African-American theater company, **Arena Players,** 801 McCulloh St., off Martin Luther King Boulevard (© **410/728-6500**), presents contemporary plays and romantic comedies.

Everyman Theatre, 1727 N. Charles St. (© **410/752-2208;** www.everymantheatre.org), is earning rave reviews for its local productions of classics and new works. The **Theatre Project** , 45 W. Preston St. (© **410/752-8558;** www.theatreproject.org), is the city's professional company presenting experimental and avant-garde work.

Center Stage   Many major American plays—including works by August Wilson and Eric Overmyer—have been developed at Maryland's state theater, which has presented new and classic work since 1963. Center Stage offers childcare at several matinees and "Nights Out" for its gay and lesbian fans. 700 N. Calvert St. © **410/332-0033.** www.centerstage.org.

Hippodrome Theatre   Located at the France-Merrick Performing Arts Center, this theater is the dazzling newcomer in town. A restored 1914 former vaudeville venue, it now stages national Broadway shows. Orchestra seats and front balcony seats are good, but pass up the back rows of the balcony—unless it's a show you absolutely have to see. A cafe serves light fare, but it's usually crowded; either arrive early or eat somewhere else downtown before heading to the theater. 10 N. Eutaw St. © **410/837-7400,** or 410/547-SEAT for tickets. www.france-merrickpac.com.

THE CLUB & MUSIC SCENE

Baltimore has a nice variety of small live-performance venues. Major national acts come to the **1st Mariner Arena** near the Inner Harbor and to the **Pier Six Concert Pavilion** at the Inner Harbor. A number of clubs welcome smaller touring acts and local performers, from rock to jazz to folk.

COMEDY

Comedy Factory   See live comedy: Thursday at 8:30pm, Friday and Saturday at 8:30 and 10:30pm. 36 Light St. (at Lombard St.). © **410/752-4189.** www.baltimorecomedy.com. Cover varies.

DANCE CLUBS

Baja Beach Club   Opposite Harborplace at the Inner Harbor, this club presents Top 40 and dance music Wednesday through Sunday from around 6pm to 2am. It's popular with locals and draws a crowd of energetic 20-somethings. 55 Market Place (at E. Lombard St.). © **410/727-0468.** No cover.

The Depot   A young crowd heads here for house and retro music. 1728 N. Charles St. © **410/685-3013.** www.thedepot.us. Usually no cover.

Sonar   Sonar has DJ or special concerts most nights, with an emphasis on techno and house music. 407 E. Saratoga St. ℂ **410/327-8333**. www.sonar.us. Cover varies.

FOLK & TRADITIONAL

Cat's Eye Pub   A Fells Point bar with an Irish feel, Cat's Eye is known for its traditional Irish music, but you'll often hear blues, bluegrass, zydeco, and jazz as well. In addition to the nightly live music at 9pm, there's a back room with chessboards and game tables. Open daily from noon to 2am. 1730 Thames St. ℂ **410/276-9085**. www.cats eyepub.com. Occasional $5 cover, mostly free.

Mick O'Shea's   If you're in a St. Patrick's Day mood on any weekend, come to this pub for traditional Irish music. There's live music Thursday through Saturday nights, and food starting at 11:30am: sandwiches, soups, and Irish specialties. 328 N. Charles St. ℂ **410/539-7504**. www.mickosheas.com. Cover for special occasions and performances.

JAZZ & BLUES

An die Musik LIVE!   This music shop schedules jazz and classical performances a couple times a week, held up on the second floor of its Mount Vernon town house. Check the schedule online. 409 N. Charles St. ℂ **888/221-6170** or 410/385-2638. www.andiemusiklive.com. Cover varies.

Bertha's   The Fells Point bar/restaurant is a great venue for live jazz and blues every day of the week. 734 S. Broadway. ℂ **410/327-5795**. www.berthas.com. No cover.

ROCK

Eight by Ten   This longtime favorite in Federal Hill has room for 400 at its two floors and two bars. The focus is live music—from rock to blues to funk. Visit the website for a schedule. 8–10 E. Cross St. ℂ **410/625-2000**. www.the8x10.com. Cover varies.

Hammerjacks   Hammerjacks features national rock acts and dance music. It's open Thursday through Saturday nights until 2am. 316 Guilford Ave. ℂ **410/234-0044**. www. hammerjacks.com. Cover varies.

The Horse You Came In On   This Fells Point bar is popular with the local college and post-college crowds. It features live rock or acoustic music nightly. 1626 Thames St. ℂ **410/327-8111**. Cover varies.

Pier Six Concert Pavilion   National acts perform on this stage right on the waterfront. 731 Eastern Ave. ℂ **410/547-SEAT** for tickets. www.piersixpavilion.com. Ticket prices vary.

Recher Theatre   North of town in Towson, this former movie theater has become a magnet for local and national musicians, mostly rock but also some ska, reggae, and blues. 512 York Rd., Towson. ℂ **410/337-8316**. www.rechertheatre.com. Cover varies; music lovers under 21 admitted.

BEER, BILLIARDS & CIGARS

Bay Cafe   This waterfront bar in Canton is Baltimore's Margaritaville, with a laidback Caribbean atmosphere. There's indoor and outdoor seating, and on weekends you'll find a DJ playing Top 40, zydeco, or something good for a party. 2809 Boston St. ℂ **410/522-3377**. www.baycafeusa.com. Cover varies; no cover in winter.

Edgar's Billiards Club & Restaurant   This upscale day-and-night club near the Inner Harbor offers 17 full-size pool tables as well as smoking and nonsmoking areas and a fine selection of cigars. 1 E. Pratt St., at Light St. ℂ **410/752-8080**. www.edgarsclub.com.

Tips   A Guy Walks into a Bar . . .

Baltimore has two distinct bar scenes: sports bars, and the Fells Point scene, which includes some bars that have live music (listed above).

Sports fans can stroll into any of a dozen bars near Camden Yards for lively game conversation. Try **Downtown Sports Exchange (DSX),** 200 W. Pratt St. (② **410/659-5844**); **Pickles Pub,** 520 Washington Blvd. (② **410/752-1784**); or the **Orioles Bar,** in the Sheraton Inner Harbor, 300 S. Charles St. (② **410/962-8300**).

Fells Point, a combination of local pubs in historic rowhouses and hip clubs in old industrial buildings, has always been a focal point of Baltimore's nightlife and a favorite among college students and young professionals—just head to Broadway and Thames Street and wander around.

But the city's bar scene has expanded, and the narrow streets of **Federal Hill** now have a number of great spots for a beer and some music. In Canton, **O'Donnell Square** is ringed with nightspots. Once you park, you can walk from place to place.

A short walk from the Inner Harbor, **Power Plant Live,** at Water Street and Market Place, packs in young singles, especially on weekend nights. Its combination of restaurants and bars includes **Babalu,** a Cuban grill with salsa music; **Havana Club,** a cigar bar; **Have a Nice Day Cafe,** a '70s-style disco; **Howl at the Moon,** a rock-'n'-roll piano bar; **McFadden's,** an Irish pub; **Mondo Bondo,** an Italian bistro; and **Ruth's Chris Steak House** (p. 81). New is the 2,000-seat live-music venue **Rams Head Live.**

Havana Club *(Finds)*   Upstairs from Ruth's Chris Steak House is this very sophisticated little spot, offering tapas, appetizers, desserts, and cigars. A DJ spins tunes on Friday and Saturday. 600 Water St. ② **410/468-0022.** www.serioussteaks.com. Cover varies.

Max's Tap Room   Max's is a Baltimore institution known for its tremendous beer selection: 118 taps and 300 bottles. It's also cigar-friendly. On the main level are several pool tables; upstairs is Max's Mobtown Lounge, a turn-of-the-20th-century lounge with leather seating and original artwork. 737 S. Broadway. ② **410/675-MAXS.** www. maxs.com.

Wharf Rat   This local favorite is also a frequent stop for conventioneers looking for a drink. It has a pool table and a dining area; it's also a brewpub. See the listing in "Where to Dine" (p. 84). The second location in Fells Point, at 801 S. Ann St. (② **410/276-9034**), is closed on Sunday. 206 W. Pratt St. (at Hanover St.). ② **410/244-8900.** www.thewharfrat.com.

THE GAY & LESBIAN SCENE

For a complete listing of nightspots, check out *Gay Life,* published by the **Gay, Lesbian, Bisexual & Transgender Community Center of Baltimore** (② **410/837-5445;** www.baltimorepride.org), and **www.outinbaltimore.com.** Below are some longtime community favorites.

The **Creative Alliance** (© 410/276-3206; www.creativealliance.org) hosts the Charm City Kitty Club, a troupe of lesbian, bi, and transgender performers. See the website for a schedule and ticket prices.

Coconuts Café   This small bar, attracting a primarily lesbian crowd, is friendly and comfortable. Weekends feature DJs and occasional live music. 311 W. Madison St. (at Linden Ave.). © 410/383-6064. www.coconutscafe.com. Cover varies.

Grand Central   This Mount Vernon pub, formerly Central Station, has six bars, a video pub, and pool tables; its happy hour (4–8pm) wins accolades. It turns into a dance club Wednesday through Sunday. 1001–1003 N. Charles St. © 410/752-7133. www. centralstationpub.com. No cover.

The Hippo ☞   This classic has three large rooms with pool, videos, and a dance floor that attracts a primarily GLBT clientele, but all are welcome. The music is mostly house and techno. Happy hour is 4 to 8pm. 1 W. Eager St. (at Charles St.). © 410/547-0069. www.clubhippo.com. Cover varies.

FILM

The Charles   The Charles, located in a historic industrial building, offers films not showing anywhere else in town—first-run independent and foreign films, in particular. It has five comfortable auditoriums with stadium seating. Cinema Sundays, when the movies come with bagels, coffee, and conversation, are presented September through December, about every other week. The Charles is also a venue of the annual Maryland Film Festival, held in April or early May. 1711 N. Charles St. © 410/727-3456. www.thecharles.com.

IMAX Theater/Maryland Science Center   Even if you have no interest in the science center, you can still see the IMAX movies. In addition to regular daytime features, there are double features each weekend on the theater's five-story-high, 75-foot-wide screen. 601 Light St. (on the harbor). © 410/685-5225. www.mdsci.org.

Little Italy Open-Air Film Festival   On summer Fridays, you can catch a free feature-length movie screened on the side of a restaurant. Bring a lawn chair, or use the ones already set up, to see films with an Italian accent like *Cinema Paradiso* and *Spartacus*. The movie is projected from the bedroom window of a nearby house. High and Stiles sts. www.littleitalymd.com.

The Senator ☞   This 1930s Art Deco movie house was rated one of the best theaters in the country by *USA Today*. It has hosted the world premieres of many Baltimore-based flicks such as *Serial Mom, Diner,* and *Ladder 49*. The Senator's regular programs include high-quality first-run features, classics, and art films, as well as occasional live-music performances. 5904 York Rd. © 410/435-8338. www.senator.com.

10 Side Trips from Baltimore

ELLICOTT CITY

Visitors have been coming to this tiny Patapsco River town, 14 miles from Baltimore, for 230 years. The town was originally built to support the Ellicott brothers' mill, the largest flour-milling center in Colonial America. In 1831, America's first railroad terminal was constructed here and still stands today. It was also here that the *Tom Thumb,* Peter Cooper's steam engine, raced and beat a horse-drawn vehicle. In addition, the country's first National Road ran through Ellicott City and gave farmers a route to the Atlantic.

Step back and look at the solid stone buildings still lining Main Street. The inns built in the 1800s remain—even the Colonial Inn and Opera House (now the Forget-Me-Not Factory), where John Wilkes Booth, it is said, got his start as an actor. Over the years, the town has endured fires, floods, and hurricanes. Through it all, it has survived, and its history and charm continue to draw visitors.

ESSENTIALS
GETTING THERE   From Route 70, take Route 29 South to Route 40 East. Turn right on Rogers Avenue and right again on Courthouse Drive, which ends at Main Street (Rte. 144). Turn left into the historic district. From the Beltway (Rte. 695), either take Route 70 West and follow the above directions or take Route 40 West and turn left on Rogers Avenue, right on Courthouse Drive, and left on Main Street.

VISITOR INFORMATION   The visitor center, at 8267 Main St., is open Monday through Saturday from 10am to 5pm, Sunday from noon to 5pm. The entrance is on the Hamilton Street side.

PARKING   If you look hard, you can find a parking space in lots marked with blue "P" signs. There are metered lots off Main Street near the visitor center, down a driveway under the railroad bridge, and down Maryland Avenue, which runs next to the B&O Railroad Museum. You can get change for the meters at the visitor center or the railroad museum. (If the parking space is yellow, you have to pay; it's free if the space is lined in white.) *Warning:* On-street parking, though not metered, has a 1- or 2-hour limit between 10am and 6pm—and you will be ticketed if you stay too long.

Some lots are free: The Oella lot is across the Patapsco River bridge near the Trolley Stop restaurant. Another free lot is down a driveway on Ellicott Mills Drive. Finally, the two lots at the Court House, 2 blocks from the historic district, have 200 free spaces. The walk is short, though uphill on the way back to your car. A good brochure from the visitor center explains where and how to park.

WHERE TO DINE
Ellicott City has 17 restaurants crammed in its narrow streets. For traditional French, don't miss **Tersiguel's French Country Restaurant,** 8293 Main St. (© 410/465-4004; www.tersiguels.com). **La Palapa,** 8307 Main St. (© 410/465-0070; www.lapalapagrill.com), serves Mexican in a gaily decorated atmosphere.

Cacao Lane Restaurant, 8066 Main St. (© 410/461-1378; www.cacaolane.net), is a casual spot with a Continental menu. Light rock musicians perform Friday and Saturday evenings. The **Ellicott Mills Brewing Company,** 8308 Main St. (© 410/313-8141; www.ellicottmillsbrewing.com), brews its own beer to accompany the German and pub-style entrees.

WHAT TO SEE & DO
"Ye Haunted History of Old Ellicott City" tours are offered April through November, Friday and Saturday at 8:30pm. Reservations are essential; call © 800/288-8747.

The **Ellicott City B&O Railroad Station,** 2711 Maryland Ave. (© 410/313-1413), America's oldest train station, now houses artifacts and model trains. Among the travelers who once stopped here were Annie Oakley and Charles Dickens. Hours are Friday and Saturday from 11am to 4pm, Sunday from noon to 4pm.

The **Thomas Isaac Log Cabin,** 8398 Main St. (© **410/313-1413;** www.thomas isaaclogcabin.net), a settler's cabin, was built about 1780—making it the town's oldest residence. Open Monday, Tuesday, and Thursday from 10am to 5pm.

A yellow 1889 building topped with a big bell houses the **City Firehouse Museum,** 3829 Church Rd. (© **410/313-1413**). Open Sunday from 1 to 4pm.

You can wander the grounds and enjoy the views of the river valley at the **Patapsco Female Institute Historic Park,** 3691 Sarah's Lane (© **410/465-8500;** www.patapsco femaleinstitute.org), which preserves the ruins of a 19th-century school for young ladies. It's open Sundays from 1 to 4pm, April through October; tours are available.

Just down Frederick Road—called Main Street in the historic district—is **Benjamin Banneker Historical Park and Museum,** 300 Oella Ave. (© **410/887-1081**). Dedicated to the first African-American "man of science," the modern museum has interactive exhibits about Banneker, who surveyed the land for construction of Washington, D.C. The park has lots of green space and nature trails. Open Tuesday through Saturday from 10am to 4pm; a $3 donation is suggested. Take Frederick Road east across Patapsco River bridge; turn left at Oella Avenue.

SHOPPING

Antiques and gift shops line Main Street and the side streets. Hours are generally 10am to 6pm; many stores are closed on Monday or Tuesday.

For antiques, stop at **Cottage Antiques,** 8181 Main St. (© **410/465-1412**); **Joan Eve,** 8013 Main St. (© **410/750-1210**); and **Taylor's Antique Mall,** 8197 Main St. (© **410/465-4444**). For home decorating, look in **Su Casa,** 8098 Main St. (© **410/ 522-7010**), and **What's in Store,** 8307 Main St. (© **410/750-2468**).

Ellicott's Country Store, 8180 Main St. (© **410/465-4482**), is worth a visit for the architecture—it's considered the oldest duplex in the country. Handcrafted gifts are featured at **Discoveries,** 8055 Main St. (© **410/461-9600**).

The **Forget-Me-Not Factory,** 8044 Main St. (© **410/465-7355**), is filled with magic wands, fairy wings, collectibles, and costumes. The **Stillridge Herb Shop,** 8129 Main St. (© **410/461-9266**), sends its own magic into the air: Lavender, rosemary, and dried fruits tumble from baskets outside the shop.

HAVRE DE GRACE

Havre de Grace—tucked up near the Mason-Dixon line, 28 miles northeast of Baltimore—is primarily a sailing town now, though it was once an important Colonial crossroads. If you're headed to or from Baltimore, this picturesque town makes an excellent stopping place, as it's known for its good restaurants, charming shops, lighthouse, and stunning views of the spot where the Susquehanna River becomes the Chesapeake Bay.

The area was originally home to the Susquehannocks, with the first European settlers arriving in 1658. It was called Harmer's Town in those days and soon became the location of a river ferry, which operated for 170 years. After the Revolutionary War, it adopted its current name from a suggestion by French soldiers who lovingly compared it to La Havre back home. This was a popular stop in the early 20th century, when a famous racetrack drew the likes of the legendary Seabiscuit, Man o' War, and Citation. Today, the town is much quieter, but it remains a crossroads: for the trains racing across the river, for the barges carrying stone down the bay, and for all the people speeding along I-95.

ESSENTIALS

GETTING THERE You could sail into Havre de Grace from the lower Chesapeake Bay. Most people, however, drive here. It's only 4 minutes off I-95 at Exit 89 (Rte. 155.) Take Route 155 east and go under the Route 40 bridge. Turn right on Juniata Street, left on Otsego Street, and right on Water Street, and you'll be heading into town along the water's edge. Parking is available on the street, at the parks and museums, and at each end of the promenade.

VISITOR INFORMATION The **Havre de Grace Tourism Commission** is at 450 Pennington Ave., between Union Avenue and Market Street (© **800/851-7756** or 410/939-2100; www.hdgtourism.com). Check the website for maps and sightseeing information. Or while you're on I-95, stop at the Chesapeake House visitor center for brochures. Wherever you stop, make sure you pick up a walking-tour guide and the handy museum guide.

SPECIAL EVENTS In early May, the **Re-enactment of the Attack on Havre de Grace in War of 1812** (© **410/942-5780**) takes place on the Lock House grounds. Mid-August brings the **Havre de Grace Seafood Festival** (© **410/939-1525**) to Tydings Park, featuring food, entertainment, auctions, and a crab-calling contest. On the weekend after Labor Day, the **Duck Fair** (© **410/939-3739**) celebrates wildlife art at the Havre de Grace Decoy Museum and grounds, with food, entertainment, and children's activities. **First Fridays,** from April to December, feature street performances and specials at restaurants and shops.

WHERE TO STAY

Since Havre de Grace is just down Route 40 from the Aberdeen Proving Ground, a military installation, there are plenty of nearby chain hotels, such as **Best Western** (© **410/679-9700**), **Days Inn** (© **410/671-9990**), and **Four Points by Sheraton** (© **410/273-1300**).

Currier House Location, location, location: This B&B is only a few steps from the promenade, lighthouse, and several museums. The 1790 farmhouse is filled with antiques reflecting the days when Havre de Grace attracted waterfowl hunters and racing fans. It's a homey place with a wide front porch, a cozy parlor, and a quiet backyard. The rooms are simply but comfortably furnished; two have balconies with water views.

800 S. Market St., Havre de Grace, MD 21078. © **800/827-2889** or 410/939-7886. www.currier-bb.com. 4 units. $95–$115 double. Rates include hearty "waterman's breakfast." AE, DISC, MC, V. Free parking. *In room:* A/C, TV/VCR, hair dryer, no phone.

The Old Chesapeake Hotel ★★ The owners have been busy turning old houses on their block into comfortable guest suites. The main building (formerly called the Crazy Swede) houses the restaurant (see "Where to Dine," below) and four suites. The inn also has rooms in nine other buildings, all on Union Avenue except for one on Girard Street. Though there's a nod to local history, the operative word here is comfort. The honeymoon suite has a 1700s brass bed and a whirlpool tub with a water view. Except for a handful of antiques, everything looks brand-new.

400 N. Union Ave., Havre de Grace, MD 21078. © **410/939-5440.** Fax 410/939-8020. www.oldchesapeakehotel. com. 30 units. $110–$185 double. Rates include continental breakfast. AE, MC, V. No children under 8. Children over 8 welcome in parent's room (up to 2 kids per room allowed); children over 16 can stay in own room. Free parking. **Amenities:** Room service from adjoining restaurant; high-speed Internet access. *In room:* A/C, TV, dataport, fridge, hair dryer, iron.

My, what an inefficient way to fish.

Ring toss, good. Horseshoes, bad.

Faster! Faster! Faster!

We take care of the fiddly bits, from providing over 43,000 customer reviews of hotels, to helping you find our best fares, to giving you 24/7 customer service. So you can focus on the only thing that matters. Goofing off.

✳ travelocity®
You'll never roam alone.℠

Spencer Silver Mansion ★★★ *Value*   This grand granite lady will take you back to Havre de Grace's gay '90s. From the wraparound porch to the 12-foot ceilings, the 1896 B&B offers an elegant yet warm welcome. All that heavy furniture and Victorian-style decor could be intimidating, but the innkeeper works hard to keep it cozy. Big windows give the bedrooms an airy feel; the Iris Room even has a whirlpool tub. A carriage house just past the garden has a sitting room, kitchenette, large bedroom with two window seats, and bathroom with whirlpool; it sleeps four.

200 S. Union Ave., Havre de Grace, MD 21078. © 800/780-1485 or 410/939-1485. www.spencersilvermansion.com. 5 units, 2 with shared bathroom. $85–$150 double. Rates include full breakfast. AE, DC, DISC, MC, V. Free parking. Pets accepted. **Amenities:** Parlor with TV/VCR, stereo, and guest fridge. *In room:* A/C, TV/DVD, Wi-Fi.

Vandiver Inn   This sprawling Victorian mansion, built in 1886, is on the National Register of Historic Places. Its location puts it right on tree-lined Union Avenue and only 2 blocks from the water. The bedrooms come in all sizes—some can even be connected to create a suite. The spacious honeymoon suite has a gas fireplace, four-poster bed, and whirlpool tub. Two guesthouses offer a little more privacy.

301 S. Union Ave., Havre de Grace, MD 21078. © 800/245-1655 or 410/939-5200. Fax 410/939-5202. www.vandiver inn.com. 17 units. $99–$149 double. Rates include full breakfast. AE, DISC, MC, V. Free parking. No children under 6. *In room:* A/C, TV, Wi-Fi, fridge, hair dryer, iron.

WHERE TO DINE

Ken's Steak and Rib House SEAFOOD/STEAKS   The three dining rooms are intimate, with a quiet and dignified atmosphere. The bar is quite small, with no TV. At dinner, the emphasis is on beef and ribs, with several chicken and seafood dishes—though the lunch menu is more casual, with sandwiches, salads, and burgers. The extensive wine list has about 280 bottles. A Sunday breakfast buffet is also offered.

400 N. Union Ave. © 410/939-5440. www.oldchesapeakehotel.com. Reservations strongly recommended. Main courses $6.95–$13 at lunch, $11–$20 at dinner; Sun breakfast buffet $9.95. AE, MC, V. Mon–Sat 11am–9pm; Sun 10am–9pm.

MacGregor's Restaurant and Tavern ★★ SEAFOOD   Set high above the water, MacGregor's boasts a view from every table. Food is served out on the deck as well as in the two-tiered dining room at lunch, dinner, Sunday brunch, and weekday happy hour. The menu is heavy on seafood items like crab dip, crab cakes, and lobster fettuccine; the Dijon-encrusted rockfish filet has won awards. This casual spot with brick walls and duck prints is a place for fun—there's live music on Fridays and Saturdays, as well as Sundays in summer.

331 St. John St. © 800/300-6319 or 410/939-3003. www.macgregorsrestaurant.com. Reservations suggested for dinner. Main courses $5.95–$14 at lunch, $15–$15 at dinner. AE, MC, V. Mon–Thurs 11am–9pm; Fri–Sat 11am–11pm; Sun 10am–9pm.

St. John Gourmet DELI   Operated out of the same building as the well-regarded Laurrapin Grille, this carryout spot offers a wide variety of salads, appetizers, sandwiches, and entrees. Selections range from crab cakes to powerhouse wraps.

210 St. John St. © 410/939-3663. www.stjohngourmet.com. Reservations not accepted. Lunch and dinner items $3.50–$18. Mon–Thurs 11am–8pm; Fri–Sat 11am–9pm.

Tidewater Grille ★★★ SEAFOOD/STEAKS   Be forewarned: You could get so caught up in the action out on the river and beyond, you might forget to eat. Trains race past on the nearby bridge, and sailboats and barges skim across the water. If you can get your mind back on the food, you're in for a treat: at lunchtime, crab cakes (with huge lumps, delicately seasoned and held together with almost too little filler), burgers, soups, salads, and sandwiches. At dinner, add prime rib, lamb chops, fresh fish, and the specialty, rich seafood au gratin. In pretty weather, eat on the deck under the awning or right in the sunshine—it's heaven.

300 Franklin St. ☎ **410/939-3313** or 410/575-7045. Reservations recommended for parties of 6 or more. Main courses $8.25–$13 lunch, $15–$26 dinner. AE, DC, MC, V Sun–Thurs 11am–9pm; Fri–Sat 11am–10pm.

WHAT TO SEE & DO

Lots of visitors to Havre de Grace come just for the water views—which you can see from the **promenade** ✿✿✿, the parks, and several restaurants. The **Millard E. Tydings Memorial Park** has room for a picnic, or you can bring your fishing rod to the **Frank J. Hutchins Memorial Park.** The half-mile promenade takes pedestrians (and bikers before 10am) on a route along the southeast edge of town. It starts (or ends) at the Concord Point Lighthouse and winds through wetlands and along the shore to Tydings Park. Along the way, you can stop at the Havre de Grace Decoy Museum or the Havre de Grace Maritime Museum.

The town boasts six small museums and historic sites: four in town and two on the outskirts. They take only an hour or two to walk through, and admission is downright cheap. In fact, an adult can visit all six for less than $20. Hours are limited to the weekends, except the decoy and maritime museums, which are open daily.

Concord Point Lighthouse ✿✿✿   This stout lighthouse at the headwaters of the bay has been watching over sailors since 1827—it's one of the oldest continuously operating lighthouses on the East Coast.

Concord and Lafayette sts., at north edge of promenade. ☎ **410/939-9040.** Free admission. Apr–Oct Sat–Sun 1–5pm. Closed major holidays.

Havre de Grace Decoy Museum ✿✿   Decoys are the star here, where the carved geese and ducks range from purely functional to fine art. The first-floor exhibits look at decoys as tools, while the second-floor decoys are exhibited as folk and even fine art. Don't miss the full-size figure of R. Madison Mitchell, one of the best-known carvers in this decoy-carving capital. The museum has re-created in 3-D a photo by the famous Baltimore photographer Aubrey Bodine.

215 Giles St. ☎ **410/939-3739.** www.decoymuseum.com. Admission $6 adults, $5 seniors, $2 children 9–18. Daily 10:30am–4:30pm. Closed Thanksgiving, Dec 25, Jan 1, and Easter.

Havre de Grace Maritime Museum   Exhibits here tell the story of Havre de Grace's maritime commerce, with most of the items donated by local residents—including a replica of a shad shack and original artifacts from the last 400 years of fishing and crabbing. The Susquehanna Flats Environmental Center offers ecology programs. The biggest attraction is the Chesapeake Wooden Boat Builders School, where students are taught how to build and restore the bay's wooden boats. Visitors can watch on Tuesdays from 6:30 to 9pm. Wooden sailboats, canoes, and other unfinished projects underway are also on display.

100 Lafayette St. ☎ **410/939-4800.** www.hdgmaritimemuseum.com. Admission $2 adults, $1 seniors and students. Guided tours $3 (reservations required). June–Aug daily 11am–5pm; Sept–May Wed and Fri–Mon 11am–5pm.

Rock Run Historic Area at Susquehanna State Park   Sure, this is a great park for hiking along the Susquehanna River, climbing the hills, and riding a bike or horse along the miles of paths through the forest—but the historic area is worth a visit, too.

It is best known for the Rock Run Grist Mill, built in 1794. Also of note are the Jersey Toll House (now an information center for the park), the Rock Run Mansion, and the Steppingstone Museum (described below).

Off Rte. 155, 3 miles northwest of Havre de Grace. © 410/557-7994. Free admission. Park daily 9am–sunset; historic buildings Sat–Sun Memorial Day to Labor Day.

Steppingstone Museum   Steppingstone, in Susquehanna State Park, celebrates the area's agricultural history with demonstrations of the rural arts from the turn of the 20th century. Visitors can see the 1771 farmhouse, blacksmith shop, carriage barn, general store, bar, and caning house. The farm is the site of a Civil War encampment in May, Scottish Festival in June, and Fall Harvest Festival in September.

461 Quaker Bottom Rd., off Rte. 155. © 888/419-1762 or 410/939-2299. www.steppingstonemuseum.org. Admission $2 adults, free for children 12 and under. May–Oct Sat–Sun 1–5pm.

Susquehanna Museum at the Lock House ⚓ *Kids*   This restored 1840 lock tender's home is now on the National Register of Historic Places. It sat at the end of the Susquehanna and Tidewater Canal, where the canal emptied into the river. The canal is no longer used, but the pivot bridge has been reconstructed so visitors can see how it worked. Inside the house are kitchen gadgets (which the kids can touch), a massive Steinway piano, a century-old bicycle with canvas tires, and even the last lock tender's wedding coat. You can also see changing exhibits and a video on the town's history. In early December, don't miss the candlelight boutique with gifts, wreaths, and food; it's part of the town's Christmas Candlelight Tour, held the second Sunday in December.

817 Conesteo St., at northern edge of town. © 410/939-5780. www.lockhousemuseum.org. Free admission. Thurs–Mon 1–5pm.

TOURS & BOAT RIDES

The *Martha Lewis* ⚓ (© 410/939-4078; www.skipjackmarthalewis.org), docked at Tydings Park, offers fun 75-minute rides on most weekends from May to mid-October. Summer visitors can learn about sailing one of the last skipjacks on the bay—the 46-year-old boat is still a working girl, spending her winters dredging for oysters in the Chesapeake Bay. Those interested in seeing a skipjack doing what a skipjack does best can take a dredging trip in November or December. Call ahead for reservations. The *Lantern Queen* (© 410/287-7217; www.lanternqueen.com) looks like it would be more comfortable on the Mississippi, but here it is, docked at Hutchins Park at the foot of Congress Avenue. Dinner cruises are offered Thursday and Friday nights at 6:30pm; reservations are required. Call for rates and sailing schedule.

SHOPPING

Havre de Grace's shops are about 7 blocks north of the promenade. Though it can be a pleasant walk along tree-lined Union Avenue or Market Street, it might be worth driving the short distance if it's a sultry day. Parking is free, but limited to 2 hours.

Antiques shops dot Franklin and Washington streets. **Bayside Antiques,** 230 N. Washington St. (© 410/939-9397), holds a wide variety of furniture in its 10,000 square feet, along with decoys for about $40. Decoy fans will definitely want to stop at **Vincenti Decoys,** 353 Pennington Ave. (© 410/734-7709), to see the numerous finely carved birds. The chocolates at **Bomboy's,** 329 Market St. (© 410/939-2939; www.bomboyscandy.com), are made right at the family-owned shop; homemade ice cream is sold at a second shop across the street. Both are closed Mondays.

OUTDOOR ACTIVITIES

BOATING   Havre de Grace has boat ramps at Millard E. Tydings Memorial Park, Frank J. Hutchins Memorial Park, and Jean Roberts Memorial Park. The launching fee is $5. **Tidewater Marine,** at the foot of Bourbon Street (© **410/939-0950**), has transient slips if you want to sail into town. Experienced sailors can charter a yacht from **BaySail** (© **410/939-2869;** www.baysail.net) for a weekend or a couple hours. It also has 3- to 5-day courses for everyone from beginners to advanced sailors.

HIKING   Trails through **Susquehanna State Park** offer pretty views of the Susquehanna River, as well as all those bridges crossing it. They're open to hikers, bikers, horseback riders, and cross-country skiers. If you go by way of the **Lower Susquehanna Heritage Greenway,** it's possible to walk the trail to the dam—which is quite a sight. The huge concrete dam holds back the mighty river, reducing it to a very shallow, rocky river bed.

6

Maryland's Two Capitals: Annapolis & St. Mary's City

Maryland's two capitals, present-day Annapolis and the state's first capital, St. Mary's City, are only 86 miles—and 3 centuries—apart. Both were founded by people seeking a place to practice their faith in a time of religious persecution.

Annapolis continues to thrive, but St. Mary's City disappeared. But the oldest city is reemerging, with archaeological digs and reconstruction of the town that was the first city of the colony.

While it's a state capital, Annapolis retains much of its Colonial heritage. The State House is where George Washington resigned as commander in chief and Congress ratified the treaty to end the Revolutionary War. More than 1,500 Colonial buildings are scattered along the narrow brick streets and alleys—more than in any other town in the country.

It's also a college town, home to the United States Naval Academy and to St. John's College, known for its "Great Books" curriculum.

Lawmakers meet in the General Assembly from January to April. Midshipmen march in "The Yard" every semester. And Marylanders arrive by land and sea year-round.

On most weekends, its streets bustle with packed restaurants, bars, and shops. Workboats still seek the shellfish for which the Chesapeake Bay is known. In spring, the pleasure boats arrive. Warm weather brings the festivities to the water's edge, and downtown takes on the air of a casual long-running party.

1 Orientation

ARRIVING

BY PLANE **Baltimore/Washington International Thurgood Marshall Airport** (© **800/I-FLY-BWI** or 410/859-7111; www.bwiairport.com) is 10 miles south of downtown Baltimore, off I-295 (the Baltimore–Washington Pkwy.). It's a major domestic and international hub. Domestic airlines serving Baltimore include **American** (© 800/433-7300), **Continental** (© 800/525-0280), **Delta** (© 800/221-1212), **Northwest** (© 800/225-2525), **Southwest** (© 800/435-9792), **United** (© 800/241-6522), and **US Airways** (© 800/428-4322).

To get to Annapolis from the airport, follow I-97 south to U.S. Route 50. Various exits will take you into town (although many chain hotels are right off Rte. 50). The Rowe Boulevard exit is the most direct one to the historic district. **SuperShuttle** (© **800/258-3826;** www.supershuttle.com) charges about $30 between BWI and Annapolis. A taxi is about $45 one-way; call **BWI Airport Taxi** at © **410/859-1103.**

BY CAR From Baltimore and points north, take I-695 (the Baltimore Beltway) to I-97 south to U.S. Route 50 east. Rowe Boulevard from U.S. Route 50 will take you into downtown. From Washington, D.C., take U.S. Route 50 east off the Washington Beltway (I-495) to Rowe Boulevard.

Parking can be a challenge in the historic district. Garages are located behind the visitor center off Northwest Street, on Duke of Gloucester Street behind City Hall, on Washington Street, and on South Street. You can also park at the Navy/Marine Corps Stadium, off Rowe Boulevard at Taylor Avenue, and ride the free downtown parking shuttle into the historic district (see "Getting Around," below).

BY BOAT   Docking at the Annapolis City Dock or moorings in the harbor are available on a first-come, first-served basis. Moorings cost $25 for boats under 45 feet. Dock fees are $6 an hour for boats up to 50 feet, $12 for bigger vessels. Electric is extra. Pay fees at the Harbormaster's Office on the City Dock. For information, call © 410/263-7973 or e-mail harbormaster@ci.annapolis.md.us.

BY BUS   Greyhound (© 800/231-2222; www.greyhound.com) offers service to 806 Chinquapin Round Rd. **Dillon's Bus Service** (© 800/827-3490 or 410/647-2321; www.dillonbus.com) runs commuter buses to D.C., with stops at the Navy/Marine Corps Stadium, Harry S. Truman Park & Ride, and West Street. It costs $4.25 one-way. The **Maryland Transit Administration** (© 800/543-9809 or 410/539-5000; www.mtamaryland.com) provides commuter bus service between Annapolis and Baltimore, as well as Washington, D.C., connecting to some of the MTA's Light Rail stops.

VISITOR INFORMATION

The **Annapolis and Anne Arundel Conference and Visitors Bureau** (© 410/280-0445; www.visit-annapolis.org) runs a visitor center at 26 West St., just west of Church Circle. Bus and walking tours (p. 139) depart from here daily. The volunteers will make recommendations and reservations for tours, dinner, and accommodations. Open daily from 9am to 5pm. The bureau also runs an information booth at the City Dock during warm weather. Pick up a free copy of *Annapolis,* a visitors' guide with a good map of the downtown area. *Inside Annapolis,* a free bimonthly magazine listing local events and area businesses, is available at most restaurants and hotels.

CITY LAYOUT

The streets of downtown Annapolis radiate from two circles: **State Circle** and **Church Circle.** The three main streets are Main, Maryland, and West. Main Street leads from Church Circle to the City Dock. Maryland Avenue stretches from State Circle to the walls of the U.S. Naval Academy. West Street runs from Church Circle to routes 2 and 50. The U.S. Naval Academy, surrounded by a high, gray wall, is in its own enclave, east of downtown.

2 Getting Around

BY SHUTTLE   The **Annapolis Department of Parking and Transportation** (© 410/263-7964; www.annapolis.gov/transport) operates two free shuttles between the historic/business district and the parking area of the Navy/Marine Corps Stadium. The State Shuttle runs Monday through Friday from 6:30am to 8pm, Saturday and Sunday from 10am to 6pm; it departs every 5 minutes during rush hour, every 15 minutes the rest of the day, with stops at Church Circle, near the visitor center, and near the State House. The Navy Bus Shuttle operates May through September, leaving the

Navy/Marine Corps Stadium on the hour and half-hour every day. It stops at the Naval Academy's visitors' gate, Main Street, and West Annapolis locations.

BY BUS   Annapolis bus service can get visitors all around town, from the historic district to West Annapolis and the shopping centers near Route 50. Base fare is 75¢; exact change is required. Buses run every half-hour, Monday through Saturday from 5:30am to 7pm, Sunday from 8am to 7pm (Brown and Gold routes only). Get a schedule at www.annapolis.gov/transport.

BY CAR   Car-rental firms in Annapolis include **Budget,** 2002 West St. (© **410/266-5030**); **Discount,** 1032 West St. (© **410/268-5955**); and **Enterprise,** 1023 Spa Rd. (© **410/268-7751**).

Parking is limited in midtown Annapolis, where streets are narrow and much of the 18th-century layout is intact. Visitors are encouraged to leave their cars in a park-and-ride lot on the edge of town, off Rowe Boulevard just west of the Navy/Marine Corps Stadium, and then take the free shuttle (see above). Parking garages can be found behind the visitor center off Northwest Street, on Duke of Gloucester Street behind City Hall, on Washington Street, and on South Street. A new lot has opened on West Street. You can also try your luck at metered parking at the City Dock or on the street. Better yet, try the new valet parking at the City Dock—look for the red awning. It's available daily in summer, weekends in the off season. If you park on a side street, look for parking restriction signs; without a permit, parking is limited to 2 hours.

BY TAXI   Call **Annapolis Cab** (© **410/268-0022**) or **Yellow Checker Cab** (© **410/268-1212**).

BY WATER TAXI   The **Jiffy Water Taxi** (© **410/263-0033**) operates from the City Dock to restaurants and other destinations along Spa and Back creeks. You can also call for a water taxi, just as you would a land taxi, and get picked up from your boat or waterfront location. If you're at a restaurant, ask the waiter to call for a ride back. It's a handy way to avoid the parking hassle as well as a pleasant sightseeing experience. Fares range from $1.50 to $4. Hours are Monday through Thursday from 9:30am to 11pm, Friday from 9:30am to 1am, Saturday from 9am to 1am, and Sunday from 9am to 11pm. Service is available in early May and in September and October.

FAST FACTS: Annapolis

American Express   The office is in the Annapolis Mall, on Bestgate Road (© **410/224-4200**). It's open Monday through Saturday.

Area Code   The area codes in Annapolis are **410** and **443**.

Emergencies   Dial © **911** for fire, police, or ambulance.

Hospitals   Go to **Anne Arundel Medical Center,** 2001 Medical Pkwy., Jennifer Road off Route 50 (© **443/481-1000**).

Liquor Laws   Places serving alcoholic beverages may stay open from 6am to 2am, except on Sunday and election days. The minimum age for buying or consuming alcohol is 21.

Newspapers & Magazines   The local daily newspaper is the *Annapolis Capital.* The *Baltimore Sun* and the *Washington Post* are also widely available. The leading monthly magazine is *Annapolis.*

Pharmacies Try **CVS,** 123 Main St. ((C) **410/295-3061**).

Post Office The main branch is at 1 Church Circle ((C) **410/263-9291**); open Monday through Friday from 9am to 5pm.

Taxes The local sales tax is 5%. The local hotel tax is an additional 7%.

3 Where to Stay

Downtown Annapolis offers a mix of big hotels, historic inns, and bed-and-breakfasts, while Eastport is blessed with several good B&Bs. Accommodations in the historic district are convenient but pricey. A number of more affordable chain hotels are located out on Route 50, a 15-minute ride or so to the historic district. These generally cost less and offer pools and larger rooms; some have shuttle service to downtown and Eastport. *Note:* All major hotels have rooms accessible for travelers with disabilities, but most inns and bed-and-breakfasts do not.

Special events—USNA's Parents Weekend in late summer and Commissioning Week in May, Army-Navy games, the Annapolis Boat Show in October, to name a few—send hotel prices skyrocketing.

EXPENSIVE

Annapolis Inn ★★★   It was good enough for Thomas Jefferson's doctor in the 18th century, and now it's perfect for a romantic getaway in the 21st century. The three bedrooms are separate and private. While the public areas are Georgian in decor, the private rooms are shrines to comfort, with plush beds, lush seating, and bathrooms with Jacuzzis and heated marble floors. There are no phones, televisions if you must, and wireless Internet access only if absolutely necessary. A three-course breakfast is served on china and crystal in the dining room and, in warm weather, on the intimate patio. Annapolis attractions are all quite close by. Want something more—perhaps a boat charter, in-room massage, string quartet, or cooking lessons? The innkeepers do what they can to make your stay just how you want it.

144 Prince George St., Annapolis, MD 21401. (C) **410/295-5200**. Fax 410/295-5201. www.annapolisinn.com. 3 units. $250–$475 double. Rates include full breakfast. AE, MC, V. Street parking only. *In room:* A/C, TV and Wi-Fi upon request.

Annapolis Marriott Waterfront ★★   The only waterfront hotel in Annapolis, and the only one with boat docks for guest use, this six-story property attracts boaters and boat-lovers. It sits in the town's best location, beside the City Dock overlooking "Ego Alley" and Spa Creek. Guest rooms are decorated in an elegant, contemporary style enhanced by floor-to-ceiling windows. About three-quarters of the rooms have water views or waterfront balconies; the rest overlook the historic district. Standard rooms are freshly renovated; some have Jacuzzis. Stop by the hotel's gallery to see the photographs and ship models, including *Old Ironsides* and the *African Queen.*

80 Compromise St., Annapolis, MD 21401. (C) **888/773-0786** or 410/268-7555. Fax 410/269-5864. www.annapolis marriott.com. 150 units. $219–$339 double; $259–$399 waterfront view. AE, DC, DISC, MC, V. Valet parking $17. **Amenities:** Indoor/outdoor restaurant and lounge; health club; boat dock; sun deck; 300-ft. waterfront walkway. *In room:* A/C, TV w/pay movies, high-speed Internet access, fridge and microwave upon request, coffeemaker, hair dryer, iron, robe.

Where to Stay & Dine in Annapolis

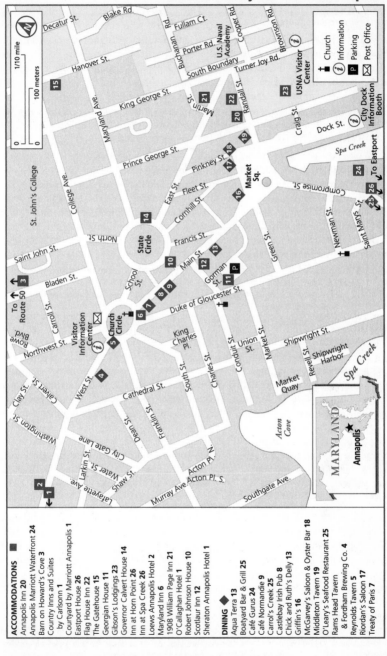

1/10 mile

100 meters

Church

(i) Information

P Parking

⊠ Post Office

U.S. Naval Academy

USNA Visitor Center

City Dock Information Booth

To Eastport

Spa Creek

Market Sq.

State Circle

Church Circle

Visitor Information Center

King Charles Pl.

Shipwright Harbor

Market Quay

Acton Cove

Spa Creek

MARYLAND

★ Annapolis

Decatur St.

Blake Rd.

Hanover St.

King George St.

Prince George St.

Pinkney St.

Fleet St.

Cornhill St.

Francis St.

Main St.

Gorman St.

Duke of Gloucester St.

Cathedral St.

Maryland Ave.

College Ave.

St. John's College

Saint John St.

Bladen St.

North St.

School St.

Carroll St.

Northwest St.

West St.

Calvert St.

Clay St.

Washington St.

Rowe Blvd.

To Route 50

Larkin St.

Water St.

City Gate Lane

Shaw St.

Dean St.

Franklin St.

South St.

Charles St.

Conduit St.

Union St.

Market St.

Green St.

Revell St.

Shipwright St.

Compromise St.

Newman St.

Saint Marys St.

Craig St.

Dock St.

Randall St.

Turner Joy Rd.

South Boundary

Porter Rd.

Fullam Ct.

Buchanan Rd.

Cooper Rd.

Brownson Rd.

Martin St.

East St.

Lafayette Ave.

Acton Pl.

Acton Pl. S.

Murray Ave.

Southgate Ave.

ACCOMMODATIONS ■

Annapolis Inn **20**
Annapolis Marriott Waterfront **24**
Barn on Howard's Cove **3**
Country Inns and Suites by Carlsonn **1**
Courtyard by Marriott Annapolis **1**
Eastport House **26**
Flag House Inn **22**
The Gatehouse **15**
Georgian House **11**
Gibson's Lodgings **23**
Governor Calvert House **14**
Inn at Horn Point **26**
Inn at Spa Creek **26**
Loews Annapolis Hotel **2**
Maryland Inn **6**
1908 William Page Inn **21**
O'Callaghan Hotel **1**
Robert Johnson House **10**
Scotlaur Inn **12**
Sheraton Annapolis Hotel **1**

DINING ◆

Aqua Terra **13**
Boatyard Bar & Grill **25**
Café Gurus **24**
Café Normandie **9**
Carrol's Creek **25**
Castlebay Irish Pub **8**
Chick and Ruth's Delly **13**
Griffin's **16**
McGarvey's Saloon & Oyster Bar **18**
Middleton Tavern **19**
O'Leary's Seafood Restaurant **25**
Rams Head Tavern & Fordham Brewing Co. **4**
Reynolds Tavern **5**
Riordan's Saloon **17**
Treaty of Paris **7**

Loews Annapolis Hotel ★★★ *Kids*   The Loews Annapolis is loaded with amenities (except for boat slips; see the Annapolis Marriott for those) and an exceedingly friendly staff. Located near Church Circle, within walking distance of the historic district, this modern six-story hotel has a redbrick facade, a tree-shaded courtyard entrance, and skylit public areas. Guest rooms, decorated in a yacht stateroom design, offer views of the skyline and historic area. Ask about packages for kids, grandparents traveling with children, or those who just need pampering.

126 West St., Annapolis, MD 21401. © 800/526-2593 or 410/263-7777. Fax 410/263-0084. www.loewshotels.com. 217 units. $139–$309 double; $239–$409 suite. AE, DC, DISC, MC, V. Valet parking $16, self-parking $11. Pets accepted. **Amenities:** Restaurant; bar; health club; plaza-level rooms. *In room:* A/C, TV w/pay movies, high-speed Internet access, fridge and microwave upon request, coffeemaker, hair dryer, iron.

O'Callaghan Hotel Annapolis   Farther down West Street from Loews is this stylish Irish-owned hotel. From the marble-floored lobby to the chic restaurant and lounge to the contemporary Euro-style furniture in the spacious guest rooms, O'Callaghan's whispers low-key luxury—it would be vulgar to shout it. Eight units have balconies, some with table and chairs. If you're here on business, note the large desks, Internet access, mini-safes big enough for a laptop, and extensive 24-hour business center. A shuttle bus will get you to and from the historic district.

174 West St., Annapolis, MD 21401. © 410/263-7700. Fax 410/990-1400. www.ocallaghanhotels-us.com. 120 units. $129–$290 double; $300–$400 suite. AE, DC, DISC, MC, V. Valet parking $15. **Amenities:** Restaurant; lounge; health club; business center. *In room:* A/C, high-speed Internet access, TV w/pay movies and video games, fridge upon request, coffeemaker, hair dryer, iron, minisafe.

MODERATE

Flag House Inn   The flags waving from the front porch offer a hint of who's staying here: The innkeepers fly the flags of their guests' home states or nations. This 1870s Victorian beauty, down the street from the Naval Academy's main gate, offers good-size rooms with either a king-size or two twin beds. Accommodations are well kept and bright, with a nice mix of modern and antique pieces. Every unit has a ceiling fan; front rooms have sound machines to soften the traffic noise outside. One room, decorated in lavender toile, is downright spacious. The innkeepers are proud parents of a 1999 USNA graduate, and the house is well located for visitors to the Naval Academy and the town itself. When you arrive, knock on the right-hand door.

24–26 Randall St., Annapolis, MD 21401. © 800/437-4825 or 410/280-2721. Fax 410/280-0133. www.flaghouse inn.com. 5 units (shower only). $150–$275 double. Rates include full breakfast. MC, V. Free parking. No children under 10. *In room:* A/C, TV, ceiling fan.

The Gatehouse   Right in the shadow of the Naval Academy, this brick town house combines Colonial style with modern conveniences. Often filled with USNA relatives, this B&B is most convenient to the Naval Academy but is still only a short walk from the historic district. It is far enough out of the way to be a bit quieter than places near Main Street. Accommodations are comfortable; the best units are the two minisuites, each with four-poster or sleigh bed, private sitting area, and bathroom. All come with fresh flowers, robes, and special soaps, as well as cookies and bottled water upon arrival. The deck offers a quiet place to relax in the sun or under the stars.

249 Hanover St., Annapolis, MD 21401. © 888/254-7576 or 410/280-0024. www.gatehousebb.com. 5 units, 1 with shared bathroom. $200–$330 double. Rates include full breakfast. 2-night minimum stay and higher rates required some weekends. Whole-house rentals available. MC, V. Street parking only. *In room:* TV.

Georgian House This B&B is in one of the oldest structures in Annapolis. Its charm is enhanced by the modern conveniences and the location. Walk through the back gate, and you're on your way down Main Street. Each unit has its own ambience: One room has a deck, one has a working fireplace, and another has a double shower.

170 Duke of Gloucester St., Annapolis, MD 21401. (✆ 800/557-2068 or 410/263-5618. www.georgianhouse.com. 4 units. $160–$220 double. Rates include full breakfast. AE, MC, V. Street parking only. **Amenities:** Video/book library; microwave; fridge on 2nd floor. *In room:* TV/VCR, Wi-Fi.

1908 William Page Inn In a town that lives and breathes Colonial style, here's a Victorian marvel, all cedar shake and wraparound porch. The first-floor bedroom has direct access to the porch; the quietest unit has a private bathroom with shower and whirlpool; and the attic suite (with whirlpool, chaise, and couch) is far enough away that guests can disappear for days—and some do. Breakfast, served in the comfortable common room, is always tempting.

8 Martin St., Annapolis, MD 21401. (✆ 800/364-4160 or 410/626-1506. www.1908-williampageinn.com. 5 units, 2 with shared bathroom. $140–$250 double. Rates include full breakfast. MC, V. Free off-street parking. *In room:* TV upon request (standard in attic unit), CD player, no phone (but all rooms wired for phones and modems).

INEXPENSIVE

Barn on Howard's Cove Just a few minutes out of town, visitors can stay in a converted 1850 horse barn. But this isn't just a barn—it's a refuge. It's a little hard to find, set back on a driveway and perched on a quiet cove. A stone fireplace dominates the common room. Climb the spiral staircase to two delightful rooms—one with a queen-size bed and pullout loveseat, the other with a queen-size bed, sleeping loft, and sitting room with balcony overlooking the water. In the hall is a kitchenette with fridge, microwave, coffeemaker, and video library. You can relax on the deck or in the gazebo, or launch a canoe and go exploring. Breakfast is served on the deck or in the solarium. If this place is booked but you want to stay on Howard's Cove, ask about **Meadow Garden,** a neighboring B&B with two rooms and a pool.

500 Wilson Rd., Annapolis, MD 21401. (✆ 410/571-9511. 2 units. $125 double. Rates include full breakfast. No credit cards. Free parking. **Amenities:** Use of canoe and kayak. *In room:* A/C, TV/VCR.

Country Inn & Suites by Carlson (Kids) This might be the most comfortable choice for those with kids. Though not downtown, the family-friendly property has the advantage of being just off Route 50, across from the Westfield Shoppingtown—and the free shuttle will get you into town quickly. One-bedroom suites come with fridge, microwave, two TVs, and pullout sofa. King suites overlook the woods rather than the highway. The whirlpool suite has a fireplace. Call the hotel directly to reserve these suites and to ask about romantic getaway packages.

2600 Housley Rd., Annapolis, MD 21401. (✆ 800/456-4000 or 410/571-6700. Fax 410/571-6777. www.country inns.com. 100 units. $99–$199 double; $159–$222 suite. Rates include continental breakfast. 2-night minimum stay may be required on weekends in summer. AE, DISC, MC, V. Free parking. **Amenities:** Coffee and snacks available anytime in breakfast area; indoor pool; health club; complimentary shuttle to historic district; fax machine; laundry service; dry cleaning. *In room:* A/C, Wi-Fi, coffeemaker, hair dryer, iron, free local calls.

Courtyard by Marriott Annapolis In a quiet setting 5 miles west of the historic district, this three-story facility is a favorite with business travelers on weekdays and families on weekends. Newly renovated in 2005, the spacious rooms follow the usual Courtyard plan and come with a separate sitting area, sofa, and desk. Some units have balconies; suites have fridges and microwaves.

2559 Riva Rd. (near Harry S. Truman Pkwy.), Annapolis, MD 21401. ℂ **800/321-2211** or 410/266-1555. Fax 410/266-6376. www.marriott.com/bwian. 149 units. $109–$169 double. Children under 12 stay free in parent's room. AE, DC, DISC, MC, V. Free parking. **Amenities:** Breakfast buffet; indoor pool; health club; whirlpool; Wi-Fi in public areas. *In room:* A/C, TV w/pay movies, dataport, coffeemaker, hair dryer, iron.

Gibson's Lodgings *(Value)* Tucked on a side street, this three-building complex is a quiet choice, yet it's only a few steps from the City Dock. Two of the buildings are historic town houses: the Patterson (a 1760s Federal Georgian with two large bedrooms) and the Berman (an 1890s house with its own porch and eight bedrooms, one equipped for disabled guests). Behind them is Lauer House, a 1988 addition with six suites, full kitchen, and sitting room that can also be used as a conference room. Filled with both antiques and reproductions, the bedrooms are of varying sizes. A central garden and courtyard serve as a common area for all three buildings.

110 Prince George St., Annapolis, MD 21401. ℂ **877/330-0057** or 410/268-5555. Fax 410/268-2775. www.gibsons lodgings.com. 21 units, 4 with shared bathroom. $59–$119 double with shared bathroom; $99–$199 double with private bathroom. Rates include continental breakfast. AE, MC, V. Free courtyard parking. Entrance is in the courtyard. **Amenities:** Dataport in Patterson House parlor; Wi-Fi in Berman House parlor and in Lauer House guest rooms.

Scotlaur Inn *(Value)* The Scotlaur is the best value in the historic district. It's housed in the top two floors of a three-story brick building; the ground floor belongs to Chick & Ruth's Delly (see "Where to Dine," below). Bedrooms are of various sizes, with the larger ones in front. All accommodations were updated in 2005. Room no. 301 has the disadvantage of two flights of steep stairs, but it's large, bright, and looks out on Main Street—the best view in the inn. A parking garage is behind the inn, which is convenient, but makes the back rooms a bit noisy.

165 Main St., Annapolis, MD 21401. ℂ **410/268-5665**. www.scotlaurinn.com. 10 units. $89–$180 double. Rates for most rooms include full breakfast. MC, V. City parking garage right behind inn ($8/day). Pets accepted. *In room:* A/C, hair dryer, iron.

Sheraton Annapolis Hotel The Sheraton is just off Route 50, a block from the Westfield Shoppingtown. It's a short trip to downtown, and the hotel offers a shuttle to the historic district. The spacious rooms are your standard Sheraton variety.

173 Jennifer Rd., Annapolis, MD 21401. ℂ **800/325-3535** or 410/266-3131. Fax 410/266-6247. www.sheraton.com/annapolis. 196 units. $99–$259 double; $159–$299 suite. AE, DC, DISC, MC, V. Free parking. **Amenities:** Restaurant; bar; indoor pool; health club; Jacuzzi; business center; shuttle to historic district; club-level rooms. *In room:* A/C, TV/VCR w/pay movies, dataport, coffeemaker, hair dryer, iron, safe, fax.

HISTORIC HOSTELRIES

Historic Inns of Annapolis Clustered around the city's two key traffic circles, the Historic Inns of Annapolis hotels offer a taste of the historic. Some of the buildings have carved wooden banisters, wide porches, and in-room fireplaces (if you prefer a specific amenity, ask when making reservations); all underwent complete renovations in 2005. Although they are separate properties, the inns are run as a single entity, and all reservations are handled through a central office in the Governor Calvert House.

Governor Calvert House, 58 State Circle, is both a conference center and a hotel. The property is made up of several restored Colonial and Victorian residences; it has underground parking and 55 bedrooms furnished with antiques.

The flatiron-shaped **Maryland Inn,** 16 Church Circle, at Main Street, has been operating as an inn since the 1770s. As pretty as the public rooms are, its 44 bedrooms are cramped. The location and helpful staff make it a good choice, though.

Tips **Renting a Home Away from Home**

During USNA's Parents Weekend or Commissioning Week, many Annapolis homeowners clear out and rent their houses to the families of midshipmen. **Annapolis Accommodations** (© **800/715-1000** or 410/263-3262; www.stay annapolis.com) offers dozens of homes in the historic district and on the waterfront, within about 12 miles of downtown, for rental of a few days, a week, or longer. They range from one to five bedrooms. All are fully furnished, including linens and well-equipped kitchens; some have pools. Rates start at *phew!* and go to *wow!* (Luxury homes can go for as much as $750 a night.) House rentals are popular, with some dates, such as boat-show weekends, very much in demand, so if you're interested, book well in advance.

The **Robert Johnson House,** 23 State Circle, between School and Francis streets, overlooks the governor's mansion and the State House. It consists of three adjoining 1773 Georgian homes. The 30 artfully restored rooms have four-poster beds and antiques; each unit also has a private bathroom.

Historic Inns of Annapolis central office, 58 State Circle, Annapolis, MD 21401. © **800/847-8882** or 410/263-2641. Fax 410/268-3613. www.annapolisinns.com. 124 units in 3 properties. $139–$239 double; rates may be higher on holiday weekends. Rates are dependent on several factors—to get the best deal, call more than once and compare the prices you're quoted. AE, DC, DISC, MC, V. Valet parking $18. Check-in at the Governor Calvert House, where free shuttle service is provided to the other inns. **Amenities:** Restaurant; 2 bars (see "Where to Dine" below and "Annapolis After Dark," later in this chapter); coffee shop; complimentary coffee and tea; privileges at nearby health club; local shuttle van. *In room:* A/C, TV or TV/VCR, dataport, coffeemaker, hair dryer, iron.

ACROSS THE SPA CREEK BRIDGE

Eastport is gaining interest as a place to live and a place to play. For centuries, it was home to Annapolis's working people: watermen, boat builders, and those who worked downtown or at the Naval Academy. Sailing schools and marinas, a handful of comfortable B&Bs, and Restaurant Row—down Severn Avenue—are making this an attractive part of town for tourists. It's easy and friendly, and can be a lot of fun.

Eastport House ♣ This is the oldest standing house in Eastport, but it's been lovingly maintained. The owner has had fun decorating the bedrooms, but she hasn't forgotten any necessities. The third-floor rooms have two double beds but sleep only two, a guideline designed to keep everybody comfortable. Breakfast is served in the dining room, or guests can elect to sit on the broad side porch.

101 Severn Ave., Annapolis, MD 21403. © **410/295-9710.** www.eastporthouse.com. 5 units, 2 with shared bathroom. $130–$175 double. Rates include full breakfast. MC, V. Free parking. **Amenities:** Fridge; free use of bicycles. *In room:* A/C, TV, Wi-Fi.

Inn at Horn Point ♣ A 1902 house with a wraparound porch has been turned into a stylish B&B, filled with bright colors and bay windows. Rooms are named for Eastport's own Trumpy Yachts. While all are spacious, the king suite on the second floor has its own private porch, two-story-high sitting area with gas fireplace, and bathroom with claw-foot tub. The first-floor room, with roll-in shower, was specifically designed to be handicapped-accessible.

100 Chesapeake Ave., Annapolis, MD 21403. © **410/268-1126.** www.innathornpoint.com. 5 units. $129–$199 double; $169–$239 suite. Rates include full breakfast. MC, V required to guarantee room; check or cash only for final payment. Free parking. *In room:* A/C, TV on request, high-speed Internet access.

Inn at Spa Creek   For something modern, try this tall gray-and-teal B&B, conveniently located across from Carrol's Creek restaurant (see below). Three bedrooms share a two-story common area with fireplace and clerestory windows. The Garden View room has an antique bed, French doors to the terrace, and soaking bubble tub—something like a whirlpool. The Port Hole room is down six stairs from the main floor, apart from the rest of the house. Breakfast is served at the dining table on the top floor of the common area, at the breakfast bar, or out on the deck under the trees.

417 Severn Ave., Annapolis, MD 21403. ℭ **877/269-8866** or 410/263-8866. www.innatspacreek.com. 3 units. $160–$250 double. Rates include full breakfast. AE, DISC, MC, V. Free parking. *In room:* A/C, TV, Wi-Fi.

4 Where to Dine

You can eat in Annapolis at Colonial dining rooms, taverns, bistros, and waterside seafood houses. Many choice spots are located in the city's hotels and inns. For families and travelers on the go, a wide selection of fast-food and family-style eateries are clustered at the intersection of routes 50, 301, and 450, about 4 miles from downtown, near the Annapolis Shopping Plaza.

EXPENSIVE

Carrol's Creek ★★★ SEAFOOD   For the best views of the waterfront and Annapolis skyline, along with imaginative food, head for this sleek waterfront spot in Eastport. Seating is available in a windowed dining room and on an umbrella-shaded porch. Start with a bowl of cream of crab soup—it's one of Maryland's best. Though this is definitely a seafood place, the kitchen is quite adventurous—pairing salmon with Parmesan polenta, for instance. Arrive by water taxi for the full waterfront experience. Come at lunch for a sunny view and the same delicious food at a fraction of the price.

410 Severn Ave., Eastport. ℭ **410/263-8102.** www.carrolscreek.com. Reservations accepted only for indoor weekday lunches and dinners; call ahead for priority seating on weekends. Main courses $7.95–$14 lunch, $14–$33 dinner, $22 brunch. AE, DC, DISC, MC, V. Mon–Sat 11:30am–10pm; Sun 10am–10pm.

Middleton Tavern ★★ AMERICAN/SEAFOOD   Established in 1750 as an inn for seafaring men, this restaurant's patrons once included Washington, Jefferson, and Franklin. Restored and expanded, the City Dock landmark offers many seafood entrees, as well as steaks and chateaubriand for two. It's a nice mix of historic location and good food. At lunch, the menu includes pasta, fajitas, and sandwiches. A drink on the tavern's front porch is a favorite summer activity for both locals and visitors.

2 Market Space (at Randall St.). ℭ **410/263-3323.** www.middletontavern.com. Call ahead for priority seating. Main courses $5.95–$16 lunch, $14–$50 dinner. AE, DC, DISC, MC, V. Mon–Fri 11:30am–1:30am; Sat–Sun 10:30am–1:30am.

O'Learys Seafood Restaurant ★★ SEAFOOD   Just over the Spa Creek Bridge, this Eastport spot has been a local favorite for over 20 years. Come here for the freshest seafood, prepared to order and served in a swank, warm dining room. The menu

The Best Crab Cake in Annapolis?

Some feel you can find it at **Crab Cake Factory,** 1803 West St. (ℭ **410/626-9900**), open daily for lunch and dinner. Regulars rave about its crab cake, which is big and flavorful.

lists other options such as duck, pork, and filet mignon. Some find the main dining room noisy; if it bothers you, come on a weekday or ask to sit in the back room.

310 Third St., Eastport. ℂ **410/263-0884.** www.olearysseafood.com. Reservations strongly recommended. Main courses $24–$33. AE, DC, MC, V. Mon–Sat 5–11pm; Sun 5–10pm.

Treaty of Paris ⌖ AMERICAN   Centrally located in the Maryland Inn, this cozy dining room exudes an 18th-century ambience with its brick walls, Colonial-style furnishings, candlelight, and open fireplace. The eclectic menu offers such dishes as rack of lamb, stuffed rockfish, a nightly game special, and beef Wellington (always a wonderful choice). Sunday brunch is luscious.

At the Maryland Inn, 16 Church Circle. ℂ **410/216-6340.** Reservations recommended for dinner and Sun brunch. Main courses $6.95–$14 lunch, $20–$35 dinner, $24 brunch. AE, DC, DISC, MC, V. Mon–Sat 7:30–9am, 11:30am–2:30pm, and 5:30–9pm; Sun 10am–2pm and 5:30–9pm.

MODERATE

Aqua Terra ⌖ INTERNATIONAL   Tucked into a storefront on Main Street, this restaurant offers a sleek and modern atmosphere, with adventurous food to match. Don't look for everyday crab cakes here. The menu always has pasta, seafood, and meat choices. But expect the fresh and inventive, too—like grilled sea bass with Indonesian-spiced rice cake, herb-crusted Australian lamb, and vegan entrees as well. Not so hungry? Try the new tapas menu.

164 Main St. ℂ **410/263-1985.** www.aquaterraofannapolis.com. Reservations recommended. AE, MC, V. Mon 5:30–9pm; Tues–Thurs 11:30am–3pm and 5:30–10pm; Fri 11:30am–3pm and 5:30–11pm; Sat noon–3pm and 5:30–11pm; Sun noon–3pm and 5–9pm.

Boatyard Bar & Grill ⌖ AMERICAN   Big and airy by day, crowded and fun by night, locals love the Boatyard—and so do visitors. You can count on the old reliable appetizers, like crab dip and garlic mussels, as well as burgers and a delightful crab-cake sandwich served on ciabatta. Dinner focuses on seafood, plus a steak or two. Brunch is served Saturday and Sunday. There's live music on Thursdays.

Severn Ave. and Fourth St., Eastport. ℂ **410/216-6206.** Reservations not accepted. AE, DISC, MC, V. Daily 11:30am–10pm (Sat–Sun from 9:30am). Bar open daily until midnight.

Café Normandie ⌖ FRENCH   This rustic storefront in the heart of the historic district offers the tastes and atmosphere of a French country restaurant. From its hearty onion soup to the delicate baked Brie, every starter is a hit. Entrees include classics like shrimp Provençal and beef bourguignon. The menu continues to include the wonderful crepes that put this place on the map years ago. Check in advance for early-bird specials from 5 to 6:30pm. Breakfast is served weekends from 8am to noon.

185 Main St. ℂ **410/263-3382.** Reservations recommended for dinner on weekends. Main courses $7.50–$13 breakfast items, $8.95–$14 lunch, $13–$28 dinner. AE, DC, DISC, MC, V. Mon–Fri 11am–10:30pm; Sat 8am–11pm; Sun 8am–10pm. Closed daily 4–5pm.

Castlebay Irish Pub IRISH   In a town full of Irish pubs, here's one that stands out. The specialties are shepherd's pie, fish and chips, and corned beef and cabbage; the beef and lamb stews are exceptional. The lunch menu is lighter, with burgers and corned beef. A children's menu lists smaller portions of the traditional fare, chicken tenders, and a few pasta dishes. Fans of home-brews should try the Three Nuns Ale. Sunday brunch includes a full Irish breakfast. Irish and pop bands play 4 nights a week.

193A Main St. ℂ **410/626-0165.** www.castlebayirishpub.com. Reservations recommended for dinner. Main courses $5.95–$12 lunch, $8.95–$19 dinner. AE, DISC, MC, V. Mon–Sat 11am–midnight; Sun 10am–midnight.

Griffin's AMERICAN   Service is swift and attentive at this busy restaurant, in keeping with the rhythm of the rock music in the background. It has a long bar specializing in microbrews, plus two dining areas with vaulted ceilings, exposed-brick walls, mounted animal heads, and several dozen tightly packed tables. The menu changes regularly, but you're likely to find the signature Griffin's Seafood Pasta—mussels and clams in an herb-tomato broth over penne—as well as steak and chicken.

22 Market Space, City Dock. ℂ **410/268-2576.** www.griffins-citydock.com. Reservations accepted Mon–Thurs only. Main courses $8–$15 lunch, $15–$27 dinner. AE, DC, DISC, MC, V. Mon–Sat 11am–2am; Sun 10am–2am. Kitchen closes at midnight.

McGarvey's Saloon & Oyster Bar PUB FARE/SEAFOOD   When you need a good sandwich, cup of chowder, or burger to go with your beer, you can't beat McGarvey's. Two narrow rooms, both dominated by bars, are set with tiny marble-topped tables. Chicken- or crab-cake-topped Caesar salads, filet béarnaise, and oyster stew are served all the time. Heartier entrees, including steaks, salmon, and crab, come out at night. The specials are usually top-notch. Brunch is served on Sunday.

8 Market Space, City Dock. ℂ **410/263-5700.** www.mcgarveys.net. Reservations accepted Mon–Thurs only. Main courses $4.25–$13 lunch, $15–$26 dinner. AE, MC, V. Mon–Sat 11:30am–1am; Sun 10am–1am. Bar open until 2am.

Rams Head Tavern & Fordham Brewing Co. ⭒⭒ INTERNATIONAL   Come for dinner in one of the cozy brick-walled dining rooms, or a drink and appetizers on the wisteria-covered heated patio. On a summer evening, the front sidewalk is the place to be. The storefront pub/restaurant serves more than 170 beers—including seasonal selections from its microbrewery, the Fordham Brewing Company. It's also a venue for live entertainment (p. 144). The menu lists a few international dishes as well as burgers, steaks, sandwiches, traditional regional fare (like crab cakes), and lots of appetizers, including a wonderful crab dip.

33 West St. ℂ **410/268-4545.** www.ramsheadtavern.com. Reservations recommended for dinner. Main courses $7.50–$13 lunch, $9–$33 dinner. AE, DISC, MC, V. Mon–Sat 11am–2am; Sun 10am–2am. Meals served until 11pm; light fare until midnight.

Reynolds Tavern ⭒ TEA   After a day of visiting historic sites, why not enjoy teatime in a lovely Colonial-era tavern? It's a genteel affair: big aromatic pots of loose tea, luscious scones piled high with jam and cream, savory tea sandwiches, and sweets. Afternoon tea is served from 11:30am to 5pm. Need something more filling? Hearty sandwiches, salads, and cream of crab soup are also on the lunch menu.

7 Church Circle. ℂ **410/295-9555.** www.reynoldstavern.org. Reservations recommended. Main courses $6.95–$13 lunch, $6.95–$29 dinner; afternoon tea $8–$23. AE, DISC, MC, V. Daily 11am–5pm; Wed–Sun 5-10pm.

Riordan's Saloon AMERICAN   Riordan's serves traditional American cuisine, including penne platters, a grilled salmon BLT, and a crab-cake sandwich. The main bar and dining area, which seem to be busy all the time, are on the first floor. For a quieter setting, sit up on the second floor. Brunch is served on Sundays.

26 Market Space, City Dock. ℂ **410/263-5449.** www.riordans.com. Reservations not necessary. Main courses $7.95–$14 lunch, $8.95–$21 dinner. AE, DC, DISC, MC, V. Mon–Sat 11am–1:30am; Sun 10am–1:30am.

INEXPENSIVE

Annapolis Ice Cream Company *Value* ICE CREAM   Super-premium ice cream stars at this little shop on Main Street. It's all made on the premises, with flavors such as Maple Walnut, Key Lime Pie, and Blackberry Cobbler. The cobblers and pies are made here and then smashed into ice cream. Sundaes and shakes are also available.

196 Main St. ✆ **443/482-3895.** www.annapolisicecream.com. Reservations not accepted. Ice cream $1.25–$6. AE, DC, DISC, MC, V. Summer Sun–Thurs 11am–10pm, Fri–Sat 11am–11pm; shorter hours off season.

Cafe Gurus AMERICAN   Eastport's got great coffee. Eat in or carry out breakfast or a lunch sandwich with your cup of java. This place specializes in coffee, in the bean or the frozen blender drink.

601 Second St., Eastport. ✆ **410/295-0601.** www.cafegurus.com. Reservations not accepted. Main courses $2.50–$6. V. Mon–Fri 7am–3pm; Sat–Sun 7am–2pm.

Chick & Ruth's Delly *(Moments)* AMERICAN   An Annapolis tradition, this ma-and-pa establishment has been run by the Levitt family for 40 years. Sit wherever you like, and a waiter will take your order in the friendly deli/restaurant, famous for its sand-wiches named after political figures and local attractions. Platters, pizzas, salads, sun-daes, and shakes are also available. Breakfast is served all day.

165 Main St. ✆ **410/269-6737.** www.chickandruths.com. Reservations not accepted. Main courses and lunch items $2.25–$9.95. No credit cards. Mon–Tues 6:30am–4pm; Wed–Thurs and Sun 6:30am–10pm; Fri–Sat 6:30am–11:30pm.

5 Historic Annapolis

Annapolis's National Historic District has more than 1,500 restored and preserved buildings. Its narrow streets are best seen on foot. If your visit is short, make sure to see the **U.S. Naval Academy,** the **State House,** the **William Paca House & Garden,** the **Hammond–Harwood House,** and the **Chase–Lloyd House.** Enjoy the stroll down pretty Prince George's Street on your way to the Paca House—it's packed with striking homes from Annapolis's 3 centuries. Tours are offered from the visitor center if you'd rather not strike out on your own.

The **City Dock,** once the destination of merchant sailing ships, now attracts pleas-ure boats from near and far. Sightseeing boats, both gas- and wind-powered, offer cruises from spring to fall. The area around the City Dock has plenty of good restau-rants, bars, shops, and a summer theater.

U.S. Naval Academy ✮✮✮   Tucked behind Annapolis's historic district, standing proudly on the shores of the Severn River, the U.S. Naval Academy has been educat-ing future naval officers for more than 160 years. Visitors to "The Yard" can tour the grounds, see a sample midshipman's room, and view the newly restored crypt of John Paul Jones in the chapel undercroft.

Enter the Naval Academy on foot at Gate 1, at Randall and King George streets (the only cars allowed are those with handicapped or DOD stickers). Start your visit at the **Armel–Leftwich Visitor Center,** just beyond the Halsey Field House. Here you can see exhibits about midshipman life, watch an orientation film, and browse the gift shop. Look for exhibits on USNA graduates in space, including the Freedom 7 space capsule flown by alum Alan Shepard. Sign up for a tour to see Bancroft Hall, the largest dorm in the world, and the magnificent chapel that is graced with unusual win-dows—blue on the outside, stained glass inside. Security is tight, so guided tours are the only way to get around. These end at the naval history museum in Prebel Hall. Please note that the museum will be undergoing renovations in mid-2007.

Try to visit during **noon formation**—held in Tecumseh Court at 12:05pm Monday through Friday, weather permitting—when the midshipmen line up in front of Ban-croft Hall before marching in for the midday meal. **Commissioning Week,** usually held the third week in May, is a colorful time of full-dress parades, parties, and a demonstration by the Blue Angels. (Plan well in advance for housing during Commissioning Week).

Armel–Leftwich Visitor Center, 52 King George St. ✆ **410/263-6933**. www.navyonline.com. Free admission to grounds and visitor center (photo ID required for those over 16). Tours $7.50 adults, $6.50 seniors, $5.50 students. Visitor center Mar–Dec daily 9am–5pm; Jan–Feb daily 9am–4pm. Closed Thanksgiving, Dec 25, and Jan 1. Tours offered daily, usually between 10am and 2:30pm; schedules vary by day and season, so call ahead or check website before coming.

Annapolis Maritime Museum Pummeled in 2003 by Hurricane Isabel, this tiny Eastport riverfront museum reopened in October 2005. The museum is based in two buildings, the McNasby Oyster Company building and the Barge House. The McNasby exhibit, fittingly enough, is "Oyster on the Half Shell," the story of the bivalve and the people who harvest them. The Barge House exhibit focuses on the Thomas Point Light and includes a 15-minute film.

Second St. and Back Creek. ✆ **410/295-0104**. www.annapolismaritimemuseum.org. Free admission; donation suggested. Sat 11am–5pm; Sun noon–4pm.

Banneker–Douglass Museum This museum focuses on African Americans of the Chesapeake region from 1633 to the Civil Rights movement. Named after two prominent local residents, astronomer/inventor Benjamin Banneker and abolitionist Frederick Douglass, the museum doubled in size in 2005, adding new gallery space.

84 Franklin St. (off south side of Church Circle). ✆ **410/216-6180**. www.bdmuseum.com. Free admission. Tues–Sat 10am–4pm.

Charles Carroll House Built in 1721 and 1722, and enlarged in 1770, this is the birthplace and home of Charles Carroll of Carrollton, the only Catholic to sign the Declaration of Independence. It sits on high ground overlooking Spa Creek, a block from City Dock. Visitors can tour the house, the 18th-century terraced boxwood gardens, and the 19th-century wine cellar.

107 Duke of Gloucester St. (behind St. Mary's Church at Spa Creek). ✆ **410/269-1737**. www.charlescarrollhouse. com. Admission $5 adults, $4 seniors, $2 children 12–17. Mar–Oct Sat 10am–2pm; Sun noon–4pm and by appointment. Closed Easter.

Chase–Lloyd House ✸✸ Home of Samuel Chase, a signer of the Declaration of Independence, this historic home (built from 1769–74) is outstanding for its brilliant interior design. Only the first-floor rooms are on view, as the house continues to be a home for retired women. It's also a good deal, at $2 for the house and garden tour. But hours are quite limited, so plan ahead if you want to see it.

22 Maryland Ave., at King George St. (across from Hammond–Harwood House). ✆ **410/263-2723**. Admission $2. Mon–Sat 2–4pm. Because docents are sometimes unavailable, call ahead to confirm.

Hammond–Harwood House ✸✸✸ If you see only one historic house in Annapolis, make it this one. A five-part classic Georgian home quite unlike the Paca mansion, it has semi-octagonal wings and carved moldings. The architecture, by William Buckland, is stunning. On exhibit are furniture, silver, and decorative arts from the last 3 centuries. The fine-arts collection, which includes works by the various Peales, is one of Maryland's finest. The collection of 18th-century items, including furniture by John Shaw, handicrafts, and textiles, is not to be missed. There are also some children's things and a few "modern conveniences" of the Colonial period.

19 Maryland Ave. (northeast of State Circle, at the corner of King George St.). ✆ **410/263-4683**. www.hammond harwoodhouse.org. Admission $6 adults, $3 children 6–17. Tours Apr–Oct Wed–Sun noon–4pm on the hour (last tour

Annapolis Attractions

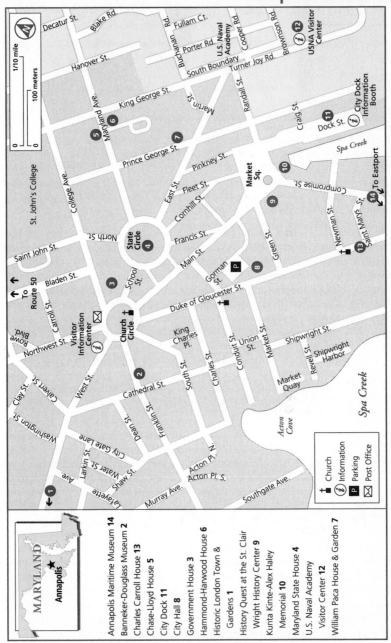

Annapolis Maritime Museum **14**
Banneker-Douglass Museum **2**
Charles Carroll House **13**
Chase-Lloyd House **5**
City Dock **11**
City Hall **8**
Government House **3**
Hammond-Harwood House **6**
Historic London Town & Gardens **1**
History Quest at the St. Clair Wright History Center **9**
Kunta Kinte-Alex Haley Memorial **10**
Maryland State House **4**
U.S. Naval Academy Visitor Center **12**
William Paca House & Garden **7**

4pm). Closed Nov–Mar except by appointment (call ext. 12) and for special events during Christmas season; check website for schedule.

HistoryQuest at the St. Clair Wright History Center

The Historic Annapolis Foundation's newest museum, located at the foot of Main Street, is a restored 1790s building. It will be home to exhibits that highlight the state capital's history, architecture, and culture. Hours and admission were not yet set at press time; call or check the website for information.

99 Main St. ✆ **410/267-7619**. www.annapolis.org. Call or check website for admission and hours.

Kunta Kinte–Alex Haley Memorial

As if frozen in time, a sculpture of Alex Haley reaches out to the Chesapeake Bay to tell the story of *Roots,* his best-selling novel, to a group of children sitting on the City Dock. This display not only memorializes Haley and his African ancestor Kunta Kinte, but also recalls an actual place where enslaved Africans arrived in the New World. The sculpture is accompanied by a series of engraved plaques that complete the story and the memorial.

City Dock. ✆ **410/841-6920**. www.kintehaley.org. Free admission. Daily 24 hr.

Maryland State House ★★★

The oldest state house in continuous use (it opened in 1779), the Maryland State House served as the U.S. Capitol from 1783 to 1784. George Washington came to the Old Senate Chamber here to resign as commander in chief of the Continental armies. The Treaty of Paris, ending the Revolutionary War, was ratified here. Today, Maryland's General Assembly still meets here from January to mid-April. Visit on your own or take a free tour at 11am or 3pm to see the old and new chambers, as well as changing exhibits. The State House dome, the only wooden one of its kind, is made of cypress beams held together by wooden pegs. The grounds, overlooking the city and shaded by old magnolias and evergreens, are a lovely spot for a break.

State Circle. ✆ **410/974-3400**. www.visitmaryland.org. Free admission. Building daily 9am–5pm. Visitor center Mon–Fri 9am–5pm; Sat–Sun 10am–4pm. Tours daily 11am and 3pm. Building closed Dec 24; visitor center closed Thanksgiving, Dec 25, Jan 1, and Easter.

William Paca House & Garden ★★★

The home of William Paca, a signer of the Declaration of Independence and a governor of Maryland, this estate was built between 1763 and 1765 and restored by Historic Annapolis. It's one of two such houses in town (another, the Brice House, is around the corner but isn't open to the public). The five-part structure is composed of a central block, flanked symmetrically with hyphens, and wings. The house tour offers a glimpse of life during Annapolis's "Golden Age." A new exhibit is the sick room, which recalls when a little girl was ill in the house. The kitchen is also undergoing restoration. The tour of the home lasts about 45 minutes, but make sure you leave time to walk around the 2 acres of formal gardens. The yard also has a pond crossed by a Chinese Chippendale bridge, plus a two-story summer house (climb to the top for a bird's-eye view of your surroundings).

186 Prince George St. ✆ **410/267-7619**. www.annapolis.org. House and garden tours $8 adults, $5 children 6–17. Mar–Dec Mon–Sat 10am–4pm, Sun noon–4pm; Jan–Feb Fri–Sat 10am–5pm, Sun noon–5pm. Tours offered on the half-hour. Closed Thanksgiving and Dec 25.

A SIDE TRIP TO LONDON TOWN ⍟

There are three reasons to set aside half a day to visit London Town: the 1760 house set high above the South River; the lush 8-acre gardens surrounding the property; and the ongoing archaeological research to uncover the lost buildings of this once thriving

Fun Fact **The Colors of Annapolis**

The Historic Annapolis Foundation has spent years identifying historic buildings throughout Annapolis. When a house meets the criteria, it receives a marker decorated with the Liberty Tree, a 400-year-old tree that once graced the grounds of St. John's College. The markers are different colors depending on the style of house, as follows:

Green   17th-century "vernacular," built 1681 to 1708

Terra cotta   18th-century "vernacular" or Georgian, built 1715 to 1800

Bronze   Georgian of national importance, built 1730 to 1800

Blue   Federal-style, built 1784 to 1840

Verdigris   Greek Revival, built 1820 to 1860

Aubergine   Victorian, built 1869 to 1901

Gray   19th- or 20-century Annapolis vernacular, built 1837 to 1921

Ocher   Distinctive homes of all styles built in the 20th century

seaport. Only remnants are left of one of Maryland's oldest towns. Although it was central to the state's trade with a busy ferry in the 1600s and 1700s, by the 1800s it was just a memory. Today, only the William Brown House remains.

The three-story brick mansion, now a National Historic Landmark, is worth a look for its 18th-century furnishings and its tavern, which covers much of the first floor. Don't miss the antique clock (with only an hour hand), leather water buckets, and prints by Elizabeth Blackwell. Children will like the basement, with its toys, clothes, and hats helping them "get into" the 18th century. Knowledgeable docents lead tours on the hour, tailoring their presentation to the ages of their guests.

In the gardens, native plants, wildflowers, and hollies cover 8 acres overlooking Almshouse Creek and the South River. Don't miss the medicinal plants and kitchen garden directly behind the house.

Reconstruction around the house is ongoing. Archaeologists have discovered a number of buildings, including a tobacco barn, along with several homes from the vanished village. They continue to sift through the soil, looking for clues about tavern life, the townspeople, and the lives they lived.

Historic London Town & Gardens (© **410/222-1919;** www.historiclondontown. com) is open year-round, except major holidays, Tuesday through Saturday from 9am to 5pm and Sunday from noon to 4pm. Guided house and self-guided garden tours cost $7 for adults, $5 for seniors, and $3 for children 7 to 12. A house-only tour or self-guided garden tour is $4. Between January and March, call ahead to arrange a tour.

To get here, take U.S. 50/Md. 301 to Exit 22, Aris T. Allen Boulevard. Exit onto Route 2 South, go over the South River Bridge, and continue ½ mile. Turn left onto Mayo Road, go ¾ mile, and turn left onto Londontown Road. Go 1 mile to the end of the road and enter the site through the gates.

6 Organized Tours & Cruises

WALKING TOURS

To hit the high points in town, take a **Historic Annapolis Walk.** Visitors carry digital audio wands, which are highly customizable to enable you to go to places of the most personal interest. Tours can focus on African-American Heritage, the Civil War, and other topics. They're available only at the **Historic Annapolis Museum Store,** 77 Main St. (© 410/268-5576; www.annapolis.org), Sunday through Thursday from 10am to 8pm, Friday and Saturday from 10am to 10pm. The tours last about 2 hours.

Annapolis Tours (© 410/268-7601; www.annapolis-tours.com) are led by guides in Colonial costume. Tours of the historic district, which include the Naval Academy, last 2 hours and don't require reservations. From April through October, they depart daily at 10:30am from the visitor center at 26 West St. and at 1:30pm from the City Dock information booth. (If you take a morning tour, guides try to get you to the Naval Academy in time for the midshipmen's noon formation.) From November through March, there is only one tour a week, Saturday at 1:30pm, departing from the City Dock information booth. The price is $11 for adults and $6 for children under 18. (*Note:* Picture ID is required for those over 16 to gain access to the Naval Academy and State House.) Other options include Ghost Tours on October evenings and Candlelight Strolls on December evenings; check the website for a schedule.

The **U.S. Naval Academy Walking Tours** depart from the Armel–Leftwich Visitor Center of the U.S. Naval Academy, Gate 1, King George and Randall streets (© **410/ 263-6933;** www.navyonline.com), daily except Thanksgiving, Christmas, and New Year's Day. In July and August, tours depart every half-hour. From September through November and April through June, tours depart every hour Monday through Friday, and every half-hour Saturday and Sunday. From December through March, tours are offered as needed. The schedule varies a lot, so call ahead or check the website before coming—or sign up when you get to the visitor center. The price is $7.50 for adults, $6.50 for seniors, and $5.50 for students. Bring picture ID.

TOURS BY BUS, TROLLEY, CARRIAGE & SEGWAY

Discover Annapolis Tours, 31 Decatur Ave. (© 410/626-6000; www.discover-annapolis.com), offers 1-hour trolley or coach tours of the city and outlying areas. An air-conditioned 25-passenger trolley takes visitors through the historic district—by the State House, the Chase–Lloyd House, the Hammond–Harwood House, and St. Johns College, to name a few—and some areas not covered by the walking tours: Eastport, the Charles Carroll House, and the Severn River Scenic Overlook. Tours operate daily April through November, departing from the lot behind the visitor center at 26 West St. Limited tours are scheduled December through March. The cost is $15 for adults, $7 for children 11 to 15, $3 for children 10 and under (free for preschoolers).

Annapolis Carriage, 77 Main St. (© 410/349-1660; www.annapoliscarriage.com), offers 20-minute carriage rides throughout the day. The coachman points out areas of interest and gives a brief history for up to four riders (six with kids). Reserve online, by phone, or in person. Tours cost $20 per person, or $80 for a private ride. Hours vary by season; check the website for a schedule.

Segs in the City, 42 Randall St. (© **800/SEGS-393;** www.segsinthecity.net), enables visitors to explore the historic district on two-wheel Segways. Guided 1- or 2-hour tours cost $45 to $70. Trained riders can rent Segways for $50 to $150. *Note:* Not every Annapolitan is thrilled with these things traveling on the busy and uneven brick sidewalks of the historic district.

CRUISES & BOAT TOURS

Watermark Cruises ⨂, at the City Dock (© 410/268-7600; www.watermarkcruises. com), offers excursions along Annapolis Harbor and beyond. Choices include a

40-minute kid-friendly narrated cruise aboard the *Harbor Queen* that covers the highlights of Annapolis Harbor, the U.S. Naval Academy, and the Severn River; a 40-minute tour aboard the *Miss Anne* of the Eastport waterfront along Spa Creek and the Naval Academy shore; a 90-minute Thomas Point Lighthouse Cruise on the Severn River; and a Day-on-the-Bay excursion to St. Michaels. The new *Lady Sarah* offers bay lighthouse cruises. Prices range from $8 to $16 for adults, $4 to $8 for children 3 to 11. Sailings are daily from Memorial Day to Labor Day, with abbreviated schedules in spring and fall.

Annapolis by Boat (© 443/994-2424; www.annapolisbyboat.com) offers more intimate trips for up to six people. Call for the daily schedule, which may include a lighthouse tour, lunch by boat, Eastport peninsula tour, Wednesday-night race cruise, sunset cruise, and trip by boat to St. Michaels. Tours last 90 minutes to 6 hours and cost $30 to $125 a person.

7 Outdoor Activities

With the Chesapeake Bay and Severn River at its doorstep, Annapolis is the pleasure-boating capital of the eastern U.S. The city offers many opportunities to enjoy sailing and watersports, as well as other outdoor activities.

BIKING Though the streets are often too crowded for a leisurely excursion, just outside the city are several parks and paths for cycling. The **Baltimore and Annapolis Trail** (© 410/222-6244) is a smooth 13-mile asphalt route that runs from Annapolis north into the suburbs. Formerly a rail corridor, it's ideal for biking, walking, or meandering. It begins at Ritchie Highway, at the U.S. Route 50 interchange, and ends on Dorsey Road at Route 648 in Glen Burnie, where it connects with the 12.5-mile BWI Trail. The trail is open daily from sunrise to sunset.

Outside the city, on the South River and Harness Creek, **Quiet Waters Park** (© 410/222-1777) has 6 miles of biking/hiking trails with an overlook along the South River. A skating rink is set up in winter. The park is open Wednesday through Monday, 7am to dusk; you'll pay $5 per vehicle, $2 per handicapped vehicle.

Visitors who want to bike the Eastern Shore can cross the Chesapeake Bay using the Annapolis Transit system. Every Annapolis Transit bus, including the Kent Island commuter bus, has a bike rack. Buses leave Kent Island and Annapolis every weekday morning and return each evening. Fare is $1.50; the bike goes for free. Call © 410/263-7964 to be sure there's room on the bus and to confirm the return trip.

SAILING SCHOOLS & SAILING TRIPS Learn to sail at the oldest sailing school in America: the **Annapolis Sailing School,** 601 Sixth St. (© 800/638-9192; www.annapolissailing.com). With more than 50 boats and a huge support staff, this school offers a wide range of programs for novices and veterans, including **KidShip** for children 5 to 15. Options range from a weekend beginner course for $325 to a 5-day advanced course in preparation for bareboat (skipper-less) charters for $950 and up. Hotel packages are also available.

Womanship, 137 Conduit St. (© 800/342-9295; www.womanship.com), is a sailing program for women. Instruction levels range from "Chicken of the Sea" to advanced, in daytime or live-aboard settings. Learning cruises range from 2 to 7 days and from $495 to $2,275. There are courses for mothers and daughters, couples, families, and youths.

There are many other sailing schools in the area, so call around for one that best suits your needs. Try **Annapolis Sailing School** (© **800/638-9182;** www.annapolis sailing.com), **J World Annapolis** (© **800/966-2038** or 410/280-2040; www.jworld annapolis.com), and **Chesapeake Sailing School** (© **800/966-0032** or 410/269-1594; www.sailingclasses.com), which offers courses for families and teens on Back Creek.

The 74-foot schooners *Woodwind* and *Woodwind II,* 80 Compromise St. (© **410/ 263-7837;** www.schoonerwoodwind.com), depart from the Marriott side of the City Dock for 2-hour sailing trips several times daily, April through November. Departure times vary, so call or check the website. Sunset cruises have a different theme each day, such as a beer tasting or eco-tour. If you like sailboat racing, you can watch the Wednesday-night races aboard the *Woodwind.* Prices are $25 to $29 for adults, $23 to $27 for seniors, and $15 for children under 12. Special destination cruises, overnight trips, and bed-and-breakfast sails are also available.

SEA KAYAKING **Amphibious Horizons** (© **888/ILUV-SUN** or 410/267-8742; www.amphibioushorizons.com) offers 3-hour sunset kayak tours in the South River on Fridays at 6pm. The cost is $30 for adults, $20 for children 5 to 16. It also offers trips in creeks on both sides of the bay, as well as instruction and kayak rentals at Quiet Waters Park south of Annapolis. Preregistration is necessary for sunset paddles. Admission to Quiet Waters is $5 per vehicle; walk-ins and bike-ins are free.

WATERSPORT RENTALS & CHARTERS To charter a sailboat, contact one of the sailing schools or call **Sunsail** (© **800/327-2276;** www.sunsail.com). **South River Boat Rentals** (© **410/956-9729;** www.southriverboatrentals.com) rents both sail- and powerboats; it's south of Annapolis by the South River Bridge on Route 2.

8 Shopping

Shops in Annapolis are filled with all kinds of gifts and nautical-themed merchandise. Navy T-shirts, the classic souvenir, are everywhere. You could redecorate your house from the shops on Maryland Avenue alone. This town is picturesque in December— with greenery draped around every window and white lights on the trees, it's a delight- ful, old-fashioned place to buy those last-minute items. Finish your day with a drink at McGarvey's or a meal at one of the casual restaurants.

In the historic district, the main shopping streets are as follows: **Main Street,** which runs from Church Circle to the City Dock, has many apparel and gift shops. **Mary- land Avenue** has shops in the block just below the State House and State Circle where you might find home accessories and antiques. **West Street** has undergone extensive redevelopment, with lots of new shops and restaurants opening since 2004. The shops around the **City Dock** itself are mostly nautical in nature.

Most stores in the historic district are open Monday through Saturday from 10 or 11am to 5 or 6pm, Sunday from noon to 5pm. Many stay open until 8 or 9pm on Friday and Saturday.

At **Plat du Jour,** 220 Main St. (© **410/269-1499;** www.platdujour.net), you'll be convinced you've walked into Tuscany or Provence. It's filled with tableware, linens, toiletries, and a cookbook or two. Lovers of the Emerald Isle should head for **Avoca Handweavers,** 141–143 Main St. (© **410/263-1485;** www.avoca.ie), for its Irish clothes, linens, and decorative items.

Handmade pottery is available in several places. **American Craft Works,** 189B Main St. (© **410/625-1583**), features the handiwork of the League of Maryland

Craftsmen. The **Annapolis Pottery,** 40 State Circle ((C) **410/268-6153**), sells wares made on the premises; you can even watch the stock being made.

For home furnishings, head for Maryland Avenue. **Peake House,** 76 Maryland Ave. ((C) **410/280-0410**), sells new stuff, including Mottahedeh, Quimper, and Herend. **Hobson's Choice Antiques,** 58 Maryland Ave. ((C) **410/280-2206**), sells the old, including 18th- and 19th-century silver, porcelain, furniture, and model trains.

For artwork to hang on the walls, check out **McBride Gallery,** 215 Main St. ((C) **410/267-7077**; www.mcbridegallery.com), or the juried exhibits at **Circle Gallery,** 18 State Circle ((C) **410/268-4566**). For something most definitely nautical, check out **Annapolis Marine Art Gallery,** 110 Dock St. ((C) **410/263-4100**; www. annapolismarineart.com). Over in Eastport, Howard L. Rogers carves teak boat signs and has a good collection of marine paintings at his **Raven Maritime Studio,** 130 Severn Ave. ((C) **410/268-8639**).

For gifts and collectibles, stop by the **Annapolis Country Store,** 53 Maryland Ave. ((C) **410/269-6773**; www.annapoliscountrystore.com); it has Pooh, Raggedy Ann, and Curious George items, plus fine scented gifts. You can get the **Christmas Spirit** at 180 Main St. ((C) **410/268-2600**) year-round. Pick up your Navy T-shirt at **Peppers,** 133 Main St. ((C) **800/254-NAVY** or 410/267-8722; www.navygear.com), or **Fit to a Tee,** 107 Main St. ((C) **410/268-6596**). Jewelry that combines elegance with nautical themes is a reality at **LaBelle Cézanne,** 117 Main St. ((C) **410/263-1996**).

MALLS & MARKETS

Annapolis Harbour Center   West of downtown at the junction of routes 2 and 665, this shopping center is laid out like a maritime village, with more than 40 stores, services, and fast-food eateries, as well as nine movie theaters. Open daily. 2512A Solomons Island Rd. (C) 410/266-5857. www.annapolisharbourcenter.com.

Pennsylvania Dutch Farmers' Market   This market is run by Amish and Mennonite families from Lancaster County, Pennsylvania. Wares range from sausages and pickles to organic produce, as well as homemade jams, fudge, cakes, pies, and soft pretzels, all ideal for a picnic or snack. Handmade quilts are available in a crafts section. Open Thursday from 10am to 6pm, Friday from 9am to 6pm, and Saturday from 8:30am to 3pm. 2472 Solomons Island Rd., opposite Annapolis Harbour Center. (C) 410/573-0770 or 410/573-0775.

Westfield Shoppingtown Annapolis   Situated off Route 50 between West Street and Bestgate Road, this mall has five department stores (including Nordstrom and Lord & Taylor), more than 175 specialty shops, a big food court, and 11 movie theaters. Open daily. 2002 Annapolis Mall (Bestgate Rd.). (C) 410/266-5432. www.westfield.com/annapolis.

9 Annapolis After Dark

Annapolis is a town of small venues. Most local bars feature live music on weekends— everything from pop to classic rock to blues and funk—and there are a few good local theater companies as well.

For up-to-date listings of concerts and other area events, check the Friday "Entertainment" section of the *Capital* newspaper. *Inside Annapolis,* a bimonthly publication distributed free throughout the city, provides a summary of upcoming events. The visitor center gives out seasonal event calendars as well.

BARS & CLUBS

Armadillo's This place offers a variety of live entertainment—jazz, blues, funk, classic rock, acoustic rock, and oldies—every night except Monday. Music usually starts at 9:30pm. 132 Dock St. ✆ **410/280-0028.** Cover around $3 Fri–Sat only.

49 West Coffeehouse, Winebar & Gallery ✿ A welcome addition to Annapolis nightlife, 49 West is located a block west of Rams Head Tavern. This coffeehouse/wine bar features live classical, jazz, and folk music every night. 49 West St. ✆ **410/626-9796.** www.49westcoffeehouse.com. Cover $6–$20.

Jazz at the Powerhouse Shows are held the fourth weekend of every month, except July and August, in a building adjacent to the Loews Annapolis Hotel. It's small, friendly, and has good music. 126 West St. ✆ **410/269-0777.**

McGarvey's Saloon McGarvey's, O'Brien's, and Riordan's, all near the City Dock, make up Annapolis's most happening nightspot. McGarvey's doesn't have live music, but draws a crowd for its oysters and beer (see p. 134 for a review). It even has its own private-label Aviator Lager. The place is loud, friendly, and fun. 8 Market Space. ✆ **410/ 263-5700.** www.mcgarveyssaloon.com.

O'Brien's Oyster Bar & Grill O'Brien's, near the City Dock, has live music nightly starting at 10pm, except Fridays when it starts at 5:30pm. 113 Main St. ✆ **410/268-6288.** www.obriensoysterbar.com. Cover $5 Thurs–Sat (free for ladies on Thurs).

Pusser's Landing The entertainment here is the boat traffic: Boaters motor up "Ego Alley" to show off their craft at the City Dock, only to turn around and head back into the harbor. Spend a summer evening on the deck with one of the specialty rum drinks. Pusser's also serves meals all day. At the Annapolis Marriott Waterfront, 80 Compromise St. ✆ **410/268-7555.** www.annapolismarriott.com.

Rams Head Tavern ✿✿✿ The Rams Head has become the top nightspot in town, hosting such acts as Crystal Gayle and Little Feat. Dinner and show packages are available. The audience usually ranges from young adult to middle-aged; you must be 21 or over. 33 West St. ✆ **410/268-4545.** www.ramsheadtavern.com. Cover varies; advance ticket purchases recommended.

Riordan's Saloon Popular with the post-college crowd, Riordan's aims to be the friendly neighborhood bar, and it is. With six TVs, if there's a game on, you can expect the usual cheers and moans. 26 Market Space. ✆ **301/261-1524.** www.riordans.com.

THE PERFORMING ARTS

The town's largest venue, the **Maryland Hall for the Creative Arts** ✿, 801 Chase St. (✆ **410/263-5544** or 410/269-1087; www.mdhallarts.org), presents performances by the Annapolis Symphony Orchestra, the Annapolis Opera, the Annapolis Chorale, and the Ballet Theater of Maryland, as well as national acts. Check out the calendar of events online. Performances are nightly at 7 or 8pm; tickets are $15 to $50.

The **Colonial Players,** 108 East St. (✆ **410/268-7373;** www.cplayers.com), stages five plays per year in a 180-seat theater-in-the-round. Shows are Thursday through Saturday at 8pm, Sunday at 2:30 or 7:30pm. Ticket prices are $10 to $15.

In summer, there are several outdoor concert series and theater productions. The **Naval Academy Summer Serenade** (✆ **410/293-0263**), held weekly at the City Dock, features the USNA groups Next Wave, the Electric Brigade, and the concert band. Concerts are free, but bring your own seating. Since 1966, the **Annapolis Summer Garden**

Theatre ✝✝, 143 Compromise St., across from the City Dock (☎ **410/268-9212;** www.summergarden.com), has staged two musicals and a comedy with local talent. Reservations are encouraged; tickets cost about $15 for adults and $12 for students and seniors.

10 Around the Capital Beltway

Baltimore, Annapolis, and Washington form a triangle filled with suburbs and small towns, connected by state roads, interstates, and beltways. The attractions below are easy day trips from Baltimore or Annapolis, though they are closer to the District of Columbia. Going counterclockwise around the Capital Beltway:

Six Flags America *Kids*   Roller-coaster fans, pay attention. Six Flags has some awesome coasters: the Joker's Jinx, Superman, and Typhoon Sea Coaster, which sends its riders through the dark and into water. Unfortunately, the lines are awesome, too. During peak times, waits can be as long as an hour. Take a break and go to Paradise Island Water Park, where the wave pool, water slides, and Outback Beach House will cool you off. *Note:* The park requires visitors to go through metal detectors. Don't take anything valuable—you'll have to put down your bags for some of the rides and to go in the water. Prices are discounted during the Halloween season's Fright Fest.

13710 Central Ave., Mitchellville. ☎ 301/249-1500. www.sixflags.com/america. Admis" $40 adults, $29 seniors and those with disabilities, $30 children (54" and under), free for kids 3 and under. Parking $10. Apr–May and Sept to early Oct Sat–10am–6pm; Memorial Day to Labor Day daily 10:30am–6pm or later. Closed mid-Oct to Mar. From Washington, D.C., take I-495/I-95 to Exit 15A to Rte. 214 east; the park will be on the left in 5 miles. From Baltimore and points north, take I-695 to I-97 south (Exit 7), then Rte. 3/301 south to Rte. 214 west to the park, 3 miles on the right. From Annapolis, head south on Rte. 3/301 to Rte. 214 west to the park.

Historic Savage Mill   This restored 1822 cotton mill has all kinds of antiques shops, as well as galleries, boutiques, and a couple of places to stop for refreshment. It's an interesting place that keeps its heritage alive by using the names of the buildings' original purposes in all signs and maps. Bonaparte Breads is in the Spinning Building. In the Carding Building and Old Weave Building, you can find Irish goodies, antique jewelry, furniture and dolls, handmade sweaters, needlework supplies, and something for your sweet tooth. It's easy to spend a day here.

8600 Foundry St., Savage. ☎ 800/788-6455. www.savagemill.com. Mon–Wed 10am–6pm; Thurs–Sat 10am–9pm; Sun 11am–6pm. Closed Thanksgiving, Dec 25, and Easter. Off Rte. 32 to Rte. 1 south. Turn right at Howard St. and follow the signs.

Brookside Gardens   It's just 50 acres, but it's a gem. The top draws are the conservatories with their tropical plantings and the summertime butterfly show, but don't overlook the rose and aquatic gardens, or the children's Fairy Folk Garden. The serenity of the Japanese Tea House is something you'll remember. Paths are accessible for wheelchairs and strollers, and some wheelchairs are available at the visitor center. There's no picnicking, but take your lunch to neighboring **Wheaton Regional Park,** 2000 Shorefield Rd. (☎ **301/680-3803**), which has lots of trees and playgrounds.

1800 Glenallan Ave., Wheaton. ☎ 301/962-1400. www.brooksidegardens.org. Free admission. Gardens daily sunrise to sunset; conservatories daily 10am–5pm; visitor center daily 9am–5pm. Closed Dec 25. From I-270 and points west, take Exit 4A, Montrose Rd. east, which turns into Randolph Rd. Go 7 miles and turn right onto Glenallan Ave. From I-495, the Capital Beltway, take Exit 31A (north on Georgia Ave./Rte. 97) toward Wheaton. Drive 3 miles north on Georgia Ave. to Randolph Rd. and turn right. At the second light, turn right onto Glenallan Ave. Park at the visitor center at 1800 Glenallan Ave. or at the conservatories at 1500 Glenallan Ave.

Clara Barton National Historic Site ⟨★⟩ ⟨*Finds*⟩   The Red Cross was everything to its founder, Clara Barton. At her Glen Echo home, the closets are filled with blankets, lanterns, and other supplies for disaster relief. Her office is no-nonsense, including her chair: She cut off the back so she wouldn't rest while working. The 1891 home is a quirky thing, its design unusual inside and out, but as you wander through the rooms that sheltered Clara and her staff, you'll get to know more about the woman who made this her mission and her life. You can see the entire house in a short, fascinating visit. The guides are great with kids and never fail to keep them interested.

5801 Oxford Rd. (at MacArthur Blvd.), Glen Echo. ⟨✆⟩ **301/492-6245.** www.nps.gov/clba. Free admission. Daily 10am–5pm; by guided tour only (given on the hour; last tour at 4pm). Closed Thanksgiving, Dec 25, and Jan 1.

Glen Echo Park   Combine a visit to Clara Barton's house with a trip to this cultural arts park—it's just across a parking lot. First a Chautauqua meeting ground and then an amusement park, its emphasis on the arts continues today. Call ahead for an up-to-date schedule. You can stop here to picnic or to ride on the hand-carved Dentzel carousel, built in 1921.

7300 MacArthur Blvd., Glen Echo. ⟨✆⟩ **301/492-6229.** www.nps.gov/glec. Free admission; tickets required for carousel; event ticket prices vary. Carousel May–Sept Wed–Thurs 10am–2pm; Sat–Sun noon–6pm.

C&O Canal Museum at Great Falls of the Potomac ⟨★⟩   This is *the* stop on the Chesapeake & Ohio Canal. The wheelchair-accessible Olmsted Island Boardwalk runs through woods to a bridge overlooking one branch of the falls, then to the overlook where the falls crash over the rocks. The boardwalk is crowded on nice days, but when you get to the falls, you'll have plenty of space to take in the view. The strenuous Billy Goat Trail is a first-rate hike. The mule-drawn *Canal Clipper* was damaged beyond repair in 2003, but fundraising is ongoing for a new canalboat, which could be on the water in 2006 or 2007.

11710 MacArthur Blvd., near Falls Rd. (Md. Rte. 189), Potomac. ⟨✆⟩ **301/767-3714** or 301/299-3613. www.nps.gov/choh. Park entry fee $5 per vehicle, $3 for walk-ins. Admission valid for 3 days. Daily 9am–4:45pm. Take Exit 41W off I-495.

11 Solomons ⟨★⟩

For more than 100 years, Calvert County—with Solomons as its centerpiece—has been a Baltimore–Washington playground. Largely agricultural, the area is becoming much more a Washington suburb, but its nearby parks, local history, outdoor activities, and marine sports continue to attract visitors.

Solomons, also known as "Solomons Island" for the island that makes up its center, is dominated by water. It's an island at the end of two peninsulas formed by the Patuxent River, Back Creek, and Mill Creek (the Patuxent's mouth into the Chesapeake is visible from the town's southern end). The island is connected to land by a bridge so short that if you blink, you'll miss it, but you'll still feel surrounded by water. A walk through town will take you past sailboats and charter fishing boats, as well as watermen's homes, the century-old Drum Point Lighthouse, and Solomons's wide public pier, the place to see beautiful sunsets over the Patuxent.

ESSENTIALS
GETTING THERE   Solomons is at the southern tip of Calvert County. Maryland routes 2 and 4 merge and run north–south across the county. To reach Solomons from

Washington, D.C., and points south, take I-95 to the exit for Route 4 south; follow Route 4 all the way to Solomons. From Annapolis and points north, take the exit for Route 4 south off U.S. Route 50; follow Route 2–4 to Solomons.

VISITOR INFORMATION Contact the **Calvert County Department of Economic Development,** Courthouse, Prince Frederick (© **800/331-9771** or 410/535-4583; www.ecalvert.com). In Solomons, stop by the information center at the base of the Governor Thomas Johnson Bridge, on Route 2–4 (© **410/326-6027**).

WHERE TO STAY

Back Creek Inn ✿✿ Housed in an expanded blue 1880 waterman's house, this inn offers travelers a relaxing stay in a waterfront setting. The innkeepers have decorated the place with antiques, quilts, flowers, and original paintings. From the cozy sitting room, you can watch boats drift by on the Back Creek. The Lavender Room is a small cottage with a Jacuzzi, fireplace, and screened porch overlooking the creek. The Tansy, Chamomile, and Peppermint rooms also enjoy water views.

210 Alexander Lane (at Calvert St.; P.O. Box 520), Solomons, MD 20688. © 410/326-2022. Fax 410/326-2946. www.backcreekinnbnb.com. 7 units. $105–$160 double; $160 suite; $210 cottage. Additional guests $25. Rates include full breakfast. MC, V. No children under 12. **Amenities:** TV; outdoor Jacuzzi (in season); bikes; picnic baskets (requires 48 hr. notice). *In room:* A/C, Wi-Fi, coffeemaker (in suites and cottage), hair dryer.

Comfort Inn Beacon Marina This two-story hotel is geared toward nautical enthusiasts as well as regular travelers. The complex includes a 187-slip marina with 40 covered slips. Guest rooms are clean, comfortable, and have been modernized throughout; some have Jacuzzis. Best of all, guests can open the windows to enjoy the breezes off Back Creek.

255 Lore Rd. (P.O. Box 869), Solomons, MD 20688. © 800/228-5150 or 410/326-6303. Fax 410/326-9492. www.comfortinn.com. 60 units. $99–$139 double. AE, DC, DISC, MC, V. Rates include continental breakfast. **Amenities:** Waterfront restaurant and bar; pool; hot tub; 187-slip marina. *In room:* Wi-Fi, fridge, microwave, coffeemaker, hair dryer, iron.

Holiday Inn Select Solomons ✿ The biggest hotel in Solomons is a standard Holiday Inn, but the rooms are comfortable and a good size. Many units have views of the marina, particularly on the second floor or above and on the southern ends of the hotel's guest wings.

155 Holiday Dr. (off Rte. 4; P.O. Box 1099), Solomons, MD 20688. © 410/326-6311. Fax 410/326-1069. www.solomonsmd.hiselect.com. 326 units. $129–$139 double; $169–$219 suite. AE, DISC, MC, V. **Amenities:** Water-view restaurant; dockside bar; outdoor pool; tennis courts; health club; sauna; volleyball courts; 90-slip marina; business center; executive-level rooms. *In room:* A/C, Wi-Fi, coffeemaker, hair dryer, iron.

Solomons Victorian Inn ✿ Known locally as the Davis House, this Victorian inn is decorated with antiques and reproductions. It has four public spaces: living room, sitting room, library, and glassed-in porch (where breakfast is served). All but one of the bedrooms enjoy a view of Back Creek Harbor or the Patuxent River. The third-floor Solomons Sunset suite features a king-size bed, microwave and galley area, whirlpool tub, and great views of the harbor on two sides. Two luxurious suites in the Carriage House have private entrances, whirlpool tubs, and harbor views.

125 Charles St. (P.O. Box 759), Solomons, MD 20688. © 410/326-4811. Fax 410/326-0133. www.solomonsvictorian inn.com. 8 units. $100–$225 double. Rates include full breakfast. 2-night minimum stay required on holidays and event weekends. AE, MC, V. No children under 13. **Amenities:** Massage available. *In room:* A/C, TV, Wi-Fi.

WHERE TO DINE

C. D. Cafe, Inc. AMERICAN   Everybody around here recommends the C. D. Cafe. People crowd into the bright, cozy spot for the rich assortment of things like savory cheesecake (walnut crust filled with herbed cheeses); Cajun shepherd's pie; and breast of chicken topped with pecans, apples, and an apple-schnapps glaze. Lunchtime salads are creative and tasty—try the curried chicken. Brunch is served on Sundays.

Behind the cafe is the **Next Door Lounge,** a laid-back place to get light fare and drinks. Open Tuesday through Friday from 4:30 to 11pm, Saturday and Sunday from 2:30 to 11pm.

Avondale Center, 14350 Solomons Island Rd. ✆ **410/326-3877.** Reservations not accepted. Main courses $4.25–$14 lunch, $8.25–$21 dinner. MC, V. Daily 11:30am–2pm and 5:30–9:30pm ('til 9pm Sun).

Solomons Pier SEAFOOD   This casual restaurant, jutting out into the water, has views of the soaring bridge and Patuxent River to accompany its fresh seafood. New owners took over after Hurricane Isabel demolished the deck in 2003; construction was ongoing through winter 2005. The new dining room has big windows overlooking the river. The menu has a new look, too, with lots of casual fare: soups, salads, sandwiches, and plenty of appetizers including a gooey crab pretzel. Entrees run from the expected crab cake to a wasabi-glazed tuna, quite unusual for these parts. If you're not hungry, get a drink and toast another sunset. Local musicians play folk or country music Friday and Saturday nights from March through October.

14575 Solomons Island Rd. ✆ **410/326-2424.** Reservations accepted only for large parties. Main courses $6.25–$20. DISC, MC, V. Mon–Thurs 11:30am–9pm; Fri–Sat 11:30am to around midnight.

ATTRACTIONS

Annmarie Garden on St. John   Where else can you go for sculpture, sylvan solitude, and art-filled bathrooms? This 30-acre retreat, now affiliated with the Smithsonian Institution, features some 20 pieces of sculpture on loan from the Hirshhorn Museum. Visitors are welcomed by the *Tribute to the Oyster Tonger,* with other sculptures installed along the walking path. Rest on one of the benches designed by local children, enjoy the 113 varieties of azaleas, and don't miss those bathrooms!

13480 Dowell Rd., off Rte. 4. ✆ **410/326-4640.** www.annmariegarden.org. Free admission. Daily 9am–5pm.

Calvert Marine Museum and Drum Point Lighthouse ★★★ *Kids*   In a state brimming with maritime museums, this is the best. It has exhibits on local industry and the environment, fossils from nearby Calvert Cliffs (see "Outdoor Activities," below), a lighthouse, and even an otter to visit. The sea-horse exhibit is intriguing—who knew they live in the bay? The Discovery Room will have kids digging for fossils and learning a little history while having fun. Then there's the Drum Point Lighthouse, one of three remaining screw-pile lighthouses on the Chesapeake. (Thomas Point Lighthouse still operates near Annapolis, and the Hooper Strait Light is the centerpiece of the Chesapeake Bay Maritime Museum on the Eastern Shore.) You can build a little boat or take a cruise on the bugeye *Wm. B. Tennison.*

Shuttle-bus tours ($3), available daily from June to August, head to the Cove Point Lighthouse, the oldest continuously operating lighthouse in the state. Nearby is the J. C. Lore and Sons Oyster House, which has exhibits on Patuxent watermen and "deadrise" workboat building. Admission is free; it's open June through August, daily from 10am to noon and 1 to 4:30pm, plus the same hours on fall and spring weekends.

Wine Tasting in Solomons

Just north of Solomons are two wineries, both small operations with limited bottling and even more limited hours. Those interested in the winemaking process will enjoy tasting the wares and talking to the winemakers.

Solomons Island Winery, 515 Garner Lane, Lusby (✆ **410/394-1933;** www. solomonsislandwinery.com), produces its own wines as well as Chapel Cellars wines, which are available in St. Mary's City. Tastings are by appointment only. To get here from Route 4, turn left on Monticello Lane and left again on Garner Lane; the winery will be on the right.

Cove Point Winery, 755 Cove Point Rd., Lusby (✆ **410/326-0949;** www. covepointwinery.com), has tastings every Saturday and Sunday from noon to 5:30pm, as well as by appointment. From Route 4, turn right on Cove Point Road.

14200 Solomons Island Rd. ✆ **800/735-2258** or 410/326-2042. www.calvertmarinemuseum.com. Admission $7 adults, $6 seniors, $2 children 5–12. Cruise tickets $7 adults, $4 children 5–12. Daily 10am–5pm. Closed Thanksgiving, Dec 25, and Jan 1. Limited docking available when visiting museum.

OUTDOOR ACTIVITIES
CHARTER FISHING ✿

Fishing is one of Calvert County's biggest draws. And for good reason: The bay waters here are filled (seasonally) with rockfish (striped bass), bluefish, Spanish mackerel, white perch, spot, croaker, flounder, sea trout, and black drum. Before you you're your trip, check with your charter-boat captain to find out what's in season.

Charter fishing is available in two ways: through organized operations and through loose affiliations of captains. It's easy to charter a boat either way. In the case of an organized operation, call the office, which will supply a boat. If all its boats are full, the company will contact a local captain and have him run the charter.

It works a little differently with captains' associations. In this case, you call a contact person for the association, usually one of the captains. If that captain has an opening, he will take you out on his boat. If he doesn't, he will arrange for another captain to take you out or give you the names of captains who might be available.

Remember to ask the captain what you'll need to bring. Most charters include fishing gear; some supply bait for free, and some don't. Bring a cooler to take your catch home. The mates on charter boats work for cash tips, which should be at least 15%. *Note:* With rising gas prices, charter captains expect higher prices in 2006.

In Solomons

Bunky's Charter Boats   Bunky's operates out of a well-stocked bait-and-tackle shop across from the walking pier on Solomons Island. It has a fleet of 10 charter boats, including one 48-foot headboat. Charter rates for up to six passengers on all boats except the *Marchelle* are $450 per half-day (6 hr.) and $550 per full day (8 hr.). Rates for six on the *Marchelle* are $500 per half-day and $600 per full day. There's a per-person charge of $60 for extra passengers. Fishing on a headboat costs $35 a person for 6 hours. Bunky's also rents 16-foot motorboats, but if you're not on a charter boat, you'll need a license to fish—which you can get here, too.

14448 Solomons Island Rd. S. ✆ 410/326-3241. www.bunkyscharterboats.com.

Solomons Charter Captains Association and *Fin Finder* Charters   The association runs many of its 40 boats out of the Calvert Marina Charter Dock, on Dowell Road (✆ **800/450-1775**). Eleven of the SCCA's boats can carry more than six people; some can carry as many as 40. Standard association rates are $500 to $600.

The *Fin Finder*, a 46-foot Chesapeake-style workboat, is Capt. Sonney Forrest's own charter boat. It carries up to 30 passengers. Rates for a full day start at $690. Cruise tours and packages are also available.

Solomons. ✆ 800/831-2702. www.fishsolomons.com or www.finfinder.com.

In Chesapeake Beach

Chesapeake Beach charters are very popular, with a fleet that takes passengers to waters filled with rockfish, blues, and flounder. To get here from Annapolis, take Route 2 south to Maryland Route 260 west, which ends just north of the harbor at Maryland Route 261. From Washington, D.C., take Route 4 west to Route 260 west and follow the directions above. It's about an hour north of Solomons.

Chesapeake Beach Fishing Charters   This association of charter captains has 15 boats. A half-day for six people costs $400; a full day goes for $550. There are evening outings and fishing trips as well.

Chesapeake Beach. ✆ 301/855-4665. www.chesapeakefishingcharters.com.

Rod 'N' Reel Charter Fishing   Rod 'N' Reel has a huge share of the charter-fishing operation in Maryland's portion of the Chesapeake. Charter rates for up to six people are $450 per 6-hour trip, $575 per 8-hour trip. Or get on a headboat for $45 per person; rod rentals are $5. Trips leave morning and evening.

4160 Mears Ave., Chesapeake Beach. ✆ 800/233-2080 or 301/855-8450. www.chesapeakebeachresortspa.com.

SPORTFISHING

Although charter fishing is this area's forte, there are also several choice locations for sportfishing, including **Bay Front Park,** in Chesapeake Beach; the **fishing pier** at Flag Pond Nature Park (see below); and **Solomons Fishing Pier,** under the Gov. Thomas Johnson Bridge (Rte. 4) in Solomons.

Bait and tackle are available at **Bunky's Charter Boats,** in Solomons (✆ **410/326-3241**); and **Rod 'N' Reel,** in Chesapeake Beach (✆ **301/855-8450**).

PARKS

Three good parks, located about 20 to 25 miles north of Solomons, are worth a walk in the woods. Two have trails finishing at the Chesapeake Bay.

Battle Creek Cypress Swamp Sanctuary   A quiet respite just off the main highway, this 100-acre sanctuary owned by the Nature Conservancy gives visitors the opportunity to walk among great bald cypress trees growing at their northernmost limit. A quarter-mile elevated boardwalk runs through a primeval environment of ferns, flowers, and 100-foot cypress. You might also spot frogs, turtles, crayfish, and raccoons. The nature loop is a good, nonstrenuous, and accessible walk.

Grays Rd., Prince Frederick. ✆ 410/535-5327. www.calvertparks.org/swamp. Free admission. Tues–Sat 10am–5pm; Sun 1–5pm. Closes a half-hour earlier in off season. Take Rte. 506 west from Rte. 2–4; turn left onto Grays Rd.; the sanctuary is ¼ mile on the right.

Calvert Cliffs State Park ✦   A 2-mile trail from the parking lot follows a brook as it travels down from the hills to a tidal marsh. It opens at a small beach on the Chesapeake Bay; on either side stand the 30-foot-tall Calvert Cliffs. These multicolored cliffs expose layers of sediment that were once at the bottom of a prehistoric ocean. As the winds and water erode them, they yield Miocene Era fossils. Though access to the bottom of the cliffs has been restricted, you can hunt on the beach for fossils and keep them.

9500 H. G. Trueman Pkwy., Lusby. ✆ **301/743-7613**. www.dnr.maryland.gov. Suggested donation $5. Daily dawn–dusk. Take Rte. 301 south to Rte. 4. Turn left on Rte. 765 (about 14 miles south of Prince Frederick). Follow signs to the park entrance.

Flag Pond Nature Park   This park, just north of the Calvert Cliffs Nuclear Power Plant, has several trails to the beach, through the freshwater ponds, and to the northern edges of Calvert Cliffs.

Off Route 4. ✆ **410/586-1477** or 410/535-5327. www.calvertparks.org/flagpond.htm. Admission Apr–Oct $4 per vehicle for Calvert residents, $6 per vehicle for nonresidents; Nov–Mar $3 per vehicle. Memorial Day to Labor Day daily 9am–6pm; rest of year Sat–Sun 9am–6pm.

Jefferson Patterson Park & Museum   Archaeology is the main attraction at this park north of Solomons. Home to the Maryland Archaeological Conservation Laboratory and its library, the park also has a visitor center, with changing exhibits on local archaeological finds, and the Riverside Trail, a 1-mile hike through Maryland history from Native American times.

10515 Mackall Rd., St. Leonard. ✆ **410/586-8500**. www.jefpat.org. Free admission. Apr 15–Oct 15 Wed–Sun 10am–5pm. From Rte. 4, turn west on Rte. 264 to Rte. 265 (Mackall Rd.)

12 St. Mary's County: Where Maryland Began

The Free State got its start here in 1634 where the Potomac River meets the Chesapeake Bay. It's a lovely but remote peninsula, still dotted with tobacco barns and laced with rivers and creeks. Lexington Park, the county's biggest town, is the home of the Patuxent River Naval Air Station. Most visitors come to St. Mary's County for the fishing or to see St. Mary's City, the state's first capital.

It's a long, lovely drive down Route 5—although pockets of suburbia are popping up all over. It's a quicker trip, though not as pretty, down Route 4. St. Mary's County makes an easy day trip from Annapolis, Washington, or Baltimore. Or combine a visit to St. Mary's with a stay in Solomons for a quintessential Chesapeake Bay vacation.

ESSENTIALS

GETTING THERE   Maryland routes 5 and 235 run the length of St. Mary's County, providing access to all the major sites of interest. You can get to Route 5 from I-495 (the Washington Beltway). From Annapolis, take Maryland Route 50 to Route 301 to Route 4 to Solomons and across the Gov. Thomas Johnson Bridge; it will intersect with Route 235 a few miles past the bridge. For a more scenic drive, take Route 50 to Route 301 to Route 5 all the way to St. Mary's City—a slow and meandering route. St. Mary's City is 86 miles from Annapolis, 69 miles from Washington, D.C., 101 miles from Baltimore, and 173 miles from Wilmington.

VISITOR INFORMATION   **St. Mary's County Tourism Office,** 23115 Leonard Hall Dr., Leonardtown (✆ **800/327-9023** or 301/475-4200, ext. 1404).

DISCOVERING MARYLAND'S FIRST CAPITAL

Historic St. Mary's City 🏆🏆🏆   St. Mary's was Maryland's capital city for a few years in the 17th century. In that time, the town and its people were responsible for some significant "firsts" for the state and the nation: The first laws establishing religious tolerance and separation of church and state were enacted; the first Catholic chapel in English America was established; and the first African American voted in a legislature. By the end of the 17th century, the capital had moved to Annapolis, and St. Mary's City began to disappear.

Though the buildings fell, they left the marks that have given archaeologists clues about the early Colonial town. Visitors can see a re-created early plantation, view the inns and public buildings, and visit a reproduction of one of the ships that brought the first Marylanders here. Allow at least 4 hours for your visit, wear comfortable shoes, and bring water, as it can get very hot and humid here.

Historic St. Mary's City is more archaeological dig than town. Once the town was abandoned, the area was developed as farmland, so lots of clues to the state's first city remain underground. The buildings that have been reproduced are small and simple—except for the State House—and look as they would have when this area was first settled. Guides will help you get a feel for 17th-century Maryland.

Once you arrive, stop at the **visitor center** to get the gear for the state-of-the-art audio tour, watch the introductory video, and see an exhibit that chronicles the rise and fall of St. Mary's City.

Don't miss the **State House** or **Godiah Spray's 17th-century tobacco plantation.** While the public building is formal, the plantation shows how hard life was for the early colonists. The house is simple, the fields rough.

The **Print Shop,** Maryland's first—and the first one south of Boston in the 17th century—is being reconstructed on its original site, and set to re-open spring 2006.

Smith's Ordinary, a reconstructed 17th-century inn, features a medieval-style fireplace and tiled inglenook. A second inn, **Farthing's Ordinary,** built in the 1600s, has prepackaged refreshments and drinks for sale to modern-day visitors.

Don't miss the site of the **Brick Chapel.** Archaeologists were surprised to discover three lead coffins here. Reconstruction of the church is well underway, with an exhibit nearby relating the archaeologists' discovery.

Walk down to the water to see the 76-foot *Dove,* a reproduction of the square-rigged merchant ship that brought some of Maryland's first settlers here in 1634. Children love to board the boat and talk with the costumed sailors.

Walking trails through woodlands and near the water stretch 3.5 miles and still recall how this area must have looked to early settlers.

Special programs are offered on **Maryland Day,** March 25; **Community and Trail Day,** in June (free admission and special events); **Tidewater Archaeology Dig,** in late June (when you can join the archaeologists); **Woodland Indian Discovery Day,** the weekend after Labor Day (with storytelling, Native American crafts, and exhibits); and **Grand Militia Muster,** in late October (a gathering of 17th-c. reenactment units).

🕿 800/SMC-1634. www.stmaryscity.org. Admission $7.50 adults, $6 seniors and students, $3.50 children 6–12. Audio guides $3. Mid-June to mid-Sept Wed–Sun 10am–5pm (all exhibits open). Early Mar to early June and late Sept to late Nov Tues–Sat 10am–5pm (all exhibits open), Sun 10am–5pm (only visitor center, exhibit hall, shop at Farthing's Ordinary, and museum grounds are open; admission reduced to $2 for adults, $1 for children). Jan–Feb Wed–Sun 10am–5pm (only museum grounds and shop at Farthing's Ordinary are open). From Rte. 4, turn left on Rte. 235 and right on Mattapany Rd. St. Mary's City will be ahead, across Rte. 5. From Washington, take Rte. 5 to St. Mary's City.

OTHER HISTORIC SITES

Sotterley Plantation (☆)   Check out this 1710 house, the only Tidewater plantation house still accessible to the public. In the 19th century, this was home to the
largest group of enslaved African Americans in the state. Restoration is ongoing at this
National Historic Landmark, but the house is fully furnished. Check the website for
a schedule of events, from wine festivals to ghost tours. *Note:* A dock is available; call
ahead if you're coming by boat. It's a 20-minute walk from the dock to the house.

44300 Sotterley Lane (off Rte. 245), Hollywood. (☎) 800/681-0850 or 301/373-2280. www.sotterley.org. Admission
to grounds $2. House tours $7 adults, $6 seniors, $5 children 6–12. Grounds year-round Tues–Sat 10am–4pm; Sun
noon–4pm. House tours May–Oct Tues–Sat 10am–4pm; Sun noon–4pm.

OUTDOOR ACTIVITIES

POINT LOOKOUT STATE PARK (☆)

At the tip of St. Mary's County, at the confluence of the Potomac River and the Chesapeake Bay, **Point Lookout State Park** ((☎) 301/872-5688) offers visitors a chance to
see both bodies of water at one time. The park's 1,046 acres offer a beach on the
Potomac, a fishing pier on the Chesapeake, Civil War monuments, docks for boating
and catching the cruise boat to Smith Island across the bay, and campsites and cabins.
The lighthouse at the tip of the peninsula, built in 1830, is now dark but open to visitors one weekend in November. Day use at the park is $5 for state residents and $6
for nonresidents on weekends and holidays, May through September. On weekdays
and out of season, the fee is $3 or $4 per vehicle. The boat-launch fee is $10.

Day-use facilities with a guarded beach for swimming are on the Potomac side, past
the fishing pier. There's a pet beach north of the causeway, too.

Visitors interested in **fishing** can cast their lines just about anywhere except the
beach swimming area. Favorite areas are the pier on the bay side and the point on
either the bay or riverside. Night fishing is the only activity allowed in the park (except
camping) after sunset. Campers can also fish at designated piers near campsites. A
fishing license is required only for the bay shoreline. Rowboat, canoe, and motorboat
rentals are available at the camp store off Route 5.

Smith Island Cruises ((☎) 410/425-2771; www.smithislandcruises.com) offers day
trips from here to Smith Island, a 1½-hour trip across the bay, on the twin-hulled
Chelsea Lane Tyler. From Memorial Day to Labor Day, boats depart Wednesday
through Sunday at 10am and return to Point Lookout at 3:30pm. Cruises continue
from September to mid-October on weekends only. Round-trip fare is $35 for adults,
$20 for children 3 to 11. Overnight packages with accommodations and meals are
also available, ranging from $315 per couple for 2 days to $499 per couple for 3 days;
reservations are essential. For details on Smith Island, see p. 179.

The park offers 143 **campsites** (26 with full hookups). The cost is $25 to $35 per
site. Cabins sleeping four cost $50 a night; one cottage that sleeps six goes for $80 a
night. Reservations can be made up to a year in advance by calling (☎) **888/432-
CAMP.** The office ((☎) **301/872-5688**) is open from 8am to 11pm in summer.

FISHING CHARTERS

Chesapeake Bay Fishing Parties ((☎) **301/872-5815**) has several charter boats and
headboats, operating out of Ridge. Charters run about $450 for six people ($40 for
extra passengers). Headboat rates are about $45, with $5 for rod rental.

For gear, snacks, and the scoop on where to eat, stop at **Rick's Marine,** on Route 5
in Scotland ((☎) **301/872-5156**), near Point Lookout State Park.

WHERE TO STAY

St. Mary's City has only one lodging option, but nearby Lexington Park has some chain hotels, including the **Hampton Inn** (© **301/863-3200**) and the **Fairfield Inn** (© **301/863-0203**).

Brome–Howard Inn The rich and famous drop in here—lots of Washingtonians have summer or retirement homes in the area—but the innkeepers will treat you with the same hospitality. The house, which looks out on the St. Mary's River, is decorated with antiques. The elegant bedrooms vary widely in decor; three have fireplaces, and two combine to make a suite for families. This is the only B&B within walking distance of the historic town.

18281 Rosecroft Rd. (P.O. Box 476), St Mary's City, MD 20686. © **301/866-0656.** Fax 301/866-9660. www.brome howardinn.com. 4 units. $125–$185 double. Rates include full breakfast or Sun brunch for Sat-night guests. AE, MC, V. **Amenities:** Restaurant; bicycles; high-speed Internet access in public area. *In room:* A/C, TV/VCR, CD player.

WHERE TO EAT

A couple of restaurants are located near one another down Route 252 (Wynne Rd.) in Ridge. They're all near the water; naturally, seafood is the specialty.

Courtney's Restaurant SEAFOOD Nothing's fancy in here. It's a cinder-block building with a simple dining room, where you'll see red tablecloths, a bar, and the TV going. But after a day of fishing or hiking, you'll be hungry for home cooking—and that's what Courtney's does best. You can get steamed crabs, crab cakes, or softshells. Want fresh fish? Courtney's husband comes home every morning with the day's catch. Carryout is available, too.

48290 Wynne Rd., Ridge. © **301/872-4403.** Reservations not necessary. Main courses $5.75–$8 lunch, $11–$14 dinner. No credit cards. Daily 7am–9pm.

Spinnakers Restaurant ITALIAN/SEAFOOD Tucked in a corner of a huge marina, Spinnakers does seafood with an Italian accent. Go for the Oysters Spinnaker, oysters on the half shell topped with spinach, prosciutto, and garlic. The decor is tropical, the atmosphere casual.

Point Lookout Marina, 16244 Miller's Wharf Rd., Ridge. © **301/872-5020.** Reservations recommended. Main courses $8–$10 lunch, $12–$15 dinner. DC, MC, V. Summer Sun–Thurs 11am–8pm, Fri–Sat 11am–9pm; winter Fri–Mon 11–9pm (call to confirm hours in cooler weather). Take Md. Rte. 5 or Md. Rte. 235 south to Ridge. Turn onto Wynne Rd. (Rte. 252) and go 1½ miles. Turn right on Miller's Wharf Rd. Restaurant is in the marina at end of road.

7

The Eastern Shore

Across the Chesapeake Bay Bridge, life slows down. Turn off Route 50 or Highway 301 and go down a country road past cornfields. Pause by rivers and marshes where birds and rustling grass are the only sounds. Stop in small towns where mom-and-pop shops still thrive. If you love to watch trees light up with fireflies on a summer night, or cycle down a country lane, or let the breeze take your boat past farms as old as America, you'll love the Eastern Shore.

Easton is the Eastern Shore's Colonial capital—its roots are evident on every picturesque street. It is the capital of Talbot County, home to three waterfront communities within easy driving distance. **St. Michaels** has the most shops as well as the Chesapeake Bay Maritime Museum. Boaters clog the harbor on summer weekends, but in spring and fall or midweek in summer, its charms are more accessible. **Oxford** is quieter, with fewer attractions, but it's attractive for its slower pace, waterfront park, and garden-bedecked streets. **Tilghman** (my favorite place!) hasn't bothered to beautify for the

tourists—but its unique waterman's lifestyle is enough to draw visitors.

Cambridge, on the Choptank River, hasn't gotten the attention it deserves. Its historic district, shopping, and nearby outdoor activities make it a place to go.

The southern areas of the Eastern Shore, including **Smith Island** and **Crisfield,** are the ultimate in waterman villages. Change comes slowly to these remote parts of Maryland, and residents like it that way. That very attitude draws visitors to these hard-to-reach spots.

North of the Bay Bridge, **Chestertown** is not only a Colonial town; it's also a college town. George Washington permitted the college founders to use his name for Washington College. A dozen miles away is **Rock Hall,** a waterfront village whose marinas and seafood restaurants are drawing more visitors.

Farther north is **Chesapeake City,** on the Chesapeake & Delaware Canal, which remains a crossroads for the marine traffic using the canal every day.

For the locations of these towns on the Eastern Shore, see the map inside the front cover of this book.

1 Talbot County ★★★

40 miles SE of Annapolis, 60 miles SE of Baltimore, 71 miles SE of Washington, D.C., 110 miles SW of Wilmington

Set in the middle of the Eastern Shore, Talbot (pronounced *Tall*-but) County has the most popular tourist towns north of Ocean City. Easton, the county seat, is filled with Colonial buildings. St. Michaels clings to its maritime tradition, and lots of visitors arrive by boat at one of the town's many marinas on the Miles River. Continue down Route 33 to Tilghman, where watermen reign. Its remote location makes it charming, but what visitors really come for are the watermen's boats and fresh seafood. Oxford was once a busy seaport, home of Revolutionary War financier Robert Morris.

The Ultimate Crab Cake, Eastern Shore Style

Finding a good crab cake on the Eastern Shore is easy, especially in warm months when crabs are in season. Even making a list can start an argument, since everybody has his or her favorite spot. Below is a sampling of good bets—just to get the discussion going.

Legal Spirits, 42 E. Dover St., Easton (© **410/820-0765**). It's is known for its cream of crab soup (which can be shipped), but the crab cakes are tops, too.

Miss Virginia's Crabcakes, 5793 Kent St., Rock Hall (© **410/639-7871**). Miss Virginia's son uses his mother's recipe with crabs caught by local watermen. Carryout only; available May through October.

Robert Morris Inn, 314 N. Morris St., Oxford (© **410/226-5111**). *Chesapeake* author James Michener always insisted the best crab cakes were made here.

ESSENTIALS

GETTING THERE   The best way to get to the Easton area is by car, via U.S. Route 50 from all directions. Follow the signs on Route 50 near Easton to get to St. Michaels, Tilghman, and Oxford, which are all reachable by boat as well, with plenty of dock space.

   Easton Municipal Airport, on U.S. Route 50 (© **410/822-0400**), serves local planes and runs a charter with three- and eight-passenger planes. **Greyhound** (© **800/231-2222** or 410/822-3333; www.greyhound.com) offers bus service to the Fast Stop Convenience Store, 9543 Ocean Gateway (Rte. 50), across from the airport.

VISITOR INFORMATION   Contact the **Talbot County Office of Tourism,** 11 S. Harrison St., Easton (© **410/770-8000;** www.tourtalbot.org). *The Tidewater Times,* a good pocket magazine with maps, is available in many shops.

GETTING AROUND   The only way to get around is by car, or, if you're lucky, by boat (though Easton itself is landlocked). Maryland Route 33 from Easton will take you to St. Michaels and Tilghman Island; Maryland Route 333 goes to Oxford.

   The shortest (in miles, not time) and most scenic route from Oxford to St. Michaels is via the **Oxford–Bellevue Ferry** (© **410/745-9023;** www.oxfordbellevue ferry.com), across the Tred Avon River. Established in 1683, this is the country's oldest privately operated ferry. The ¾-mile trip takes 7 minutes. You can catch the nine-vehicle ferry either from Bellevue, off routes 33 and 329, 7 miles from St. Michaels, or from Oxford, off Route 333. From March through November, the ferry runs every 20 minutes, Monday through Friday from 7am to sunset, Saturday and Sunday from 9am to sunset. There's no service December through February. Rates for a car and driver are $8 one-way and $12 round-trip; vehicle passengers pay $1; walk-on passengers $2; bicyclists $3; and motorcycles $4. Trailers and RVs can be accommodated, but call first. This tiny ferry offers a short, fun ride to a long country road leading to either St. Michaels or Easton. Or take the round-trip sunset ride—it costs $2 a passenger.

   To rent a car, call **Enterprise,** Route 50 and Dutchman's Lane (© **410/822-3260**). For cab service, try **Scotty's Taxi** (© **410/822-1475**).

Talbot County

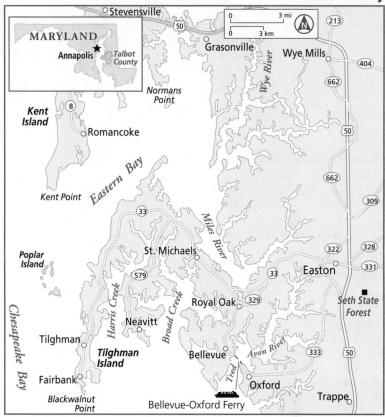

SPECIAL EVENTS   The **Waterfowl Festival** ✹✹✹ (© 410/822-4567; www.water fowlfestival.org), held the second week in November, turns Easton into a celebration of ducks, geese, and other birds. The 3-day festival draws some 20,000 visitors. You don't have to like hunting to attend. Some 400 artists' works are displayed, and venues around town display Federal Duck Stamp paintings, duck decoys, and carvings so realistic you'll want to smooth those ruffled feathers. Don't miss the duck-calling contest. Admission is $12 for adults and free for children under 12, with free shuttle buses running from site to site. If you visit wildlife refuges around Maryland, you'll see where the proceeds of this event are used—about $4.5 million has been raised over the years to protect and conserve wildlife habitats.

  Oxford Day (© 410/226-9023; www.portofoxford.com), held the last Saturday in April, is a fun local fest, with music, entertainment, and crab races.

  The **St. Michaels Food & Wine Festival** (© 800/808-7622 or 410/745-0411; www.stmichaelsfoodandwinefestival.com), held the last weekend in April or first weekend in May, offers wine tastings, cooking classes, and lots of dining opportunities. Tickets are available online or at local shops.

EASTON

Visitors to the Eastern Shore usually start at Easton. Called the "Colonial Capital of the Eastern Shore," this town values its visitors. Route 50 is filled with reasonably priced chain hotels, and good restaurants are everywhere.

WHERE TO STAY

Accommodations range from your basic chain hotels on Route 50 to high style and luxury downtown. You'll pay for the luxury, especially on busy weekends during the Waterfowl Festival or hunting season.

National chains include **Comfort Inn,** 8523 Ocean Gateway/Rte. 50 (© **800/228-5150** or 410/820-8333; www.comfortinn.com), and **Days Inn,** 7018 Ocean Gateway/Rte. 50 (© **410/822-4600;** www.daysinn.com).

Chaffinch House   This Victorian charmer sits on the corner of a residential street, but it's close to downtown. Filled with old-fashioned style, the B&B offers a variety of accommodations, from the lacy Wedding Suite with private porch to the elegant Rose Room with carved mahogany canopy bed. Breakfast is served with style—it's always a hot meal with gourmet tea service (with whole-leaf teas; no tea bags here!).

132 S. Harrison St., Easton, MD 21601. © **800/861-5074** or 410/822-5074. www.chaffinchhouse.com. 5 units. $125–$245 double. Rates include gourmet breakfast. AE, DISC, MC, V. No children under 12. **Amenities:** Parlor; Wi-Fi. *In room:* A/C, TV/VCR, coffeemaker, hair dryer (upon request), iron.

Inn at Easton   This restored 1790 house has been turned into a European-style inn with modern decor and a cosmopolitan feel. Each room has its own personality, but all share a sophisticated luxury, with down comforters and featherbeds. The Hambleton Suite has a gas fireplace, dressing room, and flatscreen TV. A porch on the second floor looks out over a street not much changed in 200 years. Make reservations for an Australian-inspired dinner here (see "Where to Dine," below).

28 S. Harrison St., Easton, MD 21601. © **888/800-8091** or 410/822-4910. Fax 410/822-6961. www.theinnateaston. com. 7 units. $175–$395 double. 2-night minimum stay required on weekends. AE, MC, V. No children under 9. **Amenities:** Restaurant. *In room:* A/C, TV.

Tidewater Inn   A hotel has stood here for 200 years—Eastern Shore hospitality was practically invented here. New owners took over in 2005, with plans to give the weathered grand dame a makeover. Nothing startling is in the works—just a return to the graciousness for which the Tidewater has always been known. The makeover should last until 2007, but look for fresh new public areas right away, with bedroom refurbishment and an upgrade of amenities to follow. If you want to stay here for the Waterfowl Festival, make reservations a year ahead. Coming to hunt? Of course there will always be room for your dogs. Check the website for the latest developments.

101 E. Dover St., Easton, MD 21601. © **800/237-8775** or 410/822-1300. Fax 410/820-8847. www.tidewaterinn. com. 100 units. $89–$186 double; $199–$499 suite. Golf and hunting packages available. AE, DC, MC, V. Free valet parking. Pets accepted (in on-site kennels). **Amenities:** 2 restaurants; bar; outdoor pool; health club; spa; business center; babysitting available; kennels for pets. *In room:* A/C, TV w/movies, VCR (upon request), high-speed Internet access, fridge (upon request), hair dryer (upon request), iron, robe.

WHERE TO DINE

Seafood lovers, rejoice: Crabs, oysters, and fish are star attractions at restaurants all around Easton. And if you're in the mood for something else, these are happy days. Easton is blessed with some sophisticated restaurants with creative menus.

Chez Lafitte Cafe & Cabaret FRENCH   Ten little tables, amusing dog art, and plenty of French delights make this an enjoyable place to stop. The cafe combines French favorites—coq au vin, quiche, French wines, cheeses, and bread made on the premises—with piano music on Saturdays and occasional special events. Brunch is served on Sundays. Look for the cafe in a new location in September 2006.

13 S. Washington St.; in September 2006 at 331 Dover St. ℂ 443/786-1366. www.chezlafitte.com. Reservations recommended. Main courses $18–$26. DC, DISC, MC, V. Fri–Sat 6pm–1am; Sun 11am–3pm and 6–10pm.

Inn at Easton PACIFIC RIM   The decor at this stylish inn mixes the best of Colonial architecture with the colors and styles of Europe. The food combines the best local seafood with contemporary Australian and Asian flavors. Where else can you get grilled Australian Moreton bay bugs as a starter, then move on to rockfish or softshell crabs? Round it all out with a sticky fig-and-ginger pudding or petite pavlova.

28 S. Harrison St. ℂ 888/800-8091 or 410/822-4910. www.theinnateaston.com. Reservations required for dinner. Main courses $24–$32; prix-fixe tasting menu $65–$85. AE, MC, V. Wed–Sun 5:30–9:30pm.

Legal Spirits *(Finds* AMERICAN   This casual tavern has lots of pub grub—burgers, French dip, and crab-cake sandwiches, as well as some meaty entrees that stand up to a beer. But whatever you have, make sure you start with the Shore Boys cream of crab soup. You're going to want to take this rich soup home—and you can. It's sold by the pint, fresh or frozen.

42 E. Dover St. ℂ 410/820-0765 or 410/820-0747. www.shoreboys.com. Reservations recommended for dinner. Main courses $8–$13 lunch, $8.25–$25 dinner. AE, DISC, MC, V. Daily 11am–10pm.

Mason's AMERICAN   The menu changes often at this delightful little eatery, where you can sit on the front porch or in the newly expanded dining room. Get a sandwich to go or stay for a full meal. Lunchtime choices range from a smoked turkey sandwich, made with Havarti and sprouts on a crusty baguette, to pan-seared salmon with grape-and-almond couscous. At dinner, look for fresh seafood and beef dishes.

22–24 S. Harrison St. ℂ 410/822-3204. Reservations recommended for dinner. Main courses $6.50–$12 lunch, $25–$34 dinner. AE, DC, MC, V. Mon–Sat 11:30am–2:30pm; Tues–Sat 5:30–9:30pm.

Old Towne Creamery ICE CREAM   Sometimes you just need an ice-cream cone. Here's a cheery place with tiny tables, pink walls, and all kinds of cones and sundaes.

9B Goldsborough St. ℂ 410/820-5223. Reservations not accepted. Ice-cream desserts $2–$6. No credit cards. Summer Mon–Sat 11:30am–10pm, Sun noon–10pm; hours may be shortened in cooler months.

Out of the Fire MEDITERRANEAN   Trendy food flavored with seasonings from around the world has made it to Easton. This chic dining room is dominated by a wood-fired oven. Lunch means soups, pizzas, and salads. Dinner choices include pasta, meats, and poultry, all with international zing.

22 Goldsborough St. ℂ 410/770-4777. www.outofthefire.com. Reservations recommended for dinner. Main courses $9–$15 lunch, $13–$24 dinner. AE, DC, DISC, MC, V. Mon–Fri 11:30am–2pm; Mon–Thurs 5–9pm; Fri–Sat 5–10pm. "Martinis & Jazz" Thurs 6–8pm.

Rustic Inn AMERICAN   A longtime local favorite, this eatery sits in the midst of a string of shops in the Talbottown Shopping Center. The tavern serves light fare. Look for it for steaks and fresh seafood, including a few $15 dinner specials each night.

Talbottown Shopping Center, 218 N. Washington St. ℂ 410/820-8212. www.rusticinnofeaston.com. Reservations recommended for dinner. Main courses $4.95–$14 lunch, $15–$46 dinner. AE, MC, V. Tues and Thurs–Fri 11:30am–2pm; Mon–Sat 5–9pm; Sun 4–9pm.

Tidewater Grille SEAFOOD   Traditional favorites, including crab cakes and a classic snapper soup, keep diners coming to this venerable eatery. The food is well prepared, the atmosphere gracious. Lunch is more casual, with sandwiches, salads, and a few entrees such as crab cakes and chicken.

At the Tidewater Inn, 101 E. Dover St. ℂ **410/822-1300**. www.tidewaterinn.com. Reservations recommended for dinner. Main courses $6.50–$17 lunch, $13–$27 dinner. AE, DC, MC, V. Daily 7–10:30am and 11:30am–3pm; Sun–Thurs 5–9pm; Fri–Sat 5–10pm.

WHAT TO SEE & DO

A walk through Easton's historic district will take you past buildings that witnessed the birth of the United States and have stood through the growth and changes of 2 centuries. The **Talbot County Courthouse,** 11 N. Washington St., was built in 1710.

The **Historical Society of Talbot County,** 25 S. Washington St. (ℂ **410/822-0773;** www.hstc.org), offers an intimate look at life in the county, including its industries such as boat building and duck decoy carving. The museum is open Monday through Saturday from 10am to 4pm; admission is free. It also offers guided tours of historic Easton and of local historic houses. Don't miss the Federal-style gardens behind the museum, a quiet haven for a spot of relaxation.

The **Academy Art Museum** ✺, 106 South St., at Harrison Street (ℂ **410/822-2787;** www.art-academy.org), transformed 18th-century buildings into a light-filled gallery with exhibits by regional and national artists, as well as a performing-arts series. Admission is $2 for adults and $1 for children; free on Wednesdays. Hours are Monday through Saturday from 10am to 4pm, until 8pm Tuesday through Thursday.

The restored Art Deco **Avalon Theatre,** 40 E. Dover St. (ℂ **410/822-7299;** www.avalontheatre.com), has been providing entertainment since 1921. Its performing-arts series draws local and national acts. For tickets, call the box office or go to www.ticketmaster.com.

Farther out of downtown is **Third Haven Meeting House,** 405 S. Washington St. (ℂ **410/822-0293**). Opened in 1684, the Quaker meetinghouse once hosted William Penn, who preached while Lord Baltimore was present. It is the oldest religious building in use in the U.S. Admission is free, donations are welcome. It's open daily from 9am to 5pm, with Sunday service at 10am and Wednesday service at 5:30pm.

Hunting Season

Maryland's Eastern Shore has long been considered the finest duck- and goose-hunting region on the Atlantic Flyway, with hundreds of thousands of migratory game birds flying through. More than 20 local organizations conduct guided waterfowl hunts for Canada geese (2 weeks in Nov and mid-Dec to late Jan), ducks (late Nov to mid-Jan), and sea ducks (early Oct to mid-Jan). Some quail and pheasant hunting are also available. White-tailed and sika deer may be hunted September through December.

The **Department of Natural Resources** publishes an annual guide with all the regulations, including bag limits, season dates, and licensing; call ℂ **877/620-8DNR** or go to www.dnr.maryland.gov. **Albright's Gun Shop,** 36 E. Dover St., Easton (ℂ **800/474-5502** or 410/820-8811; www.albrightsgunshop.com), can help plan any sort of hunting or fishing trip you have in mind.

SHOPPING

Easton's main shopping district is located along Washington, Dover, and Harrison streets. You'll find a number of galleries mixed in with the antiques, clothing, and gift shops. Hours are generally daily from 9am to 5pm; some shops close midweek, and many have shorter hours in winter.

Albright's Gun Shop   Located across from the Tidewater Inn, this shop stocks guns and accessories, sport clothing and watches, canvas goods, and tackle. It's an authorized Orvis dealer. Custom gunsmithing is done on the premises. 36 E. Dover St. ℂ 800/474-5502 or 410/820-8811. www.albrightsgunshop.com.

American Pennyroyal   Crafts aplenty, from candles and potpourri to pottery, glass, and wood. 5 N. Harrison St. ℂ 800/400-8403 or 410/822-5030.

Cherry's   Since 1926, this store has been a favored spot for ladies' and men's quality sportswear, outdoor clothing, and work and sporting shoes. It looks like a surplus store, but carries all the better brands. 26 W. Dover St. ℂ 410/822-4750.

Crackerjacks   Stop by this children's store for all sorts of books, toys, games, dolls, stuffed animals, pinwheels, crafts, and more. 7 S. Washington St. ℂ 410/822-7716.

Janet K. Fanto Antiques & Rare Books   This shop is stocked with a small assortment of rare books, 19th- and 20th-century furniture (mostly American), antiques, and odds and ends. The owners and watch-cat Sam are friendly and encourage browsing. Closed Wednesdays. 13 N. Harrison St. ℂ 410/763-9030.

Kathe & Company   There's a jumble of interior accessories, antiques, and window and wall treatments here—a fanciful treasure hunt. 20 S. Harrison St. ℂ 410/820-9153.

Troika Gallery   Artist/owners present their own work, as well as pieces by local and national artists. 9 S. Harrison St. ℂ 410/770-9190. www.troikagallery.com.

ST. MICHAELS

Since its founding in the late 1700s, St. Michaels has looked to the water for its livelihood. Shipbuilding made it famous. Log canoes were first workboats and then became better known as racing boats. Bugeyes and Baltimore clippers were built here. Watermen came to sell their catch, and canneries and oyster-packing plants sprang up. Ask a local to tell you the story of how, long ago, residents fooled the British and saved their town during the Revolutionary War.

Today, St. Michaels is a popular destination for boaters, who are crammed into the harbor on sunny weekends. It's also bed-and-breakfast heaven; many look out to the beautiful Miles River. Make time for the Chesapeake Bay Maritime Museum, where the history of the whole Chesapeake Bay is celebrated. The town's streets also offer a variety of shops and restaurants.

WHERE TO STAY

Five Gables Inn & Spa *Finds*   Get pampered with this combination B&B and spa. Every room—newly renovated with hand-decorated furniture—has a fireplace, whirlpool tub, private porch, and, since it's a spa, Aveda toiletries. A small pool, sun deck, sauna, and steam room—as well as six treatment rooms for hydrotherapy, scrubs, and massages (one is for couples)—add to the pampering. All kinds of packages add sailing or romance to the spa experience.

209 N. Talbot St., St. Michaels, MD 21663. ℂ 877/466-0100 or 410/745-0100. Fax 410/745-2903. www.fivegables. com. 14 units. $150–$395 double. Rates include breakfast. 2-night minimum stay required on weekends. AE, MC, V.

Pets accepted for a fee. **Amenities:** Indoor pool; spa treatments; sauna; steam room. *In room:* A/C, TV/VCR, whirlpool tub, hair dryer (upon request), iron (upon request), CD player.

Hambleton Inn   Location, location, location. Set right on the harbor but steps from the shopping district, every room at this immaculate Victorian-style B&B has a water view and antique furnishings. An open second-floor porch, enclosed lower porch, and small harborside deck provide three more spots from which to view the boats docked at St. Michaels. Tell the innkeeper of special needs, especially dietary, in advance.

202 Cherry St., St. Michaels, MD 21663. ℭ 866/745-3350 or 410/745-3350. Fax 410/745-5709. www.hambleton inn.com. 5 units. $195–$245 double. Rates include breakfast. 2-night minimum stay required on most weekends in high season. MC, V. No children under 13. *In room:* A/C, TV.

Harris Cove Cottages Bed 'n Boat   You can't beat Harris Cove, a throwback to a simpler, more rustic time. These cottages were built in the 1930s and look it. In fact, the owner notes they're furnished in "grandmother's attic furniture." But they are well maintained and sit beside a quiet cove, perfect for fishing or kayaking. All have kitchens and lots of windows. Gazebos and lounge chairs sit under big trees, and charcoal grills are fired up every evening so guests can grill the day's catch. Need a boat? You can rent a pedal boat, pirogue, skiff, or outdoor motor. Or bring your own—sailboats can drop anchor, and they'll taxi you in.

8070 Bozman–Neavitt Rd., St. Michaels, MD 21663. ℭ 410/745-9701. www.bednboat.com. 6 cottages, 2 units in main house. $170–$225 double. 2-night minimum stay required. No credit cards. **Amenities:** Rental boats; boat ramp; mooring anchor; crabbing equipment; gazebos; charcoal grills. *In room:* A/C, TV, kitchen.

Inn at Perry Cabin 🐾🐾   Part of the Orient Express chain, this English country–style inn on the Miles River is richly appointed and designed for stylish comfort. There are four tiers of rooms, from standard to master suite. At every level, you'll find plenty of space, river views, and luxurious towels and bedding. Some units have gas fireplaces. Amenities are fabulous and will please the most discriminating guest. But for some, the service is a bit frosty for the Eastern Shore. The inn is a short walk from the downtown area, though right next door to the maritime museum. There's access to golf, fishing, horseback riding, hunting, and a helicopter pad.

308 Watkins Lane, St. Michaels, MD 21663. ℭ 800/722-2949 or 410/745-2200. Fax 410/745-3348. www.perry cabin.com. 80 units. $295–$625 double. Ask about winter getaway packages. AE, DC, MC, V. Pets accepted for a fee. **Amenities:** Restaurant; bar; outdoor heated pool; health club; sauna; complimentary bikes; business center; massage; babysitting; laundry service. *In room:* A/C, TV/VCR, high-speed Internet access, fridge (upon request), hair dryer, iron, limited dock space.

Parsonage Inn 🐾   This redbrick Victorian home, built in 1883, is a beauty. It served as the parsonage to the United Methodist Church from 1924 to 1985. Today, it's a respite for travelers willing to exchange a water view for delicious breakfast, cozy decor, and creature comforts. All rooms have brass beds and Laura Ashley linens; three have fireplaces; and many have ceiling fans and access to a sun deck. Packages combine a stay here with a skipjack ride, dinner at a local restaurant, and visits to the maritime museum.

210 N. Talbot St., St. Michaels, MD 21663. ℭ 800/394-5519 or 410/745-5519. Fax 410/745-6869. www.parsonage-inn.com. 8 units. $100–$195 double. Rates include gourmet breakfast. 2-night minimum stay required most weekends. MC, V. Children welcome with prior approval. **Amenities:** Complimentary bikes. *In room:* A/C, TV (in some rooms), Wi-Fi, iron.

St. Michaels Harbour Inn 🐾   Here's modern convenience in the heart of St. Michaels. The Harbour Inn has kept up with the times, replacing its kitchenettes with Jacuzzis and adding an outdoor grill to the marina deck. Every room—most are suites—has a water view; almost all have terraces; and third-floor rooms have cathedral ceilings. On-site are a waterfront restaurant and a more casual eatery.

101 N. Harbor Rd., St. Michaels, MD 21663. © 800/955-9001 or 410/745-9001. Fax 410/745-9150. www.harbour inn.com. 46 units. $189–$599 double. AE, DC, DISC, MC, V. **Amenities:** 2 restaurants; outdoor pool; health club; spa; watersports equipment/rentals; boat slips; complimentary bikes; resort shuttle; business center; babysitting; Wi-Fi in some areas; ship's store. *In room:* A/C, dataport, fridge, coffeemaker, hair dryer, iron.

Wades Point Inn on the Bay ☆☆   Set high on a point, Wades Point Inn offers an easy, old-fashioned vacation outside St. Michaels. The sprawling house, built in 1819 by Thomas Kemp (builder of the famous Baltimore clipper ship), has been host to many a summer holiday over the past century. The main house and Kemp Guest House next door have spacious bedrooms decorated with period furniture. The Kemp rooms have porches or balconies; some have kitchenettes. A separate farmhouse is available for groups of up to 13. The Victorian Summer Wing, open seasonally, has cottage-style rooms with screen doors. Breakfast includes eggs and produce from the inn's organic farm. There are kayaks, a floating dock, a swim dock, and fishing rods (the fishing's great in Eastern Bay) to help guests take full advantage of the water here.

Wades Point Rd. (P.O. Box 7), St. Michaels, MD 21663. © 888/923-3466 or 410/745-2500. Fax 410/745-3444. www.wadespoint.com. 24 units. $140–$240 double. Rates include full breakfast on weekdays, continental breakfast on weekends. Children under 12 stay free in parent's room. 2-night minimum stay required on weekends and holidays. Discounts available for seniors and for stays of 3 days or more. MC, V. Located 5 miles west of St. Michaels, off Rte. 33, at end of Wades Point Rd. **Amenities:** Watersports equipment/rentals; dock; canoe/kayak launch; bike rentals; walking trails; executive-level rooms. *In room:* A/C, coffeemaker, hair dryer (upon request), iron.

WHERE TO DINE
Bistro St. Michaels ☆ FRENCH   This busy restaurant in a Victorian house captures the ambience of a Paris-style bistro. The downstairs dining room can be noisy, but the upstairs and garden patio are more intimate. On a busy night, service can be leisurely. Chef David Stein's menu is short but intriguing, with a range of choices such as grilled duck or orange-ginger-glazed salmon. The wine list is extensive.

403 S. Talbot St. © 410/745-9111. www.bistrostmichaels.com. Reservations recommended. Main courses $26–$31. AE, DC, DISC, MC, V. Thurs–Mon 5:30–9pm.

Carpenter Street Saloon SEAFOOD/PUB FARE   A noisy, friendly pub with a bar in one room and a dining room next door, this place makes a good stop for a beer and a burger—and for a family outing, too. It's got a little of everything: crab soup and crab cakes, rockfish and chips, prime rib, even a Dr. Atkins plate. It offers a kid's menu, a few games and pool tables upstairs, a model-train track circling the ceiling, live music on Tuesdays, late-night pizza, and breakfast.

113 Talbot St., at Carpenter St. © 410/745-5111. Main courses $4.75–$9.95 lunch, $6.50–$19 dinner. MC, V. Daily 8am–9pm. Bar open until 2am.

Crab Claw ☆ SEAFOOD   Many Marylanders consider this a destination restaurant. They come by the busloads for the fresh seafood, steamed crabs, and river breezes. It's casual and fun—and it's right beside the Chesapeake Bay Maritime Museum. The emphasis is crabs, served every way possible. Platters of chicken, oysters, sandwiches, and a raw bar are also available.

Navy Point, Mill St. © 410/745-2900. www.thecrabclaw.com. Reservations recommended for dinner. Main courses $14–$23. No credit cards. Mar–Nov daily 11am–10pm.

St. Michaels Crab House *Kids* SEAFOOD   Located on the marina, this casual, family-friendly restaurant offers a choice of indoor (air-conditioned) seating in a nautical setting or outdoors under an umbrella. The building is an 1830s oyster-shucking shed. The menu, which includes a children's section, features steamed crabs, crab cakes, softshells, and crab Benedict, as well other seafood, steaks, and chicken.

305 Mulberry St. (C) **410/745-3737.** www.stmichaelscrabhouse.com. Reservations recommended for dinner. Main courses $6.75–$14 lunch, $12–$23 dinner. DISC, MC, V. Mid-Mar to mid-Dec Mon–Sat 11am–11pm; Sun 11am–10pm.

Taste Gourmet Deli DELI   Sometimes you want a good sandwich or maybe a sweet roll to go with your coffee. This little deli has a delicious variety of soups, salads, sandwiches, subs, wraps, and burgers—even pizza. The place isn't fancy, but the morning pastries are sweet and light, and you'll get your fill at lunch.

105 N. Talbot St. (C) **410/745-4100.** Reservations not accepted. Sandwiches $2–$6.95. MC, V. Daily 7am–7pm.

Town Dock Restaurant 🦀🦀 AMERICAN/SEAFOOD   Waterside view, creative Eastern Shore cuisine, and intimate candlelit ambience make this one of the town's favorites. Crabs and rockfish appear on the menu, of course, but diners can also choose from sesame-seared tuna or prime rib with bourbon butter. Lunch items take advantage of the local seafood; there's also a children's menu. Foxy's Marina Bar offers a full bar, raw bar, and grill right on the harbor from May to October.

125 Mulberry St. (C) **410/745-5577.** www.town-dock.com. Reservations recommended for dinner. Main courses $9–$17 lunch, $22–$30 dinner. AE, DC, DISC, MC, V. Apr–Oct daily 11:30am–9pm (until 10pm Fri–Sat); Nov–Mar Fri–Sun 11:30am–9pm. Parking lot available.

WHAT TO SEE & DO

The **Chesapeake Bay Log Sailing Canoe Association** sponsors log canoe races—just about the oldest class of boat still sailing around here. Usually races are more exciting for the sailor than for the spectator. But these boats—big on sail, small on hull—have to be seen to be appreciated. Races are usually held on weekends from June to September. For information, contact the **Miles River Yacht Club** ((C) **410/745-9511;** www.milesriveryc.org).

The **Cannonball House,** on Mulberry Street at St. Mary's Square, may look like an ordinary Colonial-style house—but it was witness to the day the town outsmarted the British. When the British attempted to shell St. Michaels during the War of 1812, the townspeople blacked out the town and hung lanterns high in the trees, causing the British to overshoot the houses. Only one cannonball hit the town, striking the chimney of this house. The town was saved, and the "blackout strategy" was born. The house is privately owned and not open to the public.

Dockside Express ((C) **888/312-7847;** www.cruisinthebay.com) offers walking tours, land and sea tours, and Ghost Walks from mid-March to mid-November.

Chesapeake Bay Maritime Museum 🦀🦀🦀   Celebrate the Chesapeake Bay at this unusual museum. You'll know you're in for something different when you enter the driveway—under the old Knapps Narrows Bridge. The centerpiece is the picturesque Hooper Strait Lighthouse. And all around are fascinating exhibits about boat building, fishing, and oystering, and about the people who earn their livelihood on the water. Star attractions are the skipjack installed in the new Oystering Building, the boatyard where expert builders work year-round to restore historic boats, and the historic boats docked here. The grounds are open as a waterfront park after the buildings close for the day; no admission is charged then.

Navy Point, Mill St. ✆ **410/745-2916**. www.cbmm.org. Admission $10 adults, $8 seniors, $4 children 6–17. Summer daily 9am–6pm; spring and fall daily 9am–5pm; winter daily 9am–4pm. Closed Thanksgiving, Dec 25, and Jan 1. Take Rte. 33 into St. Michaels; turn right at driveway. You'll see the drawbridge.

OUTDOOR ACTIVITIES

BIKING   Rent a bike at **Wheel Doctor,** 10113 S. Talbot St., in St. Michaels Village, just before you get into town (✆ **410/745-6676**), or in town at the **St. Michaels Marina Aqua Center,** 101 N. Harbor Rd. (✆ **800/955-9001**).

BOAT RIDES ⛵   All this water, and you don't have your own boat. Not to worry: There are all kinds of ways to get on the water here. Take a ride on the **H.M.** *Krentz* (✆ **410/745-6080**; www.oystercatcher.com), a skipjack that dredges oysters in winter and earns its keep with sailboat rides from April to October. It's docked by the Crab Claw. Or perhaps you'd like a more modern sailboat? The **Lucky Dog Catamaran Company** (✆ **410/745-6203**; www.luckydogcatamarancompany.com) offers 2-hour cruises, daily from April to October, on the 36-foot *Sirius,* docked at St. Michaels Marina on Mulberry Street. A new addition is the 41-foot 1926 gaff-rigged *Selina II* (✆ **410/726-9400**; www.sailselina.com), captained by Iris Clarke; with room for just six passengers, its 2-hour sails are quite intimate.

Go in air-conditioned comfort with **Chesapeake Bay Cruises,** by the Crab Claw (✆ **410/745-3100**; www.patriotcruises.com), which offers 1-hour narrated cruises on a 65-foot tourist boat. Motorized-boat tours are also run by **Dockside Express** (✆ **888/312-7847**; www.cruisinthebay.com), with options such as 1-hour harbor tours, crabbing cruises, and eco-tours.

If you want to move on your own power, stop by the **St. Michaels Marina Aqua Center** (✆ **800/955-9001**; www.harbourinn.com) and rent a kayak, canoe, or aqua bike. **St. Michaels Harbor Tours & Water Taxi** (✆ **410/924-2198**) offers daily 25-minute tours from the town dock in season, as well as a water taxi service.

SHOPPING

Shops in St. Michaels are concentrated along Talbot Street. They're usually open from 10am to 6pm on weekdays and most weekends, with shorter hours in winter. Look for the St. Michaels/Tilghman Island visitors' guide at the visitor center, at North Talbot and Mill streets. There's a parking lot at that corner as well.

Artiste Locale   The emphasis is local crafts, but a wide range of American-made handiwork is stocked here: pottery, original-design T-shirts, soaps, candles, paintings, jewelry, gifts, and home furnishings, many with an Eastern Shore flair. 112 N. Talbot St. ✆ **410/745-6580**.

Calico Gallery   This is just the place for a local watercolor—or head upstairs and find a great toy for your favorite kid. 212 Talbot St. ✆ **410/745-5370**. www.calicogallery.net.

Corner Antiques   In a jumble of old things, you can find ancient lanterns, nautically themed knickknacks, and tools. There are lots of interesting corners to poke around in. 116 N. Talbot St. ✆ **410/745-5589**.

Cultured Pearl   Another gift shop—the town's full of them—but these are gifts from around the world, including Irish crystal, Italian inlaid boxes, and Belgian linen. 210 S. Talbot St. ✆ **410/745-0995**. www.theculturedpearlltd.com.

Keepers   Casual Orvis clothes—lots of khaki, fleece, and embroidered sweaters— share space with antique waterfowl decoys. 300 S. Talbot St. ✆ **800/549-1872** or 410/745-6388.

The Mind's Eye   The unique gift gallery is filled with folk art: woodcarvings, pottery, glassware, jewelry, cards, sculpture, and wall hangings, all by American artists. 201 S. Talbot St. (℅ **410/745-2023.**

St. Michaels Candy Company   Bring a sweet tooth here for handmade chocolates, Baltimore's own Lee's Ice Cream, and a variety of other sweet novelties and gifts. 216 S. Talbot St. (℅ **888/570-6050** or 410/745-6060. www.candyisdandy.com.

Sign of the Whale   Fine gifts, often with a nautical theme, including many an item with a witty saying. 208 S. Talbot St. (℅ **410/745-0680.**

Talbot Ship and Rail   Model ships, NOAA charts, and nautical books and art fill this store at the end of town. It also restores old models. Don't miss the model trains, from G to Z scale, from Marklin, LGB, and Micro-Trains. 211 N. Talbot St. (℅ **410/745-6268.**

A Wish Called Wanda   Handcrafted gifts for the home, including lamps and pottery, as well as jewelry. 110 N. Talbot St. (P.O. Box 855). (℅ **410/745-6763.**

TILGHMAN ISLAND

Keep driving southeast on Route 33, the road from Easton to St. Michaels, and you'll arrive on Tilghman Island. Cross the Knapps Narrows Bridge, and you'll find yourself miles from the bustle of the city. Though some development has filled a cornfield here and there—especially at the water line—this is the place for true Eastern Shore living: ospreys to wake you in the morning, stars to light the night, skipjacks and crabbing boats bobbing in the harbor. Come for fresh seafood, quiet roads, and pretty-as-a-picture water views. Tilghman is a good place to spend a day with a camera or a bike, and now even a kayak. Bring your fishing pole, as there are plenty of places on the island—not to mention charter boats for hire—to cast your line. The few hotels and B&Bs are welcoming places that help you enjoy the quiet Eastern Shore way.

WHERE TO STAY

Black Walnut Point Inn ✦   Here's a great way to escape: Drive down the main road to the very end and keep going. You'll find yourself on the southern point of Tilghman Island, with views of water on three sides, huge old trees, and an 1840s white house with wide porch to call home, at least for a while. Every room has a view of the water, but each is different: some elegant, some a bit more country style. The Tilghman Room has windows on three sides, while the Attic Hideaway is quaint but best suited for shorter people. The cottages come with living room, kitchen, and porch.

Black Walnut Rd. (P.O. Box 308), Tilghman, MD 21671. (℅ 410/886-2452. www.blackwalnutpoint.com. 4 units in main house, 3 cottages. $120–$175 double; $225 cottage. Rates include continental breakfast. 2- or 3-night minimum stay may be required on weekends or holidays. DISC, MC, V. No children under 12. **Amenities:** Pool; hot tub; wildlife sanctuary; hammocks. *In room:* A/C.

Chesapeake Wood Duck Inn ✦   The thing to remember here: Make reservations for dinner when you make reservations for lodging. Dinner is served on Saturdays—but only to inn guests with reservations. It depends on what the watermen bring over, but your meal will include seafood paired with spices and sauces from around the world. Breakfast, also cooked by one of the owners (a trained chef), is hearty and memorable: a trio of crepes, Eastern Shore eggs Benedict with smoked duck, or buttermilk pancakes with bananas Foster sauce. The inn, which has Dogwood Harbor for a backyard, is a cozy spot with gazebo and screened porch. All but one of the bedrooms have water views.

Gibsontown Rd. at Dogwood Harbor (P.O. Box 202), Tilghman, MD 21671. © 800/956-2070 or 410/886-2070. www.
woodduckinn.com. 6 units in main house, 1 cottage. $129–$229 double. Rates include full breakfast. 2- or 3-night
minimum stay may be required on weekends or holidays. Ask about winter escape packages. MC, V. *In room:* A/C.

Harrison's Chesapeake House Country Inn

Nothing about Harrison's is fancy.
Rooms are clean. Half have a water view. There's a pool, a sun porch, and a restaurant
downstairs. But the real attraction is the proximity to the fishing and hunting charters
run by Buddy Harrison—ask about the many packages. An on-site gift shop, Island
Treasures, sells apparel and Tilghman Island souvenirs.

21551 Chesapeake House Dr., Tilghman, MD 21671. © 410/886-2121. www.chesapeakehouse.com. 56 units, 4 rental
houses. $115–$130 double. MC, V. **Amenities:** Restaurant; lounge; pool; crab deck; video games. *In room:* A/C, TV.

Inn at Knapp's Narrows Marina

Every room here has a view of the Knapps Nar-
rows. They're simple, fresh, and spacious—and a good value. Third-floor units have
cathedral ceilings and Internet access. One suite can be turned into a meeting space if
necessary. Hammocks under the trees beckon. A full-service facility, boaters will find
their vessels are as welcome as they are.

Knapps Narrows (P.O. Box 277), Tilghman, MD 21671. © 410/886-2720. www.knappsnarrowsmarina.com. 20 units.
$120–$160 double. Rates include continental breakfast. DISC, MC, V. **Amenities:** Restaurant; pool; bike rentals;
marina and boat-repair services; transient slips. *In room:* A/C, TV, dataport, coffeemaker.

Lazyjack Inn

Water views, romance, and gourmet breakfasts make this a Tilghman
Island delight. The Nellie Byrd Suite, with its king-size brass bed, fireplace, whirlpool
tub, and harbor view, is hard to beat. But the other rooms are bright and comfortable,
too. The first-floor Garden Suite has a fireplace and whirlpool. The inn was completely refurbished, including air-conditioning, after Hurricane Isabel in 2003.

5907 Tilghman Island Rd. (P.O. Box 248), Tilghman, MD 21671. © 800/690-5080 or 410/886-2215. www.lazyjack
inn.com. 4 units. $139–$269 double. Rates include full breakfast. 2- or 3-night minimum stay may be required on
weekends or holidays. MC, V. No children under 12. **Amenities:** Porch; library; afternoon refreshments; turndown
service.

Sinclair House

A little white frame house on the outside, Sinclair House inside
tells a story of world travel. The owners have decorated the bedrooms with things they
collected while working in the diplomatic corps and the United Nations—you'll see
furnishings from Africa, Indonesia, Morocco, and Peru. Rooms are small, but fun and
exotic. Each has its own bathroom, though Africa's is squeezed into a closet. Morocco
is the most spacious, with king-size bed and lots of windows. Full gourmet breakfasts
are served in an airy dining room.

5718 Black Walnut Point Rd. (P.O. Box 145), Tilghman, MD 21671. © 888/859-2147 or 410/886-2147. www.sinclair
house.biz. 4 units. $119–$129 double. Rates include full gourmet breakfast. 2- or 3-night minimum stay may be
required on weekends or holidays. AE, DISC, MC, V. **Amenities:** Video library; Internet access in public area. *In room:*
A/C, TV/VCR.

Tilghman Island Inn

Here's a modern inn in the heart of old-fashioned Eastern
Shore hospitality. Set on Knapps Narrows across from a bird-filled marsh, the waterfront rooms take full advantage of the lovely setting, with French doors and balconies
or patios. Every room is decorated differently, but all have fireplaces and most have
"ultra spa baths." The inn has a cozy lounge, a restaurant with a great reputation, and
an outdoor grill at the waterfront bar on weekends and some weeknights. There's
entertainment in the lounge or outside on summer weekends. The staff will be ready
to help you find all the treasures Tilghman has to offer.

21384 Coopertown Rd. (P.O. Box B), Tilghman, MD 21671 ✆ **800/866-2141** or 410/886-2141. www.tilghman islandinn.com. 20 units. $125–$300 double. Rates include continental breakfast. AE, DC, DISC, MC, V. Pets accepted. **Amenities:** Restaurant (closed Wed); lounge; outdoor pool; tennis court; waterside deck; 9 transient slips. *In room:* A/C, TV, hair dryer, iron.

WHERE TO DINE

Bay Hundred Restaurant SEAFOOD   Just before you reach the Knapps Narrows Bridge, turn right to find this restaurant overlooking the marina and the bridge. It's the most casual of the area eateries, but the kitchen isn't so casual with its cooking. In the dining room or out on the sun-drenched deck, diners can choose from a variety of seafood, served the traditional ways or over pasta, as well as great salads, soups, and meat dishes. If rockfish is offered as a fried-fish sandwich, don't hesitate. Slips are available for boating diners.

Knapps Narrows Marina. ✆ **410/886-2126.** Reservations recommended for dinner. Main courses $5.95–$11 lunch, $12–$22 dinner. AE, DISC, MC, V. Sun–Thurs 11am–9pm; Fri–Sat 11am–10pm. Closed Mon Nov–Mar. Closed Feb.

The Bridge Restaurant   SEAFOOD   Overlooking the Knapps Narrows Bridge, this place serves traditional Eastern Shore fare along with a few choices from other regional cuisines. Get your fresh fish served California style, with mushrooms, artichokes, and a lemon-and-wine sauce, or South Carolina style, with Cajun spices, peppers, scallops, shrimp, bacon, and cream. Expect the freshest seafood and a professional, friendly staff. It's casual here, but good enough for a special occasion. A children's menu is available.

6136 Tilghman Rd. ✆ **410/886-2330.** www.bridge-restaurant.com. Reservations recommended for dinner. Main courses $5–$14 lunch, $14–$24 dinner. AE, DC, DISC, MC, V. Daily noon–10pm.

Harrison's Chesapeake House SEAFOOD   This may be the best known of the Tilghman Island restaurants, and the reason has to be its hearty Eastern Shore fare: fresh seafood served by a friendly staff. The house special combines two local favorites, fried chicken and crab cakes. But you can get anything from crab to prime rib here, served family style with plates of vegetables and homemade bread. Harrison's has water views, too.

21551 Chesapeake House Dr. ✆ **410/886-2121.** www.chesapeakehouse.com. Reservations recommended for dinner. Main courses $3.95–$16 lunch, $12–$25 dinner. AE, MC, V. Hours vary according to season, but always open Sat–Sun; call ahead to confirm. Closed Mon–Tues in Dec.

So Neat Cafe and Bakery DELI/BAKERY   At this charming eatery with soda fountain and bakery counter, you can count on a pastry, a good cup of coffee, and a generous measure of friendliness. Open early for breakfast, which includes waffles, eggs, and pastries, the cafe reopens for sandwiches and soups, even a glass of beer or wine, at lunch. On Friday and Saturday, it stays open until 5pm, scooping ice cream.

5776 Tilghman Rd. ✆ **410/886-2143.** Reservations not accepted. Breakfast items $4–$7.25; lunch items $4.50–$6.75. No credit cards. Thurs and Sun 7:30am–3pm; Fri–Sat 7:30am–5pm. Closed Oct–May.

OUTDOOR ACTIVITIES

Rent a bike and take a long ride on flat, fairly quiet roads. Hop aboard a skipjack for a ride into history, or see what's biting from a fishing boat. Rent a kayak and poke around the many coves. Whatever you do, slow down.

BIKING   Get a bike or a motor scooter (no motorcycle license required) from **Tilghman Island Marina** (✆ **410/886-2500;** www.tilghmanmarina.com). Rent for an hour or a full day. (St. Michaels is a half-hour scooter ride away.)

BOAT RENTALS **Tilghman Island Marina** (✆ 410/886-2500; www.tilghman marina.com) offers kayaks, pontoon boats, skiffs with outboard motors, sailboats, and personal watercraft, as well as fishing and crabbing gear, by the hour, half-day, day, or week. Or sign up for the Poplar Island excursion: They'll tow your kayak to this small group of islands for a 3- to 4-hour expedition, box lunch included. Reservations are required for the Poplar Island excursion, and suggested for others.

Harris Creek Kayaks (✆ 410/886-2083) rents kayaks, small sailboats, and paddleboats. It also offers kayaking tours a few miles west of the island. Look for the **Tilghman Island Water Trail** map, available at the Talbot County visitor center in Easton (✆ 410/770-8000; www.tourtalbot.org).

CRUISING Captain Murphy will take you on a 2-hour tour on his skipjack, the *Rebecca T. Ruark* (✆ 410/886-2176; www.skipjack.org), docked at Dogwood Harbor. As he sails the oldest working sailboat in the country, the captain talks about the history of his boat and tells tales about crabs and oysters.

The *Lady Patty* (✆ 800/690-5080 or 410/886-2215; www.sailladypatty.com), a 45-foot ketch, is docked at Knapps Narrows Marina. In her early days, she sailed the Pacific, the Galapagos Islands, and regularly from St. Petersburg to Havana. Now she sails the Choptank on 2-hour, half-day, or full-day trips.

Lighthouse tours are the specialty of the **MV** *Sharp's Island,* a former U.S. Navy special operations vessel. Take a 3-hour cruise and see three lighthouses up close, or spend the whole day and see 10 lights (✆ 800/690-5080 or 410/886-2215).

FISHING & CRABBING If you want to catch some really fresh seafood, try **Harrison's Sport Fishing Center** (✆ 410/886-2121; www.chesapeakehouse.com), the best known of the charters here. Capt. Buddy Harrison has 20 charter boats and room for 1 or 100. Half-day charters are available April through December, as well as packages that include breakfast and lunch or even overnight lodging. The *Miss Kim* (✆ 410/886-2176; www.skipjack.org), a Chesapeake Bay workboat, offers half-day crabbing for six-person groups. **Knapps Narrows Marina** (✆ 410/886-2720; www.knappsnarrowsmarina.com) can also hook you up with a fishing charter. Five boats offer half- and full-day fishing trips from the dock here.

OXFORD

Oxford is a refined place, with a shady park and beach in the center of town. It wasn't always so quiet, though. One of the state's oldest towns, it was the Eastern Shore's first port of entry. In the 1700s, shipping made it a busy place. It was home to many of Maryland's prominent citizens, including Robert Morris, a shipping agent, and his son Robert Morris, "financier of the Revolution," as well as Tench Tilghman, George Washington's aide who carried the news of Cornwallis's surrender to the Continental Congress. Tilghman is remembered with a monument in Oxford Cemetery.

Although Oxford is quieter than St. Michaels, it's a pretty place to visit, walk, and enjoy a picnic at the park in the center of town, under the trees on the Tred Avon River. The beach at the Strand is small and quiet enough for dipping your toes.

You can also ride the tiny **Oxford–Bellevue Ferry** <i>⚓</i>, one of the oldest in the country (see p. 156 for details). It will take you and your car across to one of the sleepiest parts of Talbot County. The country drive that follows is quiet and completely undeveloped. Of course, you can also take the ferry going the other way, making Oxford your destination. What a fun way to spend a day!

WHERE TO STAY

Combsberry   Down a country lane, this restored 18th-century manor house offers elegant and luxurious comfort. The main house has four units, while the cottages offer room to spread out. The carriage house's two bedrooms share a living room and kitchen. Six units have fireplaces; some rooms have whirlpool tubs. Gardens dotted with ancient trees surround this home, known for its fireplaces, staircase, and brickwork. Boaters, a dock awaits you here.

4837 Evergreen Rd., Oxford, MD 21654. © 410/226-5353. www.combsberry.net. 7 units. $250–$395 double. Rates include full breakfast. AE, MC, V. Pets accepted in Oxford Cottage. No children under 12. **Amenities:** Boat dock. *In room:* A/C, no phone.

Oxford Inn *Value Kids*   New owners have put a lot of TLC into this well-established inn, located beside Town Creek and close to everything. It remains a good value—all rooms have been updated, and many have window seats and/or views of the water. Two rooms can be combined to make a family suite. The gift shop is gone, so guests now have a cozy library with fireplace. And the new 40-seat restaurant serves dinner Wednesday through Sunday.

506 S. Morris St. (P.O. Box 627), Oxford, MD 21654. © 410/226-5220. www.oxfordmd.com/oxfordinn. 7 units. $110–$160 double. Rates include continental breakfast, plus hot dishes on weekends. DISC, MC, V. **Amenities:** Pope's Tavern restaurant. *In room:* A/C.

Robert Morris Inn *★★★*   Ships' carpenters built this home in 1710 for Robert Morris, Jr., a financier of the American Revolution. It retains its Colonial character with wide floorboards, the original staircase, and traditional furnishings. Each room is different in size and appointments; one has a four-poster bed and fireplace. Some bathrooms have claw-foot tubs and river views. If you like a historic setting—author James Michener favored this place while writing *Chesapeake*—the Robert Morris Inn can't be beat.

But if you're looking for a place with more emphasis on the water, the inn also runs the Sandaway Lodge, a country home built on a point jutting into the river. Among its rooms is a second-floor suite with a king-size bed that looks through French doors to the river beyond. Another unit, the Sandaway Suite, has a sitting room right on the beach. With fireplace, TV/VCR, and lots of windows, this getaway is luscious. Lots of porches, huge trees, and chaise longues make this a comfortable retreat.

314 N. Morris St. (P.O. Box 70), Oxford, MD 21654. © 888/823-4012 or 410/226-5111. www.robertmorrisinn.com. 34 units. $90–$290 double; $350 suite. Closed Dec–Mar. AE, MC, V. **Amenities:** Restaurant (see "Where to Dine," below); beach at Sandaway; morning coffee in sitting room; Wi-Fi in main building and high-speed Internet access elsewhere. *In room:* A/C, no phone.

WHERE TO DINE

Latitude 38 Bistro & Spirits SEAFOOD/INTERNATIONAL   You'll forget you saw gas pumps out front once you walk into this white-tablecloth dining room—and the creative cuisine will take you away altogether. The menu takes advantage of the area's bounty and mixes in an international style. Recent offerings included oysters poached in spinach and fennel broth, filet mignon with chile and cherry-tomato salsa, and paella with local oysters and jumbo shrimp. Lunch and Sunday brunch are a little more traditional. A smaller bar menu is also offered.

26342 Oxford Rd. © 410/226-5303. www.latitude38.org. Reservations recommended for dinner; none taken for bar area. Main courses $7.95–$13 lunch, $20–$26 dinner. AE, DISC, MC, V. Tues–Sun 11:30am–2:30pm and 5:30–9:30pm.

Golfing the Eastern Shore

Lots of nice flat land, terrific water views, and plenty of beautiful weather make the Mid-Shore an up-and-coming golf destination.

The **Hog Neck Golf Course,** 10142 Old Cordova Rd., Easton (✆ **410/ 822-6079;** www.hogneck.com), was rated among the top 25 U.S. public courses by *Golf Digest.* This par-72, 18-hole course and par-32, 9-hole executive course is north of town, off Route 50. Rates for nonresidents are $55 Monday through Thursday, $65 Friday through Sunday, carts included. It's open February through December, weekdays from 8am to sunset and weekends from 7am to sunset.

The **Easton Club,** 28449 Clubhouse Dr., Easton (✆ **800/277-9800;** www. eastonclub.com), has a par-72, 18-hole course on Route 333 that's open to the public. Greens fees, including cart, are $64 on weekends and $54 on weekdays. In peak season, the course is open weekdays from 8am to 7pm, weekends from 7am to 7pm. Call for off-season hours.

Harbourtowne Golf Resort, in St. Michaels (✆ **800/446-9066;** www. harbourtowne.com), is a par-70 course designed by Pete Dye. Greens fees are $59 for hotel guests and $69 for nonguests, including cart. Harbourtowne offers 1- and 2-night golf packages, too.

The **Upland Golf Club,** 23780 Thawley Rd., Denton (✆ **866/288-6400;** www.uplandgolfclub.com), is winning rave reviews. The par-71 Joel Weiman–designed course is open to the public for 9 or 18 holes. For 18 holes, summer fees are $60 on weekdays and $85 on weekends; in winter, $45 on weekdays and $52 on weekends.

Pier Street Restaurant SEAFOOD   It looks a little ramshackle, but it's a truism that good seafood is often best at a place like this. Views here are incredible, and the covered deck is a delight in summer. And so many choices: sandwiches and salads for lunch, seafood platters for dinner. Slips on the Tred Avon River are available for boating diners.

W. Pier St. ✆ **410/226-5171.** Reservations required for dinner. Main courses $5.95–$11 lunch, $13–$30 dinner. MC, V. Daily 11:30am–9:30pm. Closed end of Oct to Apr 1.

Robert Morris Inn ✪✪✪ AMERICAN/SEAFOOD   You can take James Michener's word for it: These *are* great crab cakes. The elegant dining room and more casual tavern of this 18th-century inn are attractions in themselves, featuring the original woodwork, slate floors, and fireplaces. The many varieties of crab cake are exceptional: Oxford crab cakes (seasoned, breaded, and fried), Morris crab cakes (baked without the breading), and baked seafood au gratin (crab and shrimp with Jack, cheddar, and seasonings). Lunch items include sandwiches, salads, and omelets. Breakfast is served, too, and people drive hours just for the Sunday Shore Platters.

314 N. Morris St. ✆ **888/823-4012** or 410/226-5111. www.robertmorrisinn.com. Reservations recommended. Dress code in dining room is "smart casual." Main courses $5–$14 lunch, $18–$36 dinner. MC, V. Apr–Nov daily 8–10am, noon–2:30pm, and 5:30–8pm. Closed Dec–Mar.

Schooner's Landing SEAFOOD   This informal spot is on a marina with great views of the water and deck seating in season. Schooner's all-day menu offers prime rib, crab, oyster, and shrimp; sandwiches; soups; and catch-of-the-day specials. It's a good place for lunch or for a boisterous evening of sailing stories, aided by several draft beer options. Bands play some summer nights. There's a kids' menu, too.

314 Tilghman St. 📞 **410/226-0160.** Reservations accepted for dining room only. Main courses $6.45–$24. AE, DC, DISC, MC, V. Daily 11am–10pm; hours vary slightly in winter.

SHOPPING

Oxford shops are usually open Saturday and Sunday from 10am to 6pm; many close midweek when the town's pretty quiet. Hours may be cut back in winter, too.

Hinckley Yacht Services   The wares here range from nautical necessities and yachting apparel to gifts and games. Transient slips and boat repair are available, too. 202 Banks St. 📞 **410/226-5113.** www.hinckleyyachts.com.

Oxford Market   Essentials are sold here: groceries, deli, ice cream, coffee, and wine. Opens at 7am daily, even in winter. 203 S. Morris St. 📞 **410/226-0015.**

Oxford Mews Emporium   This is the place for gifts, necessities, and nonessentials. 105 S. Morris St. 📞 **410/820-8222.**

2 Cambridge

Cambridge lies just across the Choptank River Bridge from Talbot. Still more of a commercial center than a tourist town, it has its charms. High Street leads to the Choptank—a lovely stroll with a great water view at the end. History buffs, especially those interested in the Civil War era, may be interested in the town's connections with the underground railroad. Nature lovers find it a nice stop on their way to Blackwater Refuge or to a hunting or fishing trip. Visitors planning a Mid-Shore visit to Easton or St. Michaels may prefer this quiet place as a base.

Since its foundation in 1684, Cambridge has drawn those who love the water. Once a harbor for trading ships taking tobacco to England and later a deepwater port for 20th-century freighters, Cambridge was also a shipbuilding town. The town still draws boaters—but now they're pleasure boaters.

In its prosperity in Colonial times and again in the early 20th century, Cambridge became the home of governors, lawyers, and landowners. Their beautiful homes line High Street, Water Street, Mill Street, and Hambrooks Boulevard. Sharpshooter Annie Oakley built her house at 28 Bellevue Ave., on Hambrooks Bay. The roofline was altered so Oakley could step outside her second-story windows and shoot waterfowl coming in over the bay. The house is now privately owned, but the owners have erected a small sign in Annie's memory.

Harriet Tubman's home no longer exists, but she often walked the streets and country roads around here as she led more than 300 slaves to freedom on the underground railroad. She is remembered in monuments, markers, a museum in Cambridge, and a driving tour.

Anyone who has read James Michener's *Chesapeake* or John Barth's *The Sot-Weed Factor* may recognize some of the places mentioned—this is one of the towns that inspired these novels.

ESSENTIALS

GETTING THERE   Come by boat (your own; there aren't any ferries)—from the Chesapeake Bay east on the Choptank River—or come by car. Cambridge is on Route 50, about 15 miles south of Easton. Once you cross the Sen. Frederick Malkus Bridge over the Choptank, you're here. The historic district is west of the highway, which is called Ocean Gateway here.

Boat slips are available at the city marina and in front of the county office building, both on the Choptank. Boats can tie up for free for 48 hours in front of the county office building, but need permission to stay longer. The city marina has slips for larger boats; reservations are required. Call © **410/228-1700** for reservations or information.

VISITOR INFORMATION   The **Route 50 Visitor Center,** 2 Rose Hill Place, just west of the bridge in Cambridge (© **410/228-1000;** www.tourdorchester.org), is full of information. The staff can tell you about Cambridge and some of the quaint, small—and I mean small—towns surrounding it, as well as the Blackwater National Wildlife Refuge south of town.

GETTING AROUND   The quickest way to get around is by car, but since the area is so flat, many prefer bicycle. Roads are fairly quiet, making it a pleasure to drive or bike. Be sure to stop at the visitor center for a couple of good brochures: *Historic Walking Tour of Cambridge* explores some of the most significant buildings, houses, and churches in town, while the museum brochure describes seven museums around town and gives directions to the outlying Spocott Windmill Complex (don't miss this, especially if you're a kid).

WHERE TO STAY

Cambridge House ☆   This Queen Anne–style sea captain's mansion, next to Long Wharf, puts visitors in the middle of Cambridge's most beautiful street. Watch the tourists go by as you sit on the front porch, or get away from it all in the Victorian gardens. The elegant rooms, some with fireplaces, feature queen- and king-size beds. A formal breakfast is served each morning.

112 High St., Cambridge, MD 21613. © **410/221-7700.** www.cambridgehousebandb.com. 6 units. $110–$140 double. Rates include formal breakfast and evening refreshments. 2-night minimum stay required on some weekends. AE, DISC, MC, V. No children under 8. *In room:* A/C, TV/VCR.

Glasgow Inn ☆☆   This whitewashed brick house on the National Register of Historic Places lies at the end of a row of reproduction Colonial bungalows. But it's the real thing: a plantation house built 16 years before the Declaration of Independence. The houses built in the intervening years have taken a bit away from the Glasgow's once-commanding views of Hambrooks Bay, but the setting in a 3-acre park is still relaxing. The inn has big, comfortable, simply furnished rooms. Quilts on the beds add a homey touch. The third floor, with slanted ceilings and dormer windows, has great views—but taller guests may want to stay on the other two floors. All units share hall bathrooms, except the only room with a king-size bed.

1500 Hambrooks Blvd., Cambridge, MD 21613. © **410/228-0575.** 5 units, 4 with shared bathroom. $100–$150 double. Credit cards accepted only to hold a reservation; bill must be paid with check, cash, or traveler's check. Rates include breakfast. *In room:* A/C, TV (in some rooms).

Holiday Inn Express Cambridge ☆   Though it's a chain hotel, the staff here brings their own Eastern Shore hospitality. There are four Jacuzzi rooms; romantic getaway packages; and fishing, hunting, and golf packages.

2715 Ocean Gateway, Cambridge, MD 21613. © **410/221-9900.** www.cambridgemd.hiexpress.com. 86 units. $84–$129 double. Rates include continental breakfast. AE, DC, DISC, MC, V. Free baby cribs; rollaway cots available for about $20. **Amenities:** Pool; health club; spa. *In room:* A/C, high-speed Internet access, coffeemaker, hair dryer, iron.

Hyatt Regency Chesapeake Bay ★★   This resort, on 342 acres on the Choptank River, has facilities beyond any other property in the area, with enough amenities to keep families busy without ever leaving the grounds—as well as a variety of packages that take advantage of the countryside. Most rooms have balconies, though of varying size (if you want one big enough to sit on, ask for it). Corner rooms seem a little bigger. Rocking chairs and hammocks invite visitors to watch the river roll by. The spa, marina, and 18-hole, par-5 Keith Foster–designed golf course are open to the public. Have your heart set on a massage? Make a reservation before you arrive.

2800 Ocean Gateway, Cambridge, MD 21613. ℂ **800/233-1234** or 410/901-1234. www.chesapeakebay.hyatt.com. 400 units, including 16 suites and 40 minisuites. $125–$400 double. AE, DC, DISC, MC, V. Pets accepted for fee. **Amenities:** 5 restaurants, with children's menus; 2 bars; indoor pool; 2 outdoor pools; 18-hole golf course; 4 tennis courts; health club; watersports equipment/rentals; bike rentals; Camp Hyatt children's program; game room; business center; general store; salon; massage; beach; 150-slip marina; jogging trails. *In room:* TV w/pay movies and games, Wi-Fi, fridge, coffeemaker, hair dryer, iron.

WHERE TO DINE

Snappers Waterfront Cafe ★★ *Kids* SEAFOOD/INTERNATIONAL   Snappers is a casual place with a friendly staff. The crab dip is served in a crusty French loaf; add a couple friends, a drink, and a deck with a view of Cambridge Creek—you're going to like it here. The huge menu lists lots of seafood, Jamaican jerk chicken, pastas, quesadillas, even an Italian night on Thursdays. Kids get their own menu and a couple of video games. Sunday brunch is served from 11am to 3pm. A new Tiki bar is open from Memorial Day to Labor Day, Thursday through Monday from 4:30pm on, with deck parties on Sundays.

112 Commerce St., Cambridge. ℂ **410/228-0112.** Reservations recommended Fri–Sat. Main courses $6.75–$15 lunch, $6.95–$29 dinner. AE, DC, DISC, MC, V. Labor Day to Memorial Day daily 11am–9pm; summer daily 11am–10pm.

Suicide Bridge Restaurant ★ SEAFOOD   This is the place to be on a Saturday night, when you'll see people waiting up to 45 minutes for their turn at seafood and crab cakes. Chicken and steak dishes are offered, but the very fresh seafood here is cooked simply and well. The restaurant overlooks the Suicide Bridge—whose sad history is printed on the menu—and has a marina for boating diners. Boats must be under 50 feet tall to fit under the Choptank River Bridge.

The restaurant operates two paddle-wheelers, the *Dorothy-Megan* and the *Choptank River Queen.* Lunch cruises are $34; dinner cruises, $45; and sightseeing cruises, $14. Call ℂ **410/943-4775** for a schedule.

6304 Suicide Bridge Rd., Hurlock. ℂ **410/943-4689.** www.suicidebridge.com. Reservations not accepted; call ahead for priority seating list. Main courses $13–$29; kids' menu $3.95–$4.95. MC, V. Apr–Dec Tues–Wed 11am–9pm, Fri–Sat 11am–10pm, Sun noon–9pm; Jan 15–Mar 30 Thurs–Sat 11am–10pm, Sun noon–9pm. Closed Thanksgiving weekend, Dec 24–26, and 1st 2 weeks of Jan.

WHAT TO SEE & DO

Historic High Street ★, which ends at Long Wharf, is lined with 19th-century homes from a variety of periods, including French Second Empire, Queen Anne, and Federal. An informative brochure offers details about the history of these homes, most of which are privately owned.

Stop in the **Dorchester Arts Center,** 120 High St. (ℂ **410/228-7782;** www.dorchesterartscenter.org), to see the exhibits and browse the gift shop. Both feature local artists and artisans. It's open Monday through Saturday from 10am to 2pm. The

Historic Ghost Walk, which departs from here, combines fun with history on Thursday, Friday, and Saturday nights. Call the center for reservations, which are a must. Or go with **Historic Guided Tours: Cambridge and Beyond,** by bus or on foot. Call ℂ **410/901-1000** to reserve; the volunteer group schedules some tours on weekends, but can arrange tours by request.

At Long Wharf, check out the *Nathan of Dorchester* (ℂ **410/228-7141;** www.skipjack-nathan.org), a living museum built by local volunteers. Visitors can sail the 63-foot skipjack; 2-hour cruises of the Choptank are offered two Saturdays a month in June, July, and August. Stop by or call for a reservation.

Brannock Maritime Museum   The museum is at a new site, its artifacts lovingly collected and displayed by former B&B owners. There are ship models, captain's caps, and books and photos that tell the story of Cambridge's shipbuilding industry from Colonial times to recent merchant marine days, along with memories of past wars. Ask about the photos of Japanese sailors planning the attack on Pearl Harbor. There's also an extensive library, often in use by people researching their families.

106 Hayward St. ℂ **410/228-6938.** Free admission. Fri–Sat 10am–4pm; Sun 1:30–4pm; by appointment.

Dorchester County Historical Society   The society operates several museums, including the Neild Museum (which focuses on industrial and agricultural history), the 1760s Meredith House, the 1790 Goldsborough Stables, and a Colonial-style herb garden.

LaGrange Plantation, 902 LaGrange Ave. ℂ **410/228-7953.** Free admission. May 1–Sept 30 Mon–Fri 10am–3pm; Oct 1–April 30 Mon–Fri 10am–1pm.

Harriet Tubman Museum   A tribute to Harriet Tubman, a former slave and conductor in the underground railroad, this small museum has exhibits on Tubman, her efforts to free slaves, and local African-American culture. It also offers tours of places in Dorchester County where Tubman lived, prayed, and worked. Only a few of the actual buildings still exist, but guides use the locations to tell stories about her life.

424 Race St. ℂ **410/228-0401.** Free admission. Tues–Sat 10am–2pm. Tours by appointment only; call ahead to make reservation.

Richardson Maritime Museum   Come here to find out what a bugeye is, how a log canoe sails, or what a skipjack was built to do. With builders' models, hand tools, and building plans, the museum focuses on all the boats used on the Chesapeake Bay for fishing, oystering, and trading.

410 High St. ℂ **410/221-1871.** www.richardsonmuseum.org. Free admission. Mar–Oct Wed and Sun 1–4pm, Sat 10am–4pm; Nov–Feb Sat–Sun 1–4pm. Closed Thanksgiving, Dec 25, Jan 1, Easter, and July 4th.

OUTSIDE OF TOWN

A self-guided brochure, available at the visitor center, leads visitors on the 105-mile **Finding a Way to Freedom** driving tour, through Dorchester and Caroline counties. It follows the footsteps of Harriet Tubman and the underground railroad.

For a worthwhile side trip, visit the **Spocott Windmill** ☆☆, 7 miles west of Cambridge on Route 343. The only existing post windmill for grinding grain left in Maryland, it's still operated at least twice a year. It's not the original—three others have been on this site since the 1700s.

There are also four historic buildings here: a **tenant house,** a humble 1½-story wood dwelling built about 1800; a one-room **schoolhouse,** built in 1870; a **country**

museum store, which evokes an old-time feeling with its potbellied stove and World War II–era merchandise (open by appointment only); and a **smokehouse,** which houses a blacksmith shop. An 1833 **doctor's office** is to be moved back to the site in late 2006. The sites are on Hudson Road (Rte. 343) and stay open daily, from dusk to dawn. Admission is free. Call © **800/522-8687** to make arrangements for a guide.

Unfortunately, the **Dorchester Heritage Museum,** 1904 Horn Point Rd. (© **410/ 228-1899**), has closed, but will still sponsor its annual fly-in. Some 200 planes from the Potomac Antique Aero Squadron fly in on a Saturday in mid-May and are on display from 8am to 5pm; check with the visitor center for the exact date. Volunteers are hoping to reopen the museum if they can muster up more staff—we hope they can. The converted aircraft hangar featured farming and fishing tools, antique toys, Native American artifacts, and an archaeological dig of a 1608 home.

A VISIT TO A NATURAL REFUGE

Blackwater National Wildlife Refuge ☆☆☆, just 12 miles south of Cambridge, gives waterfowl a place to land, provides a safe haven for bald eagles and endangered Delmarva fox squirrels, and lets humans stand in awe of nature. Some 23,000 acres of marsh, freshwater ponds, river, forest, and field were set aside in 1933 for the migratory birds that use the Atlantic Flyway.

The most popular time to visit is during the fall migration, which peaks in November. Some 35,000 geese and 15,000 ducks fill the refuge. Blackwater's free open house, held the second weekend in October, is a great time to see some of the refuge residents up close.

Winter is the best time to see bald eagles. As many as 200 eagles have been seen at Blackwater, and some 18 nesting pairs have set up homes high in the trees—the greatest number of bald eagles on the East Coast north of Florida.

Visitors in spring will see lots of birds headed north. Marsh and shorebirds arrive, as do the ospreys who set up house for their new families. The ospreys build huge nests on platforms in the middle of the marsh. They swoop and dive into the water for fish and then fly back to feed their noisy offspring. March also brings an Eagle Festival.

In summer, birders can find warblers, orioles, blue herons, and even wild turkeys. *Be prepared:* Mosquitoes and flies can be fierce here in summer. Wear a hat and be on the lookout for ticks in early summer.

GETTING THERE   From Route 50, take Route 16 southwest out of Cambridge; turn south on Route 335. Turn left onto Key Wallace Drive and right into the visitor center.

VISITOR CENTER   The new visitor center is on Key Wallace Drive (© **410/228-2677**; www.fws.gov/blackwater). It's open year-round, Monday through Friday from 8am to 4pm, Saturday and Sunday from 9am to 5pm. Staff members can provide maps, bird lists, and calendars of events. Exhibits explain who lives at the refuge, while an observation deck gives visitors a view of the waterfowl browsing in nearby fields. Look for the real-time cameras trained on the osprey and eagle nests. (The nest-cams are on the Friends of Blackwater website, too—go to www.friendsofblackwater.org.)

FEES & REGULATIONS   Entry fee at the wildlife drive is $3 per vehicle, $1 per pedestrian or bicyclist. It's free to anyone holding a Federal Duck Stamp, Golden Eagle Passport, Golden Age Passport, Golden Access, or Blackwater National Wildlife Refuge Pass. Pets are not permitted on trails, but are allowed on leashes on the drive.

A WILDLIFE DRIVE   Though the refuge belongs to the wildlife, the park has set aside hiking paths and a short drive for cars and bicycles so visitors may see and hear these amazing crowds of birds. These are open from dawn to dusk.

After paying the entry fee at a self-service pay station, visitors will reach a fork in the road about ⅓ mile into the drive. Turn left for the Marsh Edge Trail and Observation Site. Then head back up the road for the rest of the drive.

The 5-mile ride meanders through woodlands and marshes that stretch to the horizon. It's quiet, except for the insects and calling birds. Bring your binoculars and camera: You might see any number of birds, deer, or the rare Delmarva fox squirrel.

Want to stretch your legs and see everything a little more closely? You can park at one of the four walking trails. The **Woods Trail** is .5 mile long and runs through a mature forest. The 2.7-mile **Key Wallace Trail** centers on forest interior birds and forest management. For a look at how Mother Nature recovers after a tornado, take a walk on the 2-mile **Tubman Road Trail.**

The .3-mile **Marsh Edge Trail** begins in the woods and ends with an 80-foot boardwalk extending into Little Blackwater River. If you visit in spring or summer, look for the osprey. In fall, you'll see waterfowl. An observation site has been set up at the end of this part of the drive, with an information kiosk. The view over the Blackwater River with all the sights and sounds of thousands of migrating waterfowl can be awe-inspiring. A photo blind is at the edge of a pond and connected by a boardwalk to the drive overlooking the Little Blackwater River.

OTHER OUTDOOR ACTIVITIES

BIKING   The 5-mile wildlife drive is an easy ride on flat, mostly quiet roads. If you plan to bike from Cambridge (about 10 miles) or Vienna (about 15 miles), bring water—there aren't many places to stock up between Cambridge and Blackwater. Before you go, get the "Cycling Trails of Dorchester County" map (available at the visitor center in Cambridge or at www.tourdorchester.org). In addition, Blackwater has its own bike map with two suggested loops. One 20-mile loop takes cyclists from Cambridge's public high school into the refuge. A 5-mile loop crosses the refuge in two locations while winding through several miles of beautiful country roads. Ask about that at the visitor center.

BIRDING   Refuge volunteers offer bird walks on various weekend mornings from September through May. These meet at the visitor center and last about 2 hours. Call ℂ **410/228-2677** for a schedule. The visitor center also has a brochure detailing good spots to look for birds.

BOATING & FISHING   Launching ramps for canoes and kayaks are available year-round. *Caution:* Before you start paddling in fall and winter, check the waterfowl-hunting schedule. Park staff advises against getting between a hunter and a goose.

To rent a kayak, canoe, or bike, try **Blackwater Paddle and Pedal Adventures,** on the road to Blackwater (ℂ **410/901-9255**). Contact **'Peake Paddle Tours** (ℂ **410/829-7342;** www.paddletours.com) for information on kayaking tours with knowledgeable guides (one has a Ph.D.).

Fishing and crabbing are permitted from April 1 to September 30 from small boats and bridges, but note that state laws apply here. A state sportfishing license is required for fishing in the Blackwater and Little Blackwater rivers. No fishing is allowed from the shores.

Kids A Drive to Wye Mills

Three things in this hamlet make the detour worthwhile—a flour mill, the remains of a tree, and beaten biscuits. If you bring the kids, this could be one of those trips they talk about for a long time.

From Route 50, go west on either Route 404 or Route 213, about 13 miles north of Easton or 14 miles southeast from Kent Island. This tiny burg is about a mile off Route 50.

Flour ground at **Wye Grist Mill** ✸, Old Wye Mills Road (Rte. 662), off Route 50, in Wye Mills (© **410/827-6909**), was sent to George Washington's troops at Valley Forge during the Revolutionary War. The mill has been in operation since 1671. Visitors can see it at work on the first and third Saturdays of the month. Guides are good at explaining all the gear that makes the water wheel and grinding stones turn. After a visit, you can buy wheat flour or cornmeal ground here. There's no admission fee, but donations are accepted. Hours are mid-April to mid-November, Thursday through Sunday from 10am to 4pm. Because volunteers staff the mill, hours may vary; it's best to call ahead.

The 450-year-old **Wye Oak** may be gone, victim of a 2002 storm—but the stump of the largest white oak in the country and Maryland's official state tree remains, now surrounded by a fence. Also on the property is the tiny brick **Wye Oak House,** once Talbot County's oldest school. During daylight hours, you can get a peek inside the classroom.

You can't leave Wye Mills without getting a taste of an old Maryland tradition. **Orrell's Maryland Beaten Biscuits,** 14124 Old Wye Mill Rd. (Rte. 662), Wye Mills (© **410/827-6244;** www.beatenbiscuits.com), in business since 1935, has limited hours, but try to schedule a stop. The dough really is beaten—usually with a hammer, though the back of an ax works as well—to get the biscuits to rise. The method was used in a time when leavening was in short supply. You can try the finished product or buy some to bring home. Free admission. Open Tuesday (baking day) and Wednesday (call ahead for hours); tours are available.

If you bring your fishing rod, you can try your luck in the **Wye Mills Community Lake,** across the street from the mill. This 50-acre lake is home to bass, bluegill, and who knows what else. A nontidal-waters fishing license is required. There are lots of grassy spots for a picnic, too.

HUNTING   Deer hunting for both white-tailed and sika deer is allowed in the refuge, but is quite limited. Hunters must mail in applications between July 1 and September 15; locations and dates are limited. Archery permits are more readily available. Hunting licenses are required as well as valid archery, youth, muzzleloader, or shotgun hunt permits. For applications and regulations, contact **Blackwater Refuge Hunts,** 2145 Key Wallace Dr., Cambridge (© **410/228-2677;** www.fws.gov/blackwater), or pick up an application at the visitor center beginning July 1. Archery permits are available after September 15 on a daily basis, at 2145 Key Wallace Dr., off Route 335.

Muddy Marsh Outfitters (© 410/228-2770; www.muddymarsh.com) offers guided bow-hunting packages.

SHOPPING

Bay Country Shop, on Route 50 (© 800/467-2046 or 410/221-0700), offers some mementos with Eastern Shore flair. This shop, located ½ mile south of the Choptank River Bridge, sells everything with a duck or goose on it: clothing, artwork, decoys, and decor. The model boats here are built by local craftspeople. Open daily.

3 Crisfield & Smith Island ★★

138 miles SE of Baltimore, 54 miles SW of Ocean City, 135 miles S of Wilmington

The remote town of Crisfield, on the extreme southern end of the Eastern Shore, offers an insider's look at the lives of the watermen and the seafood industry. Crisfield was once known as the seafood capital of the world. Even though the industry has shrunk over time, crab and oyster packing remain major employers here, along with services for pleasure boaters. Indeed, the crab-packing houses now share the waterfront with dozens of marina slips for yachts, as well as plenty of new condominiums. For visitors, Crisfield and its neighbor, Smith Island, make a great launching point for fishing and boating trips on the deep waters of the southern Chesapeake.

ESSENTIALS

GETTING THERE   Crisfield is accessible by car via Maryland Route 413 from Route 50 or U.S. Route 13. You can also get to Crisfield by boat past Smith Island. (Before heading into shallow Tangier Sound, check your charts.)

VISITOR INFORMATION   For helpful information about Crisfield and the surrounding countryside, contact **Somerset County Tourism** (© 800/521-9189 or 410/651-2968; www.visitsomerset.com). In town, stop at the visitor center at **Somers Cove Marina,** 3 Ninth St. (© 410/968-2501; www.crisfieldheritagefoundation.org).

SPECIAL EVENTS   Crisfield's two biggest events are the **National Hard Crab Derby and Fair** ★ and the **J. Millard Tawes Crab and Clam Bake.** The Hard Crab Derby and Fair is a 3-day event, with a crab-cooking contest, a crab-picking contest, country music, and, of course, the crab race. It's held Labor Day weekend at Somers Cove Marina; admission is usually $4. Make hotel reservations well in advance. The Crab and Clam Bake, held the third Wednesday in July from 1 to 5pm, is an all-you-can-eat affair; buy tickets in advance. For either event, call © 800/782-3913 or 410/968-2500 for information.

WHERE TO STAY

Choosing where to stay is easy in Crisfield. There are a couple of motels in town, all in the moderate category with basic accommodations. The best choice, however, is a nearby country inn in Princess Anne.

Best Value Inn Somers Cove Motel   Views of the water add to the setting of this two-story facility. Each room has a balcony or patio; four have kitchenettes. An ordinary motor inn, its biggest asset is its location in the middle of everything.

700 Norris Harbor Dr., Crisfield, MD 21817. © 888/315-2378 or 410/968-1900. Fax 410/968-3448. www.crisfield. com/somerscove. 40 units. $45–$150 double. DISC, MC, V. Pets accepted for fee. **Amenities:** Outdoor pool; patio; picnic tables; grills; boat docks; boat ramps. *In room:* A/C, TV, coffeemaker (upon request), iron (upon request).

Waterloo Country Inn ★★★ About 30 miles from Crisfield, the Waterloo, a 1775 brick manor house built in the Federal style, is among Delmarva's most elegant accommodations. Listed on the National Register of Historic Places, it is surrounded by farmland and overlooks a tidal pond on Monie Creek. You can explore the area by bike or canoe. The small inn's amenities are gracious and numerous—though some quibble that decor is a bit ticky-tacky. Most rooms contain antiques or Victorian reproductions. The Chesapeake Suite features a whirlpool for two; rooms for guests with disabilities are also available. Locals claim the Waterloo offers the best fine dining in the area; the restaurant serves dinner Tuesday through Saturday, but reserve in advance.

28822 Mt. Vernon Rd., Princess Anne, MD 21853. ✆ **410/651-0883.** Fax 410/651-5592. www.waterloocountry inn.com. 6 units. May–Oct $145–$255 double; Nov–Apr $125–$235 double. Rates include full breakfast. 2-night minimum stay may be required on weekends and holidays. AE, DISC MC, V. Pets accepted with prior arrangement. **Amenities:** Restaurant; outdoor pool; bikes; canoes. *In room:* A/C, dataport, hair dryer.

WHERE TO DINE

Side Streets SEAFOOD Upstairs and down, you can get your all-you-can-eat steamed crabs here—but there are lots of other options at this waterside bistro. Seafood in this seafood capital is, of course, your best bet. There's a raw bar downstairs, too. The upstairs restaurant, open only in warm weather, is a little more formal. Outside seating is available on patios and decks by Tangier Sound.

204 S. 10th St., Crisfield. ✆ **410/968-2442.** Reservations not necessary. Main courses $8.95–$9.75 lunch, $8.95–$30 dinner. DISC, MC, V. Upstairs May–Sept daily 11am–10pm, Oct–Apr Sat–Sun 11am–10pm; downstairs daily 9am–10pm. New owners plan to start serving breakfast at 7am, but a firm date for that was not yet set at press time.

Watermen's Inn AMERICAN Although this eatery does not boast water views, the food is the prime attraction, with an adventurous menu created by owners trained at the renowned Johnson & Wales University's culinary program. Dinnertime choices range from softshell crabs and crab cakes to salmon with teriyaki glaze or bacon-wrapped filet. There's an early-bird menu for $11. The restaurant itself has been freshly decorated with a more refined atmosphere; in summer, there's alfresco dining.

901 W. Main St. (at Ninth St.), Crisfield. ✆ **410/968-2119.** www.crisfield.com/watermens. Reservations recommended for dinner. Main courses $4.50–$8.50 lunch, $9.95–$20 dinner. AE, DISC, MC, V. Summer Wed–Thurs 11am–9pm, Fri–Sat 11am–10pm, Sun 8am–9pm; winter Thurs 11am–8pm, Fri–Sat 11am–8pm, Sun 8am–8pm.

WHAT TO SEE & DO

The **J. Millard Tawes Historical Museum,** Somers Cove Marina, 3 Ninth St. (✆ **410/968-2501;** www.crisfieldheritagefoundation.org), was founded in 1982 to honor the Crisfield-born former governor of Maryland. Exhibits detail the town's history as well as its boat-building and seafood industries. Open year-round, Monday through Saturday from 9am to 5pm. Admission is $2.50 for adults, $1 for children 6 to 12. This is also the starting point for the **Port of Crisfield Escorted Walking Tour,** offered from Memorial Day to Labor Day, Monday through Saturday at 10am. To explore by trolley, take the **Ward Brothers Heritage Tour,** which includes a stop at the workshop of decoy carvers Lem and Steve Ward.

About 15 miles north of Crisfield on U.S. Route 13 is **Princess Anne,** a small country town listed on the National Register of Historic Places. All the historic homes are privately owned, except the grand neoclassical **Teackle Mansion,** 11736 Mansion St. (✆ **410/651-2238;** www.teackle.mansion.museum). It was built in 1801 by Littleton Dennis Teackle, a shipping magnate and an associate of Thomas Jefferson. It's open for guided tours April through mid-December, Wednesday, Saturday, and Sunday from

1 to 3pm; and mid-December through March, Sunday from 1 to 3pm. Inside, you'll see elaborate plaster ceilings, a 7-foot fireplace, a beehive oven, American Chippendale furniture, a Tudor-Gothic pipe organ, and an 1806 silk world map. Admission is $5 for adults, free for children under 12.

OUTDOOR ACTIVITIES

The 485-slip **Somers Cove Marina,** 715 Broadway (© **410/968-0925**), is one of the largest marinas in Maryland. It's able to accommodate both sailboat and motor yachts from 10 to 150 feet. Facilities include boat ramps, showers, laundry room, pool, boat storage, electricity, water, and fuel dock.

Fishing trips leave from the marina and the town dock each day for flounder, trout, spot, drum, blues, and rock. To book a headboat or charter, walk along the waterfront and talk with the captains, or call any of the following: **Capt. Keith Ward** (© **410/ 968-0074;** www.crisfield.com/prim), **Capt. Charlie Corio** (© **410/957-2151**), or **Capt. Larry Laird** (© **410/968-2545**). Charters cost $65 to $100 per person.

Janes Island State Park, 26280 Alfred Lawson Dr. (© **410/968-1565;** www.dnr. maryland.gov), gives nature lovers 2,900 acres of wilderness for hiking, camping, canoeing, and boating. Located on the edge of Tangier Sound, Janes Island has sandy beaches, 25 boat slips, and a canoe/boat trail, the only way to see the island portion of the park. In warm weather, the park rents canoes and kayaks. There are 104 campsites, 49 with electricity, and three backcountry sites; they go for $25 to $85 a night. Most are closed in winter, but four waterfront cabins can be rented year-round.

AN EXCURSION TO SMITH ISLAND ☞

Go for the uniqueness of the place: an island tied to the mainland only by boat, and a people tied together by the seafood industry, hard winters, and church suppers. Go for the food: crabs steamed the minute they land on the dock, homemade ice cream, multilayered Smith Island cake. Go to hear the lyrical twist Smith Islanders put on their English: If you're lucky, you'll hear a story about the good—or bad—old days that make this place "an island out of time," as Tom Horton called it in his book.

Located 12 miles west of Crisfield, at the edge of Tangier Sound, Smith Island is a cluster of islands that makes up Maryland's largest inhabited offshore community. Three towns are located here. Ewell and Rhodes Point are on one island; Tylerton is on another; and the Martin National Wildlife Refuge is on the third.

You can't bring a car, though residents have them. There are no bars, as it's a "dry" island. Walking will get you where you need to go, or you can rent a bike or golf cart. Shops are few, but make sure to stop in one for a piece of cake or a jar of preserves made from the island's pomegranate, pear, or fig trees.

Remember to bring your bug repellent and sunscreen—flies and mosquitoes are sure to plague you, and although the streets are shady, the sun can still be fierce.

One thing's for sure: If you take the ferry for a day trip, you're going to leave wishing you had at least a few more hours here.

ESSENTIALS

GETTING THERE   The excursion boats come only in summer, but you can catch the mail boat or residents' ferry if you want to visit off season. Passenger ferry boats leave from Crisfield and from Point Lookout State Park on Maryland's Western Shore. Or you can bring your own boat.

From Somers Cove Marina in Crisfield, **Smith Island Cruises** (© **410/425-2771;** www.smithislandcruises.com) sails the *Captain Tyler* at 12:30pm and docks in Ewell about an hour later, returning to Crisfield at 4pm. Service runs daily in summer, weekends only in late May and October. Round-trip fare is $24 for adults and $12 for children 3 to 11.

From Point Lookout, on the Western Shore, the twin-hulled *Chelsea Lane Tyler* makes the 1½-hour trip across the Chesapeake Bay Wednesday through Sunday in summer, plus weekends in September and mid-October. See p. 153 for details.

Capt. Otis Ray Tyler (℡ **410/968-1118**) goes to Smith Island year-round. His *Island Belle II* is the mail boat; it leaves Crisfield's City Dock at 12:30pm and departs Ewell at 4pm.

To get to Tylerton, call **Capts. Terry** and **Larry Laird** (℡ **410/425-5931** or 410/425-4471). Their *Captain Jason I* and *II* go to both Ewell and Tylerton from Crisfield's City Dock. They depart Crisfield at 12:30 and 5pm, and leave Smith Island at 7:30am and 4pm (3:30pm in winter).

You can bring your own boat, but check the charts for shallow spots: Smith Island Harbor at Ewell can be 4½ feet at low tide. Water is deeper if you come from Tangier Sound via Big Thorofare. Smith Island Marina is beside the county dock and Bayside Restaurant. The gas dock in Ewell is open Monday through Saturday from 8am to 5pm. (Avoid gassing up in late afternoon, as the watermen use the pumps then.) If you plan to stay, there is some overnight docking. (It is said that Ernest Hemingway once docked his boat here.) Call **Ruke's Store** (℡ **410/425-2311**) or **Driftwood General Store** (℡ **410/425-2111**) for dock rental.

VISITOR INFORMATION   Stop at the Crisfield visitor center at **Somers Cove Marina,** 3 Ninth St. (℡ **410/968-2500;** www.crisfieldheritagefoundation.org), or go to www.visitsomerset.com for information that includes a self-guided walking tour.

Once in Ewell, the island's largest town (pop. 100), visit the **Smith Island Center** ☆, up Smith Island Road from the Bayside Restaurant (℡ **410/425-3351**), to get a sense of how the island is laid out, learn a little history, and see exhibits about the island. Admission is $2; from May through October, it's open daily from noon to 4pm.

Visitors can also stop by the **Middleton House,** on Caleb Road, which serves as an interpretive center for the Martin National Wildlife Refuge. The refuge is too fragile for visitors, but the center's exhibits offer a look at the wildlife there.

GETTING AROUND   No cars are permitted on the island. Everything is within walking distance. You can bring your bike on the ferry or rent one right beside the County Dock. Golf carts can also be rented.

ORIENTATION   **Ewell** is the largest of Smith Island's harbor towns. It's where most cruise boats dock and has most of the island's seafood-packing houses. **Rhodes Point,** about a mile south of Ewell and the island's center for boat repair, used to be called Rogues Point because of the pirates who came here. It's a marshy place, reachable via a wooden bridge from Smith Island or March roads. **Tylerton** may be the most remote place in Maryland, accessible by only one boat. It was home to the state's last one-room school—which closed in 1996.

WHERE TO STAY & DINE

Ewell is home to two restaurants, and each of the ferries sends its passengers to a different one: **Bayside Inn** (℡ **410/425-2771**) and **Ruke's Seafood Deck** (℡ **410/425-2311**). Both are used to the sudden onslaught of hungry visitors. If you don't want to eat with a crowd, bypass the restaurants until later and pop into one of the general stores for a snack. In Tylerton, the only place to eat is the **Drum Point Market** (© **410/425-2108**). These places are all open daily, but may close from 3 to 6pm.

There are two places to stay on the island, both B&Bs.

Ewell Tide Bed & Breakfast   Just steps from the island's main dock is this country house, with four simple but comfortable rooms. Two have both a queen-size and a twin bed, one has double beds, and one has just a queen-size. The owner is also the captain of the 40-foot *Sunrise,* available to pick up guests in Crisfield and take them on a fishing charter or sunset cruise. All kinds of packages are available. With a marina out front, boaters can arrange a boat-and-breakfast package, too.

20926 Tyler Rd., Ewell, MD 21824. © **888/699-2141** or 410/425-2141. www.smithisland.net. 4 units, 2 with shared bathroom. $85–$95 double. Rates include expanded continental breakfast. Rollaway children's beds available for nominal charge. MC, V. **Amenities:** Full kitchen; marina; free use of bicycles and kayaks. *In room:* A/C, TV.

Inn of Silent Music   Visitors can find respite in this old-fashioned farmhouse, surrounded on three sides by water. All bedrooms have water views. The innkeepers pick up guests at the Tylerton dock and will cook dinner for $20 a person. Canoes, kayaks, and bikes are available.

2955 Tylerton Rd., Tylerton, MD 21866. © **410/425-3541**. www.innofsilentmusic.com. 3 units. $105–$125 double. Rates include gourmet breakfast. 2-night minimum stay required on weekends in high season. No credit cards. Closed late Nov to mid-Mar. No children under 12. **Amenities:** Dinner available; complimentary bikes, canoes, and kayak. *In room:* A/C, fridge.

4 Chestertown

55 miles E of Baltimore, 70 miles NE of Washington, D.C., 50 miles SW of Wilmington

Chestertown, north of the Bay Bridge, looks terrific for a town her age. Built in 1706 on the Chester River, this was once a thriving seaport. Residents here showed their revolutionary leanings when they tossed English tea into the harbor, just as Boston's patriots did. The sea captains' homes, many built in the mid-1700s, still line Water Street—an elegant sight as you cross the Chester River Bridge. As you cross, look for the yellow reproduction of the schooner *Sultana.* Chestertown also is home to Washington College, known for the Sophie Kerr Prize, a large cash award given to a graduating writing student each year. This picturesque riverside town makes for a good day trip or a leisurely weekend visit.

ESSENTIALS
GETTING THERE   From Easton, take U.S. Route 50 north to Route 213; then follow Route 213 north into Chestertown. From I-95 and U.S. Route 40, take the Elkton exit and follow Route 213 south into Chestertown.

VISITOR INFORMATION   For a map and brochures covering Chestertown and the surrounding area, contact the **Kent County Office of Tourism,** 400 High St., Chestertown (© **410/778-0416;** www.kentcounty.com). In town, stop at the visitor center at 122 N. Cross St. (© **410/778-9737**). It's open year-round, Monday through Friday from 9am to 4pm, Saturday and Sunday from 10am to 4pm.

GETTING AROUND   With no public transportation in Chestertown, touring by car or walking through the historic streets are the best ways to see the sights. High Street is Chestertown's main thoroughfare. Stop by the visitor center for brochures on a self-guided driving tour and a walking tour.

SPECIAL EVENTS On Memorial Day weekend, the town reenacts the **Chestertown Tea Party** 🍂🍂. On May 23, 1774, after hearing of the closing of the port of Boston, local citizens boarded a British ship in the harbor and tossed its tea overboard. The festival includes a reenactment, boat rides, Colonial parades with costumed participants, crafts, buggy rides, and ragtime bands. For information, call 📞 **410/778-0416.**

WHERE TO STAY

Brampton Inn 🍂🍂 A curving, tree-lined driveway leads to this Greek Revival plantation house, a mile southwest of town. Built in 1860 and listed on the National Register of Historic Places, it sits on 35 acres of hills and farmland. Guests enjoy the use of two sitting rooms, a wide front porch, and extensive spruce-shaded grounds with lawn furniture. Rooms are furnished with authentic period antiques; nine units have fireplaces and five have whirlpool tubs. Two cottages offer space and privacy.

25227 Chestertown Rd. (off Rte. 20), Chestertown, MD 21620. 📞 **866/305-1860** or 410/778-1860. www.brampton inn.com. 10 units. $135–$225 double; $85–$265 cottage. Rates include full breakfast and afternoon tea. 2- or 3-night minimum stay required on weekends and some holidays. DISC, MC, V. Pets accepted in Russell Cottage. *In room:* A/C, TV w/VCR or DVD, hair dryer, iron, robe.

Imperial Hotel 🍂🍂 With a fanciful gingerbread-trimmed triple-porch facade, this three-story brick building is a focal point along the main street of Chestertown. Inside, you'll find a restaurant, parlor, and lounge/bar, with a courtyard garden in back. Guest rooms are furnished with brass beds and period antiques. The third-floor suite has a private porch overlooking High Street. The new Chester River Cottage offers three bedrooms and a porch overlooking the river.

208 High St., Chestertown, MD 21620. 📞 **410/778-5000.** Fax 410/778-9662. www.imperialchestertown.com. 13 units. $95–$150 double; $150–$200 suite. Rates include continental breakfast. 2-night minimum stay required on weekends in high season. AE, MC, V. No children under 12. **Amenities:** Restaurant (see "Where to Dine," below); bar. *In room:* A/C, TV, hair dryer (upon request), iron (upon request).

Inn at Mitchell House If you're looking for a quiet old-world retreat surrounded by remote farmland and habitats for birds, migrating geese, white-tailed deer, and red fox, try this three-story 1743 manor house with a screened-in porch. Nestled on 10 acres overlooking Stoneybrook Pond, it sits midway between Chestertown and Rock Hall off routes 21 and 445. If you come by boat, they'll pick you up at the Tolchester marina, half a mile away. The guest rooms are furnished with four-poster beds, hooked rugs, antiques, and old prints; most units have a fireplace or sitting area.

8796 Maryland Pkwy., Chestertown, MD 21620. 📞 **410/778-6500.** www.innatmitchellhouse.com. 6 units. $100–$140 double. Rates include full country breakfast. 2-night minimum stay required on most weekends. MC, V. **Amenities:** Video library. *In room:* A/C, TV/VCR.

Lauretum Inn Crowning a 6-acre spot on a shady knoll outside of town, this three-story 1870 Queen Anne Victorian (listed on the National Register of Historic Places) was named Lauretum ("laurel grove" in Latin) by its first owner, Harrison Vickers. The inn has a formal parlor with fireplace, a reading room, a screened porch, and a sitting room. Hammocks hang under the trees. Bedrooms are bright and large; the third floor has two suites.

954 High St. (Rte. 20), Chestertown, MD 21620. 📞 **800/742-3236.** www.lauretuminn.com. 5 units. $115–$140 double. Rates include continental breakfast. 2-night minimum stay required on weekends in high season. AE, DISC, MC, V. **Amenities:** Extensive video library. *In room:* A/C, TV/VCR, hair dryer, iron.

White Swan Tavern 🍂🍂 (Finds) Washington may have had a drink at this tavern, but now you can sleep here. This 1730 inn has six comfortable Colonial guest rooms.

The former kitchen is the oldest room in the house, with brick floor and open-beam ceiling. The Thomas Peacock Room has rich furnishings and a view of the garden. A two-room suite on the first floor is so plush, you may never leave. The Bittersweet Guest Suites, two apartments next door, are now open and can each sleep three. Afternoon tea, served from 3 to 5pm, is open to the public.

231 High St., Chestertown, MD 21620. ℂ 410/778-2300. www.whiteswantavern.com. 6 units. $140–$240 double. Rates include continental breakfast and afternoon tea. MC, V. No children under 12. **Amenities:** Wi-Fi. *In room:* A/C, fridge, daily newspaper.

Widow's Walk Inn   In the middle of all that Colonial grandeur sits this Victorian lady, an 1877 beauty with five guest rooms, all with king-size or queen-size beds. A first-floor room with private bathroom is spacious, with big windows and fireplace. Another, with a private bathroom, has a claw-foot tub original to the house.

402 High St., Chestertown, MD 21620. ℂ 888/778-6455 or 410/778-6455. www.chestertown.com/widow. 5 units, 2 with shared bathroom. $100–$140 double. Rates include continental breakfast. MC, V. **Amenities:** Fridge; TV in parlor. *In room:* A/C.

WHERE TO DINE

Feast of Reason *Value* SANDWICHES   This airy little sandwich shop is a favorite of the college crowd and a great place to grab a bite while touring the historic district. The menu changes daily, but you can always expect tasty gourmet sandwiches, soups, and salads. They make their own bread, too.

203 High St. (across from the Imperial Hotel). ℂ 410/778-3828. Reservations not accepted. Sandwiches $3.25–$7.25. No credit cards. Mon–Sat 10am–4pm.

Imperial Hotel 🐦🐦 AMERICAN   This inn offers fine cuisine and an elegant ambience in two intimate dining rooms. Seating is also available on the patio in summer. The menu changes seasonally, but house favorites include fresh fish and rack of lamb, all accompanied by seasonal vegetables. When it's in season, the rockfish is delectable. Sunday lunch offers eggs Benedict, softshell crabs (in season), and sandwiches.

208 High St. ℂ 410/778-5000. Reservations suggested. Main courses $11–$16 lunch, $19–$30 dinner. AE, MC, V. Wed–Thurs 5:30–9pm; Fri–Sat 5:30–9:30pm; Sun noon–3pm.

Old Wharf Inn *Value* AMERICAN/SEAFOOD   Big picture windows frame views of the goings-on at the marina and down the river—the backdrop for a simply prepared seafood feast. The food's traditional: crab bisque, a rich crab and shrimp melt at lunch, and lots of seafood platters for dinner. Sunday brunch offers everything from crab cakes to eggs Benedict. Locals fill the place all the time, so come early.

98 Cannon St. (on the water). ℂ 410/778-3566. Reservations accepted only for large groups. Main courses $4.95–$14 lunch, $8.25–$20 dinner. AE, MC, V. Daily 11am–9pm.

Smith's Shallop

To mark the 400th anniversary of Captain John Smith's 1,700-mile exploration of the Chesapeake Bay, a replica 30-foot "shallop" was launched in November 2005, produced by the foundation that created Chestertown's tall ship, the *Sultana*. This small open boat is scheduled to visit harbors around the region until it embarks on a reenactment of Smith's 1607–08 voyage. Check www.johnsmith 400.org for a schedule of stops on the shallop's tour.

WHAT TO SEE & DO

Take a walk down the shady streets of Chestertown. **High Street,** the main downtown thoroughfare, takes visitors past little shops, restaurants, and inns down to the river and the 1740s Custom House. **Water Street** is lined with the brick homes built by shipbuilders, lawyers, and merchants. In midtown is the **Courthouse,** on Cross Street, the site of a 1706 court and jail.

Behind the courthouse is the **Geddes–Piper House** ✦, 101 Church Alley (✆ **410/ 778-3499;** www.hskcmd.com), home of the Kent County Historical Society and a delightful small-town museum. The house is a tall 1784 three-story charmer built by James Piper. Wander through the rooms to see fans, quilts, clothing, and toys from the 1880s. Open Wednesday through Friday from 10am to 4pm.

How big are the trees in this old town? A giant American basswood, the state champion with a circumference of almost 17 feet and height of 108 feet, is on High Street, about a block from the river.

If you like trees, check out the **Virginia Gent Decker Arboretum,** at Washington College (✆ **800/422-1782,** ext. 7726, or 410/778-7726; www.arboretum.washcoll. edu). A wide variety—from Japanese pagoda trees to American lindens—grows around these historic college buildings.

About halfway between Chestertown and Rock Hall is **St. Paul's Church,** off Route 20, erected in 1713 and one of Maryland's oldest churches in continuous use. It's open daily from 9am to 5pm; donations are welcome. The church served as a barracks for British soldiers during the War of 1812. Actress Tallulah Bankhead is buried in the church cemetery.

OUTDOOR ACTIVITIES

Just south of Rock Hall, **Eastern Neck National Wildlife Refuge,** 1730 Eastern Neck Rd. (✆ **410/639-7056;** www.fws.gov/northeast/easternneck), is well known to birdwatchers and nature lovers, who come to see migrating waterfowl all winter and the arrival of butterflies heading to South America in August and September. Like Blackwater National Wildlife Refuge near Cambridge, this 2,286-acre wooded island is a winter haven for migratory birds, including Canada geese and tundra swan. The refuge was designated a "Globally Significant Birding Area" in 2005. Waterfowl Watch, held in mid-December, takes visitors on guided tours of areas that are normally closed. The refuge has 6 miles of walking trails, an accessible boardwalk, and an accessible trail with platform. There's no entry fee.

BOATING   If the *Sultana* (✆ **410/778-5954;** www.schoonersultana.org), a reproduction 1768 schooner, is in town, call or check the website for a schedule of cruises. Reservations are a good idea.

HUNTING   You can take your gun for a walk at two nearby establishments. **Fair Winds Gun Club** (✆ **410/778-5363**) manages 2,200 acres near Chestertown for goose and dove shooting in September. **Hopkins Game Farm,** in nearby Kennedyville (✆ **410/348-5287**), has 600 acres set aside for goose, duck, pheasant, quail, chukar, and dove hunting; 2,000 acres are set aside for deer hunting. A sporting clay range is also available. Both places require reservations.

SHOPPING

High, Cross, and Cannon streets are lined with shops. Most stores are open Monday through Saturday from 9 or 10am to 5pm.

J. R.'s Antiques and Collectibles, 214 S. Cross St. (℃ **410/810-1006**), stocks quality antiques: silver, crystal, porcelain, and splendid 19th-century furniture.

Twigs and Teacups, 111 S. Cross St. (℃ **410/778-1708**), carries a huge assortment of gifts, including stationery, soaps, toys, pottery, joke items, and (of course) teacups. Have a cup of tea across the street at **Play It Again Sam,** 108 S. Cross St. (℃ **410/ 778-2688**), a popular coffeehouse that sells antiques and a few CDs.

Kerns Collection, Ltd., 210 High St. (℃ **410/778-4044**), displays contemporary prints, clocks, lamps, ties, jewelry, and accessories—much of it by artists. Pieces range from the sophisticated (sleek decorative bowls) to the humorous (papier-mâché dog-shaped wall clocks).

The **Compleat Bookseller,** 301 High St. (℃ **410/778-1480**), stocks a wide variety of books—everything from classics to bestsellers. You'll find *Chesapeake* and other Eastern Shore favorites here.

CHESTERTOWN AFTER DARK

Although Chestertown doesn't really have what could be called "nightlife," there is one local hot spot. **Andy's,** 337½ High St. (℃ **410/778-6779;** www.andys-ctown.com), features live music—everything from rock to jazz to bluegrass—on Friday and Saturday nights starting around 9pm in a back room filled with couches and a fireplace. The bar has several local microbrews on tap. The atmosphere is low-key, with most age groups represented. Andy's is closed on Sunday; the kitchen stays open until 10pm Monday through Thursday, midnight Friday and Saturday.

The restored **Prince Theatre,** 210 High St. (℃ **410/810-2060,** www.princetheatre. org), presents classic films, community theater, and live musical performances. Lots of children's favorites are offered on Saturday afternoons as well.

A SIDE TRIP TO ROCK HALL ✦

This sleepy little fishing village was once a major crossroads. In Colonial times, travelers had to stop here on their way to Philadelphia. George Washington, Thomas Jefferson, and James Madison all really did sleep here.

Now it's mostly a fishing village, squeezed onto a peninsula between the Chesapeake and Swan Creek. Water's everywhere—and so are fishing charters, marinas, and a couple of good seafood restaurants. Pleasure boaters consider this a good destination for dinner. It's an enjoyable day trip, too.

To get here, follow Route 20 west out of Chestertown, about 15 miles away. Or take the boat from Annapolis: **Watermark Cruises** (℃ 410/268-7601, ext. 104; www.watermarkcruises.com) offers 8-hour trips once a month. Tickets are about $55 for adults and $25 for children under 12.

If you come by boat and want to go into town—or if you just want to stay out of your car—get on the **Rock Hall Trolley** (℃ **866/RHTROLY;** www.rockhalltrolleys. com). It runs Friday evening and all day Saturday and Sunday between downtown and the various marinas. All-day fares are $3 for adults, $1 for children. The round-trip to Chestertown is $5 for adults, $3 for children.

WHERE TO STAY

Inn at Osprey Point ✦✦✦   One of the loveliest inns on the Eastern Shore, this place has the charm of a waterfront Colonial home and the space and necessities required by modern travelers. It's designed to look vintage, but in reality it's only 14 years old. There are high ceilings, fireplaces, and plenty of windows. Each bedroom has its own ambience: Bolero has a fireplace and window seats overlooking the water, while the waterfront Escapade suite has a whirlpool tub in its black-marble bathroom.

20786 Rock Hall Ave., Rock Hall, MD 21661. (✆ 410/639-2194. www.ospreypoint.com. 7 units. $90–$200 double. Rates include continental breakfast. DISC, MC, V. **Amenities:** Restaurant (see "Where to Dine," below); bar; pool; bike rentals; children's play area; 160-slip marina. *In room:* A/C, TV, hair dryer.

WHERE TO DINE

Bay Leaf Gourmet COFFEE/DELI   For a good cup of coffee and a quick bite, this simple cafe fits the bill. Breakfast pastries and egg sandwiches in the morning switch to soups, salads, and desserts all afternoon. Carry out or sit at a tiny table by the counter.

5757 Main St. (✆ 410/639-2700. Reservations not accepted. Main courses $5–$8. AE, MC, V. Tues–Sat 7:30am–5pm; Sun 7:30am–3pm.

Osprey Point Restaurant AMERICAN   In a small but elegant Colonial-style dining room, diners have their choice of crab cakes, fresh fish, and maybe duck or lamb, all served with creative sauces and seasonal vegetables. A recent menu offered braised short ribs and pan-seared scallops. For all the formal elegance of the setting and the food, this is a place to relax and enjoy. Brunch is served on Sundays.

At the Inn at Osprey Point, 20786 Rock Hall Ave. (✆ 410/639-2194. www.ospreypoint.com. Reservations recommended. Main courses $22–$26. DISC, MC, V. Tues–Thurs 5–8pm; Fri–Sat 5–9:30pm; Sun 8:30am–3pm.

Waterman's Crab House Restaurant & Dock Bar ✮ SEAFOOD   The dining room is a nice enough place for cracking steamed crabs, but the deck is made for it. Water views, bay breezes, and trays filled with the little gems make a picnic table the perfect dining spot. Waterman's has earned its reputation for good fresh seafood, seafood pasta, and prime rib. Save room for an ice-cream sundae or adult ice-cream drink. There's music on weekends in warm weather.

Rock Hall Harbor, end of Sharp St. (✆ 410/639-2261. www.rockhallmd.com/watermans. Reservations recommended on weekends. Main courses $2.50–$13 lunch, $12–$26 dinner. AE, DISC, MC, V. Sun–Thurs 11am–8:30pm; Fri–Sat 11am–9:30pm.

WHAT TO SEE & DO

Such a small town, but it has three museums, all with a focus on local history. **Tolchester Beach Revisited** ✮, Main and Sharp streets (✆ 410/778-5347; www.rockhall md.com/tolchester), is a two-room museum at the end of the Oyster Court shopping area. Anyone who has ever taken the ferry to the Eastern Shore beaches, or heard stories from a grandparent, will appreciate this collection of memorabilia, photos, and trinkets—all given by people who remember Tolchester Beach, the Ocean City of its day. From the 19th century until construction of the first Bay Bridge, thousands of people escaped the city heat by heading to Tolchester's beach, amusement-park rides, and hotel. Free admission; open March through December, Saturday and Sunday from 11am to 3pm, and by appointment.

The **Waterman's Museum,** Haven Harbour Marina, 20880 Rock Hall Ave. (✆ 410/778-6697; www.havenharbour.com), focuses on the people who harvest the bay. The reproduction shanty house displays photographs, carvings, and boats. It's a work in progress, with plans for construction of a pier where boats on exhibit can be tied up. Free admission; open daily from 10am to 5pm.

The **Rock Hall Museum,** located in the Municipal Museum at 5585 Main St. (✆ 410/639-7611; www.rockhallmd.com/museum), features the usual small-town exhibits: boat models, old tools, a charming sleigh, photos of all the Chesapeake Bay ferries. What makes it worthwhile is a tiny vignette in the corner, a creative display of a duck decoy carver's studio. Free admission. Open Saturday, Sunday, and holidays from 11am to 3pm and by appointment.

OUTDOOR ACTIVITIES

BIKING   This is easy biking territory, flat and quiet. Bike rentals are available at **Haven Harbour Marina** (© **800/506-6697** or 410/778-6697; www.havenharbour. com).

BOATING   There's a whole fleet of fishing charters, as well as several sailing charters, at Rock Hall's marinas—just go to www.kentcounty.com and take your pick. **Blue Crab Chesapeake Charters** (© **410/708-1803**) is one such charter, with room for six on its 36-foot *Crab Imperial.* The 90-minute sail costs $30 a person; overnight charters start at $400.

Don't know the difference between tack and jibe? Learn to sail at the **Maryland School of Sailing & Seamanship** (© **410/639-7030;** www.mdschool.com). It offers 4-day live-aboard cruises for both new and experienced sailors. Rock Hall Yacht Club hosts **Friday Night Sailing Races** on the second and fourth Fridays of the month between May and August; see www.rockhallmd.com/racenite for details.

If you like your boats smaller, see **Chester River Kayak Adventures,** 5758 Main St. (© **410/639-2001;** www.crkayakadventures.com), for kayak rentals and tours. **Haven Harbour Marina** (© **800/506-6697** or 410/778-6697; www.havenharbour. com) also rents kayaks and paddleboats; it has transient slips that can accommodate visiting boats of up to 50 feet as well.

SHOPPING

Barely a block of downtown is devoted to shops. Most are open only on weekends. For ice cream, stop at **Durding's Store,** at Main and Sharp streets (© **410/778-7957**). It sells cones, sundaes, and sodas at its 1930s-era soda counter. Before going home, stop by **Miss Virginia's Crabcakes,** 5793 Kent St. (© **410/639-7871**), to get some tasty souvenirs.

5 Chesapeake City

54 miles NE of Baltimore, 40 miles SW of Wilmington, 25 miles NE of Chestertown

Chesapeake City, on the Chesapeake & Delaware Canal, remains a crossroads for the maritime traffic using the canal every day. Technically an Eastern Shore town, it is easily accessible via I-95, and thus makes an easier Eastern Shore visit than some of the other places discussed in this chapter.

The first thing you notice when driving over the 800-foot Chesapeake and Delaware (C&D) Canal Bridge is the view of the canal. Private boats and commercial ships use this connection between the Chesapeake Bay and Delaware River. Construction of the canal brought prosperity to this town, which changed its name from the Village of Bohemia to Chesapeake City. Its inhabitants built beautiful homes, most of which still survive. Several restored Victorian dwellings now house shops and B&Bs. Boaters find it a great destination or place to stop on a cruise along the Inland Waterway.

ESSENTIALS

GETTING THERE   From Easton and other points south, take Route 301 northeast to Route 213, which leads directly into Chesapeake City. From Baltimore, take

I-95 to the Elkton exit (Rte. 279); follow Route 213 south. You can also sail into town along the canal.

VISITOR INFORMATION   For brochures, contact the **Cecil County Tourism Office,** 1 Seahawk Dr., North East (© **800/CECIL-95** or 410/996-6292; www.see cecil.org).

GETTING AROUND   Although downtown Chesapeake City lends itself to walking, the best way to see the surrounding sights is by car. New as of summer 2005 is free seasonal passenger ferry service, operated by the *Miss Clare,* connecting the north and south sides of the canal. It runs Wednesday through Sunday in summer, weekends only in spring and fall. The schedule is posted on a kiosk in Pell Gardens.

ORIENTATION   The C&D Canal divides the city into north and south sides. The main commercial and historic area is on the south side of the canal. South Chesapeake City is pedestrian-friendly; its one main street, Bohemia Avenue, has stores and businesses. Look for free walking and shopping brochures in any shop. Free parking areas under the bridge and farther in town are clearly marked.

WHERE TO STAY

Blue Max Inn   Built in 1844, this house was once occupied by author Jack Hunter while writing his book *The Blue Max.* The large bedrooms are decorated in period style. Thoughtful touches include chocolates, flowers, and complimentary beverages. Guests can enjoy a cozy parlor (with fireplace), dining room, gazebo, and, best of all, first- and second-floor porches overlooking the historic district. Breakfast can be eaten in the solarium, which offers views of the gardens and fishpond.

300 Bohemia Ave., Chesapeake City, MD 21915. © **877/725-8362** or 410/885-2781. Fax 410/885-2809. www.blue maxinn.com. 9 units. $100–$230 double. Rates include full breakfast, afternoon tea, and sodas and bottled water. 2-night minimum stay required on weekends and holidays in high season. AE, DISC, MC, V. No children under 10. **Amenities:** Health club; Jacuzzi; bikes; gift shop. *In room:* A/C, TV/VCR, dataport, Wi-Fi, hair dryer, iron, robes, CD player.

Inn at the Canal   The high painted ceilings in the public areas will remind visitors of the grand old post–Civil War days. Though the guest rooms are smaller, that style continues all the way up to the third-floor suite. Decorated with antiques, soft colors, and embroidered bedding, the 1868 house is welcoming and comfortable. Windows look out over the Back River Basin. The Upper Bay Suite fills the third floor with its own kitchenette, sitting area with trundle day bed, and tiny water-view deck. The Greenbrier Point Room, though smaller, still has a good-size sitting area and windows on two sides. The innkeepers run an antiques store, **Inntiques,** in the old milking room of the house.

104 Bohemia Ave. (P.O. Box 187), Chesapeake City, MD 21915. © **410/885-5995**. www.innatthecanal.com. 7 units. $95–$225 double. Rates include breakfast and afternoon refreshments. 2-night minimum stay required on weekends in high season. AE, DC, DISC, MC, V. *In room:* A/C, TV (most with VCR or DVD player), dataport, hair dryer, iron, robe.

WHERE TO DINE

Bayard House   AMERICAN   This 1780s house overlooking the canal has two cozy dining rooms, but who could resist the water views from the enclosed porch or brick patio? Then there's the food, artfully presented and creatively prepared. Don't miss the tournedos Baltimore: twin petite filets topped with crab cake and lobster cake, napped in Madeira cream and seafood champagne. Other options include oysters in season (prepared a number of unexpected ways), steak, and lollipop lamb chops. Lunchtime brings salads, a $10 burger, and smaller portions of the dinner entrees.

11 Bohemia Ave. ℭ **887/582-4049** or 410/885-5040. www.bayardhouse.com. Reservations strongly recommended for dinner. Main courses $10–$18 lunch, $21–$34 dinner. AE, DC, DISC, MC, V. Daily 11:30am–3pm and 4:30–9pm.

Chesapeake Inn Restaurant & Marina SEAFOOD   Walk or sail to this modern building with its own boat slips for either fine or casual dining, all with waterfront views. The deck's light-fare menu and live entertainment are offered daily, with a weekend piano bar in winter. The upper-level dining room features a well-rounded wine list and a fine-dining menu of seafood, steak, veal, chicken, and pasta, with an emphasis on seafood combinations. From the buttery bisque to the crab cakes, the crab dishes are hearty and delicious. Sunday brunch starts at 10am.

605 Second St. ℭ **410/885-2040.** www.chesapeakeinn.com. Reservations recommended for dinner. Light-fare menu $4.50–$15; lunch items $7.50–$15; fine-dining menu $21–$33. AE, DC, DISC, MC, V. Deck May–Oct Mon–Thurs noon–10pm, Fri–Sat noon–1am; fine dining year-round Mon–Thurs 11am–10pm, Fri–Sat 11am–11pm, Sun 10am–10pm.

Schaefer's Canal House ✿✿ AMERICAN   Opened in 1908 as a general store, this wide-windowed restaurant sits on the north side of the canal facing Chesapeake City's historic district. Summertime seating is available on the dockside terrace. The menu offers wonderful crab cakes, fresh fish, and surf and turf. On Thursday night, there's a seafood buffet for $25. As ships sail through the canal past the restaurant, the dining room lights dim and the ship's name, port of origin, and cargo are announced. Come by boat—there's a marina here.

208 Bank St. ℭ **410/885-2200.** Reservations recommended. Main courses $7–$14 lunch, $20–$33 dinner, $18 Sun brunch. DISC, MC, V. Mon–Sat 11am–10pm; Sun 8am–10pm (brunch served until 3pm).

WHAT TO SEE & DO
On the waterfront, the **C&D Canal Museum** ✿, 815 Bethel Rd., at Second Street (ℭ **410/885-5622**), tells the story of the giant waterway running through town. The 1829 pump house (now the museum) features the largest water wheel built in the U.S. Free admission; open Monday through Friday from 9am to 4pm.

At the water's edge is **Pell Gardens,** a grassy park with gazebo next to the town wharf. It's a good place to enjoy an ice-cream cone from the **Canal Creamery,** 9 Bohemia Ave. (ℭ **410/885-3314**), across the street (open seasonally).

Take a cruise aboard the *Miss Clare* (ℭ **410/885-5088**), captained by a fifth-generation resident who has plenty of stories and historical photos to share. Cruises are scheduled April through October on Saturday and Sunday.

SHOPPING
Shopping is one of the main attractions in Chesapeake City; most stores are open from 10am until 9 or 10pm on Friday and Saturday, and until 5pm on Sunday. Winter hours tend to be more limited.

Bohemia Avenue, the major thoroughfare, begins at the waterfront with a collection of galleries offering original and local art, as well as limited-edition prints. The oldest of these, **Canal Artworks,** 17 Bohemia Ave. (ℭ **410/885-5083**), is also the most charming. It's run by friendly staff and provides framing services.

Back Creek General Store, 100 Bohemia Ave. (ℭ **410/885-5377**), is housed in an 1861 building that's packed with throw rugs, pottery, candles, gourmet foods, soaps, and a large collection of Sheila and Byers Choice items, including ones of Chesapeake City. **Marens,** 200 Bohemia Ave. (ℭ **410/885-2475**), contains several rooms full of collectibles, cards, local folk and wildlife art, and home furnishings. Christmas ornaments and decorations are in the back room.

8

Frederick & the Civil War Crossroads

Frederick has long been an important crossroads. With the building of the National Pike in the 1700s, it was linked with the port city of Baltimore and became a stop on the road west. Young Francis Scott Key grew up and practiced law in Frederick before writing the poem that would become our national anthem. When Elizabeth Ann Seton sought a place for her new community of religious women, she looked west to Frederick, finally finding a home just north of the city in Emmitsburg.

During the Civil War, thousands of wounded soldiers arrived in Frederick to recover. The first came in August 1862, following the Battle of South Mountain. More arrived the next month after the battle at Antietam, the bloodiest day of battle during the Civil War. So many wounded arrived, they outnumbered Frederick's own citizens.

In 1862, Barbara Fritchie confronted General Stonewall Jackson and was immortalized in poetry: *"'Shoot if you must this old grey head/but spare your country's flag,' she said."* Two years later, Confederate General Jubal Early demanded ransom that saved the town from destruction. Battles at Harpers Ferry and Gettysburg brought more wounded before the Battle of the Monocacy was waged to the southeast.

Reminders of these sad days remain in the area's historic sites, museums, and four battlefields, maintained by the National Park Service.

Frederick, Maryland's third-largest city, remembers the war with its Barbara Fritchie House and the National Museum of Civil War Medicine. The growing town has drawn people to it, with suburbs extending down toward Washington, D.C., and a downtown area that shines as a place to shop, dine, and relax. Outside town are rolling fields and orchards, the foothills of the Catoctin Mountains, and plenty of green space for picnicking and hiking.

The nearby **Monocacy** site has changed little since the battle in 1864, except for a few monuments and a visitor center. **Antietam** has added battlefield guides and opened a field hospital museum. **Harpers Ferry** reminds visitors of its past in a beautiful setting overlooking the Potomac River. And **Gettysburg,** just north in Pennsylvania, draws the most crowds among these battlefields.

1 Frederick /⋆

47 miles W of Baltimore, 45 miles NW of Washington, D.C., 34 miles S of Gettysburg

Once a largely agricultural community, Frederick is now Maryland's third-largest city (behind Baltimore and Gaithersburg, a D.C. suburb). Though its downtown district is surrounded by housing developments that have given Frederick a population of

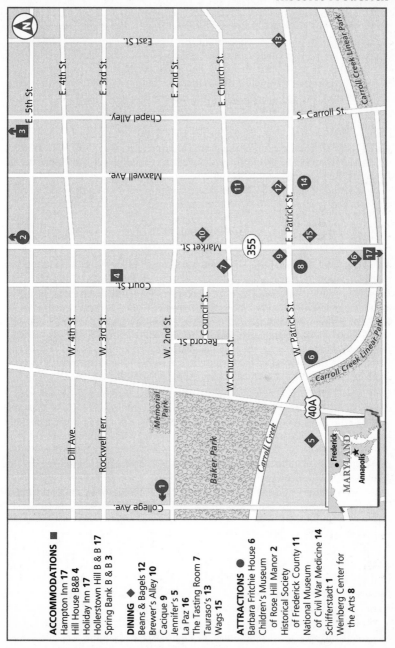

ACCOMMODATIONS ■
Hampton Inn **17**
Hill House B&B **4**
Holiday Inn **17**
Hollerstown Hill B & B **17**
Spring Bank B & B **3**

DINING ◆
Beans & Bagels **12**
Brewer's Alley **10**
Cacique **9**
Jennifer's **5**
La Paz **16**
The Tasting Room **7**
Tauraso's **13**
Wags **15**

ATTRACTIONS ●
Barbara Fritchie House **6**
Children's Museum
  of Rose Hill Manor **2**
Historical Society
  of Frederick County **11**
National Museum
  of Civil War Medicine **14**
Schifferstadt **1**
Weinberg Center for
  the Arts **8**

56,000, the 33-block historic area maintains its small-town charm. The 18th- and 19th-century buildings and cluster of church spires that make up Frederick's skyline are still a main attraction. Antiques and crafts shops dominate the downtown shopping area, and there's a vibrant restaurant and bar scene. Those who like scenic drives will be happy to know that Frederick lies at the junction of two national scenic byways, the Historic National Road (Alternate U.S. 40) and the Catoctin Mountain Scenic Byway (Rte. 15). North and west of the city, the agricultural community still thrives, with produce stands popping up among the grain fields and meadows.

ESSENTIALS

GETTING THERE   From Washington, D.C., take I-270 to Frederick, where the interstate becomes U.S. 15 and continues north to Gettysburg. From Baltimore, take I-70 west. From points west, take I-68 east to I-70.

Greyhound (© **800/231-2222;** www.greyhound.com) operates daily bus service to Frederick into its depot at the MARC train station, 100 S. East St. (© **301/663-3311**).

The MTA's **MARC** train runs between Frederick and Washington, D.C., with service Monday through Friday. Call © **866/RIDE-MTA** or go to www.mtamaryland.com for schedule and fare information.

VISITOR INFORMATION   The **Tourism Council of Frederick County** operates a helpful visitor center at 19 E. Church St. (© **800/999-3613** or 301/228-2888; www.fredericktourism.org). This office supplies maps, brochures, and listings of accommodations and restaurants; it also conducts walking tours of the historic district. The *African American Heritage Sites* brochure outlines historic African-American sites—churches, homes, and even slave quarters in both Frederick and the surrounding county. Some buildings are gone, but signs mark the place. Tourist information booths can also be found in rest areas: on I-70, west of Frederick, and on U.S. 15, south at Emmitsburg. These facilities are open daily from 9am to 5pm.

GETTING AROUND   The best way to get around Frederick is by car—that is, when you're not walking through the historic district. Parking is cheap and sometimes free: At downtown meters and garages, it's $7 Monday through Friday, $1 on Saturday, and free on Sunday. Parking garages are located at 17 E. Church St., 44 E. Patrick St., and 2 S. Court St. Stop at the visitor center to have your Church Street garage ticket validated for up to 3 hours of free parking. If you park in a residential district, check for the signs that restrict nonresident parking.

Frederick County operates **TransIT** (© **301/694-2065;** www.co.frederick.md.us/ transit), a bus service that connects outlying hotels, malls, and local colleges with the historic district and Frederick-area train stations. See the website for maps and schedules.

SPECIAL EVENTS   Fall colors are at their peak in mid- to late October—which is also the peak time for special events. Thurmont's **Catoctin Colorfest** (© **301/271-4432;** www.colorfest.org), a crafts show of enormous proportions, is held in mid-October. On the weekend before Halloween, **Haunted Rail and Trail** (© **301/696-2936** or visit www.recreater.com) takes you on the Walkersville Southern Railroad for a ride to Fountain Rock Nature Center for creepy fun.

First Saturday Gallery Walks are held every month in Frederick. Shops, galleries, and restaurants stay open until 9pm. Call © **301/698-8118** for details.

A couple of events mark the anniversaries of Civil War battles. The commemoration of the **Battle of Monocacy,** the "Battle that saved Washington," is held the weekend closest to the July 9 anniversary (call ✆ **301/662-3515** for information). The **Battle of Antietam** is recalled in September (call ✆ **301/432-5124** for information).

WHERE TO STAY

There are three B&Bs in the historic district and charming inns in the countryside. A number of chain hotels are along the city's edges, many north on Route 15.

Hampton Inn   Located 2 miles south of downtown Frederick, this modern six-story hotel has a brick facade—not the customary Hampton style. It is nestled beside an artificial lake and connected by footbridge to a replica of a lighthouse. Many guest rooms overlook the lake.

5311 Buckeystown Pike, Frederick, MD 21704. ✆ **800/HAMPTON** or 301/698-2500. Fax 301/695-8735. www.hampton innfrederick.com. 160 units. $109–$135 double. Rates include hot breakfast. AE, DC, DISC, MC, V. Take Exit 31B off I-270 at Rte. 85. Pets accepted for a fee. **Amenities:** Restaurant; outdoor pool; health club; business center; executive-level rooms. *In room:* A/C, TV w/pay movies and video games, Wi-Fi, coffeemaker, hair dryer, iron.

Hill House Bed & Breakfast   This 1870s town house is in the historic district—just enough off the beaten track to be quiet, but close enough to walk to everything. Accommodations are cheery and quite comfortable; two units have TVs. The huge canopy bed in the Victorian Room takes up most of the space, but luckily the bathroom is enormous. The Mexican Room has twin beds in a gaily painted setting, plus a huge plant-filled bathroom with chaise longue and access to the balcony. The Chesapeake Room also has balcony access. The Steeple Suite has a full kitchen and lots of sunshine streaming through its big windows.

12 West Third St., Frederick, MD 21705. ✆ **301/682-4111.** www.itlink.com/hillhouse/1.html. 4 units. $105–$125 double; $150 suite. Rates include full breakfast. MC, V. *In room:* Internet access, hair dryer, iron, CD player.

Holiday Inn *Kids*   This modern two-story brick hotel is a popular conference facility; its public areas are often bustling with activity. However, except for the handful of guest rooms overlooking the courtyard/restaurant, most units are separated from the common areas and are relatively quiet. Accommodations are slightly above the standard Holiday Inn size and decor. Attention, shoppers: The hotel is adjacent to the Francis Scott Key Mall. It's also just a short drive from the historic district.

5400 Holiday Dr. (I-270 at Rte. 85), Frederick, MD 21703. ✆ **800/868-0094** or 301/694-7500. Fax 301/694-0589. www.ichotelsgroup.com. 155 units. $94–$129 double. Children under 18 stay free in parent's room; children under 12 eat free. AE, DC, DISC, MC, V. Pets accepted. **Amenities:** Restaurant; lounge; indoor pool; health club; whirlpool; sauna; recreation center with indoor miniature golf course, table tennis, and board games; shuttle to local corporate sites. *In room:* A/C, TV/VCR w/pay movies and video games, high-speed Internet access, fridge, microwave, coffeemaker, hair dryer, iron.

Hollerstown Hill Bed & Breakfast   This rose-and-gray 1901 Victorian beauty is on a quiet lane at the southern end of the historic district. Guest rooms have small sitting areas and Victorian furnishings (some antiques, some reproductions—but all designed for comfort). One room has twin beds; the Dutro has a king-size bed and huge bathroom; another unit has its own balcony nestled in the branches of an old tree. The game room has a pool table and Civil War soldier chess set.

4 Clarke Place, Frederick, MD 21701. ✆ **301/228-3630.** www.hollerstownhill.com. 4 units. $115–$125 double. Rates include full breakfast and afternoon tea. AE, MC, V. No children under 15. **Amenities:** Sitting area w/TV; game room. *In room:* A/C, TV, high-speed Internet access.

The Inn at Buckeystown *✿*   Set in a quiet country village on the Monocacy River, this 1897 mansion is rich in Italianate Victorian details, with a wraparound porch, widow's walk, gables, bay windows, and ornate trim. The interior boasts antiques, Oriental rugs, chandeliers, and five working fireplaces. The rooms have varying amenities and unique touches—a fireplace in one, a porch in another. Lunch, Sunday brunch, dinner, and high tea are served on Victorian china with period silver and glassware (reservations required for all meals). Murder-mystery dinners are scheduled each month; check the website for details.

3521 Buckeystown Pike (Rte. 85), Buckeystown, MD 21717. © **800/272-1190** or 301/874-5755. Fax 301/831-1355. www.innatbuckeystown.com. 9 units. $110–$160 double. Rates include breakfast. MAP rates and corporate rates available. AE, DISC, MC, V. Located 4 miles south of Frederick. **Amenities:** Restaurant. *In room:* A/C, TV/VCR, dataport, robe.

Spring Bank Bed & Breakfast   Dating from 1880 and listed on the National Register of Historic Places, this redbrick Italianate and Gothic Revival B&B has three stories bedecked with gables, cupolas, double porches, bay windows, and a fish-scale-patterned slate roof. Inside are high ceilings with frescoes, stenciling, fauxmarble mantles, antiques, and William Morris wallpaper. The place is sprawling yet homey. It's located north of downtown Frederick, just off Route 15, in a country setting on 10 acres.

7945 Worman's Mill Rd., Frederick, MD 21701. © **800/400-INNS** or 301/694-0440. www.bbonline.com/md/spring bank. 3 units, 2 with shared bathroom. $100–$120 double. Rates include continental breakfast. 2-night minimum stay required on most weekends and holidays. AE, DISC, MC, V. No children under 12. *In room:* A/C, Wi-Fi, hair dryer (upon request), iron (upon request).

WHERE TO DINE

Get coffee and a bagel at the cozy **Beans & Bagels,** 49 E. Patrick St. (© **301/620-2165**). It has soups and sandwiches, plus breakfast items served all day.

Brewer's Alley AMERICAN/PIZZA   Wood-fired pizza and beer brewed on-site make this place a winner. The standard pub fare is consistently good, but the specialty pizzas are creative and fun—try one topped with barbecued chicken. The brewpub is very popular; on busy weekends, the wait for a table can be long.

124 N. Market St. © **301/631-0089.** www.brewers-alley.com. Reservations recommended on weekends. Main courses $10–$15 lunch, $7.25–$17 dinner. AE, DC, MC, V. Mon–Thurs 11:30am–9pm; Fri–Sat 11:30am–10:30pm; Sun noon–9pm.

Cacique SPANISH/MEXICAN   Diners can sit in one of the low, cozy rooms with white tablecloths and Latino music piped in, or outside on the little sidewalk patio. The Tex-Mex and Spanish favorites include paella, fajitas, and quesadillas, with a side of undeniably fresh *pico de gallo* sharp with lime and cilantro. The food is good, if not surprising, and the service is as friendly as you'd expect in Frederick.

26 N. Market St. © **301/695-2756.** Reservations recommended for dinner. Main courses $5.25–$8.95 lunch, $9.95–$18 dinner. AE, DC, DISC, MC, V. Sun–Thurs 11am–10pm; Fri–Sat 11am–11pm.

Jennifer's ⓖ AMERICAN   This neighborhood favorite is worth a venture off Frederick's restaurant row on Market Street. About a block from the county courthouse, Jennifer's is seldom crowded and attracts a mostly local crowd: lawyers and businesspeople for lunch, area residents for dinner. A slate fireplace, exposed-brick walls, and large oak bar create a warm atmosphere. Lunch brings the usual burgers, pizza, salads, and soups. Dinner is exceptional, especially the seafood. Hot and crunchy Creole catfish with honey-pecan butter is a winner, as is the crab dip. If these sound too rich or calorie-laden, order from the spa menu.

207 W. Patrick St. (C) **301/662-0373**. Reservations recommended for dinner. Main courses $5–$9 lunch, $11–$24 dinner. AE, DC, DISC, MC, V. Mon 11:30am–9:30pm; Tues–Sat 11:30am–11pm; Sun noon–9:30pm.

La Paz *Value* MEXICAN   La Paz has moved to a prime spot on newly developed Carroll Creek, with two floors of dining rooms overlooking the creek, plus a waterfront patio in warm weather. The menu remains the same good Mexican food: fajitas, flautas, vegetable burritos, and more. The margaritas are also quite good. There's a limited children's menu.

51 S. Market St. (C) **301/694-8980**. www.lapazmex.com. Reservations accepted only on weekdays for parties of 6 or more. Main courses $4–$6.25 lunch, $6–$13 dinner. AE, DC, DISC, MC, V. Mon–Thurs 11am–10pm; Fri 11am–11pm; Sat 11:30am–11pm; Sun 3:30–11pm.

The Tasting Room NEW AMERICAN   After a day of visiting museums and quaint shops on charming little streets, this minimalist cream-and-black restaurant is a breath of fresh air. Its menu is as up-to-the-minute as the decor. It changes regularly, but always lists lots of meat, salads, and some seafood, all paired with the trendiest of ingredients. At lunch, try the salmon cakes, steak salad, or pan-seared ahi tuna. At dinner, choices include fresh fish and a much-praised lobster chowder. The wine list has 150 choices, and wine suggestions are given for every dish. Martini specials are listed above the bar.

101 N. Market St. (C) **240/379-7772**. Reservations recommended for dinner. Main courses $7.95–$16 lunch, $16–$34 dinner. AE, DC, DISC, MC, V. Mon–Sat 11am–3pm and 5–10pm ('til 11pm Fri–Sat).

Tauraso's *Finds* AMERICAN/ITALIAN   Bright and busy Tauraso's, the main dining choice at the Everedy Square shopping complex, is often mentioned as Frederick's premier restaurant. There are three settings—a more formal dining room, an outdoor patio, and a casual pub—but just one extensive menu. Entrees range from Italian pastas and Tauraso's original seafood sausage to American favorites such as crab cakes and steaks. For lunch, you'll find sandwiches, frittatas, pastas, and salads. Pizzas made in a wood-burning oven are also featured throughout the day.

Everedy Sq., 6 N. East St. (C) **301/663-6600**. www.taurasos.com. Reservations recommended for dinner on weekends. Main courses $6.95–$14 lunch, $7.95–$29 dinner. AE, DC, DISC, MC, V. Sun–Thurs 11:30am–10pm; Fri–Sat 11:30am–11pm, bar open until 2am.

Wag's *Finds* AMERICAN   This basement bar is the smallest of Frederick's favorite nightspots. Its appeal can be summed up in four words: Wag's burgers and fries. Dripping with Wag's special sauce, the burgers have been voted the best in town 7 years in a row. There are other equally distressing (and wonderful) sandwiches on the menu, including the classic Reuben and ham and cheese.

24 S. Market St. (C) **301/694-8451**. http://pages.frederick.com/dining/wags.htm. Reservations not accepted. Main courses $3.75–$6.95. AE, DISC, MC, V. Mon–Sat 11am–2am.

WHAT TO SEE & DO

Head first to the **Frederick Visitor Center,** 19 E. Church St. ((C) **301/228-2888;** www.fredericktourism.org), for maps, information, and, if you parked at the Church Street garage, validation of your ticket for 3 hours of free parking. Guided walking tours of the historic district depart the visitor center at 1:30pm on Saturdays and Sundays. The cost is $5.50 for adults, $4.50 for seniors, and $2.50 for children under 12. If wineries or breweries are more your thing, or if you'd like a Candlelight Ghost Tour, the staff can suggest plenty of options. If you love covered bridges, ask for the directions to three in Frederick County.

In 2005, Frederick's 33-block historic district was honored as a **Great American Main Street** by the National Trust for Historic Preservation. This area features shops, a handful of museums, and lots of good restaurants. Some streets are filled with tiny town houses; others are lined with one mansion after another. And you can't miss the church spires: Frederick is known for its collection of steeples—in fact, the town's seal features them. (Look for a pair of ornate gray spires to find the visitor center and a parking garage.)

Kids can let loose at **Carroll Creek Park,** which runs east–west through the historic district between Patrick and Bentz streets. Redevelopment in spring 2006 has added new bridges, walkways, water features, and an amphitheater. Cross Bentz Street to get to the playground and picnic tables at Baker Park.

DOWNTOWN MUSEUMS & HISTORIC SITES

Barbara Fritchie House   This tiny house on the banks of Carroll Creek was reconstructed from the original materials of Barbara Fritchie's house after it was torn down; it's furnished with her own possessions. Reopened in 2005 after 3 years of restoration, the house recalls the feisty heroine of John Greenleaf Whittier's poem, who is remembered for waving a flag and saying "Shoot if you must this old gray head; but spare your country's flag." Some say the story isn't true, but staff here can offer written proof that although Fritchie may have been 95, she did indeed confront the Confederates and refuse an order to lower her flag. Visit the house and decide for yourself.

154 W. Patrick St. (on Carroll Creek Park). (C) 301/698-8992. Admission $2 adults, $1.50 seniors and children 5–12. Apr–Dec Fri–Sat 10am–4pm; Sun 1–4pm.

Children's Museum of Rose Hill Manor (★) (Kids)   Adults will enjoy seeing the grand architecture and decorative arts of this 1790s manor house. Kids will love looking at old-fashioned toys, trying on bonnets and hats, learning how a spinning wheel works, working a loom themselves, and touching all the labor-saving kitchen gadgets of that era. Also in the 43-acre park are an icehouse, garden, log cabin, blacksmith shop, farm museum, and carriage museum. The lawns invite picnickers to set a spell. The house tour takes about 1½ hours.

1611 N. Market St. (C) 301/694-1650. www.rosehillmuseum.com. Admission $5 adults, $4 children and seniors. House tours Apr–Oct Mon–Sat 10am–4pm; Sun 1–4pm. Tours also available Sat–Sun in Nov and by appointment Dec–Mar; call ahead. Park is always open during daylight hours.

Historical Society of Frederick County (★)   Nobody famous lived here, the guides at this 1820s Federal-style house will tell you. But, at various times, it was home to a doctor and his family; it witnessed the Civil War, with Union and Confederate troops passing through the streets just outside; and more than 100 orphaned girls once called it home. Look for portraits of Roger B. Taney, chief justice of the U.S. Supreme Court and author of the *Dred Scott* decision, and Francis Scott Key, author of "The Star-Spangled Banner." There's also a library and a formal garden.

24 E. Church St. (C) 301/663-1188. www.hsfcinfo.org. Admission $3 adults, free for children under 17. Museum Mon–Sat 10am–4pm, Sun 1–4pm; library Tues–Sat 10am–4pm. Guided tours available year-round, except 1st 2 weeks of Jan.

National Museum of Civil War Medicine (Finds)   Using the usual display cases, wall exhibits, and particularly touching life-size dioramas with wax figures and sound effects, this museum brings to life the suffering and the healing of the Civil War soldier. Exhibits focus on all aspects of Civil War medicine, from the initial treatment on the battlefield to the hospitals, hospital trains, operating rooms, treatments, and, finally, embalming practices used during that time. A new exhibit features Clara Barton and her efforts to bring supplies to soldiers on the battlefields. The building itself is where several thousand dead from the Battle of Antietam were housed and embalmed.

The museum has opened the new **Pry House Field Hospital Museum** at Antietam Battlefield (p. 203).

48 E. Patrick St. ✆ 800/564-1864 or 301/695-1864. www.civilwarmed.org. Admission $6.50 adults, $6 seniors, $4.50 children 10–16. Mon–Sat 10am–5pm; Sun 11am–5pm. Closed Thanksgiving, Dec 24–25, Dec 31, and Jan 1.

Schifferstadt   Frederick's oldest standing house is one of America's finest examples of German Colonial architecture. Built in 1756 by the Brunner family, who named it for their homeland in Germany, it has stone walls more than 2 feet thick, hand-hewn beams of native oak pinned together with wooden pegs, a vaulted cellar and chimney, and a perfectly preserved five-plate jamb stove. Guided tours are given throughout the day. Oktoberfest is celebrated in mid-October.

1110 Rosemont Ave., on the western edge of town. ✆ 301/663-3885. www.frederickcountylandmarksfoundation.org. Suggested donation $3. Apr to mid-Dec Wed–Sun noon–4pm; also open by appointment. Weekend visitors should call ahead to be sure house will be open. Closed Easter, July 4th, and Thanksgiving. Take Rte. 15 north to Exit 14, Rosemont Ave.

NEARBY MILITARY SITES OF THE CIVIL WAR & EARLIER

Fort Frederick State Park   Fort Frederick's role in Civil War history was to post Union troops, though it faced Confederate raiders in the only fighting the fort saw in December 1861. During the French and Indian War, it served as an important supply base for English campaigns; during the Revolutionary War, it was as a refuge for settlers and a prison for Hessian and British soldiers.

If you're driving through the area, the 1756 stone fort is worth a look. Daily in summer and on weekends in spring and fall, living-history reenactors show visitors about frontier life. The park also has campsites for $15 a night (✆ **888/432-2267** for group reservations only); two hiking trails through woods and wetlands; and boat rentals for Big Pool. Nearby is the Western Maryland Rail Trail, a 20-mile path that follows an old train line. The Rails to Trails Conservancy has chosen this as one of the top 12 trails in the U.S. for viewing fall foliage.

11100 Fort Frederick Rd. (40 miles west of Frederick, off I-70), Big Pool. ✆ 301/842-2155. www.dnr.maryland.gov. Admission $3 adults, $2 children 6–12. Fort exhibits Memorial Day to Labor Day daily 9:30am–5:30pm; Apr to Memorial Day and Sept–Oct Sat–Sun 9:30am–5:30pm.

Monocacy National Battlefield   This stretch of farmland was the site of a little-known but important Civil War encounter, the Battle of the Monocacy. General Jubal Early led 15,000 Confederates against a Union force of 5,800 under General Lew Wallace in July 1864. The Confederates won, but their forces were weakened so that Union troops at Fort Stevens could push them back from Washington and save the nation's capital from capture. Today, the battlefield remains virtually unchanged. The visitor center has displays and artifacts. An auto tour is 4 miles round-trip; two other trails offer historic and scenic vistas. From May through August, special events are scheduled on the first weekend of the month; a commemoration of the battle is held on a weekend near July 9.

4801 Urbana Pike, Frederick. ✆ 301/662-3515. www.nps.gov/mono. Free admission. Memorial Day to Labor Day daily 8:30am–5pm; rest of year daily 8am–4:30pm. Closed Thanksgiving, Dec 25, and Jan 1. From the north, east, or west, use I-70; take Exit 54 and proceed south on Rte. 355; the visitor center is on the left ¹/₁₀ mile south of Monocacy River Bridge. From the south, use I-270; take Exit 26 and turn left onto Rte. 80; then turn left onto Rte. 355 North. The visitor center is 3¾ miles north.

Tips Following the Path of the Civil War

At any of the visitor centers along I-70, ask for the **Civil War Trails** maps. With lots of description, some photos, and a bit of a history lesson, they offer a soldier's view of the war—only the soldiers walked, whereas visitors can drive in air-conditioned or heated comfort. Use the maps to find Antietam or Harpers Ferry or Gettysburg, or to take the roads Union or Confederate soldiers traveled. They'll lead you to some off-the-beaten-track sites of battles, skirmishes, hospitals, or strategic positions for each army. The map devoted to Antietam includes Harpers Ferry. The Gettysburg map covers much of the same territory as it describes the movement of the armies north for battle. Call ✆ **888/248-4597** or visit www.civilwartrails.org for more information.

SPECTATOR SPORTS & OUTDOOR ACTIVITIES

BASEBALL   The **Frederick Keys** (✆ **301/662-0013;** www.frederickkeys.com), an Orioles farm team, play at Harry Grove Stadium, off I-70 and Route 355 (Market St.), from May to August or early September. General admission is $5 to $11.

BIKING   Bikers and hikers can access the towpath of the **Chesapeake & Ohio (C&O) Canal** in several places in Frederick County: Point of Rocks, off Route 15 South; Brunswick, Route 79 off Maryland Route 340; and Sandy Hook, left off Route 340, before you cross the Potomac River. The canal runs along the Potomac for 185 miles from Georgetown to Cumberland. Bicycle bells are required on the towpath.

Nearby, both Antietam National Battlefield and Gettysburg National Military Park are terrific sites to tour on bike.

HIKING   The **Appalachian Trail** (www.appalachiantrail.org) runs along the border of Frederick and Washington counties, through Washington Monument State Park, South Mountain State Park, Greenbrier State Park, and Gathland State Park. You can hike the entire Maryland portion in 3 or 4 days, but any section of it makes a great 1-day excursion.

North of Frederick, **Catoctin Mountain Park** (✆ **301/663-9388**) and **Cunningham Falls State Park** (✆ **301/271-7574**) offer several miles of easy to strenuous hiking trails. Both are off Route 15 North. (See section 5, "Serenity & Apples on Route 15," p. 209.)

A final great place for a day hike is the **Billy Goat Trail,** at Great Falls of the Potomac (see the C&O Canal Museum at Great Falls of the Potomac, p. 146). The somewhat strenuous hike, through woods and over boulders, guides you along the cliff walls above Mather Gorge. Get a map online at www.nps.gov/choh.

SHOPPING

If you want antiques, vintage clothing, eye-popping jewelry, handcrafted gifts, or something that's just different, you're going to love Frederick's shopping. The historic district has plenty of interesting shops, mostly on Patrick, Market, Church, and North East streets. They're usually open from 10am to 5pm, though many close on Mondays. For **First Saturday Gallery Walks,** shops stay open until 9pm; some offer trunk shows or special merchandise, and some serve refreshments.

Everedy Square and **Shab Row,** clusters of businesses located around North East Street, have plenty of specialty shops and restaurants. Everedy Square is a block of modern buildings, while Shab Row shops are located in historic town houses and even a log cabin.

Antiques lovers should check out **Heritage Antiques,** 39 E. Patrick St. (© **301/ 668-0299**), for china, crystal, and some fine mahogany furniture. **Little's,** 102 E. Patrick St. (© **301/620-0517**), has antiques and country-style reproductions; it's closed Tuesday and Wednesday. **Emporium Antiques at Creekside,** 112 E. Patrick St. (© **301/662-7099**), has more than 130 dealers crammed into an old car dealership, selling everything from furniture and toys to silver and china. There are plenty of other antiques dealers on East, Patrick, and Carroll streets.

For home decor, try **Artful Gatherings,** 122 E. Patrick St. (© **301/682-7770**), for something old or new; **Chiffon,** 101 E. Patrick St. (© **301/228-3857**), where Shabby Chic reigns supreme; and **Molly's Meanderings,** 17 N. Market St. (© **301/668- 8075**), for vintage-look styles.

Take home a gift: perhaps handmade soap from **La Savon,** 10 E. Church St. (© **301/694-0935**); handcrafted jewelry or animation gels from **McGuire Fine Arts,** now at 110 N. Market St. (© **301/695-6567**); brightly colored tableware and crafts from **The Muse,** 19 N. Market St. (© **301/663-3632**); or items made in the Third World from **B&B International Alley,** 47 E. Patrick St. (© **301/620-2165**). For fine chocolate, head to **Candy Kitchen,** 52 N. Market St. (© **301/698-0442**).

FREDERICK AFTER DARK
BARS & LIVE MUSIC

Most of Frederick's nightspots are on or near Market Street. **Olde Town Tavern,** 325 N. Market St. (© **301/695-1454**), is the home of cheap beer and the local college crowd. Heading south on Market, **Bushwallers,** 209 N. Market St. (© **301/695- 6988**), features Irish music on Sunday and Wednesday, live bands on Friday and Saturday. **Brewer's Alley,** 124 N. Market St. (© **301/631-0089**), is a large brewpub, also described on p. 196. **Firestone's,** 105 N. Market St. (© **301/663-0330;** www. firestonesrestaurant.com), has live music on Friday and Saturday. **Wag's,** 24 S. Market St. (© **301/694-8451**), is your basic basement bar with good burgers (see p. 197 for a review).

New in town is **WestSide Café,** 1A W. Second St. (© **301/418-6886;** www.west side-cafe.com), with live acoustic music Wednesday through Sunday. The **Bentz Street Sports Bar,** 6 S. Bentz St. (© **301/620-2222;** www.bentzstreetsportsbar.com), has 30 TVs tuned to sports, live entertainment on Friday, and comedy on Wednesday.

THE PERFORMING ARTS

All kinds of events are staged year-round at the **Weinberg Center for the Arts,** 20 W. Patrick St. (© **301/228-2828;** www.weinbergcenter.org), a 1926 movie theater, including dance, music, theater, classic movies, and family entertainment.

In summer, free open-air concerts are held Sunday evenings at the **Baker Park Bandshell,** Second and Bentz streets (© **301/694-2489**). They feature local and military bands as well as touring musical acts.

The **Fredericktowne Players** (© **240/315-3855;** www.fredericktowneplayers.org) perform four shows each year at nearby Tuscarora High School. The **Shakespeare Project** (© **301/668-4090;** www.shakespeareproject.com) offers free performances each June at Hood College's Hodson Outdoor Theater.

2 Antietam National Battlefield ⊀

22 miles W of Frederick, 10 miles S of Hagerstown, 57 miles SW of Gettysburg

Antietam (or Sharpsburg to Southerners) is perhaps the saddest place you can visit in Maryland. A walk down Bloody Lane will send shivers up your spine—especially after you've seen the photographs of the corpses piled up on this road. (Photos at Antietam were the first ever taken of a battlefield before the bodies were buried.) More than 23,000 men were killed or wounded here when Union forces met and stopped the first attempted Southern invasion of the North in September 1862. It is the site of the bloodiest day of the Civil War—with more Americans killed or wounded than on any other single day of combat, including D-day. President Lincoln made a battlefield appearance shortly after the battle at Antietam to confront the Union's General George McClellan over his unwillingness to pursue the retreating Confederate army. Clara Barton, who founded the American Red Cross 19 years later, nursed the wounded at a field hospital here.

Today, the battlefield is marked by rolling hills and farmland, and attended by a visitor center, a cemetery, modest monuments, and the gentle waters of Antietam Creek. The mood is somber. Gettysburg has all the monuments and displays, but this is the place to come to consider the tragedy, rather than the triumph, of war.

ACCESS POINTS The battlefield is on Maryland Route 65, a mile north of Sharpsburg (Exit 29 from I-70). For a scenic trip from Frederick, take Alternate Route 40, which goes through Middletown and then over South Mountain ridge, where the Battle of South Mountain occurred; then turn left on Route 34 in the town of Boonsboro; this will take you into Sharpsburg.

FEES Admission to the battlefield is $4 for adults, $6 per family, and free for children under 17.

VISITOR CENTER Begin a trip to the battlefield at the **visitor center,** 1 mile north of Sharpsburg on Route 65 (© **301/432-5124;** www.nps.gov/anti). It has exhibits, documentaries, a museum, a gift shop, and an observation room overlooking the battlefield. The staff provides maps, literature, and suggestions for routes to explore the battlefield and cemetery. Open June through August daily from 8:30am to 6pm, September through May daily from 8:30am to 5pm. Closed Thanksgiving, December 25, and January 1. *Note:* The battlefield officially closes 20 minutes after sunset.

SEEING THE HIGHLIGHTS

The battlefield's quiet hills and limited number of monuments make it a stark and silent contrast to the massive memorials of Gettysburg. The park service offers an 8½-mile self-guided auto tour that can also be walked or bicycled. Tours on audiotape and CD are also

---

Moments **A Candlelight Remembrance**

On the first Saturday of December, Antietam National Battlefield is illuminated with 23,000 candles, one for each of those killed, wounded, or missing after the battle. People come from everywhere, willing to wait an hour or more, for the chance to drive past this sad but beautiful sight. Cars start moving through the park at about 6:30pm and continue until midnight or until all the cars have passed. The only entrance is on Route 34.

available. **Battlefield Guides** (℃ 800/417-9596), similar to the guides at Gettysburg, are available to take groups or families for a 2-hour tour of the battlefield; reservations are required.

Be sure to see **Burnside Bridge,** which crosses Antietam Creek near the southern end of the battlefield. Georgia snipers stalled 4,000 Union soldiers for over 3 hours as the Union tried to secure this stone arch bridge. Another must-see stop is the observation tower over a sunken country lane near the center of the battlefield. This sunken road, now known as **Bloody Lane,** was the scene of a 4-hour encounter that ended with no decisive winner and 4,000 casualties. The graceful stone arches of Burnside Bridge and the harrowing sight of Bloody Lane are among the most memorable images of the battlefield. And don't miss **Dunker Church,** which figures prominently in a number of Civil War photos.

New in 2005 is the **Pry House Field Hospital Museum** (℃ 301/695-1864; www.civilwarmed.org), just a 5-minute drive off the battlefield. This imposing brick house served as Gen. George McClellan's headquarters during the battle. Several generals were treated here; the barn was also used as a field hospital. The museum is open May through August, daily 10am to 5pm. It's closed December through April, plus 2 days in spring and fall (check the website). Donations are accepted.

Every year on September 17, and on the weekend closest to the date, the anniversary of the battle is remembered with ranger-led hikes and special events. An Independence Day concert, featuring the Maryland Symphony Orchestra and fireworks, is held on the Saturday closest to the Fourth of July.

OUTDOOR ACTIVITIES

BIKING & HIKING   The wide-open fields of Antietam Battlefield beckon both hikers and bikers. The 9 miles of paved roads are good for bicycling. Some 10 miles of hiking trails have been marked with trail maps to give visitors a chance to trek into history. The **Final Attack Trail** opened in 2005; others are in the works. For maps, go to www.virtualantietam.com, call ℃ **800/417-9506** or 240/217-3664, or stop by the visitor center.

CANOEING & KAYAKING   Antietam Creek, which flows the length of the park and then down to the Potomac, is an excellent novice-to-intermediate canoe and kayak run offering views of a small waterfall, Burnside Bridge, the ruins of Antietam Furnace, and the old C&O Canal aqueduct. **River & Trail Outfitters,** 604 Valley Rd., Knoxville (℃ **888/446-7529** or 301/695-5177; www.rivertrail.com), offers a variety of guided float trips down this scenic creek, as well as canoe and kayak rentals.

WHERE TO DINE

Because Sharpsburg is so blissfully noncommercial, you may find yourself wondering where to eat besides a fast-food restaurant along I-70. Fear not—there are some excellent alternatives.

The closest dining spot is Shepherdstown, West Virginia, just across the Potomac from Sharpsburg on State Route 64. Shepherdstown is a small college town with numerous coffee shops and cafes along its main drag, East German Street. The **Yellow Brick Bank Restaurant,** 201 E. German St. (℃ **304/876-2208**), serves lunch, dinner, and Sunday brunch in an old bank. The town's other fine-dining option is the **Bavarian Inn,** 164 Shepherd Grade Rd. (℃ **304/876-2551**), on your right just after crossing the Potomac. It's a purveyor of excellent but expensive German fare at breakfast, lunch, and dinner.

Another post-battlefield option is **Old South Mountain Inn,** 6132 Old National Pike, Boonsboro (✆ **301/371-5400;** www.oldsouthmountaininn.com), located in Maryland at the top of South Mountain ridge on Alternate Route 40 between Antietam and Frederick. It serves Saturday lunch, Sunday brunch, and dinner Tuesday through Sunday.

3 Harpers Ferry (WV) National Historical Park

22 miles SW of Frederick, 54 miles W of Baltimore, 55 miles S of Gettysburg

Though you can hardly tell today, Harpers Ferry, West Virginia, was a bustling industrial center from the 1700s until the 1930s, when it was hit by the double disasters of the Depression and a flood. It's perhaps best known for abolitionist John Brown's rebellion and the town's part in the Civil War.

On October 16, 1859, Brown—already notorious from a bloody raid against slaveholders in Kansas—enlisted 19 men to raid the federal arsenal at Harpers Ferry, intent on arming the nation's slaves and starting a rebellion. Frederick Douglass warned Brown that the arsenal, in a town wedged between mountains and the Shenandoah and Potomac rivers, would be impossible to hold with so few men, and, as Douglass had foreseen, the raid failed. Brown and his men captured the arsenal, but were unable to raise any significant number of slaves into rebellion. They were soon pinned in the arsenal's firehouse (later to be known as John Brown's Fort), and Brown was captured when U.S. Marines under Lt. Col. Robert E. Lee stormed the building. Brown was tried and convicted of "conspiring with slaves to commit treason and murder," for which he was hanged. His action polarized the nation and was one of the sparks that ignited the war. Harpers Ferry later witnessed the largest surrender of Federal troops during the Civil War; it also opened one of the earliest integrated schools in the U.S.

Today, Harpers Ferry National Historical Park is beautiful and intriguing, a delightful place to spend a day or weekend. Its narrow streets are lined with historic homes and restored shops that sell antiques and handicrafts. The National Park Service administers much of this tiny town. Historic exhibits focus on John Brown's raid, the town's industry, Storer College (an early African-American college), and the town's role in the Civil War, when it changed hands between the Union and the Confederacy eight times. Hills soar overhead and plunge down into the white waters of the Shenandoah and Potomac rivers. Walkers will find pleasant places to stroll, as well as some strenuous hikes. Water-lovers will want to sign on for a rafting or kayaking run.

ACCESS POINTS   To get here, take Route 340 west from Frederick. You will cross the Potomac River Bridge (you'll see the town off the bridge to your right) into Virginia, and then about ¾ mile later cross the Shenandoah River into West Virginia. The historical park's parking lot is about a mile past the Shenandoah Bridge, on the left.

FEES   Park admission is $6 per vehicle, $4 per pedestrian or cyclist. The fee includes the shuttle bus and is good for 3 days.

VISITOR CENTER   Start at the **Cavalier Heights Visitor Center,** 1 mile west of Shenandoah Bridge, off Route 340 (✆ **304/535-6029;** www.nps.gov/hafe). Leave your car in this parking lot (the park service has removed almost all parking from the lower town) and catch the shuttle here for the lower town. The helpful staff provides free town maps and information on ranger-led tours (available in spring, summer, and fall). The visitor center is open daily from 8am to 5pm, except Thanksgiving, December 25, and January 1. Shuttles run about every 12 to 15 minutes from 8am to 5:45pm (later in summer).

SEEING THE HIGHLIGHTS

Skip the hassles of parking and take the 6-minute shuttle ride from the visitor center. Once in the lower town, stop first at the information center on Shenandoah Street (if you didn't already get brochures and trail maps at the Cavalier Heights visitor center).

The **John Brown Museum,** on Shenandoah Street, offers exhibits and displays on the abolitionist and tracks the course of his raid, capture, and conviction. Hours for the museum are the same as the park's hours, and admission is included in the park entry fee. The **Harper House** is a restored dwelling that sits at the top of the stone stairs, above High Street. The oldest remaining structure in Harpers Ferry, it was built between 1775 and 1782 and served as a tavern for such notable guests as Thomas Jefferson and George Washington.

WALKING, HIKING & WHITE-WATER RAFTING

If you're wearing sturdy shoes, make the short but moderately strenuous climb farther up the stone stairs, past the lovely **St. Peter's Church,** to **Jefferson Rock** . At this spot, looking over the confluence of the Shenandoah and Potomac rivers, President Jefferson called the view "stupendous," and said it was worth crossing the Atlantic to see.

If you don't feel like climbing the stairs to Jefferson Rock, you might enjoy a stroll over the walking/railroad bridge across the Potomac. The view of the river is worth the walk. On the way, you'll pass the old armory fire house, known as **John Brown's Fort,** where Brown and his men took their last stand. On the other side, you'll find the bottom of Maryland Heights (see below) and the ruins of **Lock No. 33** on the C&O Canal.

Virginius Island, a long curl of land along the Shenandoah, is also worth a look. An easy stroll among trees and stone ruins, this was once a booming industrial center with a rifle factory, iron foundry, cotton mill, granary, and lumberyard. It's a silent reminder of what once was. The short history trail, about a mile long, offers some explanation of what remains, and the lovely flat site is a great place to rest or let the children run.

If you're ready for a strenuous hike, head over the railroad bridge to walk up the cliffs of **Maryland Heights,** one of the most spectacular views in the state. The hike can take 3 to 5 hours, but the view of Harpers Ferry and the confluence of the two rivers makes the effort worthwhile. The park service provides trail maps for the hike to Maryland Heights as well as to nearby **Weverton Cliffs,** which also boasts a very good view. If you're planning more than a day's hike, the **Appalachian Trail** and the **C&O Canal** join briefly and pass right by Harpers Ferry, on the opposite side of the Potomac, making the town a great stop on either route.

River & Trail Outfitters, 604 Valley Rd., Knoxville, in Maryland (© **888/446-7529** or 301/695-5177; www.rivertrail.com), offers half-day white-water rafting trips down the Shenandoah and Potomac, which pass by the town. Although this can be quite an adventure during high-water season (Feb to mid-Apr), most of the time it's a fun raft trip through beautiful scenery and a few rapids—suitable for families. Guides share local history, legends, and corny jokes. Prices depend on the season, but generally run $55 to $95 per person. River & Trail also offers guided hikes up Maryland Heights, C&O bike trips, and cross-country ski trips in winter. Experienced paddlers can rent a canoe or kayak; lessons are available for every level.

Fishing is permitted in both the Potomac and Shenandoah rivers, but adults may require licenses; check with the visitor center.

WHERE TO STAY

Harpers Ferry is about 22 miles from Frederick, which has several lodging options (p. 195). Closer to the historical park, the 50-room **Comfort Inn,** at Route 340 and Union Street (€ **800/228-5150** or 304/535-6391; www.comfortinn.com), is about a mile from the visitor center.

WHERE TO DINE

Good dining options are limited. You'll see numerous cafes and sandwich shops along Potomac and High streets. The food is fine, but patience is necessary on a busy day; note that a sandwich or salad can cost $7 to $10. Stop early for breakfast or wait until later in the day to eat. There are also plenty of places to stop for a drink or an ice cream—and the wait isn't as long.

4 Gettysburg (PA) National Military Park ★ ★ ★

34 miles N of Frederick, 50 miles NW of Baltimore

Here on the rolling green hills just north of the Maryland–Pennsylvania line, and in the streets of a tiny town that was home to a mere 2,400 people, some 160,000 brothers met in battle. For 3 days in July 1863, the 70,000 men of the Confederate Army faced the 93,000 Union soldiers under the command of Gen. George Meade. When the 3 days of fighting ended, the rebels had been driven back; some 51,000 were killed, wounded, or prisoners of war; and Gen. Robert E. Lee would never mount another campaign of such magnitude again. Most important, the tide of the war had changed. The battle would become known as the "High Water Mark of the Confederacy."

Today, the 20,000-acre battlefield is one of the most famous in the world, drawing people to its hills and valleys, beckoning them to pause for a moment before the long rows of graves in the cemeteries and monuments in the fields. They stop, too, to recall the 272 words of Abraham Lincoln as he dedicated the cemetery on November 19, 1863.

The park surrounds the small town of Gettysburg, which still bears war wounds of its own. Plenty of small privately owned museums display collections of firearms, uniforms, and other memorabilia of those dark days.

Certainly the busiest time to visit is the 3-day reenactment held every July 1 to July 3, when 350,000 people descend on Gettysburg. If you plan to come, make hotel reservations at least 8 months in advance—and make dinner reservations before arriving. It may even be a good idea to come ahead of the reenactment in order to get a good look around, take a tour, and gain some historical perspective. Remember to bring a lawn chair and comfortable shoes.

Another popular event is Remembrance Day, held the Saturday closest to November 19, the anniversary of the Gettysburg Address. Weekends in spring and fall are perhaps the most pleasant times to visit. Schoolchildren flow in during the school year, and families keep the attractions filled all summer.

GETTING THERE   Take U.S. Route 15 north from Frederick and I-70. After about 30 miles, you'll cross into Pennsylvania; then take the first exit and turn left on Business U.S. Route 15 North. The visitor center is 6 miles ahead on your right; the town is just past the visitor center.

You've got to drive here—and you've got to park. There are parking garages or lots on Race Horse Alley, at Middle and Stratton streets, and on Baltimore Street between the Jennie Wade House and the Tour Center. On-street parking is possible on most weekends. The museums and the battlefield have their own lots.

FEES & HOURS   Admission to Gettysburg National Military Park is free. The battlefield is open daily year-round: from 6am to 10pm April through October, and from 6am to 7pm November through March. The visitor center is open daily from 8am to 5pm (until 6pm in summer), except Thanksgiving, December 25, and January 1. The cemetery is open from dawn to dusk.

VISITOR CENTER   Stop first at the **Gettysburg National Military Park Visitor Center,** 97 Taneytown Rd. (© **717/334-1124;** www.nps.gov/gett), which contains worthwhile exhibits and an interesting bookstore. It's also the starting point for a number of tours, including bus tours, licensed guide tours, and ranger walks (see "Organized Tours," below). Rangers are glad to answer questions and provide maps of the hiking trails and the 18-mile self-guided auto tour, which hits all the major sites. For security reasons, backpacks and large parcels are not allowed in the visitor center. In fall 2007, a new center and museum will open ⅔ mile away, at 1195 Baltimore Pike; the old visitor center will be removed.

SEEING THE HIGHLIGHTS

Don't miss the two exhibits inside the visitor center, which offer good perspectives before a visit to the battlefield. The **Gettysburg Museum of the Civil War** contains a good collection of weaponry and uniforms from both sides. Look for the things the soldiers carried, including musical instruments, medical supplies, and personal effects. Admission is free. Also at the visitor center is the **Electric Map,** a 30-minute presentation. It's rather old-fashioned in this high-tech age, but still tells the story of those 3 days of bloodshed well. Sit high in the seating gallery to get the best perspective. Admission is $4 (but that could change when the new visitor center opens).

The **Cyclorama,** a 360-degree depiction of Pickett's Charge, the climactic battle of the Gettysburg campaign, closed in November 2005 for much-needed restoration. The 1884 painting by Paul Dominique Philippoteaux will return to public view in the new visitor center.

The battlefield and cemetery are the main reasons for a visit here. The **Gettysburg National Cemetery** gate is right across the street from the visitor center (until the center moves in 2007). Get a map at the visitor center, walk among the gravestones, and learn about the Union and Confederate soldiers now united in this place. The graves encircle the place where Abraham Lincoln gave the Gettysburg Address and where the Soldiers' National Monument now stands.

The battlefield is so large, the best ways to see it are by car, bike, or bus. Along the ridges and valleys of the park are more than 100 monuments, dedicated by various states to their military units who fought here. The largest and most often visited is the granite-domed **Pennsylvania Memorial.** Constructed of nearly 3,000 tons of cut granite, raw stone, and cement, the monument consists of a dome supported by four arched columns, topped by a statue depicting the winged goddess of victory and peace. Other monuments recall the bravery of the troops on both sides of the battle. Of the southern states, Virginia was the first to build a monument here. The **Virginia State Memorial,** dedicated in 1917, is topped by a brass sculpture of General Lee mounted on a horse. It's located where Pickett's Charge took place.

As you're visiting the monuments, look for the **John Burns Portrait Statue.** At over 70 years of age, this local constable and veteran of the War of 1812 asked Col. Langhorn Wister for permission to fight with the Union troops. Although initially mocked, he earned the soldiers' respect, fighting alongside Union regiments at Gettysburg before being wounded and carried from the field.

OTHER ATTRACTIONS

Eisenhower National Historic Site ⋆, President Eisenhower's farm, overlooks the Gettysburg Battlefield. Eisenhower first came to Gettysburg as a West Point cadet, to study the battlefields. He and wife Mamie bought their 189-acre farm south of town; as president, he entertained world leaders here. Today, visitors can catch a shuttle at the battlefield visitor center to tour the home and walk the grounds. Admission is $5.50 for adults, $4 for teens, and $3 for children 6 to 12.

Gettysburg is dotted with small, privately owned museums filled with Civil War memorabilia. The best is the **Schriver House Museum,** 309 Baltimore St. (© 717/ 337-2800; www.schriverhouse.com), which relates the story of a civilian family caught up in the terror of those 3 days of battle. Visitors can tour the home, including the attic where sharpshooters were holed up. Admission is $7 for adults, $6.50 for seniors, and $4.75 for children 6 to 12.

ORGANIZED TOURS

Park tours are offered by the **Association of Licensed Battlefield Guides** (© 717/ 334-1124), which was set up in 1915 by Civil War veterans to ensure that visitors received accurate information about the battle. These guides can tell you about everything from troop movements to who built the Pennsylvania Memorial and how much it cost. A licensed battlefield guide will ride in your vehicle—and will even drive—to give you a customized tour. Guides are assigned at the visitor center on a first-come, first-served basis. A 2-hour tour costs $40 for one to six people. Groups and those with special needs should call ahead.

Gettysburg Battlefield Tours, 778 Baltimore St. (© 717/334-6296; www.gettysburg battlefieldtours.com), offers battlefield tours in either air-conditioned or double-decker buses. Recorded, dramatized tours cost $20 for adults and $12 for children. Licensed battlefield guides lead some tours, which are $25 for adults and $15 for children. Buses leave from the visitor center; you can buy tickets there or at numerous locations around town.

There are plenty of free tours, too, offered by the **National Park Service.** In fact, there are more than 20 presentations in the cemetery and battlefield each day. These rangers' walks, talks, and tours vary—some are brief, while others include up to a 3-mile hike with lots of detail about the battles. Contact the visitor center for details.

WHERE TO STAY

With several hotels in town and more along the main routes, visitors have plenty of options—and Frederick lodgings are close enough, too. If you plan to attend the reenactment in July, reserve at least 8 months in advance.

There are two good choices within walking distance of the visitor center. The 109-room **Quality Inn Gettysburg Motor Lodge,** 380 Steinwehr Ave. (© 800/228-5151 or 717/334-1103; www.gettysburgqualityinn.com or www.qualityinn.com), just behind the visitor center, has outdoor and indoor pools, an exercise room, and doubles for $50 to $149. The 111-room **Holiday Inn Gettysburg,** 516 Baltimore St., at Pennsylvania Route 97 and Business Route 15 (© 800/315-2621 or 717/334-6211; www.ichotels group.com), has an outdoor pool, fitness room, and doubles for $80 to $200.

Outside of town, the **Quality Inn at General Lee's Headquarters,** 401 Buford Ave. (© 800/228-5151 or 717/334-3141; www.qualityinn.com), overlooking the battlefield of Seminary Ridge, has an outdoor pool and doubles for $62 to $109. A number of hotels have been built on York Road (Rte. 30), including a **Hilton Garden**

Inn, 1061 York Rd. (© **877/782-9444** or 717/334-2040; www.gettysburg.garden inn.com), with rates of $79 to $139; and a **Holiday Inn Express,** 869 York Rd. (© **800/ 315-2621** or 717/337-1400; www.ichotelsgroup.com), with rates of $90 to $129. Both have indoor pools.

If you'd like to sleep in a bit of history, the **Best Western Gettysburg Hotel,** 1 Lincoln Sq. (© **800/528-1234** or 717/337-2000; www.gettysburg-hotel.com), is right on the town square and charges $94 to $350 double. Just down the street is the small **James Gettys Hotel,** 27 Chambersburg St. (© **888/900-5275** or 717/337-1334; www.jamesgettyshotel.com), with 12 suites for $135 to $250.

A SIDE TRIP TO NEW MARKET ☞

New Market calls itself the "antiques capital of Maryland." It's a delightful place to browse in the shops along Route 144 (Main St.) and to get a bite to eat. Even the street itself is an antique: The town, 6 miles east of Frederick on I-70 (Exit 62), was founded in 1793 as a stop for travelers along the National Pike. New Market is now listed on the National Register of Historic Places.

Two weekend festivals are worth a visit. During **New Market Days,** in late September, the town celebrates autumn with local crafts, entertainment, and food. For **Christmas in New Market,** in early December, the town turns festive with carols, carriage rides, and visits with Santa. It looks especially pretty then, too.

Every shop is open on weekends, a number of them as early as 10am. Everything closes at 5pm. About half of the stores have weekday hours as well. The **New Market Antique Dealers Association** publishes a free guide and map, available around town or at www.newmarkettoday.com.

The antiques shops line Main Street (though some go around the corner a bit), offering everything from handmade furniture to estate jewelry. The **New Market General Store,** 26 W. Main St. (© **301/865-6313**), feels like a bit of an antique itself, with its 19th-century country-store atmosphere, a variety of local goods, reproduction furniture, and a lunch counter in back.

Speaking of lunch, there are only a couple of choices besides the lunch counter. The **Village Tea Room,** 81 W. Main St. (© **301/865-3450**), is a dainty little spot for sandwiches, soups, salads, and afternoon tea. It's open Tuesday through Friday from 11:30am to 3:30pm, Saturday and Sunday from 11:30am to 5pm. For an elegant meal, head to **Mealey's,** 8 Main St. (© **301/865-5488**), a fine restaurant with Colonial-style dining rooms, stone fireplaces, and a menu full of American favorites. It's open Friday and Saturday from 11:30am to 2pm, Tuesday through Saturday from 5 to 8pm, and Sunday from 10am to 8pm.

5 Serenity & Apples on Route 15

If you're planning a trip to Frederick or a drive through the Civil War sites and on to Gettysburg, reserve a day for the treasures of Route 15, now designated the **Catoctin Mountain National Scenic Byway.** Though it's a high-speed, four-lane highway with too many trucks, many delightful sites await as you drive between the orchards and farms. The two major towns, **Thurmont** and **Emmitsburg,** are charming little places. Thurmont is notable for its two main parks, while Emmitsburg was the home of St. Elizabeth Ann Seton and is still the home of Mount St. Mary's University, where a replica of the Grotto of Lourdes is located. These are great places for a weekend getaway or a day trip; both are only about 90 minutes from Baltimore.

WHAT TO SEE & DO

Catoctin Mountain Park (© 301/663-9343; www.nps.gov/cato), a national park, has several good trails and is the home of presidential retreat Camp David—whose precise location is top secret. The park's entrance is on Route 77 west of Route 15. Admission is free. Tent camping here is $20 a night; cabin rentals are $35 to $140.

Cunningham Falls State Park (© 301/271-7574; www.dnr.maryland.gov) has as its centerpiece a 78-foot high waterfall, set in a canopy of 100-year-old oaks and hickories. Stay for a few minutes or the rest of the day. The park is also the site of 43-acre **Hunting Creek Lake,** which offers swimming, canoe rentals, and picnic areas. Get a guide to the many park trails at the Manor Area visitor center, off Route 15, or at Park Central, on Route 77. Four short trails will take you to the base of Cunningham Falls. Three are in the William Houck Area, off Route 77. They range from moderate to strenuous and from .5 to 2.8 miles. The fourth trail is accessible, with a handicapped-only parking lot right on Route 77 and a .3-mile boardwalk that goes all the way to the falls on mostly flat terrain. Another trail ends at the **Catoctin Iron Furnace,** the remains of a Revolutionary War–era iron-making complex. The park is open daily from 8am to sunset. In peak season, fees run $3 to $4 per person; at other times it's $3 to $4 per car. Campsites are available for $25 a night, $30 with electric hookup; cabins are $50.

If you want to get off the beaten track—off Route 15 and onto Route 550 North—for a breathtaking mountain view, go to **Pen Mar Park,** 14600 Pen Mar High Rock Rd., Cascade (© 240/313-2700). The view is worth the short drive past Fort Ritchie and up Pen Mar Road. A dance hall and observation deck, built right on the edge of the mountain, overlook the Blue Ridge Mountains. From mid-May to mid-October, free big-band concerts are held in the dance hall on Sundays at 2pm. Hikers can head onto the Appalachian Trail from here: It's 920 miles to Georgia and 1,080 miles to Maine. Call ahead for directions and a concert schedule.

Grotto of Lourdes   If you know the story of St. Bernadette, the French peasant girl who saw Mary, mother of Jesus, in a grotto—but you aren't going to France anytime soon—then you might want to stop here. The site has been re-created on a mountain overlooking Mount St. Mary's University. You'll know you're here when you see the 95-foot tall campanile topped with a golden statue of Mary. As you wander the wooded paths, you'll see other shrines and the Stations of the Cross. Mass is offered daily.

Mount St. Mary's University & Seminary, 16300 Old Emmitsburg Rd., Emmitsburg. © 301/447-5318. www.msmary. edu/grotto. Free admission. Mar–Sept daily 7am–7:30pm; Oct–Feb daily 7am–5:30pm.

National Fallen Firefighters Memorial *Finds*   This site, at the National Fire Academy, holds special significance since September 11, 2001: The firefighters who died at the World Trade Center have their own memorial here. The service in tribute to firefighters killed in the line of duty is always held the first day of Fire Prevention Week, in October.

1682 S. Seton Ave., Emmitsburg. © 301/447-1365. www.firehero.org. Free admission. Bring photo ID to visit, as this is a federal site. Daily dawn–dusk.

National Shrine of St. Elizabeth Ann Seton ★★★   The shrine honors the first American-born saint canonized in the Roman Catholic Church. A young widow who converted to Catholicism, Mother Seton lived here with her children as she began both the Catholic parochial school system and a new order of religious women. The church is a beautiful monument, but the nearby houses—the Stone House (built about 1750) and the White House (built for her in 1810)—offer a glimpse of her life here in the mountains. The guides in these hallowed spaces are quite patient with children.

333 S. Seton Ave., Emmitsburg. ℂ 301/447-6606. www.setonshrine.org. Free admission; donations welcome. Basilica daily 10am–4:30pm; other sites Tues–Sun 10am–4:30pm. Closed last week of Jan and first week of Feb, Jan 1, Easter, Thanksgiving, and Dec 25. Mass Wed–Fri and Sun at 1:30pm; Sat–Sun at 9am (subject to change; call to verify). From Rte. 15, turn left on S. Seton Ave. The shrine is ¾ mile on the right.

SHOPPING

Don't miss the orchard stands along your drive. There are several, all selling fruits and vegetables grown right in these foothills.

Catoctin Mountain Orchard, 15036 N. Franklinville Rd. (Rte. 15), Thurmont (ℂ **301/271-2737;** www.catoctinmountainorchard.com), has locally baked pastries and McCutcheon's preserves, as well as fresh fruit. Pick your own berries in June and July, pumpkins and apples (Cameo, Pink Lady, and Honey Crisp) in fall. Open January through March, Friday through Sunday from 9am to 5pm, and June through December, daily from 9am to 5pm.

Gateway Farm Market and Candyland, 14802 N. Franklinville Rd. (Rte. 15), Thurmont (ℂ **301/271-2322**), has not only produce and fresh cider in season, but also long tables filled with boxes of penny candy. Pick out your own and fill a bag— a pound was $3.50 at press time. (Once your kids learn of this place, you can never pass it again without stopping.) Open Monday through Thursday from 8am to 9pm, Friday and Saturday from 8am to 10pm, and Sunday from 10am to 7pm.

Scenic View Orchards, 16239 Sabillasville Rd. (Rte. 550), Sabillasville (ℂ **301/ 271-2149**), truly deserves its name. Seven generations of farmers have grown the fruits, vegetables, and flowers on the farm here. It's open daily from 10am to 5pm, June through Thanksgiving, beginning with strawberries and ending with pumpkins and cider.

WHERE TO STAY ALONG ROUTE 15

Cascade Inn ⟡ This white-clapboard, turn-of-the-20th-century house is worth the drive through Sabillasville into Cascade. Formerly known as Bluebird on the Mountain, the delightful place has new owners who've been busy sprucing up the guest rooms. Two units have fireplaces, the Rose Garden Suite has its own sun porch, and the two-bedroom family suite, though not fancy, has a spacious bathroom with its own whirlpool. The B&B is a good base for visiting Frederick, Antietam, or Gettysburg.

14700 Eyler Ave., Cascade, MD 21719. ℂ **800/362-9526** or 301/241-4161. www.bbonline.com/md/bluebird or www.thecascadeinn.com. 4 units. $85–$145 double. Rates include hot breakfast. AE, DISC, MC, V. **Amenities:** Garden; massages by appointment. *In room:* A/C, TV (some w/VCR), Wi-Fi.

Cozy Inn The Cozy Inn has a certain charm. Breakfast here features homemade New Orleans bread pudding, and the premium rooms are named after presidents and decorated with things that recall them. The Reagan Cottage features a portrait of the president and horse decor, while the Roosevelt Room has a king-size bed in a style used by FDR. Every premium room has two TVs, a fireplace, and a Jacuzzi garden tub. Call ahead to reserve, especially if the president will be at Camp David—the press corps and president's staff often stay here. The Cozy Inn also hosts a German Fest in October and Christmas Open House on the Saturday after Thanksgiving. The shops here carry antiques, vintage clothing, and small specialties.

103 Frederick Rd. (Rte. 806), Thurmont, MD 21788. ℂ **301/271-4301.** www.cozyvillage.com. 21 units, including 5 cottages. $56–$165 double. Rates include continental breakfast. AE, DISC, MC, V. **Amenities:** Restaurant (see "Where to Dine," below); shopping arcade. *In room:* A/C, fridge, coffeemaker, hair dryer, iron (upon request).

Sleep Inn & Suites Emmitsburg (Kids) Emmitsburg's first and (so far) only hotel offers standard rooms, but with a detail kids will like: Nintendo games at $7 an hour. One room of note is the fireplace suite, with a gas fireplace and a Jacuzzi for two (you can even enjoy the fire and TV from the tub). Call ahead for reservations, since the place can be booked solid when nearby Mount St. Mary's University sends families and visiting athletic teams here.

501 Silo Hill Pkwy., off Rte. 15, Emmitsburg 21727. (800/SLEEP-INN or 301/447-0044. Fax 301/447-3144. www.sleepinnemmitsburg.com. 79 units. $69–$159 double. Rates include continental breakfast. Children stay free in parent's room. AE, DISC, DC, MC, V. **Amenities:** Pool; health club. *In room:* A/C, TV w/Nintendo, high-speed Internet access, coffeemaker, hair dryer, iron.

WHERE TO DINE

Carriage House Inn (★) (Kids) AMERICAN This 1857 inn once hosted Bill, Hillary, and about 20 of their closest friends. They came for the crab cakes—as many diners do. A stone fireplace dominates the dining room, which has wide plank floors and Early American–style furniture. Special enough for the president, it's also a good place for children: Kids' menus are pasted inside picture books. After your little ones choose between the burger or chicken strips for $4.95, they've got a book to keep them occupied until the food comes. There's a brunch buffet on Sundays.

200 S. Seton Ave., Emmitsburg. (301/447-2366. www.carriagehouseinn.info. Reservations recommended. Main courses $6.95–$12 lunch, $15–$31 dinner. AE, DISC, MC V. Mon–Thurs 11am–9pm; Fri–Sat 11am–10pm; Sun 10am–8pm.

Cozy Inn Restaurant (Finds) AMERICAN Just by looking at the photos and memorabilia on the walls, you can tell the Cozy's been around a long time. It features hearty buffets as well as simple fare served in the dining rooms and on the deck in summer. If you're a root-beer fan, try the house brew. If you're heading to one of the area parks, stop here for a fried-chicken picnic to go.

103 Frederick Rd. (Rte. 806), Thurmont. (301/271-7373. www.cozyvillage.com. Reservations recommended on weekends, required for candlelight fondue hideaway. Main courses $6.50–$20; lunch buffet $6.80–$9; dinner buffet $10–$15; candlelight fondue hideaway $40 for 3 courses. AE, MC, V. Mon–Thurs 11am–8:15pm; Fri 11am–8:30pm; Sat 8am–8:30pm; Sun 8am–8:15pm.

Fitzgerald's Shamrock Restaurant SEAFOOD/STEAKS This homey, friendly little restaurant proudly proclaims its Irish roots. Get a Harp or Guinness to wash down onion rings, shad in season, crab cakes, or chicken Chesapeake (an increasingly popular combination of chicken and lump crabmeat). Sandwiches are available all day. No room for dessert? Take a pie with you.

7701 Fitzgerald Rd., Thurmont. (301/271-2912. www.shamrockrestaurant.com. Reservations recommended on weekends. Main courses $6.50–$21. AE, MC, V. Mon–Sat 11am–10pm; Sun noon–9pm.

9

Western Maryland

Western Maryland is a haven for lovers of the outdoors in any season. Garrett and Allegany counties offer a wide variety of outdoor activities, and the drive there is a beautiful journey.

More than 100,000 acres of parkland stretches over mountains and into valleys. Gently rolling mountains draw visitors to their hiking and biking paths and ski slopes. Rivers and streams, particularly the Youghiogheny and the Savage, attract fly-fishermen and white-water rafters. The centerpiece is Deep Creek Lake.

Western Maryland, which begins at the state's skinniest section at Hancock and ends at the West Virginia border, is easy to reach by way of interstate highways. From Baltimore, take I-70. Washingtonians can connect with I-70 from I-270. When I-70 turns north into Pennsylvania near Hancock, it connects to I-68, which heads west into West Virginia. I-81 joins I-70 near Hagerstown to bring visitors from Pennsylvania and Virginia. U.S. Route 219 intersects I-68 and heads south to Deep Creek Lake.

For a more scenic route, the old U.S. Route 40, the nation's first national pike, connects Frederick to Cumberland and other points west and east. It's slower going, but much more interesting.

1 The Great Outdoors in Western Maryland

Western Maryland's gently rolling mountains are part of the Appalachians, with Backbone Mountain (elevation 3,360 ft.) marking the eastern Continental Divide. Outdoor enthusiasts can find forests, mountain lakes, and miles of streams and rivers. White-water rafters come to meet the challenges of the Youghiogheny (pronounced "Yok-a-*gain*-ee"; those in the know just call it the "Yock"). Boaters flock to Garrett's seven lakes. Skiers head for the hills of Wisp Resort, and cross-country skiers glide along the state parks' trails. There are also plenty of opportunities for windsurfing, snowmobiling, fly-fishing, mountain biking, golf, hunting, hiking, and camping.

Of the 100,000 acres of protected wilderness in Western Maryland, 40,000 are part of Green Ridge State Forest, east of Cumberland, while 53,000 are in the Savage River State Forest, near Deep Creek Lake. The area is great for wildlife watching and fishing. Some species, notably hawks and black bears that were beginning to disappear from the landscape, are returning in force to the region's parks and forests. Though mining runoff once threatened Garrett County's waterways, the Casselman, North Branch Potomac, and Youghiogheny rivers now boast some of the best fly-fishing around.

In other chapters of this book, the sections on outdoor pursuits are organized by activities such as biking and camping. But in Western Maryland, you can do just about anything, anywhere. So here instead is a rundown of each of the parks—except Deep Creek Lake State Park, which has its own section—and some of its unique qualities to help you decide exactly where you want to go and what you want to do. For more information, call the individual state parks for brochures and maps (see numbers below), or go online to www.dnr.maryland.gov. To reserve a campsite anywhere in Maryland, call ☎ **888/432-2267.**

ALLEGANY COUNTY

Allegany has three state parks (go to www.dnr.maryland.gov for more information), plus the terminus of the C&O Canal, which is quite popular with bikers, hikers, and history buffs. Note that all state parks allow pets on leashes in some areas.

The **C&O Canal National Historical Park** (☎ **301/722-8226;** www.nps.gov/choh) is an ideal place for a trek on the flat, wide canal towpath. Both cyclists and hikers enjoy all or part of the 184-mile route along the Potomac River, all the way from Cumberland to Georgetown, in D.C. Any portion can make a great 1-day biking trip. The canal passes by numerous sites, including Paw Paw Tunnel, Fort Frederick, Harpers Ferry, and Great Falls. The trip from Cumberland is almost all gently downhill. Because flooding can make some of the towpath impassable, check with the park service to see if the route you intend to bike is clear.

Dan's Mountain State Park (☎ **301/722-1480**), at 481 acres, is the smallest park in Western Maryland. Located about 9 miles south of Frostburg, the park is for day use only. Kids will enjoy the recycled-tire playground and the Olympic-size pool, with a water slide and views that make you feel as if you're swimming on top of the world. Take a look over Dan's Rock Overlook and see the view from 2,898 feet.

Green Ridge State Forest, Exit 64 off I-68 (☎ **301/478-3124**), at 44,000 acres, is home to abundant wildlife and scenic vistas over the Potomac River. Adirondack-style shelters are placed along the 24-mile backpacking trail. Mountain bikers have access to the park's roads, most of the 43 miles of hiking trails, and a separate bike trail and racecourse. At the oak-hickory forest's southern end, you'll find the Paw Paw Tunnel on the C&O Canal (p. 222). Primitive camping is available at 100 sites ($10 per night). The park's activities include off-road driving, hunting, canoeing, kayaking, and fishing. The shooting range is open Wednesday through Saturday and Monday from 10am to sunset, Sunday from noon to sunset.

Rocky Gap State Park ⚲, Exit 50 off I-68 (☎ **301/722-1480**), has great trails with views of 243-acre Lake Habeeb, mountain overlooks, and a stout 5-mile trail up Evitts Mountain to the remains of a 1784 homestead. Walk along Rocky Gap Run to see the mile-long gorge and hemlock forest. The lake has three swimming beaches, two boat ramps, and boat, canoe, kayak, and paddleboat rentals. Boats are permitted on the lake 24 hours a day. Fishing licenses are required. The park has 278 campsites, including 10 minicabins ($50 a night) and a family group site for up to 40 people ($225 a night). Camping is popular, so reserve your space in advance.

SUPPLIERS & GUIDES IN ALLEGANY COUNTY

C&O Bicycle, 9 S. Pennsylvania Ave., Hancock (☎ **301/678-6665;** www.candobicycle. com), rents and sells bikes in its shop, located between two good trails: the C&O Canal towpath and the 20-mile Western Maryland Rail Trail. C&O also repairs bikes and operates a general store with lodging (reservations are a good idea). Closed Tuesday through Thursday in cold weather.

Allegany Expeditions (☎ **800/819-5170** or 301/722-5170; www.alleganyexpeditions. com) rents canoes, kayaks, and cross-country skis. It offers guided experiences in surrounding parks, including hiking, rock climbing and rappelling, cave exploration, and canoeing. Call to inquire about cross-country ski packages in New Germany State

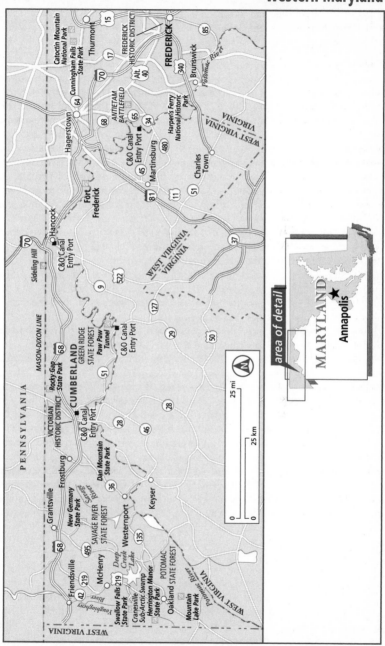

Park as well as fly-fishing and bass-fishing expeditions. The company has also developed **Upper Narrows Climbing Park.**

GARRETT COUNTY

Garrett County is covered by state forests and parks. It's the home of swimming holes, the state's highest waterfall, and an intriguing preserve owned by the Nature Conservancy. To find a park that best suits your interests, visit www.dnr.maryland.gov.

Swallow Falls State Park ✸✸✸ (© 301/334-9180) has 10 miles of hiking trails. Follow the Youghiogheny River for views of Swallow Falls and the even more spectacular Muddy Falls, which drop 63 feet. The walk through one of Maryland's last virgin forests of giant pines and hemlocks shouldn't be missed—you won't forget its quiet beauty. The park has the area's largest camping facility, with 65 improved sites and modern bathhouses with showers and laundry tubs. Camping costs $25 to $50 per night; reservations can be made up to a year in advance. Pets are permitted on leashes in designated camping areas and in day-use areas in the off season. A 5.5-mile trail good for hiking or cross-country skiing connects the park with Herrington Manor.

Herrington Manor State Park (© 301/334-9180) draws cross-country skiers to its 10 miles of groomed trails. It offers ski and snowshoe rental ($15 a day), sled rental ($6 a day), 20 furnished cabins, and stone warming rooms where skiers can grab a snack and hot cocoa. Trails and rental facilities are open from 8:30am to 4pm during good skiing conditions. In summer, the park's trails draw hikers and bikers. The 53-acre Herrington Lake has guarded beaches and canoes, rowboats, and paddleboats to rent from May through September. Bring your tennis racquet or volleyball: Courts are waiting. Campers can reserve one of 20 furnished log cabins year-round; book as much as a year ahead. Rentals range from $20 to $120 for a full-service cabin.

Savage River State Forest (© 301/895-5759), which surrounds New Germany and Big Run, is the largest of Maryland's state forests, at more than 54,000 acres. It features miles of rugged hiking trails. The longest, Big Savage, follows a 17-mile path along the ridge of Big Savage Mountain at an average elevation of 2,500 feet. Also popular is Monroe Run, which traverses the forest between New Germany and Big Run. Mountain bikers may use all trails except Big Savage and Monroe Run. Snowmobiles and off-road vehicles have their own trails; permits are required and available at park headquarters. Stop by for trail maps, including one delineating 10 miles of cross-country-ski trails. Savage River Lake was the site of the 1989 world white-water championships; only nonpowered watercraft are allowed on the water. Fifty-two primitive campsites are spread throughout the forest—you may not see another camper while you're here. Backwoods camping is also permitted, but fires are not allowed at some sites. Camping is available year-round at $10 per night, with sites offered on a first-come, first-served basis with self-registration. Pets are permitted on leashes. If you don't have the time or the inclination to stay for a while, at least drive through the park, as many motorcyclists do on weekends. The roads are public, and the feeling of escape that comes from all those acres of trees is worth the ride.

New Germany State Park ✸✸ (© 301/895-5453) has 12 miles of trails, well marked for cross-country skiing. It also offers equipment rental, cabins, and large stone warming rooms where skiers can stop and get a snack. Trails and rental facilities are open from 8am to 4pm during good skiing conditions. The park has 37 improved campsites with clean bathhouses and hot showers. All sites are large, private, and located in a wooded glen; the cost is $15 per night. These can be rented up to a year in advance for visits between April and Labor Day; September through October, the sites are offered on a first-come, first-served basis. Available year-round are 11 furnished cabins—with electricity, fireplaces, and room for two to eight persons—for $70 to $100 a night, with a 2-night minimum required. You can reserve the cabins up to a year in advance. The park also has a 13-acre lake popular with swimmers and rowboaters, with boat rentals available. The day-use fee is $2 on weekends and holidays, $3 during ski season. Note that pets are not permitted at this park.

Big Run State Park (☎ 301/895-5453), just down the road, offers fishing and hiking along Monroe Run and Big Run. You can launch your boat at Savage River Reservoir. The 300-acre park has 30 rustic campsites with chemical toilets and running water. Some are in wooded areas along Monroe Run and Big Run; others on the shore of the Savage River Reservoir. Sites at Big Run are open year-round and cost $15 per night, available on a first-come, first-served basis. Pets are permitted on leashes.

Potomac–Garrett State Forest (☎ 301/334-2038) is spread over 19,000 acres in two separate tracts in the lower westernmost corner of the county. With plenty of streams, beaver ponds, and cranberry bogs, it offers beautiful scenery, including the highest point in any Maryland state forest: Backbone Mountain, in Garrett State Forest near Route 135 and Walnut Bottom Road. There are 8 miles of mountain-biking trails, as well as trails for snowmobiles, dirt bikes, and ATVs. Off-road-vehicle permits are required and can be obtained at each park's headquarters. Hikers can choose from 30 miles of trails, many easy enough for day hike and many with mountain views that can only be seen off the road. For hunters, the park offers a 3-D bow range, open April through September. Hunting and trapping are permitted during the appropriate seasons; contact the park office for details. The fishing here is some of the best in Western Maryland, with 21 miles of first-class trout streams, including 9 miles of the North Branch of the Potomac River. Here's the place to catch the Maryland Grand Slam: brook, brown, 'bo, and cutthroat trout. Potomac–Garrett also offers five primitive camping areas, open year-round. Getting to them may take some effort, however: The sites are beautiful and generously spaced, and a few have three-sided wooden shelters, but the roads to the sites are not well maintained. The cost is $10 for regular sites, $15 for a site with a shelter. Pets are permitted off-leash if they're under control.

Jennings Randolph Lake (☎ 304/355-2346), covers 952 acres and has 13 miles of shoreline. It straddles the Maryland–West Virginia line. On the Maryland side, there's a boat ramp at Mt. Zion Road via Route 135 and a scenic overlook at Walnut Bottom Road. The lake is open for boating, fishing, and water-skiing in summer. Hiking trails on the Maryland side start at one of the overlooks. White-water rafting is available in spring. For the dam release schedule, see www.nab.usace.army.mil/recreation/jenran.htm. Pets on leashes are permitted in some areas.

Broadford Lake, near Oakland (☎ 301/334-9222), is open from March 31 to early November during daylight hours. The 140-acre park features a guarded beach as well as a boat launch and rentals. Electric boat motors only are permitted. There are picnic pavilions, playgrounds, and ball fields. Pets on leashes are permitted in some areas. Admission is $3 to $4 per car, $1.50 to walk in.

Cranesville Swamp Preserve ⚘ (☎ 301/897-8570; www.nature.org) is a vestige of the last ice age. Operated by the Nature Conservancy, it's a 1,600-acre peatland bog, home to sedges, cranberry, and sphagnum moss as well as tamarack trees—a species usually not found south of Alaska. Visitors can cross the bog on a 1,500-foot boardwalk or take one of four trails to see the unusual plants, including carnivorous ones. The entrance is in West Virginia, however, so it's a bit tricky to find. To get here, head south on U.S. Route 219; turn right on Mayhew Inn Road, left on Bray School Road, right on Oakland Sang Run Road, left on Swallow Falls Road, and right on Cranesville Road at the fork. Turn left on Lake Ford Road, right at the next fork. It's ⅕ mile on the right. The preserve is open from dawn to dusk year-round. Admission is free. Pets are not allowed.

THE WILD RIVERS OF GARRETT COUNTY

The "three sisters" area—the Youghiogheny, Casselman, and North Branch Potomac rivers—has become so popular that it's been featured on national fly-fishing shows. The Casselman is a fertile catch-and-release river; anglers here have been known to catch 40 fish a day. The Youghiogheny supports a strong population of brown and rainbow trout, but be aware that dam releases cause substantial increases in the water level below the Deep Creek Lake power plant. Call © 315/413-2823 or visit www.deepcreekhydro.com for a dam-release schedule. For a basic calendar and map, go to www.dnr.maryland.gov.

Garrett County offers myriad opportunities for white-water rafting, kayaking, and canoeing. The Youghiogheny, the North Branch Potomac, and the Savage are the area's best-known runs. Although they can be challenging all year, they're at their fiercest in the spring after snowmelt. In 1976, the Youghiogheny River between Millers Run and Friendsville became Maryland's first officially designated Wild and Scenic River. This portion, known as the Upper Yough, contains approximately 20 class IV and V rapids. Fortunately for the inexperienced paddler, outfitters have sprung up all over the area to take people down this exciting river. If you'd prefer a little less excitement, the Middle Yough offers class I and II rapids, and the Lower Yough is a class III run. There are also several rivers just across the border in West Virginia—the Cheat, Gauley, Big Sandy, and Russell Fork—that are rated class IV+.

Kayakers hoping to avoid raft traffic would do well to visit the North Branch Potomac and Savage rivers (both class III/IV); both, however, can only be run after heavy rains or snowmelt. For open canoeing, the Casselman River (class II) to the west is good in winter and spring.

Most outfitters run raft trips on several or all of these rivers; see below for options.

SUPPLIERS & GUIDES IN GARRETT COUNTY

Guided rafting trips cost $100 to $135 per person for an (expert) Upper Yough trip. Middle Yough (novice) trips cost $21 to $32; Lower Yough (intermediate) trips are $39 to $115 depending on the level of service. Family float trips cost $20 to $30. *Note:* Remember to tip your guide—$3 to $5 per person is appropriate.

Precision Rafting, in Friendsville (© **800/477-3723** or 302/746-5290; www.precisionrafting.com), offers raft trips down all of the rivers, as well as paddling lessons. Friendsville is at the intersection of I-68, Maryland Route 42, and the Youghiogheny River; from Deep Creek Lake, take U.S. Route 219 north to Maryland Route 42 into town.

Several outfitters based in nearby Ohiopyle, Pennsylvania, offer similar trips. Try **Mountain Streams & Trails** (© **800/RAFT-NOW;** www.mtstreams.com) or **Laurel Highlands River Tours** (© **800/4-RAFTIN;** www.laurelhighlands.com). To get to Ohiopyle from Deep Creek Lake, take U.S. Route 219 north to U.S. Route 40 west (just past the intersection with I-68). Go into Pennsylvania and turn right onto State

Route 381 (north), which will take you to Ohiopyle. It's about an hour from Deep Creek Lake.

Allegany Expeditions (© **800/819-5170** or 301/722-5170; www.alleganyexpeditions. com) offers equipment rentals and various guided excursions. See "Suppliers & Guides in Allegany County," above, for details.

Perhaps unique to Garrett County is its **Adventuresports Institute** ⚡, 687 Mosser Rd., McHenry (© **301/387-3330;** www.adventuresportsi.org). This division of Garrett College offers an associate's degree in adventure sports, but its classes are open to nonmatriculated students. So if you want to learn how to paddle white water rather than just ride along in a raft, enroll in a 4-day kayaking class. The institute also rents equipment and teaches classes in mountaineering, rock climbing, and ice climbing. For a list of course offerings and prices, call or visit the website.

For tackle and bait, stop by **Bill's Outdoor Center,** 20768 Garrett Hwy. (U.S. Rte. 219), McHenry (© **301/387-FISH**), or **Deep Creek Outfitters,** 32 Outfitters Way, on the lake in McHenry (© **301/387-2200**).

High Mountain Sports, 21327 Garrett Hwy., Oakland (© **301/387-4199**), sells, rents, and services bicycles. It also offers water-ski and kayak lessons and tours, and mountain-bike tours from this location. At its location next to Wisp Resort, 8527 Sang Run Rd., McHenry (© **301/387-2113**), it rents skis, snowshoes, and snowboards.

Snowshoes can be rented at **Herrington Manor State Park** (© **301/334-9180**) and **Deep Creek State Park** (© **301/387-5563**), for $15 for a full day.

2 Cumberland & Allegany County

140 miles W of Baltimore, 140 miles NW of Washington, D.C., 113 miles SE of Pittsburgh

The city of Cumberland is on a tight bend of the Potomac River in the heart of the Allegheny Mountains, with a portion of the C&O Canal as its centerpiece. Once a large industrial city, it is now quieter, with tourism a growing industry. Visitors come to see the canal, George Washington's headquarters, and the surrounding mountains.

At the turn of the 20th century, Cumberland was Maryland's "Queen City," second in size only to Baltimore. Many reminders of those days remain: its long street of Victorian mansions, the ornate storefronts of its rejuvenating shopping district, and the black smoke of the coal-powered train called *Mountain Thunder.*

Since the construction of I-68 cut right through—you might say right on top of—Cumberland, the city has become more accessible to the rest of the state. It's not only Cumberland people come to see, but also Rocky Gap State Park (known for Lake Habeeb), a new resort and golf course, and other area parks.

The Allegheny Mountains are particularly beautiful in autumn, and the area is becoming popular with bikers and hikers who find Cumberland and nearby Frostburg cheaper and closer to home than Deep Creek Lake to the west.

ESSENTIALS

GETTING THERE   I-68, which runs right through the center of Cumberland, is the fastest route by car from either the east or west. From the east and north, I-70 will take you to I-68. For a more scenic drive, you can get off I-70 or I-68 onto the Old National Pike (U.S. Rte. 40).

Amtrak (© **800/872-7245;** www.amtrak.com) serves Cumberland on its Capitol Limited train route, which travels from Washington, D.C., to Chicago. It stops at the station on East Harrison Street.

The **Cumberland Regional Airport** (© 304/738-0002; www.cumberlandairport. com) is actually in Wiley Ford, West Virginia, 2½ miles off Route 68 at Exit 43B. At press time, it offered no commercial service.

VISITOR INFORMATION   Walking-tour brochures, maps, and information about Cumberland and the surrounding area are available from the two walk-in locations operated by **Allegany County Tourism** (www.mdmountainside.com). The larger one is at the **Western Maryland Railway Station,** 13 Canal St., Cumberland (© **800/425-2067** or 301/727-2067), open daily from 9am to 5pm. If you're coming from the east, the **Sideling Hill Exhibition Center** ⚔, off I-68 about 20 miles east of Cumberland (© **301/678-5442**), is a great place to stop for brochures, information, and a view of the layers of rock exposed when the mountain was cut to build the road.

SPECIAL EVENTS   The **Heritage Days Festival** (© **301/777-0032**), held in mid-June in Cumberland and the Washington Historic District, fills the streets with arts and crafts, tours, entertainment, and scenic train rides. **C&O Canalfest** (© **301/724-3655**) takes place in mid-July at Canal Place, celebrating Cumberland's rich transportation heritage (both boat and train). Stop by for living-history demonstrations, crafts, entertainment (often by nationally known performers), and food.

WHERE TO STAY

The Cumberland–Frostburg area offers an inviting blend of historic inns, modern hotels and motels, and homey B&B lodgings. Most are moderately priced and offer very good value. All have free parking.

Best Western Braddock Motor Inn   Trees surround this two-story motel, located east of the historic LaVale Toll Gate. In fact, it's actually set right beside an I-68 exit ramp. Rooms are furnished in contemporary style. Complimentary shuttle service is provided from the airport, bus station, and train station.

1268 National Hwy., LaVale, MD 21502. © **800/296-6006** or 301/729-3300. Fax 301/729-3300. www.bestwestern braddock.com. 105 units. $69–$120 double. AE, DC, DISC, MC, V. **Amenities:** Restaurant; lounge; indoor pool; health club; spa; game room; tanning salon. *In room:* A/C, TV (w/VCR upon request), fridge (upon request), microwave (upon request), coffeemaker, hair dryer, iron.

Cumberland Holiday Inn   This modern six-story hotel sits at the east end of Cumberland's shopping promenade, providing easy walking access to the downtown area. Rooms are clean and comfortable, as you would expect from a Holiday Inn. Railroad enthusiasts might like a room overlooking the nearby tracks; everyone else will prefer the town side of the hotel, where there's less noise.

100 S. George St., Cumberland, MD 21502. © **877/426-4672** or 301/724-8800. Fax 301/724-4001. www.cumberland-dtn. holiday-inn.com. 130 units. $89–$99 double. Children under 19 stay free in parent's room; children under 12 eat free with parent. AE, DC, DISC, MC, V. Pets accepted; fees may apply. **Amenities:** Restaurant; lounge; outdoor pool; health club; billiards; high-speed Internet access; fax and copying services. *In room:* A/C, coffeemaker, hair dryer, iron.

Failinger's Hotel Gunter ⚔   Originally opened in 1897, this landmark hotel was revived several years ago by the present owners, the Failinger family. The guest rooms are masterfully done, as are the public areas and the main staircase, the hotel's centerpiece. The restoration has added modern conveniences, but hasn't altered the place's Victorian style, marked by original oak doors, brass fixtures, claw-foot tubs, vintage prints, and delicate sconces. Rooms are individually furnished, with canopy or four-poster beds, armoires, and pastel fabrics. The one exception is no. 307, starkly decorated in black and white, and named the Roy Clark Room after the country-western entertainer who stayed here during a 1990 visit.

11 W. Main St., Frostburg, MD 21532. ℂ **301/689-6511.** Fax 301/689-6034. www.failingershotelgunter.com. 14 units. $69–$74 double; $90 suite. Rates include continental breakfast. AE, DC, DISC, MC, V. *In room:* A/C, TV.

Inn at Walnut Bottom ⓖⓖ   The owners have combined the warmth and charm of a B&B with standard hotel amenities and a few niceties of their own, including delicious breakfasts featuring crème brûlée French toast, ham-and-egg biscuit pizza, or some other hot delight. You might need to borrow a bike to burn off those calories afterward. Need something more? Consider Afspaending—a relaxation therapy that combines localized massage techniques with gentle stretches and exercises. It's offered by the inn's co-owner, who is trained in the technique.

Just a block from historic Washington Street, the inn is composed of two 19th-century homes: the Cowden House (1820) and the Dent House (1890). Guest rooms are spacious, with high ceilings, large windows, antiques and period reproductions, tapestry rugs, and down comforters. The family suite has two bedrooms and a private bathroom. Children are welcome here.

120 Greene St., Cumberland, MD 21502. ℂ **800/286-9718** or 301/777-0003. Fax 301/777-8288. www.iwbinfo.com. 12 units, 4 with shared bathroom. $107–$147 double. Rates include full breakfast. AE, DISC, MC, V. **Amenities:** Relaxation therapy; bikes. *In room:* A/C, TV.

Rocky Gap Lodge & Golf Resort   Situated beside Lake Habeeb and the rolling hills of Rocky Gap State Park, Rocky Gap Lodge mixes luxury accommodations with a challenging golf course—populated by wild critters unafraid of flying golf balls—and the beauty of the Appalachians. The setting couldn't be better. Many guests come for the 18-hole Jack Nicklaus golf course, set between lake and mountains. Golf-package guests should check with the manager to extend their checkout time (tee times and golf clinics can run much later than the usual checkout time). Rocky Gap also offers a year-round program of more than 30 outdoor activities, including rappelling, rock climbing, caving, canoeing, kayaking, horseback riding, fly-fishing, cross-country skiing, horse-drawn carriage or sleigh tours, and bike and boat rentals. Or you can just pull up a lounge chair, read a book beside the lake, and choose from the many treatments offered at the new Rocky Gap Garden Spa.

16701 Lakeview Rd. NE, Flintstone, MD 21530. ℂ **800/724-0828** or 301/784-8400. Fax 301/784-8408. www.rockygapresort.com. 218 units. $79–$195 double; $325–$650 suite. Children under 18 stay free in parent's room. AE, DC, MC, V. Pets accepted for a fee. **Amenities:** 2 lakeside restaurants; lounge; indoor pool; 18-hole golf course; tennis courts; pro shop; health club; spa; numerous outdoor activities (reservations and fees required). *In room:* A/C, TV w/pay movies, Nintendo, high-speed Internet access, minibar, hair dryer, iron.

WHERE TO DINE
Au Petit Paris ⓖ *Finds* AMERICAN/FRENCH   Au Petit Paris is a find in this rural section of Maryland—a fine, intimate French restaurant, worth the drive from Cumberland. Even other area restaurateurs recommend it. The interior has a Parisian feel, with French murals and posters and bistro-style furnishings. Established 45 years ago, the restaurant is a favorite for classic French fare like chateaubriand (order 24 hr. in advance) and coq au vin.

86 E. Main St., Frostburg. ℂ **301/689-8946.** www.aupetitparis.com. Reservations recommended. Main courses $14–$28. AE, DC, DISC, MC, V. Tues–Sat 6–9:30pm. Lounge opens 5:30pm.

Giuseppe's Italian Restaurant *Value* ITALIAN   In the heart of town and a block from the Frostburg State University campus, this spot is popular with the college community and is staffed by students and locals. The first-rate food includes all the usual Italian favorites, such as pizza, pastas, shrimp scampi, and veal parmigiana, as well as a few unusual dishes like crab carbonara and a wonderful array of antipasti.

11 Bowery St., Frostburg. ℭ **301/689-2220.** www.giuseppes.net. Reservations recommended on weekends. Main courses $8–$22. AE, DISC, MC, V. Sun–Thurs 4:30–11pm; Fri–Sat 3–11pm.

Oxford House ✿ INTERNATIONAL   This restaurant is a standout in the region. The atmosphere is intimate, the food and service excellent. The chef mixes European flavors with American ones—and that makes for a menu with a lot of spice. Fish is often featured; salmon dishes, like the almond-crusted preparation, are always a winner. There are also meat and vegetarian choices. The house salad is exceptional, just as the menu claims. Be sure to check out the wine list.

129 Baltimore St., Cumberland. ℭ **301/777-7101.** www.oxfordhouse.com. Reservations recommended. Main courses $12–$23. AE, DISC, MC, V. Mon–Sat 4–9pm; brunch on the last Sun of each month, Easter, and Mother's Day 10am–3pm.

Queen City Creamery & Deli ICE CREAM/DELI   Mix nostalgia with your ice cream at this soda fountain, which has a counter, booths, and a 1952 jukebox. Coffee drinks, soups, and sandwiches are available, too. A second creamery is at Canal Place.

108 Harrison St., Cumberland ℭ **301/777-0011.** www.queencitycreamery.com. Reservations not accepted. Sandwiches $1.75–$6.25. MC, V. Mon–Thurs 7am–9pm; Fri 7am–10pm; Sat 8am–10pm; Sun 8am–9pm.

WHAT TO SEE & DO

One of the highlights of a visit to Cumberland is a stroll through the **Victorian Historic District** ✿✿✿, along Washington Street on the western side of town. This area includes the site of the original Fort Cumberland (now the Emmanuel Episcopal Church) and more than 50 residential and public buildings, built in the 1800s when Cumberland was at its peak. Listed on the National Register of Historic Places, this street is a showcase of homes with stained-glass windows, cupolas, and mansard roofs. You'll see architectural styles ranging from Federal, Queen Anne, Empire, Colonial Revival, Italianate, and English Country Gothic to Georgian Revival, Gothic Revival, and Greek Revival. Though the houses are not open to the public, a self-guided walking tour available from the visitor center offers a glimpse into their history. One exception is the **Gordon–Roberts House** (see below), which is open for tours.

Canal Place: Chesapeake & Ohio Canal National Historical Park—Cumberland Visitor Center   The C&O Canal opened here in 1850. For more than 75 years, it was an important transport line and had a major impact on the development of the town. Visit the Western Maryland Station Center at track level, check out the exhibits on the history of the canal (including a model of the Paw Paw Tunnel), and pick up a brochure. Then explore the towpath, a nearly level trail for walkers, hikers, and bikers. There are remnants of locks, dams, lock houses, and other features along the way.

13 Canal St., Cumberland. ℭ **301/722-8226.** www.nps.gov/choh. Free admission. Daily 9am–5pm. Closed Thanksgiving, Dec 25, and Jan 1.

C&O Canal Paw Paw Tunnel ✿   Paw Paw Tunnel, part of the C&O Canal National Historical Park, started in 1836 when engineers decided to build the C&O Canal right through, rather than around, an intervening mountain. The result was a tunnel lined with more than 6 million bricks and passing ¾ mile through the darkness of the hill. Today, all there is to do at Paw Paw is walk through the tunnel, which takes about 20 minutes one-way. The park service suggests bringing a flashlight. This is not for the claustrophobic or those afraid of the dark (you must walk down a narrow tow-path bounded by a guardrail, with the canal on one side and a sloping brick wall on the other). But if you're up for it, pass through the enormous brick arch into the damp darkness, then head for the light at the end of the tunnel.

Rte. 51 and the Potomac River, south of Cumberland. ✆ **301/722-8226**. www.nps.gov/choh. Free admission. Daily dawn–dusk.

Emmanuel Episcopal Church

Emmanuel Episcopal Church   This church, located in Cumberland's historic dis-trict, is built on the foundations of Fort Cumberland, where George Washington began his military career; earthworks from the fort (built in 1755) still lie beneath the church. Although the Emmanuel parish dates from 1803, the cornerstone of the cur-rent building was laid in 1849. The church contains original Tiffany stained-glass win-dows from three different periods and a scale model of Fort Cumberland. The grounds are part of the Fort Cumberland Walking Trail, signposted with plaques and detailed in a leaflet available from the visitor center.

16 Washington St., Cumberland. ✆ **301/777-3364**. emmanuel@ang-md.org. Free admission. Mon–Fri 9am–5pm, except during services. Services Wed 5:30pm; Thurs 10:30am; Sun 8am, 10am, and 6pm.

George Washington's Headquarters   This log cabin, believed to be the only remaining structure from the original Fort Cumberland, was used by then-Colonel George Washington as his official quarters during the French and Indian War. The tiny one-room cabin is not open to the public, but it does have a viewing window and an audio description.

In Riverside Park, Greene St. (at the junction of Wills Creek and the Potomac River), Cumberland. ✆ **301/777-5132**. Free admission. Daily 24 hr.; exterior viewing only.

Gordon–Roberts House   Built as a private residence in 1867 for the president of the C&O Canal, this 18-room Second Empire home is now in the hands of the Alle-gany County Historical Society. It's filled with antiques, such as a Victorian courting couch and an 1840 square grand piano. Other features include a research room, a brick-walled garden, and a basement kitchen with antique utensils, fireplace, coal stove, and pottery. It's a fascinating place to stop while strolling past all the lovely homes in Cumberland's historic district.

218 Washington St., Cumberland. ✆ **301/777-8678**. www.thrashercarriagemuseum.com. Admission $7. Tues–Sat 10am–5pm. Last tour at 4pm.

Thrasher Carriage Museum   Housed in a renovated warehouse opposite the steam-train depot in Frostburg, this museum houses an extensive collection of late-19th- and early-20th-century horse-drawn carriages, featuring more than 50 vehicles from the collection of the late James R. Thrasher. Highlights include the inaugural coach used by Teddy Roosevelt, several Vanderbilt sleighs, elaborately decorated funeral wagons, formal closed vehicles, surreys, and open sleighs.

Depot Center, 19 Depot St., Frostburg. ✆ **301/689-3380**. www.thrashercarriagemuseum.com. Admission $4 adults, $3 children under 19. Mar–Dec Wed–Sun 10am–3pm; Jan–Feb by appointment.

Western Maryland Scenic Railroad 𝆓𝆓 *Kids*   It's worth a trip to Western Mary-land to board this vintage steam train and ride the 32-mile round-trip between Cum-berland and Frostburg. The excursion—enhanced by live commentary—follows a scenic mountain valley route through the Cumberland Narrows, Helmstetter's Horseshoe Curve, Brush Tunnel, many panoramic vistas, and a 1,300-foot elevation change between the two destinations. All trains depart and terminate at Cumberland. The trip takes 3½ hours, including a 1½-hour layover in Frostburg, where you can opt to visit the nearby Thrasher Carriage Museum. The railroad also offers group excursions, dinner trains, and murder-mystery trains. Call or check the website for dates and times. Diesel trains are used May through August and in October to help meet the demand for tickets. Santa Express trips, offered Thanksgiving weekend through December, are aboard the steam train.

Western Maryland Station Center, 13 Canal St., Cumberland. © **800/TRAIN-50** or 301/759-4400. www.wmsr.com. Tickets $22 adults, $20 seniors, $11 children 12 and under. First-class tickets that include lunch $40 adults, $38 seniors, $20 children 12 and under. Reservations required. Excursions generally leave at 11:30am; dinner and special excursions leave at 6pm; 4:30pm departures added in Oct. From I-68, take Downtown Cumberland Exit 43C (westbound) or Johnson St. Exit 43A (eastbound) and follow signs.

SHOPPING

Cumberland's shopping still focuses on the needs of its residents, but a small pedestrian mall along Baltimore Street is worth a stroll. You'll find several antiques stores and gift shops here. Most are open Monday through Saturday from 10am to 5pm, with many open on Sunday, too.

Just off the pedestrian mall is the **Book Center,** 15 N. Centre St. (© **301/722-2284**), where you'll find a large selection of books on Maryland, local history, railroading, and canals. It also sells postcards, gifts, regional souvenirs, and out-of-state newspapers. It's open Monday through Friday from 8am to 6pm, Saturday from 9am to 5pm, and Sunday from 9am to 2pm.

The **Saville Gallery,** 52 Baltimore St. (© **301/777-2787;** www.alleganyartscouncil. org), is operated by the Allegany Arts Council and features the works of Western Maryland artists and craftspeople. It's open Tuesday through Friday from 10am to 4pm and Saturday from 11am to 4pm.

Canal Place, where the Western Maryland Railway Station and visitor center are located (© 800/989-9394; www.canalplace.org), is also home to several shops. You'll find **Arts at Canal Place** (© 301/777-8199), **C&O Bicycle** (© 301/678-6665), **Simply Maryland** (© 301/724-6916), **Timeless Treats** (© 301/724-7773), and **Tree House Toys** (© 301/759-4869) here. For a bite to eat, options include **Crab Alley Seafood** (© 301/724-7472), **Queen City Creamery** (© 301/777-2552), and **Wild Mountain Cafe** (© 301/759-9457). Hours vary, but expect shops to be open daily until about 8pm in summer.

CUMBERLAND AFTER DARK

There's a surprising amount of performing arts in Cumberland. Something is always going on in one of the two area theaters or at nearby Frostburg State University's **Performing Arts Center** (© **301/687-4145**). You can check with the **Allegany Arts Council,** 52 Baltimore St. (© **301/777-ARTS;** www.alleganyartscouncil.org), for a complete schedule of upcoming concerts and cultural events.

The **Cumberland Theatre,** 101–103 Johnson St. (© **301/759-4990;** www. cumberlandtheatre.com), in a renovated church, presents a professional program of musicals and comedies as well as mysteries and dramas June through November.

The **New Embassy Theatre,** 49 Baltimore St. (© **301/722-4692**), a 1931 Art Deco movie theater, hosts classic films, live music, theater, and dance. Its restoration was featured on Bob Villa's *Restore America* television program. Call for a schedule and to make reservations.

3 Deep Creek Lake ✮✮✮ & Garrett County ✮

50 miles SW of Cumberland, 190 miles W of Baltimore, 120 miles SE of Pittsburgh

Garrett County's mountain scenery has beckoned visitors for centuries. Native American hunters combed these hills a thousand years ago looking for game. In Colonial days, this was the American frontier, populated mostly by Indians and trappers. Few settled here until the coming of the Baltimore & Ohio Railroad in the 1850s. Farmers, coal miners, and loggers were the first to arrive. During the Civil War, the railroad provided a needed supply link, and Garrett towns became the targets of Confederate attack. Once peace returned to the country, Garrett became a vacation destination. Three presidents—Grant, Cleveland, and Harrison—vacationed here.

Once Deep Creek Lake was created in the 1920s and the Wisp Resort built in 1944, leisure travelers had even more reasons to make the trip to Garrett County. Deep Creek Lake is now a popular recreational area. It's the state's largest freshwater lake, nearly 12 miles in length, with 65 miles of shoreline occupied by private vacation homes and chalets. The northern end is where the action is—the commercial centers, the Wisp Resort, and the waterfront hotels and inns are all located here. Summer temperatures, averaging a comfortable 66°F, draw visitors escaping the heat and humidity of the big cities. In winter, Deep Creek Lake is Maryland's premier ski resort, with an average temperature of 28°F and a yearly snowfall of more than 100 inches.

In recent years, Garrett County has become a four-season destination as well as *the* place for mid-Atlantic residents to buy a second home. It's centrally located between Pittsburgh, Baltimore/Washington, and eastern Ohio cities, a 3- to 4-hour drive from each. Visitors can hike or bike the scenic trails; go skiing, snow-tubing, or snowshoeing; take to the waters and try boating, fly-fishing, kayaking, or white-water rafting; and visit antiques and crafts stores. Or they can do nothing but sit back and enjoy the old-time charm that this region has long been known for.

ESSENTIALS
GETTING THERE   From the east or west, take I-68 to Exit 14 and drive south on U.S. Route 219.

VISITOR INFORMATION   The visitor center is on U.S. Route 219, near the bottom of the Wisp Resort's ski runs. It's open from 9am to 5pm, with extended hours in summer. Ask for a vacation guide, which contains a calendar of events and information

---

Fun Fact **Venice in the Mountains**

Okay, nobody's *really* calling it that, but Deep Creek Lake is trying to get people out of their cars and into boats. Businesses are adding piers to their lakeside establishments and sharing them with neighbors within walking distance of the lake. Visitors can go to the store, the movies, and even to church by boat. This only works April through October, as the lake freezes pretty hard in winter. The visitor center has a "Travel by Boat" map listing all the places with piers. Call ℂ **301/387-4386** for information.

---

on local history, restaurants, hotels, and shopping. For information, call ✆ **301/387-4386** or go to www.garrettchamber.com.

For ski conditions, call ✆ **301/387-4911** or visit www.skimaryland.com.

GETTING AROUND   Businesses in Deep Creek Lake sometimes have mailing addresses in McHenry and/or Oakland. Deep Creek Lake and McHenry are, for all intents and purposes, the same place, and you can count on those addresses to be on the lake or close by.

Oakland, the county seat of Garrett County, is several miles south of Deep Creek Lake. Some businesses maintain mailing addresses there; others are actually just off the lake, outside the Deep Creek Lake/McHenry postal zone. Proximity to the lake resort areas is indicated in the listings in this section.

U.S. Route 219 runs beside the northern half of Deep Creek Lake and swings south toward Oakland. The Glendale Road Bridge crosses the middle of the lake and leads to Deep Creek Lake State Park (where you'll find the best public beach and a nature center). North of this bridge is where all the action is. South of this bridge, it's quieter and more remote. Most sailors sail their boats here; look for the weekend regattas.

SPECIAL EVENTS   Garrett County celebrates autumn with a 4-day **Autumn Glory Festival** (✆ **301/387-4386**), usually held the second weekend in October. Not only are the leaves in full fall color, but the towns are also filled with festivities. In early June, Scottish pride shows during the **McHenry Highland Festival** (✆ **301/387-3093**). Come for the traditional sounds of bagpipe, harp, and fiddle, plus dance and athletic competitions, bluegrass music, crafts, and food. The **Garrett Lakes Arts Festival** (✆ **301/387-3082;** www.artsandentertainment.org), a series of performances held March through September, includes a sampling of music and drama, as well as arts camps for kids.

WHERE TO STAY
VACATION RENTALS

The Deep Creek Lake area offers plenty of vacation properties—cabins, town homes, and mountain chalets—for rent by the week or in 2- and 3-day intervals. They come in all sizes, from a two-bedroom lakeside cottage or slopeside town house to eight-bedroom behemoths with extra everything. Fireplaces, hot tubs, decks, boat slips, and even ski-in and ski-outs are available. Many allow pets. They generally come with all the linens, appliances, and tools you'll need.

Most of the homes are individually owned and rented through agencies. Two reputable ones are **Railey Mountain Lake Vacations** (✆ **800/846-7368;** www.deep creek.com) and **A&A/Long & Foster Resort Rentals** (✆ **800/336-7303;** www.deep creekresort.com). Railey even has a guest welcome party on Mondays in summer, so visitors can get to know what's available at Deep Creek, from horseback riding to fly-fishing classes.

HOTELS, MOTELS & B&BS

Carmel Cove Inn ✶✶✶   You'll notice right away that this little B&B, with its steeples and clock tower, looks like a monastery—and it was once a Carmelite monastery. Tucked in a wooded area off Glendale Road and U.S. Route 219, you'll feel the serenity of the place as you stroll its 2 acres, down to the private cove and dock. But inside, these are no monks' cells. The luxurious guest rooms boast uncommon amenities, including flatscreen TVs and hand-held massagers. Some units have

Finds **Heading Indoors for Some Pampering**

Some of the bed-and-breakfasts listed below offer spa facilities. For the rest of us, however, there's **Sewickley Spa**, at the Wisp Resort (*C* **301/387-7000;** www.sewickleyspa.com). It offers facials, massage, body wraps, bronzing, nail services, waxing, and even spa lunches.

---

hot tubs; others have private decks or fireplaces. The parlor has a striking stacked-stone fireplace and a billiards table.

Glendale Rd. (P.O. Box 644), Oakland, MD 21550. *C* **301/387-0067.** www.carmelcoveinn.com. 11 units. $135–$195 double. Rates include full breakfast and snacks. DISC, MC, V. No children under 12. **Amenities:** Complimentary beverage bar; tennis court; billiards table; dock w/canoes, paddleboat, and inner tubes; free use of cross-country skis, snowshoes, and fishing poles; DVD library. *In room:* A/C, TV/DVD, hair dryer, robe.

Haley Farm Bed & Breakfast *☆*   If you dream of a real country vacation, surrounded by orchards, wildflowers, and horses, this could be your spot. Set on 65 acres, Haley Farm offers country living in luxurious accommodations. Rooms range from spacious to cavernous; most are suites with fireplaces, Jacuzzis, traditional furnishings, and souvenirs of the innkeepers' world travels. Three units have kitchenettes. A lakeside cottage is available by the week in summer, for 2-night minimum stays the rest of the year. If you decide to leave your room, the inn offers many spa treatments, such as sunless tanning, massages, and facials (reservations required). Ask about packages and group retreat programs, including a romantic getaway and cooking weekends; retreat topics range from yoga to conflict resolution.

16766 Garrett Hwy., Oakland, MD 21550. *C* **888/231-FARM** or 301/387-9050. Fax 301/387-9050. www.haley farm.com. 9 units. $135–$235 double. Rates include full breakfast. 2-night minimum stay required on weekends. AE, DISC, MC, V. No children under 12. **Amenities:** Garden; sauna; spa; dock w/rowboats; stocked trout/bass pond; free use of fishing tackle, bikes, cross-country skis, and tubes; high-speed Internet access; gift shop. *In room:* A/C, TV/VCR, Wi-Fi, robe.

Inn at Point View   Right on the shores of Deep Creek Lake, this lodging offers motel-style units, all with lake views—and all but one with a patio overlooking the lake. Rooms are the usual motel configuration, but spacious enough for a pile of swim rings or snowboards. Two efficiency units—one with a fireplace—are also available. Although the hotel dates to the mid–20th century, updating is ongoing. The new owners plan extensive renovations in the future. The lakeside restaurant, Sweetwater Grill, has also reopened (see "Where to Dine," below).

609 Deep Creek Dr. (P.O. Box 100), McHenry, MD 21541. *C* **301/387-5555.** www.theinnatpointview.com. 18 units. $79–$139 double. Packages available. DISC, MC, V. **Amenities:** Restaurant; lounge; boat dock; private beach. *In room:* A/C, TV, Wi-Fi, coffeemaker.

Lake Pointe Inn *☆*   Built in the 1800s, this inn has a variety of accommodations. Room sizes vary, from small to spacious enough for three. Expect dreamy beds, warm earth tones, and Arts and Crafts–style furnishings. Most units have gas fireplaces and Jacuzzis, some have steam showers, and you can count on a view of the lake. A couple units, including the spacious McCann, have balconies. South-facing rooms offer the best views, but all have comfortable amenities. The blazing fire in the living room may keep you from heading outdoors—but the lake and the ski slopes, both within walking distance, are bound to beckon. If you're allergic to down pillows and com-forters, alternatives are available. Reserve ahead for spa treatments.

174 Lake Pointe Dr., McHenry, MD 21541. ℂ **800/523-LAKE** or 301/387-0111. www.deepcreekinns.com. 10 units. $158–$259 double. Rates include full breakfast. 2-night minimum stay required on weekends. DISC, MC, V. No chil-dren under 16. **Amenities:** Sauna; steam shower; massage room; tennis court; complimentary bikes; canoes and kayaks; video library. *In room:* A/C, TV/VCR, hair dryer, robe.

Wisp Resort Hotel 👧👧 *Kids*   With accommodations overlooking the slopes and ski lockers just inside the door, Wisp makes it easy on skiers. A majority of the guest rooms are suites or efficiencies; all have queen-size beds and sofa beds. Some have kitchenettes, two have fireplaces, and some suites have Murphy beds. A learning center for kids 3 to 14, with half- and full-day skiing and snowboarding classes, makes this resort popular with families. Scenic chairlift rides and paintball are among the warm-weather activi-ties. Wisp specializes in providing vacation packages, so if there's some activity you want to try—mountain biking, white-water paddling, orienteering—let the staff know, and they'll usually be able to make the necessary arrangements.

290 Marsh Hill Rd. (off U.S. Rte. 219, on north side of Deep Creek Lake), McHenry, MD 21541. ℂ **800/462-9477** or 301/387-5581. Fax 301/387-4127. www.wispresort.com. 169 units. $79–$229 double. AE, DC, DISC, MC, V. Pets accepted for a fee. **Amenities:** Restaurant; coffee shop/pizzeria; 3 lounges; indoor pool; 18-hole championship golf course; tennis court; health club; hot tub; concierge; ski shop; ski/snowboard program for children 3–14; children's center; warm-weather mountain biking, disc golf, scenic chairlift rides, skate park, and paintball. *In room:* A/C, data-port, fridge, coffeemaker, hair dryer, iron.

WHERE TO DINE

Note: Garrett County liquor regulations prohibit restaurants from serving any alco-holic beverages, including wine, on Sunday.

Canoe on the Run DELI   This unpretentious sandwich shop serves gourmet sand-wiches, coffee, and pastries; there are even a few vegetarian options, a rarity in these parts. The dining area is spare but quiet and cozy, with a gas fireplace. In warm weather, the outdoor deck is available. Beer and wine are sold here.

2622 Deep Creek Dr., McHenry. ℂ **301/387-5933.** Reservations not accepted. Sandwiches and salads $3.95–$7.25. AE, DISC, MC, V. Mon–Fri 8am–3pm; Sat–Sun 8am–4pm.

Deer Park Inn 👧 FRENCH   For fine dining in turn-of-the-20th-century atmos-phere, it's hard to beat this lovely 1889 inn, built deep in the country as a summer home for Baltimore architect Josiah Pennington. Left dormant for many years, the 17-room "cottage" has been restored and is listed on the National Register of Historic Places. Furnished with Victorian antiques, it is now the setting for candlelit French cuisine with an American flair. The menu recently included confit of duck with braised red cabbage and garlic mashed potatoes, braised shank of lamb, and mustard-glazed salmon with rosemary. Cooking classes are occasionally offered; call for infor-mation. The inn also offers three bedrooms upstairs ($115–$145 double).

65 Hotel Rd., Deer Park. ℂ **301/334-2308.** www.deerparkinn.com. Reservations recommended. Main courses $17–$25. AE, DISC, MC, V. Summer Mon–Sat 5:30–9:30pm; winter Thurs–Sat 5:30–9:30pm. Located about 9 miles southeast of the Deep Creek Lake Bridge, off Sand Flat Rd. and Rte. 135; look for signs.

Four Seasons AMERICAN   Four Seasons is a bit more formal than many of the other eateries in Deep Creek, kind of like the restaurants you may remember from, say, the early 1960s. Furnishings in this stone-and-glass dining room have that retro flair. But the lake view is beautiful, the burgers are big and juicy, and the menu has plenty of choices. Look for traditional American fare: crab cakes, stuffed flounder, and tournedos of beef filet. It's a good place to go when you want to get away from the noise of some of the other hopping restaurants in town.

At Will O' the Wisp, 20160 Garrett Hwy. (U.S. Rte. 219), Oakland. © **301/387-5503**, ext. 2201. Main courses $5–$8 lunch, $14–$30 dinner. AE, DISC, MC, V. Reservations recommended for dinner. Daily 7am–2pm and 5–9:30pm. Located just south of the Deep Creek Lake Bridge.

Lakeside Creamery ICE CREAM/SANDWICHES If you see a crowd outside the Lakeside Creamery in the morning, you know it must be close to opening time. The homemade ice cream draws people by car, on foot, and even by boat. It offers 90 flavors, with seasonal specialties such as fresh peach ice cream. Try the handmade waffle cones, too.

20282 Garrett Hwy. (U.S. Rte. 219), Oakland. © **301/387-2580**. www.lakesidecreamery.com. Reservations not accepted. Most items $2-$6. MC, V. Summer daily 11am–11pm; off season Fri–Sat 11am–11pm, Sun 11am–10pm. Closed Jan–Feb.

Santa Fe Grill *Kids* SOUTHWESTERN Deep Creek Brewery is gone, but in its place is this Southwestern-style eatery. At first it may seem odd to be in a place that conjures up visions of the desert instead of the ski slopes, but the feeling wears off as soon as the waitstaff serves up your hearty wrap, sizzling fajita, or thick burger. Mesquite-grilled meats are a specialty. The owners just may have come up with an innovative idea here in the mountains, though it's too bad there's not a pint of Deep Creek brew anywhere in sight. Kids' and takeout menus are available, too.

19814 Garrett Hwy. (U.S. Rte. 219), Deep Creek Lake. © **301/387-4866**. Reservations not necessary. Main courses $9–$21. AE, DISC, MC, V. Mon–Sat 11am–midnight (until 11pm in winter); Sun 11am–10pm.

Sweetwater Grill AMERICAN Casual and old-fashioned, this wood-paneled restaurant has two things going for it: good food and a close-up view of Deep Creek Lake. The locals go for the crab cakes. So what if it's 100 miles from the Chesapeake Bay? The lump crab and simple preparation have created quite a stir. The menu also offers ribs, steaks, and pasta. In summer, the Friday seafood buffet has 'em lined up.

609 Deep Creek Dr., McHenry. © **301/387-5555**. www.theinnatpointview.com. Reservations recommended. Main courses $9.95–$34. DISC, MC, V. Summer daily 8am–9pm; off season Fri–Mon 8am–9pm, Tues–Thurs 4–9pm.

Uno Chicago Grill *Kids* PIZZA Everybody comes here. It's a family place, with a playground and wide lawn by the piers so the kids can wear themselves out while waiting for a table. (And there *can* be a wait, especially on weekends.) A central fireplace dominates the dining room, covered outside seating overlooks the lake, and a deck at the Honi-Honi Bar has entertainment on warm weekends. The food is the usual for Uno's: pizza, pastas, sandwiches, soups, salads, and an interesting children's menu. The chain's founder, who lives nearby, has made this restaurant a standout.

19746 Garrett Hwy., Oakland. © **301/387-4866**. Reservations not accepted. Main courses $5.75–$22. AE, DC, DISC, MC, V. Mon–Sat 11am–midnight (until 11pm in winter); Sun 11am–11pm.

OUTDOOR ACTIVITIES

BOATING Summer activities focus on watersports. You can rent just about any kind of powerboat, from a ski boat for one to a pontoon boat for 12. Paddleboats, canoes, and fishing boats are also available at many marinas around the lake. A water-ski boat costs about $90 for 2 hours; runabouts are $25 to $50; and a pontoon boat runs around $65 an hour. Some of the leading firms along U.S. Route 219 at Deep Creek Lake are **Aquatic Center** (© 301/387-8233), **Bill's Marine North** (© 800/607-BOAT or

301/387-5677), **Bill's Marine Service** (𝒞 301/387-5536), **Crystal Waters** (𝒞 301/ 387-5515), and **Deep Creek Marina** (𝒞 301/387-6977).

If you want to sail, you'll have to bring your own boat, as none are available for rent. Or you can learn to sail at **Deep Creek Sailing School** (𝒞 **301/387-4497;** www.deepcreeksailingschool.com). Courses run 5 days and cost about $235. DCSS grads can rent Flying Scots (the locally produced daysailers) for about $100 a day.

CAMPING   **Deep Creek Lake State Park** (𝒞 **301/387-5563**) offers 112 improved campsites (25 with electric hookups), plus a yurt, Adirondack-style cabin, and two minicamper cabins. Facilities include a dump station and bathhouses with showers. Rentals are $25 to $50 a night. Reservations are recommended; call 𝒞 **800/432-CAMP.** Pets are permitted in designated loops. See the Garrett County section of "The Great Outdoors in Western Maryland," earlier in this chapter, for other camping options.

CROSS-COUNTRY SKIING   Cross-country skiing is available at **Herrington Manor State Park** (𝒞 301/334-9180) and **New Germany State Park** (𝒞 301/895-5453), both described in "The Great Outdoors in Western Maryland," earlier in this chapter. **Deep Creek Outfitters** (𝒞 301/387-2200), **Allegany Expeditions** (𝒞 301/ 722-5170), and **High Mountain Sports** (𝒞 301/387-2113) all rent cross-country skis.

DOGSLEDDING   Two local outfitters offer dogsledding in area parks. The weather must be cool enough for the dogs (50°F or lower). If there's no snow, sleds on wheels are available—though the experience isn't quite the same. Reservations are required for all tours at both outfitters. They even have kennel visits available if all you want to do is get to know one of these Siberian or Alaskan beauties.

Husky Power Dogsledding (𝒞 **301/746-7200;** www.huskypowerdogsledding.com) offers kennel visits and dogsledding adventures year-round. A "mush hour" takes riders on dog sleds around local forests for $70 to $100. Very short rides (of about 10 min.) and longer tours are available as well. **Yellow Snow Dog Sled Adventures** (𝒞 **301/616-4996;** www.yellowsnowadventures.com) offers introductory tours for $50 to $65 a person, adventure tours (in which you drive your own sled team), and kennel tours for $10 per adult and $5 per child under 15. Adopt-a-husky programs give dog lovers a chance to work with young dogs for about an hour or so.

DOWNHILL SKIING   Deep Creek Lake is the home of Maryland's only ski area. With an elevation of 3,080 feet and a vertical drop of 700 feet, the **Wisp Resort,** 296 Marsh Hill Rd., McHenry (𝒞 **301/387-4911;** www.skiwisp.com)—which marked its 50th year in 2005—offers 32 ski runs and trails. New in 2005 are 10 trails on the north side of the mountain, served by two quad chairlifts. Beginners can ski on several of the long, scenic trails, while black-diamond skiers can head for the face, which is straight down the front of the mountain with lots of moguls thrown in. Trails through the forest can be fast enough for both intermediates and experts. Lift tickets range from $39 on weekdays to $55 on weekends, with reduced rates for night skiing, 2-day tickets, early- or late-season skiing, and children. Kids under 6 ski free. The ski season runs from the end of November to March or April. The Wisp also operates a ski school for kids 3 to 14, child-care facility, rental service, and ski shop.

Other activities available at the resort include the new tubing park (see below). Snowshoes and K2 snow bikes can also be rented.

ECO-TOURS   Deep Creek Lake State Park is home to the **Discovery Center** (℗ **301/ 387-7067**), which houses an exhibit on local geology, fauna, and flora. It's also the starting point for a lot of fun (and, dare I say, educational) outdoor adventures. Interpretive programs, evening campfires, hikes, and star-gazing are among the possibilities throughout the year. Activity schedules are available here and at the visitor center on U.S. Route 219.

FISHING   Deep Creek Lake is home to about 22 species of fish, including yellow perch, bass, bluegill, catfish, crappie, chain pickerel, northern pike, walleye, and trout. Four world-class rivers in the area make this fly-fishing heaven. Come for the cutthroat, rainbow, brown, and brook (wild) trout. Fishing is best April through June, but ice fishing in January and February is becoming popular. The state of Maryland requires a fishing license, which can be bought at most tackle shops.

The Casselman, North Branch of the Potomac, and Yough are good trout areas, too, of course. The Casselman is home to brook and brown, the North Branch has rainbow, and the Yough has rainbow and brown.

A trout stamp is required if you intend to remove trout from nontidal waters. Try **Bill's Outdoor Center** (℗ **301/387-FISH**) or **Deep Creek Outfitters** (℗ **301/387-2200**).

GOLF   The **Golf Club at Wisp,** Wisp Resort Golf Course, 296 Marsh Hill Rd., McHenry (℗ **301/387-4911;** www.wispresort.com), is an 18-hole, par-72 championship facility built beside (and on) the ski slopes. It's open daily from April to mid-October. Greens fees for 18 holes are $42 to $69 per person, $24 for juniors. A pro shop and driving range are on the grounds. The **Oakland Golf Club,** Sang Run Road, Oakland (℗ **301/334-3883**), has an 18-hole, par-71 championship course, also open April through October. Call ahead for greens and cart fees.

HIKING   Five trails ranging from easy to challenging are in **Deep Creek Lake State Park,** south of McHenry on State Park Road (℗ **301/387-5563**). The most scenic is Indian Turnip Trail, approximately 2.5 miles that wind along Meadow Mountain and across the ridge top. Entry fee is $2 per vehicle; the park is open daily from 8am until sunset in summer, until 4pm in winter. Hikers can head to the **Wisp Resort** (℗ **301/ 387-4911**) after the snow melts to ride up the chairlift for a mountaintop view and a downhill hike. See the Garrett County section of "The Great Outdoors in Western Maryland," earlier in this chapter, for other hiking options.

SWIMMING   Deep Creek Lake State Park (℗ **301/387-5563**) features an 800-foot guarded sandy beach with bathhouses and lockers nearby. It's one of the only public places for swimming. Entry fees to the park are $3 to $4 a person in season. Off-season fees are $3 to $4 per vehicle, with free admission for seniors and children in restraint seats. The park is open from 8am until sunset. Lifeguards are on duty from Memorial Day to Labor Day, daily from 10am to 6pm.

Tips   Ditch the Skis—Let's Go Tubing!

If you get tired of skiing, here's another way to speed down a snowy slope: The Wisp Resort offers **Bear Claw Snow Tubing Park** (℗ **301/387-4911**). It's been such a big hit that the number of runs is up to nine. Best of all, a tow rope takes you back up to the top. The fee ($15–$19 a session) is separate from the price of a lift ticket. It's a good idea to call ahead for tubing time.

OTHER ATTRACTIONS IN GARRETT COUNTY

Church of the Presidents   Presidents Grant, Harrison, and Cleveland attended services here, as did Chester Arthur (before he took office). Built in 1868 as a Presbyterian church, it's made of the same sandstone used for B&O railroad bridges and tunnels.

St. Matthew's Episcopal Church, 126 E. Liberty St., Oakland. ✆ 301/334-2510. Sun services at 8 and 10:45am.

Deep Creek Cellars   Paul Roberts and Nadine Grabania built this little winery in the basement of their home in the farthest northwest corner of Maryland. It manages to produce 12,000 bottles of light, fruity wine every year, and the owners take great pride in their work. (You can find their wines as far east as Baltimore.) At harvest time, you can see the juice as it's pressed from the fruit. Best of all, you can try the final product in the tasting room. They also produce port. It's a good 20-minute drive up Route 42, past I-68, but the scenery is worth it.

177 Frazee Ridge Rd., Friendsville. ✆ 301/746-4349. www.deepcreekcellars.com. Apr 20–Nov 20 Wed–Sat 11am–6pm.

Garrett County Historical Society Museum   This quaint museum, staffed by friendly volunteers, was revamped in 2005. It has added a pioneer cabin and rooms focusing on local history: the B&O Railroad, military life, and more. There's an amazing array of local artifacts, including those of the famous hunter Meshach Browning, plus an elegant 1908 surrey. The gift shop focuses on local history, too.

107 S. Second St., Oakland. ✆ 301/334-3226. Free admission; donations accepted. May–Dec Mon–Sat 10am–3pm; Jan–Apr Thurs–Sat 10am–3pm.

Oakland Train Station *Finds*   The restored Queen Anne–style station is striking, with its bell-shaped roof and stained glass. It was built back in 1884 for the growing resort clientele; now it houses a visitor center and the Shoppe at Heritage Square, a shop filled with local handiwork.

117 E. Liberty St., Oakland. ✆ 301/334-1243. Free admission. Daily 9am–5pm.

Simon Pearce Glass Factory *Finds*   Cross the catwalk over the furnaces and workbenches of glass artisans as they create the crystal-clear pieces for which Simon Pearce is famous. The glassblowers share the tasks of blowing orange molten glass into delicate forms. Most artisans work until 3pm, but there's always at least one team working until 5pm and on weekends. The showroom is filled with the elegant, modern wares created here and at the other Simon Pearce factories around the country.

265 Glass Dr., Mountain Lake Park. ✆ 301/334-5277. www.simonpearce.com. Daily 9am–5pm. Located south of Deep Creek Lake and Oakland: Take Rte. 219 south to Rte. 135; turn left and then turn right on Glass Dr.; the factory is on the left.

SHOPPING

A few places in outlying areas of Deep Creek Lake are worth a stop. Just north of Deep Creek Lake, off Route 42, **Schoolhouse Earth,** 1224 Friendsville Rd. (✆ **301/746-8603;** www.schoolhouseearth.com), specializes in country accessories (including some interesting garden items), artwork, gourmet food, jewelry, and home decor. Open daily from 10am to 6pm.

In Oakland, the **Book Market & Antique Mezzanine,** 111 S. Second St. (✆ **301/334-8778**), has a good selection of children's books, literary fiction, history, and biography, as well as antiques and collectibles. Open Monday through Saturday from 9:30am to 5:30 or 6pm, Sunday from 11am to 4pm. **Unfinished Business,** 114 S.

Kids Working Farms

If you like bunnies and llamas, or you want your kids to see a real farm, stop by the Deep Creek visitor center for the brochure called *Visit Our Working Farms, Share Our Heritage*, which lists 11 farms that welcome visitors. They're located all around the western half of Garrett County. Besides livestock farms, there's a hydroponic tomato farm, as well as a farm specializing in woods-grown crops such as ginseng, walnuts, and shiitake mushrooms.

At **Cove-Run Farms** (© 301/746-8161; www.coverunfarms.com), there's a corn maze built into 8 acres—Maryland's largest such autumn attraction. The corn is tall and the paths are tricky, but it's fun to hear the kids squeal as they make their way through. It's open mid-August through October, Friday from noon to 10pm, Saturday from 11am to 9pm, and Sunday from 2 to 6pm.

Second St. (© **301/533-4495**), sells unfinished furniture (which can be finished for you) and does custom framing. Open Monday through Friday from 10am to 5pm, Saturday from 10am to 1pm.

Located 8 miles south of Oakland on U.S. Route 219, just past the intersection of U.S. Route 50, is the 12,000-square-foot **Red House School Country Mall** (© **301/334-2800**). It carries antiques, crafts, local Amish wares, and furniture. It's open Monday through Saturday from 9am to 5pm, Sunday from 10am to 5pm.

AN EXCURSION TO GRANTSVILLE

The National Road, which connected the East Coast to the Ohio Valley, still comes through here. You can see the tall mile markers along the road. Plan to stop in pretty little Grantsville for some shopping and a home-cooked meal.

To get here from Route 68, take Exit 19 North (Rte. 495) to U.S. 40 East. The first stop is the **Casselman River Bridge.** This was the largest single-span stone bridge ever built when it was constructed in 1813. It was closed to traffic in 1953, but you can walk across it (for a glimpse of the Youghiogheny River) to a small park.

At one end of the bridge is the **Spruce Forest Artisan Village**, 177 Casselman Rd. (© **301/895-3332;** www.spruceforest.org). Old homes, schoolhouses, and shops were relocated here from other parts of Western Maryland; some date from Revolutionary War days. Twelve structures house studios where you can watch artisans carve wooden birds, beat iron into jewelry, and weave shreds of wood into baskets. Also produced here are stained glass, teddy bears, and handcrafted soaps. Studio hours vary, but something is always open Monday through Saturday from 10am to 5pm between Memorial Day and the last Saturday in October, plus one December weekend. Off season, you take your chances, but the artisans do work here when the weather's agreeable. Musical entertainment is offered Saturdays in summer. **Stanton's Mill** has also been restored and reopened to mill flour; it's open April through October, daily from 10am to 6pm.

If you get hungry or feel a need to shop for more crafts, head across the parking lot to the **Penn Alps Restaurant & Craft Shop** (see below). Special events are often scheduled, including concerts on Saturdays at 7:30pm, May through August, and Christmas in the Village, the first weekend in December.

WHERE TO STAY & DINE

Casselman Inn *Value* MENNONITE/COUNTRY COOKING You'll notice the wonderful aromas from the bakery as soon as you enter this 1824 inn. The dining room is usually filled with families and seniors on day trips. The food here is a bargain—and filling. You'll find homemade bread (even in the stuffing), real mashed potatoes, honey-dipped chicken, and grilled ham. A children's menu is available.

113 E. Main St. (Alt. Rte. 40, off I-68, Exit 19), Grantsville. © 30l/895-5055 for lodging; © 301/895-5266 for restaurant. www.thecasselman.com. Reservations not accepted. Main courses $1.95–$4.20 breakfast, $7.45–$10 lunch and dinner. DISC, MC, V. Mon–Thurs 7am–8pm; Fri–Sat 7am–9pm; open later in summer.

Penn Alps Restaurant & Craft Shop *Value* PENNSYLVANIA DUTCH Remember those old-fashioned restaurants with simple, homemade fare served by the kindest of waitresses? Come here for the hearty breakfasts or the substantial lunch and dinner fare. There are buffets every Friday and Saturday night, as well as a Saturday breakfast buffet and Saturday and Sunday brunch. Dishes include roast pork and sauerkraut, hickory-smoked ham, roast beef, fried chicken, steaks, and seafood. Lighter items include sandwiches, soups, salads, and burgers, plus children's and seniors' menus. You can buy fresh-baked breads or pies here, or handmade goodies from the crafts shop. The restaurant is across the parking lot from the Spruce Forest Artisan Village and an easy walk to the Casselman River Bridge. An 1818 stagecoach inn makes up part of the building. Look for the double fireplace, which has warmed visitors for nearly 2 centuries.

125 Casselman Rd., Grantsville. © 301/895-5985. www.pennalps.com. Reservations not accepted, except for large groups. Main courses $3.25–$6.95 lunch, $8–$16 dinner. AE, DISC, MC, V. Nov to day before Memorial Day Mon–Thurs 9am–7pm, Fri–Sat 9am–8pm, Sun 9am–8pm; Memorial Day to last Sat in Oct Mon–Sat 9am–9pm, Sun 9am–3pm. Closed several days at Christmas.

Stonebow Inn Set away from busy Deep Creek Lake—but close enough to get there or to Cumberland in 20 minutes—this lovely 1870 inn on 6½ acres may be the perfect getaway choice. In addition to its classic Victorian style, its location puts visitors right in the middle of the goings-on in Grantsville. You can visit Spruce Forest Artisan Village down the street, dine at Penn Alps, and take a walk or fish along the Casselman River. Guest rooms differ in size and amenities; some have a fireplace, microwave, or CD player. Two separate cottages make the escape complete. New owners have injected a little art into the place: Julyen has installed a gallery in the barn on the property, while Cathy teaches Feldenkrais classes (which she says are popular with musicians and dancers, and can help anyone move better).

146 Casselman Rd., Grantsville, MD 21536. © 800/272-4090 or 301/895-4250. www.stonebowinn.com. 9 units. $120–$185 double. Rates include full breakfast. AE, MC, V. Children under 12 accepted in cottages. **Amenities:** Sauna; massage; guest access to fridge and coffeemaker; video library; gift shop. *In room:* A/C, TV/VCR, hair dryer, robe.

10

Maryland & Delaware's Atlantic Beaches

A trip to the beach or "down the ocean," in local parlance, is the only true vacation for many Marylanders and Delawareans. And though they may choose one beach as their destination, everybody—well, it can seem that way— visits the other beaches. Bethany's vacationers can't keep away from Rehoboth's shops and restaurants or Ocean City's amusements. If you're an angler, check out both Ocean City's and Lewes's charter boats. The beaches of Delaware Seashore State Park are the quietest. If you want a party, head for the nightspots of Delaware's Dewey Beach or the boardwalk of Ocean City, Maryland.

Each town has its own character—and Delaware beaches are quite different from Maryland beaches. For one thing, all of the Maryland beaches are public, whereas Delaware has some private beaches. In this chapter, we'll give you a snapshot of each, starting at the north end of the Delaware resorts and heading south to the Maryland shore, focusing on the individual delights and differences of each.

DELAWARE BEACHES

Stretched along 25 miles of ocean and bay shoreline, Delaware's five beach towns— Lewes, Rehoboth Beach, Dewey Beach, Bethany Beach, and Fenwick Island—have their own personalities and ambience.

For information on dinner specials, coupons for fudge, and local news, grab one or two of the free publications piled up in restaurants, real-estate offices, and hotels. Look for *The Wave, Sunny Day,* and *Southern Delaware Explorer.*

LEWES   With such a quaint little town to keep your attention, you just might forget there's a beach in Lewes. You can walk to the beach on the other side of the canal. Parking is available, but you have to feed the meter. There are also bathhouses and lifeguards in season. The water is calm and the sand white. The best beach is at **Cape Henlopen State Park (② 302/645-8983;** www.destateparks.com/chsp/chsp.htm), 1 mile east of Lewes. Admission is $8 per out-of-state car—and it's worth it. The beaches are never wall-to-wall with bodies as they can be in Ocean City. Even the water at the confluence of Delaware Bay and the ocean seems calmer. You can take a walk on a nature trail here and look for shorebirds.

REHOBOTH & DEWEY   Swimming at Rehoboth's and Dewey's wide sandy beaches is one of the area's top activities. All the beaches have public access and are guarded, but there are no bathhouses.

At Rehoboth, watch out for the NO SWIMMING signs. The signs at the beach between Brooklyn Avenue and Laurel Street warn against swimming near two sunken ships. Though the ships have been cut down to the waterline, it's best to avoid this one dangerous spot. *Tip:* Rehoboth offers complimentary "Beach Wheels," wheelchairs designed specifically for beach use, at the boardwalk and Maryland Avenue or Laurel Street. They're available on a first-come, first-served basis. Call ℂ 302/227-4641 for details.

Just south of Dewey is perhaps Delaware's finest, quietest beach. A narrow strip of land between the ocean and Rehoboth and Indian River bays, **Delaware Seashore State Park** ⚜ (ℂ 302/227-2800) offers ocean waves and quiet bay waters. Besides 6 miles of beach—two of them guarded from 9am to 5pm in summer—there's a 310-slip full-service marina and boat ramp, plus 500 sites for RVs and campers. Part of the beach is set aside for surfing. Unguarded beach is available for surf fishing. With a yearly license, you can drive onto the beach. With a day pass, you can walk on. Concessions are available at the guarded beaches. Admission is $4 for Delaware cars, $8 for out-of-state vehicles. *Note:* The Indian River Inlet Bridge is being replaced; construction is expected to last until 2009. Besides creating noise, dust, and traffic snarls, this will result in the closure of some camping facilities and limit some fishing. See www.destateparks.com for updates.

BETHANY & FENWICK   Bethany's public beach is small and can be very crowded. Visitors staying in oceanside houses and condos have their own private beaches, in most cases, and don't have to worry about crowds as much. You'll hear about dolphin sightings all around the Delaware beaches, but they're quite common here. Stay a week, and you may spot dolphins several times. The beach in front of the boardwalk is free and open to the public. It is guarded from Memorial Day weekend to Labor Day, Monday through Friday from 10am to 5pm, weekends and holidays from 9:30am to 5:30pm. There are large, clean bathhouses behind the bandstand. **Bethany Resort Rental,** 201 Central Ave. (ℂ 800/321-1592 or 302/539-6244), operates a rental concession on the beach, with 8-foot umbrellas, surf mats, boogie boards, chairs, and more.

Fenwick, on the border with Maryland, has more public beach than Bethany. It's slightly more relaxed than Ocean City, but not as quiet as Bethany. Its claim to fame is the very narrow but long **Fenwick Island State Park** (ℂ 302/227-2800), where you can watch the sun rise over the ocean and later watch the sun set over Assawoman Bay. The 3-mile beach offers public space for swimming, sunbathing, surf fishing, and surfing. Facilities include showers, changing rooms, first-aid room, lifeguards, gift shop, picnic tables, nonmotorized boat rental, and refreshments. Admission is $4 for Delaware cars, $8 for out-of-state cars. Entry is free weekdays in spring and fall and all week in winter. Hours are 8am to sunset year-round.

OTHER OUTDOOR ACTIVITIES IN DELAWARE

Cape Henlopen State Park ⚜ (ℂ 302/645-8983; www.destateparks.com/chsp/chsp. htm), with its 3,143 acres bordered on one side by the Atlantic and on another by Delaware Bay, offers beach swimming, tennis, picnicking, nature trails, crabbing, and pier fishing, accessible from all the Delaware beach resorts. It's also the home of the 80-foot **Great Dune,** the highest sand dune between Cape Hatteras and Cape Cod. For those who enjoy a good climb, a refurbished World War II observation tower (115 steps) offers some of the best coastal views for miles. Walking with kids? Ask for the *Seaside Interpretive Trail Guide;* it tells about things you'd probably just walk by without noticing. The park is open year-round from 8am to sunset. Entry fee to the park is $4 for Delaware residents and $8 for out-of-state visitors from May through October; it's free the rest of the year.

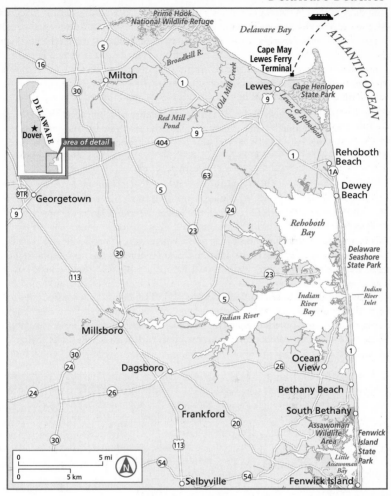

You can also camp at Cape Henlopen, an inexpensive option in a resort area. The 159 sites sit on pine-covered dunes, with water hookup and access to clean bathhouses with showers. The sites are all fairly spacious, but the ones in the center loops are not terribly private. The largest and most private are located in the back loop, but they aren't well suited for trailers or motor homes. The campground is open March 1 to November 30. Rates are $23 to $29 per night. As with all camping on the Atlantic coast, mosquitoes can be a problem, so bring bug repellent.

BIKING   Southern Delaware is a great place to bike. The terrain is flat; the views of the farmland, villages, and wetlands are pleasant; and most roads are wide, with good shoulders. The **Delaware Bicycle Council** (© **302/760-BIKE;** www.deldot.gov/static/bike) produces *Delaware Maps for Bicycle Users*. All roads are marked and color-coded according to their suitability for cyclists, so there's no guesswork involved in planning your route. Maps can be obtained online.

Bicycling on your own near the beaches is a breeze thanks to the level terrain and the wide back roads. Even a trip up Route 1 from Bethany to the Indian River Inlet is easy. For family excursions, **Cape Henlopen State Park** (see above) has lots of well-marked, paved bike trails usually away from park traffic.

Delaware state law requires that children under 16 wear helmets.

CANOEING   The creeks and ponds of Sussex County make for lovely canoe excursions. A well-maintained 5-mile canoe trail along the Hitch Pond and James branches of the Nanticoke River will take you past the two largest trees in Delaware, one of which is estimated to be 750 years old. The trail begins at **Trap Pond State Park,** 33587 Baldcypress Lane, Laurel (© **302/875-5153;** www.destateparks.com/tpsp/tpsp.htm), where you can rent canoes or kayaks for $6 to $8 an hour.

Nearby is **Trussum Pond,** which looks and feels more like the Florida Everglades or the bayou than southern Delaware. From Route 24, take Route 449, which goes by the entrance to Trap Pond State Park, to Road 72, or Trussum Pond Road. There's a small park and parking area next to the pond, where you can paddle among abundant lily pads and graceful bald cypress. (Sussex County is home to the northernmost stand of bald cypress in the country.) But you'll have to do the navigating yourself; there aren't any trail markers.

Prime Hook National Wildlife Refuge (© **302/684-8419;** www.fws.gov/north east/primehook) offers 15 miles of streams and ditches, including a 7-mile self-guided canoe trail. Electric-powered boats can also use the waterways. There's a boat launch behind the visitor center, but bring your own boat. There are no rentals at the refuge.

MARYLAND BEACHES

Ocean City has the most public beaches, and some of the most crowded. If you want to make friends, come here. The beach near the southern tip of O.C. is the widest and usually least crowded; a huge parking lot makes this a convenient place for day-trippers. The beach along the boardwalk actually gets quite narrow in a few places (though beach replenishment efforts have helped). Still, for those who love the boardwalk and all its shops and restaurants, this is the best beach. In northern Ocean City, land of high-rise condos, the beach widens. Crowds depend on the size of the building, but it's easy to find a place for your blanket here.

The inlet at Ocean City's southern end divides touristy O.C. from the wild beaches of **Assateague Island,** which doesn't have a restaurant, gas station, or hotel. It remains a pristine beach, quiet and isolated. Although you can see it across the inlet from Ocean City, it's about an 11-mile drive to the visitor center and parking lots. Most of the 30-odd-mile strip of barrier island is not open to vehicles. It's home to an enormous number of shorebirds, sika deer, and the wild ponies made famous by Marguerite Henry's books. The visitor center and campgrounds are the only buildings here.

The entire 10-mile stretch of Ocean City beach is open to the public free of charge. Lifeguards are on duty from 10am to 5:30pm all summer. Beach chairs, umbrellas, rafts, and boogie boards can be rented by the day or week. Attendants will position your umbrella and, if you rent for the week, have your umbrella and chairs ready when you arrive each day. They usually accept cash only.

Wicomico Street Bathhouse is at Wicomico and Philadelphia streets, near the southern end of O.C. It's privately operated and charges a fee. Public restrooms are along the boardwalk at Worcester, Caroline, 9th, and 27th streets.

Two stretches of beach are designated as "surf beaches" each day and announced on local radio stations. Look for signs posted on the beach or call one of the local surf shops, such as **Quiet Storm,** 74th Street (© **410/723-1313**), or **Endless Summer Surf Shop,** 38th Street (© **410/289-3272**).

Surf fishing is not permitted within 50 yards of swimmers between 9am and 6pm, so the big poles usually come out in the evening or early morning. When the swimmers go home in the fall, the surf fishermen take over.

1 Lewes

86 miles SE of Wilmington, 34 miles N of Ocean City, 107 miles SE of Baltimore, 121 miles E of Washington, D.C.

Delaware's northernmost and oldest beach resort, Lewes (pronounced *Loo*-is) is also its oldest town, founded in 1681 as a Dutch whaling station named Zwaanendael. The community maintains strong ties both to its Dutch heritage, which you can learn about at the Zwaanendael Museum, and to the sea—as a beach resort, a boating marina, and a port for dozens of fishing fleets.

Though Lewes is where the Delaware Bay meets the Atlantic Ocean, the town has grown up west of the Lewes–Rehoboth Canal, turning away from the water. Here you'll find the historic sites, small shops, restaurants, and inns. The result is a quaint, friendly little town that also happens to have a beach.

Beach fans must take an easy walk across the Savannah Road Bridge to the water. Parking is available in a paid lot. And lots of Lewes vacationers head to nearby Cape Henlopen State Park for the wide, sandy beaches there.

Lewes seems more like a Cape Cod resort than a Delmarva beach resort. With its small-town atmosphere and proximity to beaches, it's a good choice for anybody tired of the bustle of the other resorts. Ocean City and Rehoboth fans find it's a good day-trip destination, too.

ESSENTIALS

GETTING THERE   By Car   From points north, take routes 113 and 13 to Route 1 and then to Route 9 (Savannah Rd.) into town. From the south, take Route 113 to Georgetown, and then take Route 9 east to Lewes. From Ocean City or Rehoboth, take Route 1 to Route 9. From the west, take Route 50 across the Bay Bridge to Route 404 east, and then to Route 9.

By Ferry   Many visitors come to Lewes via the **Cape May–Lewes Ferry,** an 80-minute Delaware Bay minicruise that connects southern New Jersey to mid-Delaware and saves considerable driving for north- or southbound passengers along the Atlantic coast. In operation since 1964, this ferry service maintains a fleet of five vessels, each holding up to 800 passengers and 100 cars. Departures are daily year-round, from early morning until evening, with almost hourly service in the summer months from 7am to 9pm. Passenger rates are $6 off season, $8 in high season; the charge for vehicles ranges from $20 to $25, with reduced prices for motorcycles and bicycles. Reservations are recommended. In New Jersey, the **Cape May Terminal** is at the end of the Garden State Parkway. The **Lewes Terminal** (© **302/644-6030**) is by the Cape Henlopen State Park entrance, about a mile from the center of town. For reservations and information, call © **800/64-FERRY** or see www.capemaylewesferry.com. Shuttle service is available to both Cape May and Lewes every day in summer and on weekends in spring and fall for an extra $3.

By Plane   Visitors arriving by plane should fly into the **Salisbury–Ocean City Wicomico Regional Airport.** See p. 265 for details.

VISITOR INFORMATION   Contact the **Lewes Chamber of Commerce and Visitors Bureau** (© 302/645-8073; www.leweschamber.com). The chamber's office is in the Fisher–Martin House at Kings Highway, next to the Zwaanendael Museum. It's open year-round, Monday through Friday from 10am to 4pm. In summer, it's also open Saturday from 9am to 3pm and Sunday from 10am to 2pm. You can also get a visitors' guide from the **Southern Delaware Tourism Office** (© 800/357-1818; www.visitsoutherndelaware.com).

GETTING AROUND   The **Seaport Taxi of Lewes,** 1016D Hwy. 1 (© 302/645-6800), operates a taxi service from the ferry terminal to downtown, as well as local service. Ferry passengers can call from the information station at the ferry terminal.

SPECIAL EVENTS   The **Great Delaware Kite Festival** is held at Cape Henlopen State Park on Good Friday. The first weekend in October brings the Boast the Coast/Coast Day weekend. **Boast the Coast,** sponsored by the Lewes Chamber of Commerce, celebrates the town's nautical history. The highlight is the lighted boat parade in the canal. **Coast Day** (© 302/831-8083) is sponsored by and held at the University of Delaware College of Marine Studies in Lewes. The fair includes lectures, ship tours, marine aquariums, and a crab-cake cook-off. These events are free except for a small parking fee.

Nearby Milton hosts the **World Championship Punkin' Chunkin'** (© 302/684-8196; www.punkinchunkin.com), held the first weekend in November. Contestants enter their own mechanical contraptions (no explosives allowed) to see which can hurl a pumpkin the farthest—and that can be 4,000 feet or more. In addition, there are food and crafts vendors, live bands, and entertainment for kids. It's silly, rowdy, and a lot of fun. Admission is $5; parking is $1. Be prepared for traffic on routes 9 and 24— up to 35,000 people come to this.

WHERE TO STAY

Lodging options in Lewes include handsome inns as well as traditional motels. Prices range from moderate to expensive in summer—and can be a bargain in the off season. Some places require minimum stays. Reservations are mandatory in summer months and recommended at other times, since the room capacity in town barely exceeds 300. Parking is at a premium; metered parking on the street may be necessary at some local inns.

For vacation rentals, call a real-estate agent. One reputable company is **Jack Lingo,** 1240 Kings Hwy. (© 800/331-4241 or 302/645-2207). Most rentals are houses or town houses in Lewes, some with views of or frontage on Delaware Bay.

MODERATE

Blue Water House Inn 🐾🐾   Hole up at this brightly colored inn and you might feel you've been transported far beyond Delaware's shore. (In fact, the inn is a bit off the beaten track, tucked between town and beach, closer to the beach.) But its charm lies in its sense of seclusion and its beautiful rooms. Accommodations are spacious, decorated with a sense of island fun, and look out on a big balcony hung with hammocks. The sitting room has a flatscreen TV and game tables, while the "Lookout" provides panoramic views and a good place to relax. On Sundays, breakfast is delivered in picnic baskets so guests can enjoy their meal in bed. Afternoon and evening refreshments are available.

407 E. Market St. (across the canal on the bay side of town), Lewes, DE 19958. ℂ 800/493-2080 for reservations, or 302/645-7832 for information. www.lewes-beach.com. 7 units. High season $165–$275 double; off season $100–$150 double. Rates include hot buffet breakfast. 2- or 3-night minimum stay required in high season, on spring and fall weekends, and on holidays. AE, MC, V. Free parking. No children. **Amenities:** Watersports equipment rentals; free use of bikes, beach chairs, towels, and umbrellas; massage; movie library. *In room:* A/C, TV/VCR, Internet access, fridge, hair dryer, iron.

Inn at Canal Square ✚

This four-story property overlooking the canal has a casual country-inn atmosphere with the amenities of a full-service hotel. Its spacious, traditionally styled rooms come in every size, from a standard unit with two queen-size beds to a full apartment. Most have views of the canal, though two parlor suites overlook Lewes. Fourth-floor rooms have extra comforts, like an honor bar, CD players, robes, and oversize balconies. The Commodore Suite and Admiral's Quarters come with kitchen, fireplace, and sun deck.

122 Market St., Lewes, DE 19958. ℂ 888/644-1911 or 302/644-3377. www.theinnatcanalsquare.com. 24 units. $100–$270 double; $500 cottage suite. Rates include continental breakfast. Children under 5 stay free in parent's room. Ask about seasonal getaway packages. AE, MC, V. Free parking. Pets welcome in courtyard room for a fee. *In room:* A/C, TV, Wi-Fi, coffeemaker, hair dryer, iron.

John Penrose Virden House ✚

This 1888 ship's pilot's house has the best location of the B&Bs in Lewes, right in the heart of the business district. With a mix of antique and modern furnishings, it's both gracious and comfortable. Breakfast is served in the dining room, where an old ship's bar serves as a buffet, and on the patio in summer. In winter, dining by the fireplace of the sitting room is cozy, too. Two well-appointed guest rooms offer views of the town or the canal. A separate cottage off the garden offers extra privacy.

217 Second St., Lewes, DE 19958. ℂ 302/644-0217 or 302/644-4401. www.virdenhouse.com. 3 units. $165–$205 double. Rates include full breakfast and afternoon refreshments. No credit cards. Free parking. No children. **Amenities:** Complimentary use of bikes, beach chairs, towels, umbrella, and coolers; garden. *In room:* A/C, TV, dataport, fridge, robe.

Zwaanendael Inn ✚

In the heart of Lewes, this three-story hotel offers comfortable rooms and suites, all outfitted with local antiques and fine linens. Some units have TVs. The lobby and lower lobby are comfortable (and whimsical) places to rest or meet friends. Rates include breakfast at the inn's Swan's Nest Cafe.

142 Second St. (at Market St.), Lewes, DE 19958. ℂ 800/824-8754 or 302/645-6466. www.zwaanendaelinn.com. 23 units. $45–$175 double; $85–$300 suite. Rates include breakfast. Weekly rates available. 2-night minimum stay required on weekends in high season. AE, MC, V. **Amenities:** Cafe; health club. *In room:* A/C, Wi-Fi, hair dryer, iron (upon request).

INEXPENSIVE

Beacon Motel   This motel near Fisherman's Wharf, opened in 1989, occupies the top two floors of a three-story property, with the ground level devoted to shops and a reception area. Guests can spread out in the large rooms, which feature bamboo furnishings in beach colors; suites have trundle twin beds.

514 E. Savannah Rd. (P.O. Box 609), Lewes, DE 19958. ℂ 800/735-4888 or 302/645-4888. www.lewestoday.com/beacon. 66 units. $60–$180 double; $110–$230 suite. Rates include morning coffee and tea. Children under 12 stay free in parent's room. AE, DISC, MC, V. Free parking. Closed late Nov to mid-Mar. **Amenities:** Outdoor pool; sun deck. *In room:* A/C, TV, fridge, hair dryer.

Cape Henlopen Motel *Value*

This 1970s-era motel is located directly across from Fisherman's Wharf. Its wood-paneled rooms, some with beach-style furniture, may be slightly worn, but the motel is clean as a whistle and staffed by the friendliest of people. All second-floor units have balconies overlooking the canal. It's got great access to the beach, historic district, and charter boats.

106 Anglers Rd., at Savannah Rd. (P.O. Box 243), Lewes, DE 19958. © **800/447-3158** or 302/645-2828. www.beach-net. com/henlopenmotel. 28 units. $50–$140 double. 2- or 3-night minimum stay required in high season and on holidays. AE, DC, DISC, MC, V. Free parking. *In room:* AC, TV, fridge, iron (upon request).

King's Inn Outside, this is a pretty Victorian home with a wraparound porch. Inside, well, it's cluttered and a bit below the usual elegance of a B&B. But it's inexpensive—and it comes with a welcoming, well-traveled innkeeper who knows how to take care of people. Bicycles are available and there's a gazebo in the garden.

151 Kings Hwy., Lewes, DE 19958. © 302/645-6438. www.kingsinnlewes.com. 5 units, some with shared bathroom. $65–$95 double. Rates include continental breakfast. AE, DISC, MC, V. Free parking. Pets accepted for $10 fee. **Amenities:** TV in sitting room; access to fridge; complimentary use of bikes. *In room:* A/C, hair dryer, iron.

WHERE TO DINE
EXPENSIVE

The Buttery ❀❀❀ NOUVEAU FRENCH This is as close as you'll get to a Paris bistro on the Delaware shore—a restored Victorian mansion with candlelit dining rooms, a bar, and an extensive wine list. In warm weather, the porch is a lovely spot. The menu takes advantage of local seafood (crab cakes, pan-seared yellowfin tuna, bouillabaisse), with a few beef and poultry options as well. Sunday champagne brunch is delightful. The best deal is the $25 early-bird special, every night until 6:30pm.

102 Second St. © 302/645-7755. www.butteryrestaurant.com. Reservations recommended. Main courses $6–$15 lunch, $18–$32 dinner. DISC, MC, V. Mon–Sat 11am–2:30pm and 5–10pm; Sun 10:30am–2:30pm and 5–10pm.

Gilligan's SEAFOOD Gilligan's menu always includes a variety of straightforward seafood dishes, with a zing here or there. Its crab cakes have earned honors as the "best in Delaware." Other options include veal chops and cappellini pasta topped with saffron-infused *beurre blanc,* scallops, shrimp, and lump crab. An outdoor bar overlooks the canal.

134 Market St. (at Front St.). © 302/644-7230. Reservations accepted only for parties of 6 or more. Main courses $6.95–$13 lunch, $20–$26 dinner. AE, MC, V. Late May to Sept daily 11am–9pm; Apr to mid-May and Sept–Dec Tues–Sun 11am–9pm. Dinner served until 10pm Fri–Sat. Closed Jan–Mar.

Jerry's Seafood SEAFOOD Washingtonians may feel at home at this beach outlet of a D.C. institution. Jerry's has updated the decor of the place, formerly an English-style pub, with some nautical yellows and blues—and completely transformed the menu. It's now the home of the "crab bomb" (a 10-oz. crab cake), as well as a raw bar, a few salads and sandwiches at lunch, and filet mignon and chicken dishes at dinner. The reputation for crab cakes—they're jumbo lump meat bound with a whisper of filler—is well earned. Takeout is available, too.

108 Second St. © 302/645-6611. www.jerrys-seafood.com. Reservations recommended for dinner. Main courses $10–$31 lunch, $18–$31 dinner. AE, MC, V. Mon–Thurs 11am–10pm; Fri–Sat 11am–11pm; Sun 11am–8pm.

MODERATE

Notting Hill Coffee Roastery, 124 Second St. (© **302/645-0733**), roasts its coffee right here—and its baked goods are made on the premises, too.

La Rosa Negra ITALIAN This fine Italian restaurant has two very different dining rooms. The Tuscany Room is upscale, while the family-oriented Venetian Room is more casual. Look for traditional favorites as well as a few low-carb entrees. Children's entrees are $4. At lunch, choices range from subs to pizzas.

1201 Savannah Rd. © 302/645-1980. www.larosanegrarestaurant.com. Reservations recommended for dinner. Main courses $4.95–$11 lunch, $8.95–$25 dinner. MC, V. Mon–Fri 11:30am–2pm; daily 5–9pm.

Lighthouse Restaurant SEAFOOD   This place features views of the marina and a casual nautical decor. There's seating indoors and out. An all-day menu features soups, salads, sandwiches, and platters. The dinner menu has the usual selection of seafood (including seafood marinara), plus steaks, ribs, and chicken. Breakfast is served from 7 to 11:30am on weekdays, until 1pm on weekends. If you come for dinner before 5:30pm, the sunset cruise is free.

7 Anglers Rd. (at Savannah Rd.). © 302/645-6271. www.lighthouselewes.com. Reservations accepted only for parties of 8 or more. Main courses $3.95–$11 lunch, $9.95–$23 dinner. MC, V. Daily 7am–9pm. Closed Tues–Wed between Columbus Day and Apr.

Striper Bites Bistro SEAFOOD   Relax in the bright, airy dining room while you ponder the intriguing menu. The restaurant has been popular to the point of enclosing its porch and adding a new dining room. Sure, you can get beef or chicken here, but seafood reigns. You can't go wrong with the rich crab bisque or the melt-in-your-mouth pan-seared tuna to start. Grilled salmon, pistachio-encrusted grouper, or lump crab cake are all fresh and served by a most friendly waitstaff. Fifteen wines are available by the glass.

107 Savannah Rd. © 302/645-4657. www.striperbites.com. Reservations not accepted. Main courses $8–$14 lunch, $10–$24 dinner. AE, DISC, MC, V. Mon–Sat 11:30am–3:30pm and 5–9pm.

WHAT TO SEE & DO

Pretty Lewes is more than a beach and shopping town. Its historic roots are showing—in the eye-catching Zwaanendael Museum and in a complex of buildings that are part of the Lewes Historical Society. In 2006, the town celebrates its 375th birthday (and doesn't look anywhere near that old).

Lewes Historical Society ✷✷   Stop first at the **Ryves–Holt House** (© 302/645-5575), built about 1665 and the oldest house in Delaware. This also serves as the society's visitor center, where you can buy your tickets and get a map of the rest of the 12 buildings. Don't miss the Lewes Life-Saving Station or the Dr. Hiram Burton House. Guided walking tours of town are offered Mondays for $5.

218 Second St. © 302/645-7670. www.historiclewes.org. Tickets for entire complex $10; individual buildings $2 each. July–Aug Mon–Tues and Thurs 11am–4pm, Wed 1–6pm, Sat–Sun noon–3pm; June and Sept–Oct Sat–Sun noon–3pm. Hours are subject to change; call ahead to confirm, especially in spring and fall.

Zwaanendael Museum   This towering red Dutch-style building is unlike anything else in Lewes. Built for the town's 300th anniversary in 1931, it resembles the city hall of Hoorn, in the Netherlands. Lewes has been abuzz over a 1760s Colonial ship dredged up off the beach, whose artifacts washed up in late 2004. The museum has served to interpret the pieces and plans a more permanent exhibit. In the meantime, you can see a new exhibit, to mark the 375th anniversary in 2006, that focuses on the town's history from its founding to statehood. Also on display are objects recovered from the sunken ship HMS *DeBraak*—including a ketchup bottle.

Savannah Rd., at Kings Hwy. (beside the visitor center). © 302/645-1148. Free admission. Tues–Sat 10am–4:30pm; Sun 1:30–4:30pm.

OUTDOOR ACTIVITIES

BIKING   Even if you're not a serious cyclist, bring a bike to Lewes—the historic streets and shoreline paths are ideal for cycling, and it's a great way to avoid the parking problem in the shopping district. You can also rent bikes from **Lewes Cycle Sports,** in the Beacon Motel, Savannah Road (© **888/800-BIKE** or 302/645-4544).

Biking is also one of the best ways to see **Cape Henlopen State Park** (© **302/645-8983;** www.destateparks.com/chsp/chsp.htm). Paved bike routes run through the park and take you places that cars can't go. The terrain is mostly flat, with just a few hills on routes to overlooks.

BIRD & WILDLIFE WATCHING   Lewes, located between Cape Henlopen and Prime Hook, is the best base for birders on the Delaware coast. **Cape Henlopen State Park** (© **302/645-8983;** www.destateparks.com/chsp/chsp.htm) is prime breeding ground for the endangered piping plover. (Access is restricted certain times of the year to protect the nesting grounds.) Whales and dolphins appear regularly off the coast of Cape Henlopen, though usually a little farther south. About 10 miles north of Lewes, **Prime Hook National Wildlife Refuge,** off Route 16 (© **302/684-8419;** www.fws. gov/northeast/primehook), is the best place around for birding and wildlife photography. The refuge has two hiking trails and a 7-mile self-guided canoe trail (bring your own canoe); they're great places to view migrating waterfowl in spring and fall, plus shorebirds, warblers, amphibians, and reptiles in spring. Admission is free; the refuge is open daily from 30 minutes before sunrise to 30 minutes after sunset. The visitor center is open Monday through Friday from 7:30am to 4pm, plus Saturdays and Sundays between April and November from 9am to 4pm. *Note:* Bring bug repellent, especially in late summer.

CAMPING   Campgrounds at **Cape Henlopen State Park** are open March 1 to November 30. Reservations must be made at least 24 hours in advance. Call © **877/987-2757.** There are 139 sites with water and 17 without. Nonresidents pay $29 per night for water sites and $27 for sites without. Two sites are accessible for those with disabilities, and 12 are set aside for tent camping only. For more information, see "Other Outdoor Activities in Delaware" (p. 236).

FISHING   With easy access to both Delaware Bay and the Atlantic, Lewes offers a wide variety of sportfishing opportunities. The fishing season starts when the ocean fills with huge schools of mackerel in late March through April. Large sea trout (weakfish) arrive in early May and June; flounder arrive in May and remain throughout the summer, as do bluefish and shark. As the ocean warms up in June, offshore species such as tuna and marlin begin roaming the waters. Bottom fishing in the bay for trout, flounder, sea bass, and blues continues all summer, with late August through September often providing the largest catches. October and November bring porgies, shad, and blackfish. No license is required for tidal-water fishing. Surf-fishing permits are available at Cape Henlopen.

Arrange headboat ocean and bay fishing excursions and cruises at **Fisherman's Wharf,** Anglers Road (© **302/645-8862**), or at **Angler's Fishing Center,** Anglers Road (© **302/644-4533;** www.anglersfishingcenter.com). Call for full-day, half-day, or nighttime excursions.

Cape Henlopen is great for shore and surf fishing. In Lewes, try the **Lewes Harbor Marina,** 217 Anglers Rd. (© **302/645-6227**), for fishing supplies.

A Delaware Brewery & Winery

The Delaware coast now boasts both a brewery and a winery!
Nassau Valley Vineyards, 32165 Winery Way (just off Rte. 1, on Rte. 14B), Lewes (✆ **302/645-WINE;** www.nassauvalley.com), offers self-guided tours and tastings Tuesday through Saturday from 11am to 5pm, Sunday from noon to 5pm. You can see where the wine is fermenting; look at displays on viniculture, viticulture, coopering, and bottling; and then taste the locally produced chardonnay, cabernet, and rosé. It won't take long, but it's a nice break from the beach.

If a brewery tour is more your style, try the **Dogfish Head Craft Brewery,** 3 miles west of Lewes, off Route 16 in Milton (✆ **888/8DOGFISH;** www. dogfish.com). Locals are big fans of Dogfish Head's quirky brews, which also sell in 27 states and four countries. You can see this locally made ale go from grain to bottle in fragrant tours offered Monday and Friday at 3pm. An arrangement with **Quest Kayak** (✆ **302/644-7020;** www.questfitnesskayak. com) combines tours of the Broadkill River with a pint at the end of the day.

HORSEBACK RIDING   Windswept Stables (✆ **302/645-1561**) offers horseback excursions along trails or on the beach.

KAYAKING   Quest Kayak (✆ **302/644-7020;** www.questfitnesskayak.com) offers Saturday dolphin counts, as well as tours of the Lewes–Rehoboth Canal, area lighthouses, and Delaware's other coastal waterways.

SHOPPING

Lewes is the best shopping destination on the shore for arts, crafts, and antiques. All of the places listed below are in Lewes or close by. Most shops are open daily from 10 or 11am to 5 or 6pm, with extended hours in summer.

Auntie M's Emporium   Head here for kitchenware, books, furniture, and garden sculptures. 116 W. Third St. ✆ **302/644-1804.**

Garage Sale Antiques   It specializes in unusual furniture, lamps, and garden sculptures. Look for the bright-yellow house on the southbound side of Route 1. 1416 Rte. 1 (just south of Rte. 9 into Lewes). ✆ **302/645-1205.**

Kids' Ketch   Get your beach toys here—or perhaps something to while away those rainy days. 132 Second St. ✆ **302/645-8448.** www.kidsketch.com.

Lewes Gourmet (Union Jack)   This gourmet shop specializes in British goodies. Front and Market sts. ✆ **302/645-1661.**

Peninsula Gallery   Across the canal below the Beacon Hotel, this gallery displays mainly works by regional artists. Closed Mondays January through March. 520 E. Savannah Rd. ✆ **302/645-0551.** www.peninsula-gallery.com.

Preservation Forge   This blacksmith shop sells the handcrafted ironwork of John Austin Ellsworth—weather vanes, pokers, gates, door latches, and more. Stop by to see the blacksmith at work. The gallery on the second offers more display area. Open

Monday, Tuesday, and Thursday through Saturday from 10am to 4pm. 114 W. Third St.
(C) 302/645-7987.

Puzzles   Exercise your brain with the games and puzzles here, including jigsaws,
crosswords, and brainteasers. 111 Second St. (C) 302/645-8013.

Saxon Swan   Beautiful pottery, calligraphy, fabric art, fine jewelry, and lovely
watercolors fill the shelves. Don't miss the holiday items, all handcrafted. 101 Second St.
(C) 302/645-7488.

Stepping Stone   Look for American crafts here, with something new every visit.
Front and Market sts. (C) 302/645-1254.

Thistles   One of the pricier places in town, this shop carries fine, unusual furnishings, including Tiffany-style lamps, pottery, glassware, and silver. 203 Second St. (C) 302/
644-2323.

ORGANIZED TOURS & CRUISES

A good way to see the Delaware Bay and the Lewes Canal harbor is to take a tour, by
land or by sea. You can pick up a self-guided tour brochure from the visitor center in
the Fisher–Martin House, on Kings Highway. It covers more than 40 sites and gives
brief descriptions of each one. For sightseeing cruises from Lewes, call **Fisherman's
Wharf Cruises,** 217 Anglers Rd. ((C) 302/645-8862), which operates narrated excursions around the historic harbor of Lewes and the Delaware breakwater areas. Trips
include a 2-hour dolphin-watching cruise; a 4-hour whale- and dolphin-watching
cruise; a 2-hour sunset cruise; and a 2-hour buffet dinner cruise. Prices range from
$15 to $30. Most tours are offered June through September; call for details and departure times.

2 Rehoboth & Dewey Beaches (*

88 miles SE of Wilmington, 27 miles N of Ocean City, 110 miles SE of Baltimore, 124 miles SE of Washington, D.C.

Rehoboth is the most popular of the Delaware beaches. It's small-town friendly and
beach-resort casual, yet has a touch of style, too. Visitors can choose from beachfront
condominiums, boardwalk hotels, and old-fashioned cottages. On the south side of
town, grand homes overlook Silver Lake. The town's shops offer a lovely diversion,
with everything from home fashions to hippie accessories. Just outside town on Route
1, Rehoboth has become synonymous with outlet shopping (and Delaware has no
sales tax).

Rehoboth Beach is also a popular destination for gay and lesbian travelers, a mid-
Atlantic alternative to Provincetown or Fire Island, with a number of gay-owned and
predominantly gay venues.

Head south from Rehoboth and you hit Dewey Beach. It's a more casual suburb of
Rehoboth, with a trolley connecting the towns in summer. Dewey is noted for its
nightspots. Ruddertowne, in particular, draws young crowds for its party atmosphere.
But the beach is good, and the Rehoboth Bay is only a couple of blocks from the ocean.

ESSENTIALS

GETTING THERE   By Car   From the north, take routes 113 and 13 to Route 1,
and then Route 1A into Rehoboth. From the south, take Route 113 north to Route
26 east to Bethany Beach. From there, take Route 1 north to Rehoboth. From the
west, take Route 50 across the Bay Bridge to Route 404 east; then take Route 9 east

to Route 1 south. From Ocean City, continue up the Coastal Highway as it turns into Route 1 to Dewey.

By Bus   Bus service to Rehoboth is no longer available. **Greyhound** (© **800/229-9424;** www.greyhound.com) does provide service to Ocean City; see p. 265 for details.

By Plane   For visitors arriving by plane, the nearest airport is **Salisbury–Ocean City Wicomico Regional Airport.** See p. 265 for details.

VISITOR INFORMATION   Contact the **Rehoboth Beach–Dewey Beach Chamber of Commerce,** 501 Rehoboth Ave. (© **800/441-1329** or 302/227-2233; www. beach-fun.com), open year-round Monday through Friday from 9am to 5pm and Saturday from 9am to 1pm. Gay and lesbian travelers should check out www.camp rehoboth.com.

GETTING AROUND   **By Public Transportation**   From Memorial Day to Labor Day, **DART First State** (© **800/553-DART** or 302/739-3278; www.beachbus.com) operates daily shuttle service down Route 9 from Georgetown to Lewes, and down Route 1 to Rehoboth and on to the border with Ocean City. Buses go down Savannah Road in Lewes and travel along Rehoboth Avenue to the Rehoboth boardwalk, the Park & Ride Lot, and the shopping outlets. They stop at Ocean City, where passsengers can catch the Ocean City bus. A daily pass is $2.10 per person—or $7 per carload when parking at the Park & Ride Lot on Shuttle Road off Delaware Route 1. Your pass is also good for one ride on Ocean City's bus; likewise, an Ocean City pass is good for one ride in Delaware.

The **Jolly Trolley** (© **302/227-1197;** www.jollytrolley.com) operates a shuttle between Rehoboth Beach and south Dewey Beach. Buses runs Memorial Day through Labor Day, daily every half-hour from 8am to 2am; limited service is available in May and September. The fare is $2 for adults ($3 after midnight), $1 for children under 6. Bus stops are posted. Call for guided tours of Dewey and Rehoboth.

By Car   Parking in Rehoboth Beach can be difficult. Metered parking is in effect from Memorial Day weekend to mid-September, daily from 10am to midnight. The meters take only quarters. Change machines are located in the first and third blocks of Rehoboth Avenue.

To park in a nonmetered area, you need a **parking permit.** Permits for daily, weekly, or seasonal parking are available from the Parking Meter Division, 30½ Lake Dr. (behind City Hall), or from real-estate offices and downtown merchants. They cost $30 for a week, $10 for a weekend day, and $5 for a weekday. The police will explain the rules and help you get change. Call © **302/227-6181** for information. Once you've parked, leave your car and walk. Almost everything is within a few blocks of the boardwalk and the main street, Rehoboth Avenue.

SPECIAL EVENTS   Greyhound lovers converge on Dewey and Rehoboth beaches on Columbus Day weekend for the **Greyhound Reach the Beach Weekend** ⚘. This social gathering was started in 1995 by greyhound lovers who met informally over the Internet. About 3,500 ex-racers and their humans usually take part. It's a lot of fun to see and meet these graceful animals and their gracious owners.

The **Sea Witch Halloween Festival and Fiddler's Convention** is held at the end of October. This 2-day event features a costume parade, trick-or-treating, a 5K foot race, and, of course, a fiddling contest. For information, contact the Rehoboth Beach–Dewey Beach Chamber of Commerce (© **800/441-1329** or 302/227-2233).

The **Independent Rehoboth Beach Film Festival** (℃ **302/645-9095** or www. rehobothfilm.com) takes place the first weekend in November.

WHERE TO STAY

Most accommodations in Rehoboth and Dewey are moderately priced. In July and August, however, you may encounter difficulty finding any room (single or double occupancy) near the beach for under $200 a night. Even though Rehoboth and Dewey are seasonal destinations, don't expect dramatic off-season discounts like those you'll find in Ocean City. The outlets are a huge attraction for holiday shoppers, so the shoulder season extends through December (but ask your hotel about weekday packages). There are sometimes significant discounts in the later winter months of January, February, and March, but rates are subject to frequent changes. In any case, reservations are always necessary in summer and strongly recommended through the holiday shopping season.

House rentals are popular, so they can be tough to get. But for families, they can be a good idea: lots of space, kitchens, and maybe two bathrooms for about $1,000 per week and up—way up. **Crowley and Associates** (℃ **800/242-4213** or 302/227-6131) is a popular rental agent in the Rehoboth/Dewey area. Reservations should be made as early as possible—there's so much return business here, families often put in their request when they return the keys at the end of their vacation. If you'd like to rent a house or condo, be sure to call soon after Labor Day. Then again, something, probably older or farther from the beach, could be available in spring. As with other beach resorts, most condos come well equipped, except for linens, towels, and paper products; plan to bring those.

A new way to stay at the beach is to rent a cottage at the **Indian River Inlet Marina,** at the Delaware State Seashore Park. There are only 12 available—and with the amenities they offer, they're bound to be popular. Each has two bedrooms and a loft (sleeping a total of six people comfortably), full kitchen, fireplace, satellite TV, washer/dryer, and screened porch. Who called this camping? In summer, they can be rented only by the week, at rates of about $1,200. Off-season rates run about $160 a day, but 2- and 3-day minimums are required on weekends and holidays. Reserve online at www.delaware.reserveworld.com or call ℃ **877/98-PARKS.**

REHOBOTH BEACH
Very Expensive
Atlantic Sands Hotel & Conference Center ✶ The Atlantic Sands, right on the boardwalk, is Rehoboth's largest hotel. Sun worshippers love it for its spacious deck and large pool right on the oceanfront. Guest rooms, all newly refurbished, feature pickled-wood furniture and balconies with a view of the water. Some units have a whirlpool, wet bar, or microwave. In summer, the hotel operates a buffet-style restaurant, featuring all-you-can-eat breakfasts and dinners.

101 N. Boardwalk (between Baltimore and Maryland aves.), Rehoboth Beach, DE 19971. ℃ **800/422-0600** or 302/227-2511. Fax 302/227-9476. www.atlanticsandshotel.com. 182 units. $70–$490 double. AE, DC, DISC, MC, V. Free parking. **Amenities:** Restaurant; poolside bar; outdoor pool; health club; Oasis Spa w/massage therapist and nail technician; rooftop sun deck. *In room:* A/C, high-speed Internet access, fridge, coffeemaker, hair dryer, iron.

Bellmoor Inn ✶✶✶ This family-run establishment doesn't skimp anywhere. The lobby and library—with English-country decor, fireplace, and sumptuous furnishings—offer the first clue. Accommodations, though standard in layout, are richly furnished with thoughtful touches—such as curved shower-curtain rods that provide more elbowroom. Some of the units are part of a 1960s-era motel, but they are cleverly disguised and set in a soothing garden. Rooms in the newer section are equally well appointed and somewhat larger. Choose from standard rooms, junior suites, king rooms (with fireplace and whirlpool tub), or full apartments. One pool is set aside for adults only; a second one with deck is for families. A full-service spa completes the luxury.

6 Christian St., Rehoboth Beach, DE 19971. ℂ **302/227-5800.** Fax 302/227-0323. www.thebellmoor.com. 78 units. $105–$370 double; $165–$625 suite. Rates include full breakfast and afternoon tea. 2- or 3-night minimum stay required on weekends and holidays. AE, DISC, MC, V. Free parking. **Amenities:** 2 outdoor pools and sun deck; indoor hot tub (adults only); health club; full-service spa; computer room w/Wi-Fi; gift shop; concierge-level suites. *In room:* A/C, high-speed Internet access, fridge, coffeemaker, hair dryer, iron.

Boardwalk Plaza Hotel ★★   Step into the dark, ornate Victorian parlor of a lobby—complete with two tropical birds—and enjoy the old-fashioned hospitality of this friendly staff, who go out of their way to serve you in style. The fourth-floor concierge level is decorated with Victorian antiques, while the lower floors have pretty good reproductions. Most rooms are oceanfront or oceanview suites; a few have whirlpools. There are also a few standard rooms in the back of the hotel plus a spacious corner apartment. The pool is quite small, but has an abundance of whirlpool jets.

Olive Ave. and the boardwalk, Rehoboth Beach, DE 19971. ℂ **800/33-BEACH** or 302/227-7169. Fax 302/227-0561. www.boardwalkplaza.com. 84 units. $74–$519 double. Children under 6 stay free in parent's room. AE, DC, DISC, MC, V. Free parking. **Amenities:** Restaurant; bar; indoor/outdoor pool and sun deck; health club; Jacuzzi; concierge-level rooms. *In room:* A/C, TV/DVD, T-1 Internet access, coffeemaker, hair dryer.

Expensive

Avenue Inn   You might have trouble finding this place if you're on Rehoboth Avenue—step back and then you'll see it. Shops on the ground floor obscure it (though the entrance is really on Wilmington). Once inside, you'll find a comfortable, country-inn kind of place. Some rooms have TV/VCRs, fireplaces (electric, with heat optional), and Jacuzzis. Filled with dark English-country furniture and burgundy fabrics, you might forget there are hundreds of tourists outside, browsing all those shops.

33 Wilmington Ave. Rehoboth Beach, DE 19971. ℂ **800/433-5870** or 302/226-2900. Fax 302/226-7549. www.avenue inn.com. 48 units. $64–$279 double. Rates include continental breakfast, afternoon wine and cheese, and fresh cookies served by the lobby fireplace. 2-night minimum stay required on some weekends. AE, DISC, MC, V. Free parking. **Amenities:** Indoor pool and deck; health club; spa; outdoor hot tub; Wi-Fi in lobby. *In room:* A/C, Internet access, fridge, microwave, hair dryer, iron.

Brighton Suites Hotel   For families or couples traveling together, this all-suite hotel—a short walk from the beach—is a good choice. Each unit in this sandy-pink, four-story property has a bedroom with one king-size or two double beds, a large bathroom, and a separate living room with pullout sofa. The hotel's DVD library, with about 250 choices, is popular on rainy days.

34 Wilmington Ave., Rehoboth Beach, DE 19971. ℂ **800/227-5788** or 302/227-5780. Fax 302/227-6815. www. brightonsuites.com. 66 units. $69–$299 suite. Ask about packages, especially for stays of 3 or more nights. 2- or 3-night minimum stay required on summer weekends and holidays. AE, DISC, MC, V. Free parking. **Amenities:** Indoor pool; health club; rooftop sun deck; beach towels; DVD library. *In room:* A/C, TV/DVD, dataport, fridge, microwave, wet bar, coffeemaker, hair dryer.

Comfort Inn Rehoboth   Within sight of the Rehoboth outlets, this hotel is perfectly located for serious shoppers, but just 2 miles to the beach. Opened in 1996, its guest rooms are clean, comfortable, and spacious. Some have a microwave or whirlpool tub. The DART bus to the beach stops right outside.

4439 Hwy. 1, Rehoboth Beach, DE 19971. © **800/590-5451** or 302/226-1515. Fax 302/226-1550. www.comfortinn rehoboth.com. 99 units. $59–$250 double. Rates include deluxe continental breakfast. 2-night minimum stay required on summer weekends. AE, DC, DISC, MC, V. Free parking. **Amenities:** Adjacent restaurant and lounge; outdoor pool; health club; free Wi-Fi in lobby. *In room:* A/C, TV w/pay movies, Wi-Fi, fridge, coffeemaker, hair dryer, iron.

Henlopen Hotel   On the north end of the boardwalk, this beachfront lodging is a tradition dating from 1879, when the first Henlopen Hotel was built here. It's simple, plain, but nicely kept. The present accommodations are freshly remodeled. All 12 oceanfront rooms and 80 oceanview rooms have their own balconies. Families will like the suites.

511 N. Boardwalk, Rehoboth Beach, DE 19971. © **800/441-8450** or 302/227-2551. Fax 302/227-8147. www.henlopen hotel.com. 92 units. $69–$399 double. 2- or 3-night minimum stay required on weekends and holidays. AE, DISC, MC, V. Free parking. Closed Nov–Mar. *In room:* A/C, fridge, microwave, coffeemaker, hair dryer.

Moderate

Admiral Hotel   In the heart of the beach district, this modern five-story motel is a favorite with families. It has a terrific indoor pool inside a glass pavilion, plus a lovely deck with whirlpool. All units have a partial ocean view. Families can opt for six-person suites with a kitchen.

2 Baltimore Ave., Rehoboth Beach, DE 19971. © **888/882-4188** or 302/227-2103. www.admiralrehoboth.com. 73 units. $68–$359 double. Supplementary charges apply on some peak or holiday weekends. Children under 12 stay free in parent's room. 2- or 3-night minimum stay required in summer. AE, DISC, MC, V. Free parking. **Amenities:** Indoor pool; whirlpool; sun deck; complimentary coffee and tea in lobby; microwave in lobby. *In room:* A/C, TV, dataport (upon request), Wi-Fi, fridge, coffeemaker, hair dryer, iron.

Heritage Inn & Golf Club   This hotel has its own 9-hole golf course, open to nonguests. It's located just between Lewes and Rehoboth's beach—each is 3 miles away. Rooms have red, white, and blue Early American decor; three units have whirlpools; while six are family suites.

Rte. 1 and Postal Lane (P.O. Box 699), Rehoboth Beach, DE 19971. © **800/669-9399** or 302/644-0600. www.rehoboth heritage.com. 86 units. $69–$179 double. Rates include continental breakfast. AE, DISC, MC, V. **Amenities:** Outdoor pool; 9-hole golf course (greens fees $15–$35); health club. *In room:* A/C, TV w/free movies, Wi-Fi, fridge, microwave, coffeemaker, hair dryer, iron.

Oceanus Motel *(Value*   This L-shaped, three-story motel—a classic mid-1960s design—lies 2 blocks from the beach and just off Rehoboth Avenue in a quiet neighborhood. Each room shares a porch overlooking the good-size pool.

6 Second St. (P.O. Box 324), Rehoboth Beach, DE 19971. © **800/852-5011** or 302/227-8200. www.oceanusmotel.com. 38 units. $65–$199 double. Supplementary charges of $10–$20 apply on certain weekends. Children under 12 stay free in parent's room. Rates include continental breakfast. DISC, MC, V. Free parking. Closed Nov to late Mar. **Amenities:** Outdoor pool. *In room:* A/C, TV, Wi-Fi, fridge, microwave, hair dryer, iron.

Sandcastle Motel ⊛   You can't miss this motel, built in the shape of a sugary-white sand castle right off the main thoroughfare. Its location, though about 5 blocks from the beach, is ideal for shopping and walking to restaurants. Each large, well-laid-out room has a private balcony. The pool has a lifeguard on duty.

123 Second St. (off Rehoboth Ave.), Rehoboth Beach, DE 19971. © **800/372-2112** or 302/227-0400. Fax 302/226-9288. www.thesandcastlemotel.com. 60 units. $59–$179 double. 2- or 3-night minimum stay required on some weekends and holidays. AE, DISC, MC, V. Free parking in enclosed garage. Closed Nov–Feb. **Amenities:** Indoor pool; sauna; sun deck. *In room:* A/C, TV w/free movies, fridge, hair dryer.

DEWEY BEACH
Atlantic Oceanside Motel   This modern three-story structure is on the main beach highway, about equidistant from the bay and the ocean (both about a block away). The rooms are of the standard motel variety, but the motel's convenience to the beach and Dewey nightlife recommend it. It's an easy bike ride to Rehoboth.

1700 Hwy. 1, Dewey Beach, DE 19971. ✆ **800/422-0481** or 302/227-8811. Fax 302/227-4039. www.atlanticoceanside. com. 61 units. $40–$199 double. Supplementary charges apply on certain weekends. 3-night minimum stay required on summer weekends. AE, DC, DISC, MC, V. Free parking. Closed mid-Nov to mid-Mar. Pets accepted in off season for fee. **Amenities:** Outdoor pool; sun deck. *In room:* A/C, Wi-Fi, fridge, microwave, coffeemaker.

Bay Resort Motel *(Kids)*   It's a little out-of-the-way in Dewey (read: quieter), but this three-story complex, set on a strip of land between the bay and the ocean, is the ideal place to watch the sun set on Rehoboth Bay. From the 250-foot pier on the bay, you can drop a fishing line or watch the sailboats drift by. Each unit has a balcony facing either the pool or the bay.

126 Bellevue St. (P.O. Box 461), Dewey Beach, DE 19971. ✆ **800/922-9240** or 302/227-6400. www.bayresort.com. 68 units. $54–$199 double. Supplementary charges of $20–$50 per night apply on certain weekends. Children under 15 stay free in parent's room. 2- or 3-night minimum stay required on summer weekends and holidays. DISC, MC, V. Free parking. Closed Nov to late Mar. **Amenities:** Outdoor pool w/slide; 250-ft. pier. *In room:* A/C, TV w/free movies, kitchenette, coffeemaker, hair dryer, iron.

Best Western Gold Leaf   A block from both the beach and the bay, this modern four-story motel is across the street from the Ruddertowne complex and convenient to all of Dewey's attractions. Each bright, comfortable room has a balcony and a view of the bay, ocean, or both. Four king rooms feature whirlpool tubs.

1400 Hwy. 1 (at Dickinson St.), Dewey Beach, DE 19971. ✆ **800/422-8566** or 302/226-1100. Fax 302/226-9785. www.bestwesterngoldleaf.com. 75 units. $89–$229 double. Ask about reduced-rate packages Nov–Mar. 2- or 3-night minimum stay required in summer and on holiday weekends. Children under 17 stay free in parent's room. Rates include continental breakfast. AE, DC, DISC, MC, V. Free garage parking. Pets accepted in off season for fee. **Amenities:** Rooftop pool; sun deck. *In room:* A/C, TV, dataport, fridge, microwave, coffeemaker, hair dryer, iron.

WHERE TO DINE
REHOBOTH BEACH
Expensive
Back Porch Cafe *(R)* INTERNATIONAL   For more than 20 years, a Key West atmosphere has prevailed here, with an emphasis on fresh, creative fare. The flavors are global even if the food is local: spring-vegetable lasagna, prosciutto-crusted loin of rabbit, pan-seared grouper. At lunch, Jamaica, Thailand, France, and the Eastern Shore are all represented on the menu. There are three outdoor decks, decorated with eclectic plants and handmade tables. Live music on Friday night ranges from classical to world. Sunday brunch begins at 11am.

59 Rehoboth Ave., Rehoboth Beach. ✆ **302/227-3674.** www.backporchcafe.com. Reservations recommended on weekends. Main courses $9.50–$12 lunch, $29–$38 dinner. MC, V. June–Sept daily 11am–3pm and 6–10pm; early Oct Fri–Sun 11am–3pm and 6–10pm. Closed mid-Oct to end of May.

Blue Moon *(Finds)* AMERICAN/INTERNATIONAL   Located off the main drag, this restaurant is housed in an eye-catching blue-and-mango cottage. The interior features curved banquettes and exotic flower arrangements. The menu changes three times a year. You can count on rack of lamb, salmon, and duck—but the preparations are unexpected.

35 Baltimore Ave., Rehoboth Beach. ✆ **302/227-6515.** www.bluemoonrehoboth.com. Reservations recommended. Main courses $22–$39. AE, DC, DISC, MC, V. Mon–Sat 6–10pm; Sun 10:30am–2pm and 6–10pm. Closed 3 weeks in Jan.

Chez La Mer ✿✿ CONTINENTAL Rehoboth is brimming with good restaurants, but Chez La Mer skips the beach ambience for that of a French country inn. The intimate dining rooms fill up quickly with people hungry for veal Marsala, yellowfin tuna steak au poivre, and sweetbreads. Appetizers are intriguing. Special diets, such as low-sodium, can be accommodated. The solid wine list has lots of choices in the $20-to-$30 range. Dress up (in your best beach clothes) and bring your wallet and your appetite.

210 Second St., Rehoboth Beach. ℂ 302/227-6494. www.chezlamer.com. Reservations recommended. Main courses $20–$32. AE, DC, DISC, MC, V. June to early Sept daily 5:30–10pm; mid-Apr to May and mid-Sept to early Oct Thurs–Mon 5:30–9pm. Closed mid-Oct to early Apr.

La La Land ✿ INTERNATIONAL This acclaimed restaurant, on a side street off the boardwalk, blends California influence with Asian and Southwestern overtones. There's seating indoors in an art-filled pink, purple, and periwinkle dining room and outdoors on a patio set in a bamboo garden. The menu offers a variety of creative choices: plantain-crusted mahimahi or grilled-vegetable cannelloni, for instance.

22 Wilmington Ave., Rehoboth Beach. ℂ 302/227-3887. www.lalalandrestaurant.com. Reservations suggested. Main courses $19–$32. AE, DC, DISC, MC, V. Mid-Apr to mid-Nov daily 6–10pm; may close midweek in shoulder seasons. Closed Dec–Mar.

Moderate

Jake's Seafood House ✿ SEAFOOD It's spacious, with plenty of dining rooms, though still noisy. But who cares? The seafood is fresh, prepared well, and pairs with some affordable wines. Started by a Baltimore family, Jake's specializes in seafood the way locals like it. Grilled fish (including a delectable tuna), crab cakes (done Baltimore style—very traditional and very good), sandwiches, salads, and a few beef dishes are straightforward. Pair them with a salad with the house Parmesan-herb vinaigrette, and you might have room for a dessert martini.

Two locations: 29 Baltimore Ave. (at First St.), Rehoboth Beach (ℂ 302/227-6237), and 4443 Hwy. 1, Rehoboth Beach (ℂ 302/644-7711). www.jakesseafood.com. Reservations not accepted. Main courses $17–$33. AE, DC, DISC, MC, V. Daily 11:30am–10pm. Downtown location closed Jan–Feb; Hwy. 1 location open year-round.

Just in Thyme AMERICAN You might just pass by this rustic-looking place on Highway 1, but if you stop, you're in for a treat. The menu is filled with unusual pasta dishes—shrimp Orlando, Thai noodles with chicken and shrimp, crab penne Gorgonzola—and a variety of meat and fish entrees as well. These include pork loin with shiitake mushrooms and a port-wine sauce, a vegetarian medley, and catch of the day. Stop your outlet shopping early and head here for the early-bird special from 5 to 6:30pm. Or come on a summer Sunday for the sit-down brunch.

31 Robinson Dr. (at Hwy. 1), Rehoboth Beach. ℂ 302/227-3100. Reservations recommended. Main courses $12–$20. AE, DC, DISC, MC, V. Daily 5–10pm; Sun 11am–2pm.

Obie's by the Sea AMERICAN You can't dine any closer to the ocean than here beside the boardwalk. Obie's offers both indoor and open-air dining. A casual atmosphere prevails, with an all-day menu of sandwiches, burgers, ribs, salads, and "clam bakes" (steamed clams, spiced shrimp, barbecued chicken, corn on the cob, and muffins). There's DJ music and dancing on weekends.

On the boardwalk (between Virginia and Olive aves.), Rehoboth Beach. ℂ 302/227-6261. Reservations not accepted. Main courses $4.95–$19. AE, MC, V. Memorial Day to Labor Day daily 11am–1am; Apr to Memorial Day and Labor Day to early Nov Fri–Mon 11am–1am. Closed mid-Nov to Mar.

Summer House *(Kids)* SEAFOOD   Finding this place is the easy part; deciding what to eat is harder. There's an array of sandwiches, burgers, and salads, plus filet mignon, seafood, and chicken choices. One standout is the filet topped with lump crab. The restaurant is quite casual, with a party atmosphere and a children's menu for real-life kids (finger food for toddlers, PB&J, and chicken, flounder, or pizza served with applesauce and fries). Summer House doesn't close until Kate Smith sings "God Bless America" every night—recorded, of course.

228 Rehoboth Ave., Rehoboth Beach. ✆ 302/227-3895. www.summerhousesaloon.com. Reservations not accepted. Main courses $11–$30; light fare $5.95–$8.95. AE, DC, DISC, MC, V. Mid-May to mid-Sept daily 5pm–2am. Closed late Sept to early May.

Sydney's Blues & Jazz Restaurant *(Finds)* SOUTHERN/CREOLE   Located in an old schoolhouse and run by Sydney Arzt, a former schoolteacher, this classic restaurant still draws crowds for its nightly jazz and blues. Order the signature jambalaya, the shrimp and andouille over penne, or a couple appetizers as small plates. Happy hour begins at 5pm.

25 Christian St., Rehoboth Beach. ✆ 800/808-1924 or 302/227-1339. www.sydsblues.com. Reservations recommended on weekends. Main courses $18–$28. AE, DISC, MC, V. Daily 5:30–11pm. Hours vary in winter; usually Wed–Sun. Jazz sets begin at 9:30 and 11:30pm. Bar closes at 1am.

Inexpensive

Cafe Papillon *(Finds)* FRENCH   This tiny little walk-up down "Penny Lane" has plenty of inviting treats for breakfast or lunch: filled croissants, sweet or savory crepes, sandwiches, and cappuccino. The counter and tables are all outside, so this is definitely a seasonal delight.

Penny Lane, 42 Rehoboth Ave., Rehoboth Beach. ✆ 302/227-7568. Reservations not accepted. Crepes $2.75–$5.75; sandwiches $4.95–$7.25. No credit cards. June–Aug daily 8am–11pm; May and Sept–Oct Sat–Sun 8am–11pm.

Royal Treat BREAKFAST/ICE CREAM   The number of breakfast restaurants is dwindling, but you can still count on Royal Treat for eggs, French toast, and pancakes. Come back in the afternoon for ice cream. This old-fashioned Rehoboth landmark near the boardwalk must be doing something right—it's been serving breakfast for 2 decades.

4 Wilmington Ave., Rehoboth Beach. ✆ 302/227-6277. Reservations not accepted. All items $2–$7.75. No credit cards. May–Sept daily 8–11:30am and 1–11:30pm.

DEWEY BEACH

Rusty Rudder *(Finds)* AMERICAN/SEAFOOD   This California-style restaurant, right on the bay, has been a favorite of young beachgoers since 1979. It offers great views from its dining rooms, decks, and terraces. Dinner entrees include backfin crab cakes, prime rib, and enormous seafood platters. A land-and-sea buffet is offered nightly in summer, Friday and Saturday in the off season. The star of dinner, however, is the overflowing salad bar. Lunch favorites include sandwiches, salads, and seafood specialties. There's nightly entertainment, with better-known acts on weekends.

113 Dickinson St. (on the bay), Dewey Beach. ✆ 302/227-3888. www.deweybeachlife.com. Main courses $5.95–$15 lunch, $12–$49 dinner. AE, DC, DISC, MC, V. Summer daily 11:30am–10pm (Sun brunch 10am–2pm); Oct–Apr Thurs–Sun 11:30am–9pm.

WHAT TO SEE & DO

Rehoboth and Dewey offer a quieter, more relaxed alternative to Ocean City, Maryland, but both towns have nightlife and shops that stay open past 5pm, which you won't find at Bethany, Lewes, or Fenwick Island. If the sandy beaches, good restaurants, and intriguing little shops don't interest you, maybe the outlets will.

INDOOR ATTRACTIONS

The **Rehoboth Art League,** 12 Dodds Lane (© **302/227-8408**), is nestled in the Henlopen Acres section of town amid 3 acres of gardens, walking paths, and an outdoor sculpture area. The facility includes three galleries, a teaching studio, and a restored cottage. It offers exhibits by local and national artists. Admission is free, except for some special events. Open year-round, Monday through Saturday from 10am to 4pm and Sunday from 1 to 4pm.

The **Anna Hazzard Tent House,** 17 Christian St., off Rehoboth Avenue (© **302/ 226-1119**), is one of the original tiny tent buildings erected when Rehoboth was a summer retreat for Methodists. Admission is free. Open May through September, Wednesday and Saturday from 10am to 2pm; and October through December, on the first and third Wednesdays and Saturdays of the month from 10am to 2pm. Closed January through April. It's a good idea to call ahead.

ESPECIALLY FOR KIDS

Funland, on the boardwalk between Delaware and Brooklyn avenues (© **302/227- 1921;** www.funlandrehoboth.com), has rides and games. The rides for the preschool

---

Moments The Life-Saving Stations

Just south of Dewey and beside the Ocean City Inlet are two buildings that memorialize the men of the U.S. Life-Saving Service.

The pumpkin-and-brown **Indian River Life-Saving Station,** on Route 1, south of Dewey (© **302/227-6991;** www.destateparks.com), has been restored to its 1905 appearance. Built in 1876 as an Atlantic-coast outpost to look out for ships in distress, it was transferred to the U.S. Coast Guard in 1915, decommissioned in 1962, and restored in 1998. Listed on the National Register of Historic Places, its spare interior recalls the lives of the men who lived here. Guides tell the stories of heroic rescuers who saved sailors from sinking ships. Admission is $3.50 for adults, $2.50 for seniors, and $1 for children. Indian River Inlet Bridge construction is affecting operating hours, but in summer, it's open daily from 8am to 6pm, with guided tours available from 10am to 4pm. Off season, it's usually open on weekends, but call ahead to confirm.

Another station is on the Ocean City, Maryland, boardwalk. The white-and-red **Ocean City Life-Saving Station Museum,** at the Ocean City Inlet (© **410/289-4991;** www.ocmuseum.org), recalls the men who saved 4,500 sailors off these shores. Artifacts include a restored surf rescue boat and a pictorial history of storms that have raged here. Admission is $3 for adults, $1 for children 6 to 12. Hours are June through September, daily from 10am to 10pm; May and October, daily from 10am to 4pm; and November, December, and April, Saturday and Sunday from 10am to 4pm. Call ahead in winter months.

set are varied enough to keep the youngsters busy for hours; rides for kids over 8 or so are more limited. It's open from Mother's Day weekend to Labor Day; the arcade from 10am, the rides from 1pm. It closes when everybody's ready to go home.

About 1½ miles north of town is **Jungle Jim's Adventure Land,** Route 1 and Country Club Road (*©* **302/227-8444**), which offers go-carts, miniature golf, bumper boats, a rock-climbing wall, outdoor rides, and a water park with slides and rides. It's open weekends in May and September and daily from Memorial Day to Labor Day, from 10am to 11pm.

Rehoboth Summer Children's Theatre, at Epworth United Methodist Church, 20 Baltimore Ave. (*©* **302/227-6766;** www.rehobothchildrenstheatre.org), performs favorites such as *Peter Pan* and *The Emperor's New Clothes* on selected weeknights in summer. Curtain time is usually 7:30pm. The theater also offers morning acting workshops and an apprentice program. Call for reservations.

SHOPPING THE OUTLETS & THE BOARDWALK

The **Tanger Outlet Centers** *®*, stretching for 2 miles down Route 1 (*©* **302/226-9223;** www.tangeroutlet.com), have become a destination in their own right. Clothing stores include Brooks Brothers, Liz Claiborne, L.L. Bean, OshKosh, and Polo Ralph Lauren. There are over 130 outlets in all, selling accessories, housewares, china and crystal, sneakers, and handbags. Two centers are on the western side of Route 1; the third stretches between them on the east. You can't walk from center to center— and you have to be dedicated if you want to hit all the shops in a single day. Get a map so you can plan the most efficient route. Parking can be a challenge on weekends or rainy days, and Route 1 traffic can slow to a crawl. This place is so popular, New Jersey residents hop on the Cape May–Lewes Ferry to spend a day shopping in "no sales tax" Delaware. Hours are Monday through Saturday from 9am to 9pm and Sunday from 11am to 7pm. In summer, Sunday hours begin at 9am.

In downtown Rehoboth, the shopping is concentrated on the mile-long boardwalk and Rehoboth Avenue, which intersects the boardwalk at its midpoint. Most stores are open from 10am to 6pm, with extended evening hours in summer.

Azura   The owners design the stylish clothes sold here. Look for jewelry, furnishings, and accessories as well. 139 Rehoboth Ave. *©* **302/226-9650.**

Christmas Spirit   You can always find Santas, angels, and ornaments in this festive shop. 161 Rehoboth Ave. *©* **302/227-6872.**

Ibach's   Head here for chocolates: nonpareils, cashew turtles, cherry cordials. There's saltwater taffy, too. 9 Rehoboth Ave. *©* **877/270-9674** or 302/227-2870. www.dolles-ibachs.com.

Scandinavian Occasion   Sweet lace curtains, eye-catching paper cutouts to hang in a window, wrought-iron candleholders, and simple gold and semi-precious stone jewelry are just the beginning of the treasures you'll find here. 125 Rehoboth Ave. *©* **302/227-3945.**

Sea Shell Shop   This is a treasure-trove of seashell art, lamps, and jewelry, as well as loose shells, sponges, and hermit crabs. Little hands, the owners say, are always welcome. 119 Rehoboth Ave. *©* **302/227-6666.** www.seashellshop.com.

Tickled Pink   Stop in for Lilly Pulitzer's pink-and-green country-club style for women and teenaged girls. Clothes, hairbands, and accessories. 235 Rehoboth Ave. *©* **866/536-7456** or 302/227-7575.

SPAS

Sometimes you just need a little pampering. Rehoboth has become something of a spa resort, with plenty of places to choose from. **Avenue Day Spa,** 110A Rehoboth Ave. (© **302/227-5649;** www.avenueinn.com), offers European facials, waxing, makeup, and hair and nail care. It has a spa shop as well. The **Spa at the Bellmoor,** 6 Christian St. (© **302/227-5800;** www.thebellmoor.com), offers massage, facials, body treatments, waxing, and nail care. The **Spa by the Sea,** 46 Baltimore Ave. (© **302/227-8640;** www.thespabythesea.com), offers traditional massage, facials, manicures, and other treatments.

OUTDOOR ACTIVITIES

BIKING With its flat terrain and shady streets, Rehoboth is ideal for bicycling. Bikes are allowed on the boardwalk between 5 and 10am from May 15 to September 15, and anytime off season. **Bob's Bicycle Rentals,** 30 Maryland Ave., at First Street (© **302/227-7966**), has one-speed touring bikes, mountain bikes, tandems, and surreys, complete with the fringe on top. Open Memorial Day through Labor Day, daily from 6:30am to 5pm or later; hours vary the rest of the year. **Wheels Bicycle Shop,** 4100 Hwy. 1 (© **302/227-6807**), rents a variety of cruising bikes. Generally, rentals at all shops range from $5 to $7 per hour and $10 to $30 per day, depending on the type of bike. Surreys are $15 to $35 for an 11-seater.

GOLF The 9-hole course at **Heritage Inn & Golf Club,** on Route 1 in Rehoboth (© **800/669-9399** or 302/644-0600; www.heritageinnandgolf.com), is open to the public.

TENNIS There are public courts at Rehoboth City Courts, on Surf Avenue between Rehoboth Beach and North Shores; at Rehoboth Junior High School, on State Street; and in Dewey Beach on the bay at McKinley Street.

WATERSPORTS **Bay Sports,** 111 Dickinson St., Dewey Beach (© **302/227-7590**), rents kayaks, pedal boats, sailboats, Hobie catamarans, and jet skis by the half-hour, hour, or day. A kayak or pedal boat goes for $15 to $25 an hour. Hobie cats are $50 to $65, depending on size.

REHOBOTH & DEWEY BEACHES AFTER DARK

Sandwiched between the quiet family resorts of Bethany Beach and Fenwick Island to the south and Lewes to the north, Rehoboth and Dewey beaches offer the only consistent nightlife on the Delaware coast.

CLUBS & BARS

REHOBOTH BEACH Nationally known jazz and blues artists entertain year-round at **Sydney's,** 25 Christian St. (© **302/227-1339;** www.sydsblues.com). There's no cover for dinner guests (see "Where to Dine: Rehoboth Beach," above). **Irish Eyes,** 52 Rehoboth Ave. (© **302/227-5758**), schedules rock 'n roll and comedy-club entertainment in summer. There's also a pool table and 16 TVs to catch all the football action in fall and winter. **Rams Head,** 15 Wilmington Ave. (© **302/227-0807;** www.ramsheadtavern.com), offers all kinds of music in summer, from jazz to blues to folk. On winter weekends, expect jazz or open mic. People also come for the 100 beers (including locally produced Fordham brews) and hearty food. Rams Head has a brewpub in Annapolis as well.

DEWEY BEACH The *Washingtonian* has described Dewey Beach's summer nightlife as "Beach Bacchanalia." The two clubs are the **Rusty Rudder,** 113 Dickinson St., on the bay (© **302/227-3888**), and the **Bottle & Cork,** Highway 1 and Dagsworthy Street (© **302/227-7272**). The crowd tends to be 20- to 35-year-olds looking to party. The Rudder holds deck parties and has occasional bands or other activities; the cover varies. The Bottle & Cork, open only in spring and summer, is a surprisingly large rock club that hosts both local and nationally known bands; the cover varies. The music here is always good, but it can get uncomfortably crowded.

The **Starboard,** 2009 Hwy. 1 (© **302/227-4600;** www.thestarboard.com), is usually crowded with young people looking for a good time. It serves breakfast, lunch, and dinner in summer—the bloody marys are famous. Special events are listed on the website.

GAY & LESBIAN REHOBOTH

A number of Rehoboth nightspots cater to a GLBT clientele. The **Blue Moon,** 35 Baltimore Ave. (© **302/227-6515**), has a happy hour popular with the men. **Dogfish Head Brewings & Eats,** 320 Rehoboth Ave. (© **302/226-2739**), is primarily straight but draws a mixed crowd for its beer and live entertainment. Those who prefer live jazz head to **Sydney's,** 25 Christian St. (© **302/227-1339**), described above. A lesbian crowd goes to the **Frogg Pond,** 3 S. First St. (© **302/227-2234**).

THE PERFORMING ARTS

The open-air **Rehoboth Beach Memorial Bandstand,** at Rehoboth Avenue and the boardwalk (© **302/227-2233**), hosts more than 40 free concerts and other events on summer weekends, starting at 8pm. Check with the chamber of commerce office for an up-to-date schedule.

The **Henlopen Theater Project** (© **302/226-4103;** www.henlopentheaterproject. com) is a professional Equity group that offers a season of musical and nonmusical productions throughout the year. Check the website for upcoming productions.

3 Bethany Beach & Fenwick Island ⟨★

100 miles SE of Wilmington, 120 miles SE of Baltimore, 130 miles SE of Washington, D.C.

Nicknamed the "Quiet Resorts," Bethany Beach and Fenwick Island offer the most laid-back atmosphere of the Maryland and Delaware beach resorts. This pleasant stretch of condominium communities, state parks, and public and private beaches offers visitors—especially families—a calm alternative to the bustle of Ocean City to the south and the sophistication and shopping of Rehoboth to the north. It's a great place to just sit back and enjoy the beach.

These places may be quiet at night, but they offer so much during the day: swimming in the surf, bicycling along quiet roads, bird-watching in the dunes or coastal waterways, strolling on the tiny Bethany Beach boardwalk. For a little more excitement, just head up to Rehoboth or down to Ocean City, Maryland.

ESSENTIALS

GETTING THERE   By Car   Whether you're approaching from points north or south, it is best to take Route 113 and to avoid the frequently crowded Route 1—particularly in July and August. To reach Bethany Beach, at Dagsboro take Route 26 east; to reach Fenwick Island from the north, take Route 20 south (just outside of Dagsboro); and to get to Fenwick from the south, turn west on Route 54 at Selbyville. From the west, take Route 50 across the Bay Bridge to Route 404 east, then turn south on Route 113 and follow the directions above.

By Bus   Bus service is no longer available here. **Greyhound** (© **800/229-9424;** www.greyhound.com) does provide regular bus service to Ocean City; see p. 265 for details.

By Plane   Visitors arriving by plane can fly into the **Salisbury–Ocean City Wicomico Regional Airport;** see p. 265 for details.

VISITOR INFORMATION   The **Bethany–Fenwick Area Chamber of Commerce** (© **800/962-SURF** or 302/539-2100; www.bethany-fenwick.org) is on Route 1, adjacent to the Fenwick Island State Park. It publishes a helpful booklet called *The Quiet Resorts* and stocks plenty of brochures; open year-round, Monday through Thursday from 9am to 5pm, Friday from 9am to 4pm, Saturday and Sunday from 10am to 4pm. Bethany's **Town Hall,** 214 Garfield Pkwy. (© **302/539-8011**), also has brochures and a small museum telling the story of Bethany's origins.

GETTING AROUND   Since Bethany Beach and Fenwick Island are within 5 miles of each other, most people take a car, but bikes and in-line skates are also useful. All motels provide free guest parking; most restaurants also have access to parking for customers. Many Bethany and Fenwick streets are subject to metered or permit parking, and the rules are strictly enforced. Bethany's meters are enforced mid-May through mid-September from 10am to 11pm. *Tip:* Forget Bethany's meters—just stop at the kiosk for a parking permit. These run $7 a day or $47 a week and eliminate the need to keep the meters fed all day. The kiosk and a couple of change machines around town will also make change.

Once you park the car, you can get around Bethany Beach (but not to Sea Colony or South Bethany, mind you) via the **Beach Trolley.** It costs a quarter to ride and runs from 9:30am to 10pm.

ORIENTATION   If it weren't for the little signs in the median on Route 1, you'd never know there were three communities here. But officially, there are: Bethany Beach, South Bethany, and Fenwick Island. North of the town of Fenwick is the Fenwick Island State Park, all beach and parking lot with no restaurants, shops, or hotels. Fenwick Island is like a hyphen, connecting Ocean City to Delaware. Traveling north from O.C., you'll hardly know you've left the state.

Head north to Bethany Beach and its quieter, all-residential neighbor South Bethany. Bethany Beach is home to a small shopping area and boardwalk. Between the two is the huge condo resort called Sea Colony. Bethany and South Bethany have public beaches; Sea Colony's are private.

SPECIAL EVENTS   The **Bethany Beach Boardwalk Arts Festival** (© **302/539-2100**), a juried festival of fine arts and crafts, is held the Saturday after Labor Day from 10am to 5pm. In late September, join in the **Make-a-Wish Sea Colony Triathlon** (www.midatlantic.wish.org) or just cheer on the athletes. The **Fall Surf-Fishing Tournament** is held in October; the **Spring Surf-Fishing Tournament** takes place on a weekend in early May. For information, call © **302/539-2100.**

WHERE TO STAY

Bethany Beach and Fenwick Island are packed in summer, with more and more people booking a week in a condominium unit or beach house. New developments are going up on Route 24, a short drive from the beach, now that almost every oceanfront parcel has been developed.

Bethany has a variety of accommodations, from oceanfront mansions to houses in town, from duplexes and town houses to condos tucked under trees. The condo resort called **Sea Colony** ★★★ is an attractive option, with many rental units in nine oceanfront high-rises and a variety of condos on the west side of Route 1. Some of the buildings are 30 years old, while others were built in the last few years. With 12 pools, one is close to every unit. Tennis villas are surrounded by 34 courts, four indoor. There are also walking and biking paths, a fitness center, and a children's center. Shuttles take Sea Colony West guests to the beach. Guests need a recreation pass for the beach, pools, tennis courts, fitness centers, and shuttles; these cost $30 per person per week in season in 2005.

Look for your vacation rental early: Bookings are accepted beginning in January, though you might still find a nice place a few weeks before you arrive. Rentals range from $500 per week for a small unit to up in the thousands for oceanfront homes with room for extended family. Some good rental companies to call include **Century 21 Wilgus** (✆ 800/441-8118), **Coldwell Banker** (✆ 302/539-1777), **Seacoast Realty** (✆ 800/928-8800 or 302/539-8600), **Tansey-Warner, Inc.** (✆ 800/221-0070 or 302/539-3001), and **Tidewater Realty, Ltd.** (✆ 800/888-7501 or 302/539-7500). All of them will send brochures describing their rental properties.

Hotel rooms for July and August are booked months in advance, have higher rates, and often require weekend surcharges and 2- or 3-night minimum stays. Motels that would otherwise be considered in the budget category might charge between $70 and $100 for a double. To keep costs down, come midweek or visit in May, June, September, or October, when the weather can be almost as warm. June is surprisingly quiet, though the water is pretty chilly.

BETHANY BEACH

Addy Sea Bed & Breakfast ★   You'll find this romantic Victorian jewel far from the Bethany-size crowds but right by the ocean. A century-old cedar-shake cottage with wraparound porch, the Addy Sea offers quiet comfort along with a grand view from most rooms. Corner rooms (nos. 6 and 7) are brighter and have the best views. Room no. 12 has a king-size bed, Jacuzzi, and TV, while room no. 10 has a niche with windows offering a 180-degree view.

99 Ocean View Pkwy. (at North Atlantic Ave.), Bethany Beach, DE 19930. ✆ 800/418-6764 or 302/539-3707. Fax 302/539-7263. www.addysea.com. 13 units. $150–$400 double. Rates include full breakfast and afternoon tea. 2- or 3-night minimum stay required on summer weekends and holidays. AE, DISC, MC, V. Free parking. **Amenities:** TV; beach chairs and towels. *In room:* A/C, Wi-Fi, hair dryer, iron (upon request).

Bethany Arms Motel & Apartments *Kids*   Ideal for families who want to be close to the ocean, this complex offers basic motel units (with fridge and microwave) as well as apartments (with full kitchen and ocean view). Two buildings are on the boardwalk, with three more behind the first two, between the boardwalk and Atlantic Avenue.

Atlantic Ave. and Hollywood St. (P.O. Box 1600), Bethany Beach, DE 19930. ✆ 302/539-9603. www.beach-net. com/bethanyarms.html. 50 units. $75–$250 double. Surcharges may apply. 2- or 3-night minimum stay required on summer weekends and holidays. MC, V. Free parking. Closed late Oct to early Mar. *In room:* A/C, TV, fridge, microwave, coffeemaker.

Blue Surf Motel *Kids*   Families will like staying a short walk from the beach in these wood-paneled rooms, which offer plenty of space, old but sturdy furniture, small kitchens, maybe a view, and no worries. The newer annex units have more room, newer furniture, but no kitchen (only a fridge and microwave); six of these have at least some view of the ocean.

Oceanfront at Garfield Pkwy. (P.O. Box 999), Bethany Beach, DE 19930. ✆ **302/539-7531.** Fax 302/539-7605. www. beach-net.com/bluesurf.html. 35 units. $90–$220 double. 2- or 3-night minimum stay required on some weekends and holidays. AE, DC, MC, V. Free parking. Closed mid-Oct to mid-Apr. **Amenities:** Takeaway restaurant; small sun deck; bathhouse facilities. *In room:* A/C, TV (VCR available), kitchenette or fridge and microwave, coffeemaker, iron.

Westward Pines Motel   If you want comfort in a secluded setting, consider this ranch-style motel located in a residential area 4 blocks from the beach. Tall pines and flowering shrubs surround it. Guest rooms, all on ground-floor level, have standard furnishings; one has a fireplace, while another has a Jacuzzi.

10 Kent Ave. (1 block west of Rte. 1), Bethany Beach, DE 19930. ✆ **302/539-7426.** www.westwardpines.com. 14 units. $95–$145 double. Minimum stay may be required on weekends. No credit cards. Free parking. Pets accepted off season. *In room:* A/C, TV, fridge, coffeemaker, iron (upon request).

FENWICK ISLAND

Fenwick Islander Motel *(Value*   On the bay side of the highway, just north of the Maryland–Delaware state line, this bright three-story motel offers simple, clean accommodations. All units have kitchenettes; second- and third-floor rooms have balconies. Rooms in back are off the highway, quieter with a view of the canal.

Rte. 1 and South Carolina Ave. (between South Carolina and West Virginia aves.), Fenwick Island, DE 19944. ✆ **800/346-4520** or 302/539-2333. Fax 302/537-1134. www.fenwickislander.com. 62 units. $45–$159 double. Children under 9 stay free in parent's room; children 6–16 stay for $5 each per night. Surcharges and minimum-stay requirements may apply on weekends and holidays. Weekly rates available. AE, DISC, MC, V. Free parking. Closed Nov–Mar. **Amenities:** Outdoor pool; complimentary laundry facilities. *In room:* A/C, kitchenette, fridge, hair dryer (upon request), iron (upon request).

Ric-Mar Apartments *(Kids*   The homey Sea Charm is gone, but the adjacent apartments remain. The family-owned Ric-Mar offers Fenwick's closest accommodations to the beach, just 100 feet away. Guests can choose from snug studio efficiencies or one- and two-bedroom apartments. Three units that sleep six rent only by the week in summer. The units are old, but clean and "beachy."

Delaware and Bunting aves., Fenwick Island, DE 19944. ✆ **302/539-9613.** 14 units. $60–$200 double; $80–$180 apt. 3-night minimum stay required in high season. DISC, MC, V. Free parking. Closed mid-Sept to mid-May. **Amenities:** Outdoor pool; grass patio and deck w/picnic furniture and grills. *In room:* A/C, TV, kitchenette, fridge, coffeemaker.

Seaside Inn   New owners have been busy sprucing up this motel, a half-block from the beach. Rooms are simply furnished. The new linens, carpets, and upholstered furniture are certainly welcome. Larger king and two-queen units have sleeper sofas and a smidge more room. A tiny pool is tucked behind the office. The only bad news: no water views.

1401 Coastal Hwy., Fenwick Island, DE 19944. ✆ **800/417-1104** or 302/251-5000. www.seasideinnfenwick.com. 61 units. $39–$179 double. Surcharges and minimum-stay requirements may apply on weekends and holidays. AE, DISC, MC, V. Free parking. Closed mid-Nov to mid-Apr. **Amenities:** Outdoor pool. *In room:* A/C, TV, fridge, microwave, hair dryer (upon request), iron (upon request).

WHERE TO DINE

The restaurants of the Bethany Beach and Fenwick Island area provide a pleasant blend of waterside and inland dining, mostly at fairly moderate prices. Because these two resorts are popular with families, there are also some lower-priced restaurants that offer quality, ambience, and creative food. Unless otherwise noted, most restaurants serve alcohol (note that in Bethany, alcoholic beverages are available only in restaurants—there are no bars). *Note:* Hours in the "Quiet Resorts" can change at a moment's notice. Always call ahead if you're visiting in the off season—that is, before Memorial Day and after Labor Day.

Since motels in Bethany and Fenwick do not serve breakfast, you may want to check out some of the following places, particularly Frog House and Warren's Station.

BETHANY BEACH

Baja Beach House Grill MEXICAN   Fresh Mexican is on the menu at this *muy* casual eatery owned by a Bethany native. Burritos, tacos, and fajitas, as well as burgers and sandwiches, are cooked as soon as you order them at the counter. You can get carryout or stay to eat inside this sleek, California-style shop. Breakfast is served every day.

109 Garfield Pkwy., Bethany Beach. ⓒ 302/537-9993. www.bajabeachhouse.com. Reservations not accepted. You can call ahead to place carryout orders. Main courses $2.75–$11. No credit cards. Hours vary widely depending on season, but always open for breakfast, lunch, and dinner in summer, plus long weekends in the spring and fall off season; call ahead.

Cottage Cafe AMERICAN   This homey place has updated its country-cottage look but kept the comfort foods that make it so popular. The menu offers everything from old-fashioned pot roast and meatloaf to sandwiches, soup and salad combos, and pastas. In summer, a breakfast buffet is served on Saturday and Sunday from 8am to noon. Early-bird specials are offered before 6pm.

Rte. 1 at Hickman Plaza, Bethany Beach. ⓒ 302/539-8710. www.cottagecafe.com. Reservations not accepted. All items $7–$21. AE, DC, MC, V. Summer Mon–Fri 11am–1am; Sat–Sun 8am–1am.

Frog House *(Kids* AMERICAN   You can sleep in and still get breakfast at the Frog House, where it's served until 2pm. The 10 kinds of pancakes range from apple to chocolate chip. Lunchtime favorites include sandwiches, burgers, and salads; dinner brings fried chicken, steamed shrimp, and crab cakes. This is a great place to take the whole family—it's casual, friendly, and reasonably priced.

116 Garfield Pkwy., Bethany Beach. ⓒ 302/539-4500. Reservations not accepted. Main courses $3–$6.95 lunch, $7.65–$14 dinner; breakfast items $2–$8.75. DISC, MC, V. Daily 7am–9pm; call ahead in off season, as hours may vary.

Grotto Pizza PIZZA   The crowds keep coming to Grotto Pizza. There are outlets throughout Delaware, and Bethany is lucky enough to have two—which are both packed at dinnertime. It's no wonder, with the crispy crust, savory sauce, and cheese—and the perfect White Pizza, which combines spices, onions, and cheese. The menu also has salads, subs, and pastas. Grotto has branches in Dewey and Rehoboth; delivery is available, too.

793 Garfield Pkwy., Bethany Beach (ⓒ 302/537-3278), and 8–10 York Beach Mall, South Bethany (ⓒ 302/537-6600). www.grottopizza.com. Reservations not accepted. Pizza $9.75–$19. AE, DISC, MC, V. Summer Sun–Thurs 11am–11pm, Fri–Sat 11am–midnight; hours vary in off season, so call ahead.

Kingston Grille FRENCH   This new 10-table bistro is making waves among those who love traditional French cooking. Cozy but stylish, the Grille emphasizes all things French, from the foie gras to the bouillabaisse. Local seafood turns up on the menu, too, tucked into the soups or starring on their own.

14 Pennsylvania Ave. (at Campbell Place), Bethany Beach. ⓒ 302/539-1588. Reservations recommended. Main dishes $24–$35. MC, V. Wed–Sun 5–10pm. Closed Jan–Feb.

McCabe's Gourmet Market DELI   This deli and market is a local favorite for gourmet sandwiches, salads (such as a chicken-walnut option), and fresh-baked breads and pastries. It's perfect food to pack out to the beach. *Tip:* Visitors in South Bethany walk from the beach to McCabe's to pick up sandwiches for their beachside lunch—it's that close. Call ahead, and your order will be ready.

Rte. 1, in the York Beach Mall (just north of Fenwick Island State Park), South Bethany. ✆ 302/539-8550. www.
mccabesgourmet.com. Reservations not accepted. Sandwiches $4.25–$7.75. AE, DISC, MC, V. Daily 7am–5pm, with
extended hours in summer. Closed Jan–Feb.

Sedona 𝄞 AMERICAN   Offering some welcome sophistication in Bethany Beach, Sedona is a great place to sneak away from the kids and have an adult meal (although I've seen well-behaved children here, too). The sleek interior has room for 79 diners; in summer, make a reservation or be prepared to wait. A new chef has given the menu a slightly French accent; it always has something intriguing, from chicken with a lemon-thyme glaze to tuna served with Asian slaw.

26 Pennsylvania Ave., Bethany Beach. ✆ 302/539-1200. Reservations recommended. Main courses $24–$38. AE,
DISC, MC, V. Summer daily 5–10pm; hours vary in shoulder seasons, so call ahead. Closed Nov–Mar.

FENWICK ISLAND

Harpoon Hanna's 𝄞 *(Kids)* SEAFOOD   This huge, wood-paneled bayside restaurant occasionally has its ups and downs, but you can always count on fresh fish cooked in a variety of ways, along with a crisp tropical salad with mandarin orange and tiny shrimp. What *really* draws the crowds is the warm breads: sweet raisin, savory rye, and blueberry or coconut muffins. The waitstaff is young, but works hard to please. In summer, arrive really early—about 4:30pm or so—or be prepared for a long wait. The Tiki Bar has nightly parties, sometimes with live entertainment. Children are very welcome here; docks are available if you come by boat.

142nd St. (at Rte. 54), Fenwick Island. ✆ 800/227-0525 or 302/539-3095. www.harpoonhannas.oceancity.com.
Reservations not accepted. Main courses $4.95–$11 lunch, $8.95–$25 dinner. AE, DISC, MC, V. Daily 11am–9pm (Sun
brunch 10am–3pm), with extended hours in summer.

Nantuckets 𝄞 SEAFOOD   This is a place for grown-ups, with bright dining rooms, white tablecloths, and an innovative menu offering rich beef, garlicky mashed potatoes, famous quahog *chowdah,* and a lobster shepherd's pie that doesn't need a crust. If you like a more casual dining experience (although shorts are welcome in the dining rooms), try the adjacent bar, a cheerful place to grab a cold drink, appetizer, or whole meal. Service is top-notch. Early-bird specials are available before 5:45pm; there's happy hour in the taproom from 4 to 7pm.

Rte. 1 and Atlantic Ave., Fenwick Island. ✆ 800/362-DINE or 302/539-2607. Reservations recommended. Main
courses $23–$35. AE, DC, DISC, MC, V. Daily 4–10pm in tap room; 5pm–midnight in dining rooms (until 9pm in off
season).

Warren's Station *(Value)* AMERICAN   Families have been coming here since the 1960s. The big white restaurant, which resembles a lifesaving station, serves good-size portions of traditional foods, including a turkey dinner; beef, chicken, and seafood entrees; and heavenly "Crab Cutlet," a big fluffy crab cake from an old Deal Island Church recipe. Not that hungry? Try a burger, sandwich, or salad. Leave room for homemade pie. No alcohol is served.

Ocean Hwy. (Rte. 1, between Indian and Houston sts.), Fenwick Island. ✆ 302/539-7156. Reservations not
accepted. Main courses $2–$6.50 lunch, $6.75–$17 dinner; breakfast items $2–$7.25. DISC, MC, V. Mid-May to early
Sept daily 8am–9pm.

WHAT TO SEE & DO

Unlike Rehoboth Beach and Ocean City, the 1-mile-long **Bethany Beach Boardwalk** has only a few businesses on it. It's more of a promenade, perfect for a leisurely walk near the beach. Most of the shops and fast-food eateries are on **Garfield Parkway,** which intersects the boardwalk midway. **Fenwick Island** has no boardwalk between its hotels and its wide-open beach with gentle dunes. Most of the shops and businesses are concentrated along Route 1.

To see real sunken treasure, head to the **DiscoverSea Shipwreck Museum** ⊛, Route 1 and Bayard Street, Fenwick Island (© **302/539-9366;** www.discoversea. com), a small but worthwhile private museum above the Sea Shell City shop. The collection includes jewelry, coins, china, and weapons. A seashell display will help you figure out what kind of shells you found along the beach. Admission is free. Hours are Memorial Day through Labor Day, daily from 11am to 8pm; September through May, Saturday and Sunday from 11am to 4pm.

Built in 1859, the **Fenwick Island Lighthouse,** on the Transpeninsular Line, Route 54, about a quarter-mile west of Route 1, is one of Delaware's oldest. The lighthouse is still in operation today; its beams can be seen for 15 miles.

Across from the lighthouse is the **Viking Golf Theme Park,** routes 1 and 54, Fenwick Island (© **302/539-1644**), an inland amusement park with miniature golf, a water park, and go-carts. Hours vary according to weather. The water park is open from Memorial Day weekend to Labor Day, daily from 10am to 8pm. Miniature golf is open from Easter weekend to October, on warm weekends from 10am to 11pm; in summer, daily from 10am to midnight.

Bethany Beach Country Club, on Garfield Parkway, Bethany Beach (© **302/227-8660**), is actually a teeny miniature golf course squeezed between shops. It's not much to look at, but it's certainly convenient for Bethany visitors. And even without all the windmills and babbling brooks, it keeps the kids entertained. (It's fairly easy to win a free game, too.) In the summer, it's open daily from 10am to 10pm.

OUTDOOR ACTIVITIES

BIKING   The flat land along Route 1 in Bethany Beach and Fenwick Island is ideal for bicycling; however, caution is advised during peak traffic season in July, August, and summer holidays. Bethany also has bike lanes through town.

For a change of scenery, nearby **Assawoman Wildlife Area** offers several sandy but bike-accessible roads that wind through tidal marshland and forests. To get here, take Route 26 west and turn left on Road 361; then turn left on Road 363 and left on Road 364 in Bayard. The road splits, so bear left and follow the signs for Camp Barnes and Assawoman.

Bethany Cycle and Fitness Shop, 77 N. Garfield Pkwy. (© **302/537-9982**), rents beach bicycles for about $18 per day, $40 per week.

HIKING & BIRDING   During the off season, **Fenwick Island** and **Delaware Seashore** state parks, both on Route 1, are great places for a walk along deserted beaches. In high season, however, when these beaches are covered with sunbathers, it's best to head out at sunrise or venture a little inland. *Tip:* Bring bug repellent. *Note:* Burton's Island, in Delaware Seashore State Park, will be closed during replacement of the Indian River Inlet Bridge; construction is due to last until 2009.

Assawoman Wildlife Area (see "Biking," above) welcomes hikers on its few miles of dirt roads through tidal marsh and forests. An observation tower and duck blinds make it easy to view a variety of shorebirds.

KAYAKING & SAILING   To tour the quieter waters of Assawoman Bay, a salt marsh, or the nearby bald-cypress stand, stop by **Coastal Kayak** (© **877/44-KAYAK** or 302/539-7999; www.coastalkayak.com). It has a stand on the bay across from Fenwick Island State Park. Tours cost about $40 for adults and $30 for children; they last 90 minutes to 2 hours. It also rents kayaks, sailing catamarans, and windsurfers—and it delivers. (Get a coupon from the website.)

SURF FISHING   A major draw in this area, fishing in Delaware's tidal waters requires no license. Surf fishing is permitted when lifeguards are off-duty. The Bethany–Fenwick Area Chamber of Commerce sponsors two surf-fishing tournaments a year, in early May and October; for information, call © **302/539-2100.**

   Fenwick Island State Park has 3 miles of seacoast beach, most of which is open to surf fishing, and considerable tracts of open bayfront, ideal for both fishing and crabbing. There are also several dune crossings set up for off-road vehicles; a surf-fishing vehicle permit is required. Call © **302/539-9060** for vehicle permits and maps of fishing areas. Similar facilities are also available at **Delaware Seashore State Park** (© **302/227-2800**).

TENNIS   Although there's not much tennis for the general public, **Sea Colony** (p. 259) is the largest tennis resort on the East Coast, sporting 26 courts, including four outdoor lighted courts, four clay courts, and four indoor courts. If tennis is your game, contact a real-estate agent about renting a condo in Sea Colony's tennis villas.

SHOPPING

BETHANY BEACH   Most of the shopping in Bethany Beach is along or near Garfield Parkway, with a few shops on the boardwalk. They're generally open daily from 10am to 5pm, with extended hours in summer.

   Bethany Beach Books, 99 Garfield Pkwy. (© **302/539-2522**), is the perfect place to pick up some reading for the beach. For your sweet tooth, head to the **Fudge Factory,** 3 Town Center (© **302/539-7502**), or follow your nose to the delectable aromas at **Fisher's Popcorn,** 108 Garfield Pkwy. (© **888/436-6388** or 302/539-8833).

   Stop in **TKO Designs Art Jewelry,** on Garfield Parkway (© **302/539-6992;** www.tkodirect.com), for delicate, handcrafted jewelry. Bethany's premier boutique is the eclectic **Japanesque,** 16 Pennsylvania Ave. (© **302/539-2311**), which carries a wide selection of Japanese jewelry, home furnishings, and books.

FENWICK ISLAND   Shopping in Fenwick is limited, but if you like country items, visit the **Seaside Country Store** (© **302/539-6110**). This big red store on Route 1, surrounded by strip malls, has room after room of merchandise with a country feel—from gifts and clothing to home decor to candy. Closed December through February.

NIGHTLIFE IN BETHANY

Hanging out on the boardwalk is all the rage—but there really isn't much to do at night. Fifteen years ago, all the young parents brought their children in strollers for a walk before bedtime. Now young teens gather in the same spots to talk and eat.

   Bethany Beach has its own **Bandstand** with shows beginning at 7:30pm. The performances are all family-oriented, with orchestras, bluegrass bands, and puppet shows. Sometimes there are dance lessons or talent shows. The town posts a schedule on the boardwalk and at the town hall on Garfield Parkway.

4 Ocean City, Maryland ★★★

For many Marylanders, heading "downy ocean" or "to the shore" means only one thing: a summer vacation in Ocean City. It's often quite crowded on the beach, in the restaurants, and on Coastal Highway, but it's still Marylanders' favorite place to sunbathe, jump waves, eat, shop, and find friends. On a skinny stretch of barrier island less than 10 miles long, the attractions are that wide sandy beach, pounding surf, and ocean breezes. So many visitors arrive that for 3 months of the year, Ocean City is the second-largest city in the state. (Only Baltimore has more people.) Ocean City's entire beach is open to the public.

The 3-mile-long boardwalk, which stretches to 27th Street in the oldest part of Ocean City, is crowded with hotels, some of them dating back to the 1920s. Restaurants, ice-cream stands, and shops fill in the gaps. The boardwalk ends at the fishing pier, which has amusement rides and a huge Ferris wheel.

Out on Coastal Highway, shopping centers, restaurants, hotels, and condos demand your attention and your money. Miniature-golf courses are exceedingly popular: They're all crowded after dark, and there are some dandies (p. 278). The quieter waters surrounding Ocean City—the bays of Assawoman, Sinepuxent, and Montego—attract fishermen, sailors, parasailers, and kayakers.

ESSENTIALS

GETTING THERE   By Car   Route 50 goes right to Ocean City. To reach the southern end of town, continue on Route 50 to the bridge that enters O.C. at Caroline Street. For those staying at 60th Street or above, take Route 90 and cross the bridge at 62nd Street. An alternative route (but only one lane each way) is to turn on Route 404 East just past Queenstown; follow it into Delaware. Turn south onto Route 113 South. Route 26 East connects with Bethany. Turn south on Route 1 to Ocean City. Or take Route 54 to Fenwick to Route 1. However you get here, avoid Route 1 in Rehoboth—especially on summer weekends, when traffic slows to a frustrating crawl most of the day. *Tip:* New in 2005: Call ✆ **877/BAYSPAN** on your way to the Bay Bridge for up-to-date traffic reports.

By Plane   The **Salisbury–Ocean City Wicomico Regional Airport,** 30 minutes west of Ocean City, near Salisbury (✆ **410/548-4827**), handles nonstop commuter flights to and from Baltimore, Washington, D.C., and Philadelphia via **US Airways Express** (✆ **800/428-4322;** www.usairways.com). Private planes also fly into that airport, as well as **Ocean City Municipal Airport,** 3 miles west of town off Route 611 (✆ **410/213-2471**).

Car rentals are available from **Avis** (✆ **410/742-8566;** www.avis.com) and **Hertz** (✆ **410/749-2235;** www.hertz.com), both at the Wicomico Regional Airport.

By Bus   Greyhound (✆ **800/231-2222;** www.greyhound.com) has daily service into Ocean City from points north and south, with nonstop buses from Baltimore, Washington, D.C., and Salisbury. Buses stop at Second Street and Philadelphia Avenue (✆ **410/289-9307**).

VISITOR INFORMATION   The **Ocean City Convention and Visitors Bureau** operates a visitor center in the Roland E. Powell Convention Center, 4001 Coastal Hwy., at 40th Street, bay side (✆ **800/OC-OCEAN** or 410/289-8181; www.oc ocean.com). Open daily from 9am to 5pm.

If you're heading into town from Route 50, stop at the information center run by the **Ocean City Chamber of Commerce,** routes 707 and 50, 1½ miles from Ocean City (© **888/OCMD-FUN** or 410/213-0552; www.oceancity.org). It's a great place to pick up brochures and coupons for everything from restaurants to miniature golf. Open daily from 9am to 5pm.

Tip: If you have only 1 night to stay at the beach, check with the staff at either center. Although most hotels advertise 2- or 3-night minimum stays on weekend, the staff here can probably find you accommodations.

Look for coupons and event schedules in *Ocean City Visitors Guide, Sunny Day, Beachcomber,* and *Beach Guide,* available in restaurants, stores, hotels, and real-estate offices.

GETTING AROUND   By Bus   In peak season, when parking can be difficult, the bus is the fastest and most convenient way to get around. Buses run 24 hours a day year-round. They follow one route, from the Delaware border south along Coastal Highway to the inlet, returning north along Baltimore Street and Coastal Highway. In summer, buses run every 10 minutes; from October 20 to Memorial Day, they run every half-hour. The fare is $2 for a 24-hour period; exact change is required. For information, contact the **Ocean City Transportation Department,** 66th Street, bay side (© **410/723-1607**).

A **Park & Ride Lot,** on Route 50 in West Ocean City (on the western side of the bridge), has free parking. Visitors can board a shuttle to South Division Street near the inlet, to either spend the day there or catch a bus to other O.C. destinations. It costs $1 for the whole day.

By Boardwalk Tram ☝   The tram travels 2½ miles from the inlet north to 27th Street, stopping for passengers who signal the driver to pick them up. In summer, it runs every 10 minutes from 7am to midnight daily. On weekends from Easter to May, and in September and October, it runs every 15 minutes. To get off, raise your hand and the tram will stop. The fare is $2.50 one-way. It's great for parents with tired children—and a good way for first-time visitors to become familiar with the boardwalk.

By Taxi   Taxi service has expanded in recent years—serving those who've had too much to drink as well as non-drivers. Among the growing number of services are **BayShore** (© **443/783-2911**) and **Eastern Shore Taxi** (© **443/744-4497**).

PARKING   Parking is difficult, particularly at the height of the season. Most public facilities, such as shopping centers and restaurants, offer free parking for patrons. There are also eight public lots, mostly around the southern end of Ocean City. The meters must be fed $1.25 an hour, but there are change machines at several lots: Worcester Street; Somerset Street and Baltimore Avenue; Dorchester Street and Baltimore Avenue; North Division Street and Baltimore Avenue; and Fourth Street and Baltimore Avenue. These, as well as on-street meters, must be fed 24 hours a day between April 15 and October 15. They're free at other times. The largest public lot is the Hugh T. Cropper parking lot at the inlet, with 1,200 paid spaces. The first 30 minutes here are free; then the rate is $1 an hour, $1.50 on weekends. If you plan to park here for nighttime activities, be aware that hundreds of other people will have the same idea—and the wait to get in the lot, and later to get out, can be long.

ORIENTATION   Ocean City stretches for 10 miles, with one main north–south thoroughfare, Coastal Highway. It becomes two one-way streets at around 32nd Street: Philadelphia goes south, Baltimore heads north. Cross streets are designated by

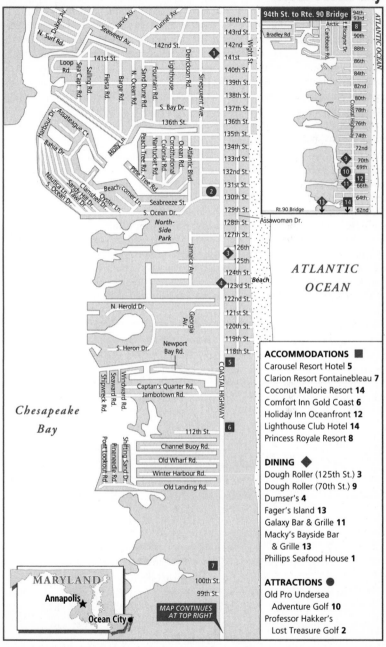

94th St. to Rte. 90 Bridge

ATLANTIC OCEAN

ATLANTIC OCEAN

Chesapeake Bay

MARYLAND

Annapolis

Ocean City

MAP CONTINUES
AT TOP RIGHT

ACCOMMODATIONS ■

Carousel Resort Hotel **5**
Clarion Resort Fontainebleau **7**
Coconut Malorie Resort **14**
Comfort Inn Gold Coast **6**
Holiday Inn Oceanfront **12**
Lighthouse Club Hotel **14**
Princess Royale Resort **8**

DINING ◆

Dough Roller (125th St.) **3**
Dough Roller (70th St.) **9**
Dumser's **4**
Fager's Island **13**
Galaxy Bar & Grille **11**
Macky's Bayside Bar
  & Grille **13**
Phillips Seafood House **1**

ATTRACTIONS ●

Old Pro Undersea
  Adventure Golf **10**
Professor Hakker's
  Lost Treasure Golf **2**

numbers (from 1st to 145th), with numbers decreasing to the south. It's vital to know the cross street when looking for a shop or restaurant (though if you have a street address, the first two numbers usually tell you the cross street). Attractions and businesses on the cross streets are designated as either ocean side (east of Coastal Hwy.) or bay side (west of Coastal Hwy.). If you see an address that says Atlantic Avenue, that means it's oceanfront.

SPECIAL EVENTS Ocean City's party atmosphere is enhanced by festivals throughout the year; below is just a selection of the largest and most popular.

Everybody in O.C. is Irish on the Sunday closest to St. Patrick's Day for the **St. Patrick's Day Parade and Festival.** Every year, more and more people decide this is the place for the "wearin' of the green." The 4-day **Springfest,** held the first week of May, brings crafts, music, and food to the inlet parking lot. Lots of businesses open now, as O.C. prepares for summer. The **Arts Alive** festival, held the first week of June, features a juried fine-art exhibit and sale, along with music and food. It takes place at the Northside Park at 127th Street and the bay.

On the **Fourth of July,** some 300,000 people crowd into Ocean City. Fireworks over Assawoman Bay top off the family-style picnic held at Northside Park beginning at 1pm. A second fireworks display takes place at North Division Street, at the south end of the boardwalk. Festivities begin with a concert at 8pm; fireworks begin at both locations at 9:30pm.

The **White Marlin Open** 𝕽 (www.whitemarlinopen.com) is usually held the first full week in August. Some 400 boats register for this annual fishing expedition. The top prize goes for the biggest white marlin, but there are other prizes for blue marlin, tuna, and shark. In 2005, the purse was set at $1.64 million. If you want to see what all the fuss is about (without actually fishing yourself), stop by the Harbor Island Marina on the bay side for the weigh-ins every night from 4 to 9pm. They reel in some whoppers. *Note:* This is not a good week to charter a fishing boat for any other fishing, as all boats are occupied. If you really want to fish, you might have a better chance of finding a boat in Lewes.

The 4-day **Sunfest** festival, held the third week of September, officially ends the summer season with crafts, music, and food at the inlet. From mid-November to New Year's, holiday displays make up the **Winterfest of Lights** 𝕽𝕽. The first takes place at the inlet, where you can drive among the lit displays. The second takes place in Northside Park. For $3 for those 12 and older, you can ride the tram through the light displays and then stop to see Santa, have hot chocolate, and browse the gift shop.

FAST FACTS: Ocean City

Area Code Ocean City's area codes are **410** and **443**.

Beach Wheelchairs Free beach-accessible chairs are available on a first-come, first-served basis from the Ocean City beach patrol. Or you can reserve your chair at the convention center or police department by calling ℂ **410/723-6610.**

Dentists Emergency work is provided at **Atlantic Dental Associates,** 12308 Ocean Gateway (Rte. 50) (ℂ **410/524-0500**).

Emergencies Dial ℂ **911** for fire, police, or ambulance.

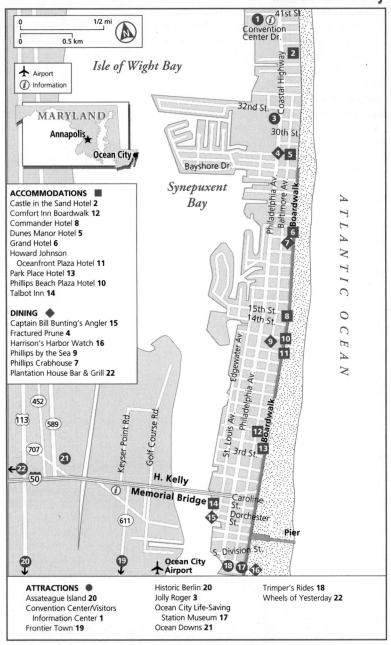

0   1/2 mi

0   0.5 km

✈ Airport
ⓘ Information

MARYLAND

Annapolis ★

Ocean City ●

Isle of Wight Bay

41st St.
● ① ⓘ
Convention
Center Dr.

②

Coastal Highway

32nd St.
③

30th St.

④ ⑤

Bayshore Dr.

Synepuxent
Bay

Philadelphia Av.
Baltimore Av.
Boardwalk

⑥
⑦

A T L A N T I C   O C E A N

ACCOMMODATIONS ■
Castle in the Sand Hotel **2**
Comfort Inn Boardwalk **12**
Commander Hotel **8**
Dunes Manor Hotel **5**
Grand Hotel **6**
Howard Johnson
   Oceanfront Plaza Hotel **11**
Park Place Hotel **13**
Phillips Beach Plaza Hotel **10**
Talbot Inn **14**

DINING ◆
Captain Bill Bunting's Angler **15**
Fractured Prune **4**
Harrison's Harbor Watch **16**
Phillips by the Sea **9**
Phillips Crabhouse **7**
Plantation House Bar & Grill **22**

15th St.
14th St.
⑧

Edgewater Av.

⑨ ⑩
⑪

Philadelphia Av.

(452)
(113) (589)
(707)
● 21
← ② 22
(50)
(611)

Keyser Point Rd.
Golf Course Rd.

St. Louis Av.
Philadelphia Av.

3rd St.
⑫ Boardwalk
⑬

H. Kelly
ⓘ
Memorial Bridge ⑭
⑮

Caroline
St.
Dorchester
St.

Pier

S. Division St.

● 20
● 19
✈ **Ocean City
Airport**

⑱ ⑰ ⑯

ATTRACTIONS ●
Assateague Island **20**
Convention Center/Visitors
   Information Center **1**
Frontier Town **19**

Historic Berlin **20**
Jolly Roger **3**
Ocean City Life-Saving
   Station Museum **17**
Ocean Downs **21**

Trimper's Rides **18**
Wheels of Yesterday **22**

Eyeglass Repair The local choice is **Accurate Optical,** 118th Street, near the Food Lion supermarket (© **410/524-0220**).

Hospitals Go to the **75th Street Medical Center,** 7408 Coastal Hwy. (© **410/524-0075**); the **Atlantic General Hospital,** 9733 Healthway Dr., Berlin (© **410/641-1100**); or the **Peninsula Regional Medical Center,** 100 E. Carroll St., Salisbury (© **410/546-6400**).

Library The Ocean City branch of the Worcester County Library is at 14th Street and Philadelphia Avenue (© **410/289-7297**).

Newspapers Ocean City's weekly newspaper is *Ocean City Today.* Dailies from Baltimore, Washington, and Philadelphia are also available.

Pharmacies Try **Bailey's,** 8th Street and Philadelphia Avenue (© **410/289-8191**), or **CVS,** Coastal Highway and 120th Street (© **410/524-7233**).

Police If it's not an emergency, dial © **410/723-6610** for Ocean City police, © **410/641-3101** for state police, or © **410/289-7556** for beach patrol.

Post Office The main post office is located at 71st Street and Coastal Highway, bay side (© **410/524-7611**).

Taxes The state sales tax is 5%.

Transit Information Dial © **410/723-2173**.

Weather Dial © **800/OC-OCEAN** or 410/213-0552.

WHERE TO STAY

More than in any other part of Maryland, lodgings here rely on a high season. Summer—especially July and early August—commands the highest rates, often with weekend supplements. In many cases, minimum stays of 2 or 3 nights are required, so check in advance. Reservations are essential for weekends. Most hotels have pools (ask if it's important to you), but those with indoor pools can fill up in the off season, especially on holiday weekends. Every hotel has rooms which are accessible for those with disabilities; nearly all have free parking.

Rates are a little lower on rooms without an ocean view or with a partial view. January rates are bargain basement (for good reason), but tariffs in spring and fall are also economical, and many hotels offer packages. Spring can be rainy, but September is terrific: The beach is nearly empty (except on weekends), lots of restaurants are still open, and the water is warm. I hate to give this secret away, but early June can also be a good time—as long as you're willing to put up with "June Bugs" (new high-school graduates celebrating their freedom). Since the grads are occupied elsewhere, you'll find lots of room in restaurants, shops, and nightspots; drive carefully. Valentine's Day and Christmas also draw a crowd; look for hotel packages and special menus for both holidays, as well as light displays and New Year's Eve parties.

For many families, renting a condo or town house is the only way to go. With several bedrooms and bathrooms, full kitchens, and living rooms, these offer a convenient way to take everybody to the beach. Most rent from Saturday to Saturday. Several real-estate companies offer hundreds of units on both the ocean and the bay; try **Coldwell Banker** (© **800/633-1000** or 800/922-9800; www.mwgbeach.com) or **Long and Foster** (© **800/843-2322**) for rentals in Ocean City, as well as in the "suburbs" of

Ocean Pines, a community of homes west of O.C. Rates start at $1,000 a week and take off from there. Every unit is different, so read the thick brochures and check the firms' websites. Generally, these units are well kept with fairly new furniture, appliances, and often a stash of paperbacks and board games for rainy days. Bring your own paper products and linens. Just about everything else is usually provided. (Check the listings to be sure.) The best units—that is, the newest and closest to the beach—are snapped up by January or February, but if you decide to go to the beach in May, there are usually condos still available.

EXPENSIVE

Carousel Resort Hotel 🐸🐸   The Carousel is an attractive option for families and couples. It's one of the oldest of northern Ocean City's high-rises and one of the most interesting. It has a year-round ice-skating rink, an indoor pool, and comfortable, if small, rooms with kitchenettes and oceanfront balconies. If those rooms aren't big enough, 93 two- and three-bedroom condo units are available in the 22-story tower behind the hotel. Carousel is a conference center and can occasionally be fully booked. Off season, the hotel offers some great values.

11700 Coastal Hwy., Ocean City, MD 21842. ⓒ 800/641-0011 or 410/524-1000. Fax 410/524-7766. www.carousel hotel.com. 332 units. $59–$339 double; $309–$499 condo. Weekly rates available. AE, DC, DISC, MC, V. Free parking. **Amenities:** Oceanfront restaurant; outdoor restaurant; deli and coffee bar; 2 bars; indoor pool; outdoor pool; lighted tennis court; health club; Jacuzzi; sauna; business center; indoor ice rink (open to the public). *In room:* A/C, dataport, fridge, microwave, coffeemaker, hair dryer, iron.

Clarion Resort Fontainebleau 🐸🐸   On the ocean, far from the boardwalk and in the midst of Condo Row in northern Ocean City, this hotel offers oversize rooms and suites, all with private balconies and views of the ocean and the bay. The cabana suites, with sitting room and huge bedroom on separate levels, are posh. The Clarion also rents 69 one-, two-, and three-bedroom units at the adjacent Marigot Beach Condominiums. The level of service here is extremely high; staff will go out of their way to make sure guests have all they need—even a wheelchair or other medical requirement.

10100 Coastal Hwy. (at 101st St.), Ocean City, MD 21842. ⓒ 800/638-2100 or 410/524-3535. Fax 410/524-3834. www.clarionoc.com. 250 units. $89–$339 double. AE, DC, DISC, MC, V. Free parking. **Amenities:** Restaurant and 2 lounges overlooking the ocean; terrace; indoor pool; health club; spa; whirlpool; sauna; steam room; gift shop; sunrooms. *In room:* A/C, TV, Wi-Fi, fridge, microwave, iron, hair dryer, safe.

Coconut Malorie Resort 🐸🐸   Stylish with a tropical flair, this Fairfield resort offers suites overlooking Isle of Wight Bay. The lobby—with waterfall, marble floors, and palm trees—is inviting. Suites are decorated with the same Caribbean style: big British colonial beds, Haitian art, luxurious bathrooms with whirlpool tubs, and plenty of space. The resort offers a variety of activities, concierge service, and good recreation facilities. A footbridge connects the hotel to **Fager's Island** (see "Where to Dine," below).

200 59th St., Ocean City, MD 21842. ⓒ 800/438-6493 or 800/767-6060. Fax 410/524-9327. www.coconut malorie.com. 85 units. $85–$278 double. AE, DC, DISC, MC, V. Free parking. **Amenities:** Outdoor pool w/bar and deck fitness room; game room w/video games, billiards, and Ping-Pong. *In room:* A/C, dataport, kitchenette, fridge, microwave, coffeemaker, hair dryer, iron.

Dunes Manor Hotel 🐸   If you like your hotels old-fashioned, the Dunes Manor is for you. On 28th Street just beyond the boardwalk, this 11-story hotel tries its best to capture days gone by. The Victorian-style facade, cupolas, and wide porch with rocking chairs are just the beginning. Tea and crumpets are offered every summer afternoon.

Each unit is up-to-date in every way, with an oceanfront view, balcony, one king-size or two double beds, and decor of light woods and floral fabrics. Rooms on upper floors have the best views; nine units have kitchenettes.

2800 Baltimore Ave., Ocean City, MD 21842. © **800/523-2888** or 410/289-1100. Fax 410/289-4905. www.dunes manor.com. 170 units. $95–$385 double; $85–$295 suite (depending on season). Weekly rates available. AE, DC, DISC, MC, V. Free parking. **Amenities:** Restaurant and lounge; indoor/outdoor pool; health club; whirlpool; sun deck. *In room:* A/C, TV, dataport, fridge, microwave, hair dryer, iron.

Lighthouse Club Hotel ✪✪✪ Empty your wallet and pamper yourself in this unique boutique hotel, perched on Isle of Wight Bay. You can't miss the inn, which resembles a gabled, red-roofed screw pile lighthouse from the Route 90 Bridge. Inside, the lobby soars to a skylight three stories up, in what is Ocean City's most luxurious hotel. A circular staircase takes guests to their rooms, decorated in tropical white and rattan. Balconies overlook the bay or nearby. Eight units have fireplaces and Jacuzzis. Lightkeeper suites offer even more spacious surroundings.

The adjacent **Edge** may be even more luxurious, with its two-story guest rooms, private Jacuzzis, wide-open sitting areas, gas fireplaces, and DVD players. Each unit has a balcony overlooking the building's own pool. The Left Bank suite has a Jacuzzi placed right by picture windows overlooking the bay. Two penthouse suites top the hotel.

201 60th St. (on the bay), Ocean City, MD 21842. © **800/371-5400** or 410/524-5400. Fax 410/524-3928. www. fagers.com. 23 units in the Lighthouse; 12 units in the Edge. $79–$339 double. Off-season packages are a good deal in winter. Rates include continental breakfast. AE, DC, DISC, MC, V. Free parking. **Amenities:** Restaurant (see Fager's Island, under "Where to Dine," below); pool; access to nearby health club; Jacuzzi. *In room:* TV/VCR, dataport, fridge stocked w/soda, coffeemaker, hair dryer, iron.

Princess Royale Resort The rooms are lovely, but what makes this the place to stay is its Olympic-size indoor pool. Even if it rains, the pool is big enough for everybody—and not all hotels can say that. It's part of a recreation center, glassed in with a sauna, Jacuzzis, and a poolside cafe that will keep your kids happy. Rooms are rented in the lower five floors; the upper floors are condo units. One-bedroom suites sleep 2 to 6 people, two-bedrooms sleep 6 to 8, and three-bedrooms sleep up to 10. The staff is gracious, and the facilities well maintained.

9100 Coastal Hwy., Ocean City, MD 21842. © **800/4-ROYALE** or 410/524-7777. Fax 410/524-1623. www.princess royale.com. 310 units, 25 condos. Double $69–$309; condo $169–$485 per night fall–spring; $2,100–$3,900 per week in summer. AE, DISC, MC, V. Free parking. Children under 12 stay free in parent's room. **Amenities:** Restaurant; seasonal outdoor restaurant for lunch; bar; comedy club; indoor pool; rooftop miniature golf; 2 tennis courts; health club; sauna; Jacuzzi; convenience store; beach volleyball. *In room:* A/C, high-speed Internet access, kitchenette (full kitchen in condos), fridge, microwave, hair dryer, iron.

MODERATE
Castle in the Sand Hotel A good choice for families who don't want to break the bank, this modern hotel with a castle-like exterior is set on the beach at 37th Street, about 10 blocks from the boardwalk. Standard rooms have all the usual amenities; if you need something bigger, check into a condo unit or one of the quaint apartments in old beach cottages. Two-bed, two-bathroom condos go for about $1,800 a week; apartments run a little less.

3701 Atlantic Ave., Ocean City, MD 21842. © **800/552-SAND** or 410/289-6846. Fax 410/289-9446. www.castle inthesand.com. 181 units. $69–$295 double (standard, suites, and efficiencies). Weekly rates available. AE, DC, DISC, MC, V. Free parking. Closed mid-Nov to mid-Feb. **Amenities:** Restaurant; bar and grill; outdoor pool; game room; children's activities in summer. *In room:* A/C, TV/VCR w/movies, fridge, microwave, iron.

Comfort Inn Boardwalk   This five-story complex has two buildings: one on the boardwalk and another behind it. All of the guest rooms, efficiencies really, are decorated with light-wood furnishings and sea-toned fabrics. Each has a sleeping area, kitchenette, sitting area with sofa bed, and private balcony. If a view is important, ask specifically for it.

507 Atlantic Ave. (at Fifth St. and the oceanfront; P.O. Box 1030), Ocean City, MD 21842. © **800/282-5155** or 410/289-5155. Fax 410/641-3815. www.comfortinnboardwalk.com. 84 units. $54–$309 double. Children under 12 stay free in parent's room. Rates include continental breakfast. AE, DC, DISC, MC, V. Free parking. Closed after Thanksgiving through mid-Feb. **Amenities:** Restaurant; outdoor and indoor pools; deck facing boardwalk. *In room:* A/C, TV, kitchenette, hair dryer.

Commander Hotel   Set right in the center of the boardwalk, this successor to one of O.C.'s oldest hotels offers lots of conveniences and comforts. A variety of accommodations—from efficiencies to suites—fits a variety of guests. The Promenade Suites lead right out onto the second-story deck and pool, while the corner Captain's Suites offer a bit more room, with lots of windows overlooking the boardwalk and beach. Cabana Suites, though a good size, overlook Baltimore Avenue.

1401 Atlantic Ave., Ocean City, MD 21842. © **888/289-6166** or 410/289-6166. www.commanderhotel.com. 110 units. $61–$243 double. Weekly rates available. Children under 5 stay free with 2 parents. MC, V. Free parking. Closed Nov to mid-Mar. **Amenities:** Restaurant; lounge; outdoor and indoor pools; oceanfront sun deck. *In room:* A/C, TV, dataport, coffeemaker, fridge, microwave (in most rooms), hair dryer, safe.

Grand Hotel   First, it's really not "grand"—more like big and comfortable. Overlooking a wide swath of beach, the Grand is a good family choice. It's right on the boardwalk, but at the quiet north end. It's got standard rooms, plus a variety of eateries and shops at the boardwalk level. If you're coming without the kids, you might prefer the 12th-floor whirlpool rooms or the bay-view suites.

2100 Baltimore Ave., Ocean City, MD 21842. © **800/447-6779** or 410/289-6191. Fax 410/289-7591. www.grand hoteloceancity.com. 251 units. $29–$299 double. AE, DC, DISC, MC, V. Free parking. **Amenities:** Restaurant; lounge; pool bar; indoor and outdoor pools w/sun deck; sauna; salon; game room. *In room:* A/C, TV, dataport, fridge, microwave, coffeemaker, hair dryer, safe.

Holiday Inn Oceanfront   Right in the center of O.C., directly on the beach, this eight-story hotel is convenient to everything. Its resort amenities make it a good choice for a weekend or a week. There are hammocks by the pool, a newly resurfaced tennis court, and a 10-person Jacuzzi. Each long, narrow room has a balcony and sitting area on one side, sleeping area in the middle, and kitchenette by the door. Units on the top three floors have fireplaces (electric, so romantic—but not hot—in summertime). Room no. 813 has views of both ocean and bay.

6600 Coastal Hwy. (oceanfront at 67th St.), Ocean City, MD 21842. © **800/837-3588** or 410/524-1600. Fax 410/ 524-1135. www.holidayinnoceanfront.com. 216 units. $54–$314 double. Weekly rates available. AE, DC, DISC, MC, V. Free parking. **Amenities:** Restaurant; poolside bar and grill; outdoor and indoor pools; tennis court; health club; Jacuzzi; sauna; children's programs in summer; game room; business center. *In room:* A/C, TV/VCR w/movies, dataport, kitchenette, fridge, coffeemaker, hair dryer, iron (upon request).

Howard Johnson Oceanfront Plaza Hotel   A moderately priced choice on the boardwalk at 12th Street, this modern seven-story hotel has a welcoming lobby with a fireplace and a fruit basket. Guest rooms are decorated with light woods, colorful furnishings, and landscape prints. Each room has a balcony with full or partial ocean views. Deluxe oceanfront units have sleeper sofas.

1109 Atlantic Ave., Ocean City, MD 21842. © **800/926-1122** or 410/289-7251. Fax 410/289-4901. www.hjocean frontplaza.com. 90 units. $44–$279 double. Children under 18 stay free in parent's room. AE, DC, DISC, MC, V. Free parking. **Amenities:** Restaurant; bar; indoor and outdoor pools; Jacuzzi; gift shop; nearby beach-chair, umbrella, and bike rentals. *In room:* A/C, fridge, microwave, coffeemaker, hair dryer, safe.

MODERATE/INEXPENSIVE

Comfort Inn Gold Coast   For value and great location, this bayside hotel is a good choice. Set back from the highway, its bayside rooms have a lovely view—and the higher rates to prove it. Not every room has a view, but all are comfortable. The hotel's location, near the Gold Coast Mall, makes it even better for the shoppers among us. Restaurants and movie theaters are right next door, too.

11201 Coastal Hwy. (at 112th St.), Ocean City, MD 21842. ✆ **800/228-5150** or 410/524-3000. Fax 410/524-8255. www.comfortgoldcoast.com. 202 units. $39–$295 double. Children under 18 stay free in parent's room. AE, DISC, MC, V. Free parking. **Amenities:** Indoor pool; health club; Jacuzzi; children's play area; bay-view sun deck. *In room:* A/C, TV, high-speed Internet access, fridge, microwave, coffeemaker, hair dryer, iron.

Park Place Hotel   Owned by a longtime O.C. hotelier family, the Park Place is designed to meet vacationing families' every need. Built in 2000, the hotel has standard rooms with space enough for all that beach paraphernalia. All have kitchenettes and pullout sofas; oceanfront rooms have balconies; and bay-view rooms are a bit bigger. Bay-view king rooms have Jacuzzis as well.

Second and Third sts., Ocean City, MD 21842. ✆ **888/212-PARK** or 410/289-6440. Fax 410/289-3389. www.ocpark placehotel.com. 89 units. $49–$259 double. Weekly rates available. Children under 12 stay free in parent's room. AE, DC, DISC, MC, V. Free parking. Closed Dec–Jan but open New Year's Eve. **Amenities:** Outdoor bar and grill; pool w/sun deck; game room; DVD/VCR rental. *In room:* A/C, TV, fridge, microwave, coffeemaker, hair dryer, safe.

Phillips Beach Plaza Hotel   Victorian chandeliers, wrought-iron fixtures, and a fireplace give this old-time hotel's lobby more elegance than you'd expect to find in O.C. But upstairs, the guest rooms are pretty standard. Still, a number of features make this place worth a second look: a variety of single rooms, 27 one- to three-bedroom apartments (some with full kitchens), a big porch with rocking chairs overlooking the boardwalk and ocean, and Phillips by the Sea restaurant (see "Where to Dine," below). If you want to stay at the beach for a week but avoid weekend traffic, you can book a week here from weekday to weekday.

1301 Atlantic Ave. (between 13th and 14th sts.), Ocean City, MD 21842. ✆ **800/492-5834** or 410/289-9121. Fax 410/289-3041. www.phillipsbeachplaza.com. 96 units. $50–$189 double; $65–$245 apt. Weekly rates available. 2-night minimum stay required on weekends. AE, DC, DISC, MC, V. Free parking. Open weekends only Nov–Dec. Closed Jan–Mar. **Amenities:** Restaurant; ice-cream parlor; piano bar; umbrella and bike rentals nearby. *In room:* A/C, TV, hair dryer (upon request), iron (upon request).

Talbot Inn *Value*   The Talbot Inn is a great spot for fishermen and those who love the boardwalk. It's an easy walk to the Talbot Street Pier (where you can find a fishing boat or take a ride on the *O.C. Rocket*), to the inlet and its rides, shops, and ice-cream stands, and to the widest part of the beach. The inn has two three-story buildings, one bayfront and the other without a view. Units range from efficiencies to two-bedroom apartments. Rooms without a view are a few feet wider and can sleep up to six. Apartments have enclosed balconies. Though this is an older property, it's well maintained and has that fantastic location. **M. R. Ducks,** the bar and clothing shop, is next door.

Talbot St., on the bay (P.O. Box 548), Ocean City, MD 21842. ✆ **800/659-7703** or 410/289-9125. Fax 410/289-6792. www.talbotstreetpier.com. 36 units. $32–$139 double. Weekly rates available. 3- or 4-night minimum stay required on summer weekends and holidays. DISC, MC, V. Free parking. **Amenities:** Restaurant; bar (M. R. Ducks); marina. *In room:* A/C, TV, kitchenette, fridge, microwave.

WHERE TO DINE

As you might expect, seafood is a favorite here. For the most part, a casual atmosphere prevails—although for the better restaurants, it's always wise to make reservations and check on the dress code. In summer, restaurants are rarely closed: Some open as early as 5am and continue serving until 10 or 11pm. Most places have full bar facilities. Just to be safe, get a copy of the Ocean City Convention and Visitors Bureau's guide to accommodations and restaurants; it gives descriptions, hours, and price guidelines for at least 50 of the best eateries.

EXPENSIVE

Fager's Island ☞ AMERICAN/PACIFIC RIM   Fager's Island plays up its bayfront location, with lots of decks, a gazebo, a pavilion, and a pier. The "1812 Overture" celebrates every sunset—it's a tradition here. The menu has an Asian flair, with dishes like wok crispy salmon, but you can also get a strip steak, crab cakes, burger, quesadilla, or sandwich. The pricey kids' menu lists beef tenderloin and crab cakes along with chicken tenders. You might want to end your meal with a fancy coffee drink—they range from Italian to Girl Scout cookie. Stay late and enjoy live entertainment at the bar. Early-bird specials are offered before 6pm.

201 60th St. (on the bay). ☎ 888/371-5400 or 410/524-5500. www.fagers.com. Reservations recommended for dinner. Main courses $6–$13 lunch, $19–$36 dinner. AE, DC, DISC, MC, V. Daily 11am–2am.

Galaxy 66 Bar & Grille INTERNATIONAL   Although it can't claim ocean or bay views, this purple-and-gold restaurant offers a sleek interior and an innovative menu that mixes familiar and exotic flavors. The menu, which changes weekly, recently included filet mignon with bleu-cheese hash and seared scallops with cranberry relish and port-wine reduction. Lunchtime features sandwiches, soups, and salads.

6601 Coastal Hwy. ☎ 410/723-6762, www.galaxy66barandgrille.com. Reservations recommended for dinner. Main courses $8–$13 lunch, $23–$36 dinner. AE, DC, DISC, MC, V. Daily 11:30am–4pm and 5–10pm. Oct–Apr dining room closes at 9pm weekdays, plus all day Mon.

Plantation House Bar & Grill ☞☞ SOUTHERN/REGIONAL   Crab houses and watering holes have been springing up in West Ocean City for a number of years. Now there's a bit of Southern elegance on Route 50 west of the bridge. Opened in 2005, this restaurant is big and bright, with windows overlooking a little pond. Start with the specialty, sweet and peppery blue-crab corn chowder, and then move on to a fresh tomato salad featuring slices of the local best. Then choose beef, pasta, or one of the six shrimp dishes. Lunch means lots of salads and sandwiches, including a burger topped with crab imperial.

12308 Ocean Gateway (Rte. 50), West Ocean City. ☎ 410/213-7786. Reservations recommended. Main courses $5.50–$21 lunch, $16–$40 dinner. AE, DC, DISC, MC, V. Daily 11:30am–9:30pm.

MODERATE

Captain Bill Bunting's Angler AMERICAN   This spacious restaurant, on the marina of Ocean City, has been a favorite since 1938. It features an air-conditioned dining room with rustic and nautical decor, plus a deck overlooking the bay—an ideal spot to see the fishermen bringing back their bounty. The extensive menu revolves around daily fresh-fish specials, prepared in one of seven ways, plus steaks and seafood platters. Dinner prices include a free ocean cruise at 7 or 9pm. Lunch focuses on raw-bar selections, fish sandwiches, salads, and burgers. *Note:* For early risers, doors open at 6am for breakfast.

Talbot St., on the bay. © 410/289-7424. Reservations recommended for dinner. Main courses $6–$13 lunch, $14–$29 dinner. AE, DISC, MC, V. May–Oct daily 6am–11pm. Bar open until 2am Sat–Sun. Closed Nov–Apr.

Harrison's Harbor Watch SEAFOOD   The vista from the top floor of this imposing restaurant makes the inevitable wait worthwhile. This place is busy, quite noisy, and the waitstaff can be a bit overwhelmed. But besides the view of the inlet and Assateague Island, there's lots of fresh seafood to choose from: stuffed shrimp, fresh fish, and crab cakes (made according to a Chesapeake Bay recipe that suits traditionalists to a T). The seafood fettuccine combines pasta with shrimp, scallops, clams, and crabmeat. At lunch, the raw bar now features oysters from around the country.

South end of boardwalk, overlooking the inlet. © 410/289-5121. Reservations recommended. Main courses $13–$23; raw bar $5.95–$12. AE, DC, DISC, MC, V. Main dining room Apr–Oct daily 5–10pm (closed Nov–Mar). Raw bar daily 11:30am–10pm.

Macky's Bayside Bar & Grill AMERICAN/REGIONAL   Watch the sun set (as Kate Smith sings "God Bless America") while you sit on the beach with a crab cake or steak. This place is like an old beach house with a great kitchen. Relax and enjoy a variety of seafood and Eastern Shore favorites—the fresh fish is always popular, as are the Angus beef dishes. The lunch menu includes sandwiches and salads.

54th St. (on the bay). © 410/723-5565. www.mackys.com. Reservations not accepted. Main courses $4.25–$11 lunch, $14–$26 dinner. AE, DC, DISC, MC, V. Daily 11am–2am (dinner served until 10pm; light fare until 1am). Closed mid-Oct to Mar.

Phillips Seafood Restaurants SEAFOOD   The Phillips family dynasty began with a small crab house at 21st Street and Philadelphia Avenue. Four decades later, that first restaurant now takes over the whole block. When it was the only location, families lined up around the block for a table. Now that Phillips has two more restaurants in O.C., the lines are a little shorter—except at around 6pm on a weekend. Carryout is available at the 21st Street and 141st Street locations—a good alternative if there's a long wait.

Phillips Crabhouse, at 21st Street, is casual: white paper on the tables and a huge menu that emphasizes crabs. The crab bisque should not be missed. The seafood buffet is also popular. Most of the tables here are nice enough, unless you get stuck in the narrow dining room behind the carryout. The food's the same, but the ambience isn't.

Phillips by the Sea ⊛⊛, a smaller operation at the Beach Plaza Hotel, drips with Victorian ambience. It offers the same crab cakes, crab imperial, and shrimp that Phillips fans love. The dining room can be noisy; when the weather is agreeable, the front porch is a better spot. A breakfast buffet and traditional breakfast are offered every morning.

Phillips Seafood House, at 141st and Coastal Highway, is situated along O.C.'s condo strip. It's designed to resemble the original and offers the same menu. The lines at dinnertime look like the original's, too.

Phillips Crabhouse, 2004 Philadelphia Ave. (at 21st St.). © 410/289-6821. www.phillipsoc.com. Reservations not accepted. Main courses $5.95–$11 lunch, $9.95–$28 dinner. AE, DISC, MC, V. Apr–Oct daily noon–10pm. Closed Nov to Palm Sunday weekend. **Phillips by the Sea,** 1301 Atlantic Ave., on the boardwalk. © 800/492-5834 or 410/289-9121. Reservations recommended for dinner. Main courses $5.95–$11 lunch, $9.95–$28 dinner. AE, DISC, MC, V. Daily 8am–1pm and 5–10pm. Closed Jan–Feb. **Phillips Seafood House,** 14101 Coastal Hwy. © 800/799-2722 or 410/250-1200. Reservations not accepted. Main courses $5.95–$11 lunch, $9.95–$28 dinner. AE, DISC, MC, V. Mon–Fri 5–9:30 or 10pm; Sat–Sun 4–9:30 or 10pm (closing time depends on season). Call for off-season hours. Closed Dec–Jan.

INEXPENSIVE

Dough Roller PIZZA   If you want pizza or a strawberry daiquiri, come to this popular local chain, with five locations in Ocean City. The restaurants are decorated with a Victorian theme, including carousel horses, but the main attraction is the terrific pizza. Also on the menu are burgers, sandwiches, subs, New England grinders, and entrees such as fettuccine Alfredo and lasagna. Pancakes are served all day.

Two boardwalk locations: S. Division St. (✆ **410/289-3501**) and Third St. (✆ **410/289-2599**). Three Coastal Hwy. locations: at 41st St. (✆ **410/524-9254**), 70th St. (✆ **410/524-7981**), and 125th St. (✆ **410/250-5664**). Reservations not necessary. Main courses $4.50–$24. AE, MC, V. Summer daily 7am–midnight; call for winter hours, which are much more limited (1 location is always open).

Dumser's *Kids* AMERICAN/ICE CREAM   An O.C. favorite since 1939, this eatery began as an ice-cream parlor but is now popular as a restaurant. The atmosphere is homey, with comfort foods like fried chicken, roast turkey, and crab cakes. Lunch choices include sandwiches, salads, subs, and soups. There's a kids' menu; no liquor is served. Save room for dessert: Dumser's is still an ice-cream parlor at heart, with more than 20 sundaes. A second location with a more limited menu, **Dumser's Drive-In,** 49th Street and Coastal Highway (✆ **410/524-1588**), is also open year-round. Both are good options for families. If you want just ice cream, there are three boardwalk locations.

12305 Coastal Hwy. ✆ **410/250-5543**. Reservations not accepted. Main courses $3.50–$8.50 lunch, $6.95–$17 at dinner, $3–$11 breakfast. MC, V. Mid-June to Labor Day daily 7am–midnight; Sept to early June daily 7am–9pm.

Fractured Prune *Finds* DONUTS/LUNCH   If you like donuts, don't come to O.C. without stopping here. In each shop, the outrageous donuts are made to order and dipped in one of a variety of glazes, toppings, and sugars. You can mix the cherry glaze with the chocolate chips, or top chocolate glaze with peanuts or coconut. Prune fans will be happy to hear that new outlets are opening in West Ocean City (on Rte. 611), Bethany, and Rehoboth.

Two locations: 28th St. and Coastal Hwy. (✆ **410/289-4131**), and 127th St. and Coastal Hwy. ✆ **410/250-4400**. www.fracturedprune.com. Reservations not accepted. Donuts $6.95 a dozen. No credit cards. Summer daily 6:30am–1pm; off season (Oct–Apr) 7am–noon at 127th St. location only.

WHAT TO SEE & DO

A fascinating self-guided walking-tour brochure of Ocean City's historic places is available at the visitor center at 40th Street.

Wheels of Yesterday   Car enthusiasts will enjoy strolling through the rows and rows of classic cars, plus a few kiddie cars and even a replica of a 1950s service station. Curator Jack Jarvis will lead you through the exhibits, most of which are part of the private collection of Granville D. Trimper, owner of many of the rides and amusements on the boardwalk. Favorites include a 1928 seven-passenger Lincoln, Jack Benny's Overland, cars used in the movies *Hoosiers* and *Tuck Everlasting,* and a shiny gold 1960 Studebaker Hawk.

12708 Ocean Gateway (Rte. 50). ✆ **410/213-7329**. Admission $4 adults, $2 children 12 and under. June–Sept Mon–Sat 9am–9pm, Sun 9am–5pm; Oct–May daily 9am–5pm. Take the Rte. 50 bridge out of Ocean City. The museum is on the left, across from the shopping outlets.

ESPECIALLY FOR KIDS

Ocean City, which claims to be the number-one family resort on the East Coast, is home to several amusement parks and child-oriented activities. Before you head for

Kids Minigolf Mania

Ocean City may have the highest concentration of minigolf courses of any barrier island on earth. Here's a rundown of the best on the island:

Jungle Golf, Jolly Roger Park, 30th Street and Coastal Highway (© 410/289-3477). Plastic lions and a rhino look on as you negotiate 18 holes that wrap around and climb the sides of a series of man-made waterfalls. Although this course has 1 lame hole early on—in essence a flat, straight 10-foot putt—most are fun. A few challenging holes on the back 9 ensure that you'll end your round with a thrill. Open Memorial Day to Labor Day.

Lost Galaxy Golf, 33rd Street and Coastal Highway (© 410/524-4FUN). Here you can play golf in outer space. Sure, the special effects are cheesy, and the water is the oddest color, but you've got to love the spaceships, aliens, and fun maze of holes. This is one of the few courses open year-round.

Old Pro Undersea Adventure Golf, 68th Street and Coastal Highway (© 410/524-2645; www.oldprogolf.com). There are seven Old Pro courses at four locations in O.C. All are good, but this is the best. It's entirely enclosed in a hangar-like barn, making it one of the most fun O.C. places to be when it's raining. The props include a submarine and a hanging plaster killer whale. If you *really* like miniature golf, get the Old Pro Pass for $12, which lets you play every Old Pro course as much as you'd like until 5pm. Open year-round.

Professor Hakker's Lost Treasure Golf, 139th Street and Coastal Highway (© 410/250-5678). You can't miss this place: It's got an airplane in the roof. There are two courses: Gold and Diamond. The decor is reminiscent of the *Indiana Jones* movies, with water traps, caves, and even a bridge. The holes are fairly easy, but the theme is what makes this one fun. Closed December through March.

the attractions, look for coupons for everything from miniature golf to go-carts, usually available at the visitor center at 40th Street.

Frontier Town ★ Kids   Frontier Town has been stuck in time for more than 40 years—it was a winner in 1959 and still is today. The cowboys and outlaws try hard to make you think you're in the Old West, with train rides, pony rides, cancan shows, bank holdups, and gunfights. In a separate park (with separate admission), there's a water park and miniature golf. Campsites on the Sinepuxent Bay are also available from April to October.

Rte. 611, 4 miles south of Rte. 50. Old West © 410/289-7877. Water park © 410/641-0693. www.frontiertown. com. Combination admission for both parks $18 children 11 and over; $15 children 4–10. Old West $12 children 11 and over; $10 children 4–10. Water park and miniature golf $12 children 11 and over; $9 children 4–10. Unlimited all-day golf $4 children 11 and over; $2 children 4–10. Night golf $4 children 11 and over; $2 children 4–10. Mid-June to Labor Day daily 10am–6pm (miniature golf until 10pm). Free parking. Take Rte. 50 west and turn left on Rte. 611 toward Assateague.

Jolly Roger   This park is home to Speedworld (the largest go-cart racing complex of its kind in the U.S.), two miniature-golf courses, a water park, and more than 30 rides and other attractions. Note that the go-cart tracks have minimum height requirements.

30th St. and Coastal Hwy. ℂ **410/289-3477**. www.jollyrogerpark.com. Water park $33. Passport entrance fees $22–$100. Daily Memorial Day to Labor Day: rides noon–midnight; Speedworld 2pm–midnight; golf 9am–5pm; water park 10am–8pm. Speedworld and golf also open Apr to Memorial Day, Sept, and weekends in Oct. Closed Nov–Mar. Free parking.

Ocean City Pier Rides   The rides here appeal mostly to older kids and teens who like centrifugal force, but the Ferris wheel is a highlight for all ages. Rising high above almost everything else in old Ocean City, it offers spectacular views of the ocean, the beach, and the boardwalk. It's a wonderful place to be at sunset. The rest of the rides seem to change every season, although the Venetian double-decker carousel is always in its place.

On the inlet in downtown Ocean City. ℂ **410/289-3031**. Rides about $2 or so each. Easter to late Sept Sat–Sun 11am–midnight; summer daily noon–midnight.

Trimper's Rides & Amusement Park   Established in 1887, this is the granddaddy of O.C. amusement areas. It has over 100 indoor and outdoor rides, including a water flume and a fanciful 1902 merry-go-round with hand-carved animals. The indoor rides are open year-round, but only on weekends in cooler months.

Boardwalk near the inlet, between S. Division and S. First sts. ℂ **410/289-8617**. www.beach-net.com/trimpers. Most rides average $1.50. A $14 wristband allows unlimited rides Sat–Sun noon–6pm and Mon–Fri 1–6pm. May–Sept daily noon or 1pm–midnight; Mar–Apr and Oct–Nov Sat–Sun noon to closing (hours vary in off season).

GOLF

Ocean City promotes itself as a major golfing destination; many courses offer vacation packages with O.C. hotels. The courses listed below welcome visitors and can be contacted directly or through the **Ocean City Golf Getaway Association,** 9935 Stephen Decatur Hwy. (ℂ **800/4-OC-GOLF;** www.oceancitygolf.com).

All courses are open year-round from dawn to dusk. Most courses in the area use a multitiered system for greens fees, which means they vary from morning to afternoon to evening. However, fees generally range from $40 to $96, with cheaper rates in the off season and on summer afternoons. Fall rates are usually the highest; if you're a January golfer, you'll find bargains then. *Tip:* Consider starting a round at about 4pm; the rates don't usually increase in the early evenings, and the temperatures have started to drop.

Bay Club   Only 8 miles from the boardwalk, the Bay Club offers two 18-hole par-72 championship courses. Features include a clubhouse, driving range, practice green, club rentals, and lessons.

9122 Libertytown Rd., Berlin. ℂ **800/BAY-CLUB** or 410/641-4081. www.thebayclub.com.

Beach Club Golf Links   A reserved tee time is recommended at this semiprivate club, which has two 18-hole par-72 championship courses. It has a clubhouse, pro shop, club rentals, driving range, and putting green.

9715 Deer Park Dr., Berlin. ℂ **800/435-9223** or 410/641-GOLF. www.beachclubgolflinks.com.

Eagle's Landing Golf Course   The scenery here may distract you from your game. This public 18-hole course also offers club rentals, lessons, pro shop, practice facilities, and clubhouse restaurant. Reservations are recommended.

12367 Eagle's Nest Rd., Berlin. ℂ **800/283-3846** or 410/213-7277. www.eagleslandinggolf.com.

Ocean City Golf Club   Founded in 1959, this club has two USGA-rated 18-hole championship courses, a seaside par-73, and a bayside par-72. Facilities include a clubhouse with restaurant, bar, and pro shop.

11401 Country Club Dr., Berlin. ℂ **800/442-3570** or 410/641-1779. www.oceancitygolf.com.

Pine Shore Golf   This is a public 18-hole mid-length course.

8219 Stephen Decatur Hwy. (Rte. 611), Berlin. (✆ **877/446-5398** or 410/641-5100. www.pineshoregolf.com.

River Run   A Gary Player 18-hole signature course, the par-71 River Run is a favorite in West O.C. Facilities include carts, pro shop, locker room, beverage carts, PGA golf pros, driving range, and putting greens. Reserving a tee time is recommended.

11605 Masters Lane, Berlin. (✆ **800/733-RRUN** or 410/641-7200. www.riverrungolf.com.

Rum Pointe Seaside Golf Links   This 18-hole par-72 championship course, designed by the father-son team of P. B. and Pete Dye, has 17 of its 18 holes overlooking Sinepuxent Bay and nearby Assateague Island. Facilities include a pro shop, driving range and practice facilities, PGA pro, clubhouse with full-service restaurant, and beverage cart. Reserving a tee time is recommended.

7000 Rum Pointe Lane, Berlin. (✆ **888/809-4653** or 410/629-1414. www.rumpointe.com.

OTHER OUTDOOR ACTIVITIES

BIKING   An early-morning ride down the boardwalk is traditional for lots of families. Boardwalk biking is allowed between 5 and 10am in summer, and anytime in the off season. Cyclists on Coastal Highway share a lane with the buses. A headlight and rear reflector are required on all bikes on the road after dark. Rental rates vary, but expect to pay $4 to $6 an hour for a two-wheeler, $12 an hour for a tandem, and $8 for "funcycles" (recumbent tricycles). Two good sources are **Continental Cycle,** 73rd Street and Coastal Highway (✆ **410/524-1313**), and **Mike's Bikes,** 10 N. Division St. (✆ **410/289-5404**).

COAST CRUISES   For sightseeing at top speed and splash, *Sea Rocket,* Dorchester Street at the bay (✆ **410/289-5887**), and the *O.C. Rocket,* Talbot Street Pier (✆ **410/289-3500**), offer a great diversion from the beach. Both are 70-foot, 150-passenger open-top speedboats zooming along the waters of Ocean City and beside Assateague Island. The trip lasts about 50 minutes; it costs $12 to $15 for adults, $5 to $8 for children 7 to 10. Departures run every hour or two from late May to September. *Tip:* People in the very back tend to get very wet (people in the front get less wet, and those in the middle get the least wet). Save this ride for a warm day, when a little sea spray is a welcome thing.

   Discovery Cruises (✆ **410/289-2700**) offers nature cruises to Assateague Island three or four times a day. These 90-minute tours, which leave from the pier at First Street and the Bay, include 30 minutes on the island, where you can scoop up aquatic life with a handnet. The cost is $8 to $12; everybody pays an additional $1 landing fee. Reservations are suggested.

FISHING   Since Ocean City is surrounded by the waters of the Atlantic and four different bays, fishing boats abound. Departures usually run from April to October. Generally, rates range from $25 (for children) to $50 (for adults) for longer headboat fishing trips. Trips leave as early as 5am, so call for departure times. Rod rentals are typically available.

   Most boats set sail from one of O.C.'s two main fishing marinas: the **Ocean City Fishing Center,** in West Ocean City (✆ **800/322-3065** or 410/213-1121; www.ocfishing.com), and the **Bahia Marina,** on the bay at 22nd Street (✆ **410/289-7438;** www.bahiamarina.com). Call either for information on the kinds of boats available, as well as their rates and departure times. Another reliable headboat is the *Angler*

(© 410/289-7424), which operates from the Talbot Street Pier on the bay, just south of the Route 50 bridge.

HORSE RACING *Kids*   Four miles west of Ocean City, **Ocean Downs,** 10218 Racetrack Rd. (Rte. 589), just off Route 50, in Berlin (© **410/641-0600;** www.ocean downs.com), features up to 10 harness races Wednesday through Sunday nights in July and August. Live racing runs from 7:25 to about 11pm. Simulcast TV racing from other tracks begins year-round daily around noon. Grandstand admission and parking are free. Clubhouse admission is extra; rates are subject to change. The race-track is very kid-friendly: Winning trotters are led to the winner's circle, where chil-dren gather around and get a close look. A parade of horses starts each evening's races, with the lead horse getting close enough for the kids to pet. Many of the horses and their drivers are local, too. It's a cheap diversion from the bustle and expense of Ocean City (until you start betting).

SURF FISHING   Surf fishing is permitted on all public beaches. However, between 9am and 6pm you cannot fish within 150 feet of swimmers or of anyone on the beach, which, in peak season, can be impossible. **Public fishing piers** are at Inlet Park (this one charges a tiny fee), as well as on the bay side at the Third Street Pier, Ninth Street Pier (which is lighted), and Northside Park (at 125th St.). Fishing supplies and tackle can be found at **Bahia Marina,** on the bay at 22nd Street (© **410/289-7438**), and at **Captain Mac's Bait & Tackle** (© **410/213-0090**).

SURFING   Lessons are offered daily at the 35th Street Beach, at 8:30am and 5:30pm. Wet suits and boards are provided. Register at **K-Coast Surfshop,** on 35th Street (© **410/732-3330**), or on 78th Street (© **410/524-8500**).

WATERSPORTS   From April through October, O.C. is a hotbed of sailing, para-sailing, windsurfing, jet-skiing, power-boating, water-skiing, and more. For informa-tion on jet skis, contact **Bay Sports,** on the bay between 21st and 22nd streets (© **410/ 289-2144**). For skiff and pontoon-boat rentals, try **Bahia Marina,** on the bay at 22nd Street (© **410/289-7438**), or **OC Parasail,** Talbot Street Pier, near the inlet and at 54th Street and the bay (© **410/723-1464**). Check the visitor center for brochures with up-to-date information.

SHOPPING

The shopping in Ocean City may not be high class, but there's a lot of it. The board-walk, the outlet center, dozens of strip malls along Coastal Highway, and small-town antiques in nearby Berlin are all happy to take visitors' money.

Fun Fact **Duck—it's a T-shirt!**

The unofficial uniform of O.C. is a shirt from **M. R. Ducks** (© **800/673-8257;** www.mrducks.com). They're available at various locations, including the Talbot Street Pier (Talbot St. and the bay), on Somerset Street, on Fifth Street, and down Coastal Highway at 140th Street. The "M. R." does not stand for "Mis-ter," but for the Eastern Shore way of speaking. Two duck hunters are talking: "M R ducks." "M R not." "O S A R. C M Wangs?" "L I B—M R ducks." (Transla-tion: Them are ducks. Them are not. Oh, yes they are. See them wings? Well, I'll be. Them are ducks.)

If you enter town from the Route 50 Bridge, you can't miss the **Ocean City Factory Outlets** (www.ocfactoryoutlets.com), a half-mile from the bridge, on the mainland at the intersection of Golf Course Road. The 41 brand-name outlets include Ann Taylor, Bass, Levi's, Jos. A. Bank, OshKosh, and Reebok. Parking is free and plentiful; a daily shuttle also stops at a variety of O.C. hotels from late July to mid-September (check the website for a schedule). The complex is open Sunday through Thursday from 10am to 6pm (until at least 8pm June–Aug), and Friday and Saturday from 10am to 9pm.

The **Tanger Outlet Centers,** in Rehoboth Beach, has a much bigger selection—and no sales tax is charged in Delaware. If you're a serious shopper, you may want to take the short trip north. See p. 255 for details.

Perhaps the most popular and populated shopping destination in O.C. is the boardwalk—27 blocks of souvenirs, candy, restaurants, snack shacks, and, of course, T-shirts. You'll find much of the same merchandise in all the souvenir shops, but there are a couple places worth visiting. **Ocean Gallery World Center,** at Second Street (© 410/289-5300), is a standout, with its mosaic-like facade of art from around the world. Its three stories are full of art posters, prints, and original oil paintings, all for sale at closeout prices. The **Kite Loft,** at Fifth Street (© 410/289-7855), has a large selection of kites (from simple to really cool), flags, windsocks, and toys. You may even see a pig fly. There's another location on 131st Street.

For something sweet, you can't miss **Candy Kitchen,** which specializes in fudge and saltwater taffy; it has numerous locations. But if you're down at the inlet end, stop in **Wockenfuss Candy** ⭐⭐, First Street and the boardwalk (© 410/289-5054), for fine chocolates. The Baltimore-based candy shop has a new outlet on Seventh Street and the boardwalk as well.

OCEAN CITY AFTER DARK

From people-watching on the boardwalk to a game of miniature golf to cocktails at the hundreds of beach and bayside bars, high-season Ocean City has almost as much nightlife as it has sand. There's something for everybody—certainly lots of places for singles to meet, as well as a few spots just to relax with a beer. Many are open on weekends year-round—and you can count on a party for New Year's Eve and St. Patrick's Day. Below are a few fun places to try.

BJ's on the Water   BJ's has live entertainment on Wednesdays and weekends in high season, plus a sports bar, raw bar, and full menu. 75th St., on the bay. © 410/524-7575. www.bjsonthewater.com.

Fager's Island   Fager's Island's bar is a popular watering hole for the well-heeled and over-30 set. There's a summer deck party on Mondays and live music most nights in high season. 60th St., on the bay. © 410/524-5500. www.fagers.com.

Greene Turtle   DJs spin the tunes most nights of the week, with the occasional live band as well. There's a second location on Route 611 in west Ocean City (© 410/723-2120). 116th St. and Coastal Hwy. © 410/723-2120. www.greeneturtle.com.

Party Block   Three clubs in 1 block—the Paddock, Big Kahuna's, and Rush—make this one of *the* places for the college-age crowd and 20-somethings to meet and dance for one cover. 17th St. and Coastal Hwy. © 410/289-6331. www.partyblock.com.

Seacrets, Jamaica   Seacrets is a Caribbean-themed mega beach bar and grill, decorated with palm trees, dangling lights, and sand (leave the high heels in your room).

At the large, covered dance area, crowds of young and old are treated to live reggae or party music. Seacrets also serves light fare, but it's best to come very early if you want to eat. Even kids are welcome early; they'll enjoy the theme-park decor. The view of Isle of Wight Bay makes this a great place to watch the sunset. *Tip:* Much of Seacrets is outside, so it might not be the best choice if rain is in the forecast. 49th St., on the bay. *©* **410/524-4900.** www.seacrets.com. Cover varies; usually $3 or more.

JUST DOWN THE ROAD IN SALISBURY

Just a few minutes away is the small shore town of Salisbury, which hosts a museum and baseball team and is just a short drive or bus ride from O.C.

Delmarva Shorebirds   The Class A South Atlantic League affiliate of the Baltimore Orioles were league champs in 1997 and 2000.

Arthur W. Perdue Stadium, Hobbs Rd., Salisbury. *©* **410/219-3112** for tickets. www.theshorebirds.com. From O.C., take Rte. 50 west to Salisbury. Turn left on Hobbs Rd. after the Rte. 13 bypass.

Ward Museum of Wildfowl Art *★★*   Named for Lem and Steve Ward, brothers from Crisfield who turned decoy carving into an art, this museum houses the world's largest collection of contemporary and classic wildfowl art. It sits on the edge of Schumaker Pond in a small wildfowl sanctuary and habitat. The huge structure contains works by the Ward brothers and galleries tracing the history of decoy making, from Native American reed figures to the most recent winners of the Ward World Championship Carving Competition, held each spring in Ocean City. Highlights include a spectacular scene of a hawk attacking ducks in which the four birds are suspended in midair among a tangle of reeds. The museum has programs for children, workshops on carving for adults, and an exceptional gift shop.

909 Schumaker Dr., Salisbury. *©* **410/742-4988.** www.wardmuseum.org. Admission $7 adults, $5 seniors, $3 students; $17 per family. Mon–Sat 10am–5pm; Sun noon–5pm. Closed Easter, Thanksgiving, and Dec 25. From Rte. 50, turn onto Rte. 13 south; turn left onto College Ave., which will veer left and become Beaglin Park Dr.; the museum is on the right.

5 Assateague Island National Seashore *★★*

Imagine yourself here on a sunny afternoon—enjoying the surf, ocean breezes, and warm sand with your family, your friends, and a fat white-and-brown pony. The famous wild horses of Assateague are not shy. The band of bachelor ponies isn't, anyway. The majority of the horses try to stay away from people, but the rest hang around the parking lot, poke their noses in open car windows, pose for pictures along the highway, or stand completely still on the beach while the wind tosses their mane.

More than 2.5 million people come to Assateague Island each year to enjoy this pristine barrier island and those ponies. On the Maryland half of this 37-mile-long island, you can see some of the 150 ponies up close. They are harder to see on the Virginia side, where they tend to stay farther from the walking trails.

Heed the warnings and don't touch or feed the ponies. They are wild and can be unpredictable. They're pretty, but they do bite and kick.

Most visitors are drawn to the guarded beaches in front of the state park's store, refreshment stands, and restrooms, or the nearby campgrounds. But you don't have to walk too far to find deserted beaches, inhabited only by the ponies and a few sika deer and shorebirds, including the endangered piping plover.

Wherever you go, be aware of Assateague's second-most-famous inhabitants—mosquitoes. They really are as bad as the brochures, guidebooks, and park rangers tell you,

Assateague Island & Chincoteague N.W.R.

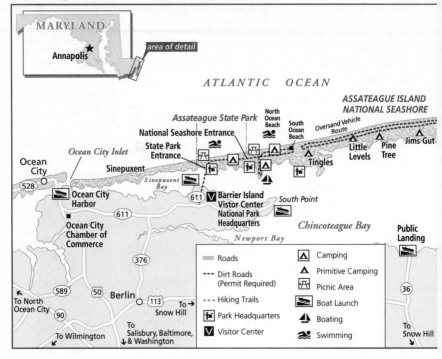

so come prepared with bug spray, citronella candles, and long sleeves. Compared to nearby Ocean City, Assateague is still wild and primitive—no hotels, restaurants, convenience stores, or gas stations. Just people. And ponies. And mosquitoes.

Assateague, in fact, is part state park and part national seashore. The descriptions of rules, regulations, and activities that follow indicate which authority has jurisdiction over which parts. For specific information on the Virginia side of the island, see *Frommer's Virginia.*

ACCESS   In Maryland, take Route 611 south from Route 50 west from Ocean City. In Virginia, take Virginia Route 175 west across Chincoteague Island. The roads do not connect in the middle.

VISITOR CENTERS   The National Park Service operates the **Barrier Island Visitor Center,** on Route 611 before you cross the bridge onto Assateague (© **410/641-1441**), and the **Campground Office,** inside the park (© **410/641-3030**). The Barrier Island Visitor Center is the place to go for brochures, exhibits, two aquariums, three videos on the island and its wildlife, and a gift shop. It's open daily from 9am to 5pm. Maryland also operates **Assateague State Park** (© **410/641-2918**), at the northern end of the island. It connects to the national park but has its own amenities, regulations, and fees.

FEES & REGULATIONS   **Assateague State Park** (© **410/641-2918**) charges an entry fee daily from Memorial Day to Labor Day: $3 per state resident, $4 per out-of-state resident. Admission is free in the off season.

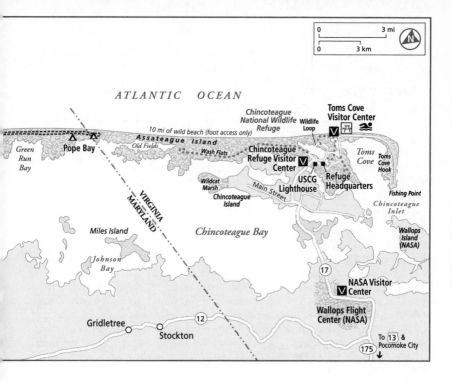

Entry to the **Assateague Island National Seashore** is $10 per car or $3 per person year-round, good for a week. Most national-park regulations apply. Permits are required for backcountry camping and off-road vehicle use. Pets are allowed only in the Maryland side of the park and must be leashed. And, of course, don't feed the ponies.

SEASONS Maryland's state park is open for day use from April 1 to December 1. Assateague Island National Seashore and Chincoteague National Wildlife Refuge are open year-round. There is no daily closing time on the Maryland side of the island, but only surf fishermen and campers who are staying in designated spots are allowed to stay overnight.

AVOIDING THE CROWDS & THE BUGS Weekends in summer are crowded. If you plan to camp, make reservations. The human population is not the biggest nuisance: Mosquitoes, biting flies, and ticks are abundant from April through September, and mosquitoes are especially a problem beginning at the end of July and following a heavy or steady rain. They're also much worse on the bay side of the island, so try to get an oceanside site if you're camping in the national park. Your best bet for avoiding the bugs is waiting until it gets cold enough to kill them all off. The good news is that sea breezes from the Atlantic keep the mosquitoes pretty much off the beach itself—so once you make it near the surf, you're safe.

RANGER PROGRAMS The National Park Service offers a wide variety of ranger-led programs on a weekly basis throughout the summer, including nature hikes, surf rescue demonstrations, canoe trips, campfire programs, and surf-fishing and shell-fishing

---

Tips **Don't Horse Around with the Ponies**

When you see the horses, remember they are wild. Do not be fooled by their gentle appearance and willingness to approach you and your car looking for handouts. The ponies are prone to unpredictable behavior—and they will bite and kick—so do not attempt to feed or pet them. Also, please drive carefully; at least one pony a year is hit and killed by a car.

---

demonstrations. For a complete rundown of these activities, pick up a copy of *Assateague Island Times,* a visitors' guide to activities and events; it's available at the visitor centers or through Assateague Island National Seashore, 7206 National Seashore Lane, Berlin (✆ **410/641-1441**).

SEEING THE PONIES

It may come as quite a surprise to learn that finding and viewing the famed wild horses takes almost no effort, especially on the Maryland side of the island, where the ponies have virtually free reign. In fact, you'll probably have to stop for a few begging ponies along the side of the road as you enter. (For your own safety, that of the ponies, and that of your car, roll up your windows and do not feed them.) If you're camping, you may hear a pack of horses stroll by your tent in the middle of the night or see the telltale signs in the morning. For a more picturesque setting, stop by the beach in the evening after the crowds have left; singly or in a band, the ponies roam the beach regularly. *Tip:* 2 miles of Bayberry Drive between the state and national park entrances offer visitors a free chance to take a drive and pull over to watch the ponies or deer. Bikers are welcome, too.

On the Virginia side, the ponies are less accessible; you can generally see them—often in the distance—along the paved road called the Wildlife Tour, in the fenced marshes south of Beach Road, and from the observation platform on the Woodland Trail.

The annual **Pony Penning and Auction** ⟨, a unique exercise in population control, is held on Chincoteague Island, a barrier island adjoining Assateague, on the last Wednesday and Thursday of July. The Chincoteague "cowboys" round up the Virginia herd on Wednesday, and thousands of spectators watch as the horses swim from Assateague to Chincoteague, where the foals are auctioned off the next day. Campsites and hotel rooms (only available on Chincoteague and the mainland) fill up fast, so reserve well in advance. If you're staying in Ocean City, get up before dawn and drive the 60 miles to Chincoteague. You'll make it in time for the pony swim and be back in O.C. for dinner.

Although it's exciting to see the ponies swim across the channel, be aware that thousands of people come to witness the annual event. You may only see the ponies as tiny dots as you wait along the shore shoulder-to-shoulder with hundreds of new friends. Traffic on the small island is almost too much to handle.

OUTDOOR ACTIVITIES

Unlike any other place on the ocean beaches in the area, **campfires** are allowed in the national park. They must be built below the high-tide mark. It's easiest to bring your own wood—sometimes you can find places to buy it right along Route 611. Fires must be extinguished until cold with water, not sand; never leave a fire unattended.

CANOEING, KAYAKING & BOATING   The only launch facility on the island is for canoes. It's at the end of Ferry Landing Road on the Maryland side. Larger boats can be launched for the day from the state park's marina just west of the bridge (across from the Barrier Island Visitor Center). The fee is $10.

Waters at the Maryland end of Chincoteague Bay are usually ideal for canoeing, though the tidal currents around Chincoteague Island are strong. The bay is generally shallow, so operators of larger boats should watch for sandbars. In summer, you can rent canoes from the concessionaire at the end of Bayside Drive. Four backcountry canoe-in campsites are located in the national park. Permits are required and can be obtained at the ranger station on the Maryland side or at the Toms Cove Visitor Center in Virginia.

Coastal Kayak (© 877/44-KAYAK or 302/539-7999; www.coastalkayak.com) offers eco-tours of the Assateague back bay. Tours cost about $40 for adults and $30 for children. (Get a coupon from the website.)

CRABBING, CLAMMING & FISHING   Pick up the *Shellfishing in Maryland* brochure at the visitor center for a map showing the best places to catch crabs, clams, and mussels. The best time to crab is late summer to early fall, in the morning or early evening. The most common approach is the string, bait, and net method: Attach a piece of bony chicken or a fish head to the string (chicken necks are the preferred bait), and cast out in shallow water. When you feel a tug, gently tow the line in. If there's a crab on the end, net it before you take it out of the water, then transfer it to a basket or other container and continue crabbing.

A single collapsible crab pot or trap may also be used, if it is attended at all times. You can purchase a crab pot at bait-and-tackle shops; they look like large chicken-wire boxes. Place bait in the center of the trap; drop it in clear, shallow water; and pull it up as soon as a crab walks in. All crabs must measure 5 inches point to point, and all egg-bearing females must be released. Limits are 1 bushel per person per day, or 2 bushels per boat per day. Crabbing is prohibited January through March.

Signing and raking are accepted methods for clamming. The mudflats at Virginia's Toms Cove are more suitable for signing. To sign for clams, walk along the mudflats at low tide and look for small keyhole openings, or "signs," indicating the presence of a clam. Then dig it out with a hand trowel or small digging tool. Raking can be done at any tide level, but you need a clamming rake, which has a basket to catch the clams. Drag the rake through the mud until the tines scrape a shell; then dig up the mud, shake it loose, and catch the clam in the basket. Clams must be 1 inch wide; the limit is 1 bushel per person per day.

Mussels and oysters are rare in the waters surrounding the island. Oysters are rarely found off the private, leased beds (and trespassing is prohibited). The park service asks that you take only what you will consume in mussels and oysters.

No saltwater license is required for surf fishing on the coast, though an after-hours permit is required on the Virginia end of the island. Fishing is prohibited on the guarded beaches and in the designated surf zones.

HIKING & BIKING   Conditions and trails for hiking and biking are better at the Virginia end of the island, but there are three .5-mile, self-guided hiking trails on the Maryland end of the national park: Life of the Marsh, Life of the Forest, and Life of the Dunes. All are short, and all require bug repellent. Cyclists can use the 3-mile paved bike path along Bayberry Drive and the Oceanside campground.

In Virginia, about 5 of the 15 miles of trails are paved for cycling. The Wildlife Tour is closed to car traffic until 3pm each day, so hikers and bikers can have it all to themselves. The Woodland Trail, which leads to a pony observation platform, is also paved. These are good, wooded paths, serene but exciting if you find the sought-after ponies.

OFF-ROAD VEHICLES   The vast majority of Assateague is not accessible by car; however, off-road (or over-sand) vehicle routes run most of the length of the island. Permits are required and are issued for a $70 annual fee. Call ℂ **410/641-3030** or see www.nps.gov/asis for information and ORV regulations.

CAMPING

Accommodations on the island are limited to a state-run campground and two campgrounds and several backcountry campsites run by the National Park Service.

The campground run by **Assateague State Park** (ℂ **410/641-2120,** ext. 22, or 888/432-2267 for state camping reservations) is open April 1 through October 31. It has 311 sites on the ocean side of the island, with bathhouses (with flush toilets and hot showers), a camp store, and a snack bar. Reservations are accepted up to a year in advance. Sites are on the ocean side of the island and cost $30 to $40 per night.

The **National Park Service** (ℂ **410/641-3030** for information, or 800/365-CAMP for reservations) operates oceanside and bayside campgrounds that are slightly more primitive than the state park facility. Both NPS campgrounds have chemical toilets, drinking water, and cold showers. There are also flush toilets and cold showers at the beach bathhouse. Reservations are recommended from April 15 to October 15—and are essential in warm weather. The rest of the year, campsites are available on a first-come, first-served basis. If possible, reserve a site at the oceanside campground for fewer pesky bugs. The cost is $20 per night from April 15 to October 15, $16 per night the rest of the year. There is no camping on the Virginia side.

In addition, the park has several backcountry or hike-in/paddle-in campsites along the Maryland end of the island. Each site has a chemical toilet and picnic table, but no drinking water. To use these sites, you must pick up a $5 backcountry permit from the ranger station during regular business hours.

If you don't mind staying off Assateague, Maryland's **Pocomoke River State Park** (ℂ **410/632-2566**), about a 45-minute drive from the Virginia or Maryland end of the island, is less crowded and more comfortable. It offers 230 improved campsites and 12 cabins (some air-conditioned) in two wooded sites along both sides of the Pocomoke River. **Shad Landing** offers a few extras: canoe, kayak, and boat rentals; a nature center; a swimming pool; and hiking and ORV trails. Its 201 campsites are available year-round: $30 for electric, $25 for non-electric, and $50 to $55 for the eight cabins. Across the river, **Milburn Landing** is smaller and open only from April to mid-December. Its 38 campsites cost $25 for electric, $20 for non-electric; the four cabins are $50 to $55. To make reservations for May through September, call ℂ **888/432-2267,** ext. 762, or visit www.dnr.maryland.gov. To get here from Assateague, take Route 611 off the island; then turn left and follow Route 376 until you reach the town of Berlin; from there, take Route 113 south. The park is 7 miles north of Pocomoke.

WHERE TO STAY NEARBY

Prefer a real bed? **Ocean City** is close, or you can try accommodations in nearby **Berlin,** about a 15-minute drive from Assateague (see above).

A SIDE TRIP TO BERLIN, MARYLAND

Barely 20 minutes away from the Ocean City boardwalk is the historic town of Berlin. Its quaint stores and antiques shops have long been a favorite side trip for vacationers in Ocean City. It also has two of the best lodgings in the area, an excellent restaurant, and a great little theater. These amenities and a location roughly equidistant from Assateague and Ocean City make Berlin a good choice for travelers looking to split their time between the islands.

To get to Berlin from Ocean City, take the Route 50 Bridge out of O.C. and follow Route 50; take a left on Route 113; from there, you'll hit Berlin in less than a mile.

WHERE TO STAY

Atlantic Hotel ✸✸   Richard Gere and Julia Roberts were here to film *Runaway Bride*. And *Tuck Everlasting* was filmed here, too. This three-story 1895 Victorian beauty has plenty of modern amenities along with old-fashioned charm. Guest rooms are furnished with mahogany pieces and local antiques. The larger units are quite comfy, while the smaller units can be a bit tight—but comfortable enough for the price. A new suite, with fireplace and DVD player, has been added to the restored 1896 Leake's Store, behind the hotel.

2 N. Main St., Berlin, MD 21811. ✆ **800/814-7672** or 410/641-3589. Fax 410/641-4928. www.atlantichotel.com. 17 units. July–Aug $95–$215 double; Apr–June and Sept–Oct $75–$155 double; Nov–Mar $65–$145 double. Rates include breakfast. AE, DISC, MC, V. Free parking. **Amenities:** 2 restaurants; bar; reading parlor; outdoor balcony. *In room:* A/C, TV.

Merry Sherwood Plantation ✸   Drive through the gates and enter a hideaway filled with fragrant flowers, butterflies, and, at the end of the drive, the 1859 plantation house. Inside, the rooms are filled with antiques, sunshine streams through the porch windows, and breezes cool the high-ceilinged rooms. Front bedrooms are sunnier, but those in back are quieter. All but two units have private bathrooms; the two that share a bathroom are spacious and well-appointed, and their claw-foot tub is equally charming. The honeymoon suite has a whirlpool tub, while the Stokes has a fireplace. And don't miss the cupola; it's a good place to catch a breeze—or ponder the universe.

8909 Worcester Hwy. (2½ miles south of Berlin on Rte. 113), Berlin, MD 21811. ✆ **800/660-0358** or 410/641-2112. www.merrysherwood.com. 8 units, 2 with shared bathroom. $125–$175 double. Rates include full gourmet breakfast. MC, V. *In room:* A/C.

WHERE TO DINE

Atlantic Hotel Restaurant ✸✸✸ INTERNATIONAL   It's worth the 20-minute drive from Ocean City to dine in this elegant Victorian restaurant. The waiters in black tie are eager to serve; the lush decor and warm welcome make you want to stay for just one more course. The creative menu changes often, but usually includes fish (such as rockfish with lump crab), oysters, and meat (such as rack of lamb). For something a little more casual, try the Drummer's Cafe, which serves some of the same excellent entrees as well as pub fare and sandwiches. On weekends, the waiters sing.

At the Atlantic Hotel, 2 N. Main St. ✆ **410/641-3589**. Reservations required in main dining room; not accepted in cafe. Main courses $24–$36 in main dining room; lunch in Drummer's Cafe $6.95–$25. AE, DISC, MC, V. Main dining room daily 6–9pm; Drummer's Cafe daily 11:30am–9pm. From Ocean City, take Rte. 50 west 7 miles to Rte. 818 (Main St.).

Globe Bistro in the Globe Theater AMERICAN/REGIONAL   This casual eatery, tucked between the bookstore and the stage at the Globe Theater, offers sandwiches, quiche, and salads at lunchtime. The dinner menu changes regularly to feature fresh produce, seafood, and other local delights. Entrees are inspired by traditional Eastern Shore cuisine. Tables are close enough to the stage that you can enjoy a meal and a performance. In fact, if you're planning to come for a concert, you can arrange to eat during the show. (Ticket prices are separate.)

12 Broad St. ℰ 410/641-0784. Reservations requested for dinner. Dinner $13–$23; lunch $4.95–$9.95. AE, DISC, MC, V. Daily 10am–2pm; Tues–Sat 5–9pm in summer (dinner usually served 3 nights per week in off season—call ahead to confirm).

WHAT TO SEE & DO

Most of the shop owners have a story to tell about the time Julia Roberts stopped by or the day the cameras moved in for a close-up of their store window. That and the shopping make this a fun place to spend a day. But don't miss the town's own museum, named for a local banker.

Calvin B. Taylor House Museum   Lovingly preserved by local residents, this Federal-style home features some fine antiques and dazzling faux-finish woodwork, as well as exhibits recalling the life of the banker/owner and the town itself. *Seabiscuit* fans will want to see the portrait of War Admiral—he was raised on a farm nearby.

208 N. Main St. ℰ 410/641-1019. Donations accepted. Memorial Day to Oct Mon, Wed, and Fri–Sat 1–4pm.

SHOPPING

Berlin is home to a variety of witty and interesting shops. Most shops are open daily from 10am to 5pm, though Sunday hours usually begin after noon.

Local artists show their work at the **Worcester County Arts Council Gallery and Shop,** 6 Jefferson St., behind the Atlantic Hotel (ℰ 410/641-0809). You'll find fun gifts at **Bruder Hill,** 925 Commerce St. (ℰ 410/629-1260), which features clothes and accessories, and **TaDa,** 18 William St. (ℰ 410/641-4430), which has plenty of striking home furnishings painted by the owner. **Town Center Antiques** (ℰ 410/629-1895), a small antiques mall, has expanded to two sites: 1 N. Main St., across from the Atlantic Hotel, and 113 N. Main St.

The **Globe Theater,** 12 Broad St., behind the Atlantic Hotel (ℰ 410/641-0784; www.globetheater.com), is a restored movie theater that serves as a cultural center for Berlin. Nationally known jazz, blues, and folk musicians play in the intimate venue. It also screens movies, holds poetry readings, and presents children's activities. The cover varies according to the artist; call or check the website for schedule. Also in the complex are **Duck Soup,** a book/gift shop, and the **Balcony Gallery,** with a collection of fine art by regional artists.

11

Wilmington

Set in a valley filled with America's castles, Wilmington celebrates its industrial side at Riverfront. A work in progress, it's a lovely 1⅓-mile walk along the Christina River, dotted with warehouses and other industrial sites reborn as a market, shops, restaurants, offices, and museums. In a whimsical touch, gaily colored cranes hover above.

Though not as flashy as Baltimore's Inner Harbor, visitors will enjoy spending a few hours walking from the train station through the Tubman–Garrett Riverfront Park to the Shipyard Shops and the urban nature preserve.

Wilmington is known for its museums, theater, restaurants, and well-appointed hotels, including the luxurious Hotel du Pont. Business-oriented Wilmington has full hotels during the week, but on weekends look for great deals: rooms at about half price as well as cheap parking. Come and spend the day in Wilmington's museums or Riverfront; head to New Castle's historic district or the Brandywine Valley's mansions and gardens; and return to the city for a delicious meal and a good night's sleep.

1 Orientation

ARRIVING

BY PLANE   Most people flying into northern Delaware use **Philadelphia International Airport** (© 215/937-6800; www.phl.org), about a half-hour ride from downtown Wilmington. Car-rental agencies at the airport include **Avis** (© 800/331-1212) and **Hertz** (© 800/654-3131).

Delaware Express Shuttle (© 800/648-5466 or 302/454-7800; www.delexpress. com) offers van service from the Philadelphia airport to Wilmington for about $34. For the most prompt service—and a better price—reserve by phone or online at least 24 hours in advance. Otherwise, look for the phone near the customer service center at baggage claim. Many Wilmington hotels also operate courtesy shuttles to and from the airport. A taxi into town will cost about $50.

BY TRAIN   **Amtrak** (© 800/USA-RAIL; www.amtrak.com) serves Wilmington on its Northeast Corridor line, with Acela, Metroliner, and regional trains stopping here several times daily. The Wilmington Amtrak station is at 100 S. French St. (at Martin Luther King, Jr. Blvd.), on the Riverfront. There's a taxi stand outside. *Note:* From 2006 to 2007, the historic train station will undergo restoration work, as well as the construction of additional office and retail space.

BY CAR   I-95 cuts across the city's center. The Delaware Memorial Bridge (part of I-295) connects Wilmington to the New Jersey Turnpike and points north. From southern Delaware and the Eastern Shore of Maryland and Virginia, Route 13 will bring you into the city.

BY BUS Greyhound (📞 800/231-2222; www.greyhound.com) and **Trailways/ Peter Pan** (📞 800/343-9999; www.trailways.com or www.peterpanbus.com) provide daily bus service into the **Wilmington Transportation Center,** 101 N. French St. (📞 302/655-6111).

VISITOR INFORMATION

Information on Wilmington, the Brandywine Valley, and New Castle is available from the **Greater Wilmington Convention and Visitors Bureau,** 100 W. 10th St., Suite 20 (📞 800/489-6664, 800/422-1181, or 302/652-4088; www.visitwilmingtonde. com). It's open Monday through Friday from 9am to 5pm. For motorists, there's a visitor center at the **I-95 Delaware Travel Plaza,** south of town between exits 1 and 3 (📞 302/737-4059), open daily from 8am to 8pm; it also has an automatic hotel reservations system.

SPECIAL EVENTS

For 10 days in June, music lovers turn out for free jazz at the **DuPont Clifford Brown Jazz Festival.** Visit www.cliffordbrownjazzfest.com for a schedule. On the second weekend in July, the **Rockwood Ice Cream Festival** (📞 302/761-4340) features hot-air balloons, baby parades, and, of course, ice cream.

CITY LAYOUT

Three rivers surround Wilmington: the Brandywine, the Christina (formerly called the Christiana), and the Delaware. The **downtown** business area, wedged between the Brandywine and Christina, is laid out in a grid system, less than 20 blocks wide and long. *Note:* Though the downtown area is relatively small, the attractions, restaurants, and hotels are spread out, with most either south of downtown or in the northern suburbs. Aside from a few museums and shops along the Market Street Mall, you can't or wouldn't want to walk between major attractions.

Two parts of Wilmington that aren't downtown are worth a visit: the revitalized Riverfront area and the more suburban north side. The **Riverfront** is about a 5-minute drive south of downtown between I-95 and the Christina River. Home to outlet shops, an arts center, and other attractions, it can be tricky to get to from downtown (take Martin Luther King, Jr. Blvd. to Madison St. and follow the signs). Or head back to I-95 and take Exit 6. Riverfront has lots of free parking.

The **north side** of Wilmington (north of Rte. 52 and northwest of I-95) features modest to lavish brick houses, parks, the trendy **Trolley Square** neighborhood, and tiny **Little Italy,** with plenty of restaurants—including **Luigi Vitrone's Pastabilities,** 415 N. Lincoln St. (📞 302/656-9822; www.ljv-pastabilities.com), featured on the Food Network. The main thoroughfares are Route 52 and Delaware Avenue; as you drive out Route 52, the city gives way to rolling hills and the Brandywine Valley. You'll be surprised how close all these wonderful attractions are.

MAIN ARTERIES & STREETS Market Street runs north–south in downtown Wilmington. The east–west cross streets are numbered from 1st to 16th, with the lowest number on the southern end. The north–south streets bear the names of presidents and local heroes west of Market, and trees east of Market. Most streets are one-way, except for Fourth Street. I-95 enters Wilmington via two main avenues: Delaware Avenue (Rte. 52) on the north end of the city, and Martin Luther King, Jr. Boulevard on the south.

Downtown Wilmington

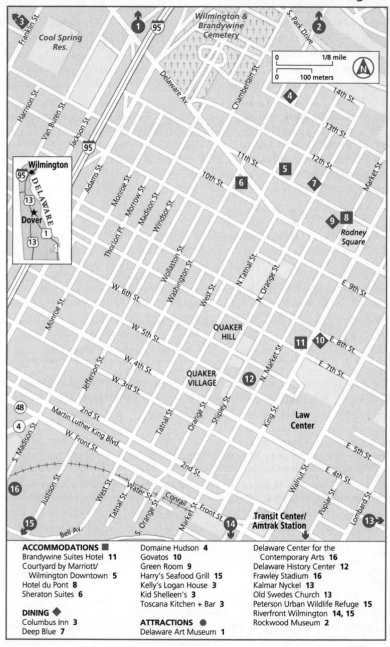

Cool Spring Res.

Wilmington & Brandywine Cemetery

Franklin St.
S. Park Drive

0 1/8 mile
0 100 meters
N

Harrison St.
Van Buren St.
Jackson St.
Delaware Av.
Chamberlain St.
14th St.
13th St.
12th St.
Market St.

Wilmington
DELAWARE
Dover

Adams St.
Monroe St.
Morrow St.
Madison St.
Windsor St.
Thorton Pl.
11th St.
10th St.

E. 9th St.
N. Tatnall St.
N. Orange St.
Wollaston St.
Washington St.
West St.
Rodney Square

W. 6th St.
Monroe St.
W. 5th St.
QUAKER HILL
E. 8th St.
E. 7th St.
N. Market St.

W. 4th St.
Jefferson St.
W. 3rd St.
QUAKER VILLAGE
Orange St.
Shipley St.
King St.
Law Center

2nd St.
Martin Luther King Blvd.
S. Madison St.
W. Front St.
Tatnall St.
2nd St.
E. 5th St.

Justison St.
West St.
Tatnall St.
S. Orange St.
Water St.
Conrail RR
Market St.
S. Front St.
E. 4th St.
Walnut St.
Poplar St.
Lombard St.

Bell Av.

Transit Center/
Amtrak Station

ACCOMMODATIONS ■
Brandywine Suites Hotel **11**
Courtyard by Marriott/
   Wilmington Downtown **5**
Hotel du Pont **8**
Sheraton Suites **6**

DINING ◆
Columbus Inn **3**
Deep Blue **7**

Domaine Hudson **4**
Govatos **10**
Green Room **9**
Harry's Seafood Grill **15**
Kelly's Logan House **3**
Kid Shelleen's **3**
Toscana Kitchen + Bar **3**

ATTRACTIONS ●
Delaware Art Museum **1**

Delaware Center for the
   Contemporary Arts **16**
Delaware History Center **12**
Frawley Stadium **16**
Kalmar Nyckel **13**
Old Swedes Church **13**
Peterson Urban Wildlife Refuge **15**
Riverfront Wilmington **14, 15**
Rockwood Museum **2**

From I-95 and downtown, approach Wilmington's north side by using Route 52, which splits into Pennsylvania Avenue (Rte. 52) and Delaware Avenue about 2 blocks north of I-95. Take Route 52 out of the city for Brandywine Valley sites.

MAPS   *Greater Wilmington and Brandywine Valley: America's Cultural Gem,* a booklet produced by the Greater Wilmington Convention and Visitors Bureau, has detailed maps of downtown and the Wilmington region with all the major attractions marked.

2 Getting Around

BY BUS   Wilmington is served by the **DART First State** (© 302/652-3278; or www.dartfirststate.com) bus system. Blue-and-white signs indicating stops are located throughout the city, and regular routes can take you to some hotels, museums, theaters, and parks, as well as the malls and historic New Castle. Fares are based on a zone system; the minimum fare for one zone is $1.15. Exact change is required. For information on schedules and fares, call or visit the website.

BY SHUTTLE   DART also operates the **Trolley,** a 25¢ bus (exact change required) that takes visitors from Rodney Square to the Amtrak station to the Riverfront. The route goes up Walnut Street north via Rodney Square and West Street to 13th Street and down Market Street and King Street to the starting point. Service is provided every 30 minutes. The whole ride takes about 10 minutes. Shuttles run Monday through Friday from 7am to 7pm. Get a schedule from the visitor center or DART.

BY CAR   Because Wilmington's attractions are scattered around town—and because so many pair a visit to the city with Brandywine Valley attractions—a car is necessary. If you aren't driving into the area, you can rent one from either **Enterprise,** 3501 N. Market St. (© **302/761-4545**), or **Budget,** 100 S. French St. (© **302/652-0629**).

BY TAXI   There's a taxi stand at the Amtrak station, across the street from the bus station. To order a taxi, call **Yellow Cab Delaware** (© **302/656-8151**).

FAST FACTS: **Wilmington**

Area Code   Wilmington's area code is **302.**

Camera Repair   For camera repair, supplies, or processing, try **Ritz Camera,** 108 W. Ninth St. (© **302/655-4459**).

Emergencies   Dial © **911** for fire, police, or ambulance.

Eyeglass Repair   Go to **Wilmington Optical,** 616 Market St. (© **302/654-0530**).

Hospitals   Downtown options include **St. Francis Hospital,** Seventh and Clayton streets (© **302/421-4100**), and **Wilmington Hospital,** 14th and Washington streets (© **302/428-4410**).

Libraries   The Wilmington Library is at 10th and Market streets (© **302/571-7400**).

Newspapers & Magazines   The city's daily newspaper is the *News-Journal.* The best monthly magazine is *Delaware Today.*

Pharmacies A local chain, **Happy Harry's Discount Drugs,** has locations at 839 N. Market St., at Ninth Street (© **302/654-1834**), and at Trolley Square, Delaware Avenue and DuPont Street (© **302/655-6397**).

Police For nonemergencies, call © **302/654-5151.** For emergencies, dial © **911.**

Post Office The main downtown post office is at Rodney Square Station, 1101 N. King St. (© **302/656-0228**).

Taxes There is no sales tax in Delaware, but an 8% lodging tax applies to stays at city hotels.

Transit Information Call **DART First State** (© **302/577-3278**).

3 Where to Stay

No matter where you go in Delaware, when you hear people refer to "The Hotel," they mean the Hotel du Pont in Wilmington. For more than 80 years, this hotel has dominated the Delaware lodging scene.

Because Wilmington is a major destination for business travelers, numerous hotels catering to them have popped up downtown. Local hotels charge top prices Sunday through Thursday—but on weekends, rates can really drop. Look, too, for packages combining accommodations with tickets to area attractions.

Tip: The suburbs offer additional choices—including the area's best. See chapter 12 for more options outside Wilmington.

DOWNTOWN
VERY EXPENSIVE
Hotel du Pont ✹✹✹   Opened in 1913 and owned by E. I. du Pont de Nemours and Company, this is the grandest accommodations in town. The 12-story Italian Renaissance structure in the heart of the city is a showcase of marble, coffered ceilings, carved walnut, oak paneling, and genteel service. Guest rooms have merited an International Gold Key Design Award. Each unit has mahogany reproductions and built-in cabinetry, original artwork, and double-glazed windows. They're spacious and luxurious, with comfortable sitting areas. Most of the fabrics, fibers, and fittings are made of the latest DuPont products.

11th and Market sts., Wilmington, DE 19801. © **800/441-9019** or 302/594-3100. Fax 302/549/3108. www.hoteldupont.com. 217 units. $199–$429 double; $650–$750 suite. Weekend packages available. AE, DC, DISC, MC, V. Self or valet parking $14. Pets under 20 lb. accepted with $100 deposit. **Amenities:** 2 restaurants; lobby lounge for cocktails and afternoon tea; coffee shop; golf course and tennis nearby; health club; concierge; business center; shopping arcade; 24-hr. room service; massage; laundry service; dry cleaning. *In room:* A/C, TV w/pay movies, Wi-Fi, minibar, hair dryer, iron, safe.

EXPENSIVE
Sheraton Suites Wilmington ✹✹   In the heart of Wilmington's corporate and financial section, this contemporary 16-story hotel offers comfortable, spacious suites. Each has a full bedroom and a separate living room with large-screen TV, wet bar, and desk. The well-lit bathrooms also have their own TVs, as well as dressing areas. The beds are so comfortable, I've never had a better pillow anywhere. **Basil's** serves breakfast, lunch, and dinner.

422 Delaware Ave., Wilmington, DE 19801. ℭ **800/325-3535** or 302/654-8300. Fax 302/654-6036. www.sheraton. com/suitesWilmington. 228 units. $139–$249 double. Weekend rates available. AE, DC, DISC, MC, V. Parking $10. **Amenities:** Restaurant; lounge; indoor pool; health club; sauna; laundry service; dry cleaning; coin-op laundry; concierge-level rooms. *In room:* A/C, 2 TVs, high-speed Internet access, kitchenette, fridge, coffeemaker, iron, 2-line phone.

MODERATE

Brandywine Suites Hotel *Value*   Although the Brandywine Suites may not look like much from the outside—just a small glass entrance wedged between two old brick buildings—this unique hotel in the heart of Wilmington is one of the area's best values. The Clarion property is made up of three vintage brick office buildings, renovated and linked together by a modern atrium and lobby. The ground-floor atrium has a sitting area with a fireplace and a small bistro-style restaurant. The European-style suites feature living areas with sofas, large TVs, and desks; well-equipped bathrooms; bedrooms with king-size beds and second TVs; and generally at least two phones. Furnishings are of the stock-hotel, dark-wood Colonial type. Some units have large cube-glass windows, which act as a source of natural light without any loss of privacy.

707 N. King St., Wilmington, DE 19801. ℭ **800/756-0070** or 302/656-9300. Fax 302/656-2459. www.brandywine suites.com. 49 units. $99–$189 suite. Rates include continental breakfast. AE, DC, MC, V. Self-parking $8.50. **Amenities:** Restaurant; health club; business center; laundry service. *In room:* A/C, 2 TVs, high-speed Internet access, minibar, fridge, microwave, coffeemaker, hair dryer, iron.

Courtyard by Marriott Wilmington Downtown   Converted from a 10-story office building, this hotel does not fit the usual mold of the Marriott chain. It does, however, offer good value for downtown. Guest rooms vary in size and configuration, but all have contemporary furniture, wet bars, and large desks designed for business travelers. Some rooms also have Jacuzzis.

1102 West St., Wilmington, DE 19801. ℭ **800/321-2211** or 302/429-7600. Fax 302/429-9167. www.marriott.com. 123 units. $139–$159 double weekdays; $59–$99 double weekends. Weekend packages available. AE, DC, DISC, MC, V. Self-parking $9.50, free parking Fri–Sat nights. **Amenities:** Restaurant (open for breakfast and dinner on weekdays, breakfast only on weekends); coffee and tea bar; health club. *In room:* A/C, TV, free high-speed Internet access, kitchenette, coffeemaker, hair dryer, iron.

SUBURBS
EXPENSIVE

Hilton Wilmington/Christiana *✦*   This hotel, nestled amid grassy grounds off Exit 4B of I-95, is a good choice in the 'burbs—it's located in a burgeoning area near Delaware's university at Newark and a variety of shopping malls. The modern four-story brick exterior is surrounded by topiary gardens, with a brick-lined courtyard, gazebo, and pond that's home to a family of swans. Bedrooms are decorated in the Old Williamsburg tradition, with dark-wood reproduction furniture and Colonial prints.

100 Continental Dr., Newark, DE 19713. ℭ **800/348-3133** or 302/454-1500. Fax 302/454-0233. www.hilton estate.com. 266 units. $94–$254 double. Weekend rates available. AE, DC, DISC, MC, V. Free parking. **Amenities:** 2 restaurants; lounge; outdoor pool; health club; concierge; free shuttle to downtown Wilmington; concierge-level rooms. *In room:* A/C, TV w/movies, Wi-Fi, fridge, coffeemaker, hair dryer, iron.

Inn at Montchanin Village *✦✦✦*   Why sleep in a hotel room when you can wake up in a historic village surrounded by autumn's glory or fragrant gardens? Just a few miles from downtown Wilmington and set among the Brandywine treasures, Montchanin Village is miles from the ordinary. It, too, is part of du Pont family history—it was once home to workers in the black powder mills and factories along the Brandywine. The whole village is listed on the National Register of Historic Places.

Eleven buildings, completed between 1870 and 1910, became the Inn at Montchanin Village in 1996. Nine of these buildings, once the workers' residences, have been converted into 28 guest rooms, including one- and two-level suites. Six superior suites have king-size beds, marble bathrooms with oversize tubs, and gas fireplaces. In fact, many units have gas fireplaces. All open onto an outdoor sitting area, and first-level rooms and suites have private gardens. The blacksmith shop houses the inn's restaurant, **Krazy Kat's** (see "Where to Dine," below), while the new health club is in the Dilwyne Barn. In 2007, a spa topped by a terrace will open behind the barn.

Rte. 100 and Kirk Rd. (P.O. Box 130), Montchanin, DE 19710. 📞 **800/COWBIRD** or 302/888-2133. Fax 302/888-0389. www.montchanin.com. 28 units (11 w/shower only). $169–$375 double; $249–$375 suite. AE, DC, DISC, MC, V. Free parking. **Amenities:** Restaurant; lounge; health club; room service. *In room:* A/C, TV/VCR or DVD, high-speed Internet access, kitchenette, fridge w/complimentary sodas and water, microwave, coffeemaker, hair dryer, iron, robe.

MODERATE

Best Western Brandywine Valley Inn ✦ *Finds*   Yes, it is very much a motor lodge, but the innkeepers have gone to great lengths to make guests forget that once they step inside. The new Court units serve business travelers with high-speed Internet access, desks with printers and cordless phones, and limousine service. The charming Country French Boudoirs, in contrast, are cozy, smaller rooms with romantic wall coverings and linens for a real bed-and-breakfast feel. For pure luxury, ask for a Winterthur Suite, outfitted with rich fabrics and fabulous Winterthur reproduction furniture—over-the-top in both decor and comfort. The location is perfect for Brandywine tourists and business travelers alike, right on Route 202 near Winterthur. Ask about museum packages, too.

1807 Concord Pike (Rte. 202), Wilmington, DE 19803. 📞 **800/537-7772** or 302/656-9436. Fax 302/656-8564. www. brandywineinn.com. 96 units. $104–$165 double; $129–$385 suite. Packages available. Rates include bagel breakfast in lobby. Children under 18 stay free in parent's room. AE, DC, DISC, MC, V. Free parking. **Amenities:** Outdoor pool and hot tub; health club. *In room:* A/C, TV, dataport, fridge, microwave, coffeemaker, hair dryer, iron.

Doubletree Hotel Wilmington   Popular with business travelers during the week and families on weekends, this modern seven-story structure is on the busy Route 202 corridor, north of downtown Wilmington and a few miles from the major museums and gardens. Its location makes it a good choice. Guest rooms have a Brandywine Valley flavor, with dark reproduction furniture and local art. Families may prefer the suites with sofa bed and fridge.

4727 Concord Pike (U.S. Rte. 202), Wilmington, DE 19803. 📞 **800/222-TREE** or 302/478-6000. Fax 302/477-1492. www.doubletreehotels.com. 244 units (45 w/shower only). $79–$179 double. Weekend packages available. AE, DC, DISC, MC, V. Free parking. **Amenities:** Restaurant; lounge; indoor pool; health club; courtesy shuttle service within 5-mile radius, including downtown Wilmington. *In room:* A/C, TV or TV/VCR, Wi-Fi, coffeemaker, hair dryer, iron.

INEXPENSIVE

Fairfield Inn Wilmington Newark/Christiana Mall *Value*   Newly renovated in 2005, this three-story property offers comfortable, attractively furnished accommodations at low prices. There are three types of guest rooms: a compact single-bed room ideal for a lone traveler, a standard double, and a larger double with king-size bed. Each unit has a full-length mirror, lounge chair, and desk.

65 Geoffrey Dr., Newark, DE 19713. 📞 **800/228-2800** or 302/292-1500. Fax 302/292-8655. www.marriott.com. 133 units. $69–$159 double. Rates include continental breakfast. AE, DC, MC, V. Free parking. **Amenities:** Outdoor pool; health club. *In room:* A/C, TV w/pay movies, Wi-Fi, coffeemaker, hair dryer, iron.

4 Where to Dine

DOWNTOWN

EXPENSIVE

Columbus Inn AMERICAN/REGIONAL   A Wilmington favorite, the Columbus Inn is in one of the area's oldest houses, atop a hill on the edge of the northern suburbs. Because it has both a comfortable semiformal dining room and a more casual pub, it draws both the business-lunch crowd and the food-savvy dinner set. There's a relaxed mood in the candlelit dining room, where the dark-wood floors and exposed-beam ceilings echo with the sounds of quiet conversation. The Columbus Inn is known for its wine list, and the menu ranges from gourmet vegetarian to steak. Sandwiches and pub fare are available in the bar.

2216 Pennsylvania Ave. (C) **302/571-1492.** www.columbusinn.com. Reservations recommended for dinner. Main courses $7–$18 lunch, $10–$32 dinner; Sun brunch $25. AE, DC, DISC, MC, V. Mon–Fri 11am–1am; Sat 5pm–1am; Sun 10am–3pm. Valet parking available at lunch and dinner. Local musicians perform in club room Thurs–Fri.

Deep Blue ✸ SEAFOOD   How do you like your seafood: sashimi, raw bar, traditional, Pacific Rim style? Deep Blue's got it all. Set in a parking garage, of all things, this noisy little restaurant draws a crowd of 30-somethings to its popular bar. (In this sleek modern setting, nothing can muffle the sound—so ask for a table away from the bar.) The menu is filled with interesting options, from the five-spice ahi tuna to the crab ravioli with lobster sauce. The wine list offers more than 170 choices. A pretheater dinner menu is available, and servers will make sure you arrive before curtain time.

111 W. 11th St. (C) **302/777-2040.** www.deepbluebarandgrill.com. Reservations recommended for dinner. Main courses $10–$19 at lunch, $20–$26 at dinner. AE, DC, DISC, MC, V. Mon–Fri 11:30am–2pm; Mon–Sat 5:30–10pm. Discounted self-parking w/validated ticket; dinner valet parking $6.

Green Room ✸✸ CONTINENTAL/FRENCH   If you want to treat yourself to a night on the town, make reservations at the Green Room. From the moment you enter these sumptuous surroundings (no, not green) of carved ceilings, paneled walls, soaring windows, and grand chandeliers, you'll know you've stepped into luxury. You'll be reminded when you see the menu, too—prices soar as high as the ceilings, but the food is exquisite. The atmosphere may be a little stiff for some, but it could also be considered refined. The tuxedoed waiters try hard to please, though service can be uneven. But the meals are perfect: with rich sauces, delightful *amuse bouche,* and artful desserts. Brunch is served on Sunday.

At the Hotel du Pont, 11th and Market sts. (C) **302/594-3154.** www.hoteldupont.com. Reservations required. Jackets required for men Fri–Sat. Main courses $12–$20 at lunch, $24–$37 at dinner; Sun brunch $36. AE, DC, MC, V. Mon–Sat 6:30–10:30am (opens and closes a half-hour later for Sat breakfast); 11:30am–2pm, and 5:30–10pm; Sun 10am–2:15pm and 5—9:30pm. Free valet and self-parking Fri–Sat evenings.

Harry's Seafood Grill SEAFOOD   The soaring dark-blue dining room of this Riverfront restaurant is dominated by a glittery sea star on the ceiling; the windows overlook the Christina River. The menu changes daily to reflect the fresh seafood available—there's everything from lobster in the nude to fish and chips. Rather than focus on Chesapeake-style seafood, the chef here has gone global, with recipes representing the Far East, Portugal, and regional American cuisine. The extensive wine list is designed for those who want to try something new—tasting flights are available.

101 S. Market St. (C) **302/777-1500.** www.harrys-savoy.com/seafood/default.asp. Reservations recommended, even for lunch. Main courses $8.95–$53 at lunch, $16–$53 at dinner. AE, DC, DISC, MC, V. Mon–Thurs 11am–10pm; Fri 11am–11pm; Sat 4:30–11pm; Sun noon–9pm (dinner only).

MODERATE

Domaine Hudson ☆☆ WINE BAR   Come here for the wine—the list, though not as extensive as at bigger restaurants, is filled with selections you won't find anywhere else in Delaware. But stay for the food, too: The chef has created dishes to pair with your wines, which come in tastes (1½ oz.) and 3- or 5-ounce servings. Oh yes, and the food: soups, salads (warm Brie atop field greens is a definite winner), small plates, and large plates. Brand-new in fall 2005, this wine bar is cozy and maybe a little noisy, but a great new addition to downtown Wilmington's evolving dining scene.

1314 N. Washington St. ✆ 302/655-WINE. www.domainehudson.com. Reservations recommended. Small plates $11–$14; main courses $21–$24. AE, DISC, MC, V. Tues–Sun 4:30–10:30pm.

Kid Shelleen's AMERICAN   Tucked in a residential area on the city's north side, just north of Trolley Square, this lively indoor/outdoor restaurant, known for its open charcoal grill, is always hopping. Inside, you'll find a pub atmosphere: exposed brick, dark wood, and walls decorated with old circus posters. But the food is better and the offerings more extensive than your average pub fare. Entrees include grilled salmon, barbecued ribs, black and bleu steak salad, and pastas. A big, friendly open bar area in the middle of the restaurant is dominated by a large-screen TV.

1801 W. 14th St. (at Scott St.). ✆ 302/658-4600. www.kidshelleens.com. Reservations recommended. Main courses $7.50–$18. AE, DC, DISC, MC, V. Mon–Sat 11am–midnight; Sun 10am–2pm and 3pm–midnight. Live music Wed–Fri at 9pm.

Toscana Kitchen + Bar ITALIAN/TUSCAN   As soon as you step into Toscana, you'll be enveloped by the excited din of the customers, the bustle of the waitstaff, and the piquant aromas flowing from the open kitchen and the wood-burning oven. The place has a Continental feel to it, with warm colors and contemporary furnishings. Freshly made pastas and exotic pizzas top the lunch menu; the dinner menu adds Italian-flavored entrees such as lamb tenderloin or fettuccine with wild boar. New is the small-plates menu, with offerings priced at $5 to $10.

1412 N. DuPont St. ✆ 302/654-8001. www.bigchefguy.com. Reservations accepted only for parties of 6 or more. Main courses $9–$15 lunch, $7–$24 dinner. AE, DC, DISC, MC, V. Mon–Fri 11:30am–5pm; Mon–Wed 5–10pm; Thurs–Sat 5–11pm; Sun 5–9pm. Live music in the lounge on Wed.

INEXPENSIVE

Govatos AMERICAN   Established in 1894, this Wilmington tradition makes an ideal midcity choice for breakfast or lunch. The menu offers sandwiches, burgers, salads, and home-style favorites. The main attractions, however, are the desserts and other confections, since this place produces Delaware's largest selection of homemade chocolates and candies.

800 Market St. ✆ 302/652-4082. www.govatoschocolates.com. Breakfast items $2.95–$5.95; lunch items $4.95–$9.95. MC, V. Mon–Fri 8am–3pm.

SUBURBS

EXPENSIVE

Krazy Kat's ☆☆☆ NEW AMERICAN   The warm, candlelit dining room set in the old blacksmith shop at the Inn at Montchanin Village has a funny name and even funnier animal "portraits" adorning its walls. But the real reason to come here is the serious food. The seasonal menu is filled with creative combinations: silky crab bisque with Meyer lemon crème fraîche or salmon with nutty brussels sprouts. The wine list is extensive, too. And the service is polished and relaxed—this is destination dining, after all. The dessert menu is as interesting as the dinner menu. A tasting menu is offered Friday through Sunday evenings.

At the Inn at Montchanin Village, Rte. 100 and Kirk Rd. (© **302/888-4200**. www.montchanin.com/dining.html. Reservations recommended, especially for dinner and breakfast on weekends. Jackets suggested for men at dinner. Main courses $10–$16 lunch, $26–$30 dinner; tasting menu $65–$85. AE, DC, DISC, MC, V. Mon–Fri 7–10:30am, 11:30am–2pm, and 5:30–9:30pm; Sat–Sun 8–11am and 5:30–9:30pm.

MODERATE

Feby's Fishery ⌖ SEAFOOD   Feby's is known for good food in a family-style atmosphere. The nautically themed restaurant—on the city's southwest side, west of the junction of Route 100 South—also has a seafood market, a sure sign of fresh fish on the premises. The menu lists as many as 18 different species of fish, plus daily specials and creative combinations. For landlubbers, there are filet mignon and Delmonico steak.

3701 Lancaster Pike (Rte. 48). www.febysfishery.com. (© **302/998-9501**. Reservations recommended for dinner. Main courses $5.95–$15 lunch, $15–$35 dinner. AE, MC, V. Mon–Thurs 11am–9:30pm; Fri 11am–10pm; Sat–Sun 4–9:30pm.

Kelly's Logan House AMERICAN   Built in 1864, this old tavern by the railroad tracks once saw the likes of Al Capone and Wild Bill Hickock. Kelly's may still draw a few characters, but now they're coming for dinner washed down by a couple of cold brews. Located right on Delaware Avenue, it's a good stop if you're on your way to Brandywine Valley attractions. The menu is varied—hearty sandwiches, wraps, pasta, salmon, and burgers, plus brunch on Sunday. Thai and Cajun seasonings add interest to the usual fare. Live music draws lots of young people Tuesday through Saturday nights (p. 306).

1701 Delaware Ave. (© **302/652-9493** or 302/655-6426. www.loganhouse.com. Main courses $6–$18. AE, DISC, MC, V. Tues–Sat 11am–1am; Sun noon–10pm; Mon 11am–midnight.

5 Attractions

Though most visitors to Wilmington head out to the Brandywine Valley attractions, the city itself has several museums and sites of interest.

Delaware Art Museum ⌖⌖   Back at home after 3 years of construction and expansion, the Delaware Art Museum, home of 12,000 works of art, has added lots of gallery space, a 9-acre sculpture garden, a children's area, a cafe, and an expanded museum store. The wait was worth it. The entrance, overlooking the sculpture garden, is crowned with a colorful Dale Chihuly glass sculpture. First-floor galleries are devoted to pre-Raphaelite art (though much of it was on loan elsewhere in 2005), local artist Howard Pyle and his fellow illustrators of the Brandywine school, and John Sloan and early American modernism. A second-floor bridge lets visitors get a closer look at the Chihuly glass as they head to galleries filled with more contemporary art, including works by Jacob Lawrence, Edward Hopper, and Jamie Wyeth.

2301 Kentmere Pkwy. (© **302/571-9590**. www.delart.org. Admission $10 adults, $8 seniors, $5 college students, $3 children 7–18. Free on Sun. Tues and Thurs–Sat 10am–4pm; Wed 10am–8pm; Sun noon–5pm.

Delaware Center for the Contemporary Arts   Housed in an impressive building on Wilmington's Riverfront, this gallery focuses on contemporary visual arts by local and nationally known artists. As a noncollecting museum, exhibits are always changing, with about 30 each year. Also featured are the works of the 26 artists who keep their studios here. There's a small gift shop, too.

200 S. Madison St. ✆ **302/656-6466.** www.thedcca.org. Admission $5 adults; $3 students, seniors, and artists; free for children under 12. Tues and Thurs–Sat 10am–5pm; Wed and Sun noon–5pm.

Delaware History Museum ✿ *Kids*
In big, bright displays with lots of artifacts right at toddler level, the "Distinctly Delaware" exhibit tells all about the 200-plus years of Delaware history. DuPont is heavily featured, of course, but visitors will also learn about agriculture, the state's role in the underground railroad, and the famous Delawareans portrayed in wax, including civil rights attorney Louis Redding and Emily Bissell, who created Christmas Seals. Grandma's Attic is a delightful place for kids to play and try on clothes. Children's programs are offered, too.

504 Market St. (near south end of Market St. Mall). ✆ **302/655-7161.** www.hsd.org. Admission $4 adults, $3 students and seniors, $2 children under 18. Mon–Fri noon–4pm; Sat 10am–4pm.

Kalmar Nyckel Foundation
A grand ship brought the first 24 Swedish settlers to the Delaware Valley in 1638. Now, on the shores of the Christina River near Old Swedes Church and Fort Christina Park, the *Kalmar Nyckel* Foundation has re-created the three-masted ship with its fine carvings and richly appointed captain's cabin. When it's not sailing, visitors can tour the 139-foot-long electric-blue ship and take a look at her 7 guns, 7,500 square feet of sail, and 10-story-high main mast. The best time to find the *Kalmar Nyckel* at home is November through April. It sails along Delaware's coast—often to Lewes—May through October. It also sometimes docks at the Riverfront Park by the train station or by the Shipyard Shops. Three-hour sailing excursions are offered in warm weather. See the website for schedule and fees.

1124 E. Seventh St. ✆ **302/429-7447.** www.kalnyc.org. Admission $5 adults, $3 children 6–12. Sat–Sun 10am–4pm. Call for sailing schedule. To get to shipyard, take Fourth st. east to Church St. Turn left on Church St.; turn right on Seventh St.

Old Swedes Church ✿
Formally known as Holy Trinity Episcopal Church, this stone-and-brick building overlooking the Christina River is the oldest church in continuous use in the U.S. It was built in 1699 as part of the Swedish Lutheran Church. Today, artifacts tell of the parish's vibrant history. Parishioners donated the black-walnut pulpit; the king of Sweden presented the altar candles in 1988; Tiffany created one of the luminous stained-glass windows; and the church chest dates from 1713. Hendrickson House, moved here and restored in 1958, contains artifacts of rural Delaware from 1690 to 1800. A labyrinth is located here, as well.

606 Church St. (at Seventh St.). ✆ **302/652-5629.** www.oldswedes.org. Donations welcome. Tours Wed–Sat 10am–4pm. Take Fourth St.; turn left on Church St.

Riverfront Wilmington ✿✿✿
On a bend in the Christina River, Wilmington has built brick and board walkways with views both urban and wild. Beginning at the train station and ending at the Russell W. Peterson Urban Wildlife Refuge, this 1⅓-mile path takes visitors past shops, museums, and a series of signs illustrating Wilmington's history. Watch a rowing team glide by, discover a Canada goose on the shore, or catch a ride on the River Taxi.

Start at the **Tubman–Garrett Riverfront Park,** at Water and South French streets; 21 placards spaced along the walkway tell the history of the Christina River and the city, beginning with the development of industry, shipbuilding, and other transportation here. The underground railroad, which ran through Wilmington, is remembered here, as are efforts to restore wetlands and excavate archaeological sites. Sometimes you can also see the *Kalmar Nyckel,* a reproduction of the ship that brought Wilmington's first settlers, near the Shipyard Shops or by the Tubman–Garrett Park. **Dravo Plaza,** with all those huge cranes, recalls the city's shipbuilding history, especially its contributions to World War II.

Hungry yet? The number of restaurants just keeps going up. Among them are **Harry's Seafood Grill,** 101 S. Market St. (© **302/777-1500**), reviewed on p. 298, and **Iron Hill Brewery,** 710 S. Madison St. (© **302/658-8200**). If you just want a sandwich, coffee, or sweets to eat now, stop at the **Riverfront Market,** 1 S. Market St. (© **302/425-4454**)—where you can also pick up meats, fish, and produce to take home. It's open Tuesday through Friday from 9am to 7pm, Saturday from 9am to 6pm. It's also fun to stroll through the stores and restaurants of the **Shipyard Shops** (© **302/425-5000**), open Monday through Saturday from 10am to 9pm, Sunday from 11am to 5pm (closes earlier in winter).

The **Delaware Theatre Company** and **Delaware Center for the Contemporary Arts** are resident arts organizations here. The Riverfront also hosts festivals and concerts at Dravo Plaza and along the walkway. Sports fans can see the Blue Rocks play minor league baseball at **Frawley Stadium,** a short walk off the Riverfront.

If you get tired of walking, the **River Taxi** (© **302/530-5069**) will take you to your next stop. From April to November, the 40-passenger pontoon boat shuttles passengers along a 30-minute loop, from the Shipyard Shops to the mouth of the Brandywine River. Call in cooler weather if you don't see the taxi running. Fare is $8.

Visitors who make it to the end of the Riverfront will reach the **Russell W. Peterson Urban Wildlife Refuge.** The 225 acres of marshland have become home to many birds and other creatures.

Madison St. (on the west) and Water St. (on the north) are the closest to the park. © 302/425-4890. www.riverfront wilmington.com. Plentiful parking available at free lots near the Shipyard Shops, 900 S. Madison St., and the Chase Center on the Riverfront, 800 S. Madison St., as well as near the Riverfront Market, 1 S. Market St. Some paid parking available near the Amtrak station, 100 S. French St. (at Martin Luther King, Jr. Blvd.).

Rockwood Museum ☀☀   Painstaking restoration of this rural Gothic mansion, furnished in 17th-, 18th-, and 19th-century decorative arts, has given Wilmington back a treasure. The grand house, built in 1850 by Joseph Shipley and set on 72 acres, was expanded by the home's only other occupants, the Bringhursts, who lived here from 1891 to 1965. Rockwood boasts a pink parlor with gilded fireplace and moldings, a conservatory filled with greenery, and spacious bedrooms, decorated as they might have been in the Bringhurst family's time. Decorative painting in many of the rooms adds a touch of whimsy to the place. Rockwood is the centerpiece of a New Castle County–owned park with hiking trails, many of them paved and lighted. A trail map is available at the museum. The Butler's Pantry, a self-serve cafe, gives visitors an opportunity to rest in one of the many colorful parlors. The house is also the site of summer concert series, a Victorian ice-cream festival (which draws 70,000 people in July), and a festival of lights in December.

610 Shipley Rd. © 302/761-4340. www.rockwood.org. Free admission. Gardens and park daily 6am–10pm; house tours on the hour 10am–3pm; Butler's Pantry 7am–3pm. From I-95 north, take Exit 9 (Marsh Rd.); follow the signs.

6 Spectator Sports & Outdoor Activities

BASEBALL   The **Blue Rocks** (© **302/888-BLUE** or 302/888-2015; www.blue rocks.com), a Class A minor league team, play at the 5,900-seat Daniel S. Frawley Stadium, off I-95 near the Riverfront. Box seats are $9; reserved seats are $8; general admission is $5; and children, seniors, and military personnel pay $2. Parking is free. Frawley Stadium is also home of the **Delaware Sports Museum and Hall of Fame** (✆ **302/425-3265**), open April through October, Tuesday through Saturday from noon to 5pm. Admission is $4 for adults, $3 for seniors, and $2 for youths 12 to 19.

GOLF   The rolling hills around Wilmington make for challenging golf. The following courses welcome visitors:

The **Delcastle Golf Club,** 801 McKennan's Church Rd. (✆ **302/995-1990;** www.delcastlegolfclub.com), located southwest of the city near Delaware Park racetrack, offers an 18-hole championship course, pro shop, and full restaurant open from 7am to dark. Nearby are a driving range and miniature golf. Greens fees range from $40 to $45.

The **Ed "Porky" Oliver Golf Club,** 800 N. DuPont Rd. (✆ **302/571-9041;** www.edolivergolfclub.com), in a residential area west of downtown and off Route 52 (Pennsylvania Ave.), has an 18-hole championship course, driving range, pro shop, and restaurant; it also provides lessons and group clinics. Tee times are accepted by phone 1 week in advance. Greens fees range from $39 to $43.

The **Three Little Bakers Country Club,** 3540 Three Little Bakers Blvd. (✆ **302/ 737-1877;** www.tlbinc.com), nestled in the Pike Creek Valley southwest of Wilmington, has a semiprivate 18-hole par-71 course open daily to the public, except after 3pm on Thursday and Friday. Facilities include a pro shop, club rental, golf lessons, and bag storage. Greens fees are $49 Monday through Friday and $54 Saturday and Sunday.

HORSE RACING & SLOTS   For half a century, racing fans have placed their bets at **Delaware Park,** 4½ miles south of Wilmington, off I-95 Exit 4B, Stanton (✆ **800/ 41SLOTS** or 302/994-2521). Thoroughbred racing is offered April through November; post time is 12:45pm. Simulcast racing is offered year-round. A wide variety of coin-operated and video slot machines are available for 5¢ to $10 per play. There are also restaurants and entertainment on weekends. Open Monday through Saturday from 8am to 4am, Sunday from noon to 4am.

PUBLIC PARKS   Wilmington's playground is **Bellevue State Park,** 800 Carr Rd. (✆ **302/761-6963;** www.destateparks.com), on the northeast perimeter of the city. This 328-acre park was once the home of the William du Pont family. Facilities include picnic areas, garden paths for walking, fitness trails for jogging, clay tennis courts, and an equestrian facility, plus ice skating in winter.

Southwest of Wilmington is **Lums Pond State Park,** 1068 Howell School Rd., off Route 71, Bear (✆ **302/368-6989;** www.destateparks.com). Stretching along the Chesapeake & Delaware Canal, this 1,790-acre park contains the state's largest freshwater pond and is home to several beaver colonies and many waterfowl. The pond offers sunbathing (no swimming), fishing, and boating. Bring your own boat or rent a rowboat, canoe, paddleboat, or sailboat during the summer and on weekends in May and September; rates range from $5 to $12 per hour. The surrounding parklands include hiking and walking trails; a nature center; picnic areas; football, soccer, and baseball fields; basketball and tennis courts; and campsites.

Entry fees to Delaware state parks are seasonal, with no admission charged from November through April. Otherwise, the fee is $6 per out-of-state vehicle and $3 per Delaware-registered car. Both parks are open from 8am to sunset year-round.

A SIDE TRIP TO FORT DELAWARE STATE PARK ⚓

Fort Delaware State Park, located on Pea Patch Island, in Delaware City (© 302/ 834-7941; www.destateparks.com), is about 16 miles south of Wilmington, in the Delaware River. Take Route 13 or I-95 south from Wilmington to Route 9 (turn left), which will take you to Delaware City. The park surrounds a five-sided granite fortress that served as a detention center during the Civil War. Inside, there's a museum, 19th-century cells and armaments, and an audiovisual presentation on the history of the island. Other facilities include an observation tower for bird-watchers (the island is a popular nesting spot for egrets, herons, and other marsh fowl) and an assortment of nature trails and picnic sites. To visit, take the ferry from Delaware City; it departs every hour from Battery Park at the end of Clinton Road. Once you arrive on the island, a tractor-pulled tram will take you from the dock to the fort, where, if you're visiting during a living-history weekend, you'll be greeted by a costumed interpreter playing the part of a Confederate prisoner.

The ferry fare, which includes admission to the park, is $6 for adults and $4 for children 12 and under. The site is open on weekends April through October, plus Wednesday through Friday from mid-June to Labor Day; call for exact hours, the ferry schedule, and the schedule of events. Reenactments and living-history demonstrations are held throughout the summer. The guided tours by Confederate and Union reenactors—and the musket, artillery, and cannon demonstrations—are great (though a bit loud) for both children and adults.

7 Shopping

Two of the Wilmington area's biggest shopping malls are **Concord Mall,** 4737 Concord Pike (© 302/478-9271), and **Christiana Mall,** 715 Christiana Mall Rd., I-95 Exit 4A (© 302/731-9815).

The downtown area offers some shopping, mostly on Ninth Street and along Market Street. **Govatos,** 800 Market St. (© 302/652-4082; www.govatoschocolates. com), has made its own chocolates and candies since 1894. The shop is open Monday through Friday from 8am to 3pm year-round; October through April, it also opens Saturday from 8am to 3pm. There's a second shop in the Talleyville Shopping Center, 4105 Concord Pike (© 302/478-5324).

On the Riverfront, **Shipyard Shops,** 900 S. Madison St. (© 302/425-5000; www.riverfrontwilmington.com), has outlets for L.L. Bean, Blair, and other shops. **Riverfront Market,** 1 S. Market St. (© 302/425-4454; www.riverfrontwilmington. com), is a great place to stop for a quick sandwich or cup of soup. Fresh seafood, meat, and produce are also available. It's open Tuesday through Friday from 9am to 7pm, Saturday from 9am to 6pm.

8 Wilmington After Dark

For the latest information on area entertainment, consult the Friday edition of the *News-Journal,* which has a weekend entertainment guide called *55 Hours.* Visit www. delawareonline.com, too. The city's *Out & About* magazine also lists entertainment events.

THE PERFORMING ARTS
CLASSICAL MUSIC & OPERA

For such a small city, Wilmington has a lively performing-arts scene, and the **Grand Opera House** ♣, 818 N. Market St. ((℃ **302/658-7897** for information, 800/374-7263 or 302/652-5577 for tickets; www.grandopera.org), is the center of it, right in the heart of downtown. Built in 1871 as part of a Masonic temple, this restored Victorian showplace is one of the finest examples of cast-iron architecture in America. The facility seats 1,100 and is home to Opera Delaware and the Delaware Symphony Orchestra. It also offers a program of ballet, jazz, chamber music, pop music, and theater.

The **Delaware Symphony Orchestra** (℃ **302/656-7442** for information, 800/374-7263 or 302/652-5577 for tickets; www.desymphony.org), celebrating its centennial in 2005 and 2006, is led by David Amado. The DSO's 90-plus performances a year range from chamber music to pops to classical. Performances are usually held in the Grand Opera House in Wilmington, but chamber music concerts are given in the Hotel du Pont or Winterthur, with other concerts at schools around Delaware. Tickets run $29 to $40; student tickets are $10.

How do you like your opera—grand Italian, light operetta, or maybe something for the kids? **Opera Delaware** (℃ **302/658-8063** for information, 800/374-7263 or 302/652-5577 for tickets; www.operade.org) offers three series with prices ranging from $27 to $40. Family tickets are $6 and $11. Supertitles are provided; those who don't like them can sit in sections where the projections can't be seen.

THEATER & DANCE

The city's other large venue, the **DuPont Theatre** (formerly the Playhouse), at 10th and Market streets (℃ **800/338-0881** or 302/656-4401; www.duponttheatre.com), has brought touring shows to downtown Wilmington for more than 80 years. Tucked into the Hotel du Pont, it has a 1,239-seat capacity amid vintage Victorian decor. In addition, local companies often stage performances here—including the Wilmington Ballet's "Nutcracker."

Delaware Theatre Company *(Finds* At the foot of Orange Street on the Riverfront, this 389-seat facility has no seat more than 12 rows from the stage. The theater is home to Delaware's only resident professional company, which presents both classic and contemporary plays. 200 Water St. ℃ **302/594-1100** for box office. www.delawaretheatre.org.

New Candlelight Theatre A big red barn in the northern suburb of Ardentown holds Delaware's first dinner theater, started more than 25 years ago. New owners, both longtime actors, have taken over the theater, added "New" to the name, and given the place a face-lift. The price of admission includes a buffet dinner. Shows are held Friday and Saturday, with a buffet at 6pm and show at 8pm; the Sunday buffet is at 1pm, with the show at 3pm. 2208 Millers Rd. (signposted off Harvey Rd.), Ardentown. ℃ **302/475-2313.** www.newcandlelighttheatre.com. Tickets $45 adults, $30 children.

Three Little Bakers Dinner Theatre Southeast of Wilmington off Route 7, this theater presents revivals of Broadway shows, as well as celebrity specials featuring stars and bands such as Shirley Caesar or the Oak Ridge Boys (not in the same show). Productions have included *Big: The Musical* and *West Side Story.* The price includes a buffet dinner, dancing, and preshow entertainment. 3540 Three Little Bakers Blvd. ℃ **800/368-3303** or 302/368-1616. www.tlbinc.com. Tickets $29–$50.

THE CLUB & MUSIC SCENE

Wilmington's Riverfront is getting to be the place to hear music. Kahunaville rocks, especially during its summer concert season. Dravo Plaza is the place for outdoor jazz, reggae, classical, and blues on Thursdays in summer. In the rest of the city, the nightlife is pretty mellow, dominated by folk music, blues, and hotel piano bars.

Catherine Rooney's Set in Trolley Square, just down the street from Kelly's Logan House, this newcomer is a welcome breath of Celtic air. Irish rock and folk are featured on Friday and Saturday from 10pm to 1am. Trolley Sq., 1616 Delaware Ave. ℂ 302/654-9700. www.catherinerooneys.com. Cover varies; sometimes no cover.

4W5 Cafe Come for jam sessions Tuesday through Thursday, live music and concerts Friday and Saturday. Open daily from 6:30pm to closing. The coffeehouse is also open daily from 7am to 3pm. 4 W. Fifth St. ℂ 302/661-0100. Cover varies; no cover for jam sessions.

Kahunaville The sprawling party bar, restaurant, and concert venue at Wilmington's Riverfront is hard to miss. It's the place to be for concerts by national acts such as the Allman Brothers, Green Day, and the Beach Boys, on the deck in warm months or in the banquet hall when it's colder. The swank **Red Room** lounge drips in red velvet. Kahunaville is open daily from 11:30am to 1am; the Red Room, Thursday through Saturday evenings; and the deck, Thursday through Sunday starting at 5pm from around mid-April to mid-October. 550 S. Madison St. ℂ 302/571-8402 for Kahunaville; ℂ 302/571-8440 for Red Room. www.kahunaville.com. Cover varies.

Kelly's Logan House This old tavern can really rock. There's acoustic music on Tuesday and Wednesday, bands Thursday through Saturday, and a DJ Friday and Saturday. The musicians play on the second floor, which makes a nice background for those on the first floor and the terrace on warm summer nights (see p. 300 for the restaurant review). Open Tuesday through Saturday from 11am to 1am, Sunday from 11am to 9pm, and Monday from 5pm to 1am. 1701 Delaware Ave. ℂ 302/655-6426. www.loganhouse.com. Cover $5–$10.

Volare Lounge Young Wilmingtonians stop at this lounge for "boozin' bingo" on Wednesday, martinis and movies on Thursday, and happy hour on Friday, as well as the occasional comedian or live music. 1010 Union St., Little Italy. ℂ 302/655-8536. www.thevolarelounge.com. Cover varies.

FILM

Theatre N. at Nemours This 221-seat theater shows independent and foreign films Friday and Saturday at 8pm, plus Sunday matinees at 2pm. A film festival is held in March. Tickets are available an hour before showtime and on the website. Nemours Building, 1007 Orange St. ℂ 302/658-6070. www.theatren.org.

ESPECIALLY FOR KIDS

The **Delaware Children's Theatre,** 1014 Delaware Ave. (ℂ 302/655-1014; www.dechildrenstheatre.org), presents plays based on fairy tales and other children's stories. Tickets are $10, with performances on select Saturdays and Sundays at 2pm. *Note:* Even for adult visitors, this ornate three-story building is worth a look for its historic and architectural value. Listed on the National Register of Historic Places, it was designed in 1892 by a woman as a women's club. Women continue to own and operate the building today.

12

The Brandywine Valley & Historic New Castle

The Brandywine Valley combines natural beauty with the best in art and craftsmanship. The valley's hills, rivers, and forests are dotted with mansions, gardens, and museums.

Here, between Wilmington and across the Pennsylvania line, you'll find the famous homes and gardens of the du Pont family—which give the Brandywine the nickname "Château Valley"—as well as the rolling hills and woodlands where three generations of the Wyeth family have lived and found inspiration for their art.

New Castle, Delaware's original capital, recalls the First State's early days. Just south of Wilmington, the town has preserved its 18th-century past with cobblestone streets, brick sidewalks, and 200-year-old homes. New Castle also offers some good antiques shops and restaurants.

1 The Brandywine Valley

10 miles N of Wilmington, 35 miles W of Philadelphia, 73 miles N of Baltimore

Meandering north from Wilmington, the Brandywine River has a long, storied history. The river and its valley provided for early settlers, powered the first du Pont industry, and inspired a school of art. To the Native Americans, the river was the *Wawset* or *Suspecoughwit,* cherished as a bountiful shad-fishing source. The Swedes and Danes later called it the Fishkill. Quakers and other English settlers renamed it the Brandywine and made it an important mill center in the 18th and 19th centuries. At its peak, more than 100 water-powered mills along the river produced everything from flour, paper, and textiles to snuff and black powder, on which the American du Ponts first made their fortune. In more recent times, the valley has been home to a school of artists and illustrators, beginning with Howard Pyle and Frank Schoonover, and including the Wyeth family—N. C.; Andrew, who still lives and paints here; and Jamie.

The Brandywine Valley begins near Wilmington and stretches into Pennsylvania. Those who wish to see Winterthur and Longwood Gardens can do both in a day, since they're only a 20-minute drive apart. Some Pennsylvania sights are included because they're part of the area; the Pennsylvania side is also explored in *Frommer's Philadelphia & the Amish Country.* Two main arteries, routes 52 and 100, were recently named the Brandywine Valley Scenic Byway—see www.byways.org for a map that works well with this chapter.

ESSENTIALS

GETTING THERE   The valley's attractions in Delaware are spread out north of Wilmington, but most are along Route 52. By car, take I-95 into Wilmington to

Delaware Route 52 North. The main attractions in Pennsylvania are along U.S. Route 1. From Wilmington, routes 52 and 100 both lead to U.S. Route 1. Alternate routes from I-95 are U.S. Route 202, which goes all the way to U.S. Route 1, and Route 141 to Route 52.

Bus service from Wilmington is available through **DART** (© **302/652-3278;** www.dartfirststate.com). See p. 294 for information on rail and air transportation.

VISITOR INFORMATION   Contact the **Greater Wilmington Convention and Visitors Bureau,** 100 W. 10th St., Suite 20, Wilmington (© **800/489-6664,** 800/422-1181, or 302/652-4088; www.visitwilmingtonde.com), open Monday through Friday from 9am to 5pm; or stop by the branch at the **I-95 Delaware Travel Plaza,** between exits 1 and 3 near Newark, Delaware, open daily from 8am to 8pm. You can also go to the **Chester County Visitor Center,** on U.S. Route 1 at the entrance to Longwood Gardens, Kennett Square, Pennsylvania (© **800/228-9933** or 610/388-2900; www.brandywinetreasures.org), open daily from 10am to 5pm.

AREA CODE   Brandywine Valley attractions located in the Wilmington suburbs use the 302 area code. Pennsylvania sights, inns, and restaurants use the 610 area code.

SPECIAL EVENTS   **Longwood Gardens** (© **610/388-1000**) has seasonal displays: The **Welcome Spring** indoor display of colorful bulbs is a favorite, as is the **Christmas Display** ✿✿✿, featuring hundreds of poinsettias and a lighted outdoor display. **Yuletide at Winterthur** (© **800/448-3883**) is always a sensation, with rooms decorated according to the customs from throughout American history.

WHERE TO STAY

Wilmington area hotels are convenient bases from which to tour the Brandywine Valley, so check p. 295 for more places to stay. Below are several inns and hotels in nearby Pennsylvania. Lots of hotels offer weekend packages that include entrance to area attractions—inquire when you call to make reservations.

Brandywine River Hotel *Value*   This hotel, on a hillside in the heart of the valley, is one of the best values in the area—lots of amenities, good location, and comfortable, stylish rooms for the price of an average chain hotel. Designed to meld with this scenic and historic region, with a facade of brick and cedar shingle, it is set beside a cluster of shops, galleries, and an artisans' cooperative. The lobby has a huge stone fireplace and a homey ambience. Accommodations include standard doubles, executive units with sofa beds, and grand and grander Jacuzzi suites with fireplaces. All are decorated in Colonial style with paintings in the Brandywine tradition.

Routes 1 and 100 (P.O. Box 1058), Chadds Ford, PA 19317. © 800/274-9644 or 610/388-1200. www.brandywine riverhotel.com. 40 units. $125–$135 double; $149–$169 suite. Rates include continental breakfast and afternoon tea. AE, DC, DISC, MC, V. Free parking. Pets under 20 lb. accepted for $20 per day; must be crated. **Amenities:** Lounge; health club; business center. *In room:* A/C, TV/VCR, high-speed Internet access, hair dryer.

Fairville Inn   This gracious 1857 inn, listed on the National Register of Historic Places, is set on 5 leafy acres near Winterthur. Its Colonial-style decor is warm and cozy. The main house has five bedrooms; if you'd like more space or a private porch (or even a fireplace), ask for a room in the Springhouse or the Carriage House. These outbuildings offer extra privacy as well.

506 Kennett Pike (Rte. 52), Chadds Ford, PA 19317. © 877/285-7772 or 610/388-5900. www.fairvilleinn.com. 15 units. $150–$250 double. Rates include full breakfast and afternoon tea. AE, DISC, MC, V. Free parking. **Amenities:** Wi-Fi in main house's public rooms. *In room:* A/C, TV w/satellite, Internet access, hair dryer, coffeemaker (upon request).

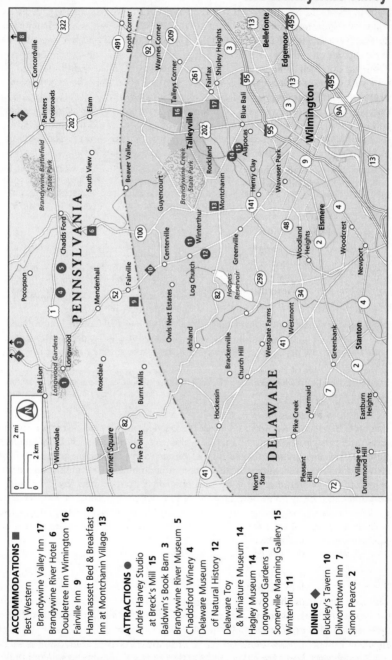

The Brandywine Valley

PENNSYLVANIA

DELAWARE

Concordville · 322 · 8 ←

Painters Crossroads · 7 ←

Booth Corner · 491 · 322 · 13 · Bellefonte · 495

Waynes Corner · 209 · 92 · Edgemoor · 495

Talleys Corner · 261 · Shipley Heights · 3 · Fairfax · 13

Elam · 202 · 16 · 17 · Blue Ball · 95 · Wilmington · 9A

Talleyville · 202 · Rockland · 15 · 14 · Alapocas · 95 · 495

South View · Beaver Valley · Guyencourt · Montchanin · 13 · Henry Clay · Wawaset Park · 9 · 13

Brandywine Battlefield State Park · Brandywine Creek State Park · 141 · 48 · Eismere · 4

Chadds Ford · 6 · 100 · Centerville · Winterthur · 11 · Greenville · Woodland Heights · 2 · Woodcrest

South View · Fairville · 52 · 10 · 9 · 12 · Log Church · Greenville · 259 · Newport · 4

Mendenhall · 5 · 4 · Owls Nest Estates · Ashland · 82 · Hoopes Reservoir · 34 · Stanton

Pocopson · 1 · Church Hill · Brackenville · Westgate Farms · 41 · Westmont · Greenbank · 2

Red Lion · 2 · 3 ← · Longwood Gardens · Longwood · 1 · Rosedale · Burnt Mills · Hockessin · 7 · Mermaid · Pike Creek

Willowdale · Five Points · 82 · Kennet Square · 41 · North Star · Pleasant Hill · Eastburn Heights · Village of Drummond Hill · 72

ACCOMMODATIONS ■

Best Western
Brandywine Valley Inn **17**
Brandywine River Hotel **6**
Doubletree Inn Wimington **16**
Fairville Inn **9**
Hamanassett Bed & Breakfast **8**
Inn at Montchanin Village **13**

ATTRACTIONS ●

André Harvey Studio
at Breck's Mill **15**
Baldwin's Book Barn **3**
Brandywine River Museum **5**
Chaddsford Winery **4**
Delaware Museum
of Natural History **12**
Delaware Toy
& Miniature Museum **14**
Hagley Museum **14**
Longwood Gardens **1**
Somerville Manning Gallery **15**
Winterthur **11**

DINING ◆

Buckley's Tavern **10**
Dilworthtown Inn **7**
Simon Pearce **2**

Hamanassett Bed & Breakfast 🌟 This romantic 1856 mansion, with Palladian windows and grand staircase, has long been a B&B. Owners Ashley and Glenn Mon, up from New Orleans, have worked to make it as luxurious as possible. You'll feel far from the crowds—though Brandywine attractions are just about 20 minutes away. Trees and flowers line the walking trails; the meadows are filled with horses. In fact, the grounds, which now feature a waterfall and koi pond, have been designated a National Wildlife Federation sanctuary. The inn itself offers a casual solarium, a library with a roaring fire in winter, and spacious bedrooms decorated with antiques and luxurious beds. An English country–style cottage with two bedrooms is available for families or those with pets. Breakfast is opulent; afternoon tea is available. And always, always expect Southern hospitality from these gracious hosts.

P.O. Box 336, Chester Heights, PA 19017. ✆ **877/836-8212** for reservations, or 610/459-3000. www.hamanassett.com. 7 units. $160–$195 double; $165–$215 suite; $250–$400 cottage. Rates include full breakfast. AE, DISC, MC, V. Free parking. Pets accepted in cottage. Children under 12 accepted in cottage. **Amenities:** Business services; game room w/billiards; video library; fridge stocked w/complimentary beverages. *In room:* A/C, TV/VCR, Internet access in some rooms, coffeemaker, iron, robe.

WHERE TO DINE

Buckley's Tavern AMERICAN This casual roadside restaurant in the quaint borough of Centreville has been feeding people since the 1800s. But the menu is up-to-date, with trendy small plates, hearty sandwiches, salads, and intriguing entrees. Lunchtime favorites include a flavorful mustard-crusted chicken sandwich, while at dinner, crab cakes are paired with roasted corn béarnaise. It's a busy place, from the porch on a sunny day to the very casual bar to the more formal Colonial dining room. Brunch is served on Sundays. The location is perfect for a Sunday drive—pair brunch with a visit to one of the local museums or some of the antiques shops that pop up along Route 52.

5812 Kennett Pike (Rte. 52), Centreville, DE. ✆ **302/656-9776**. Reservations recommended for dinner. Main courses $7.95–$12 at lunch, $7.95–$25 at dinner. AE, DC, MC, V. Mon–Wed 11:30am–9:30pm; Thurs–Sat 11:30am–11pm; Sun 10am–2:30pm and 3–9pm. Tavern fare until 11pm nightly. Live music Thurs 9pm–midnight.

Dilworthtown Inn 🌟 CONTINENTAL Located on the road that was once the principal connection between Wilmington and West Chester, this establishment was built in 1758 and restored in 1972. The 15 dining rooms include the house's original kitchen and an outside stable area for warm-weather dining. Colonial furniture, dark-wood beams, 11 fireplaces, gas lamps and candlelight, and Andrew Wyeth paintings set the mood. The menu includes an array of fine-dining options. Start with caviar or Philly cheese steak spring rolls; move on to rack of lamb or diver scallops. Pair these with an offering from the extensive wine cellar. The inn also has a demonstration kitchen for cooking classes.

1390 Old Wilmington Pike and Brinton Bridge Rd. (off Rte. 202), West Chester, PA. ✆ **610/399-1390**. www.dilworth town.com. Reservations required; jackets for men recommended. Main courses $20–$37. AE, DC, DISC, MC, V. Mon–Fri 5:30–9:30pm; Sat 5–9:30pm; Sun 3–8:30pm. Closed Wed before Labor Day to the following Tues.

Simon Pearce AMERICAN The name usually associated with fine modern crystal also has two restaurants—including this new one in the Brandywine Valley. Naturally, Simon Pearce tableware graces the tables, with creative modern cuisine served at lunch and dinner. Try the pumpkin ravioli or braised short ribs at lunch, or perhaps the duck or vegetable napoleon for dinner. The restaurant is on the second floor of the glassblowing factory, with floor-to-ceiling windows overlooking Brandywine Creek. Make sure to stop to see the glassblowers at work.

1333 Lenape Rd., West Chester, PA. © 610/793-0948. www.simonpearce.com. Reservations not necessary. Main courses $10–$15 lunch, $21–$38 dinner. AE, DISC, MC, V. Daily 11:30am–2:45pm; Mon–Sat 5:30–9pm; Sun 5:30–8:30pm.

THE DU PONT HOMES & GARDENS

If you've seen only one du Pont home, you're just getting started. Each reflects the personality of its owners and their lifestyles. For sheer splendor, a visit to **Nemours Mansion** would be required—but it's closed for restoration until May 2007. If your tastes are more of a garden variety, **Longwood Gardens** has the most varied gardens. Even if you skip the house (though it's a nice one), don't miss the conservatories. The charms of world-famous **Winterthur** are more academic; remember, this is more a museum than a house. The room with the Chinese wallpaper has earned its world-class reputation, but the house tells more about the decorative arts than about the personality who gathered them here. (Marylanders should check out the Chestertown room and the Baltimore alcove.) Leave time for the gardens, especially the children's Enchanted Woods—but if you have time for only one garden in the Brandywine Valley, go to Longwood. The **Hagley Museum** is worth visiting to see how regular Americans lived and worked when the country was new. Its grounds beside the river offer a spectacular display of autumn foliage.

Hagley Museum ✸✸✸ *Kids*   The du Pont fortune got started along this wooded riverbank. French émigré Eleuthère Irénée du Pont de Nemours built the first of his gunpowder mills here in 1802, and the first du Pont home in 1803. The mills grew in number and size, later to include workers' homes and a school. A visit to the 235-acre site can take a couple of hours or a whole day. Just the walk along the river, past the ruins of the old roll mills, will keep kids busy.

Start in the **visitor center,** which features the DuPont Science and Discovery exhibit (including a NASCAR car and a space suit). Kids will love the adjacent **Hydroelectric Plant,** where they can learn about simple machinery at the "Easy Does It!" exhibit.

Walk along the river and millrace to see the roll mills, the narrow-gauge railroad, and the dangerous steps it took to make gunpowder in the 1800s. Visit what remains of one of the workers' communities, the Gibbons House, the Sunday school, and the **Belin House Restaurant** (open 11am–4pm). Don't miss the **Millwright Shop** dioramas and live demonstration, which explain how gunpowder is made. Look for the new exhibit on the deadly 1920 explosion, right along the path of the powder yards; it serves as a bit of archaeological dig while highlighting the importance of safety.

Visitors to the family house, **Eleutherian Mills** (newly reopened in late 2005 after extensive maintenance work), catch a bus that offers a narrated tour through the powder yards to the Georgian-style residence where five generations of du Ponts lived. Rooms reflect the various periods of the house's history from the 1800s to the 1920s. The French gardens, barn, and First Office are also worth a look.

Hagley's Family Fun Events include dollar days, concerts, Christmas events, and bike and hike days; check the website for details.

Rte. 141, Wilmington, DE. © 302/658-2400. www.hagley.org. Admission $11 adults, $9 students and seniors, $4 children 6–14; visitor center exhibits only $5 adults, $2 children 6–14. Mar 15–Dec daily 9:30am–4:30pm; Jan–Mar 14 Mon–Fri 1 guided tour at 1:30pm, Sat–Sun 9:30am–4:30pm. Closed Thanksgiving, Dec 25, and Dec 31. From Wilmington, take I-95 to Rte. 52 North Turn right on Rte. 141; museum entrance is on the left.

Longwood Gardens 🎬🎬🎬 *Kids*   One of the world's most celebrated horticultural displays, Longwood Gardens marks its centennial this year. It showcases more than 11,000 different types of plants and flowers amid 1,050 acres of outdoor gardens and woodlands. For sheer size, Longwood is spectacular. But the ever-blooming displays throughout the grounds and conservatory are both creative and delightful, thanks to Pierre S. du Pont, who purchased the existing farm and arboretum in 1906, and from 1907 to 1954 designed most of what is enjoyed today.

Everybody has a favorite spot: the tropical paradise of the **Conservatory;** the eye-popping seasonal displays; the flower-garden walk that explodes in seasonal color; the understated **Chimes Tower** (with carillon); the **Idea Garden** to inspire home gardeners; the **Flower Garden Fountains,** the **Italian Water Garden,** or the **Main Fountain Garden,** whose 380 fountains and spouts rise over 130 feet high during one of the 5-minute displays throughout the day. There are also illuminated displays in the fountain garden on Tuesday, Thursday, and Saturday evenings June through September, plus fireworks displays on several evenings in summer (check the website for a schedule). The recently restored **East Conservatory,** reopened in late 2005, is filled with fresh new water features among the plantings (serious gardeners will enjoy the audio wand tours). The ballroom has also been restored; behind it is an organ museum with interactive displays for children. Construction continues: A new children's garden opens in 2007, and the conservatory's entry plaza will be completed in 2009.

Longwood's attractions also include seasonal plant displays (Christmas and Easter gardens are noteworthy) and hundreds of performances; check the website for a schedule. Facilities include the **Peirce–du Pont House,** open daily from 10am to 5pm; a large museum shop; and the **Terrace Restaurant,** which has both a cafeteria and full-service dining room. Both restaurants are open later during special events; reservations are recommended for the dining room.

Rte. 1 (just north of Rte. 52), Kennett Sq., PA. ℂ **610/388-1000.** www.longwoodgardens.org. Admission for adults: Jan–Mar $12 ($8 on Tues), April–Nov $14 ($10 on Tues), Christmas display $15; year-round for those under 20: $6 ages 16–20, $2 ages 6–15. AE, DC, DISC, MC, V. Mid-Jan to Mar daily 9am–5pm; Apr–May daily 9am–6pm; Memorial Day to Labor Day Mon and Wed–Thurs 9am–6pm, Tues and Fri–Sat 9am–10pm, Sun 9am–8pm; Sept–Oct daily 9am–6pm; early Nov to Thanksgiving daily 9am–5pm; Thanksgiving to early Jan daily 9am–9pm.

Nemours Mansion and Gardens   This 300-acre estate was the home of Alfred I. du Pont and his family. Built in 1909 and 1910, and named after the du Pont ancestral home in France, the 102-room Louis XVI–style château is a model of extravagance. Two years of restoration began in late 2005, requiring this magnificent home to be closed until May 2007. Check the website for up-to-date information about the mansion's reopening and directions to its entrance, which will be relocated. Once Nemours reopens, it should be on every visitor's must-see list.

1600 Rockland Rd., Wilmington, DE. ℂ **800/651-6912** or 302/651-6912. www.nemoursmansion.org. Closed until May 2007.

Winterthur Museum & Country Estate 🎬🎬🎬 *Kids*   Named after a town in Switzerland and pronounced "win-ter-tour," this eight-story mansion and country estate features one of the world's premier collections of American antiques and decorative arts. The estate was the country home of Henry Francis du Pont, a collector of furniture, who in 1951 turned the place into a museum for American decorative arts. The 85,000 objects made or used in America, including Chippendale furniture, silver tankards by Paul Revere, and a dinner service made for George Washington, are displayed in the 175 period rooms. The galleries include exhibits of furniture styles, life at

---

(*Finds*) **Shop off the Beaten Path**

Get off Route 52 and take a drive on Route 82 to Hockessin. The journey is more fun than the destination. Bicyclists may like this road, too, as it twists and turns alongside old railroad tracks and a lazy creek. The road forks off to the right into Pennsylvania; make sure you take the left fork. The destination in Hockessin is a little shopping center across Route 41 with one of the best crafts shops anywhere, **Creations,** 451 Hockessin Corner (*℃* **302/235-2310;** www.creationsgallery. com). The shopping center, which has several gift shops, is really just off Route 41—but Route 82 is more scenic.

Winterthur, Early American craftsmen, and the famous Campbell Collection of Soup Tureens. Look for an exhibit on film fashion from September 2006 to January 2007.

It takes more than one visit to really see Winterthur. A variety of 1-hour **Discovery Tours** focus on everything from entertaining to du Pont collections to seasonal topics. The introductory Elegant Entertaining tour, for instance, covers only one floor, highlighting the dining room, sitting rooms, and other period public rooms. The Winterthur Experience pass, good for 2 consecutive days, includes one Discovery Tour, admission to the galleries, and a tram tour of the 966-acre grounds. Additional hour-long tours can be added for $5 for adults. Reservations are recommended. An annual **Yuletide Tour** is offered from mid-November to December 31, and **iPod Tours** of the first-floor galleries are also available—Winterthur is the fourth museum in the world to have such a high-tech tour.

Children under 8 are permitted on three of the tours, as well as the Yuletide Tour. Kids (and adults, too) will love the **Enchanted Woods,** a 3-acre fairy-tale garden filled with places to play, including a Faerie Cottage and Troll Bridge. The rest of the gardens put on a new show each season. Other facilities include two restaurants (afternoon tea is a special treat), an extensive museum store, and a bookshop.

Rte. 52, Winterthur, DE. *℃* **800/448-3883** or 302/888-4600. www.winterthur.org. Admission to galleries and garden $15 adults, $13 seniors and students, $5 children 5–11. Guided Discovery Tours of house and garden $20 adults, $18 seniors and students. Special-interest tours (see website) $30 adults, $28 seniors. AE, DISC, MC, V. Tues–Fri 10am–5pm (last tour at 4pm). Closed Thanksgiving and Dec 25. Located 6 miles northwest of Wilmington on Rte. 52 and 5 miles south of Rte. 1.

OTHER ATTRACTIONS

André Harvey Studio   Housed on the second floor of an 1814 stone mill building downstream from the Hagley Museum, this studio features realistic bronze sculptures of people and animals by André Harvey. It also displays sculptural jewelry made in collaboration with goldsmith Donald Pywell. A separate gallery shows different stages of casting.

At Breck's Mill, 101 Stone Block Row, Greenville, DE. *℃* **302/656-7955.** www.andreharvey.com. Mon–Sat 10am–4:30pm and by appointment.

Baldwin's Book Barn (*Finds*)   Okay, technically this is a store—but for true bibliophiles, it's a don't-miss experience. With five floors of 300,000 rare and used books, maps, and prints in an 1822 stone barn, it's easy to while away hours getting lost among the stacks or browsing a book in the cozy reading room.

865 Lenape Rd. (routes 100 and 52), West Chester, PA. *℃* **610/696-0816.** www.bookbarn.com. Mon–Fri 9am–9pm; Sat–Sun 10am–6pm. From Rte. 1, take Rte. 52 north. The barn is 6 miles past Rte. 1 on the left, near Chadds Ford.

Brandywine Battlefield Park On these rolling hills, George Washington's troops fought with the British for control of strategic territory near Philadelphia. The September 11, 1777, defeat had its victories, too. The Marquis de Lafayette saw his first military action here, witnessed the courage and determination of the Americans, and helped convince the French to form an alliance with the colonists. House tours of two Quaker farmhouses, which served as George Washington's headquarters and the quarters of the Marquis de Lafayette, are offered on the hour. On-site are picnic areas and a visitor center with exhibits, dioramas, and a museum shop. Check the website for three driving tours.

1491 Baltimore Pike (Rte. 1), Chadds Ford, PA. © 610/459-3342. www.ushistory.org/brandywine. Free admission to battlefield and visitor center; house tour $5 adults, $3.50 seniors, $2.50 children 6–17. Tues–Sat 9am–5pm; Sun noon–5pm.

Brandywine River Museum 🎨🎨🎨 An old building in a pristine wooded setting, filled with the best of the Brandywine School's paintings, is a celebration of this picturesque part of the country. This Civil War–era gristmill—near the home and studio of three generations of Wyeth artists—has been converted into a museum that embraces not only the art, but also the setting that inspired it. Huge, sweeping windows overlook the valley and river below. Inside the galleries are the paintings of Howard Pyle and the artists he taught, including N. C. Wyeth, Frank Schoonover, and Maxfield Parrish. Works by N. C.'s children Andrew, Henriette, and Caroline are here, as well as paintings by Jamie Wyeth, the third generation of family artists. Andrew Wyeth has a gallery all his own, with his comments accompanying most of his pieces. Tours of N. C. Wyeth's house and studio are offered Wednesday through Sunday from April to November. The studio is well worth seeing: Wyeth's paint-splattered smock still hangs near his palette and the painting he was working on at the time of his death. The big museum shop and restaurant have great views, too.

Rte. 1 and Pa. Rte. 100, Chadds Ford, PA. © 610/388-2700. www.brandywinemuseum.org. Admission $8 adults, $5 seniors and students; studio tour $5. Daily 9:30am–4:30pm. Closed Dec 25. Just south of Rte. 100 on the Brandywine River.

Chaddsford Winery Walk in the door of this restored barn, and you'll be greeted with a sample of wine made in Pennsylvania's largest winery. Then take a self-guided or guided half-hour tour. For $6, buy a glass and try a wide variety of varietals, regional wines, and seasonal and sweet wines. Wine classes and festivals are held here; check the website for details.

632 Baltimore Pike (U.S. 1), Chadds Ford, PA. © 610/388-6221. www.chaddsford.com. Free admission; full tasting session $6. Tours daily noon–6pm. Located 5 miles south of Rte. 202, just past the Brandywine River Museum. Closed Thanksgiving, Dec 25, and Jan 1.

Delaware Museum of Natural History *Kids* Visitors are greeted by a giant squid "swimming" overhead in the newly constructed glass entrance—perfect for a museum known for its mollusk and bird collections. (Did you know a squid is a mollusk?) Renovations have added exhibit space for traveling displays, a canteen with vending machines, and a patio by the butterfly garden. Following a loop, visitors can look up at an Allosaurus, one of Delaware's only dinosaurs, or tiptoe over the Great Barrier Reef exhibit located under Plexiglas in the floor. The shell and gemstone and mineral cases glitter with color and light. You may see a staff member cleaning a dinosaur jawbone, happy to answer questions. The museum is bound to intrigue the kids.

4840 Kennett Pike (Rte. 52), Wilmington, DE. © 302/658-9111. www.delmnh.org. Admission $6 adults, $4 seniors, $5 children 3–17. Mon–Sat 9:30am–4:30pm; Sun noon–4:30pm. Located 5 miles northwest of Wilmington on Rte. 52. Closed Jan 1, Easter, July 4th, Thanksgiving, and Dec 25.

Tips **Wilmington & the Brandywine Valley for Kids**

Wilmington and its suburbs are home to palatial residences, elegant hotels, and immense gardens, not places you'd think of as kid-friendly. Fortunately, several sites welcome kids. All of the following are described in detail earlier in this chapter, except the Delaware History Museum and Fort Delaware State Park, both listed in chapter 11, "Wilmington."

Delaware History Museum (p. 301) This museum of First State history, housed in an old Woolworth's store in Wilmington, is bright, colorful, and has fun exhibits. Its hands-on Discovery Room lets kids touch artifacts and hear stories.

Delaware Museum of Natural History (p. 314) Children can run wild here (carefully, of course) while looking at dinosaur skeletons, lots of shells, special exhibits, and their own Discovery Room.

Fort Delaware State Park (p. 304) Kids will love this Civil War prison fort on an island in the Delaware Bay. Not only are there a boat ride to the island and a tractor-pulled tram ride to the fort, but reenactors also lead guided tours and give artillery demonstrations in summer.

Hagley Museum (p. 311) The family-friendly museum, set on the shady banks of the Brandywine River, tells the story of the du Pont family's early gunpowder mill. Kids love the gunpowder testing demonstration.

Longwood Gardens (p. 312) This is a sprawling landscape with fountains, animal-shaped hedges, and conservatories. Little ones shouldn't miss the children's garden, opening in 2007 with whimsical fountains and paths just their size. It's expensive, but adult admission is discounted on Tuesdays.

Winterthur's Enchanted Woods (p. 313) These 3 acres will delight the young ones with a labyrinth, fountains, and kid-size cottage. Pick up the amusing brochure that tells the tale of the Enchanted Woods.

Delaware Toy & Miniature Museum *(Kids)* *(Finds)* This tiny museum has collections from all over the world and from as far back as 600 B.C. Grand dollhouses, toy soldiers, and trains and trucks and planes are among the museum's holdings. Of special interest is a collection of brass dolls dressed in costumes of opera figures and in fashions representative of different countries and different designers. Kids will love the exhibits, though they can't be touched; adults will appreciate the craftsmanship—most of it anonymous, but also including works by Tiffany, Limoges, Lalique, and Fabergé.

Off Rte. 141, Wilmington, DE. © **302/427-TOYS.** www.thomes.net/toys. Admission $6 adults, $5 seniors and students, $3 children 3–12. Tues–Sat 10am–4pm; Sun noon–4pm. Located just before entrance to Hagley Museum.

Somerville Manning Gallery Also housed at Breck's Mill, near Hagley, is this gallery devoted to 20th-century art, including the works of the Wyeth family and other artists trained in the traditions of the Brandywine School.

At Breck's Mill, 101 Stone Block Row, Greenville, DE. © **302/652-0271.** www.somervillemanning.com. Mon–Sat 10am–5pm.

2 Historic New Castle

7 miles S of Wilmington, 40 miles SW of Philadelphia, 70 miles NE of Baltimore

New Castle, Delaware's original capital, was a major Colonial seaport. Peter Stuyvesant, who established a Dutch settlement named Fort Casimir, purchased the area from Native Americans in 1651. (It's said that Stuyvesant designed the town's central green by "pegging it off" with his wooden leg.) Later captured by the Swedes and then the English, who renamed it New Castle, this stretch of land along the west bank of the Delaware River remains much the way it was in the 17th and 18th centuries. Original houses and public buildings have been restored and preserved, with brick sidewalks and cobblestone streets.

Park your car (no meters here) and stroll past old homes and churches, a few tiny shops, and restaurants. Everything is close by—even the expansive Battery Park by the river. Cool breezes, green places, and playground equipment make it a nice break for both children and adults.

ESSENTIALS

GETTING THERE From Wilmington, either take U.S. Route 13 south to Delaware Route 273 east to New Castle, or follow Delaware Route 9 south directly to New Castle. From the south, take Route 301 to Route 13 North. (It's a good day trip from Baltimore or Annapolis, too.)

VISITOR INFORMATION For information, contact the **Historic New Castle Visitors Bureau** (© 800/758-1550; www.visitnewcastle.com) or stop by the visitor center in the Court House.

SPECIAL EVENTS **A Day in Old New Castle** (© 877/496-9498; www.dayinold newcastle.org), held the third Saturday in May, gives visitors a chance to tour the town's private homes and gardens, as well as public buildings, gardens, and museums. The **Historic New Castle Antiques Show** is held in Battery Park in mid-August. **A New Castle Christmas** features house tours, carolers, and carriage rides in mid-December; contact the **New Castle Historical Society** (© 302/322-2794; www.newcastlehistory.org) for details.

WHERE TO STAY

New Castle provides a convenient base for touring the Brandywine Valley and visiting Wilmington, 7 miles away.

Bridgeview Inn Close to the Delaware Memorial Bridge, this busy two-story property is set back from the main roads but within sight of traffic. Although not in the historic district, it is convenient to it. The building is done in a modernized Colonial motif, the rooms decorated with reproduction furniture and watercolors of local attractions.

1612 N. DuPont Hwy. (I-295 and Rte. 13 N.), New Castle, DE 19720. © **800/810-8511** or 302/658-8511. Fax 302/658-3071. www.bridgeviewinnde.com. 120 units. $90 double. Rates include continental breakfast. AE, DC, DISC, MC, V. Free parking. Small dogs accepted for $10 fee. **Amenities:** Outdoor pool; health club; guest laundry. *In room:* A/C, TV, dataport, coffeemaker, hair dryer, iron.

WHERE TO DINE

Air Transport Command INTERNATIONAL Air Force memorabilia sets the tone at this enormous restaurant near the runways of New Castle County Airport. The flying heroes and heroines of World War II are commemorated with old uniforms, pictures, and equipment. You can even pick up a set of headphones and listen to the

> (Finds **African-American Art in Newark**
>
> Fans of Jacob Lawrence, Hale Woodruff, or Carrie Mae Weems may want to take a detour to Newark, Delaware, to see the **Paul R. Jones Collection** at the University of Delaware (© **302/831-8088;** www.paulrjones.museums.udel.edu). The collection—the world's largest and most comprehensive of 20th-century African-American art—is housed in the newly renovated Mechanical Hall. It's open Tuesday through Friday from 11am to 4pm, Saturday and Sunday from 1 to 4pm. Admission is free.

ground-to-air instructions at the nearby control tower. Music from the 1940s adds to the vintage atmosphere. Dinner entrees include simple standards like steak, prime rib, stuffed flounder, and crab cakes.

143 N. DuPont Hwy. © **302/328-3527.** Reservations recommended for dinner. Main courses $4.95–$13 lunch, $13–$25 dinner. AE, DC, DISC, MC, V. Mon–Thurs 11am–10pm; Fri–Sat 11am–11pm; Sun 9:30am–10pm. Open cock-pit tours on Sat May–Sept.

The Arsenal AMERICAN   The same folks who operate Jessop's Tavern (see below) offer more refined dining down the street in this big brick building, which originally served as ammunition storage for the War of 1812. You have your choice of a casual tavern or more elegant dining room, both with Colonial-style ambience. Lunch choices vary from crab cakes to vegetable Alfredo. At dinner, tuck into General Sherman's salmon; for a special occasion, try the chateaubriand for two. Early-bird specials are offered Tuesday through Friday from 3 to 6pm. There's also Celtic music on the second Tuesday of the month, karaoke every Wednesday, and occasional special-event dining (check the website for details).

30 Market St. © **302/328-1290.** www.arsenal1812.com. Reservations recommended for dinner. Main courses $4.95–$14 lunch, $16–$50 dinner; three-course early-bird dinners $15; brunch $15 adults, $8.95 children under 12. AE, DC, DISC, MC, V. Tues–Thurs 11:30am–9pm; Fri–Sat 11:30am–10pm; Sun 11am–3pm.

The Chef's Table at the David Finney Inn NEW AMERICAN   A change in ownership has made this wonderful old place new again. Three elegant dining rooms—the largest dominated by a long bar—have brought the 17th-century tavern into the 21st. And so has the menu: Traditional choices are given a new twist, such as the sea scallops with almond jasmine rice or the beef short ribs braised with butter-milk and served with truffled mashed potatoes. Small plates, an artisan cheese plate, and a la carte Sunday brunch are also on offer.

222 Delaware St. © **302/322-6367.** www.chefstablerestaurant.com. Reservations recommended for dinner. Main courses $8–$14 lunch, $17–$24 dinner. AE, DC, DISC, MC, V. Tues–Sat 11:30am–2pm; Tues–Thurs 5:30–10pm; Fri–Sat 5:30–11pm; Sun 11:30am–3:30pm.

Jessop's Tavern *꿈꿈꿈* AMERICAN   Don't miss this tiny tavern tucked into a 1724 building. The menu is designed to reflect the area's history, with Colonial pot-pie (a delight), pot roast, fresh seafood, and English pub fare like fish and chips and shepherd's pie. At lunchtime, the salads, soups, and sandwiches on hearth-baked breads will keep you happy for the rest of the afternoon. Sweet-potato fries are a spe-cialty. It's a casual place, a reminder of the town's seafaring days.

114 Delaware St. © **302/322-6111.** Reservations not accepted, except for large parties. Main courses $4.95–$15 lunch, $11–$22 dinner. AE, DC, DISC, MC, V. Mon–Thurs 11am–10pm; Fri–Sat 11:30am–11pm; Sun noon–8pm.

WHAT TO SEE & DO

Many of the historic buildings in New Castle are privately owned and thus not open to the public. Stop by the visitor center in the Court House to pick up the *New Castle Guide,* which points out which ones are open to the public. *Note:* Almost everything (except a few restaurants and shops) is closed on Mondays.

If you like antiques shops, here are a couple gems: **Lauren Lynch,** 1 E. Second St. (✆ **302/328-5576**), and **Raven's Nest,** 204 Delaware St. (✆ **302/325-2510**). Most shops are open daily from 11am to 5pm. Some are closed Mondays and/or Tuesdays; call ahead to be sure.

Amstel House   Dating from the 1730s, this house is a fine example of Georgian architecture. It was likely the most elegant home in town when constructed. Today, it's furnished with antiques and decorative arts of the period.

2 E. Fourth St. ✆ 302/322-2794. www.newcastlehistory.org. Admission $4 adults, $1.50 children; combination ticket with the Dutch House $6 adults, $2.50 children. Mar–Dec Tues–Sat 11am–4pm; Sun 1–4pm. Closed holidays and Jan–Feb.

Dutch House Museum   One of the oldest brick houses in Delaware, this building has remained almost unchanged since its construction around 1700. The early Dutch furnishings include a courting bench; also on display is a 16th-century Dutch Bible. During seasonal celebrations, the dining table is set with authentic foods and decorations.

32 E. Third St., on the green. ✆ 302/322-2794. www.newcastlehistory.org. Admission $4 adults, $1.50 children; combination ticket with the Amstel House $6 adults, $2.50 children. Mar–Dec Tues–Sat 11am–4pm, Sun 1–4pm; Jan–Feb Sat 11am–4pm, Sun 1–4pm.

Frenchtown Railroad Ticket Office   A tiny white building and a stretch of track in Battery Park recall the 1820s horse-drawn railway that was once part of an important commercial route.

Battery Park. ✆ 302/322-2794. www.newcastlecity.org.

Immanuel Episcopal Church   Started in 1703 and completed in 1820, this building was the first parish of the Church of England in Delaware. Extensively damaged by fire in 1980, it has been carefully restored. The adjoining cemetery is the resting

---

Finds **Attention H.O.G. & Other Motorcycle Fans**

Is it a restaurant, a museum, or a motorcycle dealership? Actually, **Mike's Famous Harley-Davidson,** 2160 New Castle Ave., New Castle (✆ **800/FAMOUS-HD;** www.mikesfamous.com), is all three. Just off the Delaware Memorial Bridge at I-295 South and Route 9 in New Castle, motorcycle enthusiasts can eat at **Mike's Warehouse Grill;** visit the **Museum of the American Road;** and shop for a new or used Harley, parts, clothes, or baby gear. The grill describes its cuisine as "regional American roadside," serving what *Delaware Today* calls the best chili in the area. The museum (admission $4 adults; $3 children 4–10, seniors, students, and military) features the Harley ridden around the world. Store, restaurant, and museum hours vary seasonally, but all are open daily. Mike's also hosts bike runs, parties, and other events, and offers motorcycle rentals as well. Check the website for hours and special events.

place of many prominent Delawareans, including George Read I, signer of the Declaration of Independence.

Second and Harmony sts., on the green. ✆ **302/328-2413.** www.immanuelonthegreen.org. Free admission. Daily 10am–5pm; services Sun 8am and 10am, Wed 9:30am, Thurs 6pm.

Old Court House ☙   This building was Delaware's Colonial capital and the meeting place of the state assembly until 1777. Built in 1732 on the fire-charred remains of an earlier courthouse, it's been restored and modified over the years, though always maintaining its role as the focal point of town. The building's cupola is at the center of a 12-mile circle that marks the northern boundary between Delaware and Pennsylvania. Inside, you'll find portraits of men important to Delaware's early history, the original speaker's chair, and excavated artifacts. Free guided tours are available.

211 Delaware St., on the green. ✆ **302/323-4453.** www.newcastlecity.org. Free admission. Tues–Sat 10am–3:30pm; Sun 1:30–4:30pm.

Old Library Museum   This fanciful hexagonal building, erected in 1892 by the New Castle Library Society, holds exhibits by the New Castle Historical Society. Its Victorian styling is attributed to the architectural firm of Frank Furness of Philadelphia.

40 E. Third St. ✆ **302/322-2794.** www.newcastlehistory.org. Mar–Dec Sat–Sun 1–4pm. Closed Jan–Feb.

Read House & Gardens ☙   A walk through this 22-room Federal-style house overlooking the river is a walk through New Castle history. Originally the home of George Read II, son of a signer of the Declaration of Independence, it had only two other owners. Rooms from each "period" pay homage to them all. The soaring Palladian windows and intricate composition-work moldings were part of the original design. Don't miss Mr. Read's law office or the second-floor bathing room, to which servants carried hot water. The second owner added the formal gardens in the mid-1800s, now the oldest surviving gardens in Delaware. The third owner's contributions included the European-style rathskeller built in the basement during Prohibition; it's a hoot.

42 The Strand. ✆ **302/322-8411.** www.hsd.org/read.htm. Admission $5 adults, $4 seniors and students, $2 children. Mar–Dec Tues–Fri 11am–4pm, Sat 10am–4pm, Sun 1–4pm; Jan–Feb by appointment.

13

Dover & Central Delaware

To race-car fans, Dover means NASCAR twice a year. To gamblers, it's a place to play the slots. To history buffs, this town is where the U.S. Constitution got its first "yea" vote.

Set in the middle of this tiny state, Delaware's capital has its share of museums and attractions. Problem is, too many people fail to slow down on their way to the beach! What a shame.

At least the wildlife is smart enough to stop: Bombay Hook National Wildlife Refuge offers migrating visitors 16,000 acres of marsh and wetlands.

1 Dover

45 miles S of Wilmington, 84 miles E of Baltimore, 43 miles N of Rehoboth

Plotted in 1717 according to a charter by William Penn, Dover was originally designed only as the Kent County seat. By 1777, however, this rich grain-farming community's importance had increased, and the state legislature, seeking a safe inland location as an alternative to the old capital of New Castle, relocated to the more central Dover. Delaware became the "First State" on December 7, 1787, when the state's delegates assembled at Dover's Golden Fleece Tavern to ratify the Constitution of the United States, the first state to do so.

Today, Dover continues to be a hub of state government and business. Its history is showcased at a sprawling agricultural museum, a museum of American art stocked with lavish works donated by Delaware art collectors, and the Old State House. On the city's southern edge, Dover Air Force Base, the largest airport on the East Coast, is home to its own museum of aircraft.

ESSENTIALS

GETTING THERE From the north or northwest, take I-95 to Wilmington and head south on Route 1 (a toll road) or Route 13 (also known as the DuPont Hwy.) to Dover. Route 13, which runs the entire length of Delaware, is also the best way to approach Dover from the south. From Washington, D.C., and points west, take Route 50 across the Bay Bridge to Route 301 North. Follow 301 to 302 East, then take Route 454. From 454, take Route 8 into Dover.

Bus service to Dover is available through **Greyhound** (© **800/231-2222;** www.greyhound.com), which stops at 1166 S. Bay Rd. (© **302/734-1417**).

VISITOR INFORMATION Head first to the **Delaware State Visitor Center,** 406 Federal St., at Duke of York Street, Dover (© **302/739-4266**). Located on the northeast corner of the green, it offers information, exhibits, restrooms, and a gift shop. It's open Monday through Saturday from 8:30am to 4:30pm, Sunday from 1:30 to 4:30pm. Its 30-minute tours are offered Tuesday through Saturday; reservations are a must. You

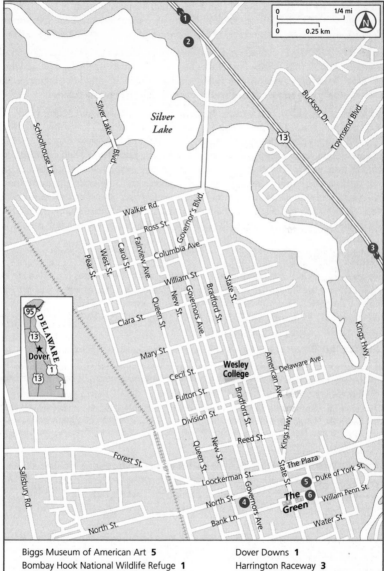

Biggs Museum of American Art **5**
Bombay Hook National Wildlife Refuge **1**
Delaware Agricultural Museum and Village **2**
Delaware Archeology Museum **4**
Delaware State Visitors Center **5**
Dover Air Force Base **3**

Dover Downs **1**
Harrington Raceway **3**
John Dickinson Plantation **3**
Johnson Victrola Museum **4**
Museum of Small Town Life **4**
State House Museum **6**

can also stop by the **Kent County Convention and Visitors Bureau,** 435 N. DuPont Hwy. (© **800/233-KENT** or 302/734-1736; www.visitdover.com), or the **Smyrna Visitor Center,** 5500 DuPont Hwy., 11 miles north of Dover (© **302/653-8910**).

GETTING AROUND   You'll need a car. To rent one, contact **Avis** (© **302/734-5550**) or **Hertz** (© **302/678-0700**). For reliable 24-hour taxi service, call **City Cab of Dover** (© **302/734-5968**). *Note:* Amish buggies are common on the area's highways and byways, usually on the shoulders. Please drive with care and pass them slowly.

SPECIAL EVENTS   The biggest events are the two **"Monster Mile"** NASCAR weekends, in June and September at Dover International Speedway (© **800/711-5882;** www.doverspeedway.com). Make your hotel reservations up to a year in advance. In late April or early May, history buffs enjoy **Old Dover Days** (© **800/233-KENT;** www.visitdover.com), when several privately owned historic homes and gardens open to the public. Costumed guides, maypole dancing, crafts demonstrations, and general merriment take place on the green. Cyclists come for the **Amish Bike Tour** (© **800/233-KENT;** www.visitdover.com); held the Saturday after Labor Day. **Christmas in Odessa** (© **302/378-4900;** www.christmasinodessa.com) is held the first Saturday in December, with house tours, music, and crafts.

WHERE TO STAY

Generally, Dover accommodations are moderately priced—but rates can skyrocket on NASCAR race weekends. (If you plan to attend, book your room when you get your tickets—hotels in the entire state fill up.) Local hotels also tend to book up on summer weekends. Most of Dover's hotels are on Route 13 (DuPont Hwy.); these are largely modern chains with ample parking.

Comfort Inn Dover   Businesspeople and families head for this Comfort Inn, just off the Route 13 corridor at Loockerman Street. The closest motel to the city's historic district, the brick-fronted inn is laid out in two adjoining wings. The decor and furnishings are typical of the chain.

222 S. DuPont Hwy. (Rte. 13), Dover, DE 19901. © **800/228-5150** or 302/674-3300. www.comfortinn.com. 94 units. $70–$300 double. Rates include continental breakfast. AE, DC, DISC, MC, V. Pets accepted. **Amenities:** Adjacent TGI Friday's; outdoor pool; health club; coffee in lobby. *In room:* A/C, fridge, microwave, coffeemaker, hair dryer (upon request), iron (upon request).

Dover Downs Hotel ✿   This 10-story luxury hotel adjacent to the slots and racetracks offers track-view rooms and plenty of pampering—whether you won or not. Most units are spacious, with standard furnishings. Jacuzzi rooms are available. The fitness center, though small, offers steam rooms and massages (call ahead to reserve a massage).

1131 N. DuPont Hwy., Dover, DE 19901. © **866/4-RESERV** or 302/674-4600. www.doverdownshotel.com. 240 units. $99–$195 double; $250–$650 suite. Children under 18 stay free in parent's room. AE, DISC, MC, V. **Amenities:** 5 restaurants; lobby bar; indoor pool; health club; shuttle service to downtown Dover; gift shop; laundry service; concierge-level rooms. *In room:* A/C, TV w/pay movies, dataport, fridge, coffeemaker, iron, safe.

Fairfield Inn & Suites Dover ✿   This Marriott franchise has room for families and amenities for business travelers. Decorated in bright colors—no solemn tans and mauves here—the inn's suites come with a pullout sofa, second TV, CD player, fridge, and microwave. Standard rooms are almost as spacious. The health center is small.

655 N. DuPont Hwy., Dover, DE 19901. © **302/677-0900.** www.marriott.com. 94 units. $72–$159 double; $119–$189 suite. AE, DC, DISC, MC, V. Rates include continental breakfast. **Amenities:** Indoor pool; health club; spa; business center w/Internet access; coffee in lobby; deck. *In room:* A/C, Wi-Fi, coffeemaker, hair dryer, iron.

Sheraton Dover Hotel ⍟ A favorite spot for business executives and conference attendees, this seven-story hotel is the most complete facility along the north–south corridor. Guest rooms are furnished in a traditional motif, with mahogany reproduction furniture. The hotel offers varied dining and entertainment choices: Tango's Bistro, a full-service, upscale restaurant with a casual atmosphere; the Starlight Lounge, a rooftop lounge with a view of Dover (open on weekends only); and the Z Bar, with light fare and nightly entertainment.

1570 N. DuPont Hwy. (Rte. 13), Dover, DE 19901. ✆ **302/678-8500.** Fax 302/678-9073. www.sheratondover.com. 156 units. $89–$169 double; $149–$495 suite. AE, DC, DISC, MC, V. **Amenities:** Restaurant; 2 lounges; indoor pool; health club. *In room:* A/C, TV w/movies, high-speed Internet access, coffeemaker, hair dryer, iron.

WHERE TO DINE

Atwood's AMERICAN New owners have taken over the old Blue Coat Inn. The Colonial-style dining rooms overlooking Silver Lake are cozy, the menu traditional. Lunchtime brings salads, soups, and sandwiches—look for the quiche and panini. At dinner, choose from pasta, pork, or fish (like salmon encrusted in pesto and Parmesan). If you can't decide, go for a "duet:" a filet with lobster or shrimp with salmon. The cream of crab soup is smooth and filled with lump meat. Service is attentive and Eastern Shore friendly.

801 N. State St. ✆ **302/674-1776.** Reservations recommended. Main courses $5–$13 at lunch, $14–$32 at dinner. AE, DISC, DC, MC, V. Mon–Thurs 11:30am–9pm; Fri–Sat 11:30am–10pm. Bar stays open later.

Spence's Bazaar MARKET No, it's not a restaurant, but if you like an old-time market, this one offers homemade sausages, breads, pies, and preserves, made by members of Mennonite and Amish communities. Hours vary, so it's best to call ahead if you have your heart set on shoofly pie. The market also houses a flea market and auction business. Auctions are at 2 and 6pm.

550 S. New St. ✆ **302/734-3441.** Tues and Fri 7:30am–5pm.

Village Inn SEAFOOD ⍟⍟ For a gracious, creative dinner, drive through the cornfields to find this lovely place in Little Creek, about 4 miles east of Dover. The outside is unremarkable, but inside is a warm dining room with fireplace, white tablecloths, candles, and welcoming staff. The new owner, who has cooked here many years, has merely tweaked the superb food. Jumbo lump meat crab cakes are a standout in a menu of seafood, steaks, and chops. A few specials are added each night. Cowboy steaks—T-bones or porterhouse steaks with a dry rub—sell out. A jazz pianist plays on Saturday nights.

Rte. 9, Little Creek. ✆ **302/734-3245.** Reservations recommended. Main courses $17–$30. AE, MC, V. Wed–Thurs 4–9pm; Fri–Sat 4–10pm; Sun 4–8pm. From Rte. 13, turn on Rte. 8 and turn south onto Rte. 9; continue 1 mile.

W. T. Smithers ⍟ INTERNATIONAL This Victorian-style eatery is dainty enough for a girls' night out, but the bar is big enough for all your friends. Stop for lunch and enjoy overstuffed sandwiches (skip the crab cake), a luscious cream of crab soup, or a salad. The dinner menu runs the gamut from fish and steak to Santa Fe fajitas to an intriguing Seafood Mosaic with shrimp, scallops, fish, and crab. Or come for the party: a DJ on Wednesdays, karaoke most Fridays, and live music on Saturdays.

140 S. State St. ✆ **302/674-8875.** Reservations recommended for dinner. Main courses $5.75–$7.25 at lunch, $8.95–$23 at dinner. AE, DC, DISC, MC, V. Mon–Sat 11am–1am; Sun noon–10pm with limited menu.

WHAT TO SEE & DO

The major museums of Dover, as well as Legislative Hall and the state archives, have been designated the **First State Heritage Park at Dover.** A "park without boundaries," the various sites, nevertheless, have varying hours. They all participate in First Saturday programs. Check the visitor center for details.

Start your visit at the green, where Delaware became the first state to ratify the U.S. Constitution in 1787. Most of Dover's historic sites, government buildings, and museums are located around or within walking distance of here. From Route 13, follow signs for the historic district and take State Street, which goes right through the center of the green.

Other attractions, along with Dover's hotels and motels, are concentrated east of the historic district, along Route 13, also known as DuPont Highway. You'll need your car to get around this strip, which is home to Dover Downs, the Delaware Agricultural Museum and Village, and the Dover Air Force Base.

MUSEUMS & HISTORIC SITES

Biggs Museum of American Art ⚘   In galleries spread over the second and third floors of the Delaware State Visitor Center, you'll see rooms filled with antique furniture; gorgeous silver tea services produced locally; and the works of Hudson River School artists, members of the Peale family, and local painters and sculptors. The collection of Sewell C. Biggs, a local art patron, spans 2 centuries and includes 20th-century Impressionist paintings.

406 Federal St. ✆ **302/674-2111.** www.biggsmuseum.org. Free admission. Wed–Sat 10am–4pm; Sun 1:30–4:30pm.

Delaware Agricultural Museum and Village   A huge barn right on DuPont Highway houses an enormous collection of tractors and other farm equipment—including a 1930s farm kitchen, log cabin, crop-dusting plane, and several changing exhibits. Outside, you'll find an 1890s village, complete with barn, farmhouses, train station, windmill, and church. The gift shop features country items.

866 N. DuPont Hwy. ✆ **302/734-1618.** www.agriculturalmuseum.org. Admission $3 adults, $2 seniors and children 6–17, $9 per family. Jan–Mar Mon–Fri 10am–4pm; Apr–Dec Tues–Sat 10am–4pm, Sun 1–4pm. Across from Dover Downs on Rte. 13.

Delaware State Museums ⚘⚘ *(Value*   Five of the states' museums are in Dover (the others are the Zwaanendael in Lewes and the New Castle Court House). The museums in Dover highlight the accomplishments of Delawareans since prehistoric times. Admission to all of these is free. *Note:* It is nearly impossible to see all of these museums in a single day at a relaxing pace. Go first to the museum you want to see the most.

Start at the **Delaware State Visitor Center,** 406 Federal St. (✆ **302/739-4266;** www.destatemuseums.org), to get a map and see the center's own exhibits. (The Biggs Museum of American Art is here, too; see above for details.) The nearby **green,** the English-style town square at Bank Lane and State Street, is an important site in Delaware's history. William Penn designed it more than 300 years ago, and soldiers gathered here to join the Revolutionary War troops of General Washington. Look for the sign remembering the Golden Fleece Tavern, where Delaware's legislators voted to ratify the U.S. Constitution.

At the **Delaware Archaeology Museum,** 316 S. Governors Ave. (✆ **302/739-4266**), look over artifacts from a Native American burial ground, peruse shards of glass and pottery from digs across the state, and learn about the methodology of archaeology. All

> (Fun Fact) **Welcome Back, Bill of Rights**
>
> Delaware's copy of the Bill of Rights is back on display in the **Delaware Public Archives,** 121 Duke of York St. (© **302/744-5000;** www.state.de.us/sos/dpa or www.dovermuseums.org), for the first time since 1789. It's one of only seven extant from the first official imprint. It is on exhibit from December 7 (Delaware Day) to July 4th; the rest of the year, it returns to its permanent home in the National Archives for conservation work. In an agreement with the National Archives, the Bill of Rights will return to Delaware annually for the next 25 years. The archives are open Monday through Saturday from 8am to 4:30pm, until 8pm Wednesday and Thursday.

of this is on view in a 1790 Presbyterian church, which shares a free parking lot with the Johnson Victrola Museum. Open Tuesday through Saturday from 10am to 3:30pm.

Next door, the **Museum of Small Town Life** ✯, 316 S. Governors Ave. (© **302/739-3261**), housed in an 1880s Sunday school, offers visitors a chance to walk down Main Street as it was a century ago. Stop by the printing office, the drugstore, the woodworking shop, and the all-important general store. Open Tuesday through Saturday from 10am to 3:30pm.

The **Johnson Victrola Museum** ✯, at New Street and Bank Lane (© **302/739-4266**), is packed with old record albums and antique phonographs that pay tribute to the man who made the Victrola a must-have at the turn of the 20th century. Eldridge R. Johnson, a Delaware boy who founded the Victor Talking Machine Company, invented a way to make the original phonograph (the one with the big horn) more compact and control its volume. His invention made the machine popular—and made him a millionaire. Open Tuesday through Saturday from 10am to 3:30pm.

The **State House Museum,** on the green (© **302/739-4266**), dates back to 1792. To mark the U.S. bicentennial in 1976, the Georgian-style State House was restored to its original appearance, with its 18th-century courtroom, legislative chambers, and deeds office where freed slaves filed their manumission papers. Although the state's General Assembly moved to the nearby Legislative Hall in 1933, the State House continues to be used for ceremonial events. Open Tuesday through Saturday from 10am to 4:30pm, Sunday from 1:30 to 4:30pm.

John Dickinson Plantation A few miles outside the historic district, the reconstructed home of John Dickinson, one of Delaware's foremost statesmen of the Revolutionary and Federal periods, was originally built in 1740. Destroyed by fire in 1804, the brick house was rebuilt in 1896. Guides dressed in period clothing give visitors a glimpse of the daily life of the Dickinson family, tenants, and slaves.

340 Kitts Hummock Rd. © 302/739-3277. www.destatemuseums.org. Free admission. Jan–Feb Tues–Sat 10am–3:30pm; Mar–Dec Tues–Sat 10am–3:30pm, Sun 1:30–4:30pm. Arrive at least 30 min. before closing time. Take Rte. 113 south from Dover to Kitts Hummock Rd., just past the Dover Air Force Base.

Legislative Hall: The State Capitol The Georgian-style building on Legislative Avenue, which has housed the state's General Assembly since 1933, is open to visitors on guided tours.

Contact 152 Legislative Ave. © 302/739-9194. www.delaware.gov. Free admission. Mon–Fri 9am–3pm when General Assembly is not in session; Mon–Fri 9am–noon on General Assembly session days.

Moments Christmas in Odessa

The quiet town of Odessa comes to life on the first Saturday of December, when 30 historic houses spanning 3 centuries open for **Christmas in Odessa** (⦿ 302/378-4900; www.christmasinodessa.com). Public buildings and private homes are open for daytime and candlelight tours. Music, carriage rides, food, and a crafts and greens shop are also available. Tickets are sold that day at the Old Academy, at Fourth and Main streets.

Even if it's not Christmas, you can still visit **Historic Houses of Odessa** (⦿ 302/378-4119), four buildings that were once the property of Winterthur; they were recently reopened by the nonprofit Historic Odessa Foundation. All but one of the buildings date back to the 18th century. Start at the visitor center, in the Historic Odessa Bank, 201 Main St. The houses are open Thursday through Saturday from 10am to 4pm (closed Jan–Feb). Admission is $10 for adults; $8 for seniors, students, and kids 12 and over.

Odessa is 23 miles north of Dover and 22 miles south of Wilmington. To get here, take Route 13 and follow the signs to the historic district.

NEARBY ATTRACTIONS

Air Mobility Command Museum (Dover Air Force Base)   This museum, located in a restored World War II hangar listed on the National Register of Historic Places, houses a collection of vintage aircraft and artifacts. Exhibits reflect the evolution and history of Dover Air Force Base, the hub of strategic airlifts in the eastern United States. The museum's first plane, a C-47A used in the 1944 D-day paratroop drop over Normandy, was rejected in 1986 by other institutions as "hopeless to repair." You'll see it here, immaculately restored.

1301 Heritage Rd. (off Rte. 113). ⦿ 302/677-5938. www.amcmuseum.org. Free admission. Tues–Sat 9am–4pm. To reach the entrance, take Rte. 9 (left from Dover) and look for the sign.

Dover Downs Slots   Dover Downs' slots casino draws busloads hoping to make a million. The 80,000-square-foot facility, adjacent to the racetrack, has 2,500 slot machines. Games range from 5¢ to $20. You can play until 4am. The adjacent **Rollins Center** hosts many concerts; recent performers have included Larry Gatlin and the Gatlin Brothers and Wayne Brady. You must be 21 to play.

1131 N. DuPont Hwy. ⦿ 800/711-5882 or 302/674-4600. www.doverdowns.com. Mon–Sat 8am–4am; Sun noon–4am. Closed Dec 25 and Easter.

SPECTATOR SPORTS & OUTDOOR ACTIVITIES

HARNESS HORSE RACING   Dover Downs (⦿ 800/711-5882; www.dover downs.com) offers harness horse racing November through April. Races run Monday through Thursday at 4:30pm, Saturday and Sunday at 5:30pm. Simulcast racing is offered year-round, daily from noon to midnight.

Harrington Raceway, Route 13, Harrington (⦿ 302/398-7223; www.harrington raceway.com), has 90 race days from late April through July and August through November. Harness racing usually runs Saturday through Thursday, with post time at 5:30pm. Simulcast is available daily from noon to midnight. Midway slot machines

---

Tips Put Yourself in the Driver's Seat

Want to ride in a Winston Cup car? Maybe even drive it yourself? **Monster Racing Driving School** (℃ 800/468-6946; www.monsterracing.com) will let you get behind the wheel to "tame the Monster" at Dover Speedway. For $89, you can ride the course for four laps with an instructor. Packages range from $359 to $919 to drive a race car for 30 laps, with shorter and less expensive alternatives in between.

---

and "video lottery" are also available year-round. The track is located on the state fair grounds, about 15 miles south of Dover.

STOCK-CAR RACING   Twice a year, NASCAR fans flock to **Dover International Speedway,** 1131 N. DuPont Hwy. (Rte. 13), Dover (℃ 302/857-3219; www.dover speedway.com). These two major races draw some of the world's top drivers to this 140,000-seat track. Ticket prices for adults range from $40 for general admission to $100 for the best seats; order online or call **800/441-RACE.** Tickets go on sale 10 months before race weekends.

DART First State (℃ 302/652-DART; www.dartfirststate.com) offers shuttle buses from the Blue Hen Corporate Center in Dover and Christiana Mall in Wilmington. Tickets are $20 per carload from the Blue Hen Corporate Center and $10 per person round-trip from Christiana Mall. Call or check the website for a schedule; bring exact change.

SILVER LAKE & KILLENS POND STATE PARK

Dover's beautiful **Silver Lake** is the core of a recreation area in the heart of the city. Biking, swimming, and picnicking draw most people, but the park also has a boat ramp, exercise circuit, volleyball court, and walking/jogging trail. The park has entrances on Washington Street and Kings Highway; it's open year-round from sunrise to sunset. Contact the **Dover Parks and Recreation Department** (℃ 302/736-7050; www.city ofdover.com/departments/parks) for additional information.

Some 13 miles south of Dover, about a half-mile east of Route 13, is Kent County's only state park, **Killens Pond State Park** ⁂, 5025 Killens Pond Rd., Felton (℃ 302/284-4526; www.destateparks.com). Covering 1,444 acres, with a 66-acre millpond, Killens Pond is a natural inland haven. Facilities include picnic areas, shuffleboard courts, horseshoe pits, biking and hiking trails, volleyball courts, boat rentals, pond fishing, camping, and the all-new Killens Pond Water Park, which has lap lanes, a mushroom fountain, and a lily-pad fun walk—something for every age. Park entry fees, applicable daily May through October, are $3 for Delaware-registered cars and $6 for out-of-state vehicles. Entrance to the water park is an additional $1.50 for adults and $1 for children under 16. The park is open year-round; the water park is open Memorial Day through Labor Day.

Also at the park are 77 campsites, including 10 cabins, 17 tent-only sites, and 1 pond-view cottage (cabin with living room). The campground is open year-round. Reservations are taken up to 7 months in advance; call ℃ 877/987-2757. Fees are $16 to $20 for tent sites and $22 to $26 for sites with water and electric hookup. *Note:* NASCAR fans fill the campsites quickly on race weekends in April and September. Be sure to reserve 7 months in advance.

THE PERFORMING ARTS

Schwartz Center for the Arts   This performing-arts venue brings back to life the beloved 1904 Dover Opera House. It plays host to a wide variety of performers, from the Second City comedy troupe to the Phil Woods Jazz Quintet to Arlo Guthrie. Film, plays, and ballet are also on the schedule, which can be found on the website. In a town where nightlife is scarce, this is big news.

226 S. State St. ℭ **800/778-5078** or 302/678-3583. www.schwartzcenter.com.

2 Bombay Hook National Wildlife Refuge ✶

Thanks to its abundance of wildlife refuges, the Delmarva Peninsula is a haven for migrating birds and those who watch them. Bombay Hook, established in 1937 as part of a chain of refuges extending from Canada to the Gulf of Mexico, is the largest of Delaware's refuges. Though the primary (and loudest) inhabitants and visitors to the refuge are wintering ducks and geese, Bombay Hook also hosts herons, egrets, sandpipers, willets, and the occasional bald eagle, as well as a more permanent mammal, amphibian, and reptile population.

If you've visited Maryland's Blackwater National Wildlife Refuge, Bombay Hook will be quite a contrast. The facilities are considerably more primitive—the roads are not paved, the trails are well marked but not well worn, and there are fewer ranger programs and visitor services. This means there are also fewer human visitors, so you may have the place all to yourself, especially in the off season.

ESSENTIALS

GETTING THERE   Take Route 13 north of Dover to Route 42; travel east (left) on Route 42 to Route 9 and then north on Route 9 for 1½ miles; turn right onto Whitehall Neck Road, which leads to the visitor center.

VISITOR CENTER   The visitor center/ranger station (ℭ **302/653-6872;** www.fws.gov/northeast/bombayhook) is open year-round, Monday through Friday from 8am to 4pm, plus spring and fall weekends from 9am to 5pm. The park is open daily from sunrise to sunset.

FEES & REGULATIONS   Entrance fees are $4 per car or $2 per family on bikes or on foot. Admission is free on hunting days—but access is limited, too. Deer, snow goose, and Canada goose hunting are permitted under special regulations in designated portions of the refuge during the regular Delaware hunting season.

SEEING THE HIGHLIGHTS

Like most wildlife refuges, much of Bombay Hook is not accessible to the public. However, the 12-mile round-trip auto route, several nature trails, and three observation towers offer opportunities to see birds and other wildlife.

The driving tour, which can also be used by cyclists, begins and ends at the visitor center and takes you by the three major wetland pools in the refuge: Raymond Pool, Shearness Pool, and Bear Swamp Pool. The roads are well marked and offer plenty of spots to pull off and park. Cyclists should note that the roads throughout the refuge are not paved—they're dirt and gravel—though they are flat. The visitor center has audiocassettes and binoculars for visitors' use. To see the most birds, come in May or June, when the shorebird population hits its peak. Or visit in October or November, when the most ducks and geese are here—they can number 150,000.

BIRD-WATCHING   Birds can be seen all along the auto tour, but for the best vantage point, hike out to one of the three 30-foot observation towers, one overlooking each of the pools. Part of the trail to Bear Swamp Observation Tower is accessible; an observation platform at ground level below the tower provides a good view, and a viewing scope at wheelchair level has been installed on the dock at the end of the path. A photography blind is available by advance request; call © **302/653-6872** or 302/653-9345.

The best times to see migratory birds are October through November and mid-February through March. Some 256 species have been counted. **Canada, tundra,** and **snow geese** begin arriving in early October, while **duck** populations—pintail, mallard, American widgeon, and others—increase through November. **Shorebird** migration begins in April; their populations in the refuge peak in May and June.

The refuge is the year-round home to **bald eagles,** though they can be difficult to spot. Eggs begin hatching in April; the baby eagles begin to leave their nests in June. Shearness Pool serves as their roosting and nesting area. Parson Point Trail will take you to the back of the pool for a closer look. During mating and nesting season (Nov–June), however, this trail may be closed. Bring binoculars or stop at the observation tower along the auto route to get a glimpse of the eagles.

HIKING   Hiking in the refuge is primarily a means of observing and photographing wildlife, so the nature trails aren't terribly strenuous or long. All of the trails are flat and range from .25 mile to 1 mile long. Bring insect repellent and wear long sleeves from July through September. The Bear Swamp Trail is partially accessible; the Parson Point Trail is the longest option. The Boardwalk Trail offers visitors a look at four different refuge habitats—woodland, freshwater pond, brackish pond, and salt marsh—and the widest variety of wildlife. Another trail leads to the Raymond Tower, set in a meadow.

Index

FROMMER'S® COMPLETE TRAVEL GUIDES

Alaska
Amalfi Coast
American Southwest
Amsterdam
Argentina & Chile
Arizona
Atlanta
Australia
Austria
Bahamas
Barcelona
Beijing
Belgium, Holland & Luxembourg
Belize
Bermuda
Boston
Brazil
British Columbia & the Canadian
  Rockies
Brussels & Bruges
Budapest & the Best of Hungary
Buenos Aires
Calgary
California
Canada
Cancún, Cozumel & the Yucatán
Cape Cod, Nantucket & Martha's
  Vineyard
Caribbean
Caribbean Ports of Call
Carolinas & Georgia
Chicago
China
Colorado
Costa Rica
Croatia
Cuba
Denmark
Denver, Boulder & Colorado Springs
Edinburgh & Glasgow
England
Europe
Europe by Rail

Florence, Tuscany & Umbria
Florida
France
Germany
Greece
Greek Islands
Hawaii
Hong Kong
Honolulu, Waikiki & Oahu
India
Ireland
Italy
Jamaica
Japan
Kauai
Las Vegas
London
Los Angeles
Los Cabos & Baja
Madrid
Maine Coast
Maryland & Delaware
Maui
Mexico
Montana & Wyoming
Montréal & Québec City
Moscow & St. Petersburg
Munich & the Bavarian Alps
Nashville & Memphis
New England
Newfoundland & Labrador
New Mexico
New Orleans
New York City
New York State
New Zealand
Northern Italy
Norway
Nova Scotia, New Brunswick &
  Prince Edward Island
Oregon
Paris
Peru

Philadelphia & the Amish Country
Portugal
Prague & the Best of the Czech
  Republic
Provence & the Riviera
Puerto Rico
Rome
San Antonio & Austin
San Diego
San Francisco
Santa Fe, Taos & Albuquerque
Scandinavia
Scotland
Seattle
Seville, Granada & the Best of
  Andalusia
Shanghai
Sicily
Singapore & Malaysia
South Africa
South America
South Florida
South Pacific
Southeast Asia
Spain
Sweden
Switzerland
Texas
Thailand
Tokyo
Toronto
Turkey
USA
Utah
Vancouver & Victoria
Vermont, New Hampshire & Maine
Vienna & the Danube Valley
Vietnam
Virgin Islands
Virginia
Walt Disney World® & Orlando
Washington, D.C.
Washington State

FROMMER'S® DOLLAR-A-DAY GUIDES

Australia from $60 a Day
California from $70 a Day
England from $75 a Day
Europe from $85 a Day
Florida from $70 a Day

Hawaii from $80 a Day
Ireland from $90 a Day
Italy from $90 a Day
London from $95 a Day

New York City from $90 a Day
Paris from $95 a Day
San Francisco from $70 a Day
Washington, D.C. from $80 a Day

FROMMER'S® PORTABLE GUIDES

Acapulco, Ixtapa & Zihuatanejo
Amsterdam
Aruba
Australia's Great Barrier Reef
Bahamas
Berlin
Big Island of Hawaii
Boston
California Wine Country
Cancún
Cayman Islands
Charleston
Chicago

Disneyland®
Dominican Republic
Dublin
Florence
Las Vegas
Las Vegas for Non-Gamblers
London
Los Angeles
Maui
Nantucket & Martha's Vineyard
New Orleans
New York City
Paris

Portland
Puerto Rico
Puerto Vallarta, Manzanillo &
  Guadalajara
Rio de Janeiro
San Diego
San Francisco
Savannah
Vancouver
Venice
Virgin Islands
Washington, D.C.
Whistler

FROMMER'S® CRUISE GUIDES

Alaska Cruises & Ports of Call

Cruises & Ports of Call

European Cruises & Ports of Call

FROMMER'S® DAY BY DAY GUIDES

Amsterdam	London	Rome
Chicago	New York City	San Francisco
Florence & Tuscany	Paris	Venice

FROMMER'S® NATIONAL PARK GUIDES

Algonquin Provincial Park	National Parks of the American West	Yosemite and Sequoia & Kings
Banff & Jasper	Rocky Mountain	Canyon
Grand Canyon	Yellowstone & Grand Teton	Zion & Bryce Canyon

FROMMER'S® MEMORABLE WALKS

Chicago	New York	Rome
London	Paris	San Francisco

FROMMER'S® WITH KIDS GUIDES

Chicago	National Parks	Toronto
Hawaii	New York City	Walt Disney World® & Orlando
Las Vegas	San Francisco	Washington, D.C.
London		

SUZY GERSHMAN'S BORN TO SHOP GUIDES

Born to Shop: France	Born to Shop: Italy	Born to Shop: New York
Born to Shop: Hong Kong, Shanghai	Born to Shop: London	Born to Shop: Paris
& Beijing		

FROMMER'S® IRREVERENT GUIDES

Amsterdam	Los Angeles	Rome
Boston	Manhattan	San Francisco
Chicago	New Orleans	Walt Disney World®
Las Vegas	Paris	Washington, D.C.
London		

FROMMER'S® BEST-LOVED DRIVING TOURS

Austria	Germany	Northern Italy
Britain	Ireland	Scotland
California	Italy	Spain
France	New England	Tuscany & Umbria

THE UNOFFICIAL GUIDES®

Adventure Travel in Alaska	Hawaii	Paris
Beyond Disney	Ireland	San Francisco
California with Kids	Las Vegas	South Florida including Miami &
Central Italy	London	the Keys
Chicago	Maui	Walt Disney World®
Cruises	Mexico's Best Beach Resorts	Walt Disney World® for
Disneyland®	Mini Las Vegas	Grown-ups
England	Mini Mickey	Walt Disney World® with Kids
Florida	New Orleans	Washington, D.C.
Florida with Kids	New York City	

SPECIAL-INTEREST TITLES

Athens Past & Present	Frommer's Exploring America by RV
Cities Ranked & Rated	Frommer's NYC Free & Dirt Cheap
Frommer's Best Day Trips from London	Frommer's Road Atlas Europe
Frommer's Best RV & Tent Campgrounds	Frommer's Road Atlas Ireland
in the U.S.A.	Retirement Places Rated

FROMMER'S® PHRASEFINDER DICTIONARY GUIDES

French	Italian	Spanish

THE NEW TRAVELOCITY GUARANTEE

EVERYTHING YOU BOOK WILL BE RIGHT, OR WE'LL WORK WITH OUR TRAVEL PARTNERS TO MAKE IT RIGHT, RIGHT AWAY.

*To drive home the point,
we're going to use the word "right" in every single sentence.*

Let's get right to it. Right to the meat! Only Travelocity guarantees everything about your booking will be right, or we'll work with our travel partners to make it right, right away. Right on!

Here's a picture taken smack dab right in the middle of Antigua, where the guarantee also covers you.

The guarantee covers all but one of the items pictured to the right.

For example, what if the ocean view you booked actually looks out at a downright ugly parking lot? You'd be right to call – we're there for you. And no one in their right mind would be pleased to learn the rental car place has closed and left them stranded. Call Travelocity and we'll help get you back on the right track.

Now, you may be thinking, "Yeah, right, I'm so sure." That's OK; you have the right to remain skeptical. That is until we mention help is always right around the corner. Call us right off the bat, knowing that our customer service reps are there for you 24/7. Righting wrongs. Left and right.

Now if you're guessing there are some things we can't control, like the weather, well you're right. But we can help you with most things – to get all the details in righting,* visit **travelocity.com/guarantee**.

*Sorry, spelling things right is one of the few things not covered under the guarantee.

I'd give my right arm for a guarantee like this, although I'm glad I don't have to.

travelocity
You'll never roam alone.